ISBN 978-1-330-05352-2
PIBN 10014098

1 MONTH OF
FREE
READING

at

www.ForgottenBooks.com

By purchasing this book you are eligible for one month membership to ForgottenBooks.com, giving you unlimited access to our entire collection of over 1,000,000 titles via our web site and mobile apps.

To claim your free month visit:
www.forgottenbooks.com/free14098

English
Français
Deutsche
Italiano
Español
Português

www.forgottenbooks.com

Mythology Photography **Fiction**
Fishing Christianity **Art** Cooking
Essays Buddhism Freemasonry
Medicine **Biology** Music **Ancient**
Egypt Evolution Carpentry Physics
Dance Geology **Mathematics** Fitness
Shakespeare **Folklore** Yoga Marketing
Confidence Immortality Biographies
Poetry **Psychology** Witchcraft
Electronics Chemistry History **Law**
Accounting **Philosophy** Anthropology
Alchemy Drama Quantum Mechanics
Atheism Sexual Health **Ancient History**
Entrepreneurship Languages Sport
Paleontology Needlework Islam
Metaphysics Investment Archaeology
Parenting Statistics Criminology
Motivational

A HISTORY

OF

MODERN PHILOSOPHY

A SKETCH OF THE HISTORY OF PHILOSOPHY

FROM THE CLOSE OF THE RENAISSANCE
TO OUR OWN DAY

BY

Dr. HARALD HÖFFDING
PROFESSOR AT THE UNIVERSITY OF COPENHAGEN

TRANSLATED FROM THE GERMAN EDITION

By B. E. MEYER

AUTHORISED TRANSLATION

VOLUME I

MACMILLAN AND CO., LIMITED
ST. MARTIN'S STREET, LONDON
1908

First Edition 1900
Reprinted 1908·

To the Memory of

MY TEACHER AND FRIEND

PROFESSOR HANS BRÖCHNER

TRANSLATOR'S NOTE

MY thanks are due to Miss M. Stawell for valuable help in the translation of the chapters on Fichte, Schelling, and Hegel; and to Miss H. Tayler, who was kind enough to read through the proofs of the latter half of Vol. II. In the case of quotations from works of which there already exist well-known English translations (*e.g* Kant's works), on which I could not hope to improve, I have quoted from these translations.

B. E. MEYER.

CONTENTS

BOOK I

THE PHILOSOPHY OF THE RENAISSANCE

A. THE DISCOVERY OF MAN

B. THE NEW CONCEPTION OF THE WORLD

BOOK II

THE NEW SCIENCE

BOOK III

THE GREAT SYSTEMS

BOOK IV

ENGLISH EMPIRICAL PHILOSOPHY

BOOK V

THE FRENCH ENLIGHTENMENT PHILOSOPHY
AND ROUSSEAU

INTRODUCTION

THE appearance of a new representation of an important period in the History of Philosophy will naturally give rise to the question as to what view of philosophy is regarded by the author as fundamental, and what is the significance, and what the value which he ascribes to its history. To which I answer that the whole aim of the studies of which the publication of this book denotes the provisional conclusion has been to shed light on the question as to what philosophy really is. As we learn to know a man from his biography, so also we must be able to learn to know a science from its history. And it is the more natural that we should adopt this path, since experience is continually showing us that, within the sphere of philosophy, contending views are advanced, each one of which claims to be valid, so that there is no one exposition of philosophy to which we can point as developing an exhaustive conception of it. It is natural, therefore, that we should here, as within the sphere of religion, employ the comparative method. The history of philosophy treats of the attempts which have been made by individual thinkers to discuss the ultimate problems of knowledge and of life. It will be a result of no small importance, therefore, if we can show clearly what are the problems with which philosophy deals, how these problems have presented themselves at different times, and what, in each case, were the conditions which determined the different statements of the problems, and the attempts at their solution. If such a result can be approximately attained, the study of the history of philosophy will be of no small importance for the future development of philosophy itself.

The investigation of the History of Modern Philosophy which I have here undertaken has confirmed me personally in the view to which I had already been led by other routes ; viz. that philosophical investigation centres in four main problems.   It may perhaps conduce to the better understanding of my book if these four problems are here briefly characterised.

1. THE PROBLEM OF KNOWLEDGE (the *logical* problem). However different the different sciences may be with regard to subject-matter and method, yet they all work by means of human thought.   Every time that they form a concept, pronounce a judgment, or draw a conclusion, they presuppose the general forms and principles of thought.   Hence the possibility of a special discipline which shall investigate the forms under which thought works, and the principles which must, from its nature, underlie it, whatever be the subject with which it is concerned. This discipline, *i.e. formal logic*, treats, however, of a part only of the problem of knowledge.   These forms and principles do not lead out beyond thought itself, but only enable it to be in harmony with itself,—to be consistent.   Every time that they are applied to given phenomena, which our thought has not itself constructed, but must take as they come, the question arises : with what right does this application take place ?—with what right do we assume that not only our thought, but also existence itself, as it expresses itself in the given phenomena, is consistent, is in harmony with itself?   Thus arises the possibility of a discipline which shall investigate the conditions for a knowledge of existence, and the limits of such a knowledge. This discipline is the *theory of knowledge.*

2. THE PROBLEM OF EXISTENCE (the *cosmological* problem) arises with the question as to what nature we must, when we deduce the consequences of everything we know, or which we can, by means of the most probable hypotheses, suppose, attribute to that existence of which we ourselves are members.   We call this the cosmological (from *cosmos*, world, and *logos*, doctrine) problem, because it leads to the discussion of the possibilities which display themselves to thought when it seeks to work up the data of experience into one general conception of the world, or, by bold speculations, to construct such a conception.   The different philosophical systems are attempts in this direction.   Their value depends upon the comprehensiveness and significance of the experience upon which they are based, and the consistency and power of combination displayed in their construction.

3. THE PROBLEM OF THE ESTIMATION OF WORTH (the *ethico-religious* question) arises because our attitude towards existence is not merely that of perceiving and understanding; it excites our feeling so that we express judgments assigning or denying it worth. Of especial significance are the judgments which we pass on human actions, our own as well as those of other men. All such judgments, like all knowing and understanding, rest on certain presuppositions, the proof and determination of which must be investigated. This is the task of ethical inquiry. If the estimation concern not only human actions and institutions, but also existence,—life as a totality,—the religious problem arises, leading to the discussion of the relation between the ethical ideal and actual existence, so that the ethical problem becomes combined with the cosmological.

4. THE PROBLEM OF CONSCIOUSNESS (the *psychological* problem). It is evident with regard to the three problems already indicated that their treatment presupposes empirical knowledge of the life of human consciousness. Psychology describes the *actual* development of human knowledge, which must be known before we can discuss the *validity* of knowledge. And since the relation between the mental and the material is one of the chief features of the problem of existence, psychology is also presupposed in cosmology. Finally, as regards the problem of the estimation of worth, psychology investigates the nature of those very feelings which lead to the setting up of a standard of worth, and also the possibilities offered by actual conscious life for further development in the direction demanded by the ethical ideal. In consequence of this close relation to the problems of philosophy, psychology must itself be regarded as a part of philosophy, and conversely, we shall have to touch upon philosophical problems in psychology. (See my *Psychology*.[1]) And if the three first problems were to be declared insoluble, or to have arisen through a misunderstanding, yet the psychological problem, the question as to the nature and laws of the life of consciousness, would remain as the last fortress of philosophy.

If it be asked what, according to the nature of the case, are the factors which influence the treatment and resolution of these problems, the first to be mentioned is the personality of

---

[1] English translation, pp. 14, 27, 54 f., 209 f., 259 f.

the philosopher. It is common to all the above-mentioned problems that they lie on the borders of our knowledge, where the exact methods can no longer help us ; hence it is impossible but that the personality of the inquirer should determine the course of his thought, although he himself may not be aware of the fact. The " personal equation " must be of greater significance in philosophy than in any other department of science. The historical and comparative method, therefore, becomes of especial value here ; by its means the personal element can most easily be detected. This personal element is not always to be put aside ; its presence is often a condition for the arising of a problem. There are thoughts which can only spring up on a particular psychological soil. Secondly, it will depend on what observations are taken as a basis. In this respect the development of natural science has been of the greatest importance for modern philosophy. As we shall see, the leading problems of modern philosophy are determined precisely by the fact that modern natural science has arisen. We must also take account, especially with regard to the problem of the estimation of worth, of historical circumstances, and intellectual movements within other spheres. Lastly, the establishment and solution of problems is determined by the consistency with which initial assumptions are laid down, and maintained.

Both the characterisation, as well as the criticism, of every philosophical essay will always turn on these three points. In the following exposition I attach most weight to the two former. An inconsequence in a great thinker is often nothing but the natural consequence of the fact that his genius displays itself in *several* lines of thought, although he may not himself have been able to follow these out far enough to discover their mutual contradiction. And it may be of the first importance that these different lines of thought should be developed. Best of all is it, of course, when depth of thought and logical consistency are united.

The attempt to establish or to solve a problem may be of twofold interest. Firstly, it may be regarded as a symptom, as the historical expression of intellectual currents. Regarded from this side, the History of Philosophy forms a part of the general history of culture. Secondly, it may be investigated with regard to the actual, definitive, clearness of the results attained. This point of view is more especially philosophical and technical. The relation between the two sides from which philosophical phenomena may be regarded varies widely, of course, in respect to different phenomena. Sometimes, indeed, the interest from the point of view of the history of culture may vary inversely with the strictly philosophic interest.

If I now briefly indicate in what my representation of the Philosophy of Modern Times differs from that of its predecessor in Danish literature,—the work of BRÖCHNER, which appeared twenty years ago,—I should name first the especial value which I attribute to the personal factor, and to the relation to empirical science, also to the importance of philosophical phenomena for the History of Culture. Further, I should point to my endeavour to give the first place to the *raising* of problems rather than to their solution. The solutions may perish while the problems live on ; were it otherwise, philosophy would never have had as long a life as that on which it can already look back. Lastly, it is obvious that a fresh study of sources, as well as the realisation of the riches of the literature of the last twenty years, must have shed a new light on many phenomena. In spite of all this, it has been no small pleasure to me to think that, in this work, I have been carrying on Bröchner's labours within the sphere of the History of Philosophy, and I trust that my book will not be found unworthy to be dedicated to the memory of this noble inquirer, whose admiration for the heroes of thought was so deep and, at the same time, so intelligent.

BOOK I

THE PHILOSOPHY OF THE RENAISSANCE

B

CHAPTER I

THE RENAISSANCE AND THE MIDDLE AGES

THAT period of the intellectual life of Europe which is known as the age of the Renaissance is characterised, on the one hand, by the breach with the shackled, disconnected, and limited conception of life of the Middle Ages, and on the other, by the extension of view to new spheres and the unfolding of new powers. Every birth includes two moments: the breaking loose from the old and the development of the new life. But that both sides of the transition to a new epoch should be represented in such a high degree as is here the case is certainly unique in the history of human intellect. In other periods of transition it is usually either negative criticism or fresh and positive fulness that acquires an overwhelming predominance. But the main characteristic of the Renaissance, in this respect, is that it is the new life which essentially involves the criticism of the old. This is the secret of its health and power. It laid the foundation of a new, free, and human conception of Nature and of human life, of which it itself could only indicate the leading features. The working-out in detail of this conception has furnished problems sufficient to occupy the thought and prompt the inquiry of centuries, although the leading features themselves have undergone no essential modification. Every attempt, therefore, to explore by means of the guidance of history the great problems of practice and of theory must start from this age, which possesses the freshness and force of a revolution, and which comprehends within it riches, dimly apprehended it is true, but of which more specialised investigation can often grasp one side only.

Before we enter upon the task of sketching the Philosophy

of the Renaissance as we find it represented in its most important thinkers, we must cast a backward glance at the Middle Ages, from which it had to cut itself loose.

It would be erroneous to regard the Middle Ages as an age of utter darkness. Not only did there unfold, within as well as without the official rule of the Church, a cheerful and natural national life which has left a memorial behind it in the revivification of national literatures, but, within the world of learning itself, it would be extremely difficult to draw any clear line of demarcation between the Middle Ages and the time of the Renaissance. In the Romance countries especially, and in Italy first and foremost, the connection with antiquity was never, strictly speaking, entirely sundered. The justification for speaking of the Renaissance as a separate period, however, is to be found in this : that a time came when the knowledge of Nature and of human life became so rich in content that it could no longer be comprehended within the limits of theological ideas. But definitely to assign the time of even this stage of development would be no easy matter. This difficulty does not affect us here more closely however, since our task is limited to the exposition of the philosophy which took shape towards the end of the Renaissance, *i.e.* in the course of the sixteenth century ; and we can therefore afford to disregard the germination and swelling of the bud, the interest of which, moreover, belongs rather to the History of Literature than to Philosophy.

Even were we to disregard the subsequent development of those germs which are contained within the intellectual life of the Middle Ages, and to restrict ourselves to the classical expression of the mediæval line of thought, we should find that the Middle Ages has rendered important contributions to intellectual development and was by no means the wilderness or the world of darkness which it is so often depicted as being. It deepened intellectual life, and sharpened and exercised its powers in no inconsiderable degree, and it certainly yields to no other period in the energy with which it used the means of culture which lay at its disposal, limited as these were by the historical circumstances of the time. In later and more favoured periods, commanding a rich wealth of content, we shall look in vain for as great a power in elaborating and closely appropriating these riches as was dedicated by the Middle Ages to its scanty material. A few individual points in which mediæval thought displays especial excellences and has prepared the way for what was to come, may be mentioned here.

The thought of the Middle Ages was theological. The theology of a monotheistic religion is based on the fundamental thought that there is one single cause of all things. Apart from the grave difficulties which this thought involves, it has the important and valuable effect of accustoming men to abstract from differences and details and of preparing them for the acceptance of an interconnection of all things according to law. The unity of the cause must correspond to the unity of the law. The Middle Ages educated men to this thought, to which the natural man, overpowered by the manifoldness of phenomena and inclined to polytheism, does not feel himself drawn. It denotes, at the same time, a preparation for a conception of the world determined by science. For all science strives to reduce phenomena to as few principles as possible, even if it must admit that the thought of one single highest law is an unattainable ideal.

For the carrying out of its ideas in detail the Middle Ages, as we have already stated, had at its disposal a miserably inadequate material. All the greater was the labour which it applied to the task. The poverty of realities must be filled up by the richness of formalities. Thought developed a formal acuteness, a skill in drawing distinctions and building up arguments, which is altogether without parallel. We may wish this skill had been better applied, but skill it was nevertheless, and its significance for intellectual development was great. It perfected organs which, in more favourable circumstances, were able to function. It was bound, in the long run, to lead to the critical investigation of precisely those presuppositions which had long been regarded as a fixed foundation, and on the examination of which no one had been bold enough to venture.

The greatest merit of the Middle Ages lies in its absorption in the inner world of the life of the soul. Classical antiquity had paused at the harmonious relation between the inner and the outer, and its interest in the inner life was limited to its relation to outer life in Nature and the State. To the faith of the Middle Ages the eternal fate of the personality was determined by the events of the inner life. Whether the growth of the soul attained sufficient development was a question of life or death. No wonder that a fine and deep sense of the inner life developed.   The self-absorption of the mystic was as important for the development of the psychological sense as the distinctions and argumentations of the schoolmen for that of the logical sense.   It dawned upon men that the spiritual world is just as much a reality as the material world, and that in the former is Man's true home.   The way was prepared for a more thorough investigation of the great problem of spirit and matter than was possible to antiquity.   Above all things, however, a sphere of experience was won for human life which was, in the strictest sense, its own property, into which no external powers could penetrate.   And this involved the possibility of a still deeper spiritual deliverance.

Nevertheless it was the great misfortune of the Middle Ages that none of these motives, in and for themselves free and fruitful, could work freely and fruitfully.   There lies in mediæval thought, as in its architecture, a striving after the great and the infinite, combined with an endeavour to introduce into its great thought-construction as, as it were, stones and pillars of support, all the elements of the world-knowledge which it possessed.   First, the world of Nature as depicted by Aristotle ; next, the world of grace which Christ had revealed to the world ; and highest of all, the prospect of the eternal world of glory.   The ideal was a harmonious, ascending series of *natura, gratia*, and *gloria*, such that the higher spheres did not interrupt, but rather completed, the lower.   This striving finds its most perfect expression in THOMAS AQUINAS (1227-74), the consummator of Scholasticism, and one of the greatest systematisers who ever lived.   He inspired Dante, was canonised in the year 1323, was known in the theological schools of the Middle Ages as the *doctor angelicus*, and still stands as the classical thinker of the Roman Church, for the present Pope decreed, in the year 1879, that his philosophy was to be taken as the basis of the teaching in all Catholic academies. Magnificent as is the system which even now, in the eyes of many, comprehends all the elements of existence and throws light on their interconnection, it yet, from the first, displayed very material shortcomings.   The elements collected from so many different sides were only artificially united.   In order to unite the physical science, believed to have been collected together by Aristotle, with the supernatural presuppositions of the Church, it had partly to be transformed, partly hindered in the development of the consequences which followed from it as a whole. The philosophy of Aristotle was, in reality, calculated to display existence as an uninterrupted ascending scale. The fundamental concepts with which Aristotle operated were taken from the phenomena of organic life. He regarded Nature as a great process of development, within which the higher grades were related to the lower as form to matter or actuality to potentiality. What on the lower stages is only possible (potential) becomes real (actual) on the higher. Aristotle himself was not able to work out this significant conception. But there can be no doubt as to the direction in which its consequences tend. As an ecclesiastical thinker, however, Thomas Aquinas had to effect an entire breach with these consequences; to suppress the monism to which they led; and to set up a dualism in its stead. This is shown characteristically in his psychology and ethics. According to the Aristotelian psychology the soul is the " form " of the body : that which exists in the body as mere possibility appears in the life of the soul in full activity and reality. But such an intimate relation between soul and body conflicts with the presuppositions of the Church, and although Thomas follows Aristotle in the letter and calls the soul the " form " of the body, yet, in reality, he treats the soul as an altogether different being from the body, as also he has no scruple in assuming " forms " without matter—in order to make room for the angels ! A similar dualism appears in his ethics. He borrows from the Greeks a number of natural cardinal virtues, *e.g.* wisdom, justice, courage, and self-mastery ; but while, with the Greeks, these constitute the whole of virtue, he introduces, as a higher grade, the three " theological " virtues : faith, hope, and love, which arise only by supernatural means. Thus the development is interrupted ; and Thomas does not even inquire if the forms of will denoted by the theological virtues could not just as well find their place among the natural virtues, as especial forms of them. As regards the conception of the world in general, the idea of a natural development appeared in sharp antithesis to the dogma of the creation, and to the assumption of a miraculous intervention. A closer inspection reveals this dualism at one point after another. Such a close inspection, however, it was the business of mediæval thought to prevent. Thought *had* to agree with the doctrines of the Church. It dared not give the world any thought or intelligence independently of theology. And when once the conviction had become established that the Aristotelian philosophy was especially suited to represent natural science in the construction of the scholastic system, any deviation from Aristotle—from Aristotle as he was known and interpreted in the Middle Ages—attracted attention and was regarded as heresy. In other words : thought and inquiry were arbitrarily checked in order that the structure which had been raised might not be shaken. The Aristotelian philosophy, which in its own time denoted such an enormous advance, was now set up as valid for all eternity. Nor did the doctrine of organic life and the life of the soul suffer most by this, for it was within this sphere that Aristotle's real merit, even in his own lifetime, lay. But it hindered the development of an exact natural science which should be able to explain by means of what elementary processes and according to what general laws the development of forms, adopted from Aristotle, had been accomplished. The fault of the Aristotelian philosophy was that it set up organic growth as the type of everything which happens in Nature. The most it could do, therefore, was to describe forms and qualities, while it could offer no real explanation of their genesis. The mechanical conception of Nature, which is both the means as well as the goal attained of modern natural science, was thus from the first excluded. Men cut themselves off from the path to progress, even though they were not able, by the help of the means at their disposal, to overcome the difficulties they encountered. The principle of authority rejected a freer and further investigation of problems and established dualism as a permanent result. But the principle of authority is itself a form of dualism, since it presupposes an irreconcilable opposition between human knowledge and its goal. Men were bidden to nourish themselves on the scanty content they already had, and by means of artificial distinctions and argumentations to interpret this content as the Church wished. Small wonder that there arose a great hunger after fulness of content, and a great enthusiasm for the new riches streaming in from all sides in the century of the Renaissance !

This evil was also apparent within the sphere in which, during the Middle Ages, men were particularly absorbed. Their self-absorption was the result of religious anxiety. It was not allowed to develop into free knowledge of the spiritual world. The dogmatist ever held watch over the mystic, so often carried by the tides of his inner life beyond the limits of the feeling sanctioned by the Church as right and true. The Church could no more venture to give inner experience its own way than she could allow free play to outer experience. She saw that it was dangerous for men to withdraw into themselves and thus come into immediate contact with the highest, for so they might become independent of the Church. She suspected that self-knowledge, no less than knowledge of Nature, offered possibilities of spiritual freedom and opened the way to a very different conception of the world from that presented by theology. It was not only, however, the timid restriction to religious introspection which checked the development of inner experience. Here, too, dualism was at work hindering the recognition, both of the actual operation of laws within the inner sphere, as well as of a natural interconnection between the psychical and the physical. The life of the soul could not rightly be understood until a freer and more comprehensive conception of Nature had been developed.

The meaning of the Renaissance, then, is that it denotes the period during which the limitations and one-sidedness of the mediæval conception of life found themselves confronted with new experiences and new points of view. However different in kind may be the phenomena presented to us in the philosophy of the Renaissance, yet common to them all is a great enthusiasm for, and confidence in, Nature, and the effort to carry through a unifying conception of existence, and to assert the law-abidingness and authorisation of natural human life. The Renaissance begins with the latter point— with the assertion of the rights of human nature—and afterwards leads to the development of a new conception of Nature, and to a new method of investigation.

A. THE DISCOVERY OF MAN

CHAPTER II

HUMANISM

It was by no accident that Italy became at once the home of the Renaissance and the cradle of modern thought. It was in Italy chiefly that the connection with antiquity had been preserved, and when the literature of antiquity once more saw the light the Italians were able to make it their own in a quite special and independent manner, since it was the work of their own past, flesh of their flesh, and bone of their bone. The Italians envisaged the Greek literature,—which, in the fifteenth century, became once more the object of enthusiastic study,— with more understanding than the nations of Northern Europe. The great importance for the history of culture of this general return to the literature of antiquity,—to the study of antique history, philosophy, and poetry,—was that it revealed to men the existence, outside the pale of the Church, of a human intellectual life, following its own laws and possessing its own history. Thus the intellectual world became enlarged and a comparative study of human relations possible. We already find this comparative method applied by several thinkers of the Renaissance. The works of antiquity, moreover, served as models for the guidance of thought until it had learnt to work independently. Many germs of thought, which had started into life in antiquity and whose further growth had been checked in the Middle Ages—that age so unpropitious for free intellectual development—were now able to unfold. After its long, deep slumber thought sought to take up its work again where it had suspended it towards the end of the classical period.

But again, it was owing to the historical circumstances of Italy that a lively understanding and an independent appropriation of the literature of antiquity was possible. The partition into many small states which were the arenas of continual political struggles, during which, usually, no stone was left unturned which could lead to the attainment and maintenance of power, brought about the dissolution of the social order of the Middle Ages. In the Middle Ages man was valued according to his union with Church and Corporation. The natural man, with his purely individual, emotional life, was of no account, and was not regarded as authorised. The political struggles in the towns all around had now, in opposition to this, evolved in men a desire to realise, at all costs, their own personality ; a desire which could naturally only lead to productive consequences in the case of those who were fortunate enough to be in power. While, on the other hand, the ruling despotisms in the Italian states could not fail to deter many individuals from entering public life, and, since the need of realising their individuality was undeniably excited, to send such persons to the relations of private life, and to artistic and literary interests for the freest possible development of their personality. Burkhardt has well shown (in his work on the Culture of the Renaissance) how the propensity to individualism and the need of a purely personal development could not fail to arise, under the influence of the historical conditions in Italy in the fourteenth and fifteenth centuries. Thus it was not only the external discovery of the literature and art of antiquity which conditioned the Italian Renaissance. For, in that case, it would have been a purely scientific movement, a preponderately receptive process. The practical discovery of human nature offered, before all things, a sphere—for every individual the sphere closest to his hand—in which there was rich opportunity and good cause both to make experiences as well as to enter upon the task of development. That which the Middle Ages had only made possible in the form of religious mysticism was now carried further, and freed from bonds and limitations. The individual life of the soul was felt as a reality, and excited interest in and for itself, quite apart from anything to which it might be attached. It was a discovery of no less importance than the discovery of a new continent on our globe and of new worlds in the heavens. It was with the poets (Dante, Petrarch), of course, that the interest in their own *ego* and the occupation with this and with inner events appeared first and was expressed in the finest language.

Humanism denotes, then, not only a literary tendency, a school of philologists, but also a tendency of life, characterised by interest for the human, both as a subject of observation and as the foundation of action. Alike in literature and in life it is a tendency which displays very many varieties. The Church, for some time, showed itself favourably disposed towards the new movement, and humanistic interest even ruled for a time from the papal chair. It may be that in causing the Crusade to be preached Pius II. virtually saved civilisation. Now that Constantinople had fallen, Rome, according to his conviction, was the last refuge of literature, and he mourned the fall of the Greek Imperial city rather more, perhaps, from humanistic than from religious motives. Humanism is somewhat indefinite in character. It denotes the discovery of the human ; but how this humanity was to be conceived and its development to be promoted, was still veiled in obscurity. For some time it seemed as though the humane and the traditionary could exist peaceably side by side. The new wine, however, soon burst the old leather bottles.

We must now show how the thinkers of the time instituted, on the basis of practical interest for humanity, a series of attempts to conceive it theoretically also—to *understand* it. To this end we must give prominence to the attempts which were made to emancipate psychology and ethics from theology.

CHAPTER III

THE collective thought of the Middle Ages had rested indeed upon an antique foundation, since it was based upon Aristotle, whose ideas it had adapted in accordance with the demands of dogma. In opposition to this "Latin" interpretation of Aristotle, however, there were not only the old Greek commentators, who gave his doctrines a naturalistic interpretation, but also the Arabian commentators, of whom Averroës stood in the first rank, who interpreted it in a pantheistic spirit. On the question as to how far Aristotle teaches the immortality of the soul, these three groups of commentators are at variance. According to the Greek commentators, who were not thought much of in the Middle Ages, Aristotle taught a natural development of the soul from the lower to the higher grades, such, indeed, that even the highest grade is not independent of natural conditions. The Averroists, on the other hand, maintained that the highest form of thought is only possible through man's participation in the eternal reason ; this participation, however, lasts for a time only, and it is not individual souls as such which are immortal, but the universal reason in which each soul, in its highest acts of thought, becomes for the moment a participant. Against this, again, the theological Aristotelians, with Thomas Aquinas at their head, asserted that the immortality of the soul is a dogma founded in the capacity of the latter to recognise and to will the universal and eternal.

PIETRO POMPONAZZI discusses this much-disputed question in a remarkable little treatise (*De Immortalitate Animi*, 1516). This work has rightly been regarded as the introduction to the philosophy of the Renaissance. It merits this place on account of the manner in which it handles the problem. It professes, indeed, merely to inquire what Aristotle's meaning really was ; but at the same time it declares the author's intention to discuss the question by the light of natural reason, and independently of all authority. Pomponazzi was famous as a teacher of philosophy first in Padua and afterwards in Bologna. Little is known about his private circumstances. He was born in Mantua in 1462, and died at Bologna in 1525. He was a distinguished disputant and orator, although his writings are not distinguished by any particular literary merit.

Pomponazzi, in opposition both to Thomas and Averroès, emphasises Aristotle's teaching, contained in his physics, of a continuous development according to law, which permits no leaps nor the interpolation of any principles which do not necessarily follow from the previous course of development. He carries these thoughts still farther than his master Aristotle, who had taught that the highest activity of Reason (" the active reason ") could not be explained out of successive development. But how, in that case, it is to be conceived and explained, Aristotle has not told us, and it is this silence which occasioned conflicting interpretations. That even the highest thought cannot be independent of natural conditions, Pomponazzi proves through the axiom expressly laid down by Aristotle, that all thought presupposes ideas which, in the beginning, must have been given through sensuous perception. And he asserts that the Aristotelian definition of the soul as the " form " of the body, or as its perfect reality, makes it impossible for us to accept the independent existence of the soul.

But does not this result involve dangerous consequences within the sphere of ethics, since the prospect of reward or punishment after death is no longer a motive to the natural man ? Pomponazzi answers that, on the contrary, it is this prospect which is ethically dangerous, since it hinders men from doing good for its own sake. The full development of the nature of man within the different spheres finds its satisfaction in itself. And while scientific and æsthetic development is not granted to all in equal degree, there is one development from which none are excluded, *i.e.* ethical development. And this carries its end and value in itself. The reward of virtue is virtue itself, while the punishment of the vicious is vice. Whether, then, man is mortal or not, yet death is of little account, and whatever may be our condition after death we dare not turn away from following after the good.   These passages, which occur in the fourteenth chapter of the book, remind us, on the one hand, of the *Apology* of Socrates, while, on the other, they point forward to Spinoza's and Kant's conception of morality.   Several Humanists, it is true, had brought forward the notion of an independent ethic, but this idea becomes especially important with Pomponazzi on account of the connection with a special religious problem in which it appears.

The question of immortality is, according to Pomponazzi, an insoluble problem (*problema neutrum*) ; we might add in his spirit, neutral too in the sense that on its solution no real moral value depends.   But with such questions the important point is to decide how far our knowledge is able to reach.   It is evident that for Pomponazzi the chief interest of his inquiry is connected with the light that it throws on the nature of our knowledge.   The problem is only the occasion for this.   He draws a sharp distinction between the standpoint of the philosopher and that of the lawgiver.   The lawgiver is concerned to find motives which may induce men to walk uprightly ; and he may, perhaps, feel justified in availing himself of the belief in immortality as an educating motive ; but the philosopher has to seek after truth only, without letting himself be led astray either by fear or hope.   A similar opposition, Pomponazzi teaches, is to be found within the individual man. With his reason he seeks to draw right conclusions from certain given premises ; the results to which reason must arrive are independent of the will of Man.   But with his will he may hold fast to a faith for which his reason can afford him no grounds.   Pomponazzi distinguishes, that is to say, between faith and knowledge ; and he is therefore able, with regard to the final decision of the problem he is discussing, to bow to the teaching of the Church.   While two centuries earlier the Scholastic, Duns Scotus, had maintained that a thing may be true for the philosopher without being true for the theologian, Pomponazzi's view may be briefly summed up in the proposition that a thing may be true for the theologian without being true for the philosopher.   It has been remarked that, as a philosopher, he concluded with a *problema neutrum.*   But that is no reason for doubting that he was quite in earnest with his doctrine of faith and knowledge, or for supposing it to be irony or a mere subterfuge.[1] He comes before us as an inquiring nature, carrying on his investigations with all earnestness. He compares the philosopher with Prometheus, because, while he is endeavouring to pierce the divine mysteries, unquiet thoughts are ever gnawing at his heart. It may be that, with him, reason was more developed than the will which should bind him to faith; nevertheless he may have been quite in earnest in his endeavours to respect the claims of both. What we miss in him is a closer explanation of the connection between will and faith. He contents himself with pointing to the will as the foundation of faith without giving any further explanation, although such an explanation would have been of great interest.

Besides the work we have mentioned Pomponazzi wrote on magic, and strove to give a natural explanation of events which were generally accounted for as the effect of a supernatural intervention. This work is interesting on account of his endeavour to assert the principle of natural causes, even though the causes which he assigns would also, according to modern ideas, be reckoned as superstitions. For instance, it is to the influence of the stars that he chiefly looks, an influence which was not regarded by his age as supernatural. In a third work he discusses the problem of divine predestination and human will. With great acuteness he exposes the contradiction involved herein. As philosopher he appeals to that which experience has established,—to the reality of the human will; but the relation of this to the divine activity he leaves as an unsolved problem, for here too he avails himself of the distinction between faith and knowledge.

This distinction did not help him elsewhere. His works were burnt in Venice by order of the Inquisition, and had he not possessed a powerful protector in Cardinal Bembo, a friend of Pope Leo X., he would probably have shared the fate of his book.

At first sight it may appear strange to place Machiavelli and Pomponazzi side by side. The Florentine statesman seems to have no connection with the Scholastic of Bologna. And yet the common enemies of these two contemporary thinkers were not far wrong in thinking them chips of the same block. Both aimed, each in his own way, at effecting the re-birth of the antique faith in human nature. And both were strongly influenced by the writers of antiquity. Just as Pomponazzi sought to carry on the naturalistic psychology and ethic of Aristotle, so Machiavelli appears, on important points, to be under the influence of the Greek historian Polybius, who harks back in his turn to the elder Greek thinkers' conception of the course of the development of States. But it was Machiavelli's own observation of contemporary events in which he was himself involved, which evoked in him the need to go back to antiquity. NICOLO MACHIAVELLI was born at Florence in 1469, of an old and respected family who had known better days. While quite young, he entered the service of the Republican government of his native town as a diplomatist, and was sent as ambassador to Pope Julius II., Cesare Borgia, the Emperor Maximilian, and King Louis XII. This afforded him excellent opportunities for gaining experience of men and things. It was fatal for the development of his views that precisely during this period of Italian history, stratagem and intrigue, malice and cruelty, were the means by which political decisions were determined. In the introduction to the fifth book of his Florentine history he himself remarks of the history of Italy in the fifteenth century, that the rule of the Italian Princes could be praised neither for "grandeur nor courage, although their history in other respects may seem as considerable when we see how many noble and great people could be restrained by their arms, however weak and ill-managed." His experiences of life could not fail to lead Machiavelli to the conclusion that prudence and power are the only qualities necessary for a statesman. He does not appear to have been a distinguished politician himself; his greatness lay in the world of thought, not in that of action. And yet it was a great grief to him when he was forced to exchange the latter for the former sphere. When the Medici overthrew the free constitution of Florence (1512), Machiavelli was discharged, and it was during the many subsequent years, which were spent in compulsory privacy, that he composed his famous work. Had he met his political misfortunes with greater dignity, his literary works might, perhaps, have been conceived in a higher style. As it was, he composed the work which has brought him most fame, *i.e.* the Book of the Prince (*Il Principe*), with the deliberate intention of procuring the favour of the Medici.

He succeeded, no doubt, to a certain degree in attaining his end, but it cannot be denied that it tarnished his character, and that—with the political power of a single House always in view—he was led to attribute more importance to individual freedom and disregard of others in politics than he might perhaps otherwise have done. It often appears from his descriptions as if, in the last instance, the nature of the aim which the ruler set before him were a matter of indifference ; and, at all events, as if he regarded it as his duty to furnish instructions for the attainment of any ends which might be desired. This is apparent not only in the " Prince," but also in what is, properly speaking, his chief work, *i.e.* the *Discorsi*, treatises on the first decade of Livy. The founder of a Republic must adopt such and such measures, of a Monarchy such and such, of a Tyranny such and such. And yet it is certain that there was *one* end which Machiavelli had at heart, and around which his innermost thoughts centred, both while carrying on his political intrigues as well as while writing his famous work ; this was the unity and greatness of Italy. Certain, too, is it that, personally, he was always a Republican ; this is evident from his advice to the Medici on the subject of the Florentine constitution. And finally ;—there hovered ever before him an ideal of human health, power, and wisdom, which was to raise men high above the wretchedness with which he felt himself surrounded, and the blight which the mediæval Church had inflicted on human nature. It was at this point that he himself turned back to antiquity, and demanded of others that they should imitate it. Although he himself was a poet and lived. amongst poets, and although he had a good deal of the unbridled man of pleasure about him, yet the æsthetic Renaissance did not suffice him any more than did the gospel of pleasure appear to him the highest. It was a Renaissance of power and of greatness that he demanded. " When I consider," he says (in the introduction to book i. of the *Discorsi*), " what veneration is shown to antiquity, how often it happens (to omit other instances) that an immense price is given by the curious for a fragment of an old statue, either to adorn their cabinets, or to serve as a model for statuaries to copy after in works of that kind ; and what pains those artists take to come up to their pattern ; on the other hand, when I observe that the great and illustrious examples of several ancient kingdoms and republics which are recorded in history, that the noble deeds of former kings, generals, citizens, legislators, and others who have consecrated their labours to the service and glory of their country, are now rather admired than imitated, and indeed, so far from being followed by any one, that almost everybody is indifferent about them to such a degree, that there seem to be hardly any traces left amongst us of the virtue of the ancients, I cannot help being both surprised and concerned at it."

In his highest ideas he is akin to the great spirit which reveals itself in Michael Angelo's finest works. But it was the tragedy of his fate that great ends had so often to yield to multiplicity of means. He was possessed to such a degree by the thought that it was of no use to have an end, however noble, without the means necessary to attain it, that he finally forgot the end in the means, or omitted to inquire whether the means which he admired were calculated, in the long run, to promote the great ends which, there can be no doubt, he always regarded as the highest. He was so disheartened by the power of the means that he ended by attributing value to them, in and for themselves, and apart from the end which was to consecrate them. Like a true child of the Renaissance, he admired the development of power in and for itself, regardless of the direction in which this power might work. Although there are utterances of his against a purely æsthetic Renaissance, yet he himself introduced it within a sphere where everything depends on the determination of power by ends. The contradiction on this point which appears in his writings, more especially in the " Prince," has often caused him to be quite misjudged. And this same contradiction was the fate—not to say the fault—of his life. When the Medici were driven out again, after the taking of Rome by the Imperial troops in 1527, his countrymen would not accept his services on the restoration of the free constitution, for they regarded him as a renegade. This embittered the last year of his life. A contemporary—who cannot be accused of partiality—said of him after his death : " I believe his own position pained him ; for at heart he loved freedom even more than most men. But it tormented him to think that he had compromised himself with Pope Clement." He died in 1527.

There is a constant under-current of comparison between

ancient and Christian morals running through all Machiavelli's works. In the *Discorsi* he set himself the task of comparing ancient with modern events, but even where such a comparison is not expressly stated it may be traced in his conceptions and manner of statement. He will not be content with narrating and describing ; he seeks at the same time to discover the causes of the difference between the old and the new, and he cannot do this without reverting to the great contrast between the ancient and the mediæval conceptions of life. Hence Machiavelli is to be regarded as the most strongly marked and conscious representative of the opposition to mediævalism.

In the Middle Ages it was regarded as the duty of the State to help men to the attainment of their highest goal— blessedness in the world to come. The Prince, if not immediately, yet certainly indirectly,—especially since on him devolved the charge of maintaining peace,—was supposed to assist in this. This is the line taken in Thomas Aquinas' conception of the State. Machiavelli, on the contrary, regards the national State as possessing its end in itself. In its health and strength at home, and its power and extension abroad, everything is summed up. And he is thinking, not of an ideal State, but of definite, actually given States. " But since it is my object," he says (*Il Principe*, cap. xv.), " to write what shall be useful to whoever understands it, it seems to me better to follow the real truth of things than an imaginary view of them. For many Republics and Princedoms have been imagined which were never seen or known to exist in reality. And the manner in which we live, and that in which we ought to live, are things so wide asunder, that he who quits the one to betake himself to the other is more likely to destroy than to save himself; since he who proposes to himself to act up to a perfect standard of goodness among all men alike must be ruined among so many who are not good. It is necessary, therefore, for a Prince who desires to maintain his position to use or not to use his goodness as occasion may require."

And in agreement with the above we find the following passage in the treatise on Livy : " When the entire safety of our country is at stake, no consideration of what is just or unjust, merciful or cruel, praiseworthy or shameful, must intervene. On the contrary, every other consideration being set aside, that course alone must be taken which preserves the existence of the country and maintains its liberty." He who cannot thus rid himself of the current notions of morality must live the life of a private individual, and not venture to become a ruler (i. 26).

It is not quite clear whether Machiavelli considers the justice and love of honour, which in certain cases hinder the requisite political action, to be real or imaginary virtues. In isolated passages (e.g. *Il Principe*, cap. viii.) he speaks of attributes which appear to be virtues, although they may bring about the destruction of princes. He does not enter any further into the great problem which here presents itself as to the relation between the ethic of the private citizen and that of the states-man. Is there a difference in principle here between two kinds of virtue? or is it not rather a misnomer to call an attribute which hindered the whole group under consideration from attaining some good, a virtue? Machiavelli is here guilty of an ambiguity of which several modern declaimers against "morals" are not free. It appears as though he would transcend the opposition between good and evil, and yet he is only aiming at a new determination of worth, *i.e.* at a new application of the concepts of good and evil. His new determination of worth, however, as we have already pointed out, remains uncertain, since the relation of the power to the end which it is to subserve is not clear. His æsthetic admiration of the development of power, regardless of all else, crowds out the thought of the end which consecrates it. He blames men because they display no energy, either for good or evil: they do not fear small sins, but they shrink back before crimes on a grand scale "whose magnitude would have blotted out the shame." In the year 1505 Pope Julius II., accom-panied by his cardinals, but without an army, ventured into Perugia for the purpose of deposing Baglioni, the despot of that town. It was certainly no moral consideration that deterred Baglioni from making use of the opportunity to over-power the rash Pope and thus, at one stroke, to free himself from his deadly enemy; to win great riches; and to teach the Princes of the Church a wholesome lesson for the future; for Baglioni was a man who did not shrink from incest and the murder of near relatives. "The inference to be drawn was that men know not how to be splendidly wicked or wholly good, and shrink in consequence from such crimes as are stamped with an inherent greatness or disclose a nobility of nature" (*Discorsi*, i. 27).

Machiavelli, then, attacks the mean, the feeble, and the fearful, and this is the real subject of the blame which he metes out to his contemporaries, as may be seen from his Florentine history. When he asks why men have so declined from the greatness of antiquity, he finds the reason to lie in their education, the effects of which are debilitation and despondency ; while education, again, is closely bound up with religion. The ancients loved honour, greatness of mind, physical strength, and health ; and the ancient religions invested the mortals who had earned renown as great generals, heroes, or lawgivers, with divine authority. Their religious ceremonies were splendid, and were often combined with bloody sacrifices which must necessarily have fostered in men's hearts a disposition to fierceness. Our religion, on the contrary, transfers the highest goal to another world, and teaches us to despise the honour of this world. It glorifies humility and self-denial, and places the quiet life of contemplation higher than the practical life, occupied with external matters. If it demand strength of us, it is rather the strength to suffer than to do. This morality has made men weak and has given over the world to reckless and violent men, who have discovered that most men are inclined, in the hope of Paradise, rather to endure than to resent offences (*Discorsi*, ii. 2). Machiavelli adds, it is true, that human cowardice is due to a false interpretation of Christianity ; but he can hardly have meant, by these words, to take back his whole comparison of ancient with Christian morality, and to which side his own sympathies leaned is clear enough. Religion is for him essentially a means in the hand of the lawgiver, to whom it is indispensable as a prop to the law. The wise man foresees much that the multitude do not anticipate and would not believe, and then the gods must be invoked to sanction the necessary laws. The history of Lycurgus and Solon attests the truth of this, and Savonarola gained his great influence over his countrymen because, rightly or wrongly, they believed that he held immediate intercourse with God. Religion is a firm foundation, especially conducive to the preservation of unity and the good customs of a nation. Numa's religious institutions played an essential part in founding the power and greatness of the Roman kingdom, and every wise prince must protect the national religion, even if, personally, he regard it as a delusion (*Discorsi*, i. 11, 12).

Machiavelli has no feeling for religion as a spiritual power, which unfolds itself according to its own necessary laws and which, therefore, does not always stand at the summary disposal of politics. He relies altogether too much on shrewd calculations, arbitrary interventions, and uniformity of circumstances, and overlooks the fact that all that is greatest in history has frequently appeared like a stream suddenly bursting forth from hitherto invisible sources. To be sure, he himself lays stress on the multitude of great and unpredictable events which his age experienced, and which might conduce to the belief that "God and Fate" rule all things. But yet he does not mean that the human will is powerless. Against a rising flood nothing, perhaps, can be done at the moment ; but when the storm is over we can dig canals and construct dykes, so that next time results may be less disastrous. Fate, that is to say, prevails where it finds itself confronted with no opposition (*Il Principe*, cap. xxv.). But he here places the involuntary in an altogether too external connection with the voluntary. A statesman standing completely outside great spiritual currents would hardly be likely to possess an understanding of them sufficient to guide him in the right construction of canals and dykes. Machiavelli lays great weight on the necessity that institutions and forms of government—religious as well as political—should from time to time be regenerated by a "return to first principles." With the lapse of time come additions and modifications which may tamper with the real source of their power. It is then that we must remember how they began and in what they originated. The occasion thereto may be afforded either by external misfortunes, as at the time when Rome was re-born after the Gallic war ; or by fixed institutions, such as the Roman tribunes and censors ; or by leaders among men whose personalities serve as examples for others, as when St. Francis and St. Dominic once more held up before men's eyes the original Christian exemplar, and thus saved the Church from the destruction with which it was threatened (*Discorsi*, iii. 1). This is one of Machiavelli's most brilliant ideas. But, at the same time, it exhibits the limitations of the wisdom which he believed himself able to systematise. The most important of all the events which he experienced was a renewal of this kind, *i.e.* according to original principles, within the sphere of religion : a renewal, however, which was no mere repetition. The course of spiritual development was turned into new channels by the Reformation, and no politician, who regarded it merely as a means, without possessing any deeper understanding of its value, was in a position to exercise lasting influence on the course of events. That by means of the " renewal " entirely new forces could be called into action, he would not understand. Speaking generally, Machiavelli was lacking in the discernment of hidden causes. Not only inner religiosity but also many other sides of life escaped his attention. The development of practical interests—of trade and commerce, mechanics and agriculture—and the way in which these interests and the new social stratification which they represented had grown strong enough to take an essential part in determining the politics of modern times,—all this escaped him, dominated and blinded as he was by his formal conception of politics as a play of intrigue and a struggle for power. His politics swam in the air because they were not bound up with the great ideas by means of which the creative forces ever at work find expression. Like so many realists he lost reality because he sought for it on the surface of events.

It was quite natural that, in his efforts to understand history, Machiavelli should dwell on the causes which he discerned or believed himself to discern. Just so Pomponazzi had to content himself with astrological explanations in his criticism of superstition. Both deserve credit for having asserted the principle of natural causes. They struck out a path and made it possible for their successors to follow it further. As regards Machiavelli in particular, he stands as the founder, not only of the scientific politics of modern times, but also of comparative ethics. He indicated the main features, and it was laid on later times, while avoiding the rocks on which he was dashed to pieces, to carry them out in detail.

Shortly after the death of Pomponazzi and Machiavelli, free intellectual life in Italy received its death-blow. The turning-point came when Florence lost her liberty for the second time (1530). A powerful reaction set in, and the Inquisition was reorganised in order to oppose the Protestant movement.   Exile or martyrdom now fell to the lot of those Italians whose religious or scientific views led them into new paths.   And yet, as we shall see later, it was precisely during this period that the new world-conception and the new scientific method—Italy's greatest contribution to the intellectual development of modern times—were developed by Italian thinkers.   We will first trace the conception of Man, and we shall have to dwell on several significant phenomena which show how the fundamental notions of the Renaissance operated outside Italy.

CHAPTER IV

MICHEL DE MONTAIGNE AND PIERRE CHARRON

No other thinker of that time exhibits the different aspects of the Renaissance as clearly and completely as MONTAIGNE. In the first place, he possessed that decided individuality which was developed in France in the sixteenth century, no less than in Italy in the preceding century, by political struggles and religious controversies, of which the latter especially affected Montaigne, since he was an eye-witness of them. Moreover, the France of the sixteenth century had a Humanism of its own. Montaigne was born in Southern France (1533) of a noble family; he received a careful and liberal education travelled in Italy, and afterwards lived, for the most part, on his own estate, in enjoyment of freedom and the pursuit of his studies, for he took good care not to become entangled in the political and religious movements of his day, which he watched unfolding before him like a drama.

His reason for thus holding himself aloof was certainly not merely because observation of the many factions and changes of opinion had bred in him a spirit of scepticism; its chief cause lay in his own personality, which he wished to preserve unchanged. This was the most important object of his studies. His *Essais* (of which the first two books appeared in 1580 and the third in 1588) are intensely personal, in content as well as in form. " I study myself more than any other subject," he says (iii. 13); "it is my supernatural Metaphysics, it is my Natural Philosophy." The book contains full particulars also of his interests, studies, habits and manner of life. It is written in free form without any systematic plan. Thinking is to him a kind of game or pastime; he lets his thoughts have free course and gives them to his readers disconnected and unclassified, as he himself received them. He explains at once in the preface that he only intends to write about himself (*je suis moy mesme la matière de mon livre*), and, if use and wont had allowed, he would willingly have given a still more detailed report of himself. In the third book of the *Essais* he goes further in this direction than in the first two, appealing to the greater freedom permitted to age. This occupation with the *ego*, in which a man gives himself up to his own thoughts and is wrapped in his own moods, is a modern trait ; it denotes that the individual is freed from traditionary assumptions and, regardless of any authority, can resign himself quietly to the currents of his own nature and let himself be guided by them.

Remarkable also is his extensive reading, especially in the literature of antiquity. His works abound in quotations, and he brings forward an enormous number of characteristic traits in elucidation of human opinions, feelings, and impulses. He employed the comparative method within the intellectual sphere still more extensively than Machiavelli, and not merely, as has often been believed, in order to draw sceptical conclusions from the multifariousness of the characters, views, and tendencies thus brought to light. He is interested in individual *nuances* while, at the same time, he feels the joy of the Humanist over the richness of his material. What fascinates him is the vision of the immeasurable world of intellectual phenomena, not merely the inner differences or conflicts which may exist within it.

His individualism, it is true, no less than his Humanism, must have rendered him antagonistic to every attempt to enforce dogmatically any one general doctrine. He attacks (see especially ii. 12) theological as well as philosophical dogmatism. If we were really in earnest with our faith in the supernatural, he says to the orthodox, — "if this ray of Divinity did in any sort touch us,"—our life would appear quite different. All its relations would be transformed in obedience to the divine commands, and religious wars, with their ignoble passions, would not be able to set us at enmity one with another. We are guided not so much by the divine powers as by custom and tradition, where indeed it is not our passions which determine our faith. In the religious wars God's cause alone would hardly be able to raise a single company. And, even in the absence of these modifying influences, it is evident that our faculty of framing ideas is not able to conceive anything lying beyond the limitations of our own nature. We can think our own qualities either augmented or diminished, but transcend them we cannot. Moreover, every being's chief interest is in himself—in his own peculiar nature. Hence we conceive the Deity in the form of man and believe that everything in the world is done for the benefit of men. But would not animals reason similarly from their nature? He who believes he knows anything of God, inevitably drags Him into the depths. Among all human conceptions of religion that one appears the most probable which recognises God to be an incomprehensible power, the author and preserver of all things, who is only goodness and perfection and who graciously accepts the homage which men pay Him, whatever be the form under which they conceive Him, and in whatever way they attest their veneration.

This refutation of orthodox assertions, however, affords no ground for boasting of human reason. Man is at once the most miserable and the proudest of all creatures. Pride is his congenital malady. He feels himself exalted high above the rest of creation, and yet the distance between him and the brutes is not so great as he believes (which Montaigne tries to prove by a detailed account of the traits which testify to the understanding and feeling of animals). He has no reason for singling himself out from the host of created beings. His knowledge is in evil case. The senses are uncertain and erring. We can never be sure that they teach us the truth. They only show us the world as modified by their nature and condition. Not external objects, but merely the condition of the sense-organs appears to us in sensuous perception (*les sens ne comprennent pas le subject estrangier, ains seulement leurs propres passions*).

In order to be able to place implicit confidence in the senses we must possess an instrument that can control them and then, again, a means of controlling this instrument, and so on *ad infinitum*. Reason, too, leads us to no final decision : every reason adduced in support of an argument itself, in turn requires a reason, and so again we could go on *ad infinitum* Add to this that both we ourselves, as well as our objects, are continually changing and shifting, that there is nothing fixed and invariable. And the wealth of differences is so great that the attempt to establish general laws or types is hopeless.   No law can exhaust the manifoldness of cases.   The more searching our examination, the more differences we shall discover. And in the attempt to bring the discovered differences under common points of view, we shall find that they stand in inner contradiction to one another, so that the comparison can lead to no result.   Continual modifications and wide differences are, in like manner, to be found within the sphere of moral and civil laws.   No natural law can be pointed out which is observed by all men.   Morals change according to time and place.   What kind of goodness is that which passed current yesterday but will not do so to-morrow, and which becomes a crime when we cross the river?   Can Truth be bounded by the hills, so that on the other side of them she becomes a lie? Doubt is thus our last resort.   But even doubt must not be regarded as definitely valid.   We dare not say that we know nothing.   Our result is : *what do I know ?*

This whole line of thought has often been counted to Montaigne for scepticism, because it has been regarded as his last word.   Such was the view of him taken by Pascal.   But it does not touch the fundamental principle of Montaigne's conception of life, the point on which for him everything finally turns and which enabled him to indicate a complete conception of the world.   Montaigne was certainly too much of a *causeur* to develop his world-conception in a purely philosophical form.   His last word, however, is not the bewildering difference of phenomena, not scepticism, not even individualism. Behind all things he descries an infinite background,—the idea of Nature in her grandeur and infinity, from whom the fulness of things flows and whose power blossoms forth in a peculiar manner in every individual creature.[2]

Thus Montaigne not only refutes puffed-up knowledge, but he even goes so far as to praise ignorance, because it gives Nature free play and does not hinder, by reflection and art, " our great and powerful mother, Nature, from guiding us."   By ignorance, however, he understands, not uncultured and thoughtless vacuity, but the ignorance which arises from an understanding of the limitations of our knowledge.   Only by knocking at a door can we convince ourselves that it is shut—not merely by standing passively before it.   Only for " a good head " (*une teste bien faiste*) is ignorance a good and healthy pillow.   In

large as well as in small matters, the concept of Nature had
significance for Montaigne.   Is it, *e.g.*, a question of illness ;
then he will know nothing of physicians, for they only squander
Nature and hinder her proper development.   Like every other
being, each illness has its appointed time of development and
close ;—interference is futile.   We must let Nature do as she
pleases ; she understands the matter better than we.   We must
submit to the order of Nature.   Like the harmony of the
world, our life is made up of opposites, of different tones, which
all—illness and death, as well as health and life—belong to
the great whole.   Is he speaking of education ; there, too, the
great thing is to let Nature have free course.   The imparting
of knowledge ought only to be the means to the development of
feeling and character, and experience of life is the best school of
self-mastery.   He virtually recants his scepticism when he gets
to the concept of Nature.   The only way, he says, in which men
can guard themselves from measuring things with a false
measure is by keeping before them " our mother Nature in all
her majesty " : she shows us a general and continual variety, in
which we discover ourselves and all that we call great to be but
a vanishing point.[8]   This will hinder us from setting arbitrary
and narrow limits.   Thus tolerance arises.   As we have seen,
Montaigne's final result with regard to religion is that the unknown Deity is worshipped by different nations under as many
different forms.   And on this reflection Montaigne founds his
conservatism.   " I have little patience with what is new," he says,
" under whatever form it may occur.   Not because existing laws
are always reasonable.   The validity of laws rests not on their
righteousness, but on the fact that they are laws : *c'est le
fondement mystique de leur auctorité !*   Custom is the mistress
of the world.   Conscience feels bound to that which it has
been accustomed to respect, and cannot part from it without
pain.   The wise man must, indeed, free his soul within, but in
external matters he must observe existing laws and customs.
To undertake to replace them by anything better is foolish presumption."   Although Montaigne does not say so in so many
words, yet it seems to be implied in his thought that Nature
reveals herself through that which has become use and wont,
and thus his conservatism is a part of his faith in Nature,
although, according to Montaigne's own view, the new must be
every bit as " natural " as the old.

In this concept of Nature the first characteristic of Montaigne which we noticed, *i.e.* his individualism, is founded. If every man will listen carefully enough to the events going on within him (*s'il s'écoute*) he will discover a nature and way peculiar to himself, a ruling character (*forme sienne, forme maitresse, forme universelle*) which offers resistance to external influences and keeps him from incompatible emotions. This character is in its innermost essence unchangeable. I may wish myself another " form "; may detest and condemn that which I possess. But that which is rooted deepest in my nature cannot really be repented of, for repentance only concerns that which can be changed. By means of this "ruling form " Nature speaks within each one of us—although to each in a different way, so that every man must be judged according to his own norm. Thus Montaigne preserves the rights both of the nature of the particular individual and of that of the great whole. While the Church demands an absolute regeneration, he maintains that a complete transformation is impossible. He disputes the reality of repentance if it involve such a transformation. Repentance is only possible where there is an inner principle which may be violated through the clear and complete picture of the evil deed which has been perpetrated. While reason alleviates all other care and sorrow, she begets the pain of repentance ; and this is the severest of all pains because it arises within us, just as the heat or cold of fever is more penetrating than any which comes from without. Similarly, we feel inner satisfaction and a noble pride when we do good and have a good conscience. To base the reward of good actions on the applause of others is to build on altogether too unsure a foundation, thinks Montaigne ; especially in such times as his own, where to enjoy the favour of the many was a bad sign. Every one must have an inner touchstone (*un patron au dedans*) by which to judge his actions.—" Only thou thyself canst judge thy actions. Others see not so much thy nature as thine art."—Even our neighbours judge our actions differently from strangers. By means of the greater insight into our nature which they possess, they are able, perhaps, to discover that our brilliant external actions are only fine jets of water springing up out of a swampy ground. We cannot conclude from externals to the inner man. (*Essais*, iii.)

How this *patron au dedans* arises, and in what relation it

stands to the *forme maitresse*, Montaigne does not explain more closely.   He thus leaves a considerable problem to subsequent thought.   But just as he only praises ignorance and the quiet surrender to Nature in the case " of a good head," so it cannot be his meaning (as may clearly be seen from his words) that we ought to leave everything to Nature in the practical sphere.   The individual nature develops its own peculiar form only under the co-operation of the deliberation and the will ; and only through attention and labour can the ruling " form " be preserved from disfigurement.   Montaigne is well aware that his is no heroic will.   If he have any virtue it is owing, he thinks, rather to the favour of fortune than to the work of the will.   He is thankful that he comes of a good stock (*une race fameuse en proud'hommie*) and has enjoyed a good education. He feels a natural detestation for most vices (especially cruelty), but will not answer for how it might have gone with him had he possessed a less fortunate nature ; inner strife and discord he cannot endure.   Reason strives ever for the mastery within him, but it is often all she can do not to let herself be disfigured by the impulses which she is not always able to reform.   And yet it was his conviction that the highest pleasure is attached to virtue ; struggle can only be a state of transition.   The lower pleasures are only momentary and fleeting and are apt to bring remorse in their train.   Perfect satisfaction, equally far removed from sensuous pleasures and from painful struggle to keep the commandments of reason, is only to be found there, where the innermost nature of the soul finds expression in good actions.   To have developed an inner nature such that every occasion to inward struggle vanishes, is what Montaigne regards as the highest.   He knows that he himself only stands in the third rank, neither among those who struggle manfully, nor among those who are high above all struggle. But he admires " the greatness of heroic souls."   His own weakness does not blind him to the strength of others. Although he himself creeps on the ground, yet he is able to follow their lofty flight.   Moreover, he regards it as no trifle that in an age when virtue appears little else than a *jargon du collège* he should have retained the power to pronounce ethical judgments (i. 19, 36 ; ii. 11 ; iii. 13).

Montaigne's defence of the concept of Nature is classical in character.   But he carries this concept beyond the limited form in which it appeared among the Greek thinkers. By its close connection with the concept of individuality it is extended to infinity. If Montaigne opposes Nature to the artificialities of men, he does so partly because the latter regard certain particular "forms" as alone justified, and thus overlook the fulness of Nature; and partly because they do violence to certain peculiar individualities, which possess the same right to develop themselves *sur son propre modèle* as do any others. The future was to unfold these two thoughts of infinity and individuality. And Montaigne's scepticism, his great powers of observation, and his Humanistic learning, gave him freedom of mind and the means to emphasise the importance of these concepts. His scepticism—which is really an assertion of the right to think —induced him to transcend artificial barriers ; and his rich experience and learning taught him what was to be found on the other side of these limits, *i.e.* new individual forms, by means of which one and the same single infinite nature finds expression.

Montaigne died in 1592. A thinker such as he could hardly hope to find disciples. His thought was altogether too subjective for that. In him were united elements which could appear in the same combination in no other mind. The man who comes nearest to being a disciple, and who may be regarded as the systematiser of his ideas, only represents a single—although a very important—side of his world of thought. It was his acquaintance with Montaigne which led PIERRE CHARRON to his philosophical ideas. Born in Paris in 1541, he was originally a lawyer, but afterwards took orders, and became a famous preacher. He published writings in defence of the Catholic faith against Protestants and free-thinkers. The most remarkable of these, however, is a work which appeared at Bordeaux under the title *De la sagesse,* in the year 1600 (three years before his death), and which contains a complete defence of the same leading thought which we met with in Pomponazzi, as well as in Machiavelli and Montaigne, *i.e.* the thought of human nature as the foundation of ethics and politics. He lays great stress on the ignorance which results from true self-knowledge. A closer examination shows us the misery, as well as the greatness, of human nature. The natural reason cannot be the measure of all things ; we must therefore abide by the old doctrines of the Church, and not become

D

entangled in new ones.—Thus Charron, like Montaigne,—only to a still greater degree,—draws conservative conclusions from the principle of doubt.   But, curiously enough, he discusses the relation of religion to morality, upon which Montaigne had not touched.   Religion and morality accompany one another, but they must not on this account be confused with one another, since each has its own spring (*ressort*).   Above all things goodness must not be made dependent on religion, for in this way it becomes an accident and no longer originates in "the good spring of Nature."   " I will," says Charron, "that a man be a good man even though there be no Heaven and no Hell.   It seems to me detestable when a man says : If I were not a Christian, if I did not fear damnation, I would do this or that.   I will that thou shouldst be good because Nature and Reason so will it— because it is demanded by the general order of things of which Reason is only a part—and because thou canst not act against thyself, thine essence and thine aim ;—what will may follow from this.   When once this stands firm, religion may follow after, but the converse relation is ruinous."

Such a decided recognition of the independence of ethics from the lips of a Catholic priest is indeed remarkable.   It remains a psychological puzzle as to how Charron, who shortly before had appeared as a zealous Catholic preacher, was led to embrace such an opinion.   It at any rate attests the fact that there existed at the time a strong tendency in that direction.

CHAPTER V

LUDOVICUS VIVES

THE great interest in everything human fostered by the Renaissance naturally and inevitably led to the eager psychological study of mental phenomena. Although, with all the above - mentioned thinkers, psychological explanation and psychological interests play an important part, yet psychological inquiry as a separate endeavour, differentiated from the more far-reaching philosophical conclusions deduced from it, had not yet emerged. At this time, moreover, all psychological study was merely theoretical. And if any one man is to be named as the representative of the pure psychology of the time, that man is the Spaniard LUDOVICUS VIVES: a quiet scholar, an eager Humanist, the friend and follower of Erasmus of Rotterdam, he is chiefly important within the spheres of psychology and pedagogics. Born in Valencia in 1492, he studied in Paris and afterwards lived till his death, in 1540, at Bruges. He was for some time tutor to the daughter of Henry VIII. of England, but the action for divorce brought about a breach between him and the English court. Vives was an earnest Catholic, but his peace-loving and healthy mode of thought led him to address an outspoken letter to Pope Hadrian VI. (1522), in which he expressed the wish that a general council should be convened to distinguish between that which is necessary to piety and morality, and that which may be handed over to free inquiry, that thus, by this means, the breach within the Church might be healed. He afterwards spoke in behalf of tolerance, and a milder and freer interpretation of Christianity. As a pedagogue, he was of very great significance for his own age. Many of the excellent ideas concerning education subsequently

put into practice by the Jesuits, really originated with Vives,
who is said to have been a personal acquaintance of Loyola's.
His interest in philological criticism and pedagogical problems
led him to undertake an examination of scientific method in
general, and he demands that experience be taken as the
ground of all knowledge.   He himself tried to comply
with this demand within the sphere of psychology, and may
be regarded as the founder of modern empirical psychology.
Like all his contemporaries, he avails himself of the rich
material afforded by antiquity, but he endeavours to confirm
everything by his own experience, and his work *De anima et
vita* (Bruges, 1538) contains many original observations.   His
description of particular mental phenomena—especially of the
emotions—is even now instructive, and his book exercised an
extraordinary influence on the psychological theories of the
sixteenth and seventeenth centuries.[4]

The clearly empirical standpoint of Vives is especially
apparent in the section of the first book of the *De anima*
entitled " What the soul is."   After he has drawn attention
to the difficulties connected with the answering of this question
(since we find it easier to say what the soul is not, than
what it is), he remarks that, properly speaking, we are interested,
not in knowing what the soul *is*, but rather *how it is active*,
and that the precepts of self-knowledge concern not the nature,
but the functions, of the soul.   We find it here asserted, with
the greatest assurance, that we have directly to deal with mental
phenomena only, and that empirical psychology can altogether
dispense with the purely speculative theory concerning the
nature of the soul.

Vives remains true to this standpoint throughout his
purely descriptive mode of treatment.   It was, indeed, almost
inevitable that he should regard much as proved by experience
which could not stand before later criticism ; but, in spite of
this, Vives did not a little towards effecting a differentiation of
the psychological standpoint, which had hitherto been confounded, on the one hand with speculative and theological
points of view, and on the other with the standpoint of physics
—which differentiation Descartes carried out still more clearly
and decidedly.   Descartes owes more to Vives than might be
thought from the very few times he mentions him.

As is apparent from the title of Vives' book, he places the

concepts of the soul and of life in close connection with one another. He regards the soul as the principle of life—not merely of all conscious life, but of all organic life. He strives to conceive the lower forms of life as the foundations of the higher. His psychology is a physiological psychology which feels itself called upon to describe phenomena as far as possible from the physiological side also. He naturally applies the physiology of his time. As an inquirer, he proves himself emancipated from the Aristotelian school by assigning know-ledge to the brain. There were still Aristotelians who maintained that the nerves proceed, not from the brain (although the later Greek anatomists had proved this), but from the heart. The vital power, on the other hand, has its seat, according to Vives, in the heart, where the first and last signs of life make themselves felt, and whose restricted or free functioning is expressed by the emotions. In agreement with a doctrine handed down from the Stoics and Galen, Vives supposes that the brain is filled with a fine air or breath (*spiritus tenuissimi ac pellucidi*). It was assumed that the vibrations of this air were connected with events in conscious-ness, but Vives does not enter more closely into the question. What the relation between the soul which is active in the brain, and that which is active in the heart, may be, he also leaves undetermined. According to his view, it is only human souls which are immediately created by God; the souls of plants and of animals (*i.e.* the principle of organic life and of sensuous perception) are generated by the power of matter. The thoughts and aspirations of the human soul find no satisfaction in the finite and sensuous, but seek an infinite object ; hence we may conclude to the divine origin of the soul, for causes must correspond to their effects. Vives here shows himself a decided spiritualist, which indeed was only to be expected from his religious presuppositions. On this point also he bequeaths weighty problems to succeeding thinkers. His psychology is confined to the description of the various mental phenomena. It was reserved to later inquiry to discover the mechanical principle, by means of which we may pass from one phenomenon to another.

CHAPTER VI

THE DEVELOPMENT OF NATURAL LAW

THE Humanism of Italy bore the stamp of an intellectual aristocracy. Its great significance lay in the founding of a free intellectual life. But as to how it was faring with human life in wider circles, it did not concern itself particularly. It left the Church, the State, and the life of the community to look after themselves, while it occupied itself almost entirely with intellectual and æsthetic problems. Even Machiavelli himself, in spite of his great interest in national and political affairs, forms no exception in this respect, for that which fascinates him most is the development of the power of the Prince, and he did not trouble himself as to the more hidden powers and conditions of social life. Humanism fell with the downfall of political freedom in Italy; but that political freedom was overthrown, and that no national life of the State could develop itself, was the fault of Humanism itself, on account of the narrow view it took of humanity, owing to its fear of facing the depth and breadth of things. It was this same fear which caused it to leave the religious question unsolved, and to content itself with merely pushing it aside. The more northern nations, amongst whom the Renaissance set in with less brilliancy, carried out their enfranchisement more deeply within, and more widely without. It was the great merit of the Reformation that it would not be contented with an evasion of the religious question, but attacked it directly, proclaiming in the sphere of religion the same principle of personality which Humanism had already proclaimed in other spheres of thought. The Reformation is the application of the thought of the Renaissance to religion, by which I do not mean that Luther and Zwingli first adopted these ideas, and then applied them. The greatness of their personality consists precisely in this ;—that they discovered these thoughts anew in their own experience of life, and clothed them in an entirely original form. They maintained that direct personal experience of life is the real foundation of religion, and taking their stand on this, they fought against the Church and the theology of the Middle Ages. Men's inner powers were freed from artificial forms. Christianity was here really brought back—to use Machiavelli's expression—to the original principle from which it had sprung. Although LUTHER did not enter upon a critical examination of primitive Christianity, yet he seized upon an important point among the doctrines held by the oldest congregation, when he took as his foundation the Pauline doctrine of justification by faith. By means of a close personal union with Christ, men are raised above all external circumstances. He develops this thought more particularly in his work *Von der Freiheit eines Christen Menschen* (1520). If personality is thus to be freed in those innermost relations on which its eternal fate depends from all external authority, a similar freedom can hardly fail to be effected in other spheres. It certainly cannot be denied that the Reformation of Luther aroused men's minds on many subjects. In his struggle with the Church, Luther became the advocate of the natural man. In opposition to the Church, he maintained the independence of the family and of the State ; and, as a natural corollary to his doctrine of justification by faith alone, he especially emphasised the importance of the impulses and workings of simple human life, in opposition to Catholicism, which despises such a life in comparison with asceticism. Luther was not yet able, however, to establish any positive connection with natural human interests. His attitude towards science, especially in his younger days, was that of mistrust, owing to his doctrine of faith ; and in public life he adhered strictly to the principle of passive obedience. In his work on " The Freedom of a Christian Man " he divides his observations into two parts : he first shows the inner freedom that a Christian possesses, but then he goes on to assign the full development of this freedom to the future life, and says that with regard to his outer man a Christian is merely " a useful servant and in subjection to every man." In this dualism of inner and outer lay the reason why Lutheranism never exerted that influence on spiritual and political development which it might otherwise, through the great and powerful personality of its founder, have acquired. The religious and the human were merely placed next to one another, like Sunday and workday, without any inner essential connection. And the same thing happened with regard to the relation of faith to knowledge. Luther took his stand at Worms on the Bible, and on the necessity of clear and evident grounds. But the mutual relation of these two principles never attained to clearness,[5] unless we call it clearness when there presently developed out of the Lutheran theology a Scholasticism less fine in conception, and even more narrow-minded, than that of the Middle Ages.

By the side of Luther stood a man who, with quiet enthusiasm, tried to unite the thoughts of the Reformation with those of the Renaissance. PHILIP MELANCTHON, " Germany's teacher," represented, as contrasted with Luther, a more rational side of Protestantism. He was not only a theologian, but also a philologist and a philosopher ; and if it was a grief to him that Luther and the Lutherans so strictly condemned all unregenerate men, this was not merely because such a view collided with his gentler conception of humanity in general, but, more particularly, because it touched his beloved Classics. At the University of Wittenberg Melancthon lectured, not only on theology, but also on natural philosophy and on such philosophical studies as psychology, logic ("dialectic") and ethics. These lectures are distinguished by the elegance of their style and the thorough acquaintance with the literature of antiquity which they display. His most interesting work is his ethics. In his natural philosophy he attacked (as we shall see later) the new Copernican learning, and as a psychologist he is not to be compared with Vives, whose work appeared at about the same time. Of great significance for his ethics was his doctrine of the *natural light,* in which he was largely influenced by Cicero's reproduction of the Stoic philosophy, though he also relied on the saying of the Apostle Paul that the law is written in the human heart. Underlying all argumentation, reckoning, and computing, every assumption of first principles in science, and every moral judgment, are certain ideas, innate in every man, and without doubt implanted by God (*noticiae nobiscum nascentes, divinitus sparsae in mentibus nostris*) ; hence it is no mere accident that scientific learning and moral judgments have never died out among the human race. (Melancthon

develops this doctrine partly in the *Liber de anima*, partly in
the *Erotemata dialectices*.) The natural light was certainly
darkened by the Fall, and it therefore became necessary that
its essential moral contents should be given again in the ten
commandments. That the ten commandments and the natural
moral law had the same content was an opinion shared by all
the Reformers. It is found in Luther as well as in Calvin, and
may be traced back to the early Middle Ages. Through this
doctrine, revived by Melancthon, it became evident that men
were arriving, by way of clearer reasons, at results identical
with those offered by Old Testament revelation. Although
Melancthon thus gave an independent, natural, and rational
foundation to the natural law, which was for him both the
moral law as well as the first principle of all theories of rights,
yet it follows from his theological assumptions that the
moral course of life based on this foundation is only concerned with external and civil life, and does not touch the innermost stirrings of the soul. He defines moral philosophy as
" the knowledge of the precepts concerning all moral actions
(*honestis actionibus*) which Reason sees to be in conformity with
human nature and necessary in civil life, so that, as far as
possible, we seek to discover scientifically the origin of these
precepts." That which is innermost and deepest in the life of
the soul, according to the conception of the Reformer, is not
" in conformity with human nature," but must first be aroused
by supernatural influences. It is true, he holds (*Philosophiae
moralis epitome*), that philosophy suffices to teach us that there
is only *one* God, that He is to be worshipped, and that the will
of God constitutes the great difference between good and evil.
The first three commandments come under the head of moral
philosophy, as much as the last seven. But yet the real
essential relation to God, " in which we have directly to do
with God," falls outside philosophy. Thus we see that it was
a mistake to regard the content of the decalogue and that of
the moral law as identical. For Melancthon could scarcely
have intended to deny to the religiousness of the Old Testament a direct and immediate relation with God. On the
other hand, this identification bears witness to the theological
prejudice that that which is most essentially human can only
be conceived under the form of religion. The humane was for
Melancthon coextensive with the civil. We meet here again,

even in this Humanist, with the old antithesis between the inner and the outer.   But his admission that human life may be ordered, in its external relations, according to fundamentally rational laws, was, nevertheless, of very great importance.   Civil life and the whole of public life were now in a position to develop themselves independently, according to purely humane principles.

And this independence was still more sharply accentuated in the school of Melancthon than it had been by the master himself.   The Danish theologian, NIELS HEMMINGSEN, called "Denmark's teacher," as Melancthon, whose instruction he had enjoyed, was called "Germany's teacher," demanded in his work *De lege naturae apodictica methodus* (1562) a strictly scientific enunciation of the natural law.   He himself states, at the conclusion of his work, that he had purposely abstained from all theological explanations, in order that it might be clearly shown "how far Reason can attain without the prophetic and apostolic writings."   By the path of inquiry he seeks to gain a clear and evident knowledge of the nature of law.   That only is a true law which does not merely depend on the authority of princes and magistrates, but which has its "firm and necessary ground"; and this is to be found only in the nature and aim of the law itself.   The germs of morality and righteousness are given in the nature of Man, as is also the power of discerning the difference between right and wrong.   Men must avail themselves of these means, if they wish to have a law in the true sense· of the word.   Hemmingsen goes on to show that human nature contains a sensuous and a rational element, and that the animal impulses aroused by sensuous perception must obey the reason which contains the true human law of nature (*lex naturae seu recta ratio*).   The goal of human life is the knowledge of truth, and the practice of good.   The spiritual life rises above family and public life (*vita spiritualis* in opposition to the *vita oeconomica* and *politica*) in its worship of God, in which the highest goal is to be found.   At this point the natural powers no longer suffice, for no man can know how to worship God in the right manner without divine revelation.   But for a knowledge of natural law itself, divine revelation is not necessary.   It is true that Hemmingsen, like Melancthon, considered the ten commandments to be a short epitome of the natural law (*epitome legis naturae*) ; but it was only after he had established the natural law that he inquired as to its agreement with the ten commandments.   We have here, then, this step in advance ; that ethics and the doctrine of rights (the " natural law " includes both) have become independent of theology, and no longer depend on supernatural authority.

But at this juncture the Lutheran movement found itself in difficulties.   Individual jurists, *e.g.* OLDENDORP and WINKLER, it is true, maintained the completely developed doctrine, but only the Reformed countries possessed the inner and outer conditions necessary for a more thorough enfranchisement of ethics and the doctrine of rights.   Neither in Zwingli, nor in Calvin, do we find that anxious distinction between the inner freedom of the individual and his limitations in all external matters.   They rejected the principle of authority to a much greater degree than did the Lutherans.   He who is made free by predestination feels his right to self-determination in all spiritual and worldly matters.   ZWINGLI, that clear and powerful nature in whom the religious sincerity of the Reformer is united with the consistency of the thinker, with the Humanist's love for antiquity, and with the demands for political freedom of the Republican, advocated self-government both in the civil as well as in the ecclesiastical sphere.   And CALVIN, although less gifted and with greater limitations, carried on his work.   It was their thought which underlay the great struggles of the sixteenth and seventeenth centuries in France, in the Netherlands and in England—struggles out of which arose the civil, religious, and scientific freedom of modern times.   The modern State and modern learning are indebted to these struggles for their existence.   That which Italian Humanism, through its effeminacy and its intellectual aristocracy, and Lutheranism, through its timorous insistence on sincerity and obedience, had not been able to accomplish, the disciples of the Swiss Reformers effected by means of intellectual weapons and of the sword.   Even here, however, a hard fight had to be fought before the confessional bonds, within which the Reformed Church, no less than all others, sought to confine the intellectual movement, could be burst asunder.   But it was of no small significance that this Church took a less prejudiced view of the relation between the inner and the outer, and drew no sharp distinction between the inner personal life and all other human interests.   It was on this account that the Reformed countries became the second home of modern philosophy, after Italy, its first home, had once more been brought under the yoke, by the powers of the reaction. Thus the modern doctrine of natural law, on which, up to our own century, all attempts at political and social reforms have been based, drew its source from these countries.

The religious wars in the Netherlands and in France, together with the political literature which they occasioned, were of great importance for the development of the idea of the freedom of the people, and the independence of the State, over against the Church. The struggle for the establishment of religious freedom was closely connected with the struggle for the maintenance of civil freedom. The right of subjects, through their legal representatives, to offer resistance to, or even, in extreme cases, to depose a prince who violated the right of the people, was very strongly asserted. The following proposition was laid down as a first principle : all sovereign power is conferred on the ruler, subject to the condition that he fulfil certain duties. Thus the principle of the sovereign right of the people was proclaimed, and the idea of an original contract between the people and the Government was made the basis of all inquiries into public law. The theory of contract had already been turned to account in the Middle Ages during the struggle between Church and State over the claims of the Church to the supremacy. The remembrance of the origin of the Roman Empire in the Roman Democracy, together with deductions drawn from the notion of a paradisiacal condition of Nature without Law or State, co-operated here. This theory was now used by the people against their Princes, while in the Middle Ages it had been a weapon in the hands of the Princes against the Church. A number of Protestant publicists, in the first rank of whom were HUBERT LANGUET and FRANÇOIS HOTMAN, made this the foundation of their polemical writings. But it was also adopted on the Catholic side. When, *e.g.*, the government of a prince was found to be cold or heretical, he was called to account by an appeal to the right of the people, as derived from an original contract. A number of Jesuit authors, many of them men of great acumen and considerable energy, discussed the question in this spirit. The Church claimed to be the only community founded above, while the State had its foundation here below. The religious wars, both physical and literary, naturally caused patriotic men, anxious for the preservation of the State which was threatened by the battle of the creeds, to fix their eyes on those conditions of the life of the State which were independent of disputable religious opinions. A party of so-called " Politicians" was formed in France in opposition to the Huguenots and Liguists ; their views found literary expression in JEAN BODIN'S work on the State (*La République*), which appeared in 1577. This remarkable man, whose superstition recalls the darkest of the Middle Ages, while his political and historical conceptions are far in advance of his age, was a French jurist, who for a time enjoyed the favour of Henry III., but afterwards forfeited it by defending the rights of the classes and the masses against the King. He was for some time closely allied with the Duc d'Alençon, the head of the " Politicians," and afterwards, he was one of the first to attach himself to Henry IV., when the latter put an end to civil wars by extending the protection of tolerance to the conflicting parties. He died, however, two years before the appearance of the Edict of Nantes. His significance in the history of the theory of rights lies in the clear and methodical manner in which he developed the *concept of sovereignty*. He makes a decided distinction between sovereignty and government.

The highest power is not identical with the sovereignty, for power may at certain times be transferred or divided, while the sovereignty is indivisible. There can no more be several gods, if God be an Absolute Being, than there can be several sovereigns in one State. Bodin distinguishes the form of the State from the form of government. The various forms of the State are determined according to how the sovereignty is vested ; the following are the marks of sovereignty,—power to make laws, the right to declare war and peace, the power to grant pardons, and to appoint the highest officers. The sovereign power may reside in the whole nation, in the aristocracy, or in the Prince. The form of government may very well be monarchical, while the form of the State is democratic ; this happens when the King is chosen by the entire nation.

Bodin felt it necessary, over against the Protestant and Catholic *Monarchomachen* [those who were opposed to an absolute monarchy], to emphasise the concept of absolute sovereignty. But yet he does not, on that account, dispute the right of the people. The sovereign power is subordinate both to the moral and to the natural law ; it cannot abolish the rights of personal property, and can, therefore, never impose

taxes. Bodin did not perceive that the legislative power cannot maintain itself for any length of time without the power to
impose taxes, and that in assigning the latter power to the
people, he was really assigning to them the sovereign power,
so that the difference between the various "forms of the State"
disappeared, and only the difference between "forms of government" remained. This conclusion from his concept of sovereignty was only drawn by his successors.

Bodin's doctrine of the State is remarkable for the emphasis
he lays on the family, and on the smaller communities or corporations. He demands that their independence and idiosyncrasy
should be preserved and developed, in so far as this is possible
in conjunction with the duties of the State in general. He has
altogether a healthy appreciation of actual human life in its
various branches, and blames Machiavelli, of whom he says
"he never sounded the depths of political science," for his
belief that tyrannical finesse is the essence of politics. In one
little work in particular (on the method of history) Bodin points
out the significance of the comparative and historical method
for the theory of right. "History," he says, "contains the
chief part of universal law, and from laws we may discover the
customs of nations, the foundation of the State, its course of
development, its forms, its revolutions and its fall—all of which
is conducive to a right estimation of laws." By this means,
he thinks, we shall be led to abandon the belief in a golden
age; "in comparison with our own the so-called golden age
would appear iron." He founds his faith in progress chiefly
on the development of industry. He emphasises strongly the
discoveries and inventions of modern times, and also the increase
of intercourse between different nations. He distinguishes,
however, between progress in culture and progress in morality;
his faith in this latter is not so hopeful. We shall speak later
of his religio-philosophical writings and their significance.

The real founder of the modern theory of natural law was
JOHANNES ALTHUSIUS. This man, whom it is Gierke's merit
to have recovered from a most unmerited neglect, was born at
Diedenshausen in 1557; he studied at Basle, probably at Geneva
also, was for some time Professor of Law in Herborn, and was
afterwards for many years burgomaster of the East Frisian town
of Emden, whose privileges he zealously defended against the
encroachments of the East Frisian counts and knights. He

was a zealous Calvinist, and followed, with enthusiasm, the struggle of the Netherlanders, who were so nearly related to the East Frisians, for religious and political freedom. He several times refers to this struggle in his books. The peasants of Friesland had retained their old freedom after it had perished in all other parts of Germany, and Althusius is careful to defend the rights of the peasantry, side by side with those of the nobles and of the burghers. His religious faith as well as his studies, contemporary events in neighbouring countries as well as social relations within his own small fatherland, therefore, contributed to the formation of his views on the philosophy of law and of the State, which he expounded in his political work, *Politica methodice digesta atque exemplis sacris et profanis illustrata*, 1603. Amongst his other works may be mentioned, in addition to several which are purely juristic, a work on the virtues which come into play through intercourse with other men (*Civilis conversationis libri duo*). He died in 1638 after a long and active life.

Althusius is agreed with Bodin that there can be only one—and that an indivisible—sovereignty. In one State there can be a single sovereign only, as in one body there is only a single soul. But he attacks Bodin's theory of several forms of the State. The sovereignty can only reside in *one* place, and can neither be transferred nor alienated. Princes and aristocrats may govern, but they can never possess the sovereignty, which must have its seat in the whole nation which never dies, and to which every ruler is answerable for his administration. The State must promote and assist the welfare and the necessities of the nation ; in this the State finds its cause and end. Individual rulers die—the whole nation never dies. And the ruler is an individual man only, while the nation consists of many men. From the people, therefore, all power must proceed, and to the people it must always revert.

Only the form of government, not the form of the State, can vary. The nation, the members of which are united by common conditions of life (*corpus symbioticum*), is the source of all power and cannot transfer it to any authority whatsoever. All who exercise the governing power do so as representatives of the people, and as soon as they exceed the limits imposed on their activity by the natural law, as it is contained in the ten commandments, and by the welfare of the community, they cease to be servants of the community, and become private persons, to whom no man owes obedience beyond the point where they transcend the limits of their power.   It is not, however, the task of every individual to restrain the power of the authorities within their limits.

In every well-ordered State, in addition to the magistrates, is another class of administrators, *i.e.* overseers (*ephori*), whose duty it is to appoint the highest magistrates, to protect the inalienable right of the people, to dismiss any magistrates who violate it, as also to protect and support every magistrate in the exercise of his rightful power.   Such ephors we recognise both in the ancient States, as senators and tribunes of the *plebs*, and, in more modern States, as members of the diet, Electors, and aldermen.   Under one form or another the controlling power must always be organised.[6]

Althusius finds historical proof of his idea of the sovereignty of the people not only in the fact that in most states some authority exists which, in the name of the people, criticises the procedure of the highest authorities, but also in the fact that a nation has been known to cast off the rule of a tyrannical prince. He points to the struggle for freedom in the Netherlands ; and in the preface to the third edition he says that his book is dedicated to the diet of Friesland, because they, like the other Netherlanders, had perceived that the sovereignty is not inseparably bound up with the person of the Prince, but that the latter only enjoys the usufruct thereof, while the sovereign rights really belong to the people, and had fought for this principle with such great bravery, insight, and perseverance.

He finds a philosophical proof when he considers the aim and cause of the State.   For the aim is not the welfare of the magistracy, but that of the whole people ; and the cause which induces men to join themselves together and form a State is the helpless and necessitous condition of the individual.   The feeling and the wants of *single* individuals are the ultimate cause of the life of the State.   At first smaller communities, *e.g.* families and neighbourhoods, are formed.   These smaller communities are the nurseries of larger communities, which arise by the union of several smaller ones.   But now it is a political, and not a merely private, community which arises.   The State is the universal community which includes within it all smaller ones.   Althusius here reminds us of Bodin, who laid such great stress on the importance of smaller communities within larger ones.   The holder of the sovereignty is the people, organised into different social groups, and represented by ephors. On this point the older authors are distinctly superior to the eighteenth century expositors of the natural law, who recognise nothing between the isolated individual, and the State as a totality. But we must remember not only that corporations had proved to be connected with many evils, but also that absolute monarchy in France, and its imitation in other places, had done their best to reduce the intermediate members between the individual and the State to the lowest possible pitch of insignificance.

Society in its simplest form, which serves as a foundation for all others, has arisen out of an agreement, which also arises out of the wants of men. In order to rightly understand the theory of contract here developed we must inquire rather more closely into Althusius' conception of the agreement which, according to him, forms the basis of all social life. It originated in men's wants, which, however, Althusius does not seem to have regarded as purely egoistic. When talking more particularly of the genesis of the family, and of the social ties arising from neighbourhood, Althusius appeals, by way of explanation, not only to " necessity," but also to " natural feeling " (*naturalis affectio*). He confirms Aristotle's statement that man is a " social animal " in a much higher degree than bees, or any other gregarious animals. How this " natural feeling " and social inclination are related to the preservation of the individual is never made clear. Althusius did not feel the need of any closer psychological `analysis. And yet such an explanation lay all the nearer to his hand from the fact that he restricted purely individual association to the simplest form of society, and derived all other forms of society from this. The belief in the natural growth of society plainly stands in a certain opposition to the direct choice of the single individual. Moreover if, as Althusius says, it is the will of the individuals forming the society that calls society into existence, yet according to his own teaching, this can only give the first impetus ; afterwards they no longer appear as individuals but as members of a corporation ; not as independent atoms but as elements of a complex molecule, whose movements are not solely determined by the individual atoms. There are no *pure* individuals ; all individuals are, involuntarily, socially determined. Thus the theory of contract, through its assumption of

pure individuals, stands, from the very beginning, in opposition
to the historical conception of social life, which regards
individuals as the *products* of social life, rather than as its active
forces. Althusius tried to unite the two points of view. But
here too the real problem was only recognised later.

In connection with this another question arises : was the
original contract which constitutes society determined consciously or unconsciously? It is evident that, if it was consciously agreed upon, we can only understand by this an actual
historical event, which took place at a definite time. But
Althusius does not seem to have conceived it in this manner.
Society, he says, arises either by an express or a tacit
contract (*pacto expresso vel tacito*). But what is meant by a
" tacit" contract? According to Althusius, it is necessary to
assume a contract, not only to explain how society has arisen,
but also to understand how the governing power became
transferred to the persons in authority. We must assume
then, first a social contract, and then a governmental contract ;
the former between individuals as such, the latter between the
whole people and those who rule over them. Now with regard
to this latter contract (and the same holds good of the former),
Althusius maintains that the people themselves retain all rights
which they have not expressly transferred to the Prince, and
that even where a people has submitted itself to an authority
without any express conditions, the general requirements of
equity and justice, and the content of the Decalogue are to be
added in thought : " for it is not probable that a people would
have unconditionally surrendered its freedom to a Prince to its
own undoing ; and even a nation has no power to rob itself of
its self-preservation or to give a power to any one individual which
would be greater than that of all others taken together." In
other words, Althusius argues from what we must *reasonably*
suppose to have been the intention of the people, to the
content of the *original* contract, and he assumes that the
people acted reasonably from the beginning, when the contract
was made. Unfortunately for this theory, neither people nor
princes always begin rationally, and there is therefore no justification for assuming a tacit reason on all occasions. It now becomes
evident that this contract (especially in its " tacit" part)
expresses Althusius' ideal of society rather than any historical
event. Natural law, particularly the theory of contract, is a

mythological expression of the ideal demand, which must be postulated in the ordering and development of society. It locates its ideal of the future in the past. It is perhaps open to question whether the majority of the expounders of natural law conceived the original contract as an actual historical event. Even Bodin saw that the idea of a golden age rested on an illusion, and the same may be said of every conception of an absolutely natural condition. The great importance of the theory of natural law consists in this: that in the idea of an original contract it possessed a form in which the right of the individual over against society and its authorities could be clearly and emphatically asserted. But it was Kant who first taught the difference between a guiding regulative idea and one actually given. With the help of this distinction we can perceive at once the deficiencies and the great importance of the theory of natural law.

Bodin and Althusius continued Machiavelli's attempt to reduce the doctrine of statecraft to a purely human science. It is true that Althusius, as may be seen from the title of his work, relies upon biblical as much as upon profane history; but he borrows only from the former purely historical examples. Unlike the *Monarchomachen* he does not employ theological arguments. He agrees with Paul that ‾ all authority is of God, but God's activity is here not direct but indirect; the forces and impulses which led to the founding of society and the instituting of authorities come through Nature from God. The power of princes and ephors proceeds *directly* from the people, and *indirectly* from God. God has transferred the care of the State not only to the Prince, but also to the ephors or to the Diet. Thus the theological hypothesis falls still farther into the background. As an ardent Calvinist, however, Althusius asserts the furtherance of religion to be one of the chief ends of the State. He expresses himself decidedly against religious freedom, referring to Deut. xiii. 5, where all who adopt ·a faith other than that of their fathers are declared punishable by death. Religious freedom, he thinks, would make faith uncertain, and disturb the unity which ought to prevail in a State;—he who is not with me is against me. The theological standpoint of Althusius also becomes apparent in his denial of the independence of the ethics of the individual over against theology. Each ·man may learn his duties from

the ten commandments, where they are not included in
the duties enjoined by the theory of law and of the State.
Thus ethics becomes nothing more than the rules for good
behaviour in speech and action which Althusius had discussed
in his work on civil intercourse (*civilis conversatio*).   He thus
holds consistently to the antithesis between the inner and
outer man asserted by Melancthon, although he takes
considerable interest in external human life and believes
it may be ordered according to purely natural laws.   His
energetic recognition of the natural forces of social life
would have excited Melancthon's indignation.   In his
Politica he formulates the Emden councillor's ideas, produced during the War of Independence in the Netherlands,
and which later, after they had been worked out and carried
to their extremest formal consequences by the passionate
spirit of Rousseau, formed the group of dogmas which dominated the French National Convention.   They constituted the
gospel of political freedom — a gospel of which Melancthon
and his school would never have admitted the existence.   In
striking contrast to this gospel is Althusius' rejection of
religious freedom—a witness to the inner conflict of the line of
thought inherited from the Middle Ages, beyond which not
even the most unprejudiced tendency of thought of ecclesiastical
Protestantism was able to advance.

   That it is HUGO GROTIUS, rather than Althusius, who has
been regarded by subsequent generations as the modern founder
of natural law, is due partly to the radical and democratic
standpoint of the author of the *Politica*, which differed entirely from that of the leading statesmen and publicists of the
seventeenth century ; partly to the wider and deeper historical
foundation assigned to the natural law by Grotius ; and
partly (and this not least) to the fact that in his famous work
De jure belli ac pacis (1625) Grotius took, as his starting-point,
the question of the justification of war, and of what law is valid
during war.   Thus he bound together the natural law and
the law of nations, and started from a phenomenon which was
occupying the thoughts of statesmen, and touched the interests
of all.   Not the inner relation between governors and people,
but the external relations of sovereign states among each other,
was the starting-point of his reflections.   He was led to
take up his pen by the sight of the many wars, often under-

taken without any sufficient reason, in which every wild passion was unchained, as though, on the outbreak of war, men became transformed into savage beasts. Hence he began to inquire how far all law must really disappear in such cases, and this question led him back to the ultimate foundation of law.

Hugo de Groot was born at Delft in 1583. While still a student at Leyden he earned a reputation for great learning. At the age of sixteen years he accompanied Oldenbarneveldt to Paris, where Henry IV. is said to have introduced him to his *entourage* as "the wonder from Holland." He soon attained high positions in his native land as a jurist and statesman. When, by the help of the orthodox priesthood, Maurice of Orange over-threw Oldenbarneveldt and put him to death, Grotius was condemned to imprisonment for life, from which he escaped by a *ruse* of his wife's. He hereupon settled in Paris, where he was supported for some time by the French Government. Here he wrote the work with which his name is connected. Afterwards he became Swedish Ambassador in Paris. He died at Rostock in 1645, on his return from a visit to Sweden.

Grotius remarks that it is easier to say what is wrong than what is right. Everything which is contrary to the nature of social life, as led by reasonable beings, is wrong. We see here that Grotius stands nearer than his predecessors to experience and history. For that the life of human society requires certain conditions, with which it stands or falls, can most easily be discovered where these conditions are lacking, so that we have, as it were, an experiment before us. Were the con-ditions always present, they would escape our observation. According to Grotius, an involuntary impulse compels men to associate with other men. Even if other men were not exactly necessary to us, yet we should seek intercourse and communion with them. As things are, indeed, we cannot dispense with the help of others, but this is not the real basis of social life. Even children display a tendency to show kindness to others, and to feel sympathy with their misfortunes. This natural appetite (*appetitus societatis*) is developed and refined when, by means of speech, communion with others becomes intellectual in-tercourse, and when men become capable of ordering their knowledge and actions according to general principles, so that they treat similar cases similarly. In the endeavour to protect a social life of this kind lies the origin of natural law. Human actions are now judged according to their agreement or disagreement with the claims of such a social life. Natural law, then, originates in principles which are contained in human nature itself (*ex principiis homini internis*), and which would be valid, even were there no God. And yet God may be called the author of natural law, since He is the author of Nature, and therefore wills this law to be valid.

The first and most important precept of natural law is that contracts and promises are to be kept. This is contained within the original will which called society into existence. Every obligation has its ground in a previous contract or given promise. Positive law (*jus civile*) here arises out of natural law. For social life could not exist, could men not enter into obligations towards each other. Thus the whole structure of civil life rests on an eternal and immutable justice, which is binding on God, as well as on all reasonable creatures. Human nature, which is the mother of natural law, thus becomes the ancestress of positive law, since the source of positive law is the necessity, according to natural law, of keeping one's word.

But what imparts to the principle of the fulfilment of promises and contracts its original force? Here we see that, like Althusius, Grotius proceeds from the theory of contract. The very principle that contracts must be kept is itself established by a contract! Only this original contract need not have been concluded with full consciousness. It may be tacit, presupposed in the nature of the case; *i.e.* it is only another expression of the will to maintain society, which is the condition of all social life. Society is regarded as the product of a free union to which every individual contributes his will as part of the common will. All individual circumstances must be judged according to this original will (*ex primæva voluntate*). The State is a body originating voluntarily (*corpus voluntate contractum*). From this follows, *inter alia*, the important conclusion that the right of the individual in his relation to the community can never entirely perish, for he certainly cannot have willed to destroy himself! He cannot forego the right of self-preservation which he possessed before entering the community.

As with Althusius, so here we find the mythological notion

of a state of nature and of its dissolution, by means of an act of will, into the life of the State. Grotius, however, is glad to avail himself, when by the help of this notion he is deducing special questions of rights (*e.g.* the unrighteousness of lying,[7] private ownership, prescriptive rights, common law), of the idea of a *tacit* compact, by which is expressed whatever is required for the best ordering of events (*aut expresse, aut ex negotii natura tacite promittere, silentio convenire*), so that it is doubtful, with regard to him also, as to how far he regarded the social contract as an historical event. But it is curious that, although he proceeds from injustice and discord as the main facts, Grotius entertained a most idyllic conception of human life, as it would appear when not organised into a society. He regards the social impulse as direct and disinterested, and its relation to self-preservation, as with Althusius, is never made clear. Hobbes was the first to start the movement which could bring out with greater clearness the psychological presuppositions of law.

Grotius differs from Althusius in maintaining that, after a nation has been constituted as such, it can, by means of the contract on which society is based, transfer the sovereignty for ever to a Prince or Diet, and also that the individual may enslave himself. He makes a direct attack on Althusius' doctrine of the sovereignty of the people, although—from what cause is not known—he does not mention him by name. He shows that the question here is not what form of the State is the best—for opinions will always differ on this point—but whose will it is which is the foundation of law (*ex voluntate jus metiendum est*). And why should the nation not be able to trust itself entirely to the power of one or of several men? Even in a democratic State the minority have to yield to the majority, and women, children, and the poor certainly take no part in any decisions, *i.e.* they do not share in the sovereignty. The original will may create a necessity which shall be binding on all times. It is idle to say that the State exists for the sake of the nation and not of their rulers, for a guardianship exists for the sake of the minor not that of the guardian, and yet the latter has power over the former. By thus ascribing to the contract by which the power is transferred to the rulers a different character from that of the contract which constitutes the nation a nation, Grotius is the forerunner of Hobbes, and makes it possible for absolute monarchy to base itself on the theory of contract. His arguments, however, do not shake Althusius' contention that it is hardly likely that a nation would have surrendered its freedom for ever. Althusius' conception is evidently most in harmony with the theory of contract, both in its mythological and in its rational sense.

As already remarked, it was war which occasioned Grotius' investigation into the concept and origin of law. War may, in the first place, be carried on between two individuals. On the presupposition of a social condition and a public life, however, the only justifiable war between individuals is limited to defence ; power to punish lies with the Government. Secondly, there may be war between individuals and the State. This is rebellion, and Grotius is quite convinced that it is inadmissible ; here again he attacks Althusius. He is of opinion that those who ascribe to the representatives of the people the right to rebel have adapted themselves too much to the conditions of a certain time and place. On the other hand, Grotius himself seems to have paid too little regard to the struggle of his countrymen, based on the law of nature. Thirdly, war may be carried on by the State against individuals. This is right when it is directed against those who have done wrong. The examination of this point thus leads to the investigation of the nature and justification of punishment. Grotius' treatment of this question is very interesting. He is decidedly opposed to the retributive theory. The end of punishment is not in itself; only a savage and inhuman mind could find satisfaction in the knowledge that any man has suffered, when the suffering brings no greater good either to himself, or to others, or to the whole community. Fourthly, there may be war between States. This theme is treated in most detail. The conditions which justify war, and the humanitarian considerations which are to be observed during war, are deduced from the principle of natural law. The main principle is that men do not cease to be men because they are enemies, and that war, since it is only carried on for the sake of peace, must be so honestly and humanely carried on as not to make peace impossible. Grotius is well aware that international law lacks the sanction conferred by the power of the State in the case of individual nations. Large States seem to be able to allow themselves anything. But even they require an ordered intercourse with other nations, and they cannot be indifferent to the opinion of humanity at large, so that war can only be effectively carried on when the nation itself believes in the righteousness of its cause. By his demands in the name of humanity, and by his analogy between the conditions of intercourse between nations and those within one and the same nation, Grotius made a quite extraordinary impression on the statesmen of the seventeenth and eighteenth centuries. Gustavus Adolphus is said to have always kept his book by him in his tent. Grotius' authority is supposed to have restrained Louis XIV. from executing his threat to grant no pardons in his war with Holland ; and it is also generally believed that the indignation caused by the devastation of the Palatinate would not have been so great, had not Grotius' work previously aroused a feeling against it. And up to this day the instructions issued by most States to their officers in time of war are to a great extent modelled on the rules laid down in Grotius' work,[8] which we cannot here follow out in detail. We have only to show that the famous jurist and expositor of international law has his place among those who discovered humanity.

It was, at that time, an important question both of civil and international law, whether men ought to be punished on account of their religious opinions, and whether one State ought to declare war against another in the cause of religion. With regard to the former point, Althusius adopted a narrow-minded, confessional attitude, and the general opinion on the latter point was shown by the religious wars. Grotius first asks what we are to understand by *true religion*. It must be that which is common to all men living at the same time, and he finds its content to be : God's unity and invisibility, God as the author of all things, and as He who cares for all. These views are susceptible of a natural proof ; and moreover their universal acceptance witnesses to ancient tradition. The existence of God, at any rate (whether of one or of several), and the rule of a providence are self-evident, generally accepted, and morally necessary truths. They who deny it injure human society and must be punished. On religious grounds, then, war must be declared with another nation only if its worship of God is immoral and inhuman in character. To the question whether war is to be declared against a nation because it will not accept Christianity, Grotius answers that, quite apart from the consideration of the nature of the Christianity presented, the rejection of a faith which rests on historical evidence, and only arises through supernatural influences, can be subject to no human jurisdiction. The horizon is wider here than with Althusius, and a natural theology is established. At this point Grotius proves himself to be in sympathy with the endeavours which we shall now pass on to discuss.

CHAPTER VII

NATURAL RELIGION

THE vigorous intellectual movement of the Renaissance, and the great extension of the intellectual horizon, could not fail to exert a deep influence on religious life. The Reformation is already a testimony to this, although, in itself, it must be regarded as attempting to limit, rather than as initiating, the religious movement. While, in opposition to it, and amongst the most remarkable phenomena of the period of the Renaissance, especially towards its close, belongs the endeavour to find a religion which shall be independent of all external forms and traditions, and shall be grounded in the very nature of man. And just as with natural right, so here, two ideas go hand in hand ; for that which is really grounded in human nature must appear again in the different historical forms under which the intellectual life of man presents itself. A comparison of the different contending confessions, whose number was just at this time on the increase, operated in conjunction with the newly awakened faith in the self-sufficing power of human nature. In the Humanism of Italy there had already arisen efforts to develop a circle of religious ideas, which should be independent of the teaching of the Church. Plato's doctrine, as understood by the Neo-Platonists, was chiefly taken as the basis. The Platonic Academy in Florence exercised great influence in this respect—an influence which extended beyond the borders of Italy. The individual could find in fervent faith in a personal God, and in the immortality of the soul, a satisfaction for his religious needs which freed him from many of the dogmas and ceremonies of the Church, while, at the same time, it enabled him to perceive in them a deeper symbolical signification. In Germany and the Netherlands this Humanistic current was united with a mystical tendency which had been quietly working, all through the Middle Ages, for a more inward and a freer religiousness. It was in this spirit that the Swabian SEBASTIAN FRANCK and the Dutchman COORNHERT protested against the new Protestant dogmatism. They pointed to an inner religious experience which could exist under very different forms of faith. Franck regarded the invisible Christ as identical with the natural light, a spark of which is found in every human spirit, and which may therefore be kindled in the heathen. It is possible, Coornhert says, to follow the laws of Christ without knowing Him by name. These two are the precursors of the religious philosophy of a later day, which sought to understand positive religion and its signification, not through external criticism of ready-made dogmas, but in the deepening of the natural spiritual foundation, and of inner experience, the ultimate source of, and the unfailing refuge from, all dogmas. They themselves were to experience the fanaticism of the creeds. The name which was generally given to those who took up an independent position over against the confessions, was applied more particularly to Coornhert, whom the Dutch preachers called a " Prince of Libertines." [9]

Natural religion developed into still more definite forms in France and England. The long and violent religious wars in France could not fail to arouse the need of getting beyond the strife of creeds, and of directing attention to the human side possessed by each one of them. In the year 1577 Henry of Navarre (afterwards Henry IV.) wrote : " Those who follow their consciences honestly belong to my religion, and I belong to the religion held by all good and honest men." Contemporaneously with this, Montaigne had, in his own way, arrived at the notion of a universal religion to be found in all men, whatever be their conception of the Deity. The most noteworthy testimony in this direction, however, is contributed by JEAN BODIN, whose ideas on the subject of the theory of politics we have already discussed. He has left us a conversation between seven men (*Colloquium heptaplomeres*), each one of whom has his own religious standpoint, which he expounds, without reserve, but with the greatest friendliness, and with the finest comprehension of the personal side of religious ideas. A rich Catholic of Venice assembles round his table a circle of friends for the purpose of discussing different subjects, amongst which, for a time, religion occupies the foremost place. Among the participants are to be found, beside the Catholic host, a Lutheran, a Calvinist, a Jew, a Mohammedan, and two men, each of whom in his own way supports a universal Theism. The objective and dramatic way in which the various standpoints are brought out is truly remarkable. Only the Lutheran, perhaps, is painted in rather sombre colours; at any rate he is not conspicuous for his acuteness. On one occasion, when the host had mixed some artificial among the natural apples that were on the table, the Lutheran is the only guest who quietly takes a mouthful of one of the former, without suspecting a trick. The host, who invariably appeals to the teaching of the infallible Church, without, however, being a fanatic, draws from this a moral: if sight, the sharpest of our senses, can be so deceived, how then can the spirit, imprisoned in the senses, be able to reach a sure knowledge of the highest things? After all the standpoints have been expounded,—in many passages with a display of great learning,—the conversation ends, although no real conclusion has been reached. A choir sings the anthem " Behold how lovely and beautiful a thing it is for brethren to dwell together in unity ! " After this the friends embrace and part. " They afterwards exercised piety and honesty in wonderful harmony; having intercourse with one another and studying in common ; but they held no subsequent debates on the subject of religion, although each one, in his religious life, kept to *his own* religion."

Bodin wrote this work in his sixty-third year, *i.e.* in 1593. It did not appear in print, but was circulated in manuscript, and was well known to the scholars of the seventeenth and eighteenth centuries. It is mentioned frequently—usually with horror. Only individuals, *e.g.* Leibniz in his riper years, expressed the opinion that it ought to be published. This was not done, however, till the year 1841, when it was published by Guhrauer in the form of a somewhat abbreviated translation, and may now serve as an example of what, a few centuries ago, was almost unanimously condemned as impiety.

Since Bodin himself has nowhere given us directly to understand which of the speakers in the *Heptaplomeres* express his own view, there has been some difference of opinion on this point. For some time the general opinion was that Bodin

sympathised with Judaism, the representative of which is depicted with especial power and knowledge. But if we take into
account what is otherwise known of Bodin's religious tendencies,
and compare this with what is brought forward in the course
of the conversation, we shall form a different opinion.
There exists a letter from Bodin to a friend, written at an earlier
date, in which he expresses himself in the spirit of the universal
Theism with which we are already acquainted. "Do not," he
says, "let thyself be led astray by different views on religion.
Hold fast in thy spirit to this only, that true religion is nothing
else than the turning of a purified soul to God. That is my,
or rather Christ's, religion." He goes on to show that men
would wander in darkness for ever if, from time to time, great
men were not raised up as examples. Among such belong,
beside the Jewish patriarchs and prophets, the Greek and
Roman sages. Plato is especially extolled for proclaiming
the ideas of God and of the immortal soul. What he initiated
Christ has completed, and after Him, chosen men have worked
in His spirit. The same idea of a progressive revelation
through a sequence of wise men, before as well as alongside
of the Mosaic, Christian, and Mohammedan religions, is now
again brought forward by one of the two persons in the
Heptaplomeres who defend universal Theism. Toralba maintains
that the best religion must be the most ancient. The first man
received his knowledge and his piety from God Himself. The
belief in *one* God, according to the testimony of the Bible, preceded the Jewish religion ; it was the religion of Abel, Enoch
and Noah ; it was Job's religion. After they had abandoned
natural religion, which is implanted in man together with his
reason (*cum recta ratione mentibus humanis insita*), men wandered
in complicated labyrinths. Natural law and natural religion
suffice ; all other religions—Christianity, Judaism, Moham-
medanism and Heathenism — are superfluous. For natural
religion no special instruction and no education is needed ;
man was created for it, it lies in his own nature. The reason
implanted within us distinguishes and judges between the good
and the bad. In a select few, this religious and moral capacity is
found to exist with greater strength than in others. Toralba
(like Bodin in the letter quoted) praises Plato because, "not
without divine help and illumination," he attained to such great
wisdom concerning divine things. The nature of the Deity is

infinite ; it cannot be comprehended in thought, far less,then,can it be expressed in words.   We come nearest to God when we call Him the eternal Being, that which is exalted above the corporeal, and is infinite goodness, wisdom, and power.   In this idea Greek philosophers are at one with Hebrews and Ishmaelites, so that it must certainly be implanted by Nature.

There is one more characteristic of Toralba which reminds us of Bodin himself.   Although in many respects so far ahead of his age, yet with regard to *one* thing he is a true child of his age.   He believes with all his heart in magic and devils, and even wrote a book against those godless men who recommended caution and mercy in the punishment of witches.   It is the devil himself, he thinks, who moves them to this mildness against those who are possessed.   In the second book of the *Heptaplomeres* this point is touched on in a discussion between Toralba and Senamus, the speaker who, on the whole, is nearest to Toralba.   Toralba says that the modern physicists have one fault, *i.e.* that they try to explain all things by natural laws, and will recognise no interference either of God or of devils.   Senamus answers that by such a recognition all natural science would be rendered nugatory, since it presupposes definite natural laws.   In proof of his view, Toralba adduces several stories of devils, and can here rejoice in the full support of the Lutheran.   Senamus rejoins that even if there were devils able to interfere in the physical world, yet it is not certain that miraculous phenomena could be explained by them ; and, on the other hand, if we assume an interference on the part of devils, why not explain everything in Nature by devils? Moreover, he emphasises the necessity of subjecting stories of witches to a critical examination.

Toralba's standpoint is Bodin's own as we know it from his utterances *in propria persona*.   And yet he puts a criticism in the mouth of Senamus which Toralba is not able to answer. Senamus is altogether the critical spirit of the *Heptaplomeres.* To the question who is to be the arbiter in religious disputes, the Lutheran answers : Christ, Who is God.   Senamus draws his attention to the fact that the dispute turns, amongst other things, on this very question of the divinity of Christ.   The Calvinist would rely on witnesses and records.   Senamus asks where the genuine witnesses and evidences are to be found ?   The Catholic points to the Church ; but Senamus asks which of the many

Churches is the true one? The Lutheran appeals to the Bible ;
the Mohammedan to the Koran ; Toralba rejects the appeal
to authorities, and is of opinion that the wise men must decide
the question ; Senamus asks, however, who the wise men are?
And when the Catholic finally demands that a distinction be
made between the essentials and non-essentials of religion,
Senamus points out that the main cause of dispute is as to
where this line of demarcation shall be drawn.

Senamus adopts the same attitude towards Toralba's
natural religion as towards the Heathen, Mohammedan, Jewish
and Christian religions. All, he thinks, are well-pleasing to
God if they are exercised with an upright heart. He himself
likes to frequent all kinds of temples, wherever they are to be
found. He will offend no one—not the most believing, the
Catholic, the " religiosissimus," any more than the man whose
religion consists only in the belief in *one* God. He does not, that
is to say, oppose natural religion to the positive religions. Bodin
has let Senamus give utterances to thoughts which contain
a corrective to dogmatism, into which, as history shows,
"natural" no less than positive religion may fall. Even if
his own standpoint coincides with Toralba's, yet he has
thrown out a suggestion which goes further than any of the
latter's. It is not impossible that, in the later years of his life,
he began to doubt his own earlier opinions within the spheres
of theology and demonology, and that he expressed this doubt
through Senamus, without being able to build up a new conception on the basis of what he makes him maintain.

The notion of natural religion was introduced to a wider
circle, and in a completely elaborated form, by Lord HERBERT
OF CHERBURY, in his work *De Veritate* (1624). Like
Althusius, Grotius, Coornhert, and Bodin, he was a statesman
who took part in the public affairs of his day, and had the
opportunity of gaining extended experience, and of instituting
comparisons. He belonged to a noble Welsh family ; his
ancestors had been sturdy knights and he himself exhibited
the same warlike spirit. War and duels are a leading theme
of his *Autobiography*. His sword sat very loose in its sheath,
although he maintains that he had drawn it in the behalf of
others only. He was born in 1582 or 1583 and received a
careful education, which he afterwards carried on himself without intermission. It was his wish to educate himself as a man of

the world.   After having, while only in his sixteenth year, married a rich heiress, he studied at Oxford, and from thence repaired to court.   He afterwards spent some time in the camp of Maurice of Orange, travelled in Germany and Italy, and was for many years English Ambassador in France.   Neither at court nor in the camp, nor while holding his diplomatic appointment, however, did he forget his " dear studies."   He finished his famous book in Paris, where he submitted it to Grotius.   Although the latter's opinion was very favourable, yet Herbert had grave doubts as to whether he ought to publish it, for he knew that it would excite considerable opposition.   One day, as he was sittting in his sunny room unable to decide, he determined to submit his doubts to a supernatural decision.   Book in hand, he threw himself upon his knees and besought God, Who is not only the author of light but also the source of all inner illumination, to give him a sign which should encourage him to publish ; if there were no sign, he would suppress the book. Immediately he heard a faint note, which came out of the clear sky and was like no earthly sound, and thereupon he confidently published his book.[10]   This event does not, as has been thought, conflict with the view developed by Herbert in his book, for he believes that God is not only active in human reason, but that He also answers the prayers of men through special manifestations.   Like Bodin's Toralba, he believes in miracles.   Shortly after the appearance of his book he was recalled from his ambassadorship, since his bold procedure did not suit the hesitating policy of James I.   He spent the rest of his life partly in London, and partly on his estate in Wales, occupied in historical and philosophical studies. At the outbreak of the Civil War his attitude was hesitating, but he finally attached himself to the Parliamentarians.   He would have preferred to combine, as in his earlier days, public activity with private study, and he never got over his political disappointments.   He died in 1648.

Herbert prepared the way for his doctrine of natural religion by means of a theory of knowledge which is not without historical interest.   If truth can be apprehended by us, there must be capacities in us for the purpose.   In addition to the critical reason and to outer and inner sense there is a natural instinct which leads to the development of certain truths, common to all men (*notitiae communes*).   We have already

met this Stoical doctrine in Melancthon and his school.   With
Herbert they serve as the foundation of universal truths
which the comparison of different religions leads us to accept.
Peculiar to himself, however, is the way in which he unites the
source of these common truths with the instincts which make
for the preservation of the individual and of the race.   The
natural instinct out of which they arise is the original force
of every man and of the whole world,—the instinct of self-
preservation in the widest sense, through which the divine prescience makes itself known.   Everything in the world strives,
without conscious reason, towards that which suits it best.
And since the "common notions" are conducive to the preservation of life and the maintenance of peace, the instinct of
self-preservation prompts to their development and recognition.
The truths most important for the individual and for
society, then, are the object of instinctive recognition.   When
freed from impure accretions, and reduced to methodical
order, they form an epitome of divine wisdom.   Such truths
are the following : mutually contradictory assertions cannot
all be true ; there is one first cause of all things ; Nature does
nothing in vain ; do nothing to others which thou wouldst not
that they should do unto thee.   The most important logical,
ethical, and religious ideas, therefore, have been established by
natural instinct in the manner indicated.   More than indications
Herbert does not give.   The relation of the original truths to
natural instinct is not made clear, and it is evident that between
the two very many intermediate psychological links must be
supplied, if we are to understand how the struggle for existence
—to use a modern form of expression—can induce us to set
up certain notions as self-evident.   These intermediate links,
however, Herbert does not seek to discover, while he sometimes
makes the natural instincts and the original truths amount to
the same thing.

Herbert makes front on three sides.   First against those
who place faith higher than knowledge, and who understand
by faith only that which their sect believes, seeking to procure
acceptance for this faith by threats of punishment in a future
life.   Together with this, generally, goes the belief in the
depravity of nature.   A godless belief, for it contradicts the
providence which expresses itself in the natural instincts !
Secondly, against those who would prove everything by

argumentation (*discursus luxuriosus*).   This scholastic pedantry does not see that natural instinct, as well as the outer and inner sense, stands higher than reason.   For natural instinct expresses itself before the reasoning faculty is aroused, and works independently of it ; it is to be found in all ; it works without hesitation, with entire certainty and is the necessary condition for self-preservation.   Thirdly, he turns against those who would deduce all knowledge from the senses and who suppose the mind to be originally an unwritten tablet (*tabula rasa*). But it is precisely these fundamental notions which are the necessary conditions of experience.   And objects themselves could certainly not cause us to react upon them.   The unanimity of men's notions exhibits the existence of a natural instinct which may also be deduced from the goodness of God, Who could not leave men helpless.

Now it is on just such a natural instinctive foundation as this that natural religion is based.   Herbert develops this incidentally in his *Autobiography*.   Faculties and impulses arise in us to which the data of experience do not afford full scope ; nor can they, by its means, attain to complete satisfaction; only the perfect, eternal, and infinite will be able to give us rest.   God Himself is their proper object.   In every sound and normal man, consequently, this same faculty of religion is to be found, even though it develop itself in the most widely different manner and never, perhaps, attain expression in any external worship.   Five propositions form the basis of all religion and are everywhere valid : there is one highest divine Being ; this Being is to be worshipped ; the most important part of His worship consists in virtue together with piety ; blasphemy and crime must be atoned for by repentance ; punishment and reward follow after this life.   Everything in the various religions which does not contradict these propositions, but serves to confirm them, is to be believed.   If there are men who dispute them, this is because so many false and unworthy notions have crept into the positive religions that some men are thereby induced to reject all, without excepting natural religion.   The five propositions in and for themselves suffice ; to these we must hold fast and leave disputable questions alone.   By means of the natural instinct on which natural religion is based an uninterrupted inner revelation to the individual is effected, so that he is independent of the counsel of priests.

We might appositely apply to Herbert the words of Senamus, *i.e.* that it is by no means easy to draw the line between the essential and the inessential in religion. To adduce a proof, too, that these five propositions are contained in all religions would be impossible. And even if it could be shown that they are universal, yet it would by no means follow that they are established by natural instinct. And supposing they had such an instinctive origin, their mode of development, as we have already pointed out, remains to be shown. Herbert's procedure is too rapid and altogether too dogmatic. On his way he passes by a whole series of epistemological, psychological and religious problems. The mode of conception, however, which he sketched in outline, is the work of a powerful hand and has come to be of great historical importance. The existence of a religious consciousness, which feels itself independent of all existing religious communities, and assumes a critical attitude over against them, was now proved.

CHAPTER VIII

LORD HERBERT occupied himself alternately with his sword and with his book, and returned from his diplomatic engagements at the court of Paris to his study, and the writing of his work *De Veritate*. But the need of the age to produce new thoughts and to burst through the stiff ecclesiastical forms in which the movement of the Reformation had so quickly congealed, expressed itself too under less brilliant circumstances. JAKOB BOEHME neglected his awl and last to write his *Morgenröte im Aufgang*. He too had seen something of the world before he took up his pen. As a shoemaker's apprentice he had had his *Wanderschaft ;* afterwards he settled in Görlitz, and in the quiet of the workshop his thoughts were no less busy than his hands. He was not an altogether uneducated man ; he calls himself a philosopher and an investigator of nature, and he had some acquaintance with works on astronomy ; curiously enough, he is so far a Copernican as to make the earth and most of the planets move round the sun ; he had read the works on natural philosophy of the physician PARACELSUS ; probably also the works, which were circulated in manuscript, of the mystic VALENTIN WEIGEL, in which the ideas of Paracelsus were combined with the teachings of earlier mystics. Moreover, he was a pious man and knew his Bible and the Lutheran doctrines. But he stated his own problems and treated them with an intellectual force and freedom which make his works valuable even now, and which carried him beyond the limits of dogmatism. While Bodin and Herbert attack the religious problem more externally, it presented itself to Boehme within the confessional circle of ideas ; he worked at these unceasingly until the current of his thought burst through all dams. In his naïve but strong self-reliance the shoemaker of Görlitz bore the stamp of the age of the Renaissance, as also the constituent elements of his thought-structure, which had found their way to him through many intermediate links and after many transformations, pointed back to the philosophical and naturo-philosophical movements of that time. He used whatever was at his disposal to solve the problem which for some time almost reduced him to despair A remarkable example of how the philosophical turn of mind is able to assert itself just where it would seem, by inner and outer circumstances, to be excluded ! So long and so hard had he wrestled with these tormenting thoughts that it seemed to him a revelation, a higher illumination, when he perceived the possibility of a solution. In the nineteenth chapter of the *Morgenröte* he has described how the light appeared to him in the midst of his doubts, and it seemed to him as though " life had pierced into the heart of death." At that time he was twenty-five years old ; the story goes that his fundamental notions first clearly revealed themselves to him while he was in an ecstatic condition, into which he had been thrown by gazing at a shining metal key. And these notions were to ripen twelve years more before he wrote his first work (*Die Morgenröte*) in 1612. That a cobbler should thus dare to philosophise so boldly was a great source of annoyance to the rector into whose hands a copy of the book had fallen. He accused Boehme of heresy from the pulpit, and persuaded the magistrates to forbid him to write ; indeed for a time this gentle-hearted man had to leave the town. Boehme respected this prohibition for a few years only. In the latter years of his life he developed a most productive activity as an author. He died at Görlitz in 1624.

The religious problem presented itself to Boehme under two leading forms. He "became quite melancholy and sore troubled" when he perceived how insignificant a place man occupies in the outer world. It is a far way up to the heavens where God, according to the learned, dwells. And the heavenly bodies and the elements which occupy space seem to wander in their courses without regarding the ways of Man ! God's remoteness and the vanishing place of Man in Nature, then, were the first stone of stumbling. But added to this came the struggle of good with evil, both in the world of men and in Nature, together with the spectacle of the godless prospering equally with the pious, and the reflection that the best parts of the world are possessed by barbarous peoples, whom fortune favours more than the devout. This was the second stone of stumbling : How is the existence of evil compatible with the existence of God ?

He solves the first problem, which arises because the world of matter is so great and the world of spirit so small and so distant, by means of the thought that God's power and essence move in all things, in us as well as in the outer masses. God is not sundered from Nature, but is related to it as the soul to the body. Heaven is not up there in the sky, but it is here, within thyself, where the divine life stirs within thee. God is not far ; thou livest in God and God in thee, and if thou art pure and holy, then thou art God. There stir within thee the same powers as in God, and in the whole of Nature. Fire, air, water, earth,—all is God. Or else thou art not God's image. Thou canst be of no other matter than God Himself. When thou regardest the stars, the earth and the depths, thou seest God, and in this same God thou art and livest. It is true the heavenly bodies and the elements are not pure Deity itself, but the force from which they derive their life reigns in thee also. The inner motions in the essence of Man are of the same nature as those which take place in God. -- In all the processes of Nature, God is concealed ; only in the spirit of Man is He recognised. Man understands nothing of God so long as his soul is separated from Him as though it were a separate being.

If any one should call this line of thought heathenish, Boehme answers : " Hear and see, and note the difference. *My writing is not heathen but philosophical.* Moreover I am no heathen, but have a deep and true knowledge of the one great God, who is all ! " And he knows how much it had cost him to reach this thought, which had made the world alive for him, and had taught him that the spirit within it is not far away and strange, but is one with that which moves at the heart of all things. He had tried to put aside such thoughts, but great fear and anxiety had led him to take them up again. (*Morgenröte im Aufgang*, chaps. xix. xxv.). The religious long-ing after inner union with God, after the annulling of the distance from Him, coincides here with the philosophical need to find an interconnection between all things ; and both find support in the naturo-philosophical doctrine of Paracelsus, that man consists of the same elements as the universe.

But Boehme does not confine his reflections to Nature as she now is. He asks himself the question, How did this outer world of sense arise? why does not everything stand in such inner and harmonious interconnection that anxieties such as those which had tormented him could not arise? Paracelsus, the revolutionary chemist and physician, who evidently exercised great influence on Boehme, must here have afforded guidance, for he had taught that the differentiation of the elements had arisen through a process of separation and cleavage. Boehme follows this track with his usual boldness, and it leads, at the same time, to the solution of the second and graver problem. The problem of the origin of evil was, however, intensified for him since he will know nothing of God apart from the world and souls, but conceives the life of these to be a part of God's own life. For Boehme, evil consists precisely in this: that we seek to separate ourselves from the whole complex,—to be a totality, although we are only a part. Thus arises the cruel disunion, the externality, the dissension and the pain of the world. Boehme throws his discussion of this question into a mythological form, using Biblical and alchymistic ideas, often in quaint, but frequently also in fine, poetical combinations. He is quite aware of the mythological or symbolical form of his exposition. That he could at all solve the high questionings which pressed themselves upon him he explains thus,—that the same spirit which stirs in the world, and has stirred from all eternity, moves in him also. In other words, he uses his own inner experiences and struggles in order to explain Nature and its history, and to understand the innermost moving force of all things. And although he depicts in sensuous images a series of processes and catastrophes, a whole world-drama, he does not mean that anything of that kind actually took place at a definite time and place. Nor does he mean that it has developed historically and successively. He is describing what goes on everywhere and at all times, the eternal fundamental relations of the world-powers, the struggle which is not over once and for all, but which is carried on unceasingly, and in the midst of which he finds himself. His utterances on this point are astonishingly clear. " My meaning is not that there is in heaven any particular place or a particular body where the fire of the divine life breaks forth . . . but *I speak in this bodily fashion for the sake of my readers' lack of understanding;* for thou canst name no place—neither in heaven nor in this world—where the divine ought not to be and is not." "And although I have written here how everything happened, and how everything became formed and shaped, and how the Deity burst forth—yet thou durst not therefore think that there is ever any rest or extinction and afterwards a fresh bursting forth. Oh no, but *I must write bit by bit for the sake of my readers' lack of understanding.*" "The birth of Nature takes place to-day, just as it did in the beginning." "With the qualities [*i.e.* the divine happenings] there is no beginning, middle, or end." "Thou must know that I do not write this as a history, which has been related to me by some one else, but that I myself must always stand in the midst of this same battle, in which I, like all other men, am often tripped up." We are therefore justified in regarding the mythological form as of minor importance in our exposition of Boehme's thoughts.

Boehme was decidedly opposed to the theory of creation out of nothing. He is convinced that nothing can be explained out of an absolute unity. In the essence of God there must lie a plurality of moments, there must be some differentiation between them which makes itself felt and which can from the beginning be produced—not arbitrarily, but which nevertheless is like a dark source of all life. Boehme expresses this in strictly logical or psychological form in his *Theosophischen Fragen.* Thus, God is not only the Yes, but this positive moment must encounter the No, otherwise there would be no joy and no sensation, nothing, in fact, which could be decidedly prominent (no *Erheblichkeit*). Without such an inner, original antithesis of a positive and a negative moment there would be no will either ; pure unity has nothing in itself that it could will. Boehme, in his mythological language, calls this original element of opposition the wrath of God and the fundament of hell. With God, wrath is original as well as love He is the fundament of hell as well as of blessedness. Where. should the anger—all that is sharp, bitter, hard, and poisonous in the world—come from, if it had not its root in God? But originally the wrath is only a moment which serves to enable love to come consciously into prominence. Life demands such an opposition ; it is only because there are different "qualities" in Nature that there is motion, growth, and impulse in

everything.   Boehme explains the word "quality" (*Qualität*)
by a naïve etymology, expressing an inspired thought, as
coming from *quallen*, *Quelle*.   "Quality is the mobility, welling
forth, or impulse of a thing."   *Qualificierung* is the same as
motion (*Bewegung*).   He is not content with ascribing to things
dead, unmoving qualities, but resolves everything into active
forces and tendencies.   That warmth, for example, is a quality,
means that it heats, illuminates, dissolves, melts.   The plurality
of qualities—*i.e.* of the original qualities—is, then, for Boehme
a matter of fact, since, without such a difference, no motion,
no life, no consciousness would be possible.   From the beginning, however, the original forces are in harmonious co-operation.
The bitterness at the root of Nature only serves to bring out
the sweetness all the more strongly.   The bitter quality is in
God also, but as the "triumphant pang of joy."

     But, even if we acknowledge this original unity of opposites,
the riddle is still unsolved.   How can such a unity be reconciled with our experience of the hardness and bitterness in the
world, and, more particularly, of the sharp struggle between
good and evil, both in the inner and outer world, which are
certainly no mere moments in an inner harmony?   Here lies
the knotty point of all religious speculation.   It is no more
possible to deduce plurality from absolute unity than it is
possible to deduce discord from absolute harmony.   Small
wonder that Boehme's mythological fancy completely overpowered his thought at this point, where his feeling is already
so violently excited.   It is impossible to give a concise
description of the drama in which the persons of the Trinity,
the primitive "qualities" and *Quellengeister*, and the host of
archangels all take part.   The chief point is that one of the
elements in the original nature of the Deity, the element
of wrath, the No, presses forward with the desire to rule the
whole.   Not content with being a moment, it will become a
totality.   It is Lucifer who, blinded by his own brilliancy, by
his power, and by his place at the centre and crown of all
things, now triumphs over the whole Deity, and will have
a prouder and more splendid *Qualificierung* than God Himself.
It is at this moment that the strife and pain of the world come
into being; a fire is kindled which since then has never been
extinguished.   The opposites are loosed from their original
harmonious union, the hard matter is thrown out into space,

and now first arises the world as we know it. Evil, then, existed before men, its germ is in Nature itself. Boehme only now arrives at the point where the story of the creation, as told in the first book of Moses, begins; a story, moreover, for which he entertains no great respect, since several things in it "run quite contrary to philosophy and reason"; on which account, too, he could never believe that "that worthy man Moses was its author." He follows his own thoughts for the most part, trusting to the inner testimony of the spirit. Neither was he overawed by the learned: "I do not need their (*i.e.* the philosophers, astronomers, and theologians) ways and formulæ, since I have learnt nothing from them; but have another schoolmaster, which is the whole of Nature."

Boehme is especially indignant with those who say that God has designedly chosen some men for blessedness while He has ordained others to condemnation. Even if Paul or Peter had written this he would not believe it. God does not will evil; neither did He foreknow that things would happen as they have happened. And yet evil must have its root in God, the author of all things. This root is the negative moment, the "fundament of Hell"—that in God which is not God, if by God we understand love only (not anger). And yet, after all, it is a divine element, broken away from the original harmony; it is "God against God," as Boehme (*Morgenröte*, chap. xiv. § 72) expressly says. It is on this account that the struggle in the world is so stern and violent; on both sides divine power is fighting! Hence the fear and pain which the struggle with self brings, and from which Boehme only saves himself by taking refuge in the thought of the heart of God which is ever at work, driving back the hardness and bitterness behind their borders.

Boehme realises in his theological speculations the psychological truth that the involuntary precedes the voluntary, and forms its foundation. He finds the origin of evil to lie, not in God's free will, but in the involuntary ground of Nature, which must contain different elements. He overlooked the great leap from difference to strife, from contrast to cleavage. How Lucifer's pride arose he cannot explain. He narrates here only, and does not establish. And yet his thought has ventured farther than the thoughts of a fervently religious man generally wander. Logically we must regard him on the

theological side as he regarded Lucifer. He set a dangerous
" quality "—*i.e.* thought—in motion, and when this source has
once begun to flow it is not easy to stop it again. It is, however, not pride but the innermost need of his understanding
which carries him on from step to step. The naïve self-
reliance of new-born thought keeps him from hesitating or
pausing. He expressly regards his task, as we have already
learnt from a characteristic utterance, as purely philosophical.
" What is still hidden ? " he asks in another place ; " the right
doctrine of Christ ? No, but Philosophy." This he will now
supply, and he attributes such great importance to the understanding he has reached, that he calls his first book " *Morgenröte
im Aufgang* " [Aurora] ; the time of consummation must now be
nigh ! The dawn is indeed in his thoughts. He felt the new
powers, even if he did not perceive whither they were leading.

Two important laws serve as the foundation of Boehme's
speculations : the law of contrast as the condition of all motion
and of all consciousness, and the law of development as a progressive unfolding of difference. With the law of contrast it is
quite clear that he starts from psychological experiences, as
may be seen from the characteristic sentence, " Nothing can
reveal itself without resistance." In the thought of development as the generation of differences he is under the influence
of Paracelsus. He introduced the concept of development
into the German language.[11] By a consistent use of this
law he carried religious thought up to its limit, a limit which
no subsequent attempt of a similar kind has succeeded in
transcending.

It might seem as if there were a great difference between
the religious speculations of Boehme and the natural religion
defended by Bodin, Cherbury and Grotius. Boehme was a
faithful believer—or thought himself to be so—in positive
Lutheranism. But he was consistent enough to perceive that
if divine light and life act as a counterpoise to the hardness
and bitterness which pervade the whole of Nature, access
to the light cannot be limited. Every man may work or
grow through the " anger " to the " love." Jews, Turks, and
Heathen, who knew nothing of Christ, have yet resembled Him.
" He who has love in his heart and leads a merciful and gentle
life, striving against evil and pressing through the anger of
God into the light,—he lives with God and is one in spirit

with Him, for God requires no other service." Bodin might quite well have put these words in the mouth of his Toralba. MARTENSEN (in a book on Jakob Boehme) finds them "curious and without foundation." But they have a secure foundation in Boehme's fundamental notions. Subsequent "speculative" theologians might envy him the sure course of his thought. Interesting for us, here, is it to notice how, in the midst of the orthodox Lutheran world, and in an ignorant artisan, we meet again in the sphere of religion with the universalistic tendency which characterises the philosophy of the Renaissance, and which is intimately connected with the circumstance that Man once more believed in his natural powers and dared to use his own thoughts.

B. THE NEW CONCEPTION OF THE WORLD

CHAPTER IX

THE ARISTOTELIO-MEDIÆVAL WORLD-SCHEME

THE conception of man can no more be separated from the conception of the cosmos than man himself can be separated from the world. Hence it is not altogether possible to follow the transformations which the conception of man underwent, unless we also take account of the modifications undergone by the conception of the world. The two conceptions act and react upon one another continuously. Thus Boehme's religious speculations are, to a certain extent, manifestly conditioned by the new cosmology (especially by the ideas of Paracelsus and Copernicus), and only become really comprehensible when taken in connection with it ; and this notwithstanding that he puts religio-psychological considerations in the first place. On the other hand, we find in several of the thinkers whom we should now regard as founders of the new world-conception, valuable ideas and discussions with regard to psychology and ethics, which, in and for themselves, entitle them to a place among the thinkers who discovered Man. Nevertheless it may perhaps be admissible to assign them their place under the point of view which constitutes their chief importance in the history of thought.

In order to understand the magnitude of the change in the conception of the world which ranks, together with its art and its discovery of man, among the greatest feats of the Renaissance, we must first get a clear idea of the main features of the world-scheme, which, as late as the fifteenth century, was regarded by learned and lay alike as beyond all question. It was descended from the Aristotelian physics and the Ptolemaic astronomy, and was interwoven with Biblical images ; a conjunction easily effected, since the whole world-scheme was based entirely on immediate sense data, merely giving these a more exact determination and a systematic carrying-out.

Even according to the current view, it was evident that there is a great difference between the motions in the heavens and those that take place on this earth. Here continual change seems to prevail. Phenomena increase and decrease, arise and pass away. Motions arise which, after a longer or shorter time, cease again. Very different is it up there : the stars continue in their regular course without any appreciable change, and that course leads them ever back again along the same path in eternal, ceaseless, circular motion. ARISTOTLE founded his conception of the world on this antithesis between the heavenly and the earthly or sublunary regions. He relies on that which perception appears to teach, pointing at the same time to the old faith of Greeks and barbarians alike, *i.e.* that the heavens are the seat of the eternal gods. The heavenly region is eternal ; the motion which takes place in it is likewise eternal, and absolutely regular. The sublunary region, on the contrary, is the home of transitoriness, where motion and rest, arising and passing away, alternate with each other.

These two regions, then, cannot consist of the same matter. The heavenly bodies must consist of matter which has its home in no one definite place, and which can therefore continue in motion throughout eternity. This matter, the " first body," Aristotle calls Æther. It fills the heavens, and in it the eternal circular motion takes place. Only circular motion can be eternal, since it alone always returns into itself, and goes from every point in the circle to every other point. In the sublunary region every motion stops at a certain point, *i.e.* when the body has reached its natural place. Here rectilinear motion prevails, which proceeds either outwards and upwards from the central point of the world, or else inwards and downwards towards this central point. That which has its natural place in or near the central point of the world is called heavy ; while that of which the natural place is situated above or near the upper regions of the sublunary world is called light. The constant changes in the earthly regions arise because the elements are not always in their natural places. The heavy element is earth, the light fire ; between these two lie water and air. For fire mounts ever aloft, while the stone that has been thrown into the air falls earthwards again. Every element strives after its appointed place in the universe. The four elements may pass into one another reciprocally, but they cannot be resolved into simpler component parts ; all bodies, on the other hand, consist of combinations of them.

There can only be one single world. If we were to suppose for a moment that there were several, we should see that the heavy elements must finally collect round one single central point, and thus we should again be reduced to one world. The earth, as perception shows us, is situated at the centre of the world, and from this, if we go outwards and upwards, we come first to the other three sublunary strata, and above these again to the region of the æther, the matter of which is purer the farther it is from the earth. The heavenly bodies, first the moon, the sun, and the other planets, then the fixed stars, are situated in solid but transparent spheres which turn on their axes. Aristotle adopted this belief from the astronomer Eudoxus. The ancients could not conceive the heavenly bodies moving freely in the heavens. All spheres revolve round the earth as the central point; the moon, the sun, and the other planets have each their sphere ; all these spheres, consequently the whole world-system, are enclosed by the " first heaven," the sphere of the fixed stars, which is itself moved directly by the Deity, while subordinate principles or spirits guide the motions of the other spheres. The highest is that which encompasses and limits. The upper or outer part of the world is the most perfect.[12]

The Aristotelian world-scheme presented a frame which apparently not only corresponded with the teaching of sensuous perception, but was also able to take up into itself the observations made by the astronomers of later antiquity. In order, it is true, to take account of the motions to and fro of the planets, it was found necessary to ascribe very complicated motions to the planetary spheres ; but this difficulty was met by conceiving every single planet as bound to several spheres at once, of which each has its own motion. Or else it was thought that the motions did not take place in simple circles, but in smaller circles, or epicycles, whose central points moved in larger circles. And with the progress of inquiry this system of epicycles became more and more complicated. Ptolemy of Alexandria (in the second century A.D.) gave an exposition of the world-system which, like Aristotle's system in philosophy, was regarded as authoritative within the sphere of astronomy throughout the Middle Ages.

Since, like the Biblical cosmology, the Aristotelio-Ptolemaic system adopted the standpoint of sensuous perception, according to which the earth stands still while the sun and stars move, it readily lent itself to combination with the religious notions prevalent in the Middle Ages. It harmonised also, as Aristotle had perceived, with the old belief that the heavens are the seat of the Deity. An essential difference emerges, however, between the antique and the mediæval conception of the world. Aristotle, it is true, placed the earth at the central point of the world; but this was not because he thought that everything else in the world existed for the sake of the earth or its inhabitants. On the contrary, for him that which surrounds and limits was the highest ; while he regarded the earth as the place of the lowest matter. But in the mediæval view of the world, it is precisely on this earth and the events which take place upon it that everything hangs. Nevertheless this view was able to avail itself of the Aristotelian schema and of the notion of the imperfection of the sublunary world, since, according to it, the heavenly powers descend in order to intervene in mundane affairs and lead them towards the right goal.

Apart from the difficulties involved in the combined spheres or epicycles, this method of conception was, as a whole, clear and comprehensible. It rested on the supposition that sensuous space is absolute space, and that within this space there are absolute places. The philosopher or astronomer took—as the practical man does to this day—the terrestrial ball on which he found himself to be the absolute centre of the world. And the world which forms itself out of the different spheres around this central point had its limits in the outermost sphere—on the other side of which nothing existed. It was an essential part of the antique conception of Nature to think of everything as formed and limited. The unlimited was the dark and unformed, if not the evil. Here, too, the schema found a support in sensuous perception and imagination, which stop at some definite point and never feel the necessity of asking what lies beyond.

G

Such a world-scheme as this was open to attack on two
sides.   Firstly, when observations and calculations should be
brought forward conflicting with it or, at least, making another
conception possible or probable.   Secondly—and this is
perhaps more interesting to us here—whenever the naïve confidence in the absolute validity of sensuous space should be
disputed.   When it has become evident that every determination of place is dependent on the place of the observer, there is
no longer any absolute distinction between the heavenly and
the earthly regions, nor between the natural places within the
earthly region.   In both these ways the Aristotelio-mediæval
world-scheme was attacked by the inquiries of the Renaissance period.   And, as we shall see, the latter way was the one
first adopted.

CHAPTER X

NICOLAUS CUSANUS

IN defiance of the sentence of antiquity, the philosophical necessity of bursting through the clearly articulated and limited world-scheme of Aristotle was already making itself felt. The founder of the Neo-Platonic school, Plotinus, expressed a thought which, when further carried out, was bound to lead beyond every dogmatic limitation and parcelling-out of Nature. Unlike Plato and Aristotle, he did not regard harmonious limitation as the highest. The highest must be something which lies on the further side of all boundaries or leads out beyond them. Thus the infinite was no longer a purely negative somewhat, but the expression of a positive, inexhaustible fulness, over against which thought and speech are, in the last resort, powerless. Finite forms, essences, and regions, then, are, each in themselves, only limited manifestations of the infinite. Although Plotinus still stands on the soil of Greek thought, yet his thought is often perilously near losing itself in mysticism. He was the ancestor of the mysticism of the Middle Ages, of a tendency which again and again protested against the conceptualistic dogmatism of the scholastics. In the conception of Nature this tendency led to the accentuation, notwithstanding the variety of external phenomena, of the interconnection of the inner forces and to a feeling of dissatisfaction with fixed forms and limits in all departments of thought. In this way mysticism cleared the way for the doctrine of development. Thus it was a fact of no small significance that during the Renaissance it was the Neo-Platonic philosophy in particular which was the object of enthusiastic study. The Academy of Florence did excellent service here.

It was not these new studies, however, which first brought
NICOLAUS CHRYPFFS, called CUSANUS after his native town,
under the influence of the Neo-Platonic ideas.   He had been
brought up at Deventer by the " Brethren of the Common
Life," on whom the German mediæval mysticism had made a
great impression.   He was born in 1401 at Cues, a small town
near Fries, but ran away while a boy from his parents' house, in
order to escape his father's ill-treatment.   A nobleman, with
whom he took refuge, sent him to be educated at Deventer.   He
afterwards studied jurisprudence, mathematics, and philosophy
at Padua.   But mysticism and the problems which it suggest are
always the key-note of his thought.   For some time it seemed
as though he would dedicate himself entirely to practical life.
Originally an attorney, he afterwards entered the Church and took
an active part in the negotiations for the purpose of Church
reform.   At first he supported the Council of Basle, but he subsequently became convinced that the only hope for ecclesiastical
reform lay in strengthening the Papacy.   Appointed Bishop of
Brixen, he had to sustain a severe struggle with the Archduke
Sigismund of Austria, and was even imprisoned for some time.
Raised to the office of Cardinal by Pius II., he was sent to
Germany on a visitation to the churches and religious houses.
Here too, in his zeal for reforming the morals of the clergy and
the convents, he had to surmount violent opposition.   The
manner in which he made war on superstition especially
witnesses to his great intellectual superiority in comparison with
the age in which he lived.   He blamed the Church for having
furthered its aims by means of superstition, and for procuring
revenues by means of relics and bleeding wafers.   Witchcraft
and magic he regarded as survivals of heathenism, which were
only encouraged by the persecutions to which they were subjected.   He found that there were most witches where there was
most belief in them.   He himself examined two old women who
were reputed to be witches ; they were half-witted, and " what
they believed themselves to have actually experienced, the devil
had sent them in dreams."   But while thus taking part in the
struggles of his age, his thoughts were occupied with his own
problems.   According to his own account, the fundamental
thoughts of his most interesting and best-known work (*De
docta ignorantia*) occurred to him as he was sailing back to
Italy from Constantinople, whither he had been sent on a papal

embassy. This was followed by a series of other works in which he partly developed, partly modified, his ideas. He died in the year 1464 at Livorno, during the preparations for the crusade, planned by his friend Pius II., against the enemies of faith, science, and literature.

Cusanus stands at the boundary-line between the Middle Ages and the Renaissance and between theology and philosophy. His deepest interest, it must be confessed, is theological. For him, the great problem to be solved was that of the Trinity. But in his treatment of this, he has incidentally worked out thoughts of great interest on questions of epistemology and natural philosophy. With his mystical tendency it was only natural that he should recognise no sharp delimitation between the different conceptual spheres. It is this intermixture which is the root of the dark and abstruse element which appears in his writings side by side with many brilliant ideas. It is of no interest to us to examine the whole philosophy of Cusanus. We need only show how he arrived at the thoughts which were to destroy the world-scheme based on the evidence of the senses, the investigations of antiquity, and the authority of the Church.

Cusanus conceives knowledge as the activity which combines and assimilates. The senses receive scattered impressions, but even on this level thought is at work, partly in collecting the separate impressions into one whole, partly in the form of an astonishment which incites us to go on. The different sense impressions are united by the imagination (*phantasia*), the different complexes of images by the reason (*ratio*) ; but on all these stages thought (*intelligentia*) is active and seeks finally to reduce all differences to an absolute unity. At this point, however, there arises the difficulty that without plurality and difference (*alteritas*) our thought can know nothing. Just at its zenith thought finds also its limit. It can only approach the absolute unity by means of a mystical intuition, in which all the radii of existence meet together in a single centre, and which annuls the process of knowledge and procures rest for thought. Thus the consummation of thought is its cessation.

This conception of knowledge (developed in his *De conjecturis*, cap. xvi.) explains what Cusanus understands by " learned ignorance " (*docta ignorantia*), an expression which had already been employed by Bonaventura. By it he means the consciousness of thought of its own limit conjoined with the mystical presupposition that the best and highest lies on the further side of this limit, although, of course, in the continuation of the process which leads up to it.   In the work entitled *De docta ignorantia* the matter is explained thus : Our knowledge seeks to rise above the oppositions and contradictions exhibited in experience.   It discovers on a closer examination that even the greatest contrasts, even the most mutually contradictory conditions, amount to one and the same thing, if once the point of unity can be discovered.   Thus by means of the concept of magnitude, maximum and minimum coincide : both are absolute quantities, each one in its direction ; both are superlatives, and this even on the same scale.   This concept of magnitude, however, embraces them both.   But our knowledge cannot discover all the members of the scale.   It cannot transcend opposites.   It advances from member to member but can never reach the perfect unity of opposites, any more than we can form a perfect circle, however many sides we add to the polygon.   Our thought is related to truth, to the perfect unity of opposites, as the polygon to the circle.

The infinite is the measure and ideal of the finite.   In it opposites are united.   An infinite curve is exactly the same as . an infinite straight line.   But every line which we can conceive is either straight or crooked.   We can never transcend finite determinations.   And yet this is necessary if there is to be a knowledge of God.   God can only be thought under the abolition of all particular determinations ; but nothing is left to us when all particular determinations are removed.   God as the unity of all things, as embracing all—even the mutually contradictory (*omnium rerum complicatio, etiam contradictoriorum*), is therefore incomprehensible.   No name can be predicated of Him.   For every name comes from a distinction and separation, where one thing is set against another.   In God, however, are no opposites, any more than there are opposites within the concept of magnitude along the whole scale from maximum to minimum.   In religious worship learned ignorance is superseded by holy ignorance (the *docta ignorantia* by the *sacra ignorantia*), negative by positive theology.   Determinate predicates and names are then attributed to God, although none of them are to be taken literally.   When, *e.g.*, God is called Light, this does not mean the light which forms the antithesis to darkness ; in the infinite light even darkness is light, just as the minimum lies within the same scale as the maximum.

The Aristotelian school mistook this truth, which affords the only entrance to a mystical theology. On this account they could not rightly understand the doctrine of the Trinity, for they did not perceive the necessity of a principle which should be able to reconcile the opposites expressed by Father and Son: *Spiritus sanctus est nexus infinitus!* And on this account too they reached no true knowledge of Nature. They halt at the difference between possibility and reality, between matter and form, between the producing and the produced, and do not seek for the bond which is able to comprehend all these opposites and express their unity. This bond is motion. Motion is neither only produced nor only producing, but both at the same time, and this is true of all other opposites. And this identification of the combining principle of the Trinity with that of Nature is no accident with Cusanus: the Holy Spirit is the bond of Nature, is one with Nature as the sum of all that motion brings about. Cusanus makes no distinction between coincidence (*coincidentia*), comprehension (*complicatio*), and union (*connexio*) of opposites, although the three terms denote very different relations. His examples are chiefly of a union of extremes through transitions and middle terms, and of their comprehension by means of the continuity thus effected. But this is something other than a complete annulling of contraries. He is lacking here in perfect clearness as to the nature of the very concept which denotes his highest point of view. This again is a result of the absence of demarcation between the different spheres of knowledge which we have already remarked.

The ease with which he passes, in his mystical contemplation, from the divine process to that of Nature, and applies the same points of view to both, is specially characteristic of Cusanus. That the two processes, the life of the Deity and the life of Nature, do not coincide is, however, clear to him. They are related to one another as the comprehending unity (*coincidentia, complicatio, connexus*) of opposites to their separate appearance in time and space. Nature is an evolution (*explicatio, evolutio*) of that which was bound together in the Deity into a perfect unity, as the line is evolved from the point (through continuous repetition), and reality from possibility. But how this trans-

formation from the complicative to the explicative form takes
place ; how this absolute coincidence of opposites is resolved
into their appearance as opposing powers ; how the confusion
of manifoldness supersedes the harmony of unity ;—all this is
a' riddle which our thought cannot solve.   Every finite existence
is a limitation, and the great problem lies precisely here : how
can the infinite limit itself?   Cusanus says somewhere that
there is no positive cause of plurality, since only the unity of
things can proceed from God.   Dost thou appeal to God in
explanation of the origin of the plurality, then thou admittest
that thou canst not understand it ? [13]

Though Cusanus, too, ends in dualism at this point (since a
deep gulf appears between his knowledge of God and his
knowledge of Nature), yet in his idea of motion as the
combining principle of Nature and as that which constitutes
the world into a totality, not less than in his idea of the
development of the world as a progressive process of " complication" and "explication,"[14] he has laid down fruitful points of view,
which anticipated the thoughts of later philosophers.   They
enabled him to defend at the same time the particularity of
individual beings (as particular complications or contractions),
and the continuous connection and transition of the same.
While both Antiquity and the Middle Ages had regarded
achieved actuality as the highest, the importance of potentialities
and of development now began to be recognised.   And this
was closely connected with the change that the concept of
infinity had undergone.   Instead of on finite and definitely
limited forms, weight was now laid on the infinite variation, the
continual transitions, which exhibit opposites as extreme cases
or stadia of a connected series.

In the religious sphere Cusanus had to meet a difficulty
which followed from the denial, according to his principles, of
the right to apply any concept whatever to the Deity.
Consistently with this he ought to have concluded that all
religious ideas are symbolical or mythological ; as a good
Catholic, however, he was not able to take this step.   In his
Docta ignorantia he helps himself over the difficulty by
making a certain distinction among predicates.   Although all
predicates of the Deity are to be denied, yet the negation of
the greatest imperfections must be " truer " than the negation of
the highest predicates.   Thus it must be truer to say : God is

not a stone, than to say He is not life or not spirit—and from this again it follows that we are more justified in calling God life or spirit than a stone. It is clear that if, in the Deity as the infinite principle, *all* opposites fall together—or away—then even the greatest difference between predicates which we are able to make from our standpoint is of entirely vanishing significance. Hence, in his later writings, Cusanus seeks for positive determinations as well as negative, and lays greater weight on positive theology in comparison with negative, without succeeding, however, in laying the difficulties which he had himself raised.

Cusanus' fundamental thoughts were applicable at several very important points to the knowledge of Nature. By his dissolution of absolute antitheses into continual transitions he was led to discover the relativity of our ideas. The epistemological law of relativity found in him one of its earliest exponents. Thus, for example, he asserted the relativity of the concept of atoms. *In our thoughts*, he says, we can always continue to divide things ; but *actual* divisibility always ceases at a particle which is for us, as a fact, indivisible. A magnitude such as this, which is indivisible on account of its smallness, is an atom. But this practical cessation is no -proof that an absolute minimum has been reached, any more than the practical cessation in the summation of magnitudes is a proof of an absolute maximum. Just as an infinite division is impossible in reality because we must always stop at a certain point in the process of division, so also a continual motion is impossible because every body, on account of its own nature and the nature of its surroundings, must always encounter opposition. A perfectly round ball on a perfectly smooth surface would continue any motion once begun for ever if nothing in its conditions were changed. It would have to be regarded as an atom, and the force imparted to it would not be able to check its activity. But a ball which is not perfectly round would be unable to take up the imparted motion in such a manner as to convert it into a natural motion which, as such, could not cease. This is one of the most important foreshadowings of the Law of Inertia which appears before Galilei. And it is due to Cusanus' great capacity for conceiving everything in the definite relations which are essential to the complete unfolding of its nature. Of still greater interest is his doctrine—which also arose from this way of looking at things—of the relativity of determinations of place and of motion. The world can have neither centre nor circumference, for it could only have these in relation to something external, by which it is limited, and would thus not be the whole world. Wherever man finds himself—on the earth, the sun or one of the stars — he will always believe himself to stand at the centre. Only combine in thought these different points of view, and thou wilt see that it is impossible to attribute any figure to the world, just as it is impossible to attribute to it motion. Every point in the world may, with equal right, be called the centre, or be set in the periphery. And since the earth does not stand at the absolute centre of the world, it cannot be at rest. But we do not perceive its motion since there is no point at absolute rest which can serve us for comparison. We are like a man on a boat sailing with the stream who does not know that the water is flowing, and who cannot see the banks : how is he to discover whether the boat is moving ? Cusanus, that is to say, denies that the earth is the central point of the world, because, on general grounds, there can be no absolute central point, and absolute rest falls with the position of absolute centrality. On the other hand, he does not teach that the earth moves round the sun ; he annuls the geocentric theory without establishing the heliocentric. Those who might think the earth thus loses in dignity he consoles with the reflection that perfection does not depend on magnitude. The inhabitants of the earth are the more perfect the more they approximate to the ideal which is in harmony with their nature ; but it does not follow that this ideal must be the same as that of the inhabitants of other heavenly bodies. Man does not strive after another nature, but only after the consummation of his own. Neither can the transitoriness which characterises this earth prove its imperfection, for nothing is absolutely transitory. It is only the particular form of a being which ceases when it is dissolved into its elements. And such processes of dissolution may take place on other planets just as well as on the earth, since we must believe that they, no less than the earth, are subjected to external influences.[15] This doctrine dealt a severe blow at the Aristotelio-mediæval world-scheme. The certainty which was a necessary condition for the undivided authority of this world-scheme had been shaken. Reflection had lifted this globe of ours from its pedestal and had set it spinning in a motion which could never afterwards be checked. Moreover, within this scheme, the sharp contrast between heaven and earth was obliterated ; the possibility that, in both regions, the same laws and relations might hold good was suggested. A valuable contribution was thus rendered to the new conception of the world—a contribution, indeed, which sprang from the innermost kernel of the system of this profound thinker. That the ancients could not arrive at the doctrine of the relativity of motion, says Cusanus, is due to their ignorance of the *docta ignorantia.* They did not see that all our concepts only hold good in certain relations and fall away with them. Thus the same thought which, according to Cusanus, made a knowledge of God impossible, enables us to know that the world-scheme can be neither so limited nor so quiescent as had hitherto been supposed.

CHAPTER XI

THE philosophy of the deep-thinking Cardinal was the greatest task undertaken by thought in the fifteenth century. It opened the way for a new conception of the world by relaxing the inflexibility which had overtaken all concepts under the rule of Scholasticism. Not only in the inner laboratory of thought, however, but also in the world of outer experience, important preparatory steps were being taken. Experience became the key-word of the sixteenth century. Men turned from the reading of ancient books to the study of the ever young book of Nature. The need for this expressed itself, as was natural at first, in a confused, but for that reason all the more passionate, manner. Men sought to drag out of the world the fulness of content which was lacking in their books. And they had not sufficient critical power either to sift out genuine experiences, or to exclude their own favourite ideas and mystical interpolations. As representatives of this Titanic craving after empirical knowledge and knowledge of Nature we may mention the German physician and chemist PARACELSUS and the Italian physician and mathematician CARDANUS. These men, both of whom were destined to chequered careers, gave utterance not only to brilliant ideas within the sphere of their own particular branches of science, but also to philosophical conceptions. They disputed the Aristotelian conception of the world at several points, more especially the doctrine of the four elements ; and, in opposition to the Aristotelio-mediæval dualism of a heavenly and a sublunary world, they maintained the unity of the different parts of the universe with respect both to matter and to force. Although they considered themselves pioneers, particularly in regard to method, yet their investigations are anything but scientific or methodical. They had yet to learn the stricter

demands on method made by natural science, which were
emphasised by Leonardo da Vinci, Galilei, and Bacon.[16]   Their
thoughts, too, do not admit of being gathered up into an easily
apprehended whole; as is the case—notwithstanding all methodological shortcomings—with BERNARDINO TELESIO, whom we·
will therefore regard as the representative of the philosophy
based on experience, which, while it was antecedent to the·
founding of modern natural science, had yet already freed
itself from the Aristotelio-mediæval conception.

    With Telesio we step on to the soil of Southern Italy, which
had produced so many of the great thinkers of antiquity, and
which was to regain its ancient fame in the age of the Renais-·
sance.   It was the home of a Telesio, a Giordano Bruno, and
a Campanella.   These three thinkers form a unique series:
their ideas run in the same direction, however characteristic
may be the differences which they otherwise present.   Telesio
influenced both the others.   Born of a noble family at Cosenza,
near Naples, he took advantage of his favourable external
circumstances to pursue comprehensive studies.   After he had
studied at Milan, he went to Rome, where he suffered ill-treat-·
ment during the taking of the town by the Imperialist troops
under Constable de Bourbon.   Afterwards he went to Padua,
and here his breach with Aristotelianism-is said to have taken
place.   This laid the foundation of a clearly-defined antagonism
between the schools of Northern and Southern Italy.   While in
Padua and Bologna they continued to reverence Aristotle and,·
more or less blindly, to swear by his words, in South Italy men's
thoughts were turning in new directions, and new paths were
being opened out, while an attempt was made to found everything
on the newly emerging science of Nature.   After staying in
Rome with Pope Paul IV., who held him in high esteem, and
even wished to make him Archbishop, Telesio returned to South
Italy.   He lectured at Naples and founded an academy at
Cosenza.   In the year 1565 appeared the first part of his chief
work, *De rerum natura* (On the Nature of Things), which was
followed (1587) by a second part, dealing with men in their
psychological and ethical aspects.   Telesio died in the year
1588.   During the last years of his life he was the object of
violent attacks on the part of the monks, who thought that
with Aristotelianism all else must fall ; and a few years after
his death his works were entered on the Index.

Telesio contrasts his endeavour with that of all his predecessors : they in their great self-confidence had hoped to
penetrate into the secrets of Nature by means of their reason,
just as though they were equal with God in wisdom ; he himself
is more humble, and will only attain to human wisdom, which
has its limits in that which the senses teach us, and in what
may be inferred from resemblance with things that we perceive
by their means.   He will build, that is to say, on sensuous
experience, and on that alone.   In this way he believes he
will be able to arrive at a surer knowledge than that of his
predecessors.   *Non ratione, sed sensu !* is his motto.   But he is
convinced that sensuous perception will never bring him into
contradiction with himself, nor (this, however, he only added—
perhaps after he had learnt by experience—in a later edition)
in conflict with the Church.   Aristotelianism, on the contrary,
contradicts experience as well as itself and the Church !

The most important feature of Telesio's natural philosophy
is his endeavour to substitute the relation between matter
and *force* for that between matter and *form*, which recurs so
constantly with Aristotle.   It was characteristic of the antique,
æsthetic conception of Nature to look for the explanation
of natural phenomena in the forms under which they occurred ;
natural processes were understood by means of the fully
developed results which they effected.   The modern conception
of Nature goes farther back, and inquires as to the active
principles.   According to Telesio there are two such principles
(*principia agentia*) : an expanding principle which he calls heat,
and a contracting principle which he calls cold.   Heat and
cold, that is to say, are for him neither matter nor mere
qualities, but forces expressing themselves in two different
modes of motion.   Telesio was thus not far from saying that
everything which goes on in Nature is to be conceived as
motion.   These two principles work on matter which is never
increased or decreased, but which under their influence assumes
the most widely different forms, according to the different
proportions of contraction and expansion, and which is everywhere uniform, so that there is no need to assume a distinction
between heavenly and terrestrial matter.

Moreover, he was also decidedly opposed to Aristotle in
his teaching that matter is something other than space ; which
teaching gave its death-blow to the Aristotelian doctrine of

the "natural places" of the different elements. Different
places in space have not different qualities. The existence of
absolutely empty space must even be possible; it was pure
imagination on Aristotle's part to say that Nature abhors a
vacuum. The Aristotelian doctrine of elements falls to the
ground, not merely because the "natural places" no longer
hold good, but also because all that remains is the one per-
sistent mass (*moles*), which assumes various forms in accordance
with the varying proportions of expansion and contraction. If
we are to assume different elements, there can at most be two,—
one in which the expansive, and a second in which the contrae-
tive principle works. The former has its central point in the
sun, the latter in the earth. Telesio accepts the Aristotelian
world-scheme to this extent, but he regards the mass of which
both the heavenly bodies are formed as uniform, and only the
forces as different; and he also assumes a more lively interaction
between the heavenly and the earthly than did Aristotle. In
addition to this, he expresses himself as distinctly opposed
to Aristotle's theory that the heavenly spheres are guided
by particular spirits. The heavens move round, not because
they are constrained thereto by an alien principle, nor because
they strive after something that lies beyond them, but because
it lies in their own nature so to do. Similarly, the earth
remains at rest because this is its nature, *i.e.* cold and dark.
God does not intervene at particular points in Nature, but has
endowed every being with its own nature and manner of
working. And the several impulses to self-preservation of
individual beings are in harmony with one another, just as
the individual organs of an organism are in harmony, for they
serve the whole when each is active in the manner peculiar to
its own nature. There are therefore no especial final causes,
but it is a satisfaction to every cause to follow its own nature,
and thus arises the harmony between individual beings. Instead
of assuming an external accommodation and an external
intervention on the part of God, Telesio believed, on the contrary, that the divine wisdom is revealed precisely in this,—that
everything which happens according to necessary laws is, in and
for itself, purposive. The heavens do not move round for the
sake of the earth, but in accordance with their own nature, and
yet their motion benefits the earth.

Telesio evidently aims at establishing truer and more

fruitful concepts than those presented in the natural philosophy of Aristotle. But he offers no methodical, inductive proof of the validity and necessity of his fundamental concepts, and in so far denies his own programme, according to which he is to build on sensuous perception only. Against these fundamental concepts themselves objections may be—and were—raised. A contemporary philosopher, the Platonist PATRIZZI, although on important points a disciple of Telesio, yet carried on an interesting discussion partly with Telesio himself, and partly with one of his pupils,[17] in which he brings forward various pertinent objections against his system ; remarking, *inter alia*, that what Telesio calls matter cannot be apprehended by means of sensuous perception, which shows us particular and changing qualities only, not absolute, passive matter. Patrizzi here touches on the important question of the relation of substance to force. He further asks how it is possible to deduce from the two forces all the manifoldness of phenomena. Both these objections are valid, and the latter, especially, is confirmed by Telesio's extremely arbitrary and naïve explanations of individual phenomena. There was as yet no material to afford a scientific explanation of particulars, and at this point Telesio does not display the critical acumen which characterises his establishment of the fundamental concepts, valid for all knowledge of Nature. Moreover it was entirely arbitrary on his part to call the original principles Heat and Cold. Amongst other things it followed logically from this that the begetting of heat through motion must always be regarded as secondary, or as the awakening of a pre-existent heat ; while the begetting of motion through heat must be the original fact ; which, as Patrizzi also pointed out, was a purely arbitrary assertion. Finally, if heat is centralised in the sun and cold in the earth, this does not, according to Telesio, exclude the production of heat by the earth under the influence of the sun ; but in that case, as Patrizzi explains, the earth would be able to move also, since heat begets motion. Telesio did not answer this objection himself, but one of his pupils remarked that there were, to be sure, some people who believed the earth moved, but they had proved nothing beyond their own sagacity. The time when the Copernican theory could exercise a decisive influence on the world-conception had not yet come. Telesio's natural philosophy had to undergo a radical change in many of its particulars before it could be harmonised with the new astronomy, according to which it is the earth, the "cold" body, which moves, and the sun, the "warm" body, which is at rest. Notwithstanding this fact, however, Telesio contributed suggestions on many important points to the new world-conception. The best evidence of this is afforded by the anger which he excited among the Aristotelians. Disputations were organised throughout Italy in which the "forces" were arrayed against the "forms," and where the battle was sometimes—*e.g.* in a disputation of 1573 at Venice, between the Telesians and the students of Padua—fought out with corporeal weapons. The philosophies of Northern and Southern Italy here confronted one another.

Mind, according to Telesio, stands in the closest relation possible to matter—it is not really, indeed, anything different from it. The material forces—"Heat" and "Cold"—must possess the capacity of feeling, otherwise they would not be able to exist; for they must feel, in order, each one for itself, to be able to offer resistance to the other opposing force, to mark its approach, and to feel satisfaction in its own existence and working. Moreover, every material thing must be able to feel with other things, in order to follow them when they withdraw; this, too, presupposes sense and feeling. But we need not, on this account, attribute special sense-organs to things; for a sense-organ is nothing but a means for passing on an impression, and can be dispensed with in immediate feeling. In this mythological and animistic fashion, Telesio finds, in the animation of bodies, the necessary presupposition of their reciprocal action. Of more lasting importance is an argument which he uses in support of his theory of animism, viz. if the original forces and original matter possessed no feeling, the genesis of this in beings which consist of the original forces and the original matter would be altogether inexplicable, for nothing can give what it does not possess. He maintains, that is to say, the impossibility of explaining the genesis of consciousness out of matter, unless we suppose matter to be originally endowed with consciousness. But in so saying he confesses that the original matter and the original forces from which he started are by no means adequate to the explanation of all things in the world. For a new force is here introduced! And yet Telesio would not have admitted the validity of this criticism. For, as he attributes consciousness to matter, so, too, he conceives the soul as a material being. For if the soul were not material, how could it be influenced by material forces? How could it become aware of expansion and contraction, were it not itself expanded or contracted? In pleasure the soul expands, in pain it contracts. And since it can contract and expand quickly and easily, it must consist of very fine matter. This soul-stuff (*spiritus*) is situated in the cavities of the brain. The proof of this lies partly in the fact that the nerves proceed from the brain and not, as Aristotle believed, from the heart, while the nerve-substance resembles that of the brain, not that of the heart; and partly in the fact that death occurs when the brain-cavities are filled with too dense matter, or if the brain is otherwise injured, and also that unconsciousness may supervene in apoplexy, fainting, and sleep, without other parts of the body suffering change. We have already encountered this vital spirit in Vives and Melancthon, which, regarded sometimes as the seat of the soul, sometimes, as here with Telesio, as the soul itself, is a notion inherited from Greek physicians and philosophers. It is evident that since Telesio conceives all matter as endowed with consciousness, he cannot be very much opposed to conceiving consciousness itself as material. It appears, however, that he distinguishes between consciousness itself and that which goes on in every "spirit" which stirs the nerves and brain and is in motion. For, when pointing out that a uniform motion of the "spirit" is associated with no sensation, but that a change in the motion of the "spirit" determined by the influence of things is necessary to arouse feeling, he remarks: "Feeling (*sensus*), then, is a perception (*perceptio*) of external impressions and of internal changes; before all things it is a perception of internal changes, since it is only by means of the latter that we can know external impressions." [18]   Feeling, that is to say, is not merely identical with the changes of motion of the internal soul-substance, but is the "perception" of them. But then arises a new question, How is this perception possible? By this interpolated *perceptio* Telesio has been betrayed into the involuntary confession that the matter is not so very simple after all. He believed himself to have solved the problem by making the soul material; but, like a mocking Jack-in-the-box, pops up the question,—

How, in that case, is that which goes on in this material soul *perceived*?

Telesio's attempt to prove that all knowledge is feeling is interesting. He denies the distinction between feeling and thought; in such a way, indeed, as to reduce all thought to feeling. For if a motion has once been excited in the "spirit" it can be subsequently recalled, since it becomes habitual, or even, perhaps, persists to a certain extent. The knowledge associated with such habitual or repeated motion is memory. When, then, a thing which has once been perceived by us in its totality afterwards presents to our immediate perception isolated qualities only, we are able, on account of its resemblance to that which we had formerly apprehended, to fill out what is missing and to grasp the thing, although given as a fragment only, in its totality. We can imagine the fire with all its qualities, even though, perhaps, we can only see its light, and cannot perceive its heat nor its consuming power. In such an apprehension as a totality of fragmentary data consists, according to Telesio, the understanding (*intelligere*), which he would therefore prefer to call a memory or a judgment. Even the highest and most perfect knowledge contains nothing more than the capacity to discover, by means of resemblance with a case with which we are familiar as a totality, the unknown qualities and conditions of things. The absolutely unknown cannot be known. There must always be a point of contact with a datum,—a connecting link, that is to say, for sense and memory, which latter is nothing more than prolonged sense-impression. To infer is only to recognise in this manner the missing qualities. Even pure logic and mathematics arise out of sensation, since sensation shows us something similar to that which is contained in the fundamental principles of logic and mathematics. Sensuous perception gives me innumerable examples that the whole is greater than the part, and that I cannot at the same time assert and deny the same thing ; as it also directly shows me that snow is white as well as cold, and that men have two legs. The simplest sensuous perceptions are connected, through all degrees of approximation,. with ideal scientific principles. There is, then, no reason to split up our faculty of knowledge into two faculties. In its essence it is single, and rests entirely on the relation of resemblance—or perhaps on several very composite relations of resemblance — between objects which are apprehended in immediate sensation, and accordingly is nothing at all but sensation.

This whole doctrine rests upon the assumption that similarity and difference can be "felt" like any other qualities. "The spirit," says Telesio, "perceives the similarity and the difference between things felt; whatever has the same effects it apprehends as one and the same thing, and whatever has different effects as different things." The question now arises whether these are quite simple sensuous acts. At any rate there is the distinction between similarity and difference on the one side, and all other qualities on the other, while the former—more than the latter—presuppose a process of comparison; so that we must distinguish, within sense, an active and a passive side. It is, then, only a question of terminology whether we shall use the term sensation of both sides, or whether (with Cusanus) we shall say that thinking enters into all sensuous perception. It sometimes happened, however, that Telsio himself set up the perception of similarity in opposition to sensation. To Patrizzi's reproach that he despised reason (*ratio*), he answers "I in no way despise reason, *i.e.* that knowledge of things which is given to us, not through sensation, but through the resemblance of things which are perceived by sensation, and I could never believe that it is to be despised. But I shall always maintain that sensation is more to be trusted than reason." To which Patrizzi very rightly answers: "You do not seem to assert of this resemblance that it can be perceived through sensation; how, then, can it be apprehended if not through the reason?" In the apprehension of resemblance, that is to say, there is something more than is contained in the simplest acts of the senses. Telesio's attempt to make knowledge at all stages absolutely identical was therefore not successful: in and for itself, however, it was a justifiable attempt—a pendant to that of Cusanus. Both schemes contain creative thoughts within the spheres of psychology and theory of knowledge.

Like all matter, the soul, too, seeks to preserve itself. It strives after many different goods and is prompted by many different impulses; but when it makes a choice and subordinates all other goods to a single one, it is very evident that the regulator of this choice is self-preservation and its conditions. The value of all goods is constituted by their connection with self-preservation, and an immediate feeling of pleasure is associated with the natural activity by which a being preserves and maintains itself. No being, not even the ' spirit," can strive after any other goal than self-preservation. It is especially evident that knowledge is a means to this end. Wisdom is the sum of all virtue, since the right knowledge for the discovery of the means to self-preservation is of the utmost importance. Only in reciprocal action with others can the individual live safely and at ease ; and, if this reciprocal action is to be fervent and fruitful, the individuals must be as closely united as if they formed a single composite being, so that they work together like the organs of an organism. In this way arise the motives of the social virtues, whose sum is humanity (*humanitas*), and the possibility of which rests on the need of social life, of confidence, and of goodwill. The highest of all virtues,[19] however, is magnanimity (*sublimitas*), which regulates love of esteem. Man will not submit to be despised : he cannot endure to be regarded as inadequate to fill his position, as impure, or as obnoxious. Hence, since his own strength does not always afford him sufficient testimony, he seeks a support in the opinion of other men. Magnanimity, then, consists in this : that only such honour must be sought after as is founded in the individual's own inner goods, and that these are precisely the goods which are to be preferred on account of the honour that may be bound up with them. Honour is for magnanimity no necessary, internal good ; the important point is to be worthy of honour ; a sufficient source of satisfaction lies in purity and integrity in and for themselves.

All this, knowledge as well as self-preservation, concerns, according to Telesio, the material soul only ; that which is developed out of the seed (*spiritus e semine eductus*). But in addition to this sense knowledge and natural self-preservation, a higher impulse and intention makes itself felt in man, which points beyond our life on this earth and its preservation, and must therefore be explained thus : God has implanted in us another soul, which, as non-corporeal form, unites with that which developed naturally, when the body became fully developed. In this way only can we explain the fact that, in contemplation, men can forget the needs of the senses ; and also that, in this earthly life,

complete satisfaction is never found.   How this form, " super-
added from above " (*forma superaddita*), is related to the natural
soul, Telesio does not explain more nearly.   By this doctrine,
which is perhaps only introduced as a concession to theology,
Telesio interrupts the finished character of his philosophy.
And he forgets that in his natural ethics he has already
described a condition of character which is exalted above
purely physical self-preservation. · Various psychological
middle terms are needed to explain to us how magnanimity
can develop out of the original impulse to self-preservation.
Telesio's endeavours ought to have been directed towards the
filling up of these lacunæ, rather than to the addition of supple-
ments which are not altogether in harmony with his foundation.

   In spite of all its imperfections, however, Telesio's system
is one of the most remarkable which the Renaissance
produced.   Born in the dust, and rooted in the senses, it yet
soars boldly aloft to the sublime.   It draws conclusions and
intimates modes of conception which were only developed
much later, on a more productive soil.   Nevertheless it
caused great excitement among his contemporaries, and
exerted no inconsiderable influence on such thinkers as
Bruno, Campanella, and Bacon.

CHAPTER XII

THE COPERNICAN WORLD-SCHEME

THE traditionary conception of the world had been shaken by Cusanus' criticism of the doctrine of absolute motion and Paracelsus' and Telesio's polemic against the Aristotelian elements and forms. But the new world-scheme of Copernicus robbed it of all foundation. He showed that there were cogent reasons for considering things in the opposite to the usual way. It was precisely this, *i.e.* that the Copernicans wanted to turn the world upside down, of which Luther complained, although he himself had in so many things put the highest lowest. No wonder that while the new world-scheme excited amongst some the greatest enthusiasm, on account of the infinite horizon it seemed to reveal, amongst others it aroused the greatest indignation, because they thought it was depriving them of the clearly defined and comprehensible frame into which, hitherto, everything which men had supposed themselves to know of the world and its forces could be fitted in. There now began a hard struggle, which cost noble blood, and what is even more precious than blood ; a struggle, not only with religious scruples, but also with the confidence in immediate, sensuous perception. Human knowledge had to learn that, in and for itself, the nature of existence may be quite different from what it immediately appears to be. This was a lesson in distinguishing between subjective apprehension and real existence which was of the greatest philosophical importance. In this matter, accordingly, freedom of mind, *i.e.* the capacity to look away from what the senses seem immediately to show us, and religious ideas to require, was especially necessary. And we find the necessity of a "free mind" constantly emphasised by the champions of the new hypothesis. Joachim Rheticus, the first pupil of Copernicus, looking back at the relation of the Master to the old astronomers, says : " He who will investigate must possess a free mind." Kepler, too, regarded the free mind (*animus liber*) of Copernicus as an essential condition for his work, and Galilei uses the same expression (*ingegno libero*) of Kepler.[20] A process of liberation had now set in.

The founder of the new world-conception grew up on the soil of Humanism. NICOLAUS COPERNICUS (his real name is said to have been Koppernigk) was born of a well-to-do family at Thorn, 19th February 1473. The Poles and the Germans have disputed as to his nationality ; he probably sprang from a German family which had for many years been settled in Poland. As far as we know, he neither wrote nor spoke Polish. In Cracow, which possessed a flourishing university, he studied the humanities, mathematics, and astronomy. Through the influence of his uncle, the Bishop of Ermeland, he was received as *canonicus*, or prebendary, in the Frauenburg Cathedral. Some degree of spiritual dignity was connected with this office, but no theological education was required, and only very few of the prebendaries were in a position to exercise spiritual functions. They lived much more like noblemen and humanists than clergy. We get quite a wrong idea of Copernicus if we think of him as a monk in his cell. The young prebendary spent ten preliminary years in Italy, where he pursued his studies in astronomy, medicine, and the humanities at Bologna, Rome, and Padua. His teacher in Bologna is said already to have doubted the correctness of the Aristotelio-Ptolemaic system. After his return from Italy, Copernicus stayed some time with the Bishop of Ermeland, partly as physician, partly as courtier. During this time, between his thirty-third and thirty-sixth years, he developed the main features of his system. He says himself that he had been sketching out the scientific exposition and foundation of his doctrine from 1506. After his uncle's death he lived for the greater part of his life at Frauenburg Castle, with the exception of a few years, during which he administered the estates belonging to the Cathedral. Thus he was not entirely occupied with astronomical studies. He was an administrator and a physician, and he also took part in negotiations connected with the reform of the currency. Nor had he entirely turned his back on his humanistic studies. In 1509 he published a Latin translation of the *Epistles of Theo-*

phylactus. In fact his activity was all-sided. Moreover, nothing that was going on in the world escaped his notice. As a physician, certainly, he belonged to the old school and followed Avicenna. But his attitude towards the religious movement, together with that of several of his colleagues, was free and sympathetic. They were anxious for reform, and wished, in any case, to ensure the battle being fought with spiritual weapons only. The spirit of Erasmus seems to have prevailed among the canons of Ermeland.

Copernicus left his work unpublished for many years. He polished it unceasingly, but he had great misgivings as to giving it to the world. Meanwhile his ideas had become widely known ; chiefly, perhaps, through a small treatise (*commentariolus*) of his, of which the MS. has lately been found. The final impetus to its publication was given by JOACHIM RHETICUS, a young and enthusiastic disciple of Copernicus, and a teacher at the University of Wittenberg. He travelled (1539) to Frauenburg and spent two years with Copernicus in order that he might study his works. From his hand the learned world received the first detailed information of the new system (*Narratio prima de libris revolutionum*, Danzig, 1539-40). Moreover he persuaded the Master to overcome his scruples and allow the book to be printed.

Copernicus' last years were not happy. The Catholic reaction set in, and the free humanistic spirit which had hitherto prevailed among the canons was checked and persecuted by the new bishop, Johannes Dantiscus, who, after having been a man of the world and an erotic poet, had become a fanatical servant of the Church. In spite of former relations of friendship with Copernicus he now seemed especially bent upon tormenting him. Copernicus was obliged to break off his intercourse with several of his intimates, because the bishop suspected them of heresy. In the spring of 1543 he was overtaken with hæmorrhage and paralysis, and he died on 24th May 1543. A copy of his work reached him on his deathbed, but he had already lost consciousness.

It would be out of place here to enter into all the astronomical questions with which Copernicus had to deal. For a general history of thought it is the presuppositions from which the reformer of astronomy started and the leading

features which the new world-scheme presented, that are of
interest. In its presuppositions his system bears the intellectual stamp of its age ; owing to the character of its world-
scheme it had no small influence on the progressive development
of the time.

Among these presuppositions two claim our interest more
especially.

The artificiality and intricacy of the old world-scheme induced Copernicus to reflect on the possibility of conceiving the
heavenly phenomena in another manner. This whole system
of innumerable connected spheres and epicycles seemed to him
to contradict the simplicity and purposiveness elsewhere revealed
by Nature. The wisdom of Nature (*naturae sagacitas*) attains its
end elsewhere by the simplest ways, without circumlocutions, and
by means of a harmonious interaction between all the elements
involved. She seeks to bind many effects to one single cause,
rather than to increase the number of causes. This faith in the
simplicity of Nature was for Copernicus and his successors not
only a methodological, but also a metaphysical principle. They
would have been embarrassed had they been asked how they
knew that Nature always proceeds according to the simplest way.
For them this was an immediate certainty, a religious faith.
They still felt themselves close to the heart of Nature. The
examination of the authorisation of such presuppositions was
one of the chief tasks of the philosophy of the following period.
For the present men fell to boldly, and in this case the
presupposition proved to have been happily chosen. It made
it necessary to find a point of view from which the order of the
world could be apprehended and the hitherto prevailing confusion
reduced to order. It could not but seem absurd, in face of the
principle of simplicity, that the whole universe should move
round the earth—the great mass round the small one. Would
it not be simpler if the great mass were to remain at rest, while
only the small masses moved?

With this principle of simplicity was combined the principle
which had already carried Cusanus beyond the old world-system
(without, however, leading him to a new one), *i.e.* the principle
of relativity. If a motion takes place in space, says Copernicus,
sensuous perception cannot immediately tell us what is moving.
It may be the thing perceived. But it may also be the percipient himself who moves. Finally, it is possible that both

the thing and the percipient are moving with different velocities or in different directions. When we are sailing it is the shore which seems to recede from us, although it is we, and not it, who are moving. Let us therefore suppose that the earth, the place from which we perceive what is going on in the universe, is in motion, and let us see if we shall not thus gain a simpler and more natural world-conception than if we assume that it is the objects perceived which move![21] Copernicus' whole work consists in the mathematical demonstration that this hypothesis would lead us to assume the occurrence of phenomena precisely as perception exhibits them to us.

The new world-scheme, then, regards the sun as the central point and source of light of the world. Round it move the planets, fixed in concentric spheres, in a series in which the earth takes its place between Venus and Mars. Moreover the earth turns on its own axis. The whole universe is comprehended within the firm and immovable heaven of the fixed stars, which is its outermost limit. Copernicus does not decide whether the world is finite or infinite ; of so much, however, he is sure ;—in comparison with the distance of the earth from the heaven of the fixed stars, the diameter of the earth's orbit must be a vanishing quantity, since we cannot perceive any such apparent motion to and fro on the part of the fixed stars as we perceive in the planets which are near the earth. This enormous extension of the universe—although for Copernicus himself it did not indicate any bursting of the old frame—was one of the greatest stones of stumbling offered by the new theory,[22] and of this Copernicus was very well aware. He consoled himself by the reflection that men would concede such an extension rather than assume such an enormous number of circles as was necessary to the belief that the earth lies in the centre. And, moreover, is it not much more probable that that which is comprehended should move, than that the all-embracing frame should be in motion? Copernicus regarded the sphere of the fixed stars as the absolute place in respect of which every other place and every other motion is determined (*communis universorum locus*). Moreover, heaven is the most honourable part of the universe ; hence immovability beseems it. And if it were to move, it would have to be with such enormous velocity that there would be much greater reason to fear its being shivered into atoms than, with Ptolemy, to entertain such a fear for the earth, if it should move. The reason why the water and air are not left behind in the earth's revolution is that they form one whole with the earth proper, and therefore participate in its motion. It is the same with objects on the earth. In this way Copernicus strove to give a brief answer to the physical objections to which his theory was open. He says nothing as to the cause of the planets moving round the earth. Like the ancients, he supposes circular motion to be the natural motion of bodies. A rectilinear motion only occurs when a part is separated from the whole to which it belongs.[23] It is always, that is to say, a sign that something is as it ought not to be. Copernicus' theory is descriptive in character. It is an attempt to show how the things of the world appear from a certain standpoint. He was, however, not able to exhibit the imperative necessity of adopting this standpoint ; and he left many difficulties on particular points to be cleared up.

Nevertheless one of the greatest of his successors has commended his courage in developing his conception undeterred by any difficulties, trusting reason rather than perception. Galilei, indeed, finds it very comprehensible that he did not enter, with more detail, into the arguments against it ; he regarded these, he says, no more than the lion regards the barking of dogs. Without such courage the new conception would neither have appeared nor have been critically investigated. Copernicanism affords a striking example in the history of thought, of the necessity of setting up ideas and hypotheses which may point out the way to investigation. Even in science chance has a place.

Copernicus, however, did not regard his doctrine as a mere hypothesis. He did not arrange for the publication of his own work. This was entrusted to Osiander of Nurenberg, a preacher, who, in order that it might excite no one's anger, wrote a preface describing the new doctrine as altogether hypothetical, adding that any attempt to work from it as a basis could afford purely mathematical pleasure only. The new views, he says, may be as good as the old ones, and no one must expect that astronomy can teach us anything certain. There is no doubt that this preface, which had all the appearance of coming from the author himself, did much at the time towards preventing the theory from exciting any great attention.   If the author did not mean it seriously, it could not be of very great interest.   Luther mocked at it in his Table-talk ; and Melancthon, in his lectures on Physics (*Initia physices*), says that men invent such wonderful things only from love of novelty, and to display their own ingenuity; but that they are un-seemly (*honestum*), and that it may set a bad example if, merely to exercise their minds, men give themselves up to such absurd opinions, instead of accepting with reverence the truth as it is revealed by God, and contenting themselves with this, especially since the new doctrine is evidently contradictory to the testimony of the Bible.   On this account Melancthon also regarded his young colleague, Rheticus, as unsettled in his opinions.   There were comparatively few who attached themselves to the new doctrine in the course of the sixteenth century.   Among the most enthusiastic of these were Giordano Bruno and Kepler, while Galilei still held back from fear of ridicule, and Tycho Brahe—partly from scientific, partly from religious reasons—took up a middle position between the old and the new systems.   Bruno had already protested in forcible language against the idea that the cowardly preface could have been written by Copernicus.   He hints that there are people who contented themselves with reading the preface, and that when they saw that it dealt with mathematical speculations only, dis-missed the matter from their minds.   Bruno asserts that the preface must have been written by some ignorant and self-satisfied ass, in the hope of setting the book right with other asses, and he appeals to Copernicus' own preface, from which it is evident that he intended his theory to be taken seriously, while, in the book itself, he speaks not only as a mathematician but also as a physicist.   Afterwards Kepler proved, from Osiander's own letters, that the preface was falsified.[24]

Even in Italy, where the ecclesiastical reaction was now in full force, some time elapsed before the new world-scheme became sufficiently well known to challenge persecution.   That it ever came to this was due not least to the great and brilliant thinker, who not only adopted the new world-scheme and wove it into his own web of thought, but also extended it and deduced from it his most important conclusions with respect to a general world-conception ; while his own life, in turn, was determined by his struggle for the new ideas.

CHAPTER XIII

GIORDANO BRUNO

(a) *Biography and Characteristics*

IN Bruno we find the ideas of Cusanus, Telesio, and Copernicus bound together into a unique whole,—into the greatest philosophical thought-structure executed by the Renaissance, and which, in several respects, was prophetic in character. It established some of the most essential features of the scientific world-conceptions of modern times. On the other hand, Bruno offered on the altar of his age and shared its superstition and fantasticalness, to which his passionate and impatient disposition made him especially susceptible. We must not go to him for clear methodical teaching ; main outlines only are clearly discernible, but these are carried out with an inspiration which stood all tests. In particulars, however, he had incomplete control both over himself and his thoughts ; he could not account to himself as to how far the latter led him away from the old faith with which he still felt himself bound up, deride and ridicule it as he might. His is a figure in which neither the intellectual nor the moral physiognomy is clearly and sharply delineated. He was himself conscious of the contradictions and struggles within him. Rooted in his nature, they were fostered by the circumstances under which he and his thought developed.

His fate was decided early. He himself says that if the first button of one's coat is wrongly buttoned all the rest are crooked. This may be applied to the step taken by PHILIPPO BRUNO (born in 1548 [25] at Nola in South Italy) when, at sixteen years of age, he entered a monastery. His family seem to have belonged to the nobility, and he enjoyed a good preliminary education. We know nothing more of his childhood—not even of what led him to become a monk. Perhaps he made this resolution in a mood of exaltation. Great oscillations between excessive enthusiasm and the deepest depression were among the idiosyncrasies of his character. He took a step which could not be cancelled, and yet his whole life was an attempt to cancel it. In the monastery, where he took the name of Giordano, it soon became evident that he was little able to bend his mind to discipline. He was repeatedly charged with heretical doings. He first incurred suspicion by removing all the images of saints from his cell, retaining the Crucifix only ; and later, after he had been ordained priest, by defending the teaching of the Arians. Later still, during the trial before the Inquisition at Venice, he announced that ever since he was eighteen he had doubted the doctrine of the Trinity. When he found that an indictment was being drawn up against him he fled to Rome to escape imprisonment, and when the indictment followed at his heels he fled, after laying aside his monastic habit, out of Rome also. This was at the end of the year 1576. He now began his restless wanderings from place to place, passionately working out his thoughts, and not less passionately fighting for the new ideas which he had won. There is much which tends to show that it was not the intellectual side of his nature only which rebelled against monastic discipline. His was a strongly sensual nature, and he has himself said that not all the snows of Caucasus could avail to allay the fires within him. He had a hard struggle, therefore, to ennoble his impulses, so that out of the "animal affects" might develop an "heroic affect." Nor was it asceticism that enabled him to reach this goal. A sequence of poems, to which he afterwards gave an allegorical explanation (in *De gl' Heroici Furori*), but which originally, there can be no doubt, were love poems, witness to this. In a comedy, the material for which must have been collected during his stay in the neighbourhood of his home, circumstances are depicted, and expressions used, which are astonishing in their coarseness, even when we remember that the inhabitants of Nola were famous for their loose tongues. Although he had entered the monastery while quite young he was never alienated from life, which, indeed, stirred so vigorously within him that it soon drove him out into the world again. Intellectual troubles, however, were the actual cause of the breach. After his flight from Rome he wandered about for some years in North Italy. For some time he kept a school for small children at Noli, near Genoa, where he also instructed some young noblemen in astronomy. He was probably at this time an adherent of Copernicus. According to his own statement he had become acquainted with him in early youth. He was at first unable to discover anything but madness in the new doctrine, but soon its truth and importance dawned upon him, especially after he had learnt sufficient mathematics to follow out in detail the reasoning on which it was based. He now felt the necessity of going farther than his teacher, who, still entangled in ancient and mediæval astronomy, adhered to the limitation of the world and the immovability of the eight spheres. For Bruno the world is limitless (since every attempt to establish an absolute limit is unauthorised), and it includes an infinity of worlds like our own, each with its central point. The Deity works at every point of this infinite universe as the inner soul which embraces and animates all. Such were the thoughts which now unfolded themselves in Bruno's mind. In addition to Copernicus, Cusanus and Telesio exercised great influence upon him. The manner in which their thoughts reappeared in him will become clear when we describe the special motivation of his teaching. We shall here only point out that this modified conception of the world set him in sharp opposition to the prevailing Aristotelian philosophy on which the theology of that time was based, and which stood or fell with the old world-scheme. Unable to find a fixed abode in North Italy, although he wandered through it as far as Venice, he crossed the Alps and arrived at Geneva in 1579. He seems here to have been regarded as belonging to the Reformed Church, although at the trial before the Inquisition at Venice he denied his apostasy. But it has been discovered that his name, in his own writing, is entered on the University books, and adherence to the Calvinistic confession of faith was a condition of this. Papers have been discovered, too, proving that he engaged in a violent quarrel with one of the professors at the gymnasium and with the clergy of the town : it was especially laid to his charge that he had called the latter " Pedagogues " ; he had also advanced heretical opinions. He was therefore excommunicated, and the excommunication was not rescinded until he had expressed his sorrow at what had occurred. This episode evidently presupposes that Bruno had, at any rate externally, given in his adherence to the Reformed Church. Thus the theocratic government of Calvinism made itself felt immediately, and we may be sure that this experience, together with others made during his residence in Protestant countries, laid the foundation of the harsh judgment which he afterwards passed on Protestantism, especially in its Calvinistic form. Bruno little guessed what was to be the historical outcome of Calvinism ; he only saw the dark side of it, and this caused him to leave Geneva after a few months and go to the south of France. In Toulouse, where he was well received, he began to give lectures at the University, and was installed as professor, an office which he held for two years. Here, too, he lectured on astronomy and the Aristotelian philosophy. This was the quietest period of his life, although here, too, he fell out with the *savants*, most likely on account of the innovations which he wished to introduce. It is worthy of note, if we are rightly to understand Bruno's relation to Catholicism, that as early as the Toulouse period he took measures towards returning into the bosom of the Catholic Church—measures which he renewed in Paris. He thought that, without returning to the cloister, he might live on good terms with the Church. He hardly regarded his relation with the Church as broken off. He believed he could reconcile the essentials of Christianity with his new ideas, and he thought that the Church could sanction that explanation of dogmatic ideas which was the necessary presupposition of this reconciliation. The unfavourable impression made upon him by Protestantism fostered his longing for union with the Church he had deserted, even though he felt it needed a radical reform. But both at Toulouse and in Paris the return to his cloister was made a first condition of reconciliation, and to this he could not consent. His wish was to live quietly, and to pursue his studies, without again subjecting himself to monastic discipline. This view of Bruno's relations to Catholicism is supported by his utterances during the trial before the Inquisition ; moreover, the fact that he returned to Italy at all is only comprehensible on this supposition.

When the Civil War put an end to Bruno's activity at the University of Toulouse he went to Paris (1581) and was here much applauded on his appearance as a teacher at the

Academy. In addition to scholastic subjects, he taught both the so-called art of Lull—a kind of thought-schematism with which he was much engrossed, and of which he has treated in a whole series of works—and also the art of Mnemonics, to which he likewise attributed great importance. King Henry III. summoned him to his court, that he might explain to him his ideas. He won the favour of the King, and on his recommendation he was received, on his going to England in 1583, in the house of the French Ambassador, the Marquis of Castelnau. In the works which he published in London he praises the hospitality and good breeding of the Ambassador and his family in the highest terms. He was less well pleased with the English, whom he thought barbarians. Even their scholars, for the most part, formed no exception. He aired his dislike of both learned and lay in *La cena delle ceneri*, the first of a series of works written in Italian which were published in London. The truth is, that it was in England that he first appeared in the *rôle* of reformer of the world-conception, and now he learnt, to use his own expression, what it was "to cast pearls before swine." Bruno was not only enthusiastic for the new ideas which were ever shaping themselves more clearly within him, and the time to announce which had now come, but he had also a great feeling of his own importance, which he expressed in a somewhat bombastic style. Others beside conservative pedants were provoked by the letter which he wrote to the Vice-Chancellor of the University of Oxford to announce his advent. He described himself as a teacher of pure and innocent wisdom ; as a philosopher famous at all the academies of Europe, with whom only barbarians and rustics were unacquainted ; as the arouser of slumbering souls, the vanquisher of ignorance, whose gaze was fastened on intellectual culture only ; hated by the stupid and the hypocritical, greeted with joy by honest and serious men, and so on, and so on. Much of this bombast must, of course, be ascribed to the taste of the time. The University of Oxford opened its doors to him, and he lectured for some time on his psychological and astronomical theories. His ideas concerning the unity of the life of the soul under the many different forms in which it appears both contemporaneously and successively in the world, and the infinity of the universe,—since the earth instead of being the absolute centre is only one of the innumerable heavenly bodies in constant motion, no one of which possesses the smallest right to claim to be the centre—were ideas well calculated to excite both bewilderment and indignation among the Oxford scholastics. The lectures had to be broken off. In one of the public disputations too, in which, according to his own report, he fifteen times reduced his opponent, "the Coryphæus of the University," to silence, he believed he had received proofs of rudeness on the part of the professional scholars. And the same thing happened in the disputation of which he has given a detailed description in his *La cena delle ceneri*. Nevertheless he did not abandon the hope that his ideas would be attended with favourable results, but used the time he spent at the French Minister's to write a series of works in Italian, in which he has given the fullest and finest presentation of his views. Restless and torn asunder as his life was, yet he had the greatest happiness which is granted to a thinker; for he succeeded in developing his ideas as fully and clearly as was possible at the stage at which he had arrived. In spite of all opposition, his visit to London was a happy time for Bruno. A few distinguished men, such as Philip Sidney and Fulke Greville, showed him friendship ; he moved in aristocratic circles and even gained the *entrée* to Queen Elizabeth, whom he eulogises in his works under the name of Amphitrite, Queen of the Sea. In his later works, moreover, he modifies his unfavourable judgment on the English. But there is no ground for supposing that there was any real comprehension of his views, even in small and select circles. At any rate no trace of it can be pointed out ; indeed we hear nothing about Bruno's residence in England except from his own report. Philosophical interest in England ran in quite another direction from that taken by Bruno, both then and in the following age. The time for the comprehension of Bruno did not come till later. The thoughts akin to Bruno's ideas, which are to be found in Shakespeare, especially in *Hamlet*, are derived in the first instance, when they do not spring from the thought of the great poet himself,[26] from Montaigne and other contemporary authors.

During his residence in London, Bruno developed an astonishing productivity. In addition to the work on Mnemonics (with the above-mentioned prefatory letter to the

Vice-Chancellor of Oxford) he here published five important
Italian dialogues, which contained an exposition of his philosophical ideas.   In the first, *La cena delle ceneri*, the Copernican
theory is discussed, together with Bruno's foundation and extension of it.   Next followed Bruno's chief work, *Della causa,
Principio ed Uno* (On Cause, Principle, and Unity), in which he
unfolded his speculative and religio-philosophical ideas.   It is
continued in the dialogue *Dell' Infinito Universo e Dei Mondi*
(On the Infinite Universe and the Worlds), which gives a more
thorough-going exposition of his doctrine of the infinite, divine
principle, which reveals itself in an infinity of worlds and beings.
After having unfolded his views on the theoretical side in these
works, he gives his moral philosophy and his practical conception
of life in the *Spaccio della Bestia Trionfante* (Expulsion of the
Brute Triumphant), to which *Cabala del Cavallo Pegaseo* and
De gl' Heroici Furori (On Heroic Affects) are sequels.   Many
sections in these works are distinguished by their thoughtfulness
and depth of feeling, as well as by their practical form of statement.   But these alternate with other sections in which either
the old Scholasticism reappears, or fancy degenerates into
fantasy, or the author struggles with speech in his efforts to
express the inexpressible.   This latter trait is perhaps the
one which is most characteristic of Bruno.   His world-conception is essentially motivated by the new way of looking at
things which Copernicus had introduced.   But Bruno saw
how far-reaching were its consequences, and that in the same
moment that we dislodge the earth from its place of rest in
the centre of the *universum* we lose all right to posit rest
and boundaries anywhere in the world.   The endeavour to
ground the world-conception on the data of experience was
now combined with a movement which led beyond the limits
of experience.   And, convinced as Bruno was that the highest
reveals itself in Nature, he was at the same time equally
convinced that any revelation or sequence of revelations
whatever is inadequate to express its fulness and its unity,
so that of it no opposites hold good, as no words are
adequate to express it.   No thought, no number, and no
measure suffice, even though Nature is determined in all parts
alike by measure, number, and thought.   He is as much
convinced of the necessity as of the inadequacy of the scientific
view.   In one of his philosophic poems he says :—

> Con senso, con raggion, con mente scerno,
> Ch' atto, misura, et conto non comprende
> Quel vigor, mole et numero, che tende
> Oltr' ogn' inferior, mezzo et superno.[1]

Thus the instructed ignorance (*docta ignorantia*), which we know from Nicolaus of Cusa is Bruno's last word also. But he stands nearer to the world of experience and devotes greater interest to it than did the theologian, who regarded the investigation of the essence and the limit of thought chiefly as a ladder to the mystical absorption in the contemplation of the Deity. Bruno does not lose himself, however, in this contemplation of the external world. He is convinced that the Deity works at the heart of the world, and is to be found at every point. The external, childish distinctions between the heavens and the earth have disappeared, but only (as later in Boehme) to make room for the feeling that the highest is everywhere, if only our mind is open to it. But then the work begins again within the sphere of the inner life. Here, too, we find sharp contrasts, a flood of waves without limit, a striving after an infinite goal. This thought occurs chiefly in the *De gl' Heroici Furori*, where it is expressed in a wealth of poems and allegories, psychological reflections and ethical ideas. Pleasure and pain are bound up together, so that we cannot choose the one without taking the other with it ; the only way to victory leads through danger and destruction ; and the danger is not only external, it is also within us ; the will must be abased that it may be able to mount aloft, and repentance is among virtues as the swan among birds. For Bruno there is a tragic relation between knowledge and truth, between the will and its aims. The highest for him was the feeling of this disproportion together with unceasing striving.

> Eh bench' il fin bramato non consegua,
> E 'n tanto studio l' alma si dilegua,
> Basta che sia si nobilmente accesa![2]

Bruno found contradictions in rich measure in his own nature and in his own fate. Ideal aspirations and a passionate

---

[1] Thought and senses alike teach me that no act of thought, no measuring, and no reckoning, are able to comprehend a force, a mass, and a number which extend beyond every limit—inferior as well as superior—and every mean.

[2] Even if the goal aimed at be never reached, even though the soul be consumed by the violence of its strivings, yet it is enough that such a noble fire should have been kindled within it.

pursuit of knowledge on the one hand; on the other, self-assertion and sensual lust; here were problems enough, and here, too, were reefs enough, on which his character, as it developed, might founder, altogether apart from external circumstances. And how complicated and varying were these ! A fugitive monk who could not feel at home in the Protestant countries through which he wandered, but who judged Protestantism still more hardly than the Church which had excommunicated him ! A thinker who would overthrow all traditionary systems for the sake of a new system which his thought strove unceasingly to frame and which met with no understanding from his contemporaries ! A Southerner, who felt in Northern Europe as though he were among barbarians in a strange land !

After spending two years in England, Bruno returned to Paris with the French Ambassador, where he made his second futile attempt at a reconciliation with the Catholic Church. He held a public disputation at the University, in which he attacked the Aristotelian philosophy and defended the new world-conception. Freedom of thought was here defended in clear and forcible language. The invitation to this disputation (*Acrotismus*, printed probably first in Paris, 1586, later in Wittenberg, 1588) is one of the clearest of Bruno's works. It gives, in a concise form, the most important of the ideas set forth in the Italian dialogues. Soon after the disputation he quitted Paris, probably on account of political disturbances. After this he wandered between several German universities. At Marburg he was refused permission to teach, which led to a violent encounter with the rector of the University, who struck his name out of the list, where it was already entered among the students. He was probably excluded as a Catholic; his writings could hardly have been known. In Wittenberg, on the other hand, he was allowed to give lectures, and here he passed two quiet years. But then came a new duke and he was obliged to withdraw. In his farewell address he praises German learning as represented by Cusanus, Paracelsus, and Copernicus, and extols Luther, because he led the struggle against the power of the Church: like a modern Hercules he had fought with Cerberus and his triple crown !

Once more he resumed his unsettled life. After staying a short time at Prague and Helmstedt he went to Frankfurt, where he devoted a quiet year to publishing a series of writings in which, partly in the form of didactic poems, he gave a systematic exposition of his doctrine. Unlike the London works these are written in Latin, probably because they were intended for the German *savants*. This series of writings is further remarkable because in them Bruno approximates to an atomistic conception of Nature (in his *De triplici Minimo*) and because, in his exposition of the new world-scheme (in the *De Immenso*), he made use of Tycho Brahe's inquiry into the paths of comets, which notably confirmed the ideas he had developed earlier. Side by side with this, however, these works contain several abstruse and symbolical arguments, which are only interesting as showing to what straits men were reduced in default of scientific data. Bruno displays in this, as in other points, a certain resemblance to Kepler, in whom, too, great scientific ideas are curiously combined with symbolical speculations.

Before these books were through the press, Bruno was obliged to leave Frankfurt. In the preface to the *De triplici Minimo*, which he was no longer able to supervise, the publishers state that the author has been torn from them by a sudden accident (*casu repentino avulsus*). He was probably expelled from the town ; papers have been found which prove that the Frankfurter magistrates regarded him with suspicion from his arrival. The expression used by the publishers indicates no voluntary journey. Moreover he had received an invitation to go to Italy which he would, we may be sure, have accepted in any case. In a sonnet he compares himself to a moth fluttering towards the candle, in allusion to the impulse towards truth, irresistible though painful. The thought of his fatherland seems to have excited a similar desire within him. In all his weary wanderings north of the Alps he had never been able to find a new fatherland. But what dangers awaited the runaway monk on his return ! The fact that the invitation came from Venice perhaps made him feel safe. A young Venetian nobleman, Giovanni Mocenigo, who had studied one of Bruno's works on Mnemonics, learnt from his bookseller that the author was living at Frankfurt. He accordingly invited him to Venice, that he might have the benefit of his instructions. He seems to have believed that Bruno was also versed in the black arts, and it was probably into these that he wished to be initiated. Bruno accepted the invitation. After his sudden departure from

Frankfurt he stayed for some time in Zurich, where he lectured
to some young men, and it was from here (in the autumn of
1591) that he started on his ill-starred journey across the Alps.
In Venice he instructed Mocenigo, and finally lived in his house.
After the lapse of some time, however, his pupil complained
that he was not learning everything he wished to learn.   He
also began to be troubled with qualms of conscience at harbour-
ing a heretic.   In obedience to his confessor he now informed
against Bruno to the Inquisition, and confined him in his house
until he was taken to their prison (23rd May 1592).

Bruno broke down at the trial.   He protested against
various wanton expressions, torn out of their context, which
were ascribed to him in Mocenigo's report; he explained that
at heart he had always remained true to the faith of the
Church, though, as a fugitive monk, he had not been able to
take part in its worship, and though he had taught in
his philosophy things which led indirectly to collision with its
dogmas.   Finally, he begged forgiveness on his knees for all
his errors and expressed a wish to do some penance, after which
he might again be received into the bosom of the Church.   To
understand how Bruno could thus deny what he had so
enthusiastically promulgated, we must remember that he himself never realised that the breach between the Catholic Church
and himself was irreparable.   His repeated attempts to obtain
a reconciliation prove this.   And the disagreeable impression
which he had received of Protestantism must also have inclined
him in that direction.   Even when in Venice, he had told
several people, who attested the fact before the Inquisition,
that he was engaged on a work which he intended to submit
to the Pope; in consideration of this book and of his literary
activity in general, he hoped he would be allowed to live in
Rome.   He also intended to lay before the Pope the works
which he had already published, trusting that he would be
granted absolution for his transgressions.   Perhaps he thought
that the symbolic truth which his philosophy enabled him
to attribute to ecclesiastical notions might cause the former to
be tolerated, especially since he could, in virtue of the *docta
ignorantia*, concede to faith an independent place, outside the
sphere of philosophy.   He accordingly gave the Inquisitors an
unreserved account of his career and of his philosophy: he told
them, *e.g.*, that what the Church called the Holy Spirit was for

him the soul of the world which held the universe together ; that while, after death, *catholicamente parlando*, souls pass into Purgatory or Hades, he taught *seguendo le raggion filosofiche*, that the life of the soul is imperishable and continually takes on new forms—a truth he found expressed in the old doctrine of metempsychosis. He did not go so far as to say with Pomponazzi that a thing might be true in theology without being true in philosophy. He believed, not in a double truth, but in a double form of the truth. The relation of his philosophy to the doctrines of the Church seemed to him rather like the relation of the Copernican theory to sensuous perception. It must, however, be admitted that he never gained complete clearness as to his own meaning. This makes it all the easier to understand how he—the man of moods, who fluctuated between states of exaltation and dejection—came to break down, and in order to secure the prospect of a quiet literary life, which he may well have longed for after the restless years of a wandering scholar, to make, like Galilei after him, the required confession, instead of opposing his own conception of Christianity to the dogmatism of the Church.

This might, perhaps, have served him ; in which case he would not have figured in the world's history as the hero whom we now know. But meantime the Inquisition at Rome had heard of the trial and demanded that he should be given up to them, on the ground not only that he was guilty of gross heresy, but also that he had taken refuge in flight from previous accusations, both from Rome and Naples. After some hesitation, the Venetian Government handed him over, and now a new trial began at Rome. Only a few fragmentary papers of the trial are now extant; the others having mysteriously disappeared from the papal archives.[27] Hence it has never been explained why Bruno spent six years in a Roman prison. Only so much is clear—that the Roman Inquisitors, amongst whom the future Cardinal Bellarmin made himself particularly conspicuous, displayed greater zeal than the Venetians. They searched through Bruno's works and made out a list of eight gross heresies, of which they demanded the recantation. At the head stood the denial of the Catholic doctrine of the Eucharist. Probably his view that there are an infinite number of worlds was also counted to him for unrighteousness.[28] This was heretical because it seemed to contradict revelation, which could not have taken place more than once. For the same reason the belief in the antipodes was considered heretical in the Middle Ages. From what little we know of the trial we see, however, that the Pope attempted to limit the recantation which was to be demanded of Bruno to such propositions as had long been condemned by the Church ; those propositions, that is to say, which were immediately connected with Copernicanism were to be left out of the question. But Bruno refused to concede to this more concise requirement. He contended that he had not been guilty of any heresy ; it was the Inquisitors who had read an heretical tendency into his views : he had nothing to recant. This attitude of his is confirmed by the view we have already expressed of his relation to Catholicism. With death before him, he held fast to his conception of Christianity in opposition to the Church's view, and he would no more abjure his philosophical than his religious views. He drew up a defence to be submitted to the Pope ; it was opened but not read.

Sentence was passed on Bruno on the 9th of February 1600. He was degraded, excommunicated, and handed over to the temporal power, the Governor of Rome, with the usual hypocritical request that he should be punished mildly and without shedding of blood. To which Bruno answered with a menacing gesture : "Ye who pass judgment over me feel, maybe, greater fear than I upon whom it is passed." He meant that they feared the truth while he himself had only to overcome the fear of suffering for truth's sake. He now saw clearly what he had not realised at Venice, *i.e.* that it was a question of defending the rights of free inquiry into truth. Now he no longer wavered. On the 17th of February 1600 he was burnt alive on the Campo di flora and met his death with firmness. He put aside a priest who would have reached him a crucifix, and died without uttering a groan. His ashes were cast to the winds. In 1889, on the place where he was burnt, a statue was erected to him, to which the whole civilised world contributed, and the Italian State now boasts of possessing the finest edition of his works.

Now that we have become acquainted with the life and personality of this the greatest of the Renaissance philosophers, we will proceed to give a detailed account of his philosophy.

(b) *Establishment and Extension of the New World-Scheme*

Giordano is one of the first thinkers to realise clearly that great thoughts are due to a long successive series of experiences. He believed himself to have uttered great thoughts, but, at the same time, he is very well aware of how much he owes to his predecessors, especially to the astronomers, on whose observations he relied. While, in the age of the Renaissance, men were still inclined to look back to antiquity as the source of all truth, just as the Church looked back to the time when the revelation took place, Bruno asserts that the men of the present time are older than "the ancients," since they have a richer experience on which to build than the latter. Eudoxus did not know so much as Hipparchus, nor Hipparchus as Copernicus. And he commends Copernicus, not only for having carried on the work of his predecessors, but more especially for his strong and magnanimous spirit, which raised him above the prejudices of the many, and the illusions of the senses, and enabled him to establish a new world-scheme. In his Latin didactic poem, " On the Immeasurable and the Countless Worlds," he breaks out into a hymn of praise in honour of Copernicus. He reproaches him, however, for having halted too soon, *i.e.* before he had deduced all the consequences of his ideas. He therefore needed a commentator, able " to think out all that was involved in his discovery," and this office Bruno claims for himself. He opened men's eyes to the infinitude of the universe, showed that this can no more have absolute limits than there can be fixed " spheres " separating the different regions of the world from one another, and that a single law and a single force prevail throughout the world, so that wherever we may find ourselves we cannot get away from God who rules throughout the same ; moreover we have no need to go beyond ourselves to find Him. Our present task is to assign the grounds on which Bruno builds in his establishment and further development of the Copernican world-scheme. These may be reduced to two main considerations—of which one is epistemological and the other religio-philosophical.

The old world-scheme, with the earth as the central point and the fixed spheres as the outermost limits, has no right to appeal to the evidence of the senses. If we examine the different sense-images which we receive when we move, we see that the horizon continually changes as we change our place. Rightly interpreted, so far from proving to us that there is an absolute centre and an absolute limit to the world, sense-perception shows us the contrary, *i.e.* the possibility of conceiving any place whatever, wherever we may be, or can convey ourselves in imagination, as the central point, and also the possibility of constantly changing and extending the limits of our world. And in harmony with this testimony of sense-perception is the capacity of our imagination and of our thought to continue unceasingly to add number to number, magnitude to magnitude, form to form ; moreover we are impelled to do this by an impulse and striving which stir within us and which are never satisfied with what we have already attained. It would be inconceivable, thinks Bruno, that our imagination and our thought should surpass Nature, and that this continual possibility of taking new views should correspond to no reality in the world. From the subjective impossibility of setting a limit and of affirming an absolute central point he now argues that there is no limit and no central point. In proof of this Bruno relies, as he himself tells us, on the fundamental condition of our knowledge (*la conditione del modo nostro de intendere*). In strict consistency with this view—a consequence, however, which he only incidentally points out—Bruno somewhere remarks that we have, properly speaking, no right to conceive the universe as a totality, if it have no limit.

Since the horizon forms itself anew round every place occupied by the spectator as its central point, every determination of place must be relative. The universe looks different according to whether we conceive it to be regarded from the earth, the moon, Venus, the sun, etc. One and the same place will, according to the different points from which it is regarded (*respectu diversorum*), be centre, pole, zenith, or nadir. Determinations such as " over " and " under " do not therefore signify, as the old world-scheme presupposes, any absolute relation. It is only when we assume definite points of view that we invest such expressions with definite significance. And as with the relativity of place so with the relativity of motion. Motion is only conceived in its relation to one fixed point, and all depends on where we suppose this fixed point to be. One and the same motion will present a different appearance according to whether I regard it from the earth or from the sun, and wherever I may place myself in thought, my own standpoint will always appear to me to be immovable. We must not demand, therefore, that absolute certainty shall attend the distinction between that which is at rest and that which is in motion. The old world-scheme takes as given exactly what has to be proved, viz. that the earth is the fixed point from which every motion is to be measured. From the relativity of motion follows the relativity of time. For no absolutely regular motion can be discovered, and we possess no records which can prove to us that all the stars have taken up exactly the same position, with regard to the earth, as those they previously occupied, and that their motions are absolutely regular. We can therefore find no absolute measure of time. Since motion appears different when regarded from different stars, there must, if it is to be taken as the measure of time, be as many times in the universe as there are stars.

Nor have the concepts of heaviness and lightness any more absolute significance than have determinations of place. For, according to Aristotle, heaviness was the tendency to seek out the central point of the world, and, since the earth was the heaviest element, it followed that it was the central point of the world. But the qualities of heaviness and lightness are predicable of the particles of every individual heavenly body in their relation to this body as a whole. When that which is heavy falls, it does so because it seeks to return to the place in which it is at home and where it can best maintain itself. The particles of the sun are heavy in relation to the sun, those of the earth in relation to the earth. With regard to the universe as a totality, the concepts of lightness and heaviness have as little validity as motion and the determinations of place and time. They only receive significance in relation to a particular heavenly body or to a particular system. This theory of weight is identical with that held by Copernicus, only that Bruno lays the chief emphasis on the fact that it is the impulse to self-preservation which causes the parts to seek out their whole. Copernicus, too, relies on the relativity of our determinations, but he pauses half-way. It is Bruno's merit to have carried out this principle, and to have shown what are the consequences following from it. In Bruno, too, we meet for the

first time with a decided answer to one of the most weighty
objections against Copernicus, *i.e.* that objects falling on to the
earth cannot fall on a spot perpendicularly below the point
from which they started, but must fall a little to the west of
this.   For Bruno shows that a stone thrown from the top of a
mast will fall at the foot of the mast because, from the
beginning of its fall, it has participated, by means of strength
imparted to it (*virtù impressa*), in the motion of the ship.   If,
on the other hand, the stone had been thrown down from a
point outside the ship, it would have fallen a little further
back.   Bruno here enters on a train of thought of very great
significance, and which afterwards led Galilei to the discovery
of the law of inertia.

Closely connected, in Bruno's theory, with the principle of
relativity is the principle that Nature is everywhere essentially the
same (*indifferenza della natura*).   From relations as we find them
with us, he concludes to relations in other places in the universe.
An experience of his childhood led him to adopt this method.
From the hill Cicada, near Nola, which lay at his feet covered
with forests and vines, he looked at the distant Vesuvius which
appeared to him small, as well as bare and unfruitful.   But
when, on one occasion, he had wandered as far as Vesuvius he
perceived that the two hills had exchanged aspects.   Now it was
Vesuvius which was high and wooded, while the Cicada was
low and bare.   The same principle which led him to establish
and extend Copernicanism through the assumption of the
infinity of the universe also led him to assume, as a matter of
course, that the same relations exist everywhere, where we have
no experience to the contrary.   He now conceives the other
heavenly bodies as similar to the earth, and the other systems
as similar to the solar system, so that the fixed stars become
suns surrounded by planets.   There is no ground for assuming
anything else but that the same force is everywhere in operation.   But, in that case, Copernicus was not justified in
following the ordinary conception and supposing all the fixed
stars to be equally distant from us, and to lie in one and the
same sphere.   Perhaps it only appears as if they always
maintained the same distance from us and from one another.
Distant ships appear immovable, and yet they are often moving
with no small velocity.   Whether this is the case with the fixed
stars can certainly only be established by observations extending

through many years, and which may even, perhaps, not yet have
been begun. But the reason that such observations have not yet
been set on foot is precisely this firm conviction that the fixed
stars never change their place, either in relation to us or to one
another! Thus it is evident that the principle of the " indifference of Nature" (or, as it is called nowadays, the principle of actuality), no less than the principle of relativity from
which it is deduced, will be productive, since it leads to new
investigations. Bruno has a much keener sense of the necessity
of confirming theoretical and subjective considerations by the
method of experience than is generally attributed to him.
"What could we think without all the observations that have
been collected?" he asks. He is certainly no mere enthusiast
for the infinite. He sought to show, by means of a thoughtful
and critical examination, what are the presuppositions on which
the old world-scheme rests, and how justifiable and natural it
is to bring forward other assumptions. And the *onus probandi*,
he thinks, lies first of all with those who assert the limitation of
the universe ; for does not experience show us that wherever
we may go the boundaries always change with our progress?
And why should the universe extend no further than to eight
spheres, as even Copernicus still believed? Why not to a
ninth, a tenth, and so on? Because our sense-perception
is limited, we have no right to conclude that the universe is
limited also. Bruno's greatest merit is the energy with which
he thought himself into the new world-conception, and
demanded its verification in detail. On this account his
teaching is more than an anticipation of genius. The epistemological foundation on which he bases it has lasting significance. Nevertheless it cannot be denied that the passionate
consistency with which he proceeded often led him to express
himself with greater certainty than he was by rights entitled to.
Small wonder if the zeal with which he laboured, and which
was necessary to the surmounting of obstacles, carried him
beyond the goal.

By means of the relativity of place-determinations Bruno
had, as we saw, overthrown the old doctrine of the elements
according to which they were characterised by heaviness or
lightness as absolute qualities, and to each one was assigned its
"natural place" in the universe. But with this doctrine the
distinction between the heavenly and the sublunary world

vanished, as also the prejudice that no change could take place in heaven. Bruno was especially anxious to over-throw the belief in the fixed spheres. He shows that this belief is a corollary from the assumption that the earth is the absolute central point. As soon as we have thoroughly grasped the idea that every heavenly body is, so to say, a central point, and can move freely in space, as the earth does, the necessity for believing in fixed spheres disappears. And why should the heavenly bodies require external forces to move them ? Each one of them, like every other creature in the world, has an inner impulse to motion which carries it forwards ; every heavenly body and every little world has in itself a source of life and motion, and space is the great ethereal medium in which the all-embracing world-soul is active ; there is therefore no need for special spirits of the spheres to set particular regions in motion. Bruno found a confirmation of his view in Tycho Brahe's investigations into the nature of comets. He may, perhaps, have composed the Latin didactic poem " On the Immeasurable and the Countless Worlds " on purpose to show how these investigations confirmed the opinions which he had deduced on other grounds in his Italian dialogue "On the Infinite Universe and the Worlds." He here eulogises the Danish investigator as the first astronomer of his day (*Ticho Danus, nobilissimus atque princeps astronomorum nostri temporis*) and as the man who put an end to the fixed spheres which were supposed to enclose our world in layers.[29] For the comets go straight through the " spheres," whose crystal masses are said to divide the different regions of the world from one another !

These are all Bruno's views that can be brought together under the point of view of an epistemological foundation of the new world-scheme. We will now pass on to what may be called the religio-philosophical foundation. This is taken from the idea of the infinity of the Deity, an idea which Bruno had, from the beginning, regarded as unquestionable ; and which he might also safely assume to be shared by his readers and opponents, even though they might not have been clear as to all it involved. To Bruno it seemed a contradiction that no infinite effect should correspond to the infinite cause. If the Deity, which in its original unity embraces all that is unfolded in the universe, is infinite, then the universe which is the un-folded form of God's essence must be infinite. No force limits itself, and the infinite force has nothing by which it can be limited. If the Deity is conceived as the principle of good, must we not then assume that it will impart all that it can ? Shall we suppose it to be envious or niggardly ? The infinite perfection must express itself in infinitely many creatures and worlds. It is not justifiable to attribute to the Deity a force or a possibility which does not become reality. This opposition between possibility and reality is only valid for finite creatures, and must not be transferred to the Deity. Otherwise we shall have two Gods,—one possible, and one real or active,—in opposition to one another ; a blasphemous theory contradictory to the unity of God. Jakob Boehme, as we saw above, was not afraid of this blasphemy. His religio-philosophical speculations remind us, in several points, of those of Bruno ; and for him too the new conception of the world had significance. But Boehme was concerned with the problem of evil, not that of the interconnection of the world. The religio-philosophical proof on which Bruno relies did not originate with himself. As he himself mentions, it had already been established by PIETRO MANZOLI of Ferrara, who, under the name of Palingenius, published a Latin didactic poem (*Zodiacus vitae*, Lyons, 1552), in which he taught the infinity of the universe ; although he conceives the world-scheme with fixed spheres in the traditional way ; in addition to the eight spheres Palingenius introduces an incorporeal and infinite world of light. It does not derogate from the originality of Bruno that he thus made use of former thinkers, *e.g.* Palingenius here, and, in other passages, Cusanus, Copernicus, and the old Atomists. In all cases he reduces their thoughts to greater coherency, and carries them out with greater consistency and on a basis of richer experience than was possible to them.

It seemed to Bruno as if he had never breathed freely until the limits of the universe had been extended to infinity, and the fixed spheres had disappeared. No longer now was there a limit to the flight of the spirit, no "so far and no farther" ; the narrow prison in which the old beliefs had confined men's spirits had now to open its gates and let in the pure air of a new life. He has expressed these thoughts in some sonnets which precede the dialogue on "the infinite Universe." The picture of reality, at the shaping of which his thought had laboured so enthusiastically and untiringly, contained for him

K

a symbolic significance.   The outer infinity was for him the
symbol of the inner.   Not all symbolism rests on so firm a basis.

(c) *Fundamental Philosophical Ideas*

Bruno's greatest achievement as a thinker is the foundation
which he assigned to the new world-scheme in the nature of
our sense-perception and of our thought, and also his extension
of this world-scheme, and the proof that such an extension was
necessary.   Closely connected with this world-conception of
his, however, are his general leading thoughts, his doctrine of
the ultimate principles of existence.   On the basis of a
thorough-going study of Bruno's Latin writings, and after a
comparison with his Italian works, Felice Tocco has attempted
to show that, with regard to Bruno's fundamental philosophical
conception, three stages are to be distinguished.   In the first
stage he stands near the Neo-Platonists, since he regards the
world as well as human knowledge as an efflux of the Deity.
This stage is more particularly represented in his *De Umbris
Idearum* (The Shadows of Ideas).   In the second stage he
conceives the Deity as the infinite substance, which persists
through all change of phenomena, as the unity of all the
opposites in existence.   This stage is represented in his chief
works, the Italian dialogues, which appeared in London.   In the
third stage he conceives that which underlies phenomena as an
infinity of atoms or monads, without, however, abandoning the
idea of the one substance moving in all things.   This stage is
expressed in the Latin didactic poem, which appeared at
Frankfurt, and more especially in his *De Minimo*.   I can, on the
whole, endorse this conception of the philosophical development
of Bruno during the last ten years (1582-92) that he spent
at liberty, especially when sufficient weight is laid on the fact,
which Tocco points out, that Bruno himself was not aware of
these transitions and differences.   There are, however, several
points of detail which, in my opinion, are susceptible of a
different interpretation from that given them by the untiring
Italian student of Bruno.

Bruno began as a Platonist.   Everything has its ultimate
ground in an eternal idea which is one with the essence of the
Deity.   It is the task of our knowledge to raise itself out of
the confused manifold of the senses to the unity which moves

in all things, even though the highest knowledge attainable by us is only a shadow of the divine ideas. But Bruno parts company from Plato in one, and that a very essential, point. While Plato understands by ideas general concepts which are common to the particular phenomena, universals, Bruno expressly explains that the concepts by means of which we raise ourselves above the confused manifold of the senses are no mere graduated series of universal concepts (*universalia logica*), but concepts which express the real connection of phenomena ; so that instead of an unformed manifold of parts, we get a firmly connected and formed whole. The particular parts thus become comprehensible as they could never be when held apart and considered each one for itself; just as we can only understand the hand in connection with the arm, the foot in connection with the leg, and the eye in connection with the head. The highest unity which is set up as the ideal of knowledge, then, is not an abstract idea, but the principle of real interconnection according to law, which alone lends existence to the particular phenomena, and makes them comprehensible to us. Bruno here expresses a thought which may be traced under different forms throughout the whole history of modern philosophy. While ancient philosophy turned its attention chiefly to the form or idea, the attention of modern philosophy is mainly directed towards the law. The interconnection of existence according to law is the fundamental fact which it strives to think out and expound. Bruno only touches on this thought in his work on the " Shadows of Ideas " ; he does not enter into it any further since his interest in it is mainly memotechnical ; he recommends for the better remembering of ideas that we should unite them with one another in the same way as the corresponding phenomena occur together in reality, since this connection will facilitate remembrance as well as practical application. It is thus not difficult to understand how Bruno passed over to the conception which he develops in the Italian dialogues in close connection with the logical consequences of the new world-scheme. What he was really seeking, even in the first stage, was the inner principle which underlies the real connection of particular things as well as the things themselves. His solution from the first is from within, not from without, or from above.

In the dialogue " On Cause, Principle, and Unity," we find

the complete working-out of this fundamental thought of Bruno's. His endeavour throughout is to conceive the universe as a whole, moved by inner forces, in which everything is inter-connected, and which is itself the unfolding of that which is contained within the infinite principle, the highest thought attainable by us. In distinguishing between cause and principle Bruno means to indicate that the infinite unity may be regarded sometimes as the antithesis to all which springs out of it,—and then he calls it the cause; sometimes as that which moves within the manifold of phenomena,—and then it is called the principle or world-soul. In the first form it is not accessible to our thought, but is an object of faith alone. The true philo-sopher and the believing theologian differ from one another in this: that while the latter seeks the Deity beyond and above, the former seeks it within Nature. As we saw in our discussion of his world-scheme, Bruno emphatically asserts that the infinity of the effect follows necessarily from the infinity of the cause. But precisely because the effect is infinite it cannot be grasped, and any knowledge of the Deity to which we can attain, must therefore always, even when it is regarded as the principle (or immanent cause) or world-soul, remain incomplete. That any knowledge at all is possible is because this principle moves in us as in all other things in the world. The new world-scheme shows how illusory it is to seek for the seat of the Deity altogether beyond our own *ego,* and teaches us that, on the contrary, it is to be sought in our innermost selves, " in a closer relation to us than that in which we stand to ourselves " (*di dentro piu che noi medesmi siamo dentro a noi*). The Deity is the soul of our soul as it is the soul of the whole of Nature.

The world-soul is for Bruno the principle which unites and orders all things, by means of space, which is not empty but forms an infinite ethereal medium ; it evokes reciprocal action between particular things. Just as space does not exclude bodies, but, on the contrary, is precisely that which renders their visible connection possible, so the world-soul, as the bearer of ideas (*mundus intelligibilis*), works not from without inwards, nor as something alien to things, but as the law of their own nature. It is an artist which produces and develops from within the forms which natural phenomena assume ; not a spirit which sets the world in motion from without, but the inner principle of motion. At every single place, in every single particle, the world-soul works as a totality. The *uni-versum* does not exist as a totality in its particular parts, but the world-soul moves as a totality in each one of these parts : *anima toto et qualibet totius parte !* [30]   There stirs in everything an inner impulse to motion, a vital force, a will, which leads things by the ways which render self-preservation possible to them.   It is this inner impulse which leads the iron to the magnet, which makes the drop of water as well as the whole earth assume the form of a ball, which is that best suited to hold the parts together.   This inner principle of motion through which the world-soul testifies of itself in every creature in the world forms, for Bruno, the antithesis to the external, moving forces of the old natural philosophy, and denotes an advance, inasmuch as external causes are rejected, where inner causes suffice.   It prepared the way for the discovery of the law of inertia which Bruno had hinted at in his dialogues.   But, for him, it was at the same time, as will be clear from what we have already said, a principle working purposively and teleo-logically.   It leads with inner necessity to self-preservation and development.   Teleology and mechanism are combined in one and the same.   The different creatures and worlds are moved by the inner principle in such wise as to secure their existence, so that the world-system does not perish out of due season.   The prescience and the active source of Nature (*la provida Natura*) are thus not different, but one and the same.   In his Latin didactic poem *De Immenso*, Bruno shows more exactly how this unity of teleology and mechanism occurs in Nature.   Those combinations of elements which are not purposive (suited to ends) quickly perish : *male adorta cito pereunt.*   Through the perpetual exagitation (*exagitatio*) of the elements, combinations must finally arise which retain existence and vitality throughout long periods.   Thus we are enabled to explain how it is that world-systems, persisting through ages, can be produced.   Although by this explanation Bruno ranges himself with the atomists of antiquity who, as may be seen from the didactic poem of Lucretius, entertained similar ideas, yet it is his firm conviction that a providence is not hereby excluded.   In the tendency which ever urges to new and ultimately victorious attempts, he sees the expression of a guiding will, he traces a *mens paterna cuncta moderans.*   This is a characteristic trait of Bruno's attempt to unite Platonic

idealism with a realistic conception of Nature. In the first
stage (in the " Shadows of Ideas ") it was in the interconnection
of Nature that he found the idea ; here he goes a step farther
and finds it in the struggle for existence itself. Bruno's conception of Nature retains a poetical character through the emphasis
which he lays on the inner force. At single points he approximates to a purely scientific mode of thought ; the impulse to
find everywhere the same motives as those he encountered in
himself hindered him, however, from actually taking this step.
He has laid down views which retain their interest even *after*
the foundation of a mechanical natural science, although they
themselves could not have led to its establishment. Among
the points on which he approximates to the mechanical conception of Nature is to be noted especially his statement that
movement in space is the principle of all change. It is on this
thought that all modern natural science rests.

Bruno's philosophy takes on a stamp of realism owing to
his polemical attack on Plato and Aristotle, who set up the
"idea" or the "form" in antithesis to matter (stuff). By this
means the former were rendered fantastic, while the latter
was degraded to an entirely passive and unfruitful principle.
Following the older Greek natural philosophers (and perhaps
influenced by Paracelsus as well) Bruno establishes the doctrine
of the conservation of matter. Out of the seed-corn arises the
blade ; out of the blade, the ear ; out of the ear, bread ; out of
the bread, chyle ; out of the chyle, blood ; out of the blood, the
sperm ; out of the sperm, the fœtus ; out of the fœtus, the man ;
out of the man, the corpse ; out of the corpse, earth ! Thus a
continual transformation of matter goes on. Matter persists
throughout all changes of form. And the forms which it
assumes in particular cases it receives, not from without, but
from within itself. Art produces forms by combination or
disintegration of matter. Nature, on the contrary, produces
her forms by the development of that to which she finds
dispositions within herself, since she explicates what is impli-
cate in the original principle of Nature. Matter, far from being
something base and of small account, is a divine thing (*cosa
divina*), author and mother of natural things, one indeed with
Nature herself. Bruno tells us that this view of the significance
and originality of matter inclined him for some time to the
opinion that forms are only something external and vanishing

in Nature.   He was probably at that time influenced by Telesio's natural philosophy.   He saw, however, that there must be an original principle through which forms can find their explanation.   Form and matter, actual activity and passive receptivity, must be originally united in the one essence which underlies all things.   The divine activity has not to go outside itself for its matter, neither has it to be set in action from without.   Possibility and reality here meet together, as do also matter and form, passivity and activity.   Bruno distinguishes two kinds of substance, which he sometimes calls form and matter, sometimes spiritual and material substance ; both persist eternally.   The world-soul is both the eternal form which comprehends the particular arising and vanishing forms, and also the infinite spirit which persists throughout the changes of finite spirits.   Everything that exists is animated and formed ;—in different fashion, certainly, at any rate as regards disposition (*secondo la sustanza*), if not in actual development (*secondo l' atto*) also.   Ultimately, however, he regards the two substances as one single substance ; they spring out of one single root, and can be reduced to one single essence.   It cannot be supposed that there are several substances in the world, but only *una originale et universale sustanza*, which underlies all the differences presented in existence.   Indeed he even explains that that which produces the differences between things does not belong to their essence, but only to their sensuous appearance.   In the highest unity, which is the goal of knowledge, then, the difference between spirit and matter is overcome, as is also the difference between form and matter, doing and suffering, reality and possibility.[31]   In short, all oppositions and differences of existence are, in the eternal essence, combined into a unity and harmony (*unità et convenienza*), such that no change in any direction is possible, nor is there anything which can set itself up in opposition to this unity, any more than there is anything which can stand in a relation of equality to it, since nothing exists beyond itself.   Because it exists eternally the difference between hour, day, year, and century disappears in it, as do also the differences between finite creatures—*e.g.* between ants and men, between Man and the stars—in relation to the infinite all-embracing essence.   On this account our thought cannot grasp this infinite unity and fulness.   We can only form a *negative* concept of it by abstract-

ing from it all differences and oppositions. Everything which
we comprehend we fashion into a unity, but the absolute unity
transcends our grasp. In his negative theology as well as in
his doctrine of the relativity of knowledge Bruno is evidently a
pupil of Cusanus. He halts (*De la causa*, ed. Lagarde, p. 268)
at the difficulty of how the Deity can be possibility *as well
as* reality, if the unity is to be absolute. Like Cusanus, he
is at some pains to invest the concept of the Deity with
life by attributing to it possibility, and not merely a reality,
finished once and for all ; but in his mystical explanation
that possibility and reality are one and the same, he cancels
this determination. And here the dualism of his system
becomes apparent, for in the finite world possibility and reality
are different, and thus there remains a strongly marked opposition between this finite world and the eternal substance, in which
the opposition between possibility and reality does not exist.
If the eternal substance, which in its unity (*complicamente et
totalmente*) embraces all the content of existence, is perfect,
what significance has the progressive process of development through the oscillation of opposites and the continual
transition from possibility to reality ? Only if we admit an
original imperfection or unreadiness (which might consist in
the content existing *only* implicitly and not explicitly) or,
with Jakob Boehme, a fall on the part of the Deity, can finite
development be compatible with the idea of God. It is
Boehme's merit to have perceived this. Bruno oscillates, without himself being aware of it, between mystical contemplation
of the unity, and enthusiastic surrender to the manifold. His
thought, however, is occupied for the most part with tracking
the eternal unity throughout the uninterrupted course of development and behind all opposites. He refers to a series of empirical confirmations (*verificationi*) of his doctrine. The continual transformation of matter into new forms is an expression
of the infinite unity which cannot be realised exhaustively in
any single form. Only by means of a common principle
underlying them can opposites like minimum and maximum,
dizzy happiness and sudden destruction, birth and death, love
and hate, pass over into one another. Through continuous
transitions the highest degree of warmth and the highest
degree of cold are connected with each other, indicating that
one single principle underlies them both (a reflection which

Bruno directs against Telesio).   He who would understand the great secrets of Nature must, above all things, take account of the way in which opposites pass over into one another in their minima and maxima.   Everywhere in Nature opposites are in operation together, and on a nearer consideration we shall always discover a common ground to which each one for itself returns.   If we remember how Bruno thus "verifies" his doctrine of the unity of opposites, we see that it loses much of its mystical character.   He exhibits the continuity of opposites; not, however, their absolute identity.   Thus his doctrine acquires a realistic character: he exhorts men to seek for all middle terms and middle causes and to find the highest in that which makes their union and co-operation possible.   This is the significance of his doctrine of the world-soul, and it is the same thought as that which had already appeared in his *De Umbris Idearum*.   This whole train of thought sets him in an optimistic mood.   Destruction, dissolution, misshapeness, and suffering have nothing to do with that which really exists.   They belong to the sensuous world where possibility and reality do not always go together, and where opposites occur in sharp conflict with one another.   They vanish when we direct our glance to that which exists eternally. But they also vanish when we conceive everything in its individual nature according to the definite manner in which it fills its place in the great whole, in which even the smallest member has its significance.   "Everything is perfect because in its own individuality (*De imm.* 11, 12 ; *in sua individuitate*) it is a being which is limited by no other ; this is the inner measure of perfection."   And that which in certain relations and for certain beings is bad, is in other relations and for other beings good.   For him who fixes his gaze on the whole complex, therefore, the conflict dissolves into harmony.   Nature is like a choir-master, who has many voices in his choir, but is able to make all sound in harmony with each other.   Yet it is only when Bruno's thought dwells in these high regions that he is able to hold fast to this harmony.   When he buries himself in the actual oppositions of life he feels these to be so contradictory to one another that his prevailing mood is more complicated, and takes on a tragic character, or, at any rate, the imprint of resignation.   It is from this side that he conceives existence in his work "On the Heroic Affects."

The passages in Bruno in which he sets up individual character as the measure of perfection, and brings into prominence the significance of small elements for great results, are to be found in the Frankfurt writings, *i.e.* in the last group of writings, which, as Felice Tocco pointed out, express Bruno's third standpoint.   He is here still further than in his London works from appealing, with the Neo-Platonists, to a supernatural principle.   And while, in the London works, it is on interconnection and reciprocal action that he lays most weight, here he emphasises the individual elements between which the reciprocal action takes place.   Prominence is given to the individual in his particularity.   He affirms, for example, that there are no two things, nor two cases, nor two times which are exactly the same ; and only the elements to which all things can be finally reduced are really substantial. That which presents itself to our senses as connected consists of corpuscles, just as number consists of units.   The atom (or the minimum, or the monad) is that which has no parts, and which is itself a primary part of a phenomenon.   We must, in every sphere, go back to the constituent elements, *i.e.* those which are not dissolved with the whole phenomenon.   A complex being cannot be substance.   Bruno here definitely asserts that division cannot be carried on *ad infinitum*, and he blames not only the physicists but also the mathematicians for believing in such infinite division.   But he does not even hold that the atoms themselves are absolute.   He conceives atoms as being of different degrees, and atoms of one degree may include atoms of another.   It is thus clear that with him the concept of the atom is a relative concept.   Of the two clauses of which his definition of the minimum consists—

Est minimum, cujus pars nulla est, prima quod est pars—

he can really only assert the latter.   The atom is the first constituent we need in explanation of a sensuous phenomenon ; but there is no ground for supposing that it itself possesses no parts ; that we do not perceive these parts is quite another matter.   Bruno now even applies the concept of minimum to great wholes ; thus the sun with its whole planetary system is a minimum in relation to the universe.   Indeed, even the whole universe is called a monad.   And further, the minimum is not only a particle of matter, but it is also active force, soul, and will. The goal is contained within it as a disposition ; by this means it is possible to preserve the unity of teleology and mechanism. From this point of view also, Bruno distinguishes between atoms (or minima or monads) of different degrees ; the world-soul too, even God Himself, is called a monad. This determination is necessary, because that which is not an individual cannot be said to exist. God is the monad of monads ; that is to say, He is the essence of all particular essences. In this way Bruno expresses what he had already said in the Italian poems, where God is called the soul of souls. Thus Bruno has not deserted the fundamental thought of his earlier stages, the thought of a single substance which moves in all things. Even after he had perceived the necessity of the concept of atoms for an exact conception of Nature, he only applies it to material phenomena, and it remains an unsolved problem how individual psychical beings are related to the spiritual substance of which they are the particular forms.[32] From his interest in the old doctrine of metempsychosis we may conclude that he assumed that, after death, individual souls pass into new bodies. Yet he did not seriously support this fantastic notion. He pauses at the thought that spiritual, like material, substance persists under continually changing forms, but that the new forms are not necessarily identical with the earlier. He attaches great importance to the impulse to the continuance of life and to uninterrupted development ; nor, he thinks, will this impulse be disappointed, even if the belief that we can know what form of existence we shall next assume be an illusion.[33]

Together with many ideas in which the poet gets the upper hand of the thinker, and side by side with many allegorical and arbitrary speculations (especially in the *De Monade*), which we have not mentioned here since they no longer possess any interest, Bruno's philosophy exhibits an attempt, very remarkable for the time, to unite a fundamentally idealistic conception with the scientific conception of the world. Bruno was not, of course, acquainted with the exact foundation of this world-conception which was introduced by Galilei and Kepler, but at several points of his thought he is not far from them.

(*d*) *Theory of Knowledge*

Bruno's main endeavour is to know Nature. And this is, for him, identical with knowing the Deity. He regarded an advance in the knowledge of Nature as a revelation. This was the cause of his enthusiasm for Copernicus and Tycho Brahe, and of his zeal in tracing out the logical consequences of their discoveries. Thought, reason, is for him only the means for discovering the essence of Nature; it must not itself be set in the place of Nature. He finds fault with Plato and Aristotle because they had set up logical differences— oppositions and distinctions of thought—as though they were real oppositions belonging to the essential being of Nature. It is, as he several times remarks, the foundation of all " natural and divine knowledge" to distinguish between logi- cal oppositions and actual unity so that we do not—as, for instance, Aristotle did, in his distinction between form and matter—separate with the Reason that which, according to Nature and to truth, is inseparable. Reason must follow Nature, not Nature Reason. It is especially and altogether arbitrary, in Bruno's opinion, to think that, in Nature, opposites are as sharply separated as they are in our thought. For in Nature opposites pass over into one another and thus show themselves to be near akin, while in a logical system they are placed as far from one another as possible.

With regard to sense-knowledge, too, Bruno enjoins a eriti- cal separation between that which belongs to our activity of knowledge only, and that which belongs to Nature. This distinction is especially prominent in his third period, where it was favoured by the atomistic trend of his mode of conception. In his *De Minimo*, which expounds his doctrine of atoms, he teaches that those minima (atoms or monads) which, properly speaking, are the only reals, are not themselves perceived as such. Sense-perception, that is to say, arises only through their united activity. The differences which are presented in our sensations, therefore, need not correspond with any equally great differences in the physical elements. Bruno does not go so far, however, as to assume a single uniform matter (*com- munis materia*), for then it would be difficult to understand how the differences of sensuous perception could arise. That light, fluids, and "dry" matter (the atoms) are one and the same matter he cannot conceive. It is consistent with this view that his atomism should be concerned only with "dry" or firm matter (*materia arida*), not with light, nor with the ethereal medium by means of which the corpuscles are united. He does not perceive that the difficulty of accounting for the differences of sensations must in any case occur with respect to the "dry" matter, since this, too, corresponds to different sensation qualities. He is not far from the principle of the subjectivity of the sense-qualities, but does not altogether accept it. Only with regard to the feeling-elements which are bound up with sensations does he teach that their significance is merely subjective and relative. Their validity rests in the perceiving subject, whose estimations of worth they express. They are valid *ex latere potentiarum*, not *ex latere objectorum* (*De Minimo*, ed. 1591, p. 59). The same observation holds good to a certain extent of the moral and æsthetic concepts. Bruno, however, asserts that there is something good in and for itself (*simpliciter*), which only thought can discover, when it must forsake the limited human point of view. The good may be so determined as not merely to express a relation to human nature (as *ad speciem humanum contractum*). The necessary logical consequence of Bruno's conception of Nature, then, seems to be that just as it is impossible that there should be any absolute determination of place in the universe, *i.e.* a place-determination without relations, so it is impossible that there should be a moral or æsthetic estimation of worth apart from a definite subjective basis. Bruno is not yet a Copernican on this point.

Bound up with this is his inability to abandon his presupposition that it is our knowledge which expresses and testifies to the innermost nature of existence. It is one and the same scale which Nature descends in her productive processes as far as particulars, and which we ascend, by means of our knowledge, as far as general laws. Production is an unfolding, an explication—our knowledge is a comprehension, a complication. The two processes correspond to one another perfectly. To understand a thing is to give it an abbreviated and simplified expression. All knowledge is a simplification because it seeks for unity; and this shows clearly that the essence of things consists in unity! It is evident that Bruno here transfers his form of thought to existence itself, only it is the form not of distinction but of unity. The latter he considers more essential than the former; but both are indispensable. The great problem here involved was not taken up again till much later.

The highest object of knowledge is also its limit, according to Bruno. The absolute unity is inaccessible to our discursive and distinguishing thought. We are not able to frame any concept which may express it. It is the object of faith. Only as revealed in Nature, only as the world-soul, is it the object of philosophy. And yet—the world-soul also, God as the soul of Nature, as the essence of all essences, must transcend all oppositions (*e.g.* between form and matter, reality and possibility, mind and matter, etc.)! It, too, must withdraw itself from knowledge. While Nicolaus of Cusa, by whom Bruno is in this matter strongly influenced, passed over at this point into positive theology, to which, as he grew older, he became more and more attached, Bruno only pauses for a moment to exclaim that " the profoundest and most pious theologians " have taught that God is honoured and loved by silence rather than by speech, and to commend the superiority of negative to scholastic theology—and then he turns back again to Nature. The ladder of knowledge which he sets up does not reach quite far enough ; moreover Bruno's own place is in the middle of the ladder, amongst the strivers.

According to Bruno, the significance of positive theology is practical only, not theoretical. He defended the new astronomical system for which he was struggling, and which encountered such great opposition from those who believed in the Bible, on the ground (afterwards taken by Galilei and Kepler) that " the sacred writings do not discuss proofs and speculations regarding natural things from the scientific standpoint, but, on the contrary, their precepts aim at guiding moral action, for the benefit of our hearts and minds." " Therefore," he adds, " they must speak a language which can be understood by all." He thus hoped to reduce to silence a somewhat "impatient and strict Rabbi." He himself is convinced that the new philosophy which he had established was far more calculated to support true religion than any other philosophy, since it taught that existence, like its cause, is infinite, and that in spite of all change, nothing perishes absolutely (*Cena*, pp. 169-173). This passage contains the clearest description of Bruno's

attitude towards positive religion which is to be found.   In
other passages (*De l'Infin.* p. 318 ; *De gl' Her. Fur.* p. 619) he
expresses himself rather more as an intellectual aristocrat : he
says, *e.g.* that faith is for rude men who need to be governed, while
thought is for contemplative natures who know how to rule
themselves as well as others.   We cannot be astonished that
this antithesis should have suggested itself to him on all sides,
especially when we consider the violent struggle which he had
to carry on with prejudices based on religious notions.   Where
he incidentally attacks or aims at Christianity, it is Protestantism rather than Catholicism which he takes as his butt.   And
this was because he feared that the useful practical consequences
of religion might be lost through Protestantism (especially
Calvinism), which produces seditious views, quarrels between
near relations, civil war, and ceaseless dogmatic polemics ; every
pedant is ready to produce a catechism of his own (if he has
not already done so), and to demand that all other men should
regulate their conduct by it.   Not least objectionable is it to
Bruno that Protestantism commends faith in opposition to
works.   This, he thought, opens the way to barbarism.   It
tends to make men appropriate and use the work of their forefathers without doing anything more themselves.   Hospitals
and poorhouses, schools and universities, are owing not to the
modern but to the ancient Church, and it would be iniquitous
if these accusers of works were to appropriate the same to
themselves.   Instead of reforming they, on the contrary, remove
what is good from religion.   These passages (*Spaccio*, p. 446
ff.) are evidently suggested by Bruno's experiences in Geneva,
France, and England.   The germ of new life contained within
the Protestant spirit escaped him ; and in the midst of all
the fermentation and mutual recriminations of the time it must
indeed have been difficult to discover it.   His sympathy is
evidently on the side of the ancient Church, and we understand
that he felt himself homeless.   The thought which moved so
freely in the large spaces of the universe made it difficult for
him to find his right place in this complicated human world.
He did not understand that Protestantism was a Copernicanism
in the spiritual sphere, that it would make every individual a
central point of the world.   The fanaticism and the pedantry of
the Protestant theologians blinded him to the process of liberation
which it ushered in.   It is true it did no more than usher it in.

In his symbolical writings (the *Spaccio* and the *Cabala*) Bruno satirises several dogmas, *e.g.* the Incarnation and Transubstantiation. And this it was which, in spite of all his protestations that, in his philosophy, the standpoints of true religion were especially prominent, brought about his condemnation. It is interesting to observe the decided distinction he draws between the Christs of history and of dogma. In the *Spaccio*, where the stars are to be reformed, Chiron the Centaur also comes under discussion. Momos the mocker cuts several jokes over Chiron's double nature which is nevertheless supposed to form one single person, but is ordered to keep his reason within bounds. Zeus reflects that during his life on earth this Chiron was the most righteous among men, that he taught them the arts of healing and of melody, and showed them the way to the stars. Accordingly, instead of being driven out of heaven, he is assigned a place at its altar, as its only priest. This trait throws light on Bruno's relation to Christianity. We are not surprised that it had no significance in the eyes of Cardinal Bellarmin.

(e) Ethical Ideas

Bruno has left no coherent system of ethics although, in the preface to the *Spaccio*, he tells us that it is his intention to write a moral philosophy " based on the inner light." We here again encounter " the natural light," which, in the sixteenth century, was to acquire an independent prominence. Bruno never arrived at carrying this plan into execution. On the other hand, he gave what he called " Preludes " in two symbolical works, the *Spaccio della Bestia Trionfante* (The Expulsion of the Beast Triumphant) and the *De gl' Heroici Furori* (On the Heroic Affects).

These two works, although there was only a short interval between them, stand in a certain opposition to one another. The *Spaccio* is optimistic ; its subject is human life in its totality, more especially social life. In the work on the heroic affects, on the other hand, Bruno introduces us to the inner struggle and opposition within each striving individual ; he emphasises the pain of unceasing striving, even though it witness to the fact that men acknowledge ideal claims upon them. It is the striving of the individual, not the striving of society as a whole, or of the race, which is here depicted. The latter work is an ethic for the select few, who experience the heights and the depths in their own inner lives ; the former is for all.

The *Spaccio* is cast in the form of a story to the effect that Zeus, by whom we are to understand, not the highest divinity, but each one of ourselves, in so far as there are divine powers within us, resolves to reform Heaven.   He addresses the gods : our scandalous stories are recorded in the stars.   Let us only return to righteousness, *i.e.* to ourselves.   Let us reform the inner world, and then the outer will also be reformed.   And this reformation is depicted under the guise of a re-naming of the stars, the different virtues taking the place of the more or less ambiguous figures of the gods and beasts.   In his inquiry as to which virtues are to be represented in Heaven, Bruno finds occasion to institute a " transvaluation," to use a modern phrase, " of all values."   The exposition is very spun-out, but contains several interesting episodes.   There is no occasion here to dwell on more than a few of its most characteristic features.

The first and highest place in the new order is assigned to Truth, who rules over all and assigns to everything its place ; all things are dependent on her.   If we were to think of something which should transcend Truth and determine her validity, then this something would itself be the real Truth !   Nothing, then, can come before Truth.   Sought by many, she is descried by few.   She is often disputed, yet she needs no defence ; on the contrary, she grows the more, the more she is disputed.   This estimation of worth evidently stands in connection with Bruno's struggle for the new world-conception, and with his conception that the new ideas extend the view and ennoble the mind.

In Bruno's world-conception the necessary interconnection of objects and their passing into one another has great importance.   He finds the same law at work within the life of the soul, especially in feeling.   If there were no change, there would be no pleasure.   And pleasure presupposes pain.   Every feeling of pleasure consists in a transition, in a movement. Hence there is no pleasure without an intermixture of sorrow. This relation of opposites makes repentance possible, and produces the desire after a higher stage of life than that hitherto attained.   This is the moving cause which induces Zeus to reform himself and the whole world of the gods.   While all else changes, Truth alone remains, and it is in the light of Truth that the reform must be undertaken.   To these two thoughts Bruno (like Heraclitus of old) always remained constant ;—the passage of all things through opposites, and the persistence of the world-law throughout all change. Hence it is only natural that Truth as well as Repentance should find a place in his ethic. Repentance, in the new order, is to take the place of the swan. Like the swan, she appears on rivers and pools, and seeks, through purification, to attain to shining purity. Repentance is grieved at her present condition, and, sorrowful at the thought that she ever found satisfaction in it, she endeavours to raise herself above the lower regions and to soar aloft towards the sun. Although error is her father, and wrongdoing her mother, yet she herself is of the divine nature ; she is like the rose which can only be plucked amongst thorns, or like the spark of fire struck out of the dull flint stone.

Among those who seek a place in Heaven under the new order is Leisure (*ocio*). She praises the happy childhood of the human race, when there was no need to work, and all care and the unquiet that comes from striving were absent, and when not only unhappiness, but also vice and sin, did not exist. To this eulogy of the golden age Zeus replies that Man has hands and thoughts in order to use them, and it is his task not only to follow the suggestions of Nature but also to produce, through the power of his spirit, a second nature, a higher order ; without which he cannot retain his dignity as the god of the earth. In the golden age, with its leisure, men were no more virtuous than are the brutes now ; indeed they may have been still more apathetic. Necessity and struggle have called industry to life, have sharpened thought, and have led to the discovery of art, hence from day to day, under the pressure of wants, new and wonderful discoveries are ever evolving themselves out of the depths of the human spirit. By this means Man quits the beast, and approaches the divine. It is true that unrighteous-ness and malice increase. But in the brute condition there is neither virtue nor vice, for we must not confuse the absence of vice with virtue. Self-mastery is only to be found where there is something to be overcome, otherwise the apathy of the brutes would be virtue. Chastity is no virtue in a cold and lethargic nature ; thus it is no virtue in Northern Europe, though it is so in France, still more in Italy, and most of all in Africa. His conclusion is that leisure is only to be acknowledged as the necessary counterpart to labour (*ocio—negocio*). Labour and rest must form a natural rhythm. To a nobly born spirit leisure becomes the greatest torment, when it does not alternate with the most arduous activity.

In his work on the heroic affects, too, he lays great emphasis on the point that the life of feeling, since its existence is composed of the greatest opposites, must, in those who have advanced beyond the limitations of the brute, be of a complex nature ; hence complexity is taken as a criterion for the development of feeling. The stupid man never gets beyond his present condition, and thinks neither of what went before nor of what is to come, of the opposite which lies so near, nor of the absent which is yet always a possibility. His joy can therefore be without sorrow, without fear, and without remorse. Ignorance is the mother of sensuous happiness and of animal enjoyment. He who increases his knowledge increases his pain. With growing knowledge we perceive a greater number of possibilities, and place a higher aim before ourselves, which is accordingly all the harder to reach. The " heroic affect " arises when a man does not let himself be detained from striving after a high aim because pain and effort are bound up with the attempt. The butterfly attracted by the flame does not know it is its death ; the heroic man knows this, and yet he seeks out the light, for he knows that pain and danger are only evil according to the limited view of the senses and not from the point of view of eternity (*ne l'occhio de l'eternitade*). It is, indeed, a necessity that all higher aspirations should be accompanied by pain, since our goal mounts ever higher the further we progress. We embark on our voyage carelessly enough, but we soon find ourselves without, on the infinite ocean, overpowered by sense and thought. The more we attain, the more clearly we see that absolute satisfaction is impossible. We discover that the object of our aspiration is infinite, and this gives rise to conflict and endeavour in finite nature. Nevertheless we feel satisfaction at the kindling of this noble fire, even though it involve pain. It is a higher form of self-preservation which induces us, in spite of jangled harmony, to continue our striving after the ideal. That which binds the will (*vinculum voluntatis*) is at all stages a love, but this love may be directed towards something which lies far beyond the finite existence of the individual.

This whole train of thought is of interest not only because it contains answers to objections which have been made, even in quite recent times, against any system of ethics which takes happiness or welfare as the criterion, but also on account of the opposition in which Bruno here stands to the classical as well as to the mediæval conception. To throw oneself into the strife of opposites, and to take ship on the sea of infinite endeavour is, for Bruno, the highest. This produces a richness and a fulness of the inner life which, in his opinion, no condition of rest could possibly effect. However much his work may remind us of Plato and Plotinus, whom Bruno himself mentions, yet it characterises him as a modern thinker. In it he is the precursor of Lessing's and Kant's idea of eternal striving as the highest ; as, too, his attitude towards the idea of the golden age reminds us of the modern conception of the history of civilisation. As in his world-conception, so here, too, in his ethical ideas, he works with a distant horizon before him, and with the belief that this will ever admit of still further extension.

CHAPTER XIV

TOMASSO CAMPANELLA

LIKE Bruno, CAMPANELLA, too, was a monk who came in contact with the new thoughts of the age and went to meet them with a receptive mind. But he already belongs to the reaction. He agrees with the philosophers of the Renaissance that there must come a new science and a new philosophy, since the book of Nature has now been opened as it has never been before. Yet he has one other reason for making this demand, and this is that the old philosophy was heathenish. It was impossible, he thought, to unite the Aristotelian philosophy with the faith of the Church, although this had been considered possible throughout the Middle Ages. A new doctrine of Nature, a new doctrine of the State, and an entirely new Philosophy must now be established if the Church is to continue in existence, and if she is not to have cause to feel ashamed before new nations in other parts of the world, when they display a culture not to be found within the Church herself. In Campanella the bold hopes of the Renaissance are united with the faithful Catholic's humility before the Church. He denies that Bruno had been burnt on account of his scientific opinions; in his defence of Galilei he exhorts the Church to grant free course to investigations based on experience, for, if thoroughly studied, the book of Nature will be found to harmonise with the sacred writings. But when the Church had condemned the new astronomy contained in Galilei's teaching, Campanella submitted. It was, indeed, somewhat of a satisfaction to him to feel that it was now not necessary for him to give up the conception of Nature which he had accepted from Telesius, and had promulgated in his earlier writings. Through his attempt to base a new philosophy on Scholasticism, however, he made bitter enemies, to which fact his long imprisonment was probably partly due. There is something tragic about his figure, for his struggle with Scholasticism was regarded with displeasure by the ecclesiastical authorities, who had learnt to look with fear on any modification of their traditionary doctrines. All his enthusiasm for the cause of the Church did not avail him. Neither was he in a position mentally to conquer the powers of the past. Thoughts full of significance arose within him, but they were clothed in scholastic and mystical form, and when he succeeded in making them public they had already been expressed by Descartes in another manner, in a clearer form, and in closer conformity with the science of the day.

Campanella was born in 1568 at Stilo in Calabria. He changed his first name Giovanno for Tomasso when he entered the Dominican order at the age of fourteen. According to his own confession, he was induced to take this step not only by religious impulse but, perhaps still more, by the hope that in the cloister he would find it easier to carry on his studies. His zeal and acuteness soon excited the attention and fear of the monks. He brought such cogent arguments to bear on the Aristotelian philosophy that it was thought he came by them by unnatural means, and this opinion may have been strengthened by his leaning towards the "occult sciences." Telesio's natural philosophy excited his enthusiasm, and it was no small grief to him that he was not allowed to visit the aged thinker ; he only succeeded in seeing him when he was on his bier. He follows the Telesian philosophy in essential points, and appeared as its zealous apologist. In order to escape from the enmity he had drawn upon himself he travelled to Rome, and from thence to Florence and Padua. He never succeeded in securing a professorial chair from which he could expound his new ideas.

Men were full of suspicions towards the new doctrine. Campanella's manuscripts were actually stolen from him, and he only found them again when he appeared before the Roman Inquisition on his return from North Italy. He seems to have got through the examination to which he was subjected fairly easily here. At home a more severe one was awaiting him. Owing to the discontent with the Spanish government, and the general fermentation of men's minds, disturbances broke out in Calabria. Campanella, who had already attracted attention by his attitude of philosophic opposition, was now to become the object of mistrust on account of the socialistic ideas which he had embraced early in life, and also because he believed himself able, from the signs of the times and of Nature, to predict that great revolutions would take place in the year 1600. Accused of heresy and of plans inimical to the State, he was several times subjected to the most terrible persecutions, and was detained in prison for twenty-seven years. The best years of his life were spent in this way. The enthusiasm of this powerful spirit was not damped, however. While in prison he wrote poems and meditated, and when the subterranean hole in which he had been confined was exchanged for somewhat better accommodation, he eagerly resumed his studies. The friends who visited him saw his manuscripts through the press. Finally he was liberated and was sent to Rome. The Pope protected him, and allowed him to take refuge in France, where, supported by the French Government, he spent his last years in peace. He died in 1639, two years after the appearance of Descartes' first and epoch-making work.

Campanella desired a philosophy based upon experience. Hence Telesio's programme inspired him with such enthusiasm that he overlooked the imperféct manner in which this programme had been carried out. This, too, was the reason why he took such a lively interest in Tycho Brahe's and Galilei's observations, and, as we have already hinted, hesitated for some time as to his conception of the universe. If Galilei's conclusions are right, he says, we shall have to philosophise in a new way. And since Galilei always relies on observations, he can only be refuted by other observations. It lay very near to the heart of Catholic Campanella that the Church should not expose herself to scorn by the condemnation of the new teaching. It was this which caused him to write from his prison his *Apologia pro Galileo*, which was published at Frankfurt in 1622 at the expense of a friend. The Church, however (as we shall explain further below), would not adopt the policy so urgently pressed upon her by Campanella, *i.e.* that she should declare that the book of Nature and the book of Revelation are each to be explained according to their own laws, in the conviction that they will ultimately be found to harmonise, especially if it is never forgotten that the Bible, as is only natural, is content to adopt the popular conception of the world, based on the senses. But when sentence was passed on Galilei, Campanella was sufficiently zealous a Catholic and Telesianite as to agree to the verdict.[84]   But he rejected, appealing to the investigations of Tycho Brahe and Galilei, the fixed spheres.   Like Telesio, he believed that there are two mutually opposing powers in the world, the expansive (warmth) and the contractive (cold), of which the former has its seat in the sun (as the *centrum amoris*) and the latter in the earth (as *centrum odii*).   The sun, together with its companions, the other stars, moves round the earth.

Campanella's natural philosophy, like that of Telesio, is animistic in character, for he thinks that the reciprocal action of things, and especially the mutual attraction of opposing forces, would be inconceivable unless they were animated.   In order to be able to work on one another they must feel one another.   He repeats Telesio's argument in more detail.   Of chief interest is his observation that sensation could not arise through the reciprocal action of the elements, since the arising of such an entirely new faculty or quality would be a creation out of nothing.   In old times it had been asserted (by Lucretius) against this, that nevertheless Nature offers many examples in which that which is produced has other qualities than those possessed by the producing elements.   Campanella answers, however, that all such cases are for us a production out of nothing, since we do not understand which among the elements contains the possibility of the new quality.   That sensation arises out of the material elements, then, is just as much a production out of nothing as that the corporeal arises out of the incorporeal.   That in the elements, which contains the possibility of the new quality must, in its essence, be akin to the latter (*ejusdem rationis*), although it need not necessarily have pre-existed in the form in which it appears in the result (*eodem modo quo nunc*).   So conceived, the notion that all things have souls has a significance altogether independent of animism, and the importance of which was first recognised just as it was yielding to the mechanical explanation of Nature.   It is the sensuous or corporeal soul only which Campanella thus means to unite with the rest of Nature.   Like Telesio, he believes the higher spiritual part of the soul to be created out of nothing.

Campanella's natural philosophy developed, like Bruno's, into a complete metaphysic, which, again, was united with religious ideas. Everything which is exists either as force (*potestas*), knowledge (*sapientia*), or impulse (*amor*). To be is, before all things, to be able, to have the power of making oneself felt. Force finds its highest infinite degree and form in the Deity ; in every finite creature is it limited, in a greater or less degree, by the *non-ens :* there is nothing which is not God ; in His essence—not in any external influence (*essentiando, non exterius agendo*)—He moves in all things ; but there is much that a finite being is not. The manifoldness of finite creatures exhibits this relative *non-ens ;* they limit and, in so far, negate one another. What is true of force is also true of knowledge and of instinct. Without knowledge, force cannot work. But this knowledge is immanent in force, is one with force. The capacity of perceiving that which is to be worked against cannot be separated from the capacity to work. The brute's instinct of self-preservation shows us this plainly ; but it is especially true of Nature. Hence knowledge must be original, and cannot first arise as an effect of outer influences. The presupposition of all other knowledge is the knowledge of oneself. Such an original self-knowledge is to be found in everything ; "hidden" (as *intellectio abdita*), however, since no opposition and no change make themselves felt. Campanella tries to show how self-knowledge is possible in opposition to Telesio's dictum that all knowledge presupposes change. This is true, Campanella thinks, only of the knowledge gained through external experience. In order to recognise other things we must be influenced and hence changed by them. But in order to know oneself it is not necessary to be influenced and changed, for what we here have to recognise, that we *are* and have not *to become*. Every individual being has an "original hidden thought" (*notio abdita innata*) of itself, which is one with its nature. That we do not at once possess clear knowledge of ourselves, but have to learn to know our nature from our acts, has its ground in this : that the self-knowledge immanent in our nature is continually hindered or checked by external influences. It is necessary for self-preservation to learn to know other things, and hence to be continually undergoing modification. In this way the original knowledge is darkened; the soul falls into self-forgetfulness or ignorance of itself. The lower animals, especially, are strangers to themselves and hence live, on account of the constant stream of external influences, in a continual delusion.   But that "hidden" knowledge of oneself is, nevertheless, the necessary presupposition to knowledge of any other things.   That I perceive warmth means that I perceive myself to be warmed.   Every recognition of other things is a special determination or modification of my consciousness and presupposes it.   Only in the infinite being can the original knowledge unfold itself clearly and freely, because here there are no external influences.   For finite beings the doctrine of self-knowledge has, however, the significance that all knowledge rests on our immediate feeling.   The sceptics may be right with regard to derived knowledge, but this always presupposes a consciousness of our immediate states and their modifications, and this consciousness is a reality which is not open to doubt.   As with our knowledge so with what we can do : that I am able to lift a weight presupposes that I can lift my arm, and hence I can only know anything of other things because I can know my own condition as it is determined through these other things.   I may be mistaken in my explanation of these states, but not that I conceive them in a particular way.   Campanella refers to Augustine who had already shown that immediate consciousness cannot deceive us.   "As for me," says Augustine, "the most certain of all things is that I exist.   Even if thou deniest that I am, and sayest that I deceive myself in this, thou confessest that I am ; for if I do not exist, I cannot deceive myself."   By this doctrine Campanella arrives at the point which, in Descartes, became the starting-point of all modern philosophy.   It is true that Campanella's "Metaphysic," in which this doctrine was expounded, did not appear until the year after Descartes' *Discours sur la méthode*, but there is no doubt that it was written for the most part while he was in prison.   Moreover the notion of immediate consciousness as the foundation of all knowledge is to be found in several of the thinkers of the Renaissance, *e.g.* Cusanus, Montaigne, Charron, and Sanchez (the latter of whom we have hitherto had no opportunity of mentioning).   Campanella, however, goes still further back.   His "hidden" knowledge is what might now be called "potential" knowledge; it is rather possibility of consciousness than actual consciousness, for Campanella teaches that it is always hindered by outer

experience. For real self-consciousness is won not by withdrawing the self from all changes (for we could not conceive an
unchanging existence to be conscious), but rather in perceiving
how our own nature is unfolded by means of changes and of our
own actions. And Campanella confesses this when he says,
" The manifold changes veil our original nature and continually
transform us into new natures, by which the comparison with
the past and the unity of our essence, as also the knowledge
of ourselves, is hindered." He here indicates a kind of self-
consciousness other than that half-mystical self-consciousness,
independent of all change.

As force and knowledge stir in all things, so, too, impulse
stirs. This is shown by the fact that everything seeks to
preserve itself. The stone seeks to remain a stone, and if it is
thrown up into the air it seeks the earth again, where it is at
home. Plants and animals seek, by means of propagation, for a
self-preservation which shall even extend beyond the life of the
particular individual. For in the need of light and warmth,
and of extending over all and in all, Campanella sees the
same eternal impulse or eternal " love " (*amor*) in operation.
And just as the power to move the self presupposes the
power to move all else, and the knowledge of the self is
the presupposition of the knowledge of all else, so love to
oneself is the presupposition to the love of all else. The
special forms which love assumes with regard to different
objects presuppose the " hidden " love (*amor abditus*), with
which every being maintains and asserts its own being. The
happiness of Man, as of every other creature, consists in such
self-preservation ; did it consist in anything else the consequence
would be self-destruction. Virtue is the rule which must be
followed in order that the highest goal may be reached ; that
which is law for society is virtue for men as individuals. Three
ways lead to the goal in this present world : preservation of
one's own personality, continuation of life in children, and
renunciation of honour and renown. A fourth way leads to
eternal life in God when Man participates in the infinite Being
(*Sein*) from which his own existence is sundered by intermixture
with the *non-ens*. Thus Campanella places all morality and
religion in close connection with self - preservation. The
relationship is closest with regard to religion ; for the unconscious or " hidden " love to self which lies at the basis of all

love to others is again, in its innermost nature, the love to the infinite Being which stirs in the limited being of all things, and only when we participate in this can we attain to eternal blessedness. There is therefore an original "hidden" religion (*religio abdita*) in all men, just as there is a "hidden" knowledge and a "hidden" impulse, and they are really all one and the same. Individual positive religions may err, but not that inner, original, religion which they share as a common presupposition. A revelation, therefore, is only necessary because positive religions (*religiones superadditae*) exhibit differences and errors.

All through his individualistic ethic, Campanella reminds us of Telesio. Like him, he makes magnanimity (*sublimitas*) the summit of virtue, since it expresses the true nobility, the inner self-preservation, looks down on external honours, and, in its endeavour to win freedom both for the self and others, never forswears itself either in the most cruel martyrdom or in the weariest imprisonment. In his socialistic ethic he reviews the different social groups, starting from the smallest, *i.e.* the family and household, and passing through the community and State up to a general society of men whose highest ruler is the Pope and whose senate is composed of the princes of the world. Campanella took part eagerly in politics. It may be that in his youth he cherished bold plans for the future of his fatherland, and believed himself called to be a religio-political reformer. We are still quite in the dark as to the conspiracy in which he is said to have taken part. Expressions which occur in his description of the magnanimous man may indicate that he had entertained great plans which he would not confess. However that may be, he afterwards planned a theocratic world-government extending throughout this earth, with the Pope at its head, in which to Spain (as is developed in detail in his work on the Spanish Monarchy) was to be assigned the task of bringing all nations of the earth within the Church, while to the "all-Christian" King of France (according to the preface in the *Universalis Philosophia*) was to fall the duty of coercing the heretics in Europe. Here Campanella's reactionary attitude comes out in politics, as we have already seen it appear in his conception of Nature. He stands in especially sharp contrast to Machiavelli, whom he regards (especially in the *Atheismus Triumphatus*, 1636) as the representative of the evil principle.

The strange thing is, however, that Campanella here,

as also in his conception of Nature, is himself most strongly influenced by precisely the thoughts which he wishes to, or ought to, dispute. His description of an ideal State, *Civitas solis* (The Republic of the Sun), was published as a companion to his ethics and politics. It was conceived in prison, with the weight of the present lying heavy upon him. Thomas More, the English Chancellor, in the preceding year, and, almost contemporaneously with Campanella, Bacon of Verulam, had sketched such ideal human societies ; all three had their common exemplar in Plato's "Republic." Campanella depicts an order of society in which science (which means natural science and philosophy) rules, and where physical labour comes by its rights. There is no priesthood and no nobility. The rulers are those who have received the best theoretical and practical education. To the inhabitants of the Republic of the Sun the idea that manual labourers belong to a less noble class than other members of the State seems laughable. No private property, no separate dwelling-houses, no private family life is allowed, for these foster egoism ; and the strong patriotism which animates the inhabitants of the Sun Republic is lessened. The magistrates regulate sexual unions according to physiological requirements, in order that the State may secure healthy and gifted citizens. For it is the State, think the citizens of the Sun, and not the individual, which is to be preserved by means of propagation. Pride is regarded as the greatest of vices. Each one is appointed to the work best suited to his capabilities, and from the produce of the labour every one gets what he requires and deserves. Accident must not decide that which concerns either procreation, vocation, or distribution. This would only lead to injustice and to many men being in need. " There dwell now seventy thousand men in the town of Naples ; of these scarcely ten to fifteen thousand labour, and they are worn out and destroyed by excessive, continuous, and daily work ; while the rest take their ease, or fall into a state of apathy, envy, weakness, sensuality, and pleasure-seeking. But in the Republic of the Sun. where menial services, arts, tasks, and occupations are shared among all men, no one need work more than a short four hours ; the rest of the time can be used in the acquirement of knowledge in pleasant ways, in discussions, reading, narrating, writing, walking, or in joyous exercise of the mind and body."

This vision of the future which swam before Campanella while he sat in prison,—"chained, yet free; solitary, but not alone; silent, and yet uttering his cry," as he says in one of his sonnets,—stands in a certain opposition alike to the philosophical and to the politico-religious conceptions which he developed in his other works. It is not in harmony with his strong emphasis of self-assertion that, as in the Sun Republic, the individual should so entirely renounce finding his own way to the goal. Among other things Campanella forgets that he had expressly declared propagation to be a form of conservation of the *individual;* but here it is *only* considered as the conservation of the race. Still more curious is the contrast between the " Republic of the Sun" and the Theocracy which Campanella regarded as the goal in his philosophical and political writings. All hierarchy and all absolute monarchy disappear here. Indeed there is no room left for positive religion. The " hidden" religion seems to suffice, and it is even expressly said that Christianity only really sanctions that which natural thought would lead us to believe; a sanction which, in such a perfect social order as that of the Sun Republic, seems no longer necessary. We can at any rate, as Sigwart remarks in his excellent treatise on Campanella and his political ideas, find no sure agreement between the scheme of a Theocracy and the scheme of a future State governed according to scientific principles; but it is characteristic of Campanella to have worked out his ideas in this double form, and in such wise, moreover, that not in the Theocracy but in the socialistic State, in which the rights of labour and of science stand in the first rank, his ultimate ideal is to be found. He regarded the powers of his age, even the representatives of the reaction in Church and State, as means and as educating forces leading up to the ideal goal, which was diametrically opposed to the existing order of things. Although Campanella is in so many ways a reactionary, yet the blood of the Renaissance runs in his veins, and his gaze ranges beyond the limits of the social world before him with no less enthusiasm than Giordano Bruno's pierced beyond the limits of the external heavens presented by the senses.

BOOK II

THE NEW SCIENCE

CHAPTER I

THE PROBLEM

PRACTICE precedes theory and art science——although subsequently a new practice may grow out of theory, as a new art
may grow out of science. Humanism, as we have seen, developed
out of the political and social relations of the Italian states, and
out of Humanism, as a tendency making itself felt in practical
life, there grew in turn a new doctrine of Man. Similarly, the
mechanical science of Nature developed out of the prosperous
industry of the Italian towns. In order to procure the means
for power and magnificence, the rulers had to support trade
and hand-industries, and the personal force and self-assertion
of the burgesses of the towns found vent in a wise and zealous
activity within the sphere of manufactures and industrial inventions. With regard to these, a rivalry sprang up between the
towns. Each sought to surpass the other in technical skill,
and jealously guarded new inventions and machines. This
practical turning to account of the forces of Nature increased
the knowledge of their mode of working and could not fail to
arouse interest in the discovery of their laws. The appearance
of a Leonardo or a Galilei is only comprehensible when taken
in connection with Italian industry, just as Pomponazzi and
Machiavelli are only comprehensible in connection with the
intellectual development and the politics of Italy.

To take a single example : Galilei begins his famous
" Inquiry into Two New Sciences " by making Salviati, the chief
speaker in the dialogue, exclaim : " The frequent resort, gentle-
men, to your most famous arsenal of Venice presenteth to my
thinking to your speculative wits a large field to philosophise
in, and more particularly to that part which is called the
Mechanicks : in regard that there are all kinds of engines and
machines continually put in use by a huge number of artificers

of all sorts." To which Sagredo answers: "You are not therein mistaken, sir, and I myself out of a natural curiosity do frequently visit that place, and the experience at the disposal of those whom, for a certain pre-eminence they have above the rest, we call 'overseers,' has often discovered to me the causal connection of wonderful phenomena, formerly considered to be inexplicable or incredible."

The development of the new world-scheme was also preparing the way in this direction. It led men to seek for an interconnection of Nature other than that immediately presented in sensuous perception, and the question could not fail to suggest itself: by what forces and laws is the world-system, which thought constructs on the basis of perception, held together and maintained in activity? The new conception of the world did not answer this question itself, or, where it attempted it, did so only in a fanciful, poetical, or animistic fashion. It was certainly an important advance when Telesio replaced the Aristotelian "form" by the concept of force. For it thus became an established principle that explanation must not be sought in quality, in the complete form of the phenomenon, as is the case with the work of an artist, which we understand as soon as we discover the ideal he has sought to realise. The concept of force, however, is still too vague to be profitable so long as it is not based on an insight into the regular interconnection of phenomena. If we know according to what laws the phenomenon B follows on the phenomenon A, we know also what force and how much force must be ascribed to A; for force in that case only means the conditions contained in A for the appearance of B. But perception and description do not suffice to discover this. We must go back to the simplest relations and examine, by way of experiment, the conditions upon which the occurrence of phenomena depends. It is no longer a question of a mere picture. The individual features of the picture must be analysed, and the connection between them investigated. Only thus can we arrive at full certainty that the picture possesses validity. Thus it came to pass that several of the investigators who are to be regarded as the founders of the new mechanical science of Nature, assisted in the construction of the new world-scheme, while they, in turn, derived some of the problems of their mechanical investigations from relations contained within the latter.

Here, too, it was a thought of antiquity which was taken up again. Archimedes, the founder of statics and hydrostatics, had as long ago as the third century B.C. uttered thoughts which contained the germ of a mechanical conception of Nature. On account of the unpropitious conditions of the times this germ was not developed till after the lapse of two thousand years. Now that his turn of mind had found more favourable conditions of life, Archimedes became, in the sixteenth century, one of the authors who were eagerly studied, published, and translated. In fact, however, a new science had yet to be founded. The philosophical interest of this event rests on its significance for intellectual life, and this significance is many-sided. In the first place, a new method was now developed and, with this, a new use for the human faculty of knowledge, which had far-reaching effects on the character and direction of intellectual development. New intellectual wants and habits arose. Experiment and analysis thrust themselves ✓ before contemplation and construction, where they did not entirely supplant them. Secondly, it was the material side of existence to which the new method was principally applicable. It was inevitable that the question should arise as to the range of the results arrived at: did they contain a knowledge of the whole of existence or, if not, in what relation did they stand to the spiritual side of existence? The revolution effected by the new conception of the world had already shown profound thinkers that the riddle of the world lies not only, or essentially—as appeared to a naïve conception—without and above us, in the great cosmical relations, but is also concealed in our own breasts, and in the most insignificant and familiar phenomena of Nature. The new method and its results brought this out still more clearly. Finally, it was inevitable that a more exact knowledge of Nature and the capacity bestowed by an insight into natural laws of foreseeing and partially controlling the course of phenomena, should strengthen men's self-reliance and further develop that which Humanism had initiated in a more æsthetic and theoretical form.

CHAPTER II

THIS great artist takes us back again to the Renaissance. His name occurs in the history of philosophy because the aphorisms selected from the manuscripts he left behind him contain the first clear utterances on the principle and method of exact science. Not only in the plastic art, but also in anatomy, in the science of engineering and in mechanics, was this many-sided child of the Renaissance at home ; and he felt called upon to give an account, in philosophical terms, of the road he had taken in his investigations, as also of the impressions which he had received from the activities of the men by whom he was surrounded. He was born in 1452, in the neighbourhood of Florence, and was instructed in the art of painting by Verrocchio, who was not only a painter, but also a weaver, a caster of metals, and a goldsmith. He was summoned by Ludovico Sforza (called il Moro) to Milan, where he founded an Academy of Sciences. It has been thought that a portion of his notes were intended for lectures to be delivered there. While in Milan, LEONARDO was active not only as a painter and sculptor, but also as an engineer, a musician, and a master of court ceremonies. After the fall of Sforza, Leonardo did splendid work in Rome and Florence. He spent his last years in France, where he died in 1519. Owing to his unsettled life and his many-sided activity he never executed the works on scientific and philosophical subjects which he had planned. They would have modified and accelerated the development of scientific thought in no small degree. Thoughts which are generally ascribed to Galilei or to Bacon had already found utterance in Leonardo, but they lay buried in his manu-scripts, which have only been studied quite recently. The thoughts which are chiefly interesting to us in this connection are those in which he lays stress on the significance of experience, and emphasises the fact that the results of our knowledge can only acquire perfect certainty by means of the employment of mathematics. Wisdom is the daughter of experience, and is therefore also a product of time. He rejects all speculations which find no confirmation in experience, the common mother of all sciences. But he is not content with mere perception. He is convinced that, with every active element (*potentia*) of Nature, effects of a definite kind, and which unfold themselves in a definite order, are connected. Necessity is the eternal bond, the eternal rule of Nature (*freno et regola eterna*). It is to this necessity we must penetrate, and— this is how Leonardo's meaning must be read—it is in virtue of this that mathematical knowledge can be applied to experience. It is necessity which makes it possible to reason from the given phenomena to those which stand to the former in a conditional relation. This can be most clearly and simply seen in mechanics, which is the " Paradise of the mathematical sciences." In the thoughts which a comparison of Leonardo's aphorisms reveal to us, the fundamental problems of the modern theory of knowledge are already contained. By his practical application of them he became one of the founders of modern mechanics and engineering science.

For the rest, Leonardo's ideas bear the stamp of a rude naturalism. He regards the soul partly as the principle of perception, memory, and thought, partly also as the formative principle of the organism. If we would know more concerning the nature of the soul, he refers us to the monks, " these fathers of the people, to whom, through inspiration, all secrets are revealed." He (like Montaigne and Bruno after him) brings forward the idea of the circulation of matter in the organic and inorganic world, and draws from this a singular conclusion, which, after the lapse of many years, appeared again in Diderot: " Life is contained in dead matter although we perceive no sign of it ; when taken up again into the nutritive organs of living creatures, it awakes anew to sensuous and mental life." In harmony with this he finds, in the continual striving and expectations of man, a witness to that which stirs in Nature herself, and of which man is a type.

Interesting though these suggestions are, yet Leonardo

owes his prominent place in the history of thought not to them, but to the idea of the combination of experience with exact thought.   After the lapse of a century this idea was destined to be still further carried out by great investigators, who had, however, to discover it in their own way.

CHAPTER III

JOHANNES KEPLER

WE have already shown how, under the form of mystical speculation, the new conception of the world was at work at the beginning of the seventeenth century, even in Boehme's quiet workshop. His contemporary and, in certain respects, kindred spirit, JOHANNES KEPLER, succeeded in finding a more exact foundation for the new conception than any on which it had hitherto rested. Through a rare combination of apparently contradictory qualities and interests he was led, by means of enthusiastic and persevering labour, from high-flying speculations to the foundation of an exact science of experience. Common to Bruno and Kepler was the need of a wider horizon and the impulse to express the thoughts stirring in their hearts. " I know," he says, " no greater torment than not to be able to express what I feel within me, let alone to have to say the opposite to what I think." The opposition of the orthodox camp made itself felt soon enough ; this, in conjunction with the low intellectual level and the great superstition of the age, threw a dark shadow on his career. His love of truth and his inexhaustible industry, however, supported him in spite of all trials.

Kepler was born in 1571, at Weil, in Würtemberg. Like so many of the most profound German thinkers, he was a Swabian. He was educated at the theological seminary at Tübingen, where he carried on extensive studies in the humanities, philosophy, mathematics, and astronomy. He was here initiated into the Aristotelian philosophy of Nature, of which he was for a long time an adherent. His teacher in astronomy was Möstlin, who, while he privately doubted the correctness of the Ptolemaic system, continued to expound it in public.

Theology was laid aside when Kepler unwillingly undertook a post as teacher of mathematics in the Gymnasium at Gratz. This appointment was decisive for his future and for that of science.   He now conceived a plan of developing a new natural philosophy, which should combine the system of Copernicus with the old doctrine of spiritual beings who moved the heavenly bodies.   He here (*Epitome Astronomiae Copernicanae*, Op. ed. Frisch. vi. p. 136 ff.) expresses his dissent from Bruno, and takes the sphere of the fixed stars to be the limit of the universe, because he thinks that, according to Bruno's theory, the fixed stars would have to lie so far apart from one another that we should never be able to see as many as we actually do.   The sphere of the fixed stars encloses a hollow space.   In the centre of this is the sun, surrounded by planets, amongst which is our earth.   Bruno here saw more truly than Kepler.   On the other hand, the latter was able to subject his ideas—in spite of their originally mystical form—to a more exact verification than Bruno.   Kepler's first work (*Mysterium cosmographicum*, 1597) proceeds from theological and Pythagorean presuppositions.   He conceives the universe as an image of the Trinity : the centre corresponds to the Father, the surrounding sphere to the Son, and the relation of the two to one another, expressed by the geometrical relations between the different spheres in which the planets move, to the Spirit ; for the divine Spirit reveals Himself in the harmonious relation of magnitudes throughout the universe. Kepler attempted to show that the five regular bodies postulated by Pythagoras, *i.e.* bodies all of whose surfaces, sides, and angles are equal, may be situated in the different spheres in which the planets move.   Thus the fundamental forms of geometry and the distribution of the heavenly bodies in space exactly correspond with one another.   This is the cosmographical mystery over which Kepler waxed so enthusiastic, and which he retained as the leading idea which partly furthered, partly checked, his subsequent investigations.   This idea was an expression of the conviction which he never abandoned that it must be possible to point to definite mathematical relations in the universe, and which incited him to ever new inquiries.   It caused him endless trouble, however, on account of the presupposition accepted by him as well as the whole of antiquity and the Middle Ages, viz. that the heavenly bodies must move in circles because the circle is the most perfect figure.

Among the men to whom Kepler submitted his work was Tycho Brahe, whom he apostrophises as " Prince of the mathematicians of his century." Tycho answered in a friendly spirit, but said that the observations of thirty-five years did not lead him to concur in Kepler's speculations, in spite of their great ingenuity. He especially directed his objections against the Copernican theory. The result of the connection thus entered upon between the two was that when, shortly afterwards, . Tycho migrated to Prague, Kepler also took up his residence there, and later still, after Tycho's death, he was entrusted with the great mass of material the latter had left behind him. He writes of this to his teacher Möstlin : " In my opinion, Tycho possessed riches which he—like so many rich men—did not put to a right use." Now he himself had inherited these riches, and by their means had acquired the possibility of further developing and confirming his ideas. Working from Tycho's observations, Kepler discovered the laws which bear his name, and—what is of more interest to us in this connection—was induced to adopt the mechanical conception of Nature in place of the animistic conception which he had hitherto supported.

Kepler spent the later years of his life at Linz, in deadly struggle with Protestant and Catholic fanaticism, and under painful difficulties in procuring means for the publication of his work. He was obliged to return for a year to his home in Würtemberg, to save his mother, who had been accused of witchcraft, from the stake. He died in 1630 at Regensburg, whither he had travelled to lay his claims to certain moneys which were owing to him before the Reichstag.

Through his idea of the significance of quantitative relations in Nature, Kepler became one of the founders of exact physical science. He arrived at this idea by way partly of theology, partly of psychology, and partly of natural philosophy. With the theological way we are already acquainted. In order that the universe should be a beautiful picture of the nature of the Deity, it is ordered in definite quantitative relations. Kepler, like Copernicus, entertained the conviction that Nature works according to simple and clear rules. Simplicity and ordered regularity (*simplicitas atque ordinata regularitas*) in a conception of Nature are therefore claims in advance to his favour. We must reduce everything to the fewest and simplest principles possible. The psychological ground lies in the fact that the human mind grasps quantitative relations the most clearly ; it is indeed, properly speaking, framed to apprehend them. With regard to quality, the activities of Nature present themselves very differently to different subjects (*pro habitudine subjecti*) ; complete certainty can only be retained by restricting ourselves to the quantitative side ; it is this therefore which shows us the real truth. Finally the naturo-philosophical foundation lies in matter itself, as we can know it from experience : " Where matter is, there is geometry also " (*ubi materia, ibi geometria*). It is shown by actual fact that the world participates in quantity (*mundus participat quantitate*).

The question as to *which* quantitative relations lie at the basis of the universe, Kepler originally (in the *Mysterium cosmographicum*) believed could be answered purely *a priori*. He abandoned this error, however, after his careful study of Tycho's materials drawn from experience and of his own observations. It is well known how indefatigably he laboured until he had found the relation which agreed with all observations, and that he was thereby induced to substitute the ellipse in place of the circle which had been deified from antiquity.

Kepler's doctrine of hypothesis clearly shows us what his conception of the nature of scientific investigations was. He was led to establish this doctrine in several ways. Tycho had abruptly dismissed the Copernican hypothesis as pure fancy (*imaginatio*), and had protested against every method which proceeded *a priori* (or, as it was then called, *ab anteriore*). Moreover, both theories—Tycho's as well as that of Copernicus —were regarded by opponents (*e.g.* Dithmarschen Ursus) as quite arbitrary opinions, the only object of which was to make fools of people, while Osiander, in his time, in order to avoid giving offence, had explained the Copernican conception to be an hypothesis which only aimed at exhibiting mathematical relations, and was not to be taken in earnest. In his un-completed *Apologia Tychonis contra Ursum* (cap. i.) Kepler discusses the whole question of the significance of hypotheses, and returns again to the subject many years later in his *Epitome astronomiae Copernicanae*. All science, he says, rests on certain presuppositions, and we do not wait to investigate until we have found the ultimate presuppositions, any more than a man waits to build his house until he has discovered whether the inside of the earth is solid. In the widest sense of the word, hypothesis means that which is taken as known in a demonstration. In this sense geometry also rests on hypothesis, and the observation on which we depend in natural science is also hypothesis. In the narrower sense of the word, an astronomical hypothesis is that assemblage of ideas by the help of which an investigator can trace the order of the motions of the heavenly bodies. Such ideas are by no means arbitrarily formed. They must be confirmed by showing that the consequences deduced from them agree with actual phenomena, and involve no physical absurdities. And they can no more be dispensed with than a doctor can dispense with the idea of an illness and consider only the separate symptoms. Science begins with observation, builds its hypotheses on these, and then seeks for the causes which effect the assumed connection. With Kepler, however, there is still some uncertainty as to the relation between the first and second members of this tripartite division. For if he means that Tycho contributed the observations on which astronomy rests, and that Copernicus supplied the best hypothesis, then the hypothesis preceded the observations._ This may very well be the case when it is an hypothesis based on a provisional investigation which leads to the comprehension of ascertained facts and to the search for fresh ones. Indeed this was the case with Kepler himself: it was his Copernican presuppositions and his ideas as to the significance of quantity in the world which showed him what lay concealed in the riches which Tycho himself did not know how to appreciate.

As regards the third member, the assignment of proofs, Kepler's demands become gradually stricter than those he had made in his first animistic period. He began (in the *Mysterium cosmographicum*) by supposing the planets were guided by souls, even, indeed, that the whole system was guided by the world-soul dwelling in the sun. Later, however, he broke with animism. In his epoch-making treatise on Mars (1609) he declares that the important point is the assignment of physical causes. He now frequently demands " true " or probable causes (*verae causae*). He is approaching the conviction that the causes assigned to natural phenomena must be such as can be shown to be active in Nature

In the second edition of this animistic work of his youth he adds, as a note to the expression " moving souls " (*animae motrices*), the following observation : " In my treatise on Mars I showed that there are no such things," and he thinks that the word " soul " should be replaced by "force." " Formerly," he continues, " I believed that the force which moves the planets was really a soul. But when I reflected that this moving force decreases at a greater distance, I concluded it must be corporeal " (*Opera*, i. p. 176). The *Mysterium cosmographicum* was now supplanted in Kepler by the idea of a *Physica coelestis*, for the execution of which, however, he had not the adequate means. It was carried an important step farther by Kepler's great contemporary GALILEO GALILEI.

CHAPTER IV

GALILEO GALILEI

WHEN, some years after Kepler's death, Galilei says in a letter that while he has always regarded Kepler's as a free (perhaps even too free) and penetrative mind, his own method of investigation differs from his,—he is, of course, in this characterisation, thinking chiefly of Kepler's earlier animistic theories. He can hardly have clearly realised the great turning-point Kepler's thought reached at the time when he instituted the investigations leading to the famous laws. As a matter of fact these two great inquirers laboured in the same spirit; they sought to unite deduction and induction, mathematics and experience, and, in virtue of this, must be regarded as the founders of exact empirical science. Only, while Kepler started rather from the *a priori* and deductive, Galilei started from the experimental and inductive side. Galilei took the really decisive step by which physical science was constituted an independent science, and a high ideal for all inquiry was set up.

Like Bruno, Galilei was a martyr in the cause of the new world-conception. It is interesting to observe the way in which his astronomical and physical investigations reacted upon each other. His experiments and his study of Archimedes showed him the difficulties of the Aristotelio-Ptolemaic system ; while, on the other hand, his eagerness for the establishment of the new world-scheme led him to discover new physical laws. It was only slowly and with hesitation that he finally decided for Copernicus. He was born at Pisa in 1564, where he studied philosophy, physics, and mathematics, and where also he cultivated poetical literature with enthusiasm. He preferred Plato and Archimedes to Aristotle ; and thus, during his student years, he laid the foundation of his later views. As professor, first at Pisa and afterwards at Padua, he expounded the old system, although, in his inmost heart, he had long been convinced of the truth of the new.   In a letter to Kepler (August 1597), he writes : " It is unfortunate that those who seek after truth and follow no false method are so rare.   Many years ago I embraced the opinion of Copernicus, and, from this standpoint, I have been able to find the causes of many natural phenomena which are certainly inexplicable on the ordinary hypothesis.   I have written down many principles and many refutations which, however, I have not dared to make known, as I have been deterred by the fate of our teacher Copernicus. He, it is true, won undying fame amongst some few, but amongst the multitude (there are so many fools in the world) he was only an object of scorn and laughter."   Not until after he had constructed a telescope and discovered the satellites of Jupiter, did he openly (1610) confess his adherence to the Copernican system.   This was the signal for persecution.   Although Galilei made discovery after discovery which confirmed his hypothesis— thus *e.g.* he discovered the sun-spots and the phases of Venus— yet monks and theologians expressed themselves against him with increasing violence.   Aristotelian philosophers would not even look through Galilei's telescope, lest they should see the vexatious spectacle of the changes in the heavens, and thus lose their faith in the old world-scheme.   Galilei was right in saying that were the stars themselves to descend from heaven to bear witness, his opponents would refuse to be convinced. In vain did he seek to show that his views were not in contradiction with the Bible.   Had he stayed in Padua, which was under the rule of Venice, his person would no doubt have remained in safety.   But in order to get more leisure and a better pecuniary position, he accepted the office of " Mathematician " to the Grand Duke of Florence, and here he came within easy reach of Rome.   The College of the Inquisition now (1616) took the significant step of entering the work of Copernicus on the list of forbidden books (" until it is amended ") and of declaring its teaching heretical.   Galilei was summoned before Cardinal Bellarmin, and, according to the Catholic version, received express orders not to defend or spread the heretical doctrine.   Proof that such a command was really given cannot, however, be produced.   Galilei did not abandon his inquiries on this account, however.   His investigations of comets involved him in a quarrel with the Jesuits, and this mighty Order rose against him as one man. In addition to this, he worked unceasingly at a complete exposition of the conflict between the two world-systems, which he had several times announced in his earlier works. As long as he expressed himself hypothetically there would be no danger, he thought. He employed the method adopted by Osiander when he published Copernicus' work. In the year 1632 appeared Galilei's famous work, described on the title-page as "A Dialogue on four successive days, in which are discussed the two most important world-systems—the Ptolemaic and the Copernican—while the philosophical and natural grounds, both of the one and the other, are brought forward, without any decision being arrived at between them (*indeterminatamente*)." The dramatis personæ of the dialogue are Salviati and Sagredo, two of Galilei's friends, and Simplicio, the representative of the Aristotelian philosophy. Salviati is the cautious critical inquirer ; he brings forward principles, but draws no definite conclusion at all, and seeks to restrain the fiery Sagredo, through whom Galilei airs his freest ideas, in order, when necessary, to revoke them through Salviati. But the side to which the author's sympathies lean is plain enough to every reader, and they were not to be deceived in Rome. The book was prohibited, and Galilei was summoned thither. He was probably not actually tortured, only threatened. On 22nd June 1633, however, he had to go down on his knees and abjure "the false doctrine that the sun is the central point of the universe and immovable, while the earth, on the contrary, is not the central point, and is in motion"; and to swear upon oath "that, in the future, he would neither by word of mouth nor in writing utter anything from which this doctrine might be inferred ; but, on the contrary, would notify to the Inquisition if he encountered a heretic, or any one suspected of heresy"! That he perjured himself is not open to doubt. He did not abandon his conviction. Instead of burning his body, they punished him with the burning pain which the forced concealment of his own conviction caused him. If Galilei's nature were not such as to make him feel this pain so keenly as would have been the case with a Kepler, yet it was keen enough to embitter his life. In addition to this came trouble and blindness. He lived, under constant surveillance, in the neighbourhood of Florence, unceas-

ingly occupied with scientific ideas.   The life which he saved
by his false oath acquired extraordinary value by the publication of his second great work, "Investigations (*Discorsi*) into Two
New Sciences," which, in order to escape the censor, was printed
in Holland (1638).   This work, which contains the foundation
of modern science, was obliged, as has been well remarked, to
steal its way into literature.   Galilei died in 1642 ; his mind was
active to the last moment.   We will now pass on to consider
the principal points of view which constitute Galilei's importance for the general history of thought.[35]

(a) *Method and Principles*

Galilei advances against formal logic the objection that,
though excellent for the purpose of regulating and correcting
the course of thought, it is not a means to the discovery of new
truths.   Such discovery, he says, takes place when, from certain
experiences, we deduce a postulate and then seek to show deductively that the said postulate agrees with other experiences.
Thus the analytic method (*metodo risolutivo*) and the synthetic
method (*metodo compositivo*) are mutually complementary.   If by
induction we are to understand an examination of all possible
cases, then inductive reasoning is either impossible or useless :
impossible when we cannot include all cases, useless if we could
summon all cases before us.   It is therefore only a question
of the investigation of the most characteristic cases ; from these
we infer to others.   But we must lay down the proposition as an
hypothesis before we can discover its real proof.   Confidence in
the correctness of the proposition contributes much to the discovery of its proof.   On the other hand, that which is inferred
from general principles must be confirmed by trial in particular
cases.   Thus Galilei proved by experiments on inclined planes
the postulate which he had assumed *a priori*, viz. that orbits
described with equally accelerating velocities must be as the
squares of the times.

But if deduction and induction are thus to co-operate, a
difficulty arises in the fact that, in our deductive reasonings we
assume the relations to be simpler than is really the case.
Mathematical axioms only hold good for ideal figures.   It is
no fault in real things that their configuration never exactly
coincides with any one of the figures constructed by geometry.

The irregular configuration of the stone is, in it, a perfection. In the application of abstract reasoning to concrete relations the manifold and complex conditions of the latter must also be taken into account. It is our arithmetic, not the configuration of things, which is imperfect. In empty space all bodies, so we assume, would fall to the ground with the same velocity. But since we are never able to produce absolutely empty space, we notice how the proportion varies in denser and rarer media, and since we see that the rarer the medium the more the velocities approximate to one another, we regard the proposition as proved. That a body thrown along a horizontal surface will continue its motion if all obstacles be removed is proved by the fact that the more we are able to exclude hindrances the longer the motion persists.

In order to find in experience links by which to connect deductions, and to be able to show to what extent experience approximates to the ideal presuppositions on which deduction rests, Galilei, like Kepler, lays great stress on quantitative relations. Only through measurement of phenomena is it possible to decide how far the claims of deduction are satisfied. Hence it was a principle with Galilei to measure everything measurable, and to bring within reach of measurement whatever is not susceptible of direct measurement.

Galilei's chief method is the one which long afterwards Stuart Mill called the method of concomitant variations, and which might also be called the method of limits. It enables us to combine abstract thought with concrete perception. By approximation, concrete cases participate in the ideality of abstract rules. As for Plato the "idea" was the archetype of the real thing, so for Galilei the law is the ideal expression of the connection of things.

If, then, the law is to be found by means of analysis of the data of experience, it is self-evident that those causes by which the phenomena are explained must be the very ones which are given in experience. Galilei acknowledges the same principle which Kepler expressed in his demand for *verae causae*. He shows very strikingly that the appeal to the divine will explains nothing, just because it explains everything equally easily. It is just as easy for God to make the universe move round the earth as to make the earth move round the sun. On such an assumption the former is as easy

N

as the latter. But if we restrict our consideration to that which is self-moving only, then the two views, in respect of simplicity, are obviously very different ; the one demands a much greater expenditure of force than the other. Before the infinite finite differences vanish, but they remain when we compare two finite beings with one another. Science has to deal with this latter sort of comparison only. If we appeal to miracle, then we can accept the one just as well as the other ; we are left with no criterion. Moreover, we forget that all the productions of Nature and God are miracles, even though they may admit of natural explanation.

Not only the theological but also the animistic explanation of Nature is excluded by the employment of this method. To explain the mutual influence of things upon one another—*e.g.* the attraction of the magnet—through " sympathy " is only to dismiss a host of questions with a comfortable word. So, too, gravity is only a name. We no more know what attracts the stone to the earth than we know what keeps the moon in its circular path round the earth, or carries on the movement of the stone after it has left the hand that projected it. Galilei therefore rejects the assumption that the moon influences the tides. Here his dread of " hidden qualities " leads him astray.

(b) The New World-System

In spite of Galilei's frequent assertions in his Dialogues that he wishes to decide in favour of neither view, yet his own standpoint is clear enough, even if we did not know it from his letters. He admires Copernicus because, in spite of the evidence of his senses, he was able to gain and to hold the conviction that the earth moves. And he himself, by means of his astronomical discoveries, adduced a series of proofs that the universe cannot, as Aristotle believed, be divided into two worlds, one unchangeable and heavenly, and the other changeable and terrestrial ; the spots on the sun and the new stars show that, even in the heavens, changes take place. And, remarks Galilei, with what right do we attribute to the unchangeable greater worth than to the changeable? " It is my opinion," he makes Sagredo say, "that the earth is very noble and admirable by reason of so many and so different alterations and generations which are incessantly made therein " ; to which Simplicio rejoins, that while changes on the earth may take place for the benefit of men, changes in the heavens would be quite aimless. He brings forward a similar argument against the enormous extension conferred (as Tycho Brahe had already remarked) upon the universe by the Copernican system; what use could the immeasurable space between the outermost planets and the sphere of the fixed stars be? In his answer, Salviati observes of final causes, as Simplicio elsewhere observes of natural causes, that we must not presume to know the ends of the Almighty! Is there not even in our own body so much of which we cannot know the significance? how then can we hope to know the significance of that which is more remote? And how are we to discover what power a thing exerts on its whole environment when there is no possibility of seeing what effects its elimination would bring about? We impose limits on the divine power when we believe that the enormous dimensions of the universe would render its· activity at all points impossible. The sun shines on the grapes and ripens them as if it had nothing else whatever to do; and, in the same way, God and Nature can care for every individual, even if the content of the universe be infinite. Galilei is almost inclined to assume (with Bruno) the infinity of space; he is doubtful as to the correctness of speaking of a central point of the world; if he does not express himself decidedly on this point it is probably because Bruno's fate made him cautious.

We may well be surprised that, in his discussion of Kepler's world-system, Galilei should have left unmentioned laws which, when deduced by Newton from the law of gravity, were of such cardinal importance in supporting the new system. It is probable that he assigned to them a purely mathematical interest, and that it had not occurred to him that they might witness to the physical interconnection of the universe.

(c) *First Principles of the Doctrine of Motion*

In support of the new world-scheme, Galilei, like Copernicus before him, appeals to the principle of simplicity. Nature does nothing in vain, hence she always takes the simplest way and seeks through few and simple causes to attain a manifold of effects. This principle of simplicity, which Galilei opposed to the complicated systems of Ptolemy and of Tycho, led him, within the sphere of physics, to the formulation of the first laws of the changes of material phenomena. It seemed to him the simplest that, when no change occurs, a thing should remain in the condition in which it already is. Kepler had already established the proposition that a body cannot of itself pass from rest to motion. Galilei now discovered further that a body can neither change its motion of itself, nor pass from motion to rest. This is the law which was afterwards (in accordance with an expression of Kepler's) called the law of inertia. Galilei, however, does not establish it as a general proposition. That both the direction as well as the velocity is preserved he has nowhere stated. In the Dialogues he dwells principally on the preservation of velocity ; he is here thinking especially of horizontal motion, and he assumes that circular as well as rectilinear motion persists. In the *Discorsi* the proposition is stated more clearly. A motion, he here says, can increase only when fresh force (*impeto, momento*) is introduced, and can decrease only when it meets with an obstruction (*impedimento*) ; in both cases, that is to say, under the influence of external causes. If external causes are excluded (*dum externae causae tollantur*), the motion will continue with the velocity which it has once acquired.[36] That this is an experiment of thought Galilei expressly admits ; but he proves the correctness of the proposition by trials which show that the more external causes are excluded, the longer the motion continues unchanged. Here we see the interplay between induction and deduction in the method of limits, and Galilei himself affords an illustration of his assertion that the way of demonstration is other than that of discovery. For to appeal to the simplicity of Nature is no proof, even though this thought may lead to important discoveries.

In his investigation of the movement of falling bodies too, Galilei starts from the principle of simplicity. " In the study of naturally accelerated motion we have been assisted, and, as it were, led by the hand by that observation of the usual method and common procedure of Nature herself in her other operations, wherein she constantly makes use of the first, simplest, and easiest means there are. . . . Why, therefore, shall I not be persuaded, when I see a stone to acquire continually new additions of velocity in its descending from its rest out of some high place, this increase is made in the simplest, easiest, and most obvious manner that we can imagine? And we shall find no increase more intelligible than that which ever increaseth after the same manner." Here too, however, the general principles are only used in discovery and assumption, not in demonstration proper.

Galilei opens his inquiry into motion with the words, "From a very old subject I produce an entirely new science." He especially points out that hitherto no one had investigated the quantitative variation of the motion of projectiles or of freely falling bodies. Galilei is conscious of having, through the discovery of the laws of these variations, founded a new science, "to penetrate into the deep secrets of which superior minds are required."

The founding of this science was a step of extraordinary significance. The later history of natural science has shown that the laws of motion contain the key to all scientific knowledge of material nature. Galilei himself had a premonition of this. He says in the Dialogues that he has never been able to understand how a transformation of one stuff into another could be possible. When a body exhibits qualities which it has never possessed before, he thinks it not impossible that this may be owing to a change in the disposition of the parts only, in which nothing perishes and nothing arises. He thus clearly asserts that it is only possible to understand the qualitative changes in Nature when these can be traced back to quantitative changes, which means here to motions in space. Modern philosophy had now to face the great question as to what attitude it should assume over against the great principle thus established, and which triumphantly proved its applicability to one sphere of Nature after the other.

(d) The Subjectivity of the Sense-Qualities

It was evident, even with Copernicus and Bruno, that the new conception of the world would lead to a new statement of the problem of knowledge, since the picture of the world given by immediate perception could not fail to be replaced by one very different, when thought proceeded to draw its conclusions. With Galilei this comes out even more strongly.

Though in so many important questions he regards the principle of simplicity as fundamental, yet he expressly distinguishes between the ease and simplicity with which Nature works, and the often involved and difficult procedure which we are forced to adopt in order to convince ourselves of her simplicity. What we find difficult to understand, Nature finds very easy to perform.   Thus there here emerges a decided opposition between existence and knowledge.   Galilei was of opinion that this opposition disappears to a certain degree in the clearest knowledge we possess, *i.e.* mathematical knowledge.   Here human knowledge participates in the necessity with which God thinks the truths which underlie the content of existence—but that which we think successively, advancing laboriously from conclusion to conclusion, God knows through simple intuition (*di un semplice intuito,* in opposition to *con discorsi*).   To this extent the opposition between simplicity and manifoldness remains, even at this point.   Further, it is only in intensity, strictness, and necessity, that human knowledge, even here at its zenith, touches the divine knowledge.   In range it stands infinitely far below, and it is beyond the possibility of the deepest inquiry to penetrate into even the most insignificant occurrence in Nature.   Socrates saw this imperfection of our knowledge clearly, and yet he is praised as the wisest of the wise.   Both on account of its simplicity, as well as of its infinity, existence forms a contrast to our knowledge.   Galilei, no less than Cusanus and Bruno, teaches the *docta ignorantia.*

The opposition between existence and knowledge comes out no less clearly in the sharp distinction which, like all Copernicans, Galilei makes between absolute and relative motion. We can only conceive motion in relation to something which is itself at rest.   The motion which is common to several things is—as regards their mutual relations—as though it did not exist.   While the antique conception of the world quietly took for granted that visible and absolute space are one and the same, thought had now to force a new path for itself and to realise that absolute space, as the immovable supporter of all material things, is not an object of sensuous perception at all, for this apparently unmoved frame may itself, in relation to some point lying beyond, be in motion, and so on.   Copernicanism in general, especially when treated with the acuteness of a Galilei, afforded opportunities for practice in the application of the epistemological law of relativity.   Though the Peripatetic philosophy would recognise no other change in the heavens, yet it admitted the rising, and setting of the sun and of the stars, the change between day and night, to be real changes.   Galilei's representative in the Dialogues remarks on this : " All these are only changes from the standpoint of the earth.   Think away the earth and there is neither sunrise nor sunset, no horizon, no meridian, no day, and no night ! "

Just as, in this way, a whole series of changes in the heavens lost their absolute character and were explained through the standpoint of the spectator only, so also Galilei found occasion, with regard to terrestrial phenomena, to effect a transference of differences from the objective to the subjective sphere.   We have already seen that he disputed the transformation of matter, and would only allow a fresh disposition of its particles ; in this the principle of the subjectivity of the sense-qualities was already contained.   But Galilei has expressed this principle in a still more definite form.   In a remarkable section of a polemical work on astronomy (*Il Saggiatore*, 1623) he declares that the only qualities which we are necessarily obliged to attribute to things are figure, magnitude, and motion or rest.   These qualities, which he accordingly called the first and real qualities (*primi e reali accidenti*), we cannot, by any exertion of our imagination, however great, separate from things.   On the other hand, it is only owing to a prejudice fostered by the senses that we regard taste, smell, colour, warmth, etc., as absolute qualities of things.   These are only names which we give to things because they excite certain sensations in us.   In fact, they have their seat, not in the things, but in the sensitive body (*nel corpo sensitivo*).   Take away the sensitive being and all these qualities would at once disappear.[37]   The parallelism of this view with the line of thought employed in defence of the new world-scheme is easy to see.   It became of great importance for the modern theory of knowledge, as soon as the latter was able to free itself entirely from the swathing-bands of dogmatism.

CHAPTER V

(a) Predecessors

THE new science, founded as it was under the influence of the experiences and inventions of practical life, could not but lead to an enlargement of the traditional logic. But even among those who had not especially come under the influences which had given birth to the new science, *i.e.* in Humanist circles, the need for a new logic had made itself felt with increasing strength throughout the fifteenth and sixteenth centuries. Out of this need sprang a whole series of attempts at reform,— programmes and promulgations were issued containing many different forecasts of what was to be put in the place of the scholastic logic, now that the latter was seen to be only fit to draw formal conclusions from premises previously established by authority. For, in the Middle Ages, logic was pressed into the service chiefly of theology and the doctrine of rights, and both these started from premises which were established by authority. The whole series of attempts at reform culminated in FRANCIS BACON OF VERULAM. This man, who has been so often described as the founder of empirical science, does not even merit the name of a Moses who has seen the promised land. He possessed, it is true, a certain prophetic insight, and he often gave inspired utterance to thoughts which illuminated the course and conditions of human inquiry. He was, moreover, perfectly conscious of his attitude of opposition towards scholasticism ; but the promised land had already been conquered, though he was not aware of it, by Vinci, Kepler, and Galilei. He modestly declares himself to be no warrior, but merely a herald inciting to the combat. The inquirers who founded modern empirical science, however, did not require the sound of his blast to inspire them for the struggle. Nevertheless, this does not deprive Bacon of his importance in the history of philosophy. He assimilated, in no common degree, the thoughts and hopes which were stirring in the age which saw the birth of modern science. If he did not contribute to its foundation, yet he dwelt in the medium in which it developed, and he prognosticated the profound effect on human life which such a science must necessarily exercise. He had a clearer consciousness of the fundamental re-shaping of the course of thought and of interests than any other thinker of the transition period. On this account he will always retain his great name, even though we must discount the adoration offered him by his countrymen, which neither his works nor his personality deserve. Before we proceed to consider this man and his works more closely we must spend a few moments with his predecessors in the sixteenth century.

PIERRE DE LA RAMÉE (Petrus Ramus) came from among the ranks of the Humanists. He engaged in a violent struggle with the Aristotelian logic in the middle of the sixteenth century. It is true that in so doing he was only continuing the efforts [38] of the preceding century to bring logic nearer to practical application, especially to rhetoric. And he himself confesses his indebtedness to Agricola and Sturm, the German Humanists and pedagogues. The whole tendency, however, found in him its most gifted and most eloquent representative, and he carried on the struggle with an energy which largely contributed to shake the sovereignty of Scholasticism in the universities of Western Europe.

Ramus, born in 1515, was the son of a charcoal-burner in the north-east of France. That he was the son of a charcoal-burner was often—after the polemical fashion of those days—cast in his teeth by his opponents. He was not ashamed of the fact, however. And this not because his family—although come down in the world—belonged to the nobility, but because, through his passionate love of learning he had raised himself to a high position in the world of learning. He began as servant to a rich student in Paris. After his day's work was accomplished he studied at night. At first he was attracted by the scholastic logic; but he did not find it satisfying, and great was his enthusiasm on meeting with Plato's Dialogues, which seemed to him to describe far more truly the real living activity of thought. In his disputation for the degree of Master of Arts in 1536, he defended the radical thesis that everything that Aristotle had said was false. The exasperation of the Aristotelians was great ; but it grew still greater after his detailed criticism of the ancient logic. The University demanded the suppression of Ramus' books on the plea that he was an enemy of religion and of the public peace, who inspired the young with a dangerous love of novelty. Francis I. accordingly issued an edict against the books of Ramus, and also forbade their author to attack Aristotle and other ancient authors ! Under Henry II. Ramus was once more allowed to teach, and he commenced his labours at the Collège de France, where his lectures drew an audience of 2000. This was a movement such as had not been known since the days of Abelard. In 1555 Ramus published his *Dialectic* in French. The fundamental thought of his doctrine is that we must first discover how Nature uses thought, before we can establish rules for the same. He goes back, therefore, to the earliest philosophers, who had no artificial logic. And not only these philosophers, but also great statesmen, orators, poets, and the mathematicians of antiquity display in their works the spontaneous use of the faculty of thought. Here we find rules unconsciously applied. The Humanistic interest of Ramus was satisfied, since the study of the ancient authors could thus be made of service to logic. Like his Humanistic predecessors, he, too, ascribes to logic two leading functions : the discovery (*inventio*) of arguments, and the application of these arguments made by the judgment (*judicium*) in establishing and deter-mining the thesis more nearly. The judgment is, therefore, in the language of the schools of the following age, frequently called *secunda pars Petri.* Ramus occupied himself chiefly with the latter function, and, more particularly, with the doctrine of syllogism ; and here we are astonished to find that he does not after all deviate much from the Aristotelian logic. The purely formal character of his reform is shown in the great stress which he lays upon dichotomy. Without regard to the nature of the subject-matter, the exposition is divided at every point into two members, since (according to the doctrine of the logic) a certain given predicate must be either valid or not valid. Thus it was really a new scholasticism which he introduced. There was stirring in Ramus, however, a strong desire to go back to Nature, and he did good service by simplifying exposition and by emphatically pointing out that art always rests on Nature. But he looked for Nature in the writings of antiquity instead of in ever-living thought. He was no deep student of the psychology of thought, and his description of the method of thought was not fit to serve as a model for the procedure of modern science.

Ramus, who had become a convert to Protestanism, was murdered in the massacre of St. Bartholomew in 1572. It is not impossible that the hatred of a fanatical scholastic showed his murderers the way. His corpse was mutilated by the Catholic students.

His reform of education in the liberal arts opened the way for him in foreign countries also. Ramism flourished in Germany, Scotland, and Switzerland. At the University of Cambridge, it was attacked by the zealous scholastic and mystic, EVERARD DIGBY, who was probably Bacon's tutor ; but it found in England a warm defender also in WILLIAM TEMPLE (the elder), who gained the victory for it, and who, by his polemic against Scholasticism, laid the foundation of that freer tendency in philosophy which, from that time on, has always been characteristic of Cambridge in contradistinction to conservative Oxford. Digby's and Temple's violent dispute as to method could not fail to excite great attention, and must have exercised considerable influence on the course of Bacon's development.[39]

While Ramism was running its victorious course in Northern and Western Europe there was stirring in the minds of many a deep need of exact knowledge, a thirst for a well-established science of actual Nature. This is evidenced by the writings of Telesio and Campanella, partly also by those of Bruno. A remarkable example of profound criticism of the traditional knowledge, of a clear notion of how much it means to know anything rightly, but, at the same time, of impotence to find a positive realisation of this ideal, is offered by FRANZ SANCHEZ, author of *Tractatus de multum nobili et prima universali scientia quod nihil scitur* (A Treatise on the Noble and High Science of Nescience), which appeared in 1581. Sanchez was the son of a Spanish doctor who had settled in Bordeaux, and was himself Professor of Medicine, first at Montpellier, afterwards at Toulouse. Although it might seem as if the title of his chief work stamped Sanchez as a sceptic, yet it would be a grave error to regard him from this point of view only. He entertained a lively feeling of the imperfection of human nature—especially of human knowledge. Doubt is for him not an end but a means. His sceptical work only forms the introduction to a series of empirical works on particular subjects. It was his intention also to write a special treatise on method. He commends observation and experiment, in conjunction with the exercise of the judgment, as the best way to knowledge. His motto is : Go to things themselves ! But he has not that great hope in further progress in this direction which inspires his contemporary Bacon. He sees how many riddles even the smallest thing contains, that all things in the world are intimately connected with one another, and that the world itself is infinitely extended ; on this account he regards a complete knowledge of things as an unattainable ideal. The attempts which he himself made in the direction of natural philosophy, and which remind us of those of Telesio and Bacon, brought him no such satisfaction as their own similar attempts afforded these two inquirers.

At one single point Sanchez goes deeper than Bacon and Ramus. He goes back, namely, to the source of all knowledge in the human mind. No external knowledge, he says, can be more certain than that which I possess of my own states and my own actions ; the latter is immediate as the former can never be. I have greater certainty that a thought, a desire, a will, stirs within me than I can have that I perceive a certain object or a certain person without me. On the other hand, inner experience is inferior to outer in clearness and exactitude. In virtue of this line of thought Sanchez ranks as a predecessor of Campanella and of Descartes. But he, no more than Campanella, was able to make it fruitful. This was reserved for Descartes.

Bacon not only pointed out the shortcomings of knowledge, but also showed the way to a right method, with far greater clearness than any of the humanists and empiricists before him who had attempted to effect a reform in logic ; and this has rightly been explained not only through Bacon's peculiar personality, but also through his position in the midst of the richly pulsating life of England. As has been truly said of him, he had, as his precursors, not only philosophers and men of science, but also practical investigators of nature, engineers, sailors, and adventurers.

(*b*) Bacon's Life and Personality

Bacon's character has long been a subject of dispute. His honour not only as a thinker, but also as a man, has been alternately impugned and defended. But the question is no longer an open one for the attentive reader of his *Essays*, and of the diaries which were published a few years ago. In these he has been so straightforward that we cannot misunderstand him, especially when we compare these direct or indirect self-confessions with the traits of character which are displayed in his philosophical works.

Francis Bacon was born in 1561. He was the son of Nicholas Bacon, keeper of the great seal under Queen Elizabeth, and nephew of the prime minister Burleigh. After he had studied at Cambridge, where Digby was probably his tutor in Scholasticism, he accompanied an embassy to Paris. The brilliant prospects open before him were closed by the early death of his father. As a younger son he had to make his own way in life ; his powerful uncle would do nothing for him. He was animated by a strong desire for power, riches, and honour, although this was not his only impelling motive. In one of his early treatises (*Conference of Pleasure*, 1592) he says : " Are not the pleasures of the affections greater than the pleasures of the senses, and are not the pleasures of the intellect greater than the pleasures of the affections ? Is that only a true and natural pleasure whereof there is no satiety, and is it not that knowledge alone that doth clear the mind of all perturbations ? " Not only were the longing for knowledge and the desire for power, riches, and honour united in Bacon, but he found a justification for the latter motive by subjecting it to the former ; he sought to gain power and riches only as a means to the execution of the great scientific schemes—consisting in nothing less than a complete renovation of the sciences (*instauratio magna*)—over which he brooded. And here we must notice a third factor in his character which comes out especially in his writings, namely his great sanguineness, and his not less great self-confidence. He saw before him a great work which needed great means. Hence he excused to himself the moral subterfuges to which he had recourse,—even baseness itself disappeared in the brilliant light in which he saw his endeavour. In order to carry out his plan, leisure, and means to collect observations, and make experiments, were necessary. He therefore threw himself into a political career. But with him, as with Machiavelli, the means gained the upper hand over the end which was to consecrate them. Had he, instead of planning his work in respect to ends as well as to means, on so ambitious a scale, attentively studied the works of his great contemporaries, Tycho Brahe, Gilbert, Kepler, and Galilei, he would have found matter enough for reflection, and a sufficient foundation for the working out of a programme for the future. His sense for the grandiose led him astray and, in conjunction with his love of power, involved him in circumstances which ruined his character, and plunged him into misfortune. He was lacking in the keen moral sense which might have served as a regulative counterpoise to other motives. In the *Essays* he says : " The best composition and temperature is to have openness in fame and opinion, secrecy in habit, dissimulation in reasonable use, and a power to feign if there is no remedy." And in another passage : " And certainly there be not two more fortunate properties than to have a little of the fool and not too much of the honest."

Bacon's ambition led him into political and worldly life, and here he found the materials for observation and for knowledge of men which are embodied in his works (especially in the *Essays* and in the 7th and 8th books of his work, *De dignitate et augmentis scientiarum*). He commends Machiavelli for having described so openly and honestly what men are *wont* to do rather than what they *ought* to do. This knowledge is necessary in order that to the harmlessness of the dove may be added the wisdom of the serpent. Here again his means have become his end. For, in order to rise in the world, a man must order his behaviour according to the actual behaviour of men ; hence Bacon enters a warning against remaining the same under changing circumstances ; we must accommodate our feelings to the occasion and the opportunity (*ut animus reddatur occasionibus et opportunitatibus obsequens, neque ullo modo erga res durus aut obnixus.*) Moreover, he recommends men to keep several ends in view, so that if they fail to secure their . chief end they may at any rate attain some subordinate one. A very dangerous piece of advice, especially for his own character !

Bacon first attempted to make a career for himself at the Bar. In this he was not successful. He opposed a project of the Government's in Parliament, and thus fell into disfavour with the Queen. His friendship (if it can be called friendship) with Essex helped him over serious pecuniary difficulties for some time. But when Essex was nearing his fall, Bacon withdrew himself from him. Indeed he went so far as to offer his services to the Queen (who accepted them) while the trial of his sometime friend was proceeding, and as Essex had made a desperate attempt at a rebellion, Bacon appeared as a witness against him, and after his execution wrote a treatise in justification of the line of action taken by the Government—a zeal which cannot be explained by anxiety to let justice take its course, but which becomes comprehensible when we read the following passage from an essay (*Of Followers and Friends*), which was published in 1597, *i.e.* a few years before the fall of Essex : " There is little friendship in the world, and least of all between equals, which was wont to be magnified. That that is, is between superior and inferior, whose fortunes may comprehend the one the other." Such was Bacon's " friendship " for Essex, and he took care betimes that the fate of his " friend " should not " comprehend " his own to any compromising degree. Whether men are really wont to act thus may be left an open question. William Temple, at any rate, whom we have already mentioned, and who had been Essex's secretary, did not see fit to adopt such a course, and met with exile as his reward.

In spite of all Bacon's attempts to sail with the wind, he had no success under Queen Elizabeth. His fortunes improved in James I.'s reign, especially as he was clever enough to insinuate himself into the good graces of the King's different favourites. But here the dark side of his character worked unhappy and far-reaching historical effects. He himself was convinced that the King ought not only to comply with the constitutional wishes of the Lower House, but also to employ his sovereign power to effect the codification of the laws, and the colonisation of Ireland, as well as to take up an energetic attitude with regard to foreign affairs, by making himself supreme head of a Protestant league. In this way the attention of the nation would be distracted from constitutional questions. It was impossible, however, to maintain such an attitude with a fickle and weak king, puffed up by the sense of his own power.   Herbert of Cherbury's similar views on foreign politics soon afterwards lost him his post as ambassador to France.   Bacon suited himself to the caprices of the King, whether quite unconsciously (as Edwin Abbott, his biographer, thinks) or not, is the great question.   There can be no doubt that an energetic protest on his part would have carried great weight.   His compliance met with its reward.   He ultimately became Lord Chancellor, Bacon of Verulam, and Viscount St. Albans.   In order to reach this high goal he had not only to change his political views, but also to advance the fortunes of the royal favourites.   This caused his precipitate fall (1621). Bacon had pronounced some monopolies granted to Bucking- ham's relations to be constitutional and profitable.   When Parliament rose in indignation against them, the King laid the blame on his counsellor.   The attack was now directed against Bacon, and he was accused of having taken bribes.   He pleaded guilty at once, was deprived of his dignities by the Upper House, sentenced to pay a large sum of money, and to be imprisoned during the King's pleasure.   Since—apart from his own guilt—he had fallen a victim to the practices of the King and his favourites, he was let off easily.   He was only imprisoned for a few days, and he never payed the fine. He spent his last years in seclusion, occupied with scientific pursuits.   This privacy he might have won earlier, and at a cheaper price.   He now attained what he had stated in his *Essays* to be most enviable, *i.e.* to die "in an earnest pursuit, which is like one that is wounded in hot blood, who, for the time, scarce feels the hurt."   He died in 1626.   His friends and servants loved and admired him.   Together with this, we may mention his great interest in study, and his firm belief that the future development of human culture would be rich and glorious beyond all expectation.   These traits throw a redeeming light upon his character in spite of all there is to be said in his disfavour.

In the midst of his active life as judge, statesman, and courtier, he had never forgotten his studies.   The outlines of his chief work took shape quite early in his life.   A work dated 1607 (*Cogitata et Visa*) is the first sketch of Bacon's most famous work, the *Novum Organum* (The New Logic), which appeared in 1620, after Bacon had revised it twelve times.   It investigates the reasons of the imperfection of the sciences, sets forth the hindrances to true knowledge which have their ground in the constitution of the human mind and the circumstances under which the latter develops, and then proceeds to describe the inductive method.   The work is un-finished, and planned on a scale for the execution of which Bacon's time did not afford the necessary means.   It was not till two centuries later that Stuart Mill completed in his Logic the work upon which Bacon had ventured with such imperfect material.   A work of the year 1605 (*Advancement of Learning*) is the first sketch of a larger work, *De dignitate et augmentis scientiarum* (On the Value and Progress of the Sciences), which appeared in 1623.   This is an encyclopædic review of the sciences, and contains many striking observations, especially on the lacunæ which had still to be filled up.   Bacon's other works are, for the most part, collections of material which are of hardly any interest now.

As a writer, Bacon's style is powerful and trenchant, and he is often extremely happy in his choice of metaphors.   But that he should ever have been compared to Shakespeare is quite incomprehensible.[40]   His imagination is abstract and symbolical, and he lacks Shakespeare's fiery energy, as well as his fineness of shading and his rich emotional inwardness.

(c) Hindrances, Conditions, and Method of Knowledge

Science, says Bacon, has only been pursued a very short time, and this is especially true of natural science, the mother of all the sciences.   The Greeks devoted themselves chiefly to moral philosophy, the Romans to the philosophy of law, and after the appearance of Christianity, the most highly-gifted minds threw themselves into theology.   Only their leisure hours did they devote to its handmaid (as it was regarded), natural science, and, even then, the main problem was neglected, and they did not set that aim before them by which alone it can be made really fruitful, *i.e.* the amelioration and enriching of human life.   Moreover their methods were erroneous.   The human mind was thought to be far too exalted to occupy itself with experiments, especially since to it was ascribed the faculty of being able to spin the truth out of itself.   Men were content with what had been handed down to them.   They entertained all too great a veneration for the past with its great thinkers, whom we call "old," although that term more properly applies to ourselves, since we can look back on a much longer experience than they could. Added to all this, came a mistaken religious zeal, which did not perceive that natural science teaches us to know God's power, as religion teaches us to know God's will. As faith gives us back the innocence lost at the fall, so science gives us back the power over Nature which we lost at the same time. Most injurious of all, however, have been men's pusillanimity and doubt in their own power. Hope, and courage to face great problems, have been wanting.

Now we are justified in being of good courage precisely *because* the imperfection under which we suffer is due to our own faults. The right method must be discoverable. This will not, like the spider, spin webs out of itself, nor, like the ant, collect material only, but, like the bee, it will assimilate and transform. If once material is collected, and we can exclude prejudices and preconceived opinions, the right explanation of Nature will soon be found. Accordingly, the most important step to be taken is to procure as rich and many-sided a collection of facts as possible. The human mind will then, by the spontaneous promptings of instinct, work up and explain them. In this assertion of the involuntary activity of mind which is to come into play directly the necessary material has been collected, Bacon was perhaps influenced by Ramus, whom he mentions with respect, although he reproaches him for his too simple method. The difference between them rests on this, that Bacon realised that if invention and judgment are to be able to work fruitfully they must have a great mass of empirical material at their disposal. The most dangerous fault which we can commit, according to Bacon, is to proceed too quickly — to leap to general propositions instead of ascending to them gradually through many middle terms. The human mind requires lead rather than wings. The goal is the enrichment of human life by means of the experiences afforded us by a knowledge of Nature. Knowledge is power ; for we are able to produce things when we know their causes. By the help of inventions and of mechanical skill men have gradually raised themselves out of barbarism, and have won for themselves a civilised life. Only so can the misery and unhappiness, under which men still suffer, be cured. We must aim at gaining greater power over Nature ; but if we are to do this we must obey her. We should be doing Bacon an injustice, however, if we attributed to him the opinion that science is only to be pursued for the sake of its practical advantages. Higher than any external booty which knowledge may procure for us, he places the contemplation of things (the *contemplatio rerum* higher than the *inventio fructus*). We rejoice in light because, by its help, we can work, read, and see one another ; yet the sight of light is still more glorious than any of its manifold uses.

But we can only hope to reach this great goal if we lay aside all prejudices. As into the kingdom of heaven, so also into the human kingdom founded on science, we can only be received if we become as little children. Prejudices and preconceived opinions must be laid aside. We must aim at *explaining* Nature, not at *anticipating* her ; at an " *interpretatio*," not an " *anticipatio*." Bacon accordingly attempts to give a complete doctrine of incorrect anticipations. This is his famous doctrine of illusions or " idols " of the mind (*idola mentis*), which must be rooted out in order that the mind may become a perfectly blank tablet (*tabula abrasa*), on which things may be able to write their real nature. Bacon distinguishes four classes of such " idols."

Some illusions (*idola tribus*) are grounded in human nature, and are therefore common to the whole race. Such idols include those which arise because we apprehend things in their relation to, and in analogy with, ourselves (*ex analogia hominis*), instead of in relation to, and in analogy with, the universe (*ex analogia universi*). But our mode of conception, our mode of perception and thought, cannot be the measure of things ! We are particularly inclined to presuppose greater order and regularity in things than is really to be found. We anticipate in things the uniformity (*aequalitas*) of our own minds. And we are inclined to overlook anything which runs counter to an opinion we have once formed. We are apt to pass over negative instances in arguing from experience. We attribute too great importance to that which affects us suddenly and immediately, since we are disposed to attribute the same nature to things farther away. On the other hand, we read into Nature the restlessness and constant striving of our minds, so that we will impose no limits to

its extension or to the causal series. Or else we content ourselves with finding the explanation in an end, and we postulate
final causes (*causae finales*)—an explanation which is evidently
taken from our own nature, not that of the universe. Finally,
our results are very apt to be determined by our feelings and
impulses, our hopes and fears ; and this influence of feeling
on knowledge often operates quite imperceptibly.

Another class of illusions arises from the particular nature
of individuals. Bacon calls these (referring to an image of
Plato's) " idols of the cave " (*idola specus*), since the individuality
of every particular man is like a cave from which he regards
the universe, and in which the light of Nature is refracted
in a peculiar manner. These illusions of individuality are
determined by original disposition, education, intercourse, and
reading. Some men are more disposed to dwell on the
differences of things, while others are more inclined to seek
out their resemblances, some love the old best, others turn, by
preference, to the new, some seek the elements of things,
others do not go beyond complex phenomena, as they are
immediately given.

But the worst illusions of all—Bacon thinks—are those
which are due to the influence of words on thought. He calls
them " idols of the market-place " (*idola fori*). Words are formed
according to the needs of practical life and popular understanding (*ex captu vulgi*), and the boundary lines between
things which they lay down must often be rejected by more
exact thinkers. There are words for non-existent entities,
while, on the other hand, words are lacking for real things
presented in experience. This gives rise to many verbal
disputes.

While the first three classes of "idols" are grounded in human
nature, the last class, " the idols of the theatre " (*idola theatri*)
arise through the influence of transmitted theories. These
theories may be very ingeniously and acutely thought out, and
yet they may miss the goal. He who takes the right road,
although less gifted, reaches the goal more quickly and surely
than the best runner who has once left the right path ; indeed
his very skill carries the good runner ever farther from the
goal. The empirical method which Bacon opposes to the
brilliant speculations of earlier times leaves, in his opinion,
very little room for the exercise of ingenuity and intellectual

power.   The right method equalises the difference between
minds.   If a circle is to be drawn by hand, difference of natural
endowment may be important, but with the use of a compass
such difference ceases to exist.   It is difficult to keep this
fourth class of idols distinct from the second, since Bacon
names reading, tradition, and authority, as factors in the
production of individual peculiarity.

Bacon's doctrine of "idols" is a piece of critical philosophy
—an attempt to distinguish between that which belongs to the
subjective nature of knowledge, and that which belongs to the
universe.   We meet with attempts in the same direction in
Montaigne, Cusanus, Bruno, and Galilei.   Unfortunately, Bacon
lacks that commanding point of view which is especially
remarkable in Galilei, owing to the Copernican theory with
its emphasis on the relativity of standpoint.   And Bacon
is inclined to regard the modes of conception which we involuntarily employ as altogether deceptive.   Thus he regarded
it as a deception of the senses (*fallacia sensuum*) that they
show us things otherwise than as science explains them.
Beyond this he has not entered into any closer inquiry as to
how it is possible to purify the mind, so that it should be like
an unwritten tablet.   Even if we could discover them, we
cannot do away with the conditions and forms lying in our
original individuality, and in our common human nature.   At
this point Bacon is self-contradictory.   For, as we saw, it is his
conviction, that when once the material has been arranged, it
will be elaborated by the mind involuntarily, and according to
its own inner capacity (*vi propria atque genuina*).   But is not
something added to the matter here? and with what right is
this added?   What guarantee do we possess that our mind's
own inner power can determine us to regard things no more
in their relation to ourselves, but in their relation to the
universe?   How shall we convince ourselves that we have
really attained to the *analogia universi?*   This was the question
attacked by subsequent theories of knowledge.   Bacon is their
predecessor in virtue of his doctrine of "idols."   Specially
interesting is the thought that the presupposition which
Copernicus, Bruno, and Galilei assumed as a matter of course,
viz. that Nature always takes the simplest way, is perhaps of
purely human and subjective origin, so that its authorisation
has yet to be investigated.

The method to be followed in elaborating material is that of induction.   This method had indeed long been in use, but Bacon found an essential fault in its ordinary employment, which he reckons among the illusions of the race (*idola tribus*), viz. that men had contented themselves with those instances in which a phenomenon occurred, and had considered such instances a sufficient basis for the understanding of the nature of phenomena.   Bacon calls this kind of induction "induction by means of simple enumeration" (*inductio per enumerationem simplicem*).   He demands that it should be supplemented by an examination of "negative instances," *i.e.* those cases in which the phenomenon does not occur, although the circumstances resemble those under which it occurs.   And, in addition to this, he demands a graduated scale showing under what circumstances the phenomenon increases or decreases. By this method of procedure we can arrive at a provisional conception of the nature or, as Bacon calls it, the "form" of the phenomenon.   By "form" Bacon understands the "nature" which is always present when the phenomenon is present, and always absent when it is absent, and which increases or decreases with it in the same degree.   After setting aside such conditions as do not satisfy these demands, we have the "form" left.   In the investigation of the nature of death, *e.g.* we must abstract from whether it is caused by drowning, burning, the sword, apoplexy, consumption, etc.   When we are examining heat we must abstract from the special mode of its production, from the composition of the warm substance, etc.

Bacon has often been accused of conceiving induction as a mere collating of material, but it must be noted that he lays great weight on the formation of provisional hypotheses as a means of survey and orientation.   The first explanation is only an attempt, it is the "first vintage," which serves merely as a trial (*Nov. Org.* ii. 20).   It is undertaken because truth is more easily reached through error, if only this is clearly thought out, than through a chaotic accumulation of material.   This is one of Bacon's most famous aphorisms: *citus emergit veritas ex errore quam ex confusione*.   As one of these provisional hypotheses, Bacon lays down the following proposition in regard to the "form" of heat; heat is motion.   His inductive method proceeds, after the establishment of these provisional hypotheses, using them as finger-posts.   We must next find or discover by means of experiment such cases as are particularly suited to throw light upon the view postulated, and to establish it more exactly. Of such "prerogative instances" Bacon cites a great number. Among others he quotes cases (as *instantiae solitariae*) in which the "nature" in question is exhibited under circumstances which have otherwise nothing in common with all the other cases in which it occurs, or which do not exhibit it although they possess all the other characteristics common to the cases in which it does occur. These are the methods which Stuart Mill afterwards called the methods of agreement and difference. As "*instantiae viae*" Bacon mentions cases and experiments which show us the phenomenon "on the way," as it is coming into being, when its nature ("form") is most easily discoverable. As "*instantiae irregulares et deviantes*" he mentions cases in which, conversely, the phenomenon is discovered "in by-paths," assuming varied or irregular forms. By such variations the thing discovers its real nature more easily. Akin to these are the transitional forms (*instantiae limitaneae*), which exhibit some qualities which are traceable to one "form" and others to another.

Bacon intimates that a whole series of more extensive operations are necessary for the complete carrying out of the inductive method. But the *Novum Organum* ends with the enumeration of the different kinds of prerogative instances.

The detailed description of the inductive method which Bacon gave was a real step forward for his time. It betrayed a clear understanding of essential points. The subordinate position which he assigns to quantitative determination, and to deduction, puts him in the shade in comparison with the founders of modern science. Exact empirical science was first made possible when, by means of the exact measurement of phenomena, a foundation of mathematical deduction could be laid. It is true he assigns a place to quantitative determination in the inductive process ; *instantiae quanti*, also called *doses naturae*, form an especial kind of prerogative instances. Nevertheless he did not perceive their pre-eminent importance. Hence, too, his depreciation of deduction. The most brilliant deductions are mathematical. Although Bacon does not, as he has often been accused of doing, altogether overlook the importance of deduction (" the first vintage " proves this), yet he gives it quite a subordinate place in his empirical method.

It had not dawned on him that it is a deduction which affords the real proof of the correctness of the inductive conclusion.

Bacon seeks by way of induction, to find a definition of the nature or " form " of things, to determine the essential nature of each one. Properly speaking, however, such a definition is no induction in the modern sense of the word. It does not give the dependence of one phenomenon on another ; it gives not a law but a concept. It ought rather (as FRIES in his History of Philosophy has already remarked) to be called abstraction than induction. And Bacon himself points to Plato as his model here. There is, he says, a difference between the " idols " of the human mind and the ideas of the divine mind. It is these latter that he seeks : they are the eternal " forms " of things. The " form " is the definition of the thing, is the thing itself (*ipsissima res*). He commends Plato because he perceived that the " form " is the real object of science. Plato committed the mistake partly of separating the "forms" or "ideas" from the things themselves,—whereas it is precisely in the particular phenomena that they are to be sought,—partly of not resolving complex " forms " or " natures " into their simplest elements. According to Bacon it is precisely the simplest irreducible qualities of things[41] (*naturae simplices*) which must be established. Such qualities are colour, weight, dissolubility, extension, etc.

Regarded from this side, Bacon's concept of " form " points backwards to ancient and scholastic philosophy. But his view of this concept varies considerably. In isolated passages the "form" does not mean a definition or determination of the nature of the thing, but the law according to which the activity, in which the phenomenon consists, proceeds. " The forms," he says somewhere, " are fictions (*commenta*) of the human mind, if we cannot call them the laws of activity or of motion of the forms." The form of heat therefore is the same as the law of the phenomena of heat. In this way he strives to distinguish his " forms " from those previously set up. We must know the law in order to be able to produce the phenomenon. Both in theory, then, as well as in practice, it is important to discover it. This practical side it is, of course, which makes itself felt when Bacon speaks of the " form " as the expression of the essence of things, calling it the active nature (*natura naturans*) of the thing, the source out of which spring its particular qualities (*fons emanationis*). Plato, too, regarded ideas as true causes. The different shades of meaning which—without Bacon himself being aware of it—are contained in the concept of "form," since it is sometimes regarded as the essence of the thing, sometimes as the law of its genesis, are, however, not without significance for the characterisation of his doctrine of method. It here becomes evident that he stood on the boundary line between the old and the new philosophy. He assumes with Plato and the Scholastics that there are a certain number of "simple natures" which, in combination, form the different phenomena. But that things are subject to definite laws is a premise which he neither establishes nor investigates.

Bacon unites the two significations of the concept of "form" by means of his emphatic assertion that we can only discover the essence of things by examining the process by which they are produced, as well as the inner connection of the facts of which they are made up. Both these, however, lead us beyond the senses. For the changes in Nature take place by degrees, by means of small transitions (*per minima*), so small that we can no more notice them than we can perceive the molecules out of which things are probably made up, and whose mode of combination (*schematismus*) produces the qualities (forms!) which they present to us. The task for investigation, therefore, is to find the hidden process (*latens processus*) which binds together continuously the different stages of development which our interrupted and periodic perception apprehends, and the hidden order (*latens schematismus*) which lies at the root of the sensuous qualities. Nature is too subtle for our senses. We are unable to perceive, in and for itself, the motion of which the essence of warmth consists. The hidden process here eludes us. The same thing happens with the development of the organism, with the process of nutrition (if we are to include all stages, "from the first reception of the food to its complete assimilation to the recipient"), and with voluntary movement (if we are to include all stages, "from the first impression of the imagination, and the continuous effects of the spirits, up to the bending motion of the joints"). And the solution of the problem becomes particularly difficult if, at every point, we are to find what has been lost, what remains, and what is added ; for Bacon regards it

as certain that the total sum of matter is neither increased nor
diminished.   This doctrine (*Nov. Org.* i. 10, 50; ii. 5-7;
40, 41) of the continuous process and of its individual members
as transformations into new forms of that which was given in
another form, without any loss of, or addition to, the quantity,
belongs to Bacon's most brilliant anticipations—although his
own method would exclude "anticipation" and replace it by
"interpretation."   He established the principle of continuity
which was afterwards to prove so productive.   Bacon here
makes the involuntary confession that every explanation must
proceed from certain principles.   He establishes the whole
doctrine of the hidden continuous process and of the hidden
order purely dogmatically, since he only illustrates it by
individual examples.

If we seek to draw logical conclusions from the doctrine of
the hidden process, we discover that Bacon's two meanings of
the concept of "form" contradict one another.   According to
the first meaning (form = simple nature = quality, which constitutes the essence of the thing) we start from the assumption
that the qualities presented through perception belong also to
the things themselves.   According to the second meaning
(form = law of the process by which things arise) it is
evident that things really consist of atoms and are produced
by minute changes which cannot, when taken separately, be
perceived.   The subjectivity of the sense-qualities agrees with
the latter meaning (since heat either in itself or *in ordine ad
universum* is motion), while it is in contradiction to the first
meaning (where heat, like colour, etc., is *natura simplex*).
As Bacon's first meaning reminds us of Plato and the
Scholastics, so his second reminds us of Democritus, without,
however, being exactly atomistic.   It is characteristic of him
that the passage quoted above to the effect that "forms" are
inventions and *idola tribus*, if by "form" we do not mean
law, occurs immediately after his commendation of Democritus
for his exhortation to dissolve Nature into its elements,
rather than to set about making abstractions.   Here again
it is the relation between quality and quantity at which Bacon
stops short.   Entangled in Platonic and scholastic presuppositions, he could not consistently carry out what was
contained in his notion of a continuous process, by which
qualitative differences are dissolved into quantitative ; on this

account, too, his recognition of the subjectivity of the sense-qualities is less distinct than Galilei's.

(d) "First Philosophy," Theology, and Ethics

The inductive method is valid for all sciences ; not only for the natural but also for the mental sciences (ethics, politics, logic). Bacon everywhere lays great stress on the unity of science, in spite of its division into separate branches. Complete isolation of the individual branches would condemn all to sterility. If we ask where the common foundation of the different sciences is to be found, we discover that the answer given in his two chief works is not identical. In the *Novum Organum* it is natural philosophy which is said to be the great mother of all the sciences. In his work on the Advancement of Learning (*De augmentis scientiarum*), however, that science which contains the principles common to all the different sciences is honoured with the title of "Mother of the Sciences." This science of common principles Bacon calls the *prima philosophia.* But no such science has as yet been developed, although it would be of first-class importance, since a system of such common principles would afford a witness to the unity of Nature. Bacon names as examples of these common principles (*Nov. Org.* i. 80, 127 ; *De aug.* iii. 1) : Equals added to unequals give unequals ; things which agree with one and the same third thing agree with each other ; Nature reveals herself especially in minima ; everything changes, but nothing passes away. Some of these are propositions with which Bacon operates as a matter of course in his doctrine of method. He does not discuss their origin and foundation more fully ; but in his opinion, of course, they are themselves the fruit of an induction. There can be no doubt that his thought runs in a circle here, for, while on the one hand he employs these principles as the presuppositions of the inductive method, on the other, he regards them as results of induction ; a circle which is unavoidable in all forms of pure empiricism. And as we saw, Bacon would make the mind like an unwritten tablet before the work of knowledge can begin.

He does not discuss the establishing of first principles by induction in his doctrine of the *prima philosophia*, but in quite another connection, viz. where he is drawing the

boundary line between philosophy and theology. Bacon
enters a special warning against confusing philosophy with
theology ; in this way we get a fantastical philosophy and an
heretical religion. Their sources are quite distinct. Philosophy
proceeds from sensuous perception, while theology rests upon
divine inspiration. In science, the human mind is under the
influence of the senses ; in faith, under the influence of another
mind ; faith, therefore, is nobler than science. And the more
improbable and incredible a divine mystery is, the greater
honour we show God in believing it, the more glorious is the
victory of faith. But when once we have accepted the principles of religion we can proceed to draw logical conclusions
from them, just as we do from first principles in philosophy.
The important difference between them is, that in philosophy
the principles themselves, like all other propositions, are subjected to a closer critical examination by means of induction ;
while in religion, in virtue of their divine authorisation, the
first principles stand firm and cannot be moved, just as the first
rules of the game of chess are not open to discussion. Bacon
thinks, however, that a closer examination into how far reason
is to be applied within the sphere of religion, and also a
discussion of the question to what extent unity in religious
opinions is necessary, are much to be desired.

Beside the positive theology of which Bacon was mainly
thinking in the above discussion, he held that a natural theology,
although limited in scope, was possible. It could only serve to
refute atheism and to show the necessity of assuming a first cause.
When we begin to discover natural causes (*causae secundae*) we
often feel so overpowered by them that we think a first cause is
not necessary. But afterwards we see that it is precisely this
firm interconnection of causes which witnesses to the existence
of a god. Akin to this is the further consideration that even if
natural philosophy needed no final causes—although, on the
contrary, the assignment of a purely human motive to Nature
is degrading to science—we should still be authorised in
assuming final causes, and they can very well be combined
with the continuous process, the discovery of which is the task
of natural philosophy. The final cause is like a nun,—sterile
in philosophy, but of religious significance.

In his *Essays* Bacon examines the relation between atheism
and superstition. Here, too, he says that though a little inquiry

leads to atheism, deeper inquiry leads to the acceptance of a god. "The chief causes of atheism," however, he says, "are divisions in religion, . . . scandal of priests . . . a custom of profane scoffing in holy matters, and learned times especially with peace and prosperity" (for unhappiness and misfortune make the mind receptive to religion). Atheism degrades man, whose spiritual nature requires re-inforcement in order that his corporeal nature should not drag him down too far towards the brute, and because man is ennobled by his connection with a higher nature, as the dog is by his connection with man. Superstition, however, is still worse than atheism. Rather no belief in God at all than a belief which is unworthy of Him; the former is only unbelief, the latter an insult. Superstition begets immoral qualities far sooner than unbelief The former is dangerous to the State, since it establishes a power in the nation which may exceed the power of the Government; in which case wise men are forced to follow fools. It is chiefly in barbarous times that superstition arises.

The doubleness which appears in Bacon's doctrine of faith and knowledge, and which bears upon it the very evident stamp of a compromise, is consistently reflected in his psychology and his ethics. The sensible soul of man is material, like that of the animals. It consists of a fine, fiery air (*aura ex natura flammae et aërea conflata*) which streams from the brain through the nerves and is nourished by the blood. Bacon is here in agreement with Telesio. He fails, however, to give any further proof of how this fine air is able to move the dense and hard body. He also agrees with Telesio in attributing to everything sensibility to impressions, which he prefers to call perception (*perceptio*), rather than sense (*sensus*). He desires that a closer investigation should be made as to how the former can pass over into the latter, as also how general susceptibility to impressions can pass over into sensation, and unconscious psychical life become conscious. Besides the sensible and material soul Bacon, like Telesio, admits a spiritual soul, implanted by God; but only religion—not philosophy—can instruct us about this. The special psychological observation of the phenomena of psychical life, which pursues its course independently of materialism and spiritualism alike, was unknown to Bacon. In this respect he is inferior to Sanchez and Campanella, not to speak of

Descartes.   He only mentions it incidentally in the statement that we learn to know Nature by means of direct light, God by means of a light refracted in the medium of the world, and Man, who is his own object, by means of reflected light (*radio reflexo*).

As regards ethics, Bacon distinguishes between the doctrine of "exemplars" and the doctrine of ways and means by which we may approach to these "exemplars." The latter doctrine (*de cultura animi*) has been to a great extent neglected from the same reasons which account for the imperfection of the sciences in general; men have preferred revelling in imaginings of the ideal to diligently studying how ideals may be realised. As regards the "exemplar";—in its highest form its home is religion, not philosophy, since it is revealed by divine inspiration.   The philosophic doctrine of the "exemplar" has already been well expounded by the ancient philosophers. Bacon looks in vain, however, for an inquiry into the original sources of ethics (*fontes ipsi rerum moralium*).   He demands, that is to say, a doctrine of the psychological development of ethics.   And he himself supplies the main outlines of such a theory.   In everything we may discover a double impulse : the one moves the thing to assert itself as a whole ; the other causes it to work as part of a larger whole.   The former has as its object the good of the individual, the latter the general good. The ancient philosophers were wrong in laying greater stress on the individual good and in setting up knowledge and contemplation as the highest life, for active life ought to be placed still higher.   It is not our duty in this life to play the part of onlookers only.   Bacon refuses to discuss politics.   For the work (*De augmentis scien.*) of which such a discussion would form a part, was dedicated to King James I.—and before such a master in statecraft, silence best becomes him !

Here at the end we meet Bacon as a courtier again.   His adoption of this career was the misfortune of his life, as his entrance into a monastery was the undoing of Bruno.   Nevertheless Bacon succeeded in unfolding thoughts which served to express the new way which inquiry was preparing to take, and which foreshadowed the philosophical inquiry which was to contribute largely towards procuring for his fatherland a prominent place in the history of intellectual development in modern times.

BOOK III

THE GREAT SYSTEMS

INTRODUCTION

AFTER an age of new ideas and discoveries comes the season of endeavours to order and systematise this wealth of thoughts and facts, and to reduce them to simple, well-established, fundamental notions. These attempts were undertaken in the firm persuasion that the right foundation had already been found. Analysis was replaced by construction. The great importance of this for thought was that it now became possible to see clearly what exactly was involved in the points of view to which the Renaissance and the new science had led. These positions were established with a dogmatic certainty unknown to the intellects of a former age, who had never taken exact account of individual principles and their bearings. That which previously had only floated, more or less vaguely, before men's minds was now formulated with express consciousness. And out of the principles thus formulated systems were constructed, each of which claimed to replace the old scholastic system, and to give it its death-blow at last. But yet the very endeavour to arrive at an absolute goal for knowledge, to bring thought to rest by means of a principle involving in itself no further problem, was an inheritance from scholasticism. The new structures were to reach as high as those which had been pulled down. The natural impulse, always more or less active in the human spirit, to synthesise all ideas established as valid, expressed itself here with a vigour and energy, coupled with an originality, to be found in no other period in the history of modern philosophy. Problems were stated, moreover, with a freshness and distinctness unparalleled either before or since. The new world-scheme and the new science had now to be interwoven with those other intellectual contents which appeared to consciousness as indisputable. The problem of existence thus came into the foreground. Bruno had already treated it from the point of view of the new world-scheme. But, since then, the modern mechanical explanation of Nature had arisen, and with this, thought found itself confronted with the great problem of the relation between the physical and the mental. The most important of the possible hypotheses regarding this relation were exhibited in the systems of the seventeenth century with a clearness and energy which lend lasting value to these essays of thought. Other problems became interwoven with this, however. For some time, indeed, that of the relation between God and the world occupied the first place. Connected with this, again, is the question of the unity or multiplicity of existence. And finally, it became an important question as to how far the mechanical explanation of Nature renders it possible to attribute real significance to the teleological concept.

The problems of knowledge and of worth were thrust into the background by the problem of existence, although they exercised a continuous, and more or less recognised, guiding and impelling influence. In Descartes, the first on the list of great system-makers, the endeavour to find the way to con-structive thought through analysis is evident even in his manner of statement. With Hobbes and Spinoza, analysis is darkened by construction. With Leibniz, the analytical tendency begins once more to assert itself—a transition to the predominant importance which the problems of knowledge and of worth were to exercise in the eighteenth century. The history of culture during the seventeenth century presents features analogous with the definitive, systematic tendency which con-stituted the main stream of philosophical thought during this period. One and the same fundamental disposition pervades the spheres of politics, of the Church, and of thought. It is the age of the absolute sovereignty of the State. The State has freed itself from the guardianship of the Church, and demands in its turn, from men as individuals, as well as from smaller societies, unconditional subjection. Indeed the principle of sovereignty is to be found in its most accentuated form in the two thinkers who formed the zenith of the constructive movement. The individual man now sought rest and certainty after the storms of the Renaissance and the Reformation. Intellectual contem-plation and mysticism attracted many. A tendency to quietism made itself felt. In the philosophical systems, however, these inclinations were satisfied by the thoughtful working-out of the new ideas and discoveries. They thus become important as experiments by which the range of important lines of thought could be tested.

CHAPTER I

RENÉ DESCARTES

(a) *Biography and Characteristics*

THIS man, the founder of modern philosophy, was born 31st March 1596, of a noble family of Touraine. The delicate boy early displayed unusual talents, and his father used to call him " the philosopher " on account of his many questions. In order that he might receive a careful education he was sent to the Jesuit College of La Flèche, which had been recently founded by Henry IV. In after life he always remembered his Jesuit teachers with gratitude, and it was a cause of great grief to him that the Jesuits opposed his philosophy. At La Flèche he studied physics and philosophy according to the scholastic system, but he devoted himself chiefly to mathematics, and seems to have occupied himself very early with the ideas which led him to his great mathematical discovery — the foundation of analytic geometry by the application of algebra to geometry. He has himself described his development during youth in his epoch-making work *Discours de la méthode*, which is also the history of the birth of his philosophy.

On leaving school he felt unsatisfied in spite of all that he had learnt. He was acquainted with many facts, and had been instructed in many beautiful thoughts, and he especially admired the stringent method of mathematics. But these facts and thoughts seemed to him disconnected fragments, and mathematics only an idle fancy of the brain. He now abandoned all his studies and threw himself into the whirl of Paris life. But he was not able altogether to deny his theoretical interests ; among his papers was found a treatise on the art of fencing, written at this time. He soon tired, however, of this unintellectual life and, suddenly disappearing from among his friends, he withdrew to a lonely part of the town, where he could study in peace.

It became more and more his great desire to lead a retired life, dedicated to meditation and study. His motto was : " Happy he who lives in seclusion " (*Bene vixit qui bene latuit*). At the end of two years he was discovered by his friends and torn away from his solitude. He now determined to study the " great book of the world." Perhaps practical life, which puts all ideas to the test, has taught men truths which are not to be discovered by learned speculation. Moreover he wanted to try himself among the chances of life. He took military service as a volunteer under Maurice of Orange, paying his own expenses, and still devoting every quiet hour he had to study—to mathematies more particularly. From Holland he went to Germany, then on the brink of the Thirty Years' War. He joined the army which the Elector of Bavaria was collecting against the Bohemians, who were in revolt.

While in winter-quarters at Neuburg on the Danube (1619-20), he experienced a mental crisis, during which he discovered the general method which afterwards guided him in his philosophical as well as in his mathematical studies. In a record of this time which he has left behind he even assigns a definite date to the birthday of this ruling thought : " the 10th November 1619, when filled with enthusiasm, I discovered the foundations of a wonderful science!"[42] He shut himself into his room and gave himself up to thoughts which led him to his general doctrine of method.

It occurred to him that just as the common work of many men is, in general, more imperfect than that which is executed by one man only, so our imperfect knowledge comes to us from many different teachers, each of whom communicates to us his own opinions, from the influence of the different instincts, and from the different and contradictory judgments which we hear pronounced by learned persons and practical people. We must therefore, if we are to get rid of this imperfection, begin again from the beginning, disregarding tradition and raising our edifice slowly on one single foundation. The right method consists in accepting only what is clearly and evidently thought, in separating every difficulty into its component parts, so that, starting from what is simplest and most easily comprehensible, we may gradually reach the most complex questions. This was the general analytical method, as it unfolded itself within his mind.   Within the region of mathematics this method led him to the idea of a science which should be wider than any single mathematical science, since it would deal with relations and proportions in general, whether these existed between figures, or numbers, or other things.   This was the general doctrine of magnitudes or functions, of which analytic geometry was a special application.   His mind was occupied so eagerly with these ideas that he fell into an over-strained condition, had strange dreams, and on the following day he vowed to the Virgin that he would make a pilgrimage to Loretto if only she would assist his thoughts.   (He waited to fulfil this vow till a convenient opportunity offered itself.)   A vow to make a pilgrimage is a curious introduction to modern philosophy—a counterpart to the supernatural voice, in which Herbert of Cherbury a few years later was to find the sanction for his "natural religion"!   In Descartes' opinion it was still too soon to proceed to the working out of his philosophy.   After he had assisted at the taking of Prague and accompanied an expedition into Hungary, he returned to France and took over the estates which he had inherited.   His family wished to see him married and settled in an official position, but his in-clinations did not lead him in that direction.   He determined to devote his life to learning, and in order that he might give himself undisturbedly to this, he withdrew (1629) to Holland. He had previously had frequent opportunities of expound-ing his philosophical ideas, more particularly on method, in the literary circles of Paris.   Two remarkable unfinished treatises, which did not appear till long after his death, "Rules for the Direction of the Mind" and "An Inquiry after Truth by means of the Natural Light," must have been written at this time.   They are important as giving a description of the analytical method.   At the beginning of his stay in Holland he was occupied (as we see in the *Discours de la méthode*, third and fourth parts) with the speculative ideas which he afterwards exhibited in detail in the *Meditationes*.   Here he founded his theology and his psychology, and discovered a way which led him, through doubt itself, to the starting-point of all connected philosophical knowledge.

That Descartes settled in Holland was due, most assuredly, not merely to the fact that he wanted rest or because—as he said—he could philosophise better in a cooler climate. A co-operating cause is to be found in the fact that he expected to be able to prosecute his inquiries there with greater freedom. The reactionary movement, which brought Bruno to the stake and subjected Galilei to the torture of the Inquisition, had spread to France. When a young inquirer wished to defend the atomic theory against the Aristotelian physics in a public disputation at Paris (1624), the theological faculty denounced as heretical the doctrine that everything consists of atoms, since it contradicted the Catholic doctrine of the Eucharist. The disputation was forbidden at the last moment, after nearly one thousand people had assembled to hear it. The author was arrested and expelled from the town, and on the 6th of September 1624 the Parliament forbade, on pain of death, the declaration of any principles which clashed with the old, tried, authors, and the institution of any disputations other than those sanctioned by the theological faculty. This must certainly have rendered the air of Paris most unhealthy for a philosopher! In Holland he might expect to find a freer atmosphere. In addition to the purely philosophic speculations already mentioned, Descartes occupied himself, in his new retreat, with the study of natural science, and he completed a treatise which was to have been called *Le Monde*, and in which he hoped to prove that the world had developed and built itself up according to purely mechanical laws. He imagined that God had created matter as chaos, and had afterwards ordered it according to the same laws which He still continues to observe in its preservation. In this way he reconciled the belief in the dogma of creation with the idea of a development according to natural, and finally demonstrable, laws, through the application of which to our world-system Descartes may be regarded as the forerunner of Kant and Laplace. But then came the news that Galilei was sentenced and that the College of the Inquisition had condemned the Copernican theory, on which Descartes had founded his hypothesis—and the work was withdrawn. He wished to teach nothing, he wrote to his friend Father Mersenne, which contradicted the faith of the Church ; moreover his motto was that he lives best who lives quietly *(Bene vixit qui bene latuit)* ; before all things he sought to enjoy peace and to shun fear and annoyance, and he would, there-fore, under existing circumstances, restrict himself to studying for himself alone. Thus Descartes' beautiful motto was turned to an ugly use, and the whole affair is rightly considered as a stain on his character. It is evident from his letters that he was in thorough agreement with Galilei's conclusions, and even were there every reason to suppose Descartes to have been a good Catholic, yet there can be no doubt that it was fear, and still more, perhaps, the need of quiet, which were the chief causes of his withdrawal. He afterwards (in the *Principia philosophiae*) presented his history of cosmical evolution, but in a disguised form. He threw dust, as his first biographer said, in the eyes of the Inquisition.

Although Descartes had as yet printed nothing, his ideas on philosophy and natural science were widely known, both in Paris and in Holland. The Cartesian philosophy, as has been truly said, was taught, long before it could be studied in books. Several of his pupils propounded it at the Dutch universities, where it occasioned violent disputes, to the great disquiet of its author. At last, in the year 1637, he yielded to the solicitations of his friends and published four treatises (*Essaies philosophiques*, Leyden, 1637), which he regarded as characteristic examples of his inquiries and their results. In the first treatise (*Discours de la méthode*), the only one of immediate philosophical interest, he sketched the history of his ideas and of the leading features of a new theory of knowledge and metaphysic ; in the second and third treatises (*Dioptrique Météores*) he gave examples of a strictly mathematical explanation of Nature, and in the fourth (*Géométrie*) he founded analytic geometry.

The complete presentation of his philosophy followed some years later in the *Meditationes* (1640) and in the *Principia philosophiae* (1644). He had previously submitted copies of the " Meditations " to several of the thinkers of the time, *e.g.* the famous Jansenist, Antoine Arnauld, Gassendi, and Hobbes ; and their objections, together with Descartes' answers, were printed as a supplement to the original work, which thus acquired the character of an interesting dialogue. The discussion with Gassendi was continued for a considerable time, and assumed a somewhat bitter tone. While the opposition of Gassendi and Hobbes was strictly philosophical, and therefore always instructive, the new philosophy had to encounter objections, based on quite other grounds, both from the Jesuits and from the orthodox Protestants.   Violent discussions took place at Utrecht, Groningen, and Leyden, where the theologians clung to the scholastic philosophy as the bulwark of faith. Finally, a prohibition of the new philosophy was published. The Dutch, said Descartes in a letter, honour the beard, the voice, and the face of theologians more than their integrity. He thought the Protestant worse than the Catholic theologians. He found himself between two fires : the Protestants charged him with scepticism, atheism, and the dissolution of the Universities, the Church, and the State ; the Catholics accused him not only of holding heretical opinions—*e.g.* the earth's motion (a fact which he had vainly tried to conceal)—but also of an inclination to Protestantism, and of taking part in Protestant worship.

The last work of Descartes which appeared during his life was his interesting treatise on the emotions (*Les passions de l'âme*, 1649).   The existence of this is due to the Princess Elizabeth von der Pfalz (a daughter of Friedrich von der Pfalz, the unhappy King of Bohemia), with whom he kept up a vigorous correspondence.   In the letters addressed to her he developed his ideas on ethics.   He also entered into correspondence with another gifted princess, *i.e.* Queen Christina of Sweden.   On Christina's invitation he travelled to Stockholm in order to personally initiate her into his philosophy.   This sojourn " in the land of bears, ice, and rocks " (as he says in a letter), as well as the life at court, were prejudicial to his health.   A year after his arrival he contracted an illness which ended in his death (1650).

The chief features of Descartes' character come out clearly in his life.   His love of study and of thought, to which he remained true throughout his whole life, and which, in moments when new ideas dawned upon him, rose to passion and enthusiasm, was the finest and most salient feature of his nature. Favourable and independent circumstances rendered it possible for him to carry out the plan of life he had laid down for himself, which was mainly directed to ensuring the rest and tranquillity of mind necessary to the prosecution of his studies. That he was not lacking in courage may be seen from his journeys, but his attitude towards authority was too timorous and apprehensive.   His most disagreeable trait was his incapability of recognising the merits of others.   He had

a high idea of the novelty of his standpoint, and emphatically denied having learnt anything from his predecessors, maintaining that even the views which he held in
common with them had been arrived at by him from different
premises.   He names Plato, Aristotle, Epicurus, and among
the moderns Telesio, Campanella, and Bruno, as authors with
whom he was acquainted, but from whom, in spite of all agreement, he had learnt nothing, since his principles were quite
other than theirs.   He only owns to having learnt from
Kepler; the German inquirer's mechanical conception of Nature,
the emphasis which he laid on the significance of the concept
of quantity, and his partial discovery of the law of inertia,
all exercised great influence on Descartes' natural philosophy.   But this idiosyncrasy is a part of his entire absorption
in his own thoughts.   As a thinker he is chiefly characterised
by sharp distinctions, and clear reductions to simple points
of view.   His work thus acquired a lasting importance, making
a final end of all caprice and imagination within the sphere of
method.   If his thinking contain errors, it is at any rate easy
to discover where they lie.   He is at his best in destructive
criticism, and in analysis leading back to first principles,
although his aim was the construction of a positive system
which should include the whole of our knowledge.   In virtue
of his over-hasty transition from analysis to construction he
ranks as a dogmatist ; but yet he was conscious, to a much
greater degree than is generally supposed, of the hypothetical
character of his ideas.   Although his intellect was his most
strongly developed side, yet his correspondence witnesses to
lively and deep feeling.

(b) Method and Presuppositions of Knowledge

Since in all knowledge, whatever be its object, we use our
understanding, Descartes is of opinion that it is of the greatest
importance to inquire closely into the nature of this.   The
understanding works everywhere in the same way ; therefore
the science of the understanding must be the universal science,
and there can be only one true method.   The essence of the
true method is to proceed only from what is clear and evident
and, starting from this, to try to understand the complex and
obscure.   Above all things, we must collect by means of

experience (*induction* or enumeration) all that is necessary to the explanation of the problem under consideration. This material must then be so arranged that the simplest and most directly evident circumstances form the foundation. To find an immediately evident proposition is *the first* condition of all knowledge. Every transition of thought takes place through immediate perception, i.e. *intuition*. Through intuition I learn that a triangle is bounded by three lines, that a ball has only one single surface, and that I must exist because I think. By means of such immediate perceptions we obtain first principles. There are some propositions so simple that we cannot think them without believing them to be true. Such propositions are ;—one and the same thing cannot both be and not be ; out of nothing, nothing comes ; the effect cannot contain more than the cause. Descartes does not mean that such propositions are immediately *given*. He expressly says that intuitions depend on particular cases ; but a general truth may be contained in individual examples, and we recognise this as immediately self-evident (*simplici mentis intuitu*) even before it is formulated as a general proposition. On the great question as to how general principles can be deduced from individual cases, Descartes does not enter. He merely exhorts to great carefulness in the laying down of principles.[43]

From these clear and self-evident propositions we derive further consequences by means of *deduction*. This consists in taking a succession of intuitions, and advancing from link to link of the chain so formed by means of a continuous movement of thought, thus joining together that which did not immediately appear to be connected. If, in so doing, we light on something which cannot be understood we must pause, for it would be useless to proceed. Either our experience is insufficient, or we have chanced upon questions which are unanswerable from the nature of the human mind. If we succeed in carrying out our deduction we shall have reduced the unknown to the known, and the validity of the first simple truth is extended over a larger sphere. The sciences accessible to us are joined to one another in a wonderful bond of union, and may be reached by the way of argument from one to another, so that they may all be discovered if we only proceed step by step from the most simple knowledge we possess.

It is evident, from the manner in which deduction is conditioned by simple empirical intuition, that Descartes is no
enemy of the empirical method. This may be seen also from
the unfailing assiduity with which he collected empirical instances and instituted experiments. But he insists that
scientific knowledge is only to be attained by means of
rigorous thought, and that the real significance of experience
lies in the fact that it gives rise to such thought. On the
other hand, he undervalues the necessity of verifying the results
of deduction. Science arises, according to him, from conclusions drawn from empirical data, and consists in logically
deduced hypotheses.

But how far must I go back to find that which is most
simple? Where shall I find a fixed foundation for my knowledge? Descartes answers these questions in the *Discours de
la méthode* (chap. iii.), and, in more detail, in the " Meditations."
We may doubt all contents and objects of knowledge. All
opinions and perceptions may rest on deception of the senses.
Supposing an evil being has created us who continually fills
our minds with error! Even then there would be *one* thing
that we could not doubt ;—our own thought, our own existence.
All doubt, even all error, is a thought, an activity of consciousness. However many erroneous and unreal things I
may imagine, yet the power of imagination (*vis imaginandi*)
is itself a proof of its reality. In so far as I think (or am
conscious) I am : *Je pense, donc je suis.* (*Cogito, ergo sum.*)
As already remarked, this is an immediate intuition which we
cannot prove any more than we can define thought or existence. This intuition possesses immediate clearness and distinctness, and is the pattern and measure of every other judgment. Descartes declares it to be a misunderstanding to
regard this proposition as an inference, but there is no doubt
that he himself occasioned this misunderstanding by his use
of the word " *donc* " (*ergo*).

But this simple, indubitable intuition is not as yet knowledge. How do we advance? How are we able to establish
the objective validity of our knowledge, the reality of that
which we imagine and think? In answering this question,
Descartes avails himself of the axiom of causality, or rather
the axiom that cause and effect must correspond with one
another. As we have already seen, this proposition is, accord-

ing to Descartes, one of those which can be discovered by intuition. The natural light teaches us that the effect cannot contain more than was in the cause. It follows from this that nothing can come out of nothing, and that the perfect cannot proceed from the imperfect. If we apply this to our ideas it becomes clear that some of them arise from external causes, while others must be explained as arising within us. But neither of these explanations are sufficient to make the idea of God as the infinite Being, the essence of all perfection and reality, comprehensible. Since I myself am a finite being (and of this I am convinced by my doubts and my desires) I cannot have produced any such idea. Neither can it have arisen by any combination of particular, perceived, perfections, for it would not then contain the unity and indivisibility which are the marks of the idea of God. Moreover every external cause is finite. There is therefore nothing left but to suppose that God Himself is the author of the idea. It is innate in us in the sense that, as soon as our power of thinking awakes to clearness, it can comprehend this idea by its own power. By an innate idea (*idea innata*) Descartes understands, then, not an idea *given* from the beginning, but one which we are capable of developing. The idea of God, he says, is innate in the same sense as is the idea of myself. "Innate ideas proceed from the capacity of thought itself." [44] The word "innate," however, was fatal ; it occasioned many misunderstandings.

The reality of the idea of God being thus assured (by means of the axiom of causality, be it noted), we have won, according to Descartes, a sure foundation for the reality of our knowledge. All that I know is a part of the infinite reality which that idea expresses ; it is one of the perfections which the conception of God contains, and is therefore firmly established for me. Only a finite being can err ; the possibility of error disappears in the infinite Being, in whose perfection, in virtue of my clear and distinct ideas, I participate. Descartes expresses it in popular language thus : God, the final cause of all our feelings and ideas, cannot err, since He is a perfect Being. But, if we look a little closer, we see that he points to a less external connection between the idea of God and the reality of our knowledge. Since I can only perceive my own imperfection by means of a more or less distinct idea of perfection, and since the idea of God is the idea of the highest, all-embracing perfection, this idea serves me as an ideal by which I can measure and correct my imperfect knowledge.[45]   If Descartes introduces the conception of God into his theory of knowledge, he certainly has not God, in the religious sense of the word, before his eyes ; the idea of God is for him the idea of a continuous, all-embracing, unity of existence, in which everything that possess reality must be able to find a place.   In the Sixth Meditation he says : "By Nature in general" (*natura generaliter spectata*) "I understand nothing else than either God Himself or the co-ordination (*co-ordinatio*), ordained by God, of all created things."   Everything that I am to recognise as true must be able to find a place in this unity, which may therefore be equally well called Nature or God.   The particular acquires reality for me through its connection with everything else.   The criterion of the difference between dreaming and waking is this;—that I can, without interruption, unite the experiences of my waking life with all my other experiences and recollections (*perceptionem earum absque ulla interruptione cum tota reliqua vita connecto*).   This is the deeper meaning which underlies Descartes' theological foundation of the validity of knowledge.   Interesting though this line of thought is, yet he might have altogether avoided an appeal to theology, for the axiom of causality, which he had already presupposed in his proof of the reality of the idea of God, would have sufficed to mediate between the knowing subject and the universe. Descartes expressly excepts (in the *Responsiones secundae*) the axiom of causality and the other first principles from the knowledge which depends on the idea of God as its foundation.   Had he developed the implications of the axiom of causality farther, he would have seen that this itself leads to the positing of a unity in which all particular phenomena have their definite place.   But the time for a closer examination of the causal relation and the axiom of causality did not come till a century after Descartes' time.

(c) Theological Speculations

Descartes began with analysis and criticism, but he very soon passes over to theological and spiritualistic speculations. In his *Je pense, donc je suis* he finds the starting-point for both. We will dwell, by way of preliminary, on his theological ideas, the interest of which, for us, lies in the fact that they offer a more logical development and foundation of the contents of "natural religion." Descartes denies that the existence of God can be proved from the world as given in experience. The chain of causes may extend to infinity, and we ought not to confound the impotence of our understanding to follow such an infinite chain with the necessity of positing a first cause. Moreover, it is only on the assumption that the concept of God is already known that I can exhibit the justification for calling such a first cause God. Descartes' own proof is more direct. He insists, as we have already seen, on the impossibility of a finite being conceiving the idea of an infinite Being. On the contrary, this latter idea is the presupposition of the idea of myself as a finite, limited being ; for the finite presupposes a limit to the infinite ; the infinite is the positive, the limitation of which gives rise to the finite. The conception of God, then, is formed by the removal of limitations (that is to say, through the negation of a previously existing negation). In this last definition, Descartes is not far from saying that the conception of God is formed in the same manner as all our ideals (except those which arise through the combination of elements taken from different complexes), *i.e.* through the extension and abolition of limitations. Gassendi, in replying to this, reminds Descartes that, as a matter of fact, we form ideal constructions by extension and combination ; but Descartes replies that this very capacity of extending ideas by means of the relative perfection given in experience presupposes that we had our origin in God. Instead of studying with Gassendi the psychology of the *forming* of ideals (a subject to which, even in the present day, very little attention is paid), Descartes was content with the *ready-made* idea of God : since this deals with the infinite it cannot have been produced by a finite being. But this conclusion would only be valid if the idea itself, and not merely its object, were infinite.

Descartes had, however, one further proof, *i.e.* the ontological. While, before, he had gone from the idea of God back to the cause of this idea, he here tries to show that if we think the conception of an infinite and all-perfect Being clearly and distinctly, we must also posit the existence of such a Being ; for we should deny Him a perfection if we denied Him existence, and so arrive at a contradiction with ourselves. Against this reasoning (which is to be found in the Fifth

Meditation) Gassendi objects that existence is assuredly the condition of a thing possessing either perfection or imperfection, but that in and for itself it is no perfection. Descartes continued to maintain, however, that we attribute existence to things in the same way that we attribute to them other qualities.

Descartes is now clear that the concept of God, the validity of which he has, in his opinion, established by the two proofs already quoted, differs from the popular conception. Most men do not conceive God as the sublime and infinite Being, the sole author of all things ; under the word God they conceive a finite being, who can be worshipped by men. It is therefore no wonder that there are men who deny the existence of such a God. Descartes develops his own higher conception of God more fully when he defines Him as the absolute Substance. To say that God is a substance is to say that He is a being who is capable of existing of Himself (*per se*), and does not require any other things in order to exist. It is true that Descartes also uses the concept "Substance" of finite beings (*e.g.* of the soul and the body, which we shall have to consider more fully later) ; but he explains that it cannot be used in one and the same meaning (*univoce*) of the infinite Being and of finite beings. Since all finite beings are dependent on the infinite Being, they can only be called unreal substances.[46] Descartes carries out this notion of Substance in the strict sense more particularly in his letters. "One cannot prove," he writes, "the existence of God without considering Him as the all-perfect Being ; but He would not be this if anything happened in the world which did not proceed from Him." Even natural philosophy teaches us that not even the most insignificant thought can arise in the human spirit unless God wills, and has willed from eternity, that it should do so. This is one of the reasons, too, which led Descartes to reject the atomic theory ; an atom claims to be something which can exist of itself ; but only one single Being, the highest of all beings, can be independent of every other. In his works Descartes expresses himself more vaguely, introducing, side by side with his strict definition of the concept of substance, a wider and more popular one. According to the laxer usage of speech, Substance means the same as thing or being. Substance is that which possesses certain attributes. In this sense (as the bearer of attributes) a finite being may very well be a substance. It is evident that much confusion will arise if the two meanings of these words are not sharply distinguished from one another. But Descartes conceives soul and body as substances also in the sense of absolutely independent beings. And as he applies the stricter concept of substance to finite beings, so he also applies the laxer concept of substance to the infinite Being, since this concept contains all possible reality and perfection— that is to say, all possible attributes. It was, therefore, a truly penetrative criticism of Descartes' system, when Hobbes and Gassendi objected against him, that we have no positive concept of substance as the bearer of attributes, since we know attributes only (accidents, qualities, or, as we should now say, phenomena). Descartes acknowledged that we do not directly perceive substance, but infer it from its attributes ; but he maintains that we can think it, even though we can form no picture of it in our minds.[47] Here was another problem which acquired great importance in later philosophy.

By means of the axiom of causality Descartes was able to posit the existence of God. But it may seem as though this same axiom would lead beyond the idea of God, for must not God Himself have a cause? Descartes tried to evade this difficulty by distinguishing between that which has its cause outside itself, and that which has its cause within itself. God must be, with regard to Himself, what the cause is with regard to its effect, i.e. He is self-caused (causa sui). As the infinite Being, God has an inexhaustible power within Himself, so that He needs no other thing than Himself in order to exist. In this way the concepts of substance and cause became very closely united. Antoine Arnauld, the great Jansenist theologian, who afterwards became an ardent Cartesian, objected that the expression " self-caused " contradicts itself, and in any case cannot be predicated of God. For, said he, no one can give what he does not possess ; and if any one can generate himself he must have existed previously. And if God is cause, He must also be effect, for a cause precedes its effect in time, but with God there is no distinction between the past and the future, or between possibility and reality. Descartes replied that if we prove the existence of God by means of the axiom of causality, we must also apply this axiom to God Himself, and it is only possible to do this if we conceive Him as the cause of Himself. He adds, moreover, that the expression "cause" can only be used by analogy of God, on account of the imperfection of human knowledge, and that though we may say God is the cause, we must not say He is the effect of Himself, otherwise one part of God will be lower than the other. Further, the temporal relation has no sort of validity of God, since it is only the product of human thought—a *modus cogitandi*. It seems indisputable that there is very little left of the concept of causality in the theological application. The Cartesian philosophy of religion could not fail to beget the need for an examination into the justification and significance of our fundamental notions in regard to their application in theology.

The statement that the temporal relation is not valid of God is especially remarkable where Descartes teaches that the eternal truths (*e.g.* a thing can not be and not be,—the sum of the angles of a triangle are equal to two right angles) are dependent on the absolute will of God. God's reason and will are not separate. He did not first conceive the eternal truths, and then establish them. His will is as eternal and unchangeable as His Being. Here, too, we see the great difference between Descartes' and the popular conceptions of God. There is, indeed, no psychological attribute which can be predicated of God. This was a result, however, at which Descartes had not yet arrived. Some difficulties still remain, even if we were to allow all Descartes' opinions. Our doubt shows us our imperfection, and the concept of this pre-supposes the concept of perfection. So we rise to the concept of God. But after we have attained to this height, imperfection still continues—moreover, how was it possible for imperfection ever to arise, when the Being in whom are all things is ideally perfect? Descartes answers that imperfection necessarily clings to the finite, and that all created things are finite. Moreover, it is only a negation which brings about imperfection, and this negation makes the world more perfect than it would otherwise be, since through it the manifoldness of the world is increased. And even if the eye is the most excellent part of the body, yet the other parts of the body have no ground of complaint, since the body cannot consist entirely of the eye. Descartes here hints at a *théodicée* similar to that afterwards exhibited in detail by Leibniz.

(d) Philosophy of Nature

By means of the criterion of truth which he had found, Descartes concludes that our sensations must be caused by something other than our consciousness. But this something —according to Descartes—need not in itself be as the senses present it to us. The importance of sensuous perception is, before all things, practical; it has to teach us what is useful or injurious to us. And even if we regarded it as the office of sensuous perception to help us to a knowledge of things, it is not necessary that our sensations should *resemble* the things, as long as they correspond to them, as the word corresponds to the thought. If we consider the manner in which sensuous perception takes place we shall perceive that all sense-impressions are touches; so that we only come in contact with the surface of things. If we try to think how things—apart from the way in which they affect us—are constituted, the only qualities which we are not able to think away in our imagination are extension, divisibility, and mobility. These are the simplest and clearest ideas which we can have of matter, and it is evident that if we hold fast to these, *i.e.* to the ideas of the purely geometrical qualities, we shall be able to arrive at a simple and clear understanding of all that goes on in the material world. The phenomenon of motion contains the explanation of all other phenomena. On the other hand, we shall be able to explain nothing if we attribute forms or qualities to matter. Qualities belong to our consciousness, but all that really takes place in the physical world are motions without or within our organisms. In science we must conceive the material world as it would be apart from all sensuous perception. Thus the principle of simplicity, which had played such an important part in the struggle for the new world-scheme, is now used to establish the reduction of all qualities of matter to extension and motion. As a consequence of this reduction, qualities were relegated to the subjective sphere. As Descartes could hardly have known Galilei's *Saggiatore*, he must have arrived at the principle of the subjectivity of the sense qualities independently, in his attempt to think out the conditions of a purely objective and strictly necessary explanation of material events. From some of Descartes' notes, written in the year

1619-20, it is evident that at that time he had not embraced the mechanical explanation of Nature. He must have been led to adopt this view during the years 1620-29. In addition to Kepler, it is probable that he was influenced by a group of young French inquirers who held atomic views, and were much impressed by SEBASTIAN BASSO, the real reformer of the atomic theory in modern times. Descartes himself names Basso among his predecessors. It was two of these young men who wanted to hold the disputation in Paris mentioned above, and thus occasioned the terroristic decree against new opinions. Since Sebastian Basso seems, in his turn, to have been influenced by the writings of Giordano Bruno, we here get an historical connection between Descartes and the philosophy of the Renaissance. HARVEY'S discovery of the circulation of the blood also, as we shall see later, had great influence on Descartes' line of thought.

In his attempt to explain all material phenomena by means of extension, divisibility, and mobility as the ultimate qualities of matter, Descartes adopts a deductive mode of procedure. He proceeds from cause to effect. He is perfectly well aware that, in this way, we can only arrive at an hypothesis, since it is always possible that the given phenomena may have been produced by other causes than those from which we started. Experiment and experience must supply confirmation, and Descartes says that the necessary experiments are so numerous and costly as to far exceed his own powers, and to require the co-operation of many men. Unlike Galilei, Descartes is also interested in general principles and deductions. He regards deduction as the really scientific mode of procedure, and he is lacking in Galilei's power of throwing light on great and far-reaching problems by the examination of particulars—although he himself, in his doctrine of method, takes intuition, which depends on the perception of particulars, as the starting-point of his thought. His task was other than Galilei's. His mission was to show, clearly and explicitly, that the time had gone by when an explanation of Nature could be reached by faith in mysterious powers, or by supernatural interposition. His ideal of all natural science is the deduction of phenomena from their causes, with the same transparent necessity with which a mathematical conclusion follows from its premises. The principle of simplicity to which he appeals, is indeed, at the same time, the principle of transparency. He was not mistaken with regard to the principles so established ; but he attributed greater importance to the deductive application of general principles and to the hypotheses founded upon them than they really possessed, and thus his philosophy of nature acquired a dogmatic character, which became still more strongly developed in the hands of the Cartesians. Thus, in many cases, a mechanical scholasticism took the place of the scholasticism of substantial forms and qualities.

It follows, from the ultimate qualities of matter, that there can be no such thing as an absolute atom, since a limit to divisibility is unthinkable ; that there can be no empty space, for space means extension, and extension presupposes an extended being, *i.e.* matter ; that the material world is infinite, for it is impossible to set limits to extension, and where there is extension there is also matter. It further follows that the changes which take place in matter must always be explained according to the laws of motion which are, therefore, the highest natural laws. Descartes tried to arrive at these laws also by deduction ; he found the premises for this deduction in the concept of God, which receives a significance in his philosophy of nature analogous to its application in his theory of knowledge. From God's immutability, which is a part of His perfection, Descartes concludes that the sum of motion generated at the creation remains unaltered during its conservation (which, according to Descartes, is an uninterrupted continuous creation). Motion may be distributed differently in different parts of the world, but no motion is lost, and none can begin anew. In the theological foundation which Descartes gives to his principle of the constancy of motion lies the involuntary confession that the ultimate attributes of matter, from which he starts in his philosophy of nature, are too simple and too abstract. For it is evident that what is really constant is the divine power continuously active in the world ; the constancy of motion is derived from the constancy of this power. Had Descartes clearly seen this, he would have discovered a proposition of greater validity than the one he laid down ; for it is not motion, but force or energy, that is constant. At every transition from motion to rest, or the converse, Descartes' proposition lands him in difficulties. But even in this imperfect form it is interesting as a precursor of the modern principle of the conservation of energy. Descartes also derives special laws of motion from the immutability of God, of which the most important is the law of inertia, which he was the first to establish consciously and systematically. It would, thinks Descartes, be inconsistent with the divine immutability if a thing, which is to be regarded as one and indivisible, could change its condition without external cause. He also denies the possibility of such a thing being able to pass of itself (*sua sponte*) from motion to rest, or the converse. Descartes probably arrived at the law of inertia under the influence of Kepler (who established half of it), but independently of Galilei, for he had already asserted it in his *Monde*, which was finished before Galilei's Dialogue appeared. Descartes makes a reservation in his statement of the law of inertia, since he leaves it an open question whether spirits and angels can affect matter. This reservation is made in the interest of his spiritualistic psychology, which we shall examine later.

Descartes' concept of matter bears the stamp of simplicity and clearness, it is indeed founded on the principle of simplicity. This is a natural result of the tendency, also visible in Kepler and Galilei, to seek to reduce all qualities to quantitative relations, by means of which an exact science of nature would be possible. But just as Descartes is inclined to overlook the hypothetical character of his deductive results, so also he is inclined to look upon his definitions formed by abstraction, and according to the principle of simplicity, as exhaustive. He believes it possible to arrive at a complete knowledge of the nature of matter by means of the determinations extension, divisibility, and mobility, although he can give no guarantee for the truth of this. When he speaks of matter as extended substance he does not perceive that he has converted an abstraction into a being, existing in and for itself. Nor did he ever give any justification for considering the geometrical qualities of things as absolute. It does not, for instance, necessarily follow that these qualities are the most important for the knowledge of Nature. Qualities such as extension, divisibility, and mobility may very possibly be due to the influence of things on us (just as much as colour, taste, smell, etc.) without their bearing any resemblance to the things themselves. Moreover, as already pointed out, there is **one**

determination which is even more fundamental than the three
qualities beyond which Descartes did not go, *i.e.* force or energy.

It was the task of later inquiry to discuss the questions
here indicated.   At the time, and in spite of its onesidedness,
Descartes' philosophy of Nature denoted an immense advance
in clearness.   We will now briefly examine his most important
applications of his general principles, concerning ourselves
only with his fundamental notions.   Some of his individual
explanations are arbitrary, and anything but happy.   His
weakness lay in the multiplication of hypotheses ; his greatness
in his happy knack of seizing general points of view.

If everything in material nature is to be explained by
extension, divisibility, and mobility, it is evident we can have
no use for finite causes; yet Descartes founded his rejection
of the teleological explanation of Nature on theological, rather
than epistemological, grounds.   Since God is an infinite Being,
much that He does must be beyond our comprehension ; to
attempt to discover His aims would be presumption.   There is
infinitely much in this limitless world which does not affect us
at all ; what sense is there, then, in saying that it must all have
been created for us?   The only conceivable end of all that
happens is God Himself.   Thus the teleological view is rejected,
since we dare not set limits to the nature of the world and the
nature of God.

If we wish to understand Nature in detail, we must,
according to Descartes, proceed from the simplest and most
easily understood phenomena,—from the events which we
have ever before us,—and by means of these explain what is
hidden from us, and the events of the past.   Thus in Descartes'
hands the principle of simplicity turns into the principle of
actuality, which demands that the far and unknown should
be explained by the near and known.   Above all things we
should take, as our fundamental notions, the construction and
working of our machines, for these are the clearest ideas we
have.   He therefore describes the world as though it were a
machine(*terram totumque hunc mundum* instar machinae *descripsi*).
We should be able to explain the present condition of the
world if we conceived the parts of matter as having been from
the beginning (for matter and motion arose simultaneously) in
whirling motion round fixed centres.   The smaller parts, which
arise during the whirling motion by the mutual friction of the

larger, necessarily collected into these centres. In this way the different larger and smaller heavenly bodies have come into existence. Some of these heavenly bodies gradually lost their independence, and were carried into the eddy which surrounds the larger heavenly bodies. This is what has happened with the earth. Descartes thought that, according to his theory, he could call the earth immovable, since it does not change its place within the medium in and with which it is whirled round the sun, and since, in addition to those parts of the universe which lie open to our perceptions, there may also be stars, in relation to which the earth remains immovable ! By such far-fetched applications of the concept of relativity Descartes sought—in vain, as it proved—to escape the reproach of being a Copernican heretic. Weight is explained as a consequence of the pressure of the whirling eddies against the parts in space, in which they are pressed against the heavenly bodies, or, at any rate, kept in close proximity to them.

Descartes is the first of the moderns who attempted to give a mechanical theory of the evolution of the world-system. He showed, it is true, polite consideration for theology, by allowing that the world was created perfect and complete, and saying that he only wishes to point out the *possibility* of the present condition of the world having been developed according to natural laws out of a less perfect original condition. If any one asks how we are to conceive this original condition he answers it matters very little whether we conceive it in this way or in that ; for in virtue of the natural laws, matter passes through all the states which it is capable of assuming, so that after the exhaustion of a greater or lesser number of more imperfect conditions, the present condition would, in any case, have been reached. This explanation (*Princ. Phil.* iii. 47), which contains the programme of all mechanical theories of evolution, is of greater interest as Descartes' attempt to describe in detail the cosmogonical process.

Just as he had attempted to explain the unity and development of the world according to the general laws of Nature, so Descartes tried to explain the organism and organic life according to purely mechanical laws. Not only astronomy but also physiology ought, according to his conception, to be a purely mechanical science. As he had left out theology in his cosmogonical hypothesis, so he leaves out psychology in his organic mechanics, and conceives the human body to be put together out of material parts, and to be active according to the laws of heat and motion without the intervention of any soul at all (whether "vegetative," "sensitive," or "rational"). This conception, a result of the general principles of Descartes' natural philosophy (since the organism as a material being must fall under the general laws of Nature) received what he considered to be an empirical confirmation in WILLIAM HARVEY'S discovery of the circulation of the blood (1628). Harvey stands in the first rank of the founders of modern natural science ; he is to physiology what Galilei was to physics. He gave the death-stroke to mystical powers in the sphere of physiology when he showed that the movement of the blood is due neither to its own force nor to the force of the soul, but is determined by the contraction of the heart, which forces it out into the body. The general laws of motion, therefore, are valid within, as well as without, the organism. Among leading men, Descartes was one of the first to assent to Harvey's teaching, and his acceptance of it, expressed in the *Discours de la méthode* (chap. v.), was a great support to the new doctrine, which had so much resistance to encounter, sharply opposed as it was to the old conception of organic life.[48] Descartes describes in several of his works (more particularly in *Traité de l'homme*), how the human body may be conceived as a mere machine. Here, too, his general method of conception was conducive to clearness, even when his particular explanations were not happy. NIELS STEENSEN. one of the greatest anatomists of the age immediately following, admitted that the method introduced by Descartes served to expose the inadequacy of earlier teachings concerning the significance of the different organs, and to exhibit in a clearer manner the problems involved. Descartes extended the mechanical conception, which Harvey had justified with respect to the circulation of the blood, to the physiology of the nerves. In agreement with the physiology of the time he believes there are currents of animal spirits (*esprits animaux*) in the nerves, which currents are caused by the finer parts of the blood, after they had been warmed in the heart, streaming up to the brain and filling its cavities, while the rest of the blood continues its way through the veins. From the brain, these currents make their way through the nerves, into the muscles. They may be set in motion by impressions of which we are not conscious ; this happens in involuntary movements, *e.g.* in stretching out the hands when falling, or when we continue to walk without thinking about it. Such involuntary movements may take place entirely mechanically, and even against our will (*mente invita et* tanquam in machina). Descartes expresses this by saying that the animal spirits are reflexed (*esprits réfléchis*), and he gives a clear description and explanation of what is now called reflex movement.

We are obliged to assume that all the functions and actions of animals occur entirely in this involuntary and mechanical manner. There is no ground for supposing them to have a soul. That the lamb flees at the sight of a wolf happens because the rays of light from the body of the wolf strike the eye of the lamb, and set the muscles in motion by means of the "reflex" currents of the animal spirits ; and that the swallows appear in the spring may be explained by analogy with a clock which strikes the hour at definite times. Moreover, we know that animals cannot adapt themselves to new and complicated circumstances, any more than can machines. The view that animals are nothing but machines recommended itself to Descartes because otherwise, according to his principles, we must attribute to them immortality ; and shall an oyster or a fungus be immortal ?

It is different in the case of human beings, where, by reason of the consciousness which makes itself felt in each one of us, we must assume a soul, a thinking substance in reciprocal action with the material substance, capable of interfering with and guiding the "animal spirits." According to Descartes, the soul only stands in immediate connection with a single part of the brain, *i.e.* the pineal gland (*glandula pinealis*), which attracted Descartes' attention, because it is not a re-duplicated organ, as is the case with so many other parts of the brain, and because it seemed to him to be situated in about the middle of the brain, above the channel through which the "animal spirits" from the anterior and posterior cavities commune with each other. The "animal spirits" come into contact with the pineal gland, and thus excite sensations, feelings, and impulses in the soul ; the soul answers—also by pushing the pineal gland !—and in this way guides the "animal spirits" in a particular direction. Often (for example, in self-control) shock and counter-shock act in opposite directions, and then the issue depends on which is the stronger of the two![49]

Descartes has the merit of having thrown much light on involuntary activity by his description and analysis of reflex movement. He has the further merit of having maintained that the activity of the soul depends on the brain, and is connected immediately with this only. Finally, in spite of the imperfect anatomical knowledge at his disposal, he has the merit of having expounded the spiritualistic psychology with great penetration and in all its consequences.

We will now look somewhat more closely at his theory of psychology.

(e) *Psychology*

Descartes attributes souls to human beings only, and by soul he understands a substance distinguished from body as a peculiar substance, the bearer of all spiritual attributes, as body is the bearer of all material attributes. Since, as we saw, he carries over his mechanical conception of Nature into the sphere of organic life, he is obliged to assume that motion, which is not the continuation of previous motion, can no more arise in the organism than in any other part of material nature, and similarly, that no motion can disappear without being continued by a subsequent motion; for the principle of the constancy of motion is one of the chief principles of his natural philosophy. But when, according to his theory, the soul pushes the pineal gland in order to set the "animal spirits' in motion, whereupon the soul in its turn receives a shock through the working of the "animal spirits" on the pineal gland, motion must here both arise and vanish without any subsequent compensatory motion! Moreover, if we can read any sense into the soul pushing or being pushed, Descartes' spiritualistic psychology here comes into open contradiction with his natural philosophy. He is really thinking of the soul as a material being, when he makes it push and be pushed, and this is always the fate of spiritualism if only it is thought out with perfect clearness. Descartes' gifted correspondent, Princess Elizabeth von der Pfalz, very rightly remarked that it is easier to conceive the soul as material than to understand how, without being material, it is able to move matter, and to be set in motion by it. In one passage Descartes seems to want to

restrict the influence of the soul, so that it only causes a change
of direction of the animal spirits, which in themselves might
take one direction or another equally well ; but such guidance
would conflict with the law of inertia, and could only be
established as an arbitrary exception to it.

If Descartes conceives the soul as an altogether peculiar
being, different from the body, this is because consciousness and
extension are such radically different attributes that he can only
suppose them to belong to different beings. *Je pense, donc je
suis !* was his starting-point, and by thought he understands, as
he expressly states, consciousness in general (*omnia quae nobis
consciis in nobis fiunt*). He might, therefore, as he remarks, have
just as well said : I feel, therefore I am ; or I will, therefore I
am. What he wants to emphasise is the ultimate fact of consciousness. And the merit of his psychology lies in the fact that
he takes consciousness (*mens*) as his starting-point; for the
concept of the soul (*anima*) is, and still more was, equivocal
and mystical. He thus prepared the way for modern empirical
psychology. It is not impossible that he was influenced in
this by Vives, who distinguished clearly between psychical
phenomena as actually given, and the nature of the soul in itself.
Vives' work on psychology is several times quoted by Descartes.
Descartes believed, however, that in thought or consciousness
he had an entirely clear and exhaustive concept of the
nature of the soul, as he also believed that extension furnished
an entirely clear and exhaustive concept of the nature of
matter. If, says Descartes, I am able to think the concept of
the soul clearly and perfectly without having to presuppose
the concept of body, and if I can think the concept of body
clearly and perfectly without having to think the concept
of the soul, is not this a proof that we have here before us
two distinct beings or substances entirely independent of one
another? As we have already pointed out, the concept of
substance has a twofold signification with Descartes. It does
not only mean a bearer of attributes, a something which has
the properties presented in experience. Even in this vague
signification of the word Descartes concludes too much when
he makes the " something " of thought differ from the " something " of extension ; one and the same something might very
well have both qualities ! But, in the stricter sense of the
word, substance is a *self-sufficient* and independent being. It

lies in the nature of substances, says Descartes, *to be mutually exclusive.* And he assumes this of soul and body, because he is able to think each one of them without thinking the other with it. Man consists, therefore, of two mutually exclusive natures. But, if so, reciprocal action between these two becomes incomprehensible. If one substance works upon the other, they cannot be entirely independent of one another : for, in that case, something goes on in the one which I cannot understand unless I think of the other. The situation then becomes incomprehensible, and Descartes confesses this himself. He who never philosophises, he says in a letter, never doubts but that soul and body act and react upon one another and form one single being ; philosophically, however, it is impossible to think the difference and the union between body and soul at the same time. No inference and no comparison, he says elsewhere, can teach us how consciousness, which is incorporeal, is able to set the body in motion ; sure and evident experience, however, teaches us this daily ; it is one of the things which must be understood of itself, and which becomes obscured by comparison with other things. Descartes here talks as if he had seen how the soul moves the pineal gland, and is moved in return by it ! But the whole difficulty of the problem lies in the fact that immediate experience can *not* decide the matter, but that, on the contrary, inference and comparison are the only means by which we can hope to arrive at a comprehensible and incontestable hypothesis.

It is generally admitted that the mediæval dualism lurks in Descartes' theory of soul and body. Descartes own contribution to the theory, however, is his effort to form clear and evident conceptions. From the mutual independence of the concept he goes on to infer the mutual independence of the corresponding beings. His greatest merit is his clear and sharp characterisation of the difference between mental and bodily phenomena ; but it is this very thing also which leads him astray. As a dogmatist, he relies upon the perfection of his concepts, and concludes that existence must agree with them.

Descartes carried out, in a more extreme form, the psychological dualism which we met with in Telesio, Bacon, and Campanella, and, in so doing, did much to lead out beyond it. He formulated the popular metaphysic of the soul and body so sharply as to bring into prominence its difficulties

and contradictions.   Gassendi and Arnauld rightly objected
against him that, because consciousness and extension are the
chief attributes of the soul and body, we cannot therefore
conclude that they exhaust their nature.   And here they
touched upon the crucial point of Descartes' theory.

The consequences of Descartes' separation between soul
and body are noticeable in his psychology proper.   He
carefully examines which mental activities and phenomena
belong to the soul itself, and which are due to the influence of
the body on the soul.

Sensuous perception is due to the body ; it arises by means
of the influence exercised by the " animal spirits," through the
pineal gland, on the soul.   Descartes here points out that in
popular usage much more is reckoned as perception than is
really included within it.   We ought, *e.g.*, to distinguish between
the motion arising in the brain through stimulation (which is also
found in animals); the effect of this motion in the brain on the
soul, which gives rise to sensation (*e.g.* of colour) ; and, thirdly,
the judgments which, in consequence of the motions of the
bodily organs, we involuntarily pass on external things.   It is
in virtue of one of these involuntary judgments that we conceive things to be without us, and situated at definite places in
space.   It is the motions of the eye and the head which, by
means of corresponding motions of the animal spirits, excite
the soul to the deliverance of such a judgment.   The third
moment of perception is due to the soul alone.

There are also two kinds of memory : one of material
things, which depends on after-effects or traces of preceding
excitations of the brain, and the other of mental things,
depending on permanent traces in consciousness itself.
Thought proper (*intellectio*) and imagination (*imaginatio*) may
be distinguished from one another by this, that in thought
proper the soul alone is active, while in imagination it makes
use of sensuous images.   Imagination, like perception and the
material remembrance of the soul, only belongs to the soul in
as far as it is united with the body ; but the soul in its
pureness (*anima pura*) can be thought without either imagination or perception.   The difference between instinct and will
similarly rests on the fact that while the former arises in the
body, the will belongs to the soul itself.

Descartes attributes to us direct consciousness of the

freedom of the will, although he acknowledges that the indifference of the will is rather an imperfection of our knowledge than a perfection of our will.   The scope of the will
is greater than that of the understanding ; we may choose and
assert that which we do not understand.   The will is unlimited,
the understanding limited ; thus Descartes explains the possibility of error.   The emotions (*passions*) are due to the influence
of the body upon the soul ; but the inner feelings (*émotions
intérieures*) arise in the soul as a consequence of its own thoughts
and judgments.   Inner and purely intellectual feeling is, it is
true, accompanied by an emotion, a sensuous feeling ; but this
arises from the influence of the soul on the brain, as, *e.g.*, in
intellectual love, when the disposition of the soul affects the
pineal gland.   In emotion, joy precedes love ; the reverse is the
case in the inner feeling.   Although by this dualistic conception
Descartes really cut himself off from any theory of a connected
continuous development of the feelings, yet the psychology
of feeling owes not a little to him, on account of his attempt to
trace the different feelings back to certain elementary forms,
through combinations of which they arose.   His elementary
feelings are wonder, love, hate, desire, joy, and sorrow.   His
account both of them and their combinations is purely descriptive and analytic, and constantly brings in his physiological theory.
In order to explain the physiological side of the emotions, he
lays chief stress upon the reciprocal action between the brain
and the heart.   Only in the case of wonder, which he considers
to be a purely intellectual feeling, does he believe there to be
no influence of the brain on the heart.   He emphasises the
connection of the emotions with the instincts ; they incline the
soul to will the useful and to shun the injurious ; it is also
without the influence of the soul that the motion of the animal
spirits, which causes the emotions, effects the carrying out of
purposive actions.   But this purposiveness is by no means
absolute ; experience and reason must therefore interfere and
correct.   Of importance for the development of feeling is the
connection between a representation in the soul and a certain
condition of the " animal spirits " ; only by means of such a
representation, and not directly, can the will intervene to guide
the motions of the body.   The struggle between reason and
the senses is not carried on, according to Descartes, within the
soul, but is a struggle between the soul or the will, on the one

side, and the body (*i.e.* the animal spirits) on the other, and all depends upon which of the two can give the most violent push to the pineal gland (*Passions de l'âme*, i. 47). Here, too, we find the spiritualistic theory carried out by Descartes with the most admirable consistency.

(*f*) *Ethics*

When Descartes chose universal doubt as the starting-point for his philosophy, he made a provisional exception of the moral sphere, although he was aware that his philosophising must have effect in this sphere also. That he might not be left without guidance in his way through life whilst he was analysing everything theoretically, he drew up the following temporary rules (*Discours de la méthode*, chap. iii.) of conduct, 1. to observe the religion and customs of his fatherland, 2. to carry out resolutely what he had once decided upon, 3. to seek to conquer himself rather than fate, to subordinate his wishes to the world-order, and to bear ever in mind that our thoughts are all that we have entirely in our own power.

Later, after he had developed and published his philosophical views, he hesitated to venture into the sphere of morals. The theologians, he said, who were already so angry with him on account of his physics, would certainly not leave him unmolested if he wrote on ethics. With the exception of some expressions in his *Passions de l'âme*, we find his ethical ideas in his letters to the Princess Elizabeth, to Queen Christina, and to Chanut (the French Ambassador to Sweden). They are little more than a further development of the provisional rules given in the *Discours de la méthode ;* they betray the influence of the Stoic philosophers, especially of Seneca. What means, asks Descartes, does philosophy enable us to point out, by which we may reach that highest happiness which vulgar minds vainly expect from the course of events, but which is only really to be found in ourselves? Three means offer themselves: clear knowledge of the right, a firm will to do the same, and a repression of all wishes and desires directed towards objects beyond our reach. Only by the intervention of the will can knowledge gain the mastery in us, and the animal spirits become obedient to it. While without this, the sensuous feelings or the emotions confuse our thoughts, and cause us to overestimate external goods, it enables us to dwell in the inner pleasures of the soul, which are eternal like the soul itself, since they are built up on the firm foundation of the knowledge of truth. The most important knowledge is the knowledge of God as the author of all things, as the all-perfect Being, of whom our mind is an efflux, and the knowledge of the soul as a being differing from body. With this comes the knowledge of the infinitude of the world, which destroys the belief that everything exists for the sake of the earth, and the earth for our sakes. Knowledge teaches us to regard ourselves as parts of a whole (family, society, state), and to prefer the interests of the whole to our own. Most important of all is it to distinguish between what does and what does not lie in our own power. Only the use of our will stands entirely in our power. The feeling of this constitutes *magnanimity (générosité)*, the key to all the virtues. The magnanimous man feels his own power to perform great things, and at the same time is conscious of his own limitations. Instead of the idea of a capricious fate, which is a mere phantasm, he must hold firm to the conviction that everything rests on the eternal and immutable will of Providence. Thus the passions will be purified, and there will be room for the intellectual love of God (*amor intellectūalis*), the most lovely and profitable of all feelings which we can have in this life (although the decision is left to the theologians as to whether this love, in so far as the natural man may possess it, is sufficient to procure for men eternal blessedness). With sufficient exertion of the senses and thoughts, this may become the strongest of all feelings. As in his theory of knowledge and his natural philosophy, so too in his ethics, Descartes leads thought up to the idea of the infinite Being as its ultimate foundation. A blending of rationalism and mysticism is characteristic of Descartes, as of the seventeenth century in general. This side of Descartes' philosophy was especially developed by his successors.

THE Cartesian philosophy could not but exercise a great influence on the age, for, by its demand for methodical doubt and analysis, and by its disregard for all traditional pre-suppositions, it could not fail to arouse free inquiry and in-dependent thought. In this lay its chief importance ; for, by this means, it exercised an influence over a far larger circle than that of the Cartesians, in the strict sense of the word. By its demand for a purely mechanical explanation of Nature it worked a reform in natural science, especially in physics and medicine, even though several of its particular hypotheses were soon found to be untenable. It taught the principle of mechanism with an energy which has retained a lasting im-portance. Its spiritualistic psychology and theological specula-tions commended it to current opinion, to which the decided and absolute distinction between soul and body appeared very clear and attractive, and which, at the same time, found in the Cartesian proofs a new foundation for the harmony between theology and science, in place of that which seemed threatened by the fall of the scholastic philosophy. Thus, in the latter part of the century, we find BOSSUET and FÉNÉLON, the finest minds in the French Church, eager Cartesians. Amongst prominent Jansenists also it had its adherents, *e.g.* ARNAULD and NICOLE ; while PASCAL, the greatest figure amongst the Jansenists, took up a singular position, of which we shall speak later. Under the guidance of Arnauld, an excellent treatise on Logic (*La logique ou l'art de penser*, 1662), which is still of interest and value, was written by this school. Among the learned priests of the Oratory, too, Cartesianism met with great support. It was promulgated in wider circles, by means of popular lectures in Paris and the provinces. It may be seen from the letters of Madame de Sévigné how great was the interest it excited amongst the aristocracy, including women. It was not less widely known in Holland, where it was taken up by several of the younger teachers at the universities. But both in France and Holland it met at once with violent opposition. The Jesuits and the orthodox Protestant clergy sought, each in their own fashion, to suppress it. The new philosophy granted too much to the free human reason, and assigned a dangerous importance to doubt; it taught the subjectivity of the qualities given by the senses, which was not reconcilable with the dogma of the Eucharist (especially in its Catholic form), and besides all this, it believed in the motion of the earth and the infinity of the universe. The cause of theology seemed bound up with the old scholastic teaching. Cartesianism was prohibited in several of the Dutch universities, and its adherents were excluded from theological chairs and from the ministry. Descartes' works appeared (1663) on the Index of forbidden books at Rome, and in France repeated royal decrees forbade the exposition of Cartesian doctrine at the universities. But all this could not hinder it from becoming the ruling philosophy, whose power only came to an end in the new direction given to thought by Locke and Newton, a direction for which it itself had prepared the way.

The difficulties and contradictions contained in Descartes' teaching could not fail, from the nature of the case, to stimulate the more independent Cartesians to attempt further developments of their master's teaching. There were two points in the dogmatic portion of the Cartesian system which were sure to excite criticism. One was the relation between the absolute substance (of such great importance for Descartes' theory of knowledge, natural philosophy, and ethics) and the finite substances, more especially the finite world. How can an absolute Being have a finite world outside himself? and what reality can such a world possess? This problem was bound to become especially prominent in an age which inclined to mysticism and to the recognition of absolute powers; for this was the age of absolute sovereignty in politics and, by a natural analogy, it became so in philosophy also. The Cartesian philosophy soon melted into mysticism. The second

point was the relation between the soul and body as substances which, though mutually exclusive, are yet said to be
in reciprocal action one with another.   The master himself
had declared that this could only be understood so long as
men abstained from philosophising.   Some of his disciples
continued his philosophy from this point, and found here an
incomprehensible something, which reappears everywhere in
experience where different things are said to influence one
another.   Hence Cartesianism was led to limit knowledge
to the explanation of succession and the external connection
of phenomena, whilst the inner connection was pronounced to
be incomprehensible.   Thus the way was prepared for the
treatment of the problem of causality by a later epistemology.
Both these points co-operate in what is known as *Occasionalism*
in such a manner as to render the mystical element, the inclination to centre all reality and all causality in the absolute
substance, predominant.   We will briefly consider the most
important representatives of this tendency.

LOUIS DE LA FORGE, a French physician, pointed out that
it is not more difficult to understand how the mind can move
the body than it is to understand how one body can move
another.   This thought may have been previously expressed by
another Cartesian, GÉRAUD DE CORDEMOY, a Parisian lawyer
who afterwards became tutor to the Dauphin ; and if that is
so, it is he who must be looked upon as the founder of Occasionalism.   And while de la Forge declares the relation
between soul and body can only be explained if we suppose
them to have been originally united by God, Cordemoy goes
further and teaches that, unless God intervene, it is just as
impossible for the soul to receive new ideas as it is for the
body to receive new motions.   Finite beings, souls as well as
bodies, are only occasions for God's interference.   Thus, for
example, our will is the occasion for God to move our arm.
How much the tendency to concentrate all activity in an
absolute Being contributed to the development of Occasionalism may be seen from the following quotation from the
Cartesian SYLVAIN RÉGIS : " In order, properly speaking, to be
able to produce actions, a man must act outside himself and
through himself, *i.e.* by his own power ; and it is certain that
God alone can act in this manner.   From this it follows that
God is the only truly efficient cause."

This thought was logically developed by ARNOLD GEULINCX, a Cartesian of the Netherlands. Geulincx was born at Antwerp, of Catholic parents, in 1623. He studied at Lyons, where he became professor. As a Cartesian he was regarded with small favour, and means were found to drive him from his post. He next went to Leyden, where he became a Protestant. After a succession of calamitous years, during which he was active as a teacher of philosophy, he died at Pesth in 1669, shortly after he had been appointed to a professorship at the university. The most important among the works of Geulincx which appeared during his lifetime is his *Ethica* (which, however, was not published in complete form till 1675). His occasionalistic teaching appears partly as the background of his *Ethica*, partly—and in more detail—in his *Metaphysic* (1695), published after his death.

The chief characteristic of Geulincx's philosophy is a curious blending of rationalism and mysticism. At the same time, we may see clearly in him how the problem of causality grew up out of the Cartesian doctrine of substance.

Geulincx developed his system of ethics in sharp contrast to the prevailing Aristotelian ethics which starts from man's striving after happiness, and lays great stress on practice and unconscious habit. According to Geulincx, morality consists in obedience to the law of Reason which God has deposited within us. Not in obedience to God's will, for this will be fulfilled whatever we may do, moreover everything, however exalted and holy, is subject to the decision of Reason. Ethics presupposes knowledge of Nature, for Man must learn to know his place in the world in order to be able to act rightly. Self-examination (*inspectio sui*) is the foundation of ethics. It teaches me that only my thoughts and my will belong to me, while my body is a part of the material world. Now in the material world I have produced nothing, and am not able to produce anything; for by what right do I dare to assert that I produce something, when I do not know at all how it has arisen? And moreover my activity cannot extend beyond the limits of my being; it cannot exercise itself on other things. My will has significance for my own soul only. Neither can things affect each other or me. How can the action of a thing, which is its own inner condition, be significant for other things? It does not know itself how changes external to it are brought about ; its inner condition certainly does not extend to other things ! If thou thinkest that thou thyself movest thy limbs, although thou knowest not how this happens, thou mightest just as well believe thyself to have written the *Iliad*, or to have set the sun in its course in the heavens ; and the child in the cradle might, with equal right, think that its will sets the cradle in motion directly, when its mother fulfils its wish to be rocked. If my willing and doing are to reach beyond my own being, God, who is the only true and efficient cause, must interfere. Finite beings are only occasions or instruments for the activity of the Deity. He who imparts motion to matter and invests it with laws, forms my will also, and unites it in such a way with the material body that will and movement must correspond to one another like two clocks, which follow the same course and strike at the same time, not because the one affects the other, but because they are made by one and the same maker. More striking than this simile, which had been already used by Cordemoy, and has become classical in the discussion on the relation between soul and body, is one which Geulincx uses in his *Annotata majora in principia Cartesii.* If, in return for money, I can procure food and clothing, this is not brought about by the metal's own natural power, for the worth of this is determined by human institution (*ex hominum instituto, quo valor iste ei consignatus est*) ; similarly, it is not material motion which is able to produce sensations and ideas n me, but this happens by divine institution (*nulla vi sua, sed instituto quodam decretoque divino*).

Through the sharp accentuation of the diversity and ex- clusiveness of individual beings, the problem of causality, which is concerned with the possibility of a transition and connection between them, is brought into prominence. And since the divine will is conceived as the one and indivisible power which embraces all individual beings and is active in them, it is at the same time indicated that the problem is altogether insoluble unless we believe in the unity of existence behind all differences, in a continuity which extends through and beyond all these differences. When it is finally said that not motion itself but an element contained in it or bound up with it brings about psychical states, we get a hint of a solution of the problem of the relation of soul and body deeper than that offered by Cartesianism. It is true that everything appears with Geulincx under a theological or mythological form, which precludes perfect clearness and consistency. Nevertheless his philosophy is of great interest on account of his emphatic assertion of the inseparability of the activity and the nature of a thing. Geulincx himself draws from his doctrine the ethical conclusion that we stand over against the world, or rather God, as spectators. For the world itself can produce no world-picture in me ; only God can do that; and as a spectator of that which goes on in the world I am a continual wonder : *ego ipse spectator mundi maximum sum et juge miraculum !* We are absolutely dependent on God's will. Thus the highest principle of ethics is : where I can do nothing I ought not to will anything (*ubi nihil vales, ibi nihil velis*) ! The cardinal virtue, therefore, in the ethics of Geulincx, is humility. A characteristic antithesis to the magnanimity of Descartes, as well as of Telesio and Campanella. The emphatic self-assertion of the Renaissance has given place to its opposite ! I have no right to anything, says Geulincx, not even to myself My task can therefore never be to promote my own happiness, but only to do my duty. In this way it is possible that my happiness may be best advanced, for, says Geulincx, our unhappiness really comes from our too eager striving after happiness. We cannot here enter into the details of this ethic of complete resignation. In many of his ethical reflections Geulincx shows tender and deep feeling.

We meet with an extreme form of Occasionalism in NICOLAS MALEBRANCHE, with whom the mystical side of Cartesianism occupies a very prominent position. Malebranche, the son of a high official in Paris, entered the Oratory in 1660, at the age of twenty-two years. His delicate health had, while he was still a child, fostered in him the love of a quiet, contemplative life, and he spent the greater part of his last years alone in his cell. He one day accidentally lit upon one of Descartes' works (*Traité de l'homme*), and the clearness with which the thoughts contained in it were developed interested and excited him to such a degree that he could hardly finish his perusal of the book. From that moment his life was dedicated to philosophy. His chief work is *La recherche de la vérité*, the first volume of which appeared in 1674. Among his other works his *Entretiens sur la métaphysique* (1687) deserves especial mention, and is considered by many to be his best work. As a writer Malebranche is clear, elegant, and ingenious, though at the same

time somewhat prolix.   Religious and philosophic interests go
hand in hand with him, and he believed he had found the way
to their complete reconciliation.   He did not see that his
thought led to results similar to those already arrived at by
Spinoza, whom he calls "le misérable Spinoza."   Like Spinoza,
too, he seems to have been unacquainted with the preceding
Occasionalists (Cordemoy and Geulincx); a proof that a
natural evolutionary tendency was here active.   Malebranche
retained his intellectual freshness to a great age, and died in
1715.

Malebranche begins his *Recherche de la vérité* with an inquiry
into the causes of error and the means by which we can free
ourselves from it.   A chief source of error is the belief that
the senses, which are given us to serve practical ends, are able
to reveal to us the nature of things ; these qualities given us
by sensuous perception we then transfer to the things themselves.   Material things in themselves are only extended, not
coloured, hard, soft, etc.   Imagination leads us astray since it
is under the influences of the senses and is, at the same time,
dependent on our feelings.   Malebranche institutes an interesting inquiry into the psychological and physiological nature of
feeling, and expresses opinions (especially on the part played
by the influence of the nervous system on the blood-vessels)
which even now attract attention.   The errors of perception, as
of imagination, arise through the influence of the body.   But
the reason also, although in and for itself it belongs to the
soul, must be subjected to criticism.   The chief question is :
From whence do we get our ideas?   We are only immediately
conscious of our mental states and activities ; other things we
know only by means of the presentations or ideas we have of
them.   Now these ideas can be produced neither by the things,
nor by us, for no finite being can be an absolute cause.   To be
the cause of anything is to be divine, and therefore it is paganism
to attribute causality to finite things.   There can only be
one single cause, and that is God ; natural causes are only
occasional causes (*causes occasionelles*—hence the name of this
whole school of thought).   When a ball is set in motion because
it is struck by another ball, this other is not a cause.   Between
the motions of the two balls there is no necessary connection.[50]
The concussion of the balls is, for the author of all material
motion, only the *occasion* for carrying out the disposition of His

will, by imparting to the ball that was struck part of the motion of the striking ball. The power which moves bodies is simply and entirely the will of Him who preserves bodies. And it is the same with the human mind ; apart from God it can neither perceive nor will. It would not help us to suppose God to have given bodies and souls the power to act, by investing them with some of His own power. For God cannot do that : God cannot create gods ! As true religion teaches that there is only *one* God, so true philosophy teaches that there is only *one* cause.

Our knowledge then can only be explained by the fact that, in respect of all our thoughts, we are dependent on God. God stands in immediate relation with every spirit ; He is *le lieu des esprits.* By means of this union with God, the author of all things, our spirit perceives created things, for the ideas of these must be in God, otherwise He could not have created them. Properly speaking all the particular ideas we have are only limitations of the idea of God, the infinite Being. Every act of thought is the nearer determination of an undetermined idea of the existing Being, from which we can never detach ourselves. Similarly all our striving is really a striving after God ; only in union with Him lies true happiness, and He it is who awakes in us the need of happiness ; but we often halt at a finite, limited good, and regard this as the highest good—as when we take finite beings for real causes. Malebranche's ethics is thus completely analogous with his theory of knowledge.

Malebranche's doctrine that we see all things in God, meets with a difficulty in the question : why then is it necessary to believe in an actual material world ? Our knowledge of Nature, according to Malebranche, is fully explained by God's working in us, and the actual material world is entirely unnecessary : God's ideas of it (intelligible extension, as Malebranche calls it) are enough. It is said that when he visited Malebranche shortly before his death, Berkeley raised this objection. The same difficulty appears in a correspondence carried on between Malebranche and MAIRAN, the mathematician, who was formerly a pupil of his. Mairan confronts Malebranche with the following alternative : either material extension does not exist (since, according to Malebranche, it is not necessary as an explanation of our knowledge of it) or else material extension belongs itself, as Spinoza taught, to the nature of God (so that we see in God not only intelligible extension, not only the idea of extension, but actual extension). The aged mystic and philosopher was much hurt by these objections, and the correspondence with Mairan was brought to a close by Malebranche's appeal to religious faith as the ultimate ground of all certainty.

While, among the thinkers above mentioned, Cartesianism led over to a theological idealism, in another circle of thinkers it contributed to the production of a new form of scepticism It contained several elements which might lead in this direction. First, there was the principle of methodical doubt, the entirely critical tendency with which Descartes' philosophy started. Not every one could pass with the same swiftness as did the founder of Cartesianism from doubt and analysis to dogmatic certainty. Secondly, the dogmatism of Descartes must itself have challenged criticism, especially since the dogmatic results presented new problems or old problems in a new form. Thirdly, Descartes had himself asserted the antithesis between positive religion and scientific knowledge ; an antithesis which might, if still more emphasised, cause men to deny any real value to whatever philosophic results Descartes might have reached, since they could never lead to the highest truth. Towards the end of the seventeenth century these motives worked in different degrees and under different forms on a succession of men who, in spite of all differences, have this in common ; that they were for some time at least under the influence of the Cartesian philosophy, and that they afterwards adopted a position of more or less decided philosophic scepticism.

JOSEPH GLANVIL (1636-80), while still young, thought himself out of and beyond Puritanism and the scholastic philosophy which prevailed during his student days at Oxford. He became a great admirer of Bacon and Descartes (especially the latter) and entertained great hopes for the future of empirical science. In his chief work (*Scepsis scientifica*, 1665), dedicated to the Royal Society, he spoke in behalf of unrestrained inquiry ; he only considered himself a sceptic in the original sense of the word, in which it means one who seeks. He is entirely at one with Descartes in his demand for a mechanical explanation of Nature (the mechanical hypothesis), in opposition to the scholastic doctrine of forms and qualities. To him Nature is the great automaton. But he

was more emphatic than Descartes in his assertion that all
our knowledge of Nature is hypothetical ; he traces out with
great zeal all the reasons indicating that imperfection must
always infect our knowledge ; and he shows how the progress
of experience itself must reveal to us fresh phenomena which
may oblige us to alter our previously constructed hypotheses.
No less strongly than the Occasionalists (although independently of them) did he bring out the difficulties which arise
in connection with reciprocal action between the soul and
the body, and he saw no less clearly, although earlier, than
Geulincx and Malebranche, the difficulties involved in any
causal relation whatever.   "We know causes," he says (*Scepsis
scientif.* chap. xxiii.), "not by immediate intuition, but by
their effects only.   If we infer that one thing is the cause of
another, we are only depending on the fact that the former
always accompanies the latter ; for *causality itself is unsensible.*
But the inference from accompaniment to a causal relation
is not necessary."   Glanvil here anticipates Hume.   He lays
particular stress on those cases in which cause and effect are
very dissimilar, and where we are therefore unable to obtain
any clear and necessary view of their mutual relation.   That,
in spite of all his critical and empirical leanings, he defended
the belief in witches was because he considered it dogmatic
to wish to quarrel with magic, since we cannot know *a priori*
what causal relations there may be in the world.   His scepticism inclined him also not to put complete trust in the "mechanical hypothesis."   In this respect he furnishes a proof,
as do also those men of intellectual kinship with him who
immediately succeeded him, that the new thought had not
yet succeeded in scaring away all mediæval notions.

High above the men who formed this group, and distinguished among distinguished men of all times, rises the
figure of BLAISE PASCAL.   Pascal (1623-62), too, came under
the influence of Descartes, and always retained some of the
Cartesian conceptions among his ideas.   His agitated and
troubled inner life caused him, however, to turn his back on
philosophy.   And yet there is always a certain relationship
between Pascal's religious thinking and the philosophising of
Descartes : both pronounce for independent conviction.   In
his *Fragment d'un traité du vide* Pascal expresses himself ad-
verse to the power of authority in the province of science, and

in his treatise *De l'esprit géométrique* he gives clear indications
of a doctrine of method which expressly recognises Descartes'
Discours de la méthode.   Later, after he had passed through
a religious crisis, he fought on the side of the Jansenists
against the validity of the papal authority with respect to
facts.   He appealed from Rome to Heaven.   And, with regard
to the condemnation of Galilei, he makes (in the eighteenth
Provincial Letter) the remark, which has since been so often
quoted, that if the earth really turns she will not be hindered
from doing so by any decree, but, together with all the men
upon her, will go on turning whether the latter believe it or
not.   Like Bruno and Descartes he believed in the infinitude
of the universe ; and, in his religious agitation, he dwelt on
this thought, that his soul might grow faint at the realisation
of its own impotence.   He is at one with Descartes in his
conception of soul and body.   The body is for him only a
machine, an automaton.   He uses the sharp antithesis between
thought and extension in order to bring out the spiritual
dignity of Man ; as a material being, indeed, Man is nothing
in respect of mere bulk ; he is only a reed—but a *thinking*
reed !   This is a truly Cartesian thought.   Though this
thought could fill Pascal with enthusiasm, yet in his eyes it
did not embrace the highest.   Above the world of matter
and of spirit he found the supernatural world of love, which
is immediately revealed to men by God.   Religion is the
heart's direct experience of God (*dieu sensible au cœur*).   The
philosophic adducement of proofs may, under favourable circumstances, lead to the God of truth, but never to the God
of love, the one true God.   Deism and atheism are all one
and the same for Pascal.   What he desires is to have his
heart satisfied, and no intellectual inquiry can help him to
this.   Besides this direct impulse to unite his feeling with an
infinite object, there is another psychological motive at work
in Pascal which caused him to differ widely from a man such
as Malebranche.   This is the fear which he feels at finding
himself in a world without limits and without constancy, in
a world about which knowledge can give us no certain results.
Sceptics and dogmatists dispute with one another, and neither
side can gain the ascendency—and yet one or other must
be right ; their dispute itself shows that the sceptics are really
right.   It is no good to try and found the first principles of

knowledge in human nature; for where is human nature to be found? It is either constantly changing or is dominated by custom. In practical life men are either hurried onwards by restlessness and vanity, or they observe traditional customs.

Man is full of inconsistencies and contradictions; doubt and uncertainty reign within him. " He who is to rule all things is as yet nothing but a miserable worm; he who is to be the bearer of truth is a sink of uncertainty and error; he is at once the glory and the shame of the universe." Pascal only finds one way of deliverance from all these contradictions, *i.e.* the refuge afforded by historically revealed religion. In this his loving and anxious soul found rest. In order to lead other men to this, he had thought out an exposition which was founded on the Bible story, and was to show how all the inconsistencies and contradictions in Nature and in the circumstances of human life vanish in the light of the revelation given in the Scriptures. It is certainly fortunate for Pascal's after-fame that the positive part of his apology for Christianity was never completed, so that his thoughts (*Pensées*) on human nature and its conditions, which were to have formed the pre- liminary portion only of the apology, can have full range. Pascal is inspired by a strong feeling of the importance and value of life. In opposition to the rationalistic tendency which found so much support in Descartes' philosophy, Pascal appeals to the living personality, to the heart, to the con- science, as the ultimate, decisive motive in the conception of life. A century before Rousseau, he raised the question as to the value of scientific knowledge for personal life. In his need for love and his anguish of soul he found the answer—" the whole of philosophy is not worth an hour's study"! And he formed a plan to write against those who were too much absorbed in science (*qui approfondissent trop les sciences*). That he himself found the solution in the Christian, particularly in the Catholic, more particularly in the Gallican, and most parti- cularly of all in the Jansenist, doctrine he would not regard as the effect of custom or tradition; he would not see that he thus left a weak spot open to the attacks of the sceptical argument which he himself had introduced. And when any one asked him what he ought to do, how he was to set about silencing sceptical thoughts, he always answered like a good Cartesian : We are automaton as well as spirit; both must be brought to believe, the latter through conviction and the former by habit. And if the conviction will not come, then begin with habit ; act as though thou believedst ; sprinkle holy water and let masses be said ; that will stupefy thee and make thee believe. This is to cut the knots—by means of the philosophy which he used even while attacking it.

PIERRE DANIEL HUET, Bishop of Avranches (1630-1721), was another who wished to suppress free inquiry in the interests of religious faith, which was for him, still more than for Pascal, the faith of the Church. He held firmly also to essential parts of the scholastic philosophy. He was a Cartesian for some time, and felt great enthusiasm for the clear and simple method of the new philosophy. But afterwards he began to doubt whether there could be any rational criterion of truth ; for, if so, we should require a criterion to show us that this was the right criterion of truth and so on *ad infinitum !* Descartes requires us to begin with what is simple, and from that to proceed to the complex ; but there is nothing so easy and simple that it can claim to be indubitable ! Descartes thinks that we cannot doubt thought itself ; but why not ? We only know our thoughts in the same way that we know everything else—by directing our attention to them, *i.e.* by a new thought. We can never reach an absolute beginning in this way. The *Cogito ergo sum* of Descartes is an inference, the validity of which is open to doubt, and his proof of the existence of God falls to the ground when we see that existence is not a quality. Only the authority of tradition and of the Church can afford a foundation for knowledge, and Huet, the learned Humanist, who was repelled by the Cartesians' want of appreciation of the ancients, tried to show that the religions and the philosophical systems of antiquity were due to a tradition of Jewish origin.

PIERRE BAYLE (1647-1706) had become acquainted with Cartesianism while studying at Geneva, where it supplanted in his mind the scholastic philosophy which he had pursued in a Jesuit college. He especially admired the Cartesian exhortation to use clear and distinct concepts and to trace back complicated questions to simple and immediately evident propositions. Later, during the years in which he was active at the universities of Sedan and Rotterdam, he adopted a critical attitude towards several of the Cartesian doctrines. He was, properly speaking, a man of learning and literature rather than a philosopher ; he took an interest in literary phenomena and speculative views in all their many-hued variety, and the impulse to seek for clear and distinct concepts caused him to still more accentuate already existing differences of standpoint, to bring into prominence the point of a problem, and to reveal illusory solutions.   LUDWIG FEUERBACH, in his masterly characterisation of Bayle, points out that he was anything but a systematic doubter, but that the difficulties and diversity of individual problems produced doubt in his mind. He looked upon philosophy as criticism ; its importance as negative rather than positive.   Its results are distinctly at issue with those of theology.   Bayle proves this in the case of one particular dogma (that of the fall of man) by placing side by side a series of theological and philosophical principles which evidently admitted of no reconciliation.   By means of this comparison (which occurs in the *Réponse aux questions d'un provincial*) Bayle started the most important discussion on the problem of evil which had taken place since Jakob Boehme's *Aurora*.   He had already asserted, in his *Dictionnaire historique et critique*, and more particularly in his article on the Manichæans, that the admission of two principles in the world, a good and a bad, would be very difficult to dispute if it were defended by unprejudiced and acute thinkers.   Had Augustine not abandoned the teaching of the Manichæans, he would, Bayle thought, have been able to make something out of it which would have brought much confusion into the ranks of the orthodox.   This doctrine cannot be refuted by way of the reason.   Man has the choice between reason and faith, and faith appears all the more glorious in proportion as the dogma to be believed is contrary to reason.   Bayle had, of course, made his own choice, and was quite sincere in drawing this sharp distinction.   Nevertheless this choice did not prevent him from recognising a humanity independent of all dogmatism.   He lays great weight (especially in the *Pensées diverses à l'occasion de la comète*) on the natural instincts which, without conscious reasoning, preserve the individual and the race.   And with regard to men's way of acting in general, both in public and private life, he affirms that it is determined far more by their natural temperament and character than by any beliefs or non-beliefs.   He therefore declares himself (which gave great offence) quite well able to conceive a State made up of atheists.   LUDWIG HOLBERG remarked later, in respect of this very line of thought of Bayle's, that it rendered futile the whole dispute as to how far freethinkers could live a moral life (*Ep.* ii. 10).   This line of thought connects itself naturally with Bayle's eager struggle for tolerance, and not less with his assertion that ethics preserves its independence over against theology.   The Cartesian method is here applied by him in the most interesting manner : as the axiom that the whole is greater than its part is so clear and distinct that we should not dare to believe any revelation which contradicted it, so also are the simplest ethical judgments by which we distinguish good from bad so clear that no revelation could annul them ; on the contrary, indeed, they serve as the criterion by which the validity and the worth of all revelation must be tested.   If we reject the natural light here, we are left without any standard at all.   At this point in Bayle's argument a possibility presents itself, by means of which the struggle between faith and knowledge would lose its significance : the possibility, namely, that the natural instincts and the immediate sense of the true and good suffice to support life !   It was the task of the eighteenth century to develop this possibility which had already been grasped by the Renaissance in its discovery of Man, but which, owing to the victorious reaction, had not been able to penetrate beyond a narrow circle of thinkers.   Moreover it was a thought which required still further development.

CHAPTER III

PIERRE GASSENDI

PIERRE GASSENDI formed the counterpoise, in the French world, to Descartes, although in virtue rather of his method than of his results. His ideal was to be an empirical philosopher and to defend perception against Descartes' intuitive and deductive method. While Descartes soared, with greater haste than even his own method permitted, to the highest ideas of all, and was inclined to consider these as founded immediately in the human mind, Gassendi asserted the empirical origin of our ideas. The polemic which he published against Descartes (*Disquisitio metaphysica*, Amsterodami, 1644) ranks among the most interesting records of the controversy between·the empirical and deductive schools. That Gassendi nevertheless ends with spiritualistic conclusions is due to his clerical office, which obliged him to unite theology with his empirical philosophy. Born at Digne, in the south of France, in 1592, he became first a preacher (1617), and afterwards a professor of philosophy at Aix, which post he abandoned in order to undertake a mathematical professorship in Paris, where he was active till his death (1655).

Gassendi published in his youth a sharp criticism of the scholastic philosophy ; but, afterwards, the strict decree of 1624 against the new doctrines and, later, the condemnation of Galilei, caused him to keep in the background. He occupied himself with physical and astronomical studies, but did not dare declare himself in favour of Copernicanism. In his later writings he developed atomism, partly under the form of a revival of Epicureanism. He defended the personality and philosophy of Epicurus against the usual charges. These works were of great importance, since the atomistic theory for which Bruno and Basso had prepared the way was especially

S

suited to the requirements of the modern science of Nature. Gassendi was an admirer of Galilei's, and his principles of natural philosophy betray the latter's influence. Starting from the axiom that nothing can become nothing, or can arise out of nothing, and that therefore, throughout all changes, a something must persist, he asserts that if change is to be explained at all, the something which persists through all changes, *i.e.* matter, must be made up of a manifold of solid and indivisible elements, *i.e.* atoms. Mathematical division can be continued *ad infinitum*, but physical divisibility has a definite limit. Through the motions of the atoms all changes in Nature are to be explained: all causes are motions. Between the atoms lies empty space, otherwise it would not be possible for them to move. Space, like time, is a thing *sui generis*, which cannot be termed either being or quality. Motions can only arise and cease by means of contact; all causes therefore must be material. The soul only moves the body in so far as it is itself material (as the vegetative and sensuously perceiving soul). Gassendi differs from Descartes in asserting that we must attribute more than extension and mobility to matter; and also in his limitation of physical divisibility. At the same time he teaches (clearly under Galilei's influence) that it is not motion itself, but the impetus to motion which is constant; the impetus does not cease to exist when motion passes into rest. These modifications of the new mechanical conception of Nature indicate a decided advance. On the other hand, Gassendi reminds us of the predecessors of Descartes and Galilei, especially Telesio, when he assumes that all atoms possess feeling, and this view, as well as the notion of a world-soul, is carried out in his natural philosophy. A similar incompleteness arises through his attempt to unite spiritualistic ideas with atomistic and mechanical doctrines. Atoms are created by God: God and the supernaturally given soul or part of the soul (*anima rationalis* or *intellectus*) form exceptions to the axiom that all causes are material. This compromise was still more inconsequent than the Cartesian, since it split up the soul itself into two parts, one material and the other immaterial. But it had this advantage: it accustomed people in the learned and especially the theological world, to no longer regard atomism as an absolutely godless doctrine. Natural Science might now undisturbedly avail herself of the atomistic hypothesis.

CHAPTER IV

THOMAS HOBBES

(a) *Biography and Characteristics*

THE alarming rumours of war, occasioned by the news that the Spanish Armada was putting out to sea (1588) for the purpose of invading England, so affected the wife of the Vicar of Malmesbury that she was brought to bed prematurely of a son. "She bore twins," said Hobbes later, in a versified autobiography, " namely myself and fear." He attributed his timorous and peace-loving disposition,—which, however, as his life shows, did not preclude energetic thought and a taste for literary polemics,—to this circumstance. He received his earliest education in his native town ; at the age of fifteen he went to Oxford, where he studied scholastic logic and physics, which, however, failed to excite his interest. While still a youth, he left the University and became tutor to a young nobleman, of the Cavendish family. With this family he remained in friendly relations throughout his life. His position occasioned repeated journeys in different countries of Europe, and he thus gained experience of the world. He also devoted himself, with much ardour, to the study of literature, more especially to the classic historians and poets. At the same time, he attentively observed the course of events in his own country, and there can be no doubt that he had in his mind the thunder-clouds, which, even in the early years of Charles I.'s reign, were threatening the political horizon, when working at his translation of *Thucydides*, published in 1629. For some time, however, his interest was diverted into quite another channel. He accidentally came upon Euclid's Geometry, and thus discovered the existence of a strictly deductive science. Up till now he had been in complete ignorance on the subject, for mathematics did not then form part of the ordinary educational curriculum in England; indeed it was looked upon as devilry. He had now found a model for his thought. Mathematician by profession he never was. His later attempts in this direction turned out anything but happily, and involved him in tedious literary disputes, in which he was decidedly worsted. But the foundation of his philosophy was now laid. The great importance which he attributes to deductive thought places him near Descartes, while it sets him in direct contrast to Bacon, with whom, in the last years of his life, he had been in personal contact, acting as his secretary and assisting him with the translation of his works into Latin. Bacon, however, exercised no marked philosophical influence upon him, though single passages can perhaps be pointed out in which, after he had been started on his own particular line of philosophic thought by influences coming from elsewhere, he adopted Baconian ideas and wove them into his system. The problem which first set him thinking occurred to him, according to the account given by his earliest biographer, in the course of a conversation, probably held among a group of scientific men in Paris, in which the question as to what sensuous perception really is was incidentally raised. As this question remained unanswered, Hobbes began to turn it over in his own mind. It now became evident to him that if material things and all their parts were always either at rest or in uniform motion, all difference (*discrimen*) between things and, with this, all sensuous perception, would cease to exist. From this he inferred that change of motion (*diversitas motuum*) is the cause of all things. From that moment, as he himself has told us, day or night, waking or dreaming, he had no thought for anything but motion. He perceived that the deductive method with which he had lately become acquainted in its most perfect form, was eminently suited to the application of his fundamental principle that everything is motion. It was probably at this time too (*cir.* 1630) that he arrived, independently, at the conviction of the subjectivity of the sense-qualities.[51] That Galilei had already, in 1623, asserted this principle, Hobbes was not aware. Not until some years later, when on a journey in Italy, did he make the acquaintance of the man of whom (in the dedication to the *De Corpore*) he has said: "He has been the first to open to us the door to the whole realm of Physics, *i.e.* the nature of motion." The train of thought upon which he had already entered now acquired a more definite form and a firmer basis. It is said that it was Galilei, too, who drew his attention to the possibility of a deductive treatment of ethics, analogous to physics. If this be true, we may say that Hobbes had already arrived at the conclusion of his system, although for a long time it existed only in his own mind and thoughts, and in the confidential exchange of ideas which took place among a group of men whom Mersenne, a monk, and a friend of Descartes and Gassendi, drew around him, and to which Hobbes, too, belonged. "From the moment," says Hobbes, in his *Autobiography*, "in which I imparted my ideas to Mersenne, and he again made them known to others, I, too, was reckoned among the philosophers. His cell was better than all the schools." It was Mersenne, too, who afterwards put Descartes' "Meditations" into the hands of several thinkers, amongst them Gassendi and Hobbes, and thus evoked one of the most remarkable discussions of the seventeenth century. Hobbes's criticism of Cartesianism is interesting for the light that it throws on his philosophy, before it had been developed into systematic form. Hobbes, who had been left in pecuniary independence by the late Lord Cavendish, now hoped, on his return to England after an absence of several years, to be able to elaborate his ideas in a threefold system, Corpus—Homo—Civis, *i.e.* a doctrine of the laws of Matter, Man, and the State, carried out as far as possible by the deductive method, and founded on the general laws of motion. The execution of this plan, however, was delayed for a long time, owing to the outbreak of civil war in England. A man of his temperament could not but observe the mounting passions of the political struggle with the gravest anxiety. It was a quarrel which seemed to him to threaten entire destruction to all orderly civil life. He anticipated with horror the unbridled ascendency of the elementary impulses. His experience of life had taught him that the egoistic and self-preserving instincts may work for ill as well as for good, and that only a great power can confine these forces within their proper channel. He was ultra-conservative precisely because his theory was ultra-radical and went back to strictly elementary principles. His intercourse with the aristocracy had also, no

doubt, exercised great influence in the determination of his
political sympathies. He misinterpreted, therefore, the significance of the English Revolution, although he condemned it
on entirely naturalistic grounds ;—a motivation which was
diametrically opposed to that which was held by the adherents
of the Stuarts. For Hobbes, the principle of authority was a
derived principle, while the Stuart party regarded it as absolute,
divine, and supernatural: the significance of this difference
became evident enough when Hobbes elaborated his political
theory. And it is the motivation, rather than the results, of this
theory which has given it a permanent and, in a certain sense,
unique importance in modern ethics and political theory. In
the year 1640 he completed the work which contains the
leading features of his psychological and ethico-political
theories. This work, copies of which were circulated in manuscript, afterwards appeared in two parts, *Human Nature* and *De
Corpore politico*, and has recently (1888) been edited by Tönnies
after the oldest MS. and under the original title of *Elements
of Law*. It is one of Hobbes's freshest and most instructive
works, and should form the foundation of every study of his
philosophy. Written as it was with the disturbed state of
public affairs before his eyes, it has all the force of an exhortation. Hobbes believed he would have been exposed to personal danger from the Opposition, had the King not dissolved
Parliament. As disturbances increased and the new Parliament began to take strong measures against the adherents of
the King, Hobbes fled (end of 1640) to France, that he might
be able to continue his studies in peace. But the grave events
that were taking place left him no quiet in which to divert his
mind from political problems, and he now elaborated the last
part of the *Elements of Law* into an independent work (*De
Cive*), which appeared in 1642 in a smaller, and in 1647 in a
larger, edition. This was to form the third part of the complete system. It differs from the earlier treatise in the much
stronger emphasis which is laid on the contrast between the
condition of Nature and civil life, and in its insistence on the
necessity of handing over the supreme power in religious
matters to the State. Hobbes was radically opposed to all
hierarchies, Protestant as well as Catholic, a circumstance
which rendered his sojourn in a Catholic country and in a
circle of banished clerical Royalists anything but secure. A

formal breach occurred when he laid aside his study of natural philosophy in order to write a political work. This was his famous book, *Leviathan ; or the Matter, Form, and Power of a 'Commonwealth, Ecclesiastical and Civil*, which appeared in London in 1651. It is called after the powerful sea-monster, mentioned in the Book of Job, of whom it is said : " Upon earth there is not his like, who is made without fear." Hobbes compares the absolute power of the State to this powerful monster. He carried out the doctrine of sovereignty founded by Bodin and Althusius to its extremest consequences—though on a naturalistic basis, and in an anti-hierarchical spirit. That he did not specially assert the absoluteness of the kingly power, but rather that of the State, has been interpreted (without any justification) as a sign that he hoped to gain Cromwell's favour by this work. He offended the ecclesiastical Royalists, too, by saying (in the concluding section omitted in the later Latin edition of 1670) that as Elizabeth had overthrown the Catholic hierarchy, so the Presbyterians had overthrown the Episcopalians, to be in their turn overthrown by the Independents, " and thus we are brought back to the independency of the early Christians." In consequence of this, Hobbes lost his post as teacher of mathematics to the young king, Charles II., and was denied admission to the Court. Affairs were now settling down in England ; there was once more an established and ordered power in the State, an executor of the sovereignty, and Hobbes thought it would be safest for him to return home. After a troublesome winter journey he arrived in England towards the end of 1651, and the perfect freedom of the press was now of great service to him, allowing him to carry out undisturbedly the publication of his works, which he had always kept in view. In 1655 appeared the *De Corpore*, which contains the logic, the doctrines of first philosophy (*philosophia prima*), of motion and magnitudes, and of physical phenomena ; and, in 1658, the *De Homine*, which is chiefly a treatise on optics (in order to elucidate the nature of the sense of sight) and only contains beyond this a short sketch of the psychology of speech and feeling. This second part is not to be compared, either in content or form, with the first part of the *Elements of Law*, or with the opening chapters of the *Leviathan*. The third part consists of the work which had already appeared as the

De Cive, and with this the whole system was completed. Then came the Restoration, which Hobbes greeted with joy. He won the favour of his former pupil, Charles II., who often entered into conversation with him. He passed a studious old age in the Cavendish family, busily engaged in mathematical and theological controversies. His anti-hierarchism was taken for atheism, and a "Hobbist" was identical with a freethinker. Although he assigned to the State the sole right to decide what should be taught, yet he himself expounded the Bible in a critical and rational spirit. For him, the primitive faith of Christianity was simply that Jesus was the Messiah, and contained no speculative doctrine at all. He repudiated eternal punishment and did not believe in disembodied spirits. Generally, however, he falls back on the incomprehensibility of the dogmas of faith, and advises that they should be accepted uncritically, just as it is best to swallow bitter pills whole, without chewing them. Hobbes preserved his physical and mental vigour to a great age, and was ninety-one years old when he died (1679).

Hobbes is an acute and energetic thinker. He instituted the best thought-out attempt of modern times to make our knowledge of natural science the foundation of all our knowledge of existence. The system which he constructed is the most profound materialistic system of modern times. Moreover Hobbes's works, which are distinguished by their powerful and clear exposition, contain many interesting observations on logic and psychology. He may be called the founder of English psychology, that is, of the English school of philosophy. It was his ethical and political views, however, which exerted the greatest influence upon his contemporaries. His sturdy, although one-sided, naturalism, challenged men's opinions, and brought them into a state of flux. In the sphere of mental science he effected a breach with Scholasticism similar to that instituted by Copernicus in astronomy, Galilei in physics, and Harvey in physiology. Hobbes, with justifiable pride, ranges himself alongside of these men as the founder of sociology : this science (as he remarks in the preface to the *De Corpore*) is no older than his own *De Cive*. The naturalistic basis which he gave to ethics and politics originated a movement which has been strikingly compared to that inaugurated by Darwin in the nineteenth century.

(b) *Primary Assumptions*

Science, according to Hobbes, stands in antithesis partly to sensuous perception and memory, partly to theology. Unlike sensation and memory it does not stop short at particular phenomena but seeks to know these through their causes; sometimes it passes from cause to effect, sometimes from effect to cause. It follows from this that science is only concerned with that which has a genesis; hence theology, the doctrine of the eternal "ingenerable" God, is excluded. So at least, says Hobbes, do I define science. Other men may perhaps prefer another definition:—that is their affair. Definition is free and arbitrary; it is only an explication of the meaning of a name, and the use of a name is arbitrary. Science begins with the definition of its fundamental concepts. These concepts are discovered by an analysis (*resolutio*) of that which is given to the senses (*a sensibus ad inventionum principiorum*). The validity of the principles of the fundamental concepts cannot itself be a subject of proof, but only of definition. They are known in and for themselves—otherwise they would not be principles at all. Since they are established by the arbitrary imposition of names it is we ourselves who produce them. Not science, but artificial construction, establishes principles; here we ourselves create truth : " *ratiocinationis prima principia, nempe definitiones, vera esse facimus nosmet ipsi per consensionum circa rerum appellationes*" (*De Corpore*, cap. 25, 1 ; cf. cap. 3, 8-9).

Strictly speaking it is not until we come to the *De Corpore* that we find any distinct emphasis laid by Hobbes upon the purely arbitrary element in the establishment of first principles ; in the *Elements of Law* it appears much less distinctly. It is due to the constantly increasing prominence given to the deductive method ; if all true science is deduction, the premisses of the deduction, which cannot themselves be deduced, must be purely arbitrary. But then it is not easy to understand what is meant by saying that principles must be "known in and for themselves" (*per se nota*), if this is to mean anything more than that we are aware of the meaning of the words. And even

this immediate consciousness is a premiss which itself needs
to be established.   It is a kind of intuition, or, as Hobbes
himself somewhere calls it,[52] a " reflection."   Hobbes, indeed,
goes on to explain that we arrive at principles through resolution
or analysis (*resolutio analysis*) of the given ; but then we are
no longer free to choose what principles we shall establish, and
there is more in their establishment than a mere imposition of
names.   Hobbes expressly says that analysis is a conclusion
from the given to principles or definitions (" *analysis est ratio-
cinatio a supposito ad principia, id est, ad definitiones,*" *De
Corp.* cap. 20, 6): that is, the first principles of inference are
themselves established by means of an inference, inasmuch
as they are established by analysis !   It thus appears that
the establishment of principles is not such a simple matter
as the theory of arbitrary naming would have us believe.

Hobbes has limited freedom of choice in the establishment
of principles or the imposition of names in yet another way.
We must not give one and the same thing two names which
contradict each other.   Hobbes (*De Corp.* cap. 28) declares this
principle to be the principle of all inference, that is, of all
science.   At the same time, there is nothing arbitrary in the
principle itself ; it implies a limitation of my choice,—for, if I
have once given a thing a name, I cannot go on to give it
any other at will.   The same holds good wherever we construct : the first step may be purely arbitrary, but the others
are determined by the first.   Notwithstanding the vacillation
and one-sidedness which Hobbes here displays, much credit is
due to him for the prominence into which he brought the
active and constructive element in knowledge.   This was not
sufficiently brought out either by Descartes or by Bacon, and
they accordingly give no adequate indication of the crucial
point at which thought turns from induction and analysis to
deduction.

When once we have arrived at first principles by way of
analysis, the next step is to deduce phenomena from them.
Hobbes takes as his general principle : there is only one cause
of all the properties presented to us by phenomena, and that is
motion.   This assertion requires no proof, he says : it will be
admitted by all who think the matter out without prejudice
(*De Corp.* cap. 6, 5).   After this proposition, that all change
is motion, follows a series of other propositions which Hobbes

incidentally introduces, without examining their precise relation either to each other or to the first. Such are the general law of causation (given in his work *On Liberty and Necessity*), the law of inertia, the proposition that the cause of motion is always contact with a moving body, and the law of the conservation of matter. In one single passage, however, Hobbes demonstrates the proposition that all change is motion, by means of the laws of causality and inertia. We further find occasional demonstration of these two propositions, although a closer scrutiny shows that they presuppose the very thing which was to be proved.[53]

On the proposition that all change is motion, and on the laws standing in more or less close connection with this, Hobbes attempts to build up his system by the deductive method. First of all, logic must examine the method and first philosophy (*philosophia prima*), the most important fundamental concepts. After this, geometry has to discuss the mathematical laws of motion, mechanics the effects of the motion of one body upon another, physics the effects of the motions which take place in particles of bodies, and the doctrine of man and the State (or the mental sciences, as we should say), the motions which go on in the minds of men, and which determine their behaviour to one another. If the system admitted of a purely deductive development we ought to find in all these different branches simply a more and more special application of the general laws of motion : beginning with the initial postulates of our own construction we should pass through the graduated series of Corpus—Homo—Civis, and this is evidently the ideal which Hobbes had before him. But we saw, on Hobbes's own showing, that the doctrine of the free construction of postulates only holds good with important reservations, and we find him further admitting that there are two points of his system where the strict deductive argument suffers interruption ; the conditions are too complicated to be elucidated by a single progressive method.

Although, according to Hobbes, science proceeds partly from effects to causes and partly from causes to effects, yet he is quite clear that we only have strictly necessary knowledge when we pass from cause to effect. If we begin with a given phenomenon and regard this as an effect, the knowledge of the cause can never be more than hypothetical : we can then only

discover the way in which the phenomenon *may* be produced ;
but whether it really *is* produced in this way cannot be
decided by a purely deductive method.   If we start from the
given, and ask for its real causes, we are not ourselves producing
principles, but are obliged to try and find those which are
employed by the author of Nature in its production.   Here lies
the point of divergence between physics on the one hand, and
geometry and mechanics on the other (*De Corp.* cap. 25, 1 ;
De Hom. cap. 10, 5).   When, then, we pass over from
mechanics to physics we have to pause in our deduction to ask
what the given phenomena are, and to frame our hypotheses
by an analysis of them.   The question now arises whether
something analogous is not also true with respect to the
· presuppositions of logic, of first philosophy, of geometry, and
of mechanics, in which case these presuppositions would also
not be apodeiktic, but merely of a hypothetical nature.   This
seems to be shown by the fact that they can only be discovered
by analysis.[54]

The other point at which the continuous procedure of the
system is inadequate to the increasing complexity of conditions is at the beginning of the mental sciences.   For
deduction from the laws of mechanics and physics is not the
only way, Hobbes says, to discover the causes of psychical
motions; every one of us, by means of self-observation (*per
unius cujusque proprium animum examinantis experientiam*), can
know the principles, *i.e.* human feelings and impulses and
their tendencies, on which civil philosophy rests.   Accordingly
we can arrive at civil philosophy not only through the long
series of deductions which begins in geometry and passes
through mechanics and physics, but also directly and induc-
tively, from the facts of self-observation, taken as new starting-
points for deduction (*De Corpore*, cap. 6, 7).

Hobbes recognises here the independence of empirical
psychology over against the science of material nature.   He
has the greater reason to draw attention to this point, since
he had himself published works on psychology and civil
philosophy (*Elements of Law, De Cive,* and *Leviathan*) before
publishing the work which, in the system, precedes the mental
sciences (*De Corpore*).   He ought to have gone one step
farther.   For what, on the physical side, could be deductively
understood, could never be more than the physiological events

in connection with mental phenomena.   As phenomena of
consciousness, mental phenomena can only be known by means
of induction, *i.e.* through self-observation : the interruption of
the deductive process is therefore more serious than Hobbes
perceived.

A closer examination, moreover, shows that these two
points are connected together.   For the reason why we must
interrupt deduction in passing from mechanics to physics is
really this,—that physical phenomena, though they present
themselves to us as qualities, are, in truth, only due to the
perceiving subject.   The data of physics are therefore subjective
phenomena, the objective cause of which we have to seek ;
and this cause, on Hobbes's assumptions, must necessarily be
motion (*De Corpore*, cap. 25, 3).   Hence it is, at both points,
mental phenomena which interrupt the uniformity of his
method and of his system.

(c) *The Object of Science*

In accordance with his fundamental principle that all
change is motion, Hobbes explains that the object of knowledge is the corporeal.   By body (*corpus*) every one will
understand that which is independent of our thought and
which fills a portion of space.   As independent of us it is
called substance.   Body and substance are one and the same.
An incorporeal substance is for Hobbes a contradiction.   We
do not, however, conceive substance and body immediately,
but only by means of ratiocination.   We perceive qualities
(accidents) only ; of substance as such we really have no
presentation, although we infer a something underlying these
qualities.   The essential attributes of body are extension and
motion.   All other qualities are only subjective phenomena
occurring in a perceiving consciousness.   Space and time, too,
are subjective for Hobbes, for under space and time he includes
such ideas as are begotten in us by the extension and motion
of bodies, and which we could preserve even if all bodies were
to disappear.

This might be interpreted to mean that Hobbes renounced
all knowledge of the nature of things and only considered
their qualities, in so far as these can be grasped by the help
of sensuous perception.   And it is true that Hobbes was very

well aware that precisely the fact that something can appear
to us, and can be grasped by us, is the most remarkable of all
facts for the philosopher. " Of all the phenomena or appearances which are near us, the most admirable is apparition
itself (*id ipsum*, τὸ φαινεσθαι). So that if the appearances be
the principles by which we know all other things, we must
needs acknowledge sense to be the principle by which we
know those principles, and that all the knowlege we have is
derived from it. And as for the causes of sense, we cannot
begin our search of them from any other phenomenon than
that of sense itself" (*De Corpore*, cap. 25, 1).

Here perceiving consciousness is taken as the original
starting-point of all knowledge—a deliverance which calls to
mind Descartes' *Cogito, ergo sum*. Tönnies and Natorp
have contended, on the strength of it, that Hobbes's philosophy
should, rightly speaking, be called materialism. But Hobbes
can only be called a materialist when he is arguing strictly
deductively from his original postulates or definitions. His
materialism disappears wherever the strictly deductive procedure, which aims at deducing everything from the proposition,
change is motion, is interrupted. That Hobbes desires such
a deduction is indeed certain, although it is equally certain
that he could not attain to it, and that he was aware that
it was unattainable. Whether, then, he is or is not to be
called a materialist may easily degenerate into a merely
verbal dispute. Edw. Larsen (in his Monograph on Hobbes,
Copenhagen, 1891, p. 186) treats the matter as if Hobbes
were only a materialist in his doctrine of method (since, in
his opinion, our knowledge is adequate only to the explanation
of motion), while, on the other hand, he never attempts to
give a materialistic metaphysic. But this is, in my judgment,
to attribute to Hobbes a distinction between method and
system with which he was quite unacquainted, and which he
is far too much of a dogmatist to make. He assumes, as a
matter of course, that things are what our definitions declare
them to be. He is a materialist in the same sense that
Descartes is a spiritualist. The views of both involve them
in contradictions ; contradictions, however, of which they themselves were neither of them conscious.

Accordingly we find Hobbes, immediately after he has so
energetically pointed out how great a problem is involved in

the fact that anything can be a fact for us, passing on with perfect equanimity to the question of how sensuous perception, the principle of all knowledge, arises, and answering this question in the light of his first principle. Since all change is motion, sensuous perception, which arises by means of change, must also be motion. "Sense" (*Empfindung*) he says, "can be *nothing else but* motion in some of the internal parts of the sentient" (*De Corpore*, cap. 25, 2 ; cf. *Leviathan*, cap. 6). And what he here says of sense he asserts, in his objections against Descartes, of consciousness in general (*mens nihil aliud erit praeterquam motus in partibus quibusdam corporis organici*). Thus, for Hobbes, psychology is really nothing but a part of the doctrine of motion. And even where he distinguishes between motion itself and its appearance ("apparition") for us, *e.g.* when he insists on the subjectivity of the sense-qualities, he still maintains that *what really exists*, when we have feelings and sensations, is only motion. "Pleasure," for example, "is nothing *really* but motion about the heart" (*Elements of Law*, vii. 1). "Apparition," conception, feeling, consciousness, are for Hobbes, when he is speaking strictly deductively, merely an appearance (*Schein*) ("nothing really," *Elements of Law*, i. 2, 5), an appearance, however, we must add, which gives rise to a great problem ; for motion, according to Hobbes, can only produce motion, and hence it remains an inexplicable miracle how at a certain point in addition to motion the "apparition" arises which we call consciousness.

Hobbes is important mainly for the clearness with which he has exposed the limitations of the materialistic hypothesis. His energetic deductive mode of thought led him to the crucial point here. No subsequent materialistic essay has been carried out with such clearness and impartiality as his. He has thus rendered a contribution of permanent value to the elucidation of the problem as to the place which psychical phenomena occupy in the plan of existence. Perfect consistency never goes unrewarded !

With reference more particularly to Hobbes's physics we can only mention here that, like Descartes, he did not believe in empty space, but assumed that the smallest indivisible particles move in a fluid ether, and, with Gassendi, he did not believe that motion ceases to exist when it passes into rest. He conceives space and time to be composed of small parts, each one of which is smaller than any part that experience is able to show us (*minus quam datur*); even in these infinitely small parts of time and space, motion, although in the form of tendency (*conatus*, endeavour), is present, and this endeavour does not cease to exist when it encounters an equal endeavour in the opposite direction ; it then becomes pressure (*nixus*). By the help of this concept (given in *De Corpore*, 15, 2 ; 22, 1) Hobbes, who here (as Gassendi in his corresponding ideas) is under Galilei's influence, is able to maintain, far more completely than was possible for Descartes, the continuity of matter.

(d) *Limitations of Knowledge.   Faith and Knowledge*

Every idea we are capable of framing is, according to Hobbes, finite and limited. Knowledge of the infinite is therefore excluded. When we hear the words "eternal and infinite" says Hobbes, we must be prepared for absurdities. "Infinite" can only be used in a negative sense of that to which we can set no limits. This word does not signify a something in the thing itself, but a want of power (*impotentia*) in our minds. By it we express our own limitations, not a positive quality of any being whatever. For Descartes, on the contrary, the infinite was the positive conception, and the finite arose through limitation of the infinite. This antithesis is characteristic of the different views of life entertained by these two thinkers.

There can no more be a knowledge of the infinite than there can be a knowledge of the world as a totality. With regard to the universe only a few questions can be asked—and none of them can be answered. Science can say nothing about the magnitude, the duration, or the beginning of the world, nor even, indeed, whether it had a beginning at all. Knowledge of first things, the first-fruits of wisdom (*primitiae sapientiae*) are reserved to the theologians, as in Israel the first-fruits of the harvest were offered to the priests. So Hobbes expresses himself in the *De Corpore* (cap. 26, 1). He says here, too, that we can never complete the chain of causation in such wise as to know for certain that it is impossible to proceed. For, even if we suppose a first cause, this cannot be unmoved, for nothing is moved by that which is not itself in motion ; so that where we stop, there must be something eternally in motion.   In and for itself, however, the view that the world has no beginning contains no contradiction whatever ; " therefore," says Hobbes, " I cannot commend those that boast they have demonstrated by reasons drawn from natural things that the world had a beginning." In striking contradiction to this is the way in which he expresses himself in his works on civil philosophy (*De Cive*, cap. 14-16, and *Leviathan*, cap. 11, 12). It is true he here acknowledges that God is incomprehensible, but he finds no difficulty in reasoning back from the world to God : if we went back far enough we should necessarily reach an eternal cause which did not in its turn have a cause ! Yet it is not only theoretical, but, more especially, practical reasons which lead to natural religion, for man yields obedience to God on account of his weakness and dependence.   This contrast is all the more striking since it cannot be explained by the fact that the works on civil philosophy were written before the *De Corpore*. For in the objections against Descartes, which were written nearly at the same time as the *De Cive*, it is expressly stated that the creation of the world is not susceptible of proof.   The matter can hardly be explained otherwise than by supposing that, in his political writings, Hobbes attributed, from practical motives, greater significance to rational grounds than by right belongs to them.   But he always consistently maintains that we can form no idea of God.   In this respect we are like a blind man warming himself at a fire ; of the cause of the warmth he can form no idea.   We must not transfer our qualities and states to God — neither pain, nor desire, nor understanding, nor will ; for all these, if they are to have significance, presuppose a limited being.   Only negative, superlative, and indefinite expressions are admissible, and they serve merely as an indication of our obedience and our admiration, and not as determinations of what God is, in and for Himself.   The word " incorporeal," too, can only be applied to God as a term of respect.   For since everything that exists is corporeal, God must be so also—a view which agrees with that of the old doctors of the Church.   Natural religion is not sufficient, for the reason is imperfect and the passions strong. A revelation is therefore necessary.   The place to discuss this, however, is in the philosophy of the State.   For, since it surpasses man's powers of comprehension, it can only be supported by authority, and a private individual can only gain

authority by the working of miracles: now that the time of
miracles has gone by the State must decide all religious
questions.   Religion is not philosophy, but law ; she demands,
not discussion, but obedience.

(e) *Psychology*

Hobbes is the first of that series óf eminent investigators
within the sphere of psychology who are the pride of English
philosophy.   With his usual powerful grasp and his eye for
great elementary lines, he has rendered valuable contributions
to the understanding of mental phenomena.   It was his
endeavour to find an empirical foundation for ethics and the
theory of politics that led him to psychology ; this latter has,
however, an independent interest of its own in his exposition.
We will first consider Hobbes's physiological theory, as far as
it concerns his conception of consciousness.   That which goes
on in the external world is, as we saw, nothing but motion.
When this motion has propagated itself through the sense
organs and the nerves to the brain, and from that to the heart,
it there meets with a certain opposition and counter motion,
since the internal organs themselves are always in a certain
state of motion.   On account of this counter motion, which is
a sort of endeavour outwards, we locate the object of our
sensuous perceptions in the outer world.   Hobbes gives no
explanation as to how these inner events (action and reaction)
are more nearly related to one another.   It is evident that he
is somewhat nearer than Descartes to the antique and scholastic
physiology, since he regards the heart as the seat of sensation
(although not till the *De Corp.* cap. 25, 4, and not in the
Elements of Law, i. 2, 8).   This opinion no doubt originated in
those emotional effects of feeling which are bound up with
sensations, and in which the heart plays so large a part.   The
" original " of life is in the heart, and according to the way in
which the external stimulus changes the vital motion (which is
the same as the motion of the blood), that is to say, according
to whether it helps or hinders it, arises either pleasure or pain.
By this, again, an involuntary endeavour either to continue the
pleasurable or to check the painful motion is set up.   Even
in the movements of the embryo this original endeavour (*conatus
primus*) makes itself felt.

All that really goes on in the world, according to Hobbes, is motion—motion within and without us. The subjectivity of the sense qualities is therefore, for Hobbes, a consequence of his metaphysic of motion. But he attempts to prove the subjectivity of qualities, not only by way of deduction, but also by the inductive method. Thus he points out that we see images of things in places at which they do not actually exist, e.g. in reflections, in dreams, and in illusions of the senses ; that different people conceive the same things to be differently coloured; that we sometimes see things double; that light arises from a blow on the eye or a pressure on the optic nerve, when there is no real external light. From all these he concludes that the content of our sensation is never anything but the "apparition" of motions in the brain and nerves, and is nothing real.

If the sense stimulus [55] disappear without any after effect, no sensuous perception, properly speaking, can arise. In that case we only have a fleeting *phantasma*, no *sensio*. To sensation proper belongs a judgment on objects, based upon a comparison of stimuli (*Nam per sensionem vulgo intelligimus aliquam de objectis per phantasmata judicationem, phantasmata scilicet comparando et distinguendo*). Sensation, therefore, presupposes memory and comparison. Individual sensations must be distinguishable from one another. It is therefore a necessary condition of sensation that the sense stimuli should vary. If the stimulation is entirely uniform all sensation ceases. A man who should go on looking at one and the same thing without moving would no more experience sensation therefrom than I am sensible of the bones in my arm, notwithstanding that they are surrounded by a very sensitive membrane. "To be always sensible of one and the same thing, and not to be sensible at all of anything, is almost all one." This was, as we saw, the starting-point of Hobbes's whole philosophy: without change there would be no sensation. Starting from this, and by means of the proposition that all change is motion, he reached his philosophy of motion, from which, however, the return to sensation was difficult—a difficulty which he himself, certainly, never remarked. No wonder that he so emphatically asserted that the fact that we can perceive anything (or that anything can be a phenomenon for us) is itself the most remarkable of all phenomena ; his whole philosophy turns on this, as it constructs now the causes and now the effects of sensation.

As several different sense excitations obscure one another, so also memory-images, which are nothing else than sensations weakened by the absence of their objects, are still further weakened by fresh sense excitations. In dreams, where no such fresh excitations arise, memory-images appear to be expressions of the present, and are often accompanied by features and qualities taken from other ideas. Memory-images arise according to fixed laws. They observe the order of succession of the original sensuous impressions. The motions in the brain are connected together in such wise that, on repetition of the first, the others follow after by force of cohesion, just as water on a smooth table runs after my finger, which guides a portion of it in a certain direction. Thus the idea of the apostle Andrew may make us think of the apostle Peter ; the name of the latter, again, may call up a stone, etc. This is the law now known as the law of contiguity. But Hobbes lays just as much weight on the law of interest. The course of ideas is not only regulated by the connection of the original sense impressions, but also by the influence of feeling and impulse. A certain order and a certain connection arise in our thoughts owing to the fact that we are always striving to reach an end, and that we accordingly seek for the means to its attainment. Continual regard for our end (*frequens ad finem respectio*) brings system into our thoughts. Dreams are lacking, not only in external stimuli, but also in this conscious-ness of an end ; thus the capriciousness of dream ideas becomes more comprehensible. The origin of speech, according to Hobbes, is not sufficiently accounted for by involuntary association between an object which excites feeling and an audible exclamation or an action, by means of which the feeling finds vent. Speech arises, in Hobbes's view, as al-ready mentioned, in the arbitrary imposition of names. Men make a mark by which to know a thing again, just as seafarers mark a rock when they sail past it, that they may know the place again. Speech is a mark (*nota*) for the individual before it becomes a sign (*signum*) by which he can communicate with others, and not until signs of communication have thus been established can a society arise. In Hobbes' own doctrine of association lay the conditions of a more natural and more correct psychology of speech than this theory which ascribes too much to conscious reasoning and choice. The arbitrary imposition of names is, as we saw, of great importance in his theory of knowledge. It makes the construction of first principles or definitions possible ; and when once such a construction has been carried out, all thinking, according to Hobbes, consists in the addition or subtraction of names. He tries to make all thinking a sort of algebra with names. A judgment, for example, expresses the fact that one name denotes the same thing as another name. Since Hobbes never perceived the importance of similarity in the involuntary association of ideas, he was consistent in stopping short at this entirely external conception of thought, a conception which, moreover, harmonises well with his deductive tendency.

Pleasure and pain are, as already remarked, closely connected with the furtherance or hindrance of the vital process. The impulse to self-preservation is the fundamental impulse of man. Pleasure and pain arise from its satisfaction or dissatisfaction at the moment. When we have gained experience, and, with this, the possibility of forming ideas of the future, the complex feelings arise. These, according to Hobbes, can all be traced back to the feeling of power or of impotence. If I feel pleasure in something which can afford me pleasure in the future, this presupposes that I possess the power to procure it for myself. This power may be my own mental or bodily force, or it may be the power of my friends on whose assistance I rely, or an authority by whom I feel protected ; it is possible that God Almighty alone disposes the power which causes me to be able to feel pleasure at the idea of the future. The feeling of pain, on the other hand, arises from the idea of lack of power to gain future goods, or to provide against future ills. All men have this continuous and restless endeavour after power, to which only death puts an end. We do not always expect greater joy than that which we already possess, but that which we have we wish to hold with increasing security. The special feelings arise in the course of this struggle or race between men. Exultation arises in those who surpass others, humility in those who are left behind, hope when a man is on the way, despair when he is exhausted, anger when he perceives an unexpected obstacle, the feeling of pride from overcoming a serious hindrance, weeping from a sudden fall, laughter at the sight of another's fall, compassion when we see some one, whom we wish well, left

behind, indignation when we see some one, whom we wish ill,
making progress, love when we are of service to some one on
the way, happiness when we are continually catching up those
in front of us, unhappiness when we are always left behind—
and only death puts an end to the race! As long as we
live we set ends before ourselves, and are conscious of striving.
All feeling of pleasure is bound up with the striving after an
end. Supposing the ultimate end were attained, not only all
endeavour, but also all sensation would come to an end. For
life is continual motion; if this cannot proceed in a straight
line it revolves in a circle!

In his more detailed explanation of compassion and love
Hobbes traces these feelings back to the impulse to self-
preservation and the feeling of power. Compassion arises
when the sight of the misfortunes of others causes us to think
of our own possible misfortune; love consists in the feeling of
our own power which we have when we are able to help another.
Delight in knowledge, too, is no less a species of the feeling of
power than delight in riches and rank; only knowledge gives
very little power since so few understand it. Hobbes, however,
believes also in an immediate delight in knowledge, but to this
he is not logically entitled; cruelty, he explains, is contempt
for the pains and sorrows of others; it arises from the conviction
that we ourselves are in security; on the other hand, Hobbes
thinks it unlikely that in the absence of the expectation of
personal benefit therefrom, any one could feel direct pleasure in
the sufferings of others. Hobbes's explanation of all feelings as
arising out of the impulse to self-preservation becomes, in
detail, artificial and one-sided. But he has always firm and real
ground under his feet when he regards the feelings as caused
and regulated by the struggle for existence and for advancement. He was not subtle, like LA ROCHEFOUCAULD, his contemporary, who, in the "Maxims" in which he gave utterance
to the "experiences" gathered in the Fronde and the salons of
the time, had the knack of tacking on to every feeling a conscious *arrière-pensée*. Hobbes had much more sense of the
involuntary. He was not the man to write down such a statement as this of La Rochefoucauld's: "men only weep in order
that they may gain the reputation of deep feeling, or to be
pitied, or to escape the disgrace of not weeping."

Regarding the psychology of the will, we find in Hobbes

valuable observations on the relation between instinct, deliberation, and will, directed against the scholastic psychology which
makes the will a special abstract faculty, without connection
with the more elementary expressions of activity. Hobbes's short
treatise *On Liberty and Necessity*, too, elicited by a discussion
with an English bishop, is a valuable contribution to the defence
of determinism. The bishop was of opinion that if the will
is not free, laws are unjust in so far as they forbid actions;
deliberation useless; exhortation, praise, blame, and punishment futile; and books, weapons, instruments, and medicines
of no service! Hobbes answered that law is deterrent, and
thus supplies a motive; that punishment does not torment a
man for what cannot be undone, but in order to impress him,
and to deter others; that without deliberation, action would
often be bad, or not what it might be; and that, for the same
reason, instruments, remedies, etc., are indispensable; while
praise and blame are conditioned by the utility or injuriousness of actions, and have nothing to do with necessity or
non-necessity.

(f) Ethics and Theory of Politics

With the same energy with which he founded his whole
conception of existence on the laws of mechanical motion,
Hobbes grounds his whole conception of moral and social life
on the impulse to self-preservation. If we inquire as to the
relation between Hobbes's ethics and politics on the one hand,
and the rest of his system on the other, we learn, from his own
confession, that we can reach ethics and politics in two ways;
either by deduction from physics, or by immediate psychological experience. He never, however, attempted the way
of deduction, perhaps because his ethico-political works were
written previously to those on natural philosophy.

He made no attempt to deduce the instinct towards self-
preservation from mechanics; unlike Telesio and Bruno before
him, and Spinoza after him, he did not look upon self-mainten-
ance as the general tendency of everything which exists. He
was content to assert it as a fact. But there is still a third
way in which, according to Hobbes, ethics and politics may be
approached, *i.e.* through arbitrary definition, arbitrary establishment of first principles. In ethics and politics we are

concerned with our own life, the estimation and ordering of which depends on our will. It follows, therefore, according to Hobbes, that ethics and politics, no less than geometry and mechanics, may be constructive sciences. For all moral and political laws presuppose a contract entered into by men of their own free-will, the object of which is to make social life under certain conditions possible. From this contract the particular moral and political laws may be deduced. But just as with general scientific presuppositions, so also here, regard for experience is of essential importance in the establishing of principles; the choice is not unmotived. On the contrary, not the least interesting part of Hobbes's ethico-political theory is his attempt to show how men came to construct a social life for themselves.

Experience of bitter need and danger moved them to it. It is false to believe (with Aristotle and Grotius) that men feel an original desire and need for social life. Quite the contrary. Since want and the feeling of power moves each individual to acquire as much as possible of that which Nature offers, he will be brought into collision with others, who have a similar need and feeling of power. Fear may even cause men to seek to surpass one another in deeds of violence, in order not to be overtaken themselves. That this is the case may be seen from the records of our barbaric forefathers and of savages, as also in the precautions to secure safety which we all take, as well as in the attitude of States towards one another. The condition of Nature, *i.e.* the condition of man in the absence of any social life, is that of *a war of all against all* (*bellum omnium contra omnes*). The necessities and the power of the individuals are the only rule here. If the power be small, it is supplemented by cunning. This does not mean that all men are by nature bad. Human nature itself is not bad; nevertheless injurious actions may spring from it. And even if there were fewer bad than good men, the latter would still have to take measures for security against the former.

There would be no escape from this dismal condition if it were not that reason, as well as passion, is rooted in human nature. Right reason moves men to seek for better means to preservation than those which they can reach when each man fights for himself. They discover that the evil is common and that it can be fought by common means. Thus arises the *first and fundamental moral law of Nature ;* peace must be sought, and if it cannot be attained, then occasion for war must be sought. There is this condition, however: each individual must renounce the unconditional right he possessed in the state of nature. The impulse to self-preservation dictates this renunciation. From this it follows further that fidelity, gratitude, courtesy, forbearance, and justice must be practised, and pride and arrogance avoided ; that what cannot be divided must be shared in common; that internal strife is to be settled by arbiters; that every individual must preserve his mental faculties unimpaired (for otherwise right reason and its precepts cannot prevail). All these consequences are comprehended in the old saying : Do not that to another which thou wouldest not have done to thyself. Should any one object that the laws of reason could not control the passions, Hobbes confesses that fear and hope, anger and ambition, covetousness and vanity may certainly hinder their recognition ; but yet there is no one who does not sometimes have a mind at rest (*sedatus animus*), and he will then recognise them in their necessary connection with the impulse to self-preservation. All duties and virtues proceed from the one law that peace must be procured ; they are the means to peace. For this reason the natural moral law is also the will of God ; reason is bestowed by God ; and Christ, the apostles, and the prophets proclaimed laws identical with those which can be deduced from right reason.

It is not impossible that, at this point in his thought, Hobbes was under the influence of Herbert of Cherbury, who also perceived the importance of the natural law to lie in the fact that it hindered reciprocal destruction, and who saw in the right establishment of common ideas a means to peace. It is known, from Hobbes's biography (*Vitae Hobbianae Auctarium*), that he was personally acquainted with Lord Herbert.

When Hobbes appeals to right reason he is perfectly well aware that he does not believe, with Plato and the schoolmen, in a particular mystical faculty which can supply a common measure in all decisions as to what is good and what evil. He expressly denies (*Elements of Law*, ii. 10, 5) that there can be any such perfect " recta ratio " in this world. The only constant is the goal towards which all living beings strive, and when reason awakes to clearness it will find the necessary means to the attainment of this end. Tönnies is therefore

282 THOMAS HOBBES BK. III

hardly justified in considering the use made by Hobbes of the concept of *recta ratio* as an after-effect of Scholasticism. Hobbes ascribes to reason, as its basis and content, self-preservation and the means to this end, and is quite clear that reason can only work when the mind is quiet (*De Cive*, iii. 26 : *sedato animo*). He starts from such a quiet state of mind in his construction of the principles of ethics and politics. Experience, too, had taught him that only when the impulse towards self-preservation is united with that quiet of the mind which makes deliberation possible, can there be any question of ethical rules of human conduct. An idealisation of the given, that is to say, is necessary ; for passionate excitement, as well as short-sightedness and inconsequence, must all be held aloof if we are to have "right" reason. The ideal and consistent claims made by peace must, at the same time, be sustained by a steadfast will. It is not only a question of external observation of the laws, but also of willingness to obey them for their own sakes. The natural moral law summons every individual before the bar of his own conscience (*in foro conscientiae*). Hobbes was certainly unaware of the extent to which he is here idealising. If the impulse to self-preservation in its elementary form is to be the only motive, such a conscience as Hobbes conceives,—a feeling or a will that observes the necessary conditions of peace for *their own sakes*,—becomes an impossibility. He is as illogical here as he is when he makes love of knowledge an immediate feeling of pleasure ; this, too, cannot be deduced from the impulse to self-preservation. Hobbes lacks the notion of the displacement of motives by means of which what was at first a means may afterwards become an end. Such a metamorphosis is quite conceivable on the basis of the impulse to self-preservation : it may even be that we use means best when we do not use them *as* means !

It is of little use, however, for the individual to recognise the natural law before the bar of his own conscience. An authority must be instituted, to whom all submit. The individual must transfer his natural right to such a power, on the understanding that all other men in like manner transfer theirs to the same power. This power, *i.e.* the power of the State, then concentrates in itself all the right that, in the natural condition, was divided among the many. This contract, by means of which civil life takes the place of the condition of nature, includes an agreement made by individuals between each other, and, at the same time, the common recognition of a higher power (whether this be vested in a single person or in an assemblage of several). Hobbes's teaching here differs from that of Althuşius, who separates the social contract from the institution of authority ; with Hobbes these coincide. Hobbes, however, believes no more than earlier teachers of natural law, that this contract was entered into with full consciousness ; it might have been tacit or supposed ("a supposed covenant," *fractum subauditum*), and need not have been express (*fractum expressum*). Examples of tacit contracts are to be found in the relations between the conqueror and the conquered whose lives have been spared ; if the former did not rely on the obedience of the latter, he would not have granted them their lives. There is, similarly, a tacit agreement between the tender infant and its guardian and protector, generally its mother. Hobbes *infers* from the nature of the relation that the contract was made. If the contract is supposed or tacit, it is really nothing more than a point of view which serves for explanation, and the determination of worth. But it is characteristic of Hobbes to take precisely this point of view. The contract (if it be express) presupposes that individuals, each with his impulse to self-preservation, stand over against one another as independent beings, and that society is the product of their reciprocal action. This point of view enables Hobbes to deduce the life of the State from individual self-preservation. He thinks of men as mushrooms, each of whom has shot up in his place on the earth, and who then unite together—a mental experiment necessary in the constructive method. Hobbes, however, made no express inquiry as to the relation of experience to this idea ; he never, in fact, gave any clear explanation of the relation of experience to the arbitrary presuppositions of constructive thinking.

It is evident from the theory of contract that enlightened self-interest will prompt each individual to render obedience. The power which is to be obeyed must be unconditioned. The power of the State must be as strong as possible, so that each individual shall be entirely impotent against it. The State must possess the right to inflict punishment and to declare war and conclude peace; it must have the free disposition of all property, and the deciding voice as to what opinions and doctrines are to be disseminated. Absolute power on the one side corresponds to absolute obedience on the other. Only that which is worse than death, *e.g.* to kill oneself or one's neighbour, the State cannot command. An abuse of this prodigious power constitutes a transgression of the moral law of Nature, according to which those invested with the sovereign power are also subject to the judgment of their own consciences, but it is not a transgression of the law of the State, which cannot bind the power by whose will it is administered. If it be objected that these are hard conditions, Hobbes answers that the power to protect is inseparably associated with the power to oppress. Human life can never be without un- pleasantness. The freedom of the condition of nature is combined with insecurity and strife, the bondage of civil life with security and peace. It is impossible to limit the sovereign power, for power can only be limited by power, and therefore to limit power is to divide it. If the power of the sovereign is limited, then the sovereignty really resides in the person or persons who can punish or set aside the so-called sovereign. Hobbes has here in view the attempt to distinguish between spiritual and temporal, or between executive and conferred power. Hobbes considers monarchy to be the best form of government. Democracy is, as a matter of fact, an aristocracy of orators. The advantage of monarchy is that there is only one person to misuse the power, and, more particularly, that party strife is avoided, and secrets more easily kept. As a matter of fact, it is the people (by virtue of the original con- tract) who rule; their will is executed by the monarch, to whom on account of the original contract, every man's natural right is transferred.

The decision of all religious and moral questions rests with the sovereign. The sovereign must decide how God is to be worshipped ; otherwise what is worship to one man will be blasphemy to another, and there would thus be a constant source of strife and dissolution. Neither can individuals decide what is good and right in practice ; this would occasion con- tinual rebellion. For it is evident that only when definitions are held in common can there be any security that the con- clusions will also be common. If Hobbes called ethics and politics constructive sciences, because "we ourselves" establish their first principles, in practice this "we ourselves" is identical with the sovereign.   Here the strangeness of Hobbes's stand-point comes out clearly.   His free naturalistic inquiry has led him to perceive the necessity of an absolute authority, whose reason must be recognised as the *recta ratio ;* but yet he him-self proceeds to give a foundation to this *recta ratio*, founding it in his own *recta ratio*, and availing himself in doing so of the very freedom of thought and speech whose eradication he demanded.   He employs the fruits of knowledge which he himself had plucked to emphasise the prohibition to eat of the tree of knowledge.   He availed himself of the freedom of the press during the ascendency of the Independents to publish the first edition of his *Leviathan* (1651), and later, under the Restoration, he took advantage of the absence of censorship in Holland to bring out a second edition (1670).   It must be remembered, in connection with this, that Hobbes, like so many of the best men of the seventeenth century, united in himself the strong self-esteem and love of freedom of the Renaissance with the conviction of the absoluteness of the great sustaining powers. His teaching witnesses to the strong reaction against the Renais-sance and the Reformation.   He attributes the seditious belief in the freedom of the conscience, and in the rights of individual knowledge within the sphere of morals and politics, partly to the study of Roman and Greek authors (especially Aristotle) at the universities, partly to the free reading and exposition of the Bible instituted by the Reformation.   In opposition to this he teaches the most rigid Cæsarism ; Christ's kingdom does not begin until His second coming at the last judgment ; till then God speaks only by means of his vice-gods, the executors of the political power.   He declares himself as opposed to Catholics as he is to Anglicans and Puritans.   If the Pope is to be the shepherd of the faithful, he becomes the virtual sovereign, and the State will be dissolved.   If every individual believer is to be regarded as a participator in the divine wisdom there will ensue a strife of all against all.   If the bishops are to have greater power than is granted them by their sovereigns at their installation (" the Anglicans believe they have some-thing more, they know not what, of divine right "), there will arise dissension between Church and State—and at the same time, a spiritual tyranny.   The Protestant clergy believe the

Papacy to have been overthrown that they may step into its
place. But what should we have gained by our deliverance
from the tyranny of the Pope if these petty men are to succeed
him ! especially since the mental qualities of these people are
not conducive to a peaceable civil life (*quorum ingenium paci
et societati aptum non est*)! Thus, though Hobbes begins
with a polemic against free inquiry, he ends with a polemic
against those smaller authorities who had pushed themselves
into the places of the greater. They it was at whom he was
really aiming, and the explanation of his peculiar position is to
be found in this circumstance.

Hobbes shares in the tendency to unity, concentration, and
resignation, peculiar to the seventeenth century, and which
finds expression in philosophy not only in his theory of politics,
but also, with analogous features, in the mysticism of Fénélon
and Malebranche and the pantheism of Spinoza. He has
rendered great service to the theory of politics by showing
that there can be only one centre of gravity in a State. But
this centre of gravity leads him astray : he loses sight of all
other forces except gravity, and accordingly all masses collect
round this centre. Power and obedience are everything for
him. The involuntary content of life, manners and customs,
public opinion, those still and hidden ways on which even the
executors of power are dependent, that which moves in the
hearts of the many, and on the other side, the whole development of life, the fostering and protection of which is the duty of
the State, and for which it must provide a serviceable foundation—all these things escaped Hobbes's attention. His gaze is
fastened on the one point, and his thinking is executed in the
style of a lapidary,—the finer *nuances* evade him. He has all
the more sense, however, for the great elementary conditions of
life in human society. He belongs to that particular side of
the English mind which has produced Malthus and Darwin,
both of whom may be said to have carried on Hobbes's line of
thought.

And yet, as already mentioned, Hobbes lets drop remarks
which open out a wider horizon. The duty of the ruler is
summed up in the proposition that the welfare of the people is
the highest law ; for the State was not founded for the benefit
of the ruler, but of the citizens. The despotism which Hobbes
advocates is identical with that which we meet with again in

the enlightened and reformed statesmen of the eighteenth
century (Friedrich II., Joseph II.). He is strongly opposed,
not only to all forms of hierarchy, but also to all kinds of class-
rule which are to be found even in "free" countries. By
means of the absolute centre of gravity he hopes to abolish
the lesser centres, so that all the elements may move in
their natural orbits. And this absolute authority is itself
established by reason. Hobbes hopes to profit by free discussion. He trusts his *Leviathan* "will fall into the hands of a
sovereign who will consider it himself without the help of
any interested or envious interpreter ; and by the exercise
of entire sovereignty, in protecting the public teaching of it,
convert this truth of speculation into the utility of practice."[56]
He hopes, however, not only for the enlightenment of princes,
but also for that of the people. As regards the hierarchy, he
depends not only on jealousy of political power but also on
the progressive education and criticism of the people : "paulatim
eruditur vulgus!" (*De Homine*, xv. 13). Contradiction between the different axioms of a doctrine, or between the
doctrine and the conduct of its promulgator must, sooner or
later, be discovered. A wide horizon opens here, wider even
than that which dawned on the heroes of the enlightenment of
the eighteenth century ; for Voltaire and Diderot were distinctly
averse to the notion of an enlightenment of the people (*vulgus*) ;
moreover, if we thoroughly master Hobbes's presuppositions, we
shall see that this wider outlook is not the result of inconsequence.
For the "contract" by means of which individuals resign their
own wills does not really cause them to disappear, but only takes
them up into a higher union. What we miss in Hobbes is any
indication as to how the isolated will, when it is thus interwoven
into a greater totality, can suffer a metamorphosis. With his
first and last word Hobbes points to the imperfection of his own
doctrine, an imperfection which is outweighed by the native
power and acuteness with which he founds and constructs his
theory.

(g) *Contrasting Tendencies in English Philosophy*

The history of English philosophy during the seventeenth
century is not exhausted in Bacon, Herbert of Cherbury, and
Thomas Hobbes, and in the line of thought initiated by them.
Besides this line of thought, which takes as its foundation

the data of external or internal nature, and seeks, starting from these, to arrive, by means of induction or deduction, at further results, there is another tendency connected historically with Neo-Platonism, which believes there is a foundation for the highest ideas, more especially ethical ideas, which is exalted above all experience.   To this school belongs ROBERT GREVILLE, LORD BROOKE, who fell at Lichfield, in the thirty-fifth year of his age, fighting for the Parliamentary cause (1643).   In his work on *The Nature of Truth*, which appeared two years before his death and which was perhaps evoked by the writings of Herbert of Cherbury, he protests against the view that knowledge is only a human faculty, which, in and for itself, is empty, and has to seek its content: only light is susceptible to light, and knowledge is a ray of the divine nature.   True knowledge raises us above sense—of this the Copernican system is an example. All plurality, all spatial and temporal relations are nothing but appearance ; thought only finds rest in the knowledge of the one cause of all things.   The knowledge of the unity of all things in God delivers me from envy, shows me other men's happiness as my own, destroys the darkness of the soul, and heals all pain.   Experience, on the other hand, can show us no real causes ; it can only tell us that one phenomenon precedes another.[57]

The Platonic school to which Lord Brooke belonged found shelter, in the middle of the century, at Cambridge, while Oxford adhered to Scholasticism.   A year after Hobbes's *Leviathan*, appeared (1652) NATHANIEL CULVERWEL'S *Treatise on the Light of Nature*.   Culverwel died in 1651.   He was an M.A. of Cambridge, and a Fellow of his college.   His work is as strongly Platonising in tendency as that of Brooke's, but it is less mystical, and he attributes greater importance to psychological experience.   He believes, however, in eternal truths, valid alike in the spheres of practice and theory.   These truths are one with the being of God, and are maintained in the world by God's will.   Thus with him, as with Brooke, philosophy and theology merge into one, while, with Bacon and Hobbes, they are sharply distinguished from one another.[58] In a more systematic form, this same tendency, which is characterised by the close union of Platonic philosophy with Christian theology, appears in RALPH CUDWORTH (*d.* 1688) and HENRY MORE (*d.* 1687), both of whom were active at the

University of Cambridge. While for Bacon and Hobbes the
main point is that truth must fight its way upward in the
world, and can only arise in human consciousness by means of
strenuous exertion, these men turned back to the Platonic
doctrine of eternal truth, which has no beginning, and which
the consciousness of men has only to acknowledge in order
to become participant in. This school ran counter both to
Puritanism, with its antagonism to philosophic thought, and to
Hobbes (More was also opposed to Spinoza), in whose opinion
philosophy was opposed to theology. The fact that Henry
More was moved to the study of philosophy by doubts as to
the truth of Calvinism was not without significance for his subsequent opinions ; he had been brought up as a strict Calvinist,
and the very fact that he had been able, by the energy of his own
thought, to rise above the doctrines which had been inculcated
upon him, seemed to him to witness to the independence of
thought over against all external things. This independence
he proceeded to turn to account, not only against the narrow
theology of the Puritans, but also against the realistic tendency
of Bacon and Hobbes. More was in touch with Descartes, and
adopted several of his ideas ; not, however, his sharp separation
between mind and matter. The mental in his opinion is extended, although not an object of touch. In his work *De Anima*
(Rotterdam, 1677, cap. 1) he defines the mind as a substance
which can be penetrated but not divided (*substantia penetrabilis
et indiscerpibilis*), while body is a substance which can be
divided but not penetrated (*substantia impenetrabilis et dis-
cerpibilis*). In this way he mediates between Hobbes and
Descartes and believes himself to have refuted Hobbes's objection against spiritualism, *i.e.* that we could not form any idea
of an immaterial substance. Extension must be common to
both kinds of substances ; More, indeed, goes a step farther,
since he, in common with several of the philosophers of the
Renaissance, regards space as a divine attribute ; that God
possesses extension follows from His omnipresence ! The
difference between God and individual souls consists in this
only : that God is unlimited while the soul is limited. In this
daring mysticism More is evidently influenced by the doctrines of
the Cabbala. His mystical conception of space reappears again
in Newton, who was very much influenced by More. More
differs from Descartes not only in his view that all substances

possess extension, but also in including activity (in regard to the mind, original activity ; in regard to matter, imparted activity) in the concept of substance. Thus he, like Hobbes and Gassendi, prepared the way for Leibniz' natural philosophy. We must not dwell longer on this tendency of thought, which must be regarded rather as a learned mysticism than as modern philosophic thought. For mental development in England it was of great importance ; to the history of philosophy, however, it contributed no new thoughts.

Greater interest, in this respect, attaches to an author who met Hobbes on his own ground, *i.e.* examination into the psychological basis of ethics and social life. RICHARD CUMBERLAND (born in 1632, studied at Cambridge, died in 1715 as Bishop of Peterborough) published in 1672 a work remarkable in the history of ethics : *De legibus naturae disquisitio philosophica* (A Philosophical Examination of Natural Law), which is expressly directed against Hobbes. He declares his intention of continuing the work of Hugo Grotius, although in a manner other than that adopted by the famous Netherlander. Instead of examining how the moral laws of Nature exhibit themselves in experience and history, he intends to investigate their origin and causes. In this investigation he means to start from experience, and from causes near at hand, and to reason back to those more remote. In this way he is confident that he will ultimately arrive at a divine origin of these laws ; but he scorns the " comfortable " method of the Platonists, who consider this high origin to be directly revealed by innate ideas: " I have not been so fortunate," he says, "as to gain the knowledge of natural laws in so comfortable a fashion." At any rate he will not found his ethics on such an hypothesis, although he acknowledges the healthy and good influence of "our Platonists" within the sphere of morals. In opposition to Hobbes, he emphasises the involuntary tendencies of human nature, while Hobbes had taken as his foundation the voluntary accommodation of the will. From the moment of birth there ensues a development of human capacities and powers, an involuntary use of the organs connected with immediate satisfaction. The sense-stimuli meet with an involuntary inclination to take them up, to turn towards them. In this way the first experiences are made, and the first mental operations, remembering, comparing, and counting, undertaken. In this immediate impulse (*impetus*), which is not produced, but

only evoked, by stimuli, the natural and self-evident truths
of reason (*naturalia rationis dictata*) are founded. And such an
immediate impulse lies at the root, too, of the first endeavour to
do good and to avoid evil—and this without any separation of
the particular good and evil of the individual from that which
is common to all. On the contrary, it is involuntarily acknowledged that a good common to all reasonable beings is higher than
that which falls to a single individual, and that individual beings
attain their own happiness precisely by striving for the good of
the community to which they belong. Clear consciousness
and voluntary will are only able to develop more fully what
the involuntary tendencies supply ; art may work on the basis
of nature, but it can never take its place. While, in opposition
to Hobbes, who constructed society out of fully conscious
independent individuals, Cumberland thus emphasises the
original, natural instincts, he asserts, on the other hand, that
the natural is not only that which appears in the first stages of
life, but also those ripe fruits which we find after the completion
of growth and development. The nature of man, therefore, is
not only to be sought in the elementary impulses, but also in that
which is exhibited in the highest mental development we know.
Even if men from the beginning limited their interests to themselves, it would still be natural for them to be interested
in what brings happiness to all. The state of nature is not
abandoned because a self-esteem (*generositas*) arises, for which
the good is that which promotes the preservation and perfection of the whole human race, perhaps even of the whole
universe, so far as we can have any notion of this last. Cumberland brings out firstly, the possibility of a gradual development of self-esteem (*generositas*) from the elementary impulses,
without the mediation of the notion of an external and mechanical contract ; secondly, the harmony between the individual
and the general good. In respect of both these points he
originated thoughts which were more firmly established and
further developed in the English philosophy of the eighteenth
century, and which, in his lifetime, were being quietly elaborated in Spinoza's ethics and Leibniz' philosophy of right.
Although Cumberland's exposition is confused and imperfect,
yet it contains important points. Written (according to the
title-page and preface) as an immediate attack on Hobbes, his
work has an independent importance in the history of ethics.

CHAPTER V

BENEDICT SPINOZA

(a) *Biography and Characteristics*

SPINOZA is the central thinker of the seventeenth century. In him all lines of thought converge : mysticism and naturalism, theoretical and practical interests, which, with other thinkers of his century, stand in more or less opposition to one another, and, where they occur in the same personality, excite internal conflict,—he sought to carry out logically and to show that it is precisely by means of this logical carrying out that their reconciliation is to be effected. While the majority of thinkers know of no other way in which to bind together the different strands of thought than to cut each one severally, and then to weave them together in a merely external union, the greatness of Spinoza's thought lies in this : that he imposes no arbitrary limits, but relies entirely upon the harmony founded in the innermost nature of the thoughts themselves. By dedicating his life to the labour of quiet contemplation he hoped to fashion a work, which, taking up into itself the new conception of the world and the new science, should develop their consequences, at the same time preserving the reality and independence of the spiritual,—a work in which the diversity and the individuality of phenomena should find full recognition, whilst the unity, the all-embracing world-order, should be seen to be the power which supports the innermost nature of all things and is active in all. Nor did Spinoza regard this work as of purely theoretical interest. For him it was the satisfaction of an urgent personal need for clearness and self-comprehension, and through it he gained that steadfast cheerfulness of mind which is won by soaring above the unrest and darkness of this present life to the understanding of the eternal laws. His chief work (the *Ethica*) is thus not a merely speculative work, but a work of art. It has been strikingly compared, with its five books, to a drama in five acts, a comparison which admits of being carried out in detail. In the first book are given the most general propositions, which disclose to view a grand and infinite background to human life. In the second book we have a series of auxiliary propositions taken from natural philosophy, by means of which the strictly mechanical conception of Nature is established ; then follows an examination of human knowledge. The latter part of the second book offers a provisional conclusion, and there is some ground for the hypothesis that these first two books originally formed a whole in themselves. The goal which Spinoza had set before himself, *i.e.* a knowledge of the connection between our minds and the whole of nature is in sight. This knowledge (according to an autobiographical fragment) he perceived to be the only good intimately united with his own personality of which external events could not rob him. This early close of the drama, however, is hindered by a cloud which appears on the horizon ; true knowledge is frustrated not only by want of thought and false association of ideas, but also, and above all, by the feelings and passions which dominate us. Here is a new and serious difficulty to be overcome—and if we are to overcome it, it is before all things necessary that we should learn to know it. Accordingly in the third book, Spinoza gives a masterly scientific account of the feelings. He points out the connection between the passions and the impulse to self-preservation, and shows how the former become transformed under the influence of ideas. His chief effort is directed towards finding a firmly established causal connection in the sphere of mind as well as in that of matter. He seeks for the law of the ebb and flow in which we are tossed, and it is in this law that he finds deliverance. In the fourth book light begins once more to dawn. It is true that no passion can be directly eradicated, but it may be checked by another and stronger passion. Once this is recognised, it is evident that we must let the knowledge of the good, *i.e.* the conditions for the preservation of our nature, become a ruling power within us ; this is possible since this knowledge excites pleasure in us both because it shows us the end and also because it is itself a mental activity, an expression of our power. This knowledge will unite us with individuals of

like nature with ourselves, since it shows us that we are
subjected to common conditions, and that only by a common
striving can each one of us attain the goal.   With this the
drama approaches, for the second time, its conclusion.   There
remains, however, one question, *i.e.* how can the individual
thr ugh the union of scientific knowledge (the possibility of
which is shown in the first two books), with the practical course
of development, with the education gained in the struggle for
existence (described in the third and fourth books), fully work
out his own personality ?   The fifth book shows that the clear
understanding of our passions in their natural connection raises
us above them, and unites with all the rest of our knowledge of
nature in the immediate intuition of our being as one of those
forms under which the eternal God, who works in the world of
mind as well as of matter, unfolds His nature.   Since in this
way we see ourselves—and all things—*sub specie aeternitatis*,
the unrest and darkness of time and finitude vanish away, and
with the mental freedom, the development of which is described
in the fourth book, is now united the inner feeling of union with
the eternal and infinite Being.   In this way Spinoza finds room,
within one frame, for the philosophy of religion, physics, theory of
knowledge, psychology and ethics ; moreover this development
of realism by means of the strict application of the causal law
does not in his case hinder, but, on the contrary, makes possible,
the mystical union with God.   If we bear in mind also that this
grand and complex structure of thought is presented in mathematical fashion (*more geometrico*), under the form of theorems
and proofs, we have before us the picture of a work unique in
its kind.   Small wonder that his contemporaries did not understand it ; that, indeed, the time for the comprehension of it on
the idealistic side did not dawn till one hundred years after its
appearance ; while, only in our own day, has its meaning on the
realistic side been understood.   It is the first duty of the history
of philosophy, in the case of a work of this kind, to discover how
it arose and what are its historical presuppositions.   We see it
as a polished crystal ; we should like, if possible, to discover
something of the process of crystallisation.   To this perhaps
the personality of Spinoza, his circumstances, and his philosophical development, may help us.   For it can hardly be
doubted that the varied context which is here presented in so
unique a setting is held together mainly by the personality of

the author.   An analysis of the system will then show us how the premisses and elements which the author adopted were realised by him, and whether, and, if so, how far, he attained the end he set before him.

BARUCH SPINOZA was born 24th November 1632, at Amsterdam, where his parents, Spanish Jews, had found a refuge from the Inquisition.   The gifted boy received his first instruction at the Jewish Academy in this town, where he was initiated into the doctrines of the Talmud and of mediæval Jewish philosophy.   Thus was laid the foundation of an essential side of his thought, *i.e.* of the endeavour to assert and maintain the thought of God as the one infinite Being, as He is presented in the higher national religions, more particularly in Judaism.   This oriental and mystical tendency forms the basis of all his thought, and gives it that finish and definite direction towards one single point by which it is distinguished.   He very soon began to doubt the Mosaic theology ; this aroused the suspicion of the Jewish theologians, and this, in turn, caused him to hold himself aloof from the synagogue.   He felt the need of widening his mental horizon, and began to study the humanities and natural science.   He received in- struction in Latin from Van Ende, a physician who had the reputation of being a freethinker.   The most important source for Spinoza's biography, *i.e.* the pastor COLERUS, who, in spite of his great detestation of Spinoza's doctrine, has collected, with great regard for truth, all the details of his life, hints that Spinoza learnt something more than Latin in this " school of Satan."   According to Colerus, Spinoza loved Van Ende's talented daughter who helped her father in his teaching, but was rejected in favour of a comrade, more skilled than himself in the art of wooing.   It has since been discovered that Clara van Ende could only have been twelve years old at the time here alluded to, so that this report seems somewhat improbable (although, as has been remarked, Beatrice was not more than nine years old when Dante first saw her).

Colerus says that Spinoza abandoned theology at this time and gave himself up entirely to physics.   It is probable that, among the authors whom he studied in order to become acquainted with the new conception of Nature, Giordano Bruno was one of the most important.   It is true that Bruno is never mentioned by Spinoza, yet the latter's first work (especially a

little dialogue which is embodied in the "Short Tract concerning
God and Man and the latter's Happiness") distinctly reminds us
of Bruno. Spinoza here found a philosophical conception which
enabled him to unite those religious ideas which he considered
essential with a scientific understanding of Nature. Bruno's
doctrine of the infinitude and divinity of Nature made it possible for Spinoza to bind closely together the concept of God
and the concept of Nature. This influence of the philosophy
of the Renaissance on Spinoza was only suspected on the discovery (about thirty years ago) of his first work. Up till that
time Colerus's account had been received without question, i.e.
that after Spinoza had abandoned theology for physics, he
had wavered for a long time as to which teacher he should
follow; that Descartes' works had then fallen into his hands
and had attracted him on account of their endeavour to give
clear and distinct reasons for everything. It was believed
that Spinoza began by being a Cartesian, and only gradually
assumed a critical attitude towards Cartesianism. Against this
we find that the very first work known to be by Spinoza's
hand contains a criticism of some of the cardinal points of
Cartesianism. A Cartesian Spinoza never was; but he learnt
much from Descartes and made use of several of his ideas, as
he also, to a certain extent, employed his terminology. During this transition period too, before his own system was
definitely sketched out, he must have studied the later
scholastic authors who at that time—before the philosophy of
Bacon and Descartes had won general recognition—controlled
philosophical instruction in Germany and the Netherlands.
Many of the expressions and theorems in the later as well as
in the earlier works of Spinoza, point to such a scholastic
influence, and he himself alludes to the scholastics in several
places. It becomes evident—when we take all this into
account—that, during his philosophical development, Spinoza
explored a very wide and varied field of thought, and a by
no means contemptible literature. Detached and complete in
itself as his chief work may appear to us, yet its roots branch
out on many sides within philosophical tradition.[59] But this
does not detract from his originality; it is a sign of genius
that it can assimilate and elaborate as nothing else can. The
originality and individual character of a building do not suffer
because the stones have been brought together from many

places. Under the influence of these intellectual tendencies streaming in upon him from all sides, Spinoza's views led him farther and farther from the synagogue. His public defection was anticipated and, in order to avert it, an attempt was made to detain him by the offer of a yearly pension. But neither this, nor the attempt of a fanatic to assassinate him, could hinder him from proceeding with his line of thought. He was now (1656) solemnly expelled from the Jewish congregation. His enemies even succeeded—since the Protestant clergy also considered him to be a dangerous man—in procuring his temporary banishment from Amsterdam. He lived for a time with a friend in the country, not far from Amsterdam. He gained his livelihood by polishing optical glasses, a skill which he owed to his rabbinical education, as every young Rabbi is obliged to learn a trade. His friends from the town fetched his glasses and sold them for him. It appears that, even at this time, a group of younger men gathered round him and his thoughts. His work " On God and Man " (*Tractatus brevis de Deo et Homine ejus-que Felicitate*) and perhaps the first sketch of his later "Theologico-political Treatise" (*Tractatus Theologico-politicus*) belong to this time. Spinoza turned indignantly away from the fanaticism of positive religious societies to find, with ever deepening conviction, and growing self-comprehension, the task of his life in independently working out a group of thoughts which were to throw light upon the nature of man and his place in existence. Experience had taught him (as he says at the beginning of his unfinished treatise "On the Amendment of the Understanding") that neither riches nor sensuous enjoyment nor honour can be a true good for man ; but, on the contrary, that the only thing which is able to fill the mind with ever new satisfaction is the continual striving after knowledge, by means of which the mind is united with that which remains constant while all else changes. Spinoza's thought—however speculative and abstract the form it assumed, and however remote it may seem from ordinary human life—has a distinctly personal and practical motive. Complete intellectual clearness was for him a vital necessity.

In the year 1661 he moved to Rhynsburg, a small town near Leyden. Here he began to formulate his famous work. He mentions it in letters to his friends (especially to Oldenburg and Fries). Copies of the completed part of the work appeared quite early, and Spinoza's young friends at Amsterdam, most of whom were medical students, studied the book together, and, in doubtful cases, applied to the master for explanation. His life was not so lonely as has often been described. His correspondence, which was not thoroughly known until after the find of manuscripts, about thirty years ago, when the "short treatise" was also discovered, shows him to us in contact with a not inconsiderable group of men of different positions in life and different turns of mind. The study of this correspondence is of the greatest interest for the understanding both of Spinoza and his thoughts, and also of the intellectual conditions of his time. He had several friends, too, in the neighbouring University town of Leyden. Thus he was on intimate terms with Niels Steensen (Nicolaus Steno), a Danish natural philosopher, who was studying at this time at Leyden. Subsequently, after his conversion to Catholicism, Steensen addressed a letter of invitation to Spinoza (*Epistola ad novae philosophiae reformatorem*), whom he calls his late familiar friend (*admodum familiaris*), to follow him into the bosom of the one saving church. A. D. Jörgensen, the Danish state-archivist and Niels Steensen's biographer, gives the following explanation of the silence with which Spinoza received his former friend's invitation : " The restless spirit of love characteristic of Christianity, induced Steno to attempt to make his friend a participator in the happiness of this spirit; the infinite indifference of philosophy towards the personality of the individual with its desires and griefs showed Spinoza that this man was hopelessly lost to the knowledge of truth, and that silence was the right answer to his address." In my opinion, this excellent historian (who was the first to call attention to the interesting relation between Steno and Spinoza) does a grave injustice here, both to Spinoza and to philosophy. I entertain the greatest respect for Steno, for his religious as well as for his scientific personality ; nevertheless I believe that in every propaganda, however noble a name it may adopt, other motives besides the spirit of love (if indeed this be always a factor) are at work. This spirit of love at any rate has prevented neither Steno nor very many others from rejoicing in a salvation from which, as they believe themselves to know, very many are excluded. At any rate it is unjust to deny the spirit of love to Spinoza because he would not force his views upon others. His loving faith embraced all men, and he found the human under very different forms of faith. An unbiassed witness, Pastor Colerus, relates how sympathetic he was towards others, and how he consoled and cheered his housemates when they were visited by sorrow or illness. To the question of his landlady at the Hague as to whether she could be saved by the religion to which she belonged, he answered her that her religion was good, that she should seek for no other, and that she would certainly be saved by it if she led a quiet and pious life. He had most sympathy with the freer tendencies of Protestantism. He regarded the significance of Protestantism from a different point of view to that taken by his kindred spirit Bruno ; and this was indeed only natural, for he lived in the freest country in Europe, where the importance of the struggle for religious freedom made itself felt on all sides. Afterwards, when Albert de Burgh, a young man who had lived in the same house with Spinoza, and who had gone over to Catholicism, repeated Steno's attempt to convert him, Spinoza answered him with a letter in which he maintained the lawfulness of free knowledge, and declared justice and love to be the essence of all true religion. It must not be forgotten that Steno was not in the least affronted by Spinoza's defence of religious freedom. To labour for religious freedom was for Steno to court his soul's destruction ! May not Spinoza's conviction that a true faith can be imposed neither by spiritual nor by physical force, and his care not to shake the faith of other men, as long as they were in earnest with it, show a greater and truer concern for individual personality, than that which expresses itself in a passionate propaganda ?[60]

After a residence of some years at Rhynsburg, Spinoza moved (1663) to Voorburg, near the Hague, and later (1670) to the Hague itself. Here, too, he had many friends, some of them men in high position, as, for instance, the brothers De Witt. He lived simply, and displayed great disinterestedness in pecuniary matters towards his relations and friends. His way of looking at life is characterised by a gay and glad tone of mind. " Why," he asks in his *Ethica*, " is it more seemly to extinguish hunger and thirst than to drive away melancholy ? My reasons and my conclusions are these—no God and no human being, except an envious one, is delighted by my impotence or my trouble, or esteems as any virtue in us tears, sighs, fears, and other things of this kind, which are signs of mental impotence ; on the contrary, the greater the joy with which we are affected, the greater the perfection to which we pass thereby, that is to say, the more do we necessarily partake of the divine nature. . . . It is the part of a wise man, I say, to refresh and invigorate himself with moderate and pleasant eating and drinking, with sweet scents and the beauty of green plants, with ornament, with music, with sports, and with the theatre."[1]   In spite of his vein of mysticism, Spinoza was no ascetic.   In his life, as in his philosophy, the effort to work out everything from one thought went hand and hand with a sense of the manifold reality, whose inner law it is, according to his conception, which this one thought expresses.   We shall get a false idea both of his life and his philosophy if we allow ourselves to lose sight of the different tendencies by which he was actually impelled, although perhaps he never (as he believed) found the key-word by means of which each of these tendencies were to receive their due, and be reconciled one with another.

The first work published by Spinoza was an exposition of the Cartesian philosophy (1663), originally undertaken for a young man (the Albert de Burgh already mentioned) whom he did not yet wish to initiate into his own philosophy.   Very characteristic is this way of looking upon Cartesianism as an introduction to his own doctrine.   He occupied himself unceasingly with his *Ethica*, elaborating it more and more.   Only with great caution did he communicate it to others : before he allowed his disciples to show his MS. to strangers he instituted strict inquiries as to the latter's character and circumstances. Thus, for instance, he refused his friend Tschirnhausen leave to show the *Ethica* to Leibniz : it was not till after long personal intercourse with the latter that he himself showed him his great work.   According to an hypothesis of Tönnies [61] the first two books of the *Ethica* were worked out independently, while the realistic psychology of the third book, betraying the influence of Hobbes, which is also apparent in his civil philosophy, appears to have been written later.   This would explain several contradictions between the exposition of the second and third books.   In comparison with the "short treatise," the *Ethica* denotes this advance, that Spinoza no longer conceives the relation between mind and matter as a causal relation, but as a relation of identity.   Spinoza had taken measures for the publication of this

[1] [Hale White's translation.]

his chief work, but he abandoned them again, since the rumour of its publication was enough to cause great excitement. Since the appearance of the " Theologico-political Treatise " (1670) he had been looked on with suspicion, although it does not contain the development of his own system. This book defends religious freedom as a right of man, with special reference to the fact that difference of personality must involve difference of belief. It contains, further, a purely historical examination of the Biblical writings (especially of the Old Testament, the later origin of which is maintained) and a psychological character- isation of the authors. A definite distinction is made between religion, with its practical aim of leading the minds of men to obedience and morality, and science, the aim of which is purely theoretic ; and on the basis of this distinction, perfect freedom is awarded to science. It concludes with a polemic against the belief in miracles, for the laws of Nature are the laws of God's own essence. This work, which contains so many germs of future thought, was regarded as the quintessence of godlessness. His experiences on this occasion led Spinoza not only to keep back his *Ethica*, but also to refuse a call to a professorial chair in Heidelberg : he feared, in spite of all promises, that he would not be granted sufficient freedom in his teaching. An inherited disease of the chest, which had undermined his health for many years, caused his death on February 21, 1677. Over his death, as over his life, wild rumours were spread abroad, which the truth-loving Colerus, after adequate inquiry, has refuted— although he himself is astonished that a freethinker could lead such a beautiful life and die so quiet a death, and finds it scandalous that Spinoza's barber should have sent in a bill after his death in which he alludes to his late customer as " Mr. Spinoza of blessed memory."

Thus we see, in Spinoza's personal development, the different elements of his system appearing on different sides. It must now be our task to discover, by an analysis of his completed system, how he proposed to unite these elements, and whether and if so, to what extent he really succeeded in this union.

(*b*) *Theory of Knowledge*

If we are to follow Spinoza's own *Ethica* in our exposition of his system, we must begin with certain definitions and primary assumptions, and, from these again, deduce a series of theorems. But then the question how Spinoza came by his definitions and primary assumptions, which contain within them his whole system, would remain unanswered, and it is precisely this question which is of greatest interest historically. If we begin on the bare ground, as did Spinoza himself, with definitions and principles, we shall naturally suppose either that these principles are purely arbitrarily established (as Hobbes believed), or that they are the object of immediate intuition. Neither of these views was Spinoza's. By following the fashion of his day, which demanded a strictly deductive procedure, he has given occasion for the misunderstanding of his system. It may be seen, from the, alas! unfinished treatise " On the Amendment of the Understanding," that he had devoted serious consideration to scientific method, and intended to write a kind of inductive logic. In a certain sense it is true to say that Spinoza arrived at the principles on which he grounds the deductive exposition of his *Ethica* by searching out and constructing the presuppositions on which our empirical knowledge of the world rests.

If we understand by experience the mere perception of things as these are involuntarily and accidentally presented to us, then, indeed, it gives us no true knowledge. It contents itself with the given, as this occurs at a definite time and in a definite place, and an opinion is only established in consciousness because, so far, we have met with no facts which contradict it, although we are without guarantee that no such facts exist. Spinoza calls this kind of experience *experientia vaga ;* it corresponds to Bacon's *inductio per enumerationem simplicem.* True knowledge must be a reasonable knowledge which does not rest in a particular given phenomenon as such, but regards it as the consequence of a general law, as the particular expression of a general order of things, which extends far beyond the given phenomenon. Reason (*ratio*) regards empirically given phenomena in their definite inner connection, and finds in this the explanation of every particular phenomenon. Reason starts from the given. Spinoza emphasises the necessity "that we should always deduce our concepts from real things, by following, as far as possible, the sequence of causes." An exposition of matters of fact must therefore first be given, and from this our fundamental concepts and principles must be deduced. In his "Theologico-political Treatise" Spinoza draws an analogy between the exposition of a book (the Bible) and the explanation of Nature. First of all there must be a statement of the given content. Then certain general relations and laws, which are involved at every point, must be secured. These are, on the physical side, the laws of motion ; while, on the mental side, Spinoza could point to the laws of the association of ideas. In a word : the idea of conformity to law governing all things reveals itself in particular and changing phenomena, and it is this ·idea only which makes each particular phenomenon comprehensible to us. In this conformity to law the true, eternal, nature of things revealed itself to Spinoza. Some confusion has been caused by the fact that he called the general laws of phenomena "the constant and eternal things on which mutable individual things are so innerly and essentially dependent that, without them, they can neither exist nor be understood." These laws are revealed just as perfectly in Nature as a totality as in its single parts. It is to them we must go back if we want to reach a conclusion for knowledge. The series of phenomena is unending, inexhaustible ; we may go on for ever from member to member. But true knowledge is concerned with that which unites the members, *i.e.* that which is everywhere present. And as Spinoza makes a definite distinction between the causal series consisting of "the constant and eternal things" which are one with the laws of phenomena, and the series of phenomena, which in their mutual relations are also called causes and effects, so he makes no less decided a distinction between the general laws, which are to him just as much a reality (*entia realia*) as individual phenomena, and general ideas (*abstracta et universalia*), which possess no objective reality.

The truth and validity of our knowledge rest, according to Spinoza, not upon any external characteristic, not upon agreement with something beyond itself. It is the clearness and distinctness resulting from perfect consistency which give us the certainty of truth. An error always arises from taking what is limited and isolated to be a whole in itself. Error disappears if only we continue, with the strictest consistency, to make our way onwards out of the incorrect presuppositions in which we are entangled : *Intellectio fictionem terminat.* In strict logical consistency, then, our thought possesses a norm of truth which it can apply everywhere, even where it is in error. Truth, says Spinoza, measures itself as well as error (*veritas norma sui et falsi est*), just as light manifests itself as well as darkness. Thus the starting-point of all our inquiry will naturally be an examination of the principle of truth given us in the nature of our understanding itself. This is the foundation on which we build when we inquire after the eternal and necessary among things, after that which lies at the root of all things (*res omnium prima*).

Spinoza here intimates that it is only by means of our subjective reason that we can discover "the eternal things," "the first of all things," in Nature. Had he further pursued the line of thought here suggested, the problem of knowledge, in all its distinctness, would have presented itself to him: with what right do we believe that existence itself observes the norm which is valid for the mutual relation of our thought? This problem, however, did not occur to him. He regarded it as certain that the presuppositions of our reason are also those of things; yes, even that the eternal things correspond to them; an objective world-order corresponds to the subjective order of thought.

Between the objective objects of our thoughts (which Spinoza designates by the scholastic term *essentiae formales*) the same relation holds good as between our thoughts among themselves. To that which is our first thought, and from which all other thoughts are derived, corresponds that which is the first thing in existence, and the origin and source of all other things. Closely connected with this is the fact that Spinoza calls those laws which explain particular phenomena "things" or "beings." By this he means to express (putting his view into modern language) that the connection which makes things comprehensible is just as much a reality as each single thing, taken apart from its surroundings; indeed, that since it is eternal and all-embracing, it deserves the name of reality in a far higher degree. But since Spinoza calls the laws or constant relations between phenomena, "things" or "beings," without which particular phenomena could neither exist nor be comprehended, we here find the origin and meaning of what he, in his deductive exposition, calls substance. For by substance he understands what exists in and for itself and can be understood of itself, and by means of which everything else exists and is comprehensible. Spinoza's substance, the fundamental concept of his whole philosophy, is thus, properly speaking, causality, considered as a thing or being. For, according to Spinoza, causality, the relation of causation, is self-evident and makes all else comprehensible to us. And as the causal relation is the presupposition for the knowledge of real existence which is revealed to us in experience, we see that Spinoza's whole philosophy may be called a construction of the presuppositions valid for all scientific experience, by means of which these presuppositions become identical with the innermost nature of things. Causality or causation, which Spinoza conceives as real power, on which particular things are dependent, and in which they exist, corresponds again, with him, to the necessity with which we deduce conclusions from their premisses ; or, in other words, Spinoza makes no difference between ground and cause ; the causal relation, according to him, is not a temporal relation in which the cause precedes and the effect follows after, but an eternal and ultimate relation ; the relation between the "constant and eternal things" (or "the first of all things") and particular phenomena is not such that the former exist first and that the latter arise afterwards as their effects. According to Spinoza the temporal relation falls away in true knowledge. Reasonable knowledge is, according to him, a conception of things "under the form of eternity" (*sub specie aeterni*): it fixes its gaze only upon that in things by which they reveal the eternal necessity within them, and regards them only as examples of this necessity. Spinoza considers the principle of causality to be itself a necessary principle of reason. In his *Ethica* he takes as his fundamental principle : 'a thing must have its cause either in itself or in something else. _ Now since substance, *i.e.* that which exists and can be understood of itself, cannot have its cause in something else it must have its cause in itself, *i.e.* must exist with necessity. If we deny this principle we must also deny the principle that everything must necessarily have a cause (either within or without itself). And that it is a principle of reason proceeds likewise from the fact that the relation of two things to one another as cause and effect means that the idea of the one can be deduced from that of the other ; knowledge of the effect is only knowledge of a special quality of the cause ; the two ideas have something in common

with one another.   Only when, in this way, the temporal
relation and, generally speaking, *the difference between cause and
effect* falls away, so that the effect is seen to be the logical
consequent of the cause (which would certainly be the ideal
consummation of knowledge), can substance or "the eternal
things" be called the cause of phenomena.   And only on the
assumption of this convertibility of ground and cause is it
comprehensible how Spinoza could hope to construct a purely
rational knowledge of Nature ; or, in other words, to recognise
existence as rational in its inmost nature.   We get the
antithesis to this view of Spinoza's in the conception—already
hinted at by Brooke and Glanvil (as also by the Occasionalists)
and carried out later by Hume—that cause and effect are *quite
different* things ; a view which must lead to doubt as to the
rationality of existence.

Reasonable knowledge (*ratio*) leads us, it is true, to the
perception of the eternal and necessary in things ; but it is not,
according to Spinoza, the highest form of knowledge.   It still
shows us general laws and particular phenomena in antithesis
to one another, and thought is still discursive, arriving at its
results by means of comparison and inference.   The highest
form of knowledge, according to Spinoza, is the intuitive,[62] in
which the particular phenomenon is immediately perceived to
be, as it were, interpenetrated by the general order of things,
as *e.g.* I immediately perceive that two lines are parallel to one
another if they each run parallel to one and the same third
line ; or as I, in the knowledge which I have of a subject, at
the same time immediately perceive what it is to know a
subject.   The difference between the universal and the individual has here entirely disappeared ; the unity of the two is
perceived at a single glance.   It is Spinoza's highest aim to
understand as much as possible in this immediate and intuitive
manner.   In the last book of his *Ethica* he seeks to understand individual minds in their inner unity with the eternal
essence : an intuition which forms the consummation of
his theoretical and practical endeavours.   The chief thing
necessary, in order to rise to this intuition, is to free ourselves
from external and accidental experience and, with the help of
reason, to discover the necessary interconnection.   It is difficult,
however, to maintain any sharp distinction between reason and
intuition for both show us things " under the form of eternity " ;

moreover, in his description of intuitive knowledge, Spinoza says that it "*progresses* from a perfect idea of the nature of certain divine attributes to the perfect knowledge of the essence of things": so that the discursive has not completely disappeared here. Spinoza aims at nothing less than the highest aim of all knowledge, viz.: the most intimate union possible of individuality with continuity, of the particular with the sum of constant relations. He only succeeds in this when postulating an intuition which reminds us now of the artist's conception, now of the mystic vision, according to whether stress is laid on the individual or on the universal moment.

It is much to be regretted that Spinoza never completed his theory of knowledge. The fragment that we possess, however, shows that his fundamental definitions and axioms did not come to him in a flash from heaven, but were constructed on the basis of a reflection on the assumptions involved in all understanding of existence. Spinoza's dogmatism consists in the certainty with which he lays down these assumptions and treats them as realities ; not, however, in entirely overlooking their existence.

(c) Fundamental Concepts of the System

(a) If Spinoza begins his deductive exposition with a definition of that which he understands by the cause of itself and by substance, and with the establishment of his fundamental principle, that that which has not its cause in anything else must have it in itself, he has in so doing, strictly speaking, only postulated the possibility of a definitive knowledge of existence. Existence would not be knowable if the causal principle were not valid, and causal knowledge could never reach a conclusion if there were not Something which has its cause in itself and does not refer inquiring thought to something beyond itself, as does every particular phenomenon. Although Spinoza defines Substance as "that which is in itself and is conceived by itself ; that is, whose concept needs not the concept of another thing for it to be formed from" (*per substantiam intelligo id, quod in se est et per se concipitur, hoc est id, cujus conceptus non indiget conceptu alterius rei, a quo formari debeat*), yet in so doing he conceives himself to have given no mere

subjective determination of a concept, but to have formulated an
objective fact, a given reality. He has no doubt that substance
exists. Its existence is given ; but if we would think over
what substance is, we should see that its existence is also
necessary, because there is nothing which it can exclude, since
it has its cause in itself. It follows, too, from the nature of
substance that it cannot arise or pass away; that it can neither
be divided nor limited ; that there can only be one single substance. All other things to which we attribute existence can
thus only be attributes (*attributa*) of the one substance, or particular phenomena (*modi*, modes), in which it reveals itself.
The fact that in existence we meet with different qualities
(*attributa*), *e.g.* consciousness and extension, which we are not
able to reduce to a common form, does not (as Descartes
thought) justify the belief in different substances : they must
be conceived as different qualities or attributes of one and the
same substance. Nor are we any more justified, because experience shows us a manifold of finite things, or of phenomena
temporally and spatially divided, in believing in a manifold of
substances. The existence of finite things or phenomena is
conditioned throughout, and true existence (substantiality) can
only be attributed to the general order of things, to the all-
embracing nature, which is the supporter of all things.

(β) The concept of God and the concept of Nature are for
Spinoza identical with the concept of Substance. His concept
of Substance looks back towards Cartesianism and the Scholastics, his concept of Nature towards Bruno and the Renaissance,
and his concept of God towards the religious ideas which
were the first to set his thought in motion. As the infinite
nature, which reveals itself under an infinitude of attributes,
substance is called God. Everything which is predicated of
substance must also be predicable of God, so that everything
which is, is in God and, without God, can neither exist nor be
understood. Consequently both matter (extension) and mind
(consciousness) are divine attributes ; they do not denote a
being outside God ; neither do particular things nor phenomena
(*modi*) exist outside God. It is no more possible that any
differences or oppositions should exist within the nature of
God, than that anything should exist outside Him. In Him is
no difference between possibility and reality, no temporal distinction. Everything which follows from the nature of God,

follows with eternal necessity ; it is precisely in this necessity, which is determined by His nature, that God's freedom consists. When God is called the cause of things, it must be carefully noted that cause and effect are not two different things here, but that the effect is a revelation of the nature of the cause. God's work is not different from Himself, as is the work of a human master. God is the cause of things in the same sense in which He is the cause of Himself ; He is the immanent (*immanente*) but not the transitive (*transcendente*) cause ; His work remains in Him and He in His work ; beyond the circumference of His nature He cannot come. It is true we must distinguish between God and the totality of all particular phenomena (*modi*) : phenomena make up Nature as it is begotten (*natura naturata*); God is Nature as it begets (*natura naturans*). But there is no external separation. According to Spinoza it is a purely abstract mode of thought which looks at particular phenomena in isolation from the "whole order of Nature," *i.e.* from substance, from *natura naturans*. By so doing it rejects the conditions necessary to the understanding of them. To regard existence superficially and in the abstract, as it presents itself to the senses and the imagination, on the occurrence of isolated phenomena, is for Spinoza the very opposite of regarding it as substance, and by means of the understanding. Every particular phenomenon is but a limited form of the one infinite substance, arising through a negation, through the renunciation of all other forms under which substance occurs. Every particular determination is a negation.[63]

(γ) Substance, God or Nature, appears under different qualities or attributes. " By attribute," says Spinoza, " I understand that which the intellect perceives concerning substance, as constituting the essence thereof." Of the infinitely many attributes which the infinite being called God or Nature possesses, we only know two, mind and matter. The essence of God or of Nature appears to us only under these two forms, as it is active partly in the world of material and partly in that of mental phenomena. Spinoza's attitude towards experience may here be clearly seen. Not only is it a matter of experience that we know only two attributes, but the definition of the concept of attribute also rests upon experience, namely on the fact (which Spinoza must have perceived in the interval between the " short treatise " and the definitive working out of the *Ethica*) that

the mental and the material are each to be understood according to their own laws.   The difference between these two
worlds is thus irreducible ; we cannot deduce the mental from
the material, nor the material from the mental ; but within the
mental world for itself, and within the material world for itself,
we can point to coherence and causality.   Spinoza expresses
the fact that the mental and the material are irreducible differences in existence by calling them attributes, and by defining
attribute as that which expresses the essence of substance : [64] for
substance is that which exists in itself and can be conceived
through itself.   We must not leap from the one attribute to
the other.   "So long," says Spinoza, "as things are regarded
as mental phenomena (*modi cogitandi*) we must (*debemus*) explain
the order of Nature or the causal connection by the attribute of
thought alone ; and so long as we regard them as material
phenomena (*modi extensionis*), we must (*debet*) explain the whole
order of Nature by the attribute of extension alone."   There is,
that is to say, only one single substance, only one single causal connection, but this may be regarded in a twofold manner.   Spinoza
can hardly have meant by this that the attributes are only
points of view from which *we* regard substance.[65]   Indeed he
says expressly that attribute is that which the intellect perceives *as constituting* the essence of substance, and we have no
reason to think that Spinoza entertained any doubt that what
our intellect perceives as constituting really constitutes.   When,
therefore, he says that we *must* explain the mental by the
mental and the material by the material, this is a necessity
which is, for him, like all necessity, an expression of the eternal
essence of existence.

   If we ask for the real reason why the mental side of
existence cannot be explained by the material, nor the
material by the mental, we shall find the answer in Spinoza's
ideal of explanation through causes, according to which
cause and effect must resemble one another (axioms 4 and 5
in the first book of the *Ethica*).   In a letter (*Ep.* 4 in Land
and Van Vloten's edition) Spinoza says, still more clearly : "If
two things have nothing in common with one another the one
cannot be the cause of the other ; for, since there would be
nothing in the effect that was also in the cause, everything that
was in the effect would have arisen out of nothing."   If we
keep this fundamental principle consistently before us we shall

have the key to Spinoza's whole system. From this principle, for instance, follows the doctrine of God or substance as the immanent cause of all phenomena (*modi*), that is to say, the abolition of the theological dualism of God and the world. From it, too, follows the impossibility of the cause being material and the effect mental, and the reverse; *i.e.* the doctrine that mind and matter are expressions of one and the same existence, of one and the same causal connection—and this involves the abolition of the spiritualistic dualism of soul and body. As considerations of *general* epistemological value concerning the conditions which make the comprehension of that which is given in experience possible led Spinoza to the establishment of his concept of substance (as the concept of hypostatised causality), so the consideration of the *special* problem of the possibility of understanding the mental and material led him to his doctrine of attributes. This doctrine is essentially conditioned by the conviction of the possibility of conceiving the material side of existence as a continuous whole, and by the further conviction of the impossibility of deducing the mental side of existence from it. Spinoza makes front against Descartes as well as against Hobbes. His attribute theory is an attempt to solve the difficulties which beset both Cartesianism and Hobbism (spiritualism and materialism). He meets both spiritualism and materialism with a new and original hypothesis.

Spinoza has not strictly maintained this meaning of the doctrine of attributes. With the problem of the relation between mind and matter he confounded, in several places, the problem of the relation between knowledge and its objects. It is easy to see that these are two separate problems; for mind as well as matter (existence on its mental as well as on its material side) is the object of knowledge, and the problem of knowledge arises with respect to all sides, the existence of which may be perceived. But since Spinoza, as a dogmatic philosopher, took for granted the agreement of our reason with the essence of things, he was obliged, as we have already seen, to believe that every relation of thought corresponds to a relation in existence. And this epistemological doctrine of identity he confused with the psycho-physical doctrine of identity, which is expressed in his doctrine of attributes. When he asserts that "the order and connection of ideas is

the same as the order and connection of things" (*Ethica*, ii. 7)
this proposition is ambiguous, since it may be understood in
an epistemological or in a psycho-physical sense. Spinoza
himself took it in the main epistemologically. This may be
seen from his example: to my concept of a circle there corresponds a circle existing in Nature (*Ethica*, ii. 7 Schol.). Had he
regarded it psychologically he must have said: my image of a
circle corresponds to the condition of my brain when I have this
image. But when Spinoza, in immediate connection with this,
asserts that mental phenomena must be explained by mental,
and material by material phenomena, he is discussing quite
another problem. In the third book of the *Ethica*, where the
point of view is psychological and not epistemological, he
makes a strictly psycho-physical application of the doctrine of
attributes. This confusion stands in natural connection with
the fact that, with Spinoza, the problem of knowledge never
appeared as an entirely independent problem. Only in a
critical revision of our knowledge, with regard to its capacity for
knowing the mental as well as the material side of existence,
did the difference between these two problems clearly emerge.[66]

As, according to Spinoza, an inner relation (an indwelling,
immanent relation) exists between substance (God or Nature)
and particular phenomena, so also the great fundamental
forms and qualities which existence exhibits must, for him, be
attributes of substance. Accordingly, with daring consistency,
Spinoza declares matter or extension to be a divine attribute. According to the usual theological conception, matter
is secondary, a product of the mental. But no more
than Bruno and Boehme could Spinoza content himself
with this conception, which is, indeed, especially opposed to
his fundamental thought of an immanent causal relation. In
Spinoza's doctrine of matter as a divine attribute it must be
carefully remarked that under matter he here understands the
substantial in material phenomena,—that in them which persists
through all change and in spite of all division, and that can
neither suffer, nor arise, nor cease to be. The material side of
existence, no less than the mental, is a revelation of God or
substance; the "infinite power of thought" (*potentia infinita
cogitandi*) of the latter answers to the infinite material extension, of which particular phenomena are parts. That which
lies at the foundation of the world, from whatever side it may

be regarded, is the causal connection and the unity of which the causal connection witnesses.

Particular phenomena are, as already mentioned, the various forms under which, within the different attributes, substance occurs. Since, then, the attributes are predicable of substance, they are also predicable of the particular modes (*modi*); every particular phenomenon, therefore, may, like existence as a whole, of which it is a member or a part, be viewed from an infinite number of sides, only we are not able to know more than two of these sides. The definition of mode (*modus*) is: "the affections of substance, or that which is in somewhat else, through which also it is conceived." As *affectio substantiae* the mode is only understood through substance, and has in it its existence—in the same way, it might be said, as the particular wave only exists as a part of the sea, and can only be understood when it is regarded as part of that sea. In every particular phenomenon there is an impulse towards self-preservation, which is a part of the divine force active in all things. But in every particular phenomenon this force is active only in a limited manner; we cannot, therefore, understand how the particular mode works or suffers if we do not regard it in its reciprocal action with all other modes. The condition of the particular mode can therefore only be understood through something other than itself. Here an external (transcendent) cause comes into force. However external the relation in which particular phenomena stand to one another, yet collectively and individually they are nothing but determinations (*affectiones, modificationes, determinationes*) of the one infinite substance. The *natura naturans* is active in the *natura naturata* at all points.

In the *natura naturata* Spinoza distinguishes between the necessary and infinite modes which follow immediately from the eternal nature of God, and the finite modes which can only arise by means of other modes. Within the attribute of extension he mentions, as infinite modes, motion and rest; he seems to be thinking more especially here of the conservation of motion, or of the law that under all modifications of matter the same proportion between motion and rest persists,—this law which shows that every particular body is only a part of the whole universe. Within the attribute of thought he mentions the "infinite intellect" (*intellectus infinitus*) or the

" idea of God " (*idea dei*) which is an immediate effect of the
infinite divine power of thought, and which—since it is taken
as analogous to the constancy of motion—must mean the
mental energy which always remains constant in the world,
however much particular mental phenomena may change. Here,
too, we notice that Spinoza speaks of beings where we should
only speak of laws.

(δ) In further characterisation of the system here sketched
we can only hint at a series of problems and difficulties to
which it gives rise.   God or substance is spoken of as that
which works, although the form of time is said to be valid only
of the modes (the *natura naturata*) and not of substance
(the *natura naturans*).   This follows from the confusion
between ground and cause mentioned above.   Two kinds of
causal relation exist : one between the modes among themselves, which is external and transitive ; and another between
the substance and the modes, which is immanent.   How are
these two to be reconciled ?   The unity of the substance and
the multiplicity of the attributes and the modes are not
harmonised ; we are not told how the one and only substance
can appear under different points of view, nor how, out of one
single substance, an infinite number of effects can follow.   And
if, with Spinoza, the concepts, Substance, God, and Nature are
coextensive, yet in the term "God" he introduces an estimation of worth, the only foundation for which is his definition of
perfection as reality ; the question whether this definition can
be maintained is not entered upon, and at a later point in his
exposition, as we shall see, he even gives a concept of perfection according to which not all reality is perfect.   So that
even the boldest speculative system leaves behind it unanswered
questions !   Spinoza's greatness consists in the resolute carrying out of the thought that existence must be rational ; from
this he concludes that its essence must be identity,—absolute
unity.   Logically therefore, instead of having several fundamental concepts in his system, he ought to have had only one,
i.e. Substance.   To this concept we can perhaps rise, but
having once reached it, we can certainly never descend from it
again.   These objections against Spinoza's system, however,
do not affect his fundamental endeavour, nor the main tendency
of his thought, but are for the most part occasioned by the
dogmatic procedure which he adopted.

(d) Philosophy of Religion

It will be of interest to pause for a moment in order to see in what relation Spinoza's philosophy stood to the current views on religion. By calling his highest concept (Substance) "God" he has himself provoked the comparison. We find this question already being discussed in his correspondence. On a certain occasion he writes (*Ep.* 73): "I embrace a view of God and Nature very different from that which modern Christians usually defend. I assert, namely, that God is (as it is called) the immanent, not the external cause of all things. That is to say, I assert with Paul, that in God all things live and move. . . . But if any one thinks that the 'Theologico-political Treatise' assumes that God and Nature,—where by Nature is understood mass or corporeal matter,—are one and the same, he is entirely mistaken." Spinoza's doctrine differs from the ordinary theological view on two points, *i.e.* more especially in not looking upon God and Nature as two different essences, and in not attributing to God any human qualities. At first his opinions were denounced, without more ado, as atheism and materialism. Henry More, *e.g.* says in a work in which he attempts to refute the "crass atheism" (*atheismus crassimus*) of Spinoza, that God and Nature are, according to him, identical. Thus, says More, stones, mire, lead, dung, are God, for all these things are Matter! Spinoza is accordingly an "unclean and foul atheist" (*sordidus et lutulentus atheus*).[67] A little specimen of seventeenth-century polemics! The new system was embarrassing on account of its peculiarity ; it was not easy to bring it under any of the usual heretical rubrics, and, by its sharply defined form, it excited indignation at many points. Later we meet with the term "Pantheism" (probably first used by Toland). Spinoza's critics were now provided with a word more likely to hit the mark. And yet they are not agreed in their use of it. According to some it denotes a view which conceives the relation of God to the world as an immanent one ; while, according to others, the essence of Pantheism is that in it God is not conceived as a personal being.[68] According to the first of these interpretations there can be no doubt that Spinoza's system is pantheistic, while, according to the latter, it is not quite clear how we ought to characterise it.

In one of his letters (*Ep.* 54) Spinoza says that in order not to confuse the divine with human nature he attributes no human qualities such as will, reason, attention, hearing, etc., to God. Reasons for this are given in several places in the *Ethica*. It is evident that psychological determinations are no longer applicable if the temporal relation falls away, and, according to Spinoza, this is predicable only of the *natura naturata*, not of the *natura naturans*. With the temporal relation all other change disappears : God cannot pass over either to a greater or less state of perfection, and can therefore feel neither joy nor sorrow, love nor hate. Moreover God as substance has nothing outside Himself; there is no external object, towards which He can direct His feeling or will. Our consciousness, our reason as well as our feeling and will, is determined by such external objects, and if these fall away our consciousness ceases also. If we use such expressions as " reason " and " will " of God we must make it clear to ourselves that the meaning of each must undergo such a change that the word in its two applications has only about as much in common as the word " dog " when it is used both of the dog-star (Sirius) and of the barking mundane animal. The impulse to carry over human qualities to God has therefore no objective validity whatever. Could triangles think, they would conceive God as three-cornered ; could circles think they would conceive Him to be round.

On the other hand, however, Spinoza acknowledges the mental as an independent side of existence. God is *substantia cogitans* as well as *substantia extensa ; cogitatio* (thought, mind) is one of the attributes of God, that is to say, it expresses the nature of God ! Reason and will belong to the *natura naturata* only, not to the *natura naturans ;* in this latter, however, must lie a ground for the arising of the former, and if the " infinite reason " or the " idea of God " persists eternally, throughout the change of all mental phenomena, it too must have its ground in the nature of God. We might perhaps express Spinoza's conception thus : God is mind, but not personality, because only a limited being can be personality. Spinoza only employs the expression personality in one place ; he pronounces it to be indistinct. It is to be remarked here that Spinoza himself, since he declares *cogitatio* to be a divine attribute, and, as we shall see later, speaks of God's infinite love to himself (of which the love of man to God is only a part), undertakes a sublimisation of psychological qualities similar to that which at other points he rejects. Against *cogitatio* as a divine attribute the same objections may be raised as those urged by Spinoza himself against the ordinary view. Whoever tries to reduce a philosophical system to any kind of " ism " will find himself in the same sort of difficulty as Spinoza, especially since every thinking Theism must undertake a sublimisation of the same kind as Spinoza's.

(e) *Natural Philosophy and Psychology*

Since Spinoza declares extension to be one of the attributes of existence and (in strict accordance with his definition of attribute) demands that in the explanation of a phenomenon we shall abide by the attribute under which it appears to us, he has already pronounced for the purely mechanical as the only scientific conception of Nature. As coming under the attribute of extension all corporeal phenomena are to be explained by corporeal causes only ; through causes, that is to say, which work from points in space other than those at which the phenomena to be explained occur. It is therefore very easy for Spinoza to demonstrate the law of inertia : it is indeed really contained already in the establishment of extension as an attribute. Spinoza assumes, no less dogmatically than Descartes and Hobbes, that the first principles of mechanics are eternal truths,—although he is obliged to admit that he is not able to deduce motion from extension itself.[69]

There can be no difference of essence between bodies ; they differ only in respect of motion and rest, quickness or slowness. The laws of motion are eternal laws of Nature and Reason. The doctrine of attributes also involves the rejection of all belief in ends of Nature. Since the one attribute cannot determine the other, no material phenomenon as such can have its ground in a thought, as the teleological explanation supposes. In a lengthy note to the first book of the *Ethica*, Spinoza attempts to show that the teleological view is due to the practical needs and wishes of men, to their impulse towards self-preservation, together with their original ignorance regarding real causes. Man assumes that everything is arranged in his behoof, and that the gods, too, work for him ; where no acceptable end can be assigned, he contents himself with finding the explanation in God's will,—that "asylum of ignorance" which

is always at his service.   Had not mathematics pointed out a
rational way to knowledge, the teleological conception would
always have stood in the way of the knowledge of Nature.
The teleological conception, however, not only hinders the
knowledge of Nature, but also sets up unworthy notions of
God : if God works for ends He cannot be perfect, but only
becomes so on the attainment of His end !   Men are arrogant
enough to apply moral and æsthetic concepts to Nature, and
to find in it order and confusion, beauty and ugliness, good and
evil, because they believe that it is only arranged to give them
pleasure.   They do not see that the perfection and power of
Nature are identical, and that this power is infinite, so that it is
able to produce all possible grades and forms of existence,—
those which stand lowest in our estimation as well as those
which we look upon as the highest.

Spinoza indicates in a series of physical propositions, in
the second book of the *Ethica*, the way in which he conceives
a mechanical conception of Nature should be carried out.
According to the law of inertia the motion or rest of a body is
determined through that of a second body, this through a third,
and so on.   The manner in which a body is determined,
depends partly on its own nature, partly on the nature of the
body influencing it.   When bodies of the same or of different
magnitudes are so held together by other bodies that they
touch each other, or when they impart to one another their
motion in a certain proportion, we say that they are reciprocally
united, and that together they form one single body or one
single individual, which differs from other individuals through
the definitive connection of the single bodies of which it consists.
Such an individual remains the same,—even if new parts are
taken up and others separated off, or if the magnitude of the
parts and the direction of their motions change,—if only the
general form of the combination remains the same.   Several of
such individuals may be united to form an individual of the
second order, and several individuals of the second order may
form an individual of the third order, and so on, till at last the
whole of Nature appears to us as a single individual, whose
particular parts differ in infinite ways without any change of
the whole individual.

Through all its grades and degrees Nature is animated.
This, too, follows from the doctrine of attributes ; for, since

every attribute expresses the whole of substance, every form under the one attribute must correspond to a certain form under the other attribute. Thus the different grades of individuality in material Nature correspond to the different grades of psychical life in mental Nature. As the human body consists of many combined individuals of different kinds, so, too, thought, which constitutes the human mind, is put together out of many different thoughts. Mind and body are one and the same substance, or rather, one and the same mode of substance, and that which, under the attribute of extension, appears as more or less composite forms of motion, appears under the attribute of thought as more or less composite forms of thought. When I feel an impulse, or make a resolution, then at the same time, under the attribute of extension, a corporeal determination, according to the general laws of motion and rest, takes place ; which is indeed so to be understood that we see it to be one and the same thing that is happening. Through this view, as Spinoza points out, we avoid asserting the influence of the mind over the body, or the reverse,—of which no one can form a clear idea. If we say the mind sets the body in motion, we really mean that we do not know how such motion arises. At the same time this view possesses the advantage of setting no arbitrary limits to the activity of material Nature. Up till now, indeed, no one has been able to discover the limits to that which can be effected through the laws proper to material Nature ; so that we have no right to appeal to the intervention of the mind because the body appears to work in a marvellous manner. Neither can an appeal to the "freedom" of the will serve us. This so-called "freedom" (true freedom, according to Spinoza, consists in following the necessity of one's own nature) is a delusion which arises because men do not know the causes of their own actions. The loquacious man believes himself free to act when he uses his glib tongue, in the same way as a stone, if it could think, would believe that it fell "of free will" to the ground. Resolution, moreover, is dependent on memory, and of that we are not always master !

Although Spinoza rejects every explanation of mental phenomena through material causes, yet he uses—as he is fully justified in doing according to his own premises—the parallelism between the material and the mental to throw light upon

mental phenomena, where these cannot be immediately understood. Every sensation answers to a bodily condition. Now
this condition, it is true, has its cause in the influence of other
bodies, but this influence is modified by the condition of our
own body ; from this it follows that sensation corresponds not
only to the nature of external bodies, but also and principally to
the nature of our own body. Yet we involuntarily regard every
sensation as an expression of a reality until other sensations or
ideas arise in us which exclude the assumed reality. According to Spinoza, that is to say, our conception of reality is
clarified and determined by the inner struggle between sensations
and ideas. Sensations call up ideas of that which is similar
to the object of sensation, or has been presented with it.[70] The
laws of the association of ideas are, for Spinoza, mental laws of
Nature—a counterpart to the laws of motion in the attribute
of matter. Spinoza makes a sharp distinction between the
association of ideas and thought proper ; to this distinction we have already alluded in our section on the problem
of knowledge. Sensuous perception and the association of
ideas express the condition of Man as a member in the series
of phenomena, in the infinite *natura naturata*. The higher
grades of knowledge—rational and intuitive knowledge—will
be reached if we go back to that which stirs in all things as
their common law and essence, *i.e.* to the infinite substance,
and perceive how everything is comprehended in it ; or, in
other words, regard everything *sub specie aeterni*. Hobbes's
psychology possesses an advantage over Spinoza's here, in that
it shows how it is possible for thought proper to develop itself
out of the involuntary association of ideas through concentration on an end or problem. Spinoza, according to the scholastic
manner, still treats thought proper as an entirely distinct activity,
differing in its essence from ordinary ideas. All the more
remarkable is it that, in his doctrine of attributes, he should
have confounded the epistemological with the psycho-physical
point of view ; although, on the other hand, this confusion would
scarcely have arisen had he seen that the laws of the association
of ideas are not, as a matter of fact, suspended by thought
proper.

Spinoza's treatment of the psychology of the feelings ranks
among the most excellent work which has been done not only
by him, but also within the whole sphere of psychology. In

the first place, he has the merit of having asserted the necessity and justification of a purely scientific examination of human feelings and passions. As a scientific inquirer he neither mocks nòr despises nor bewails them, but seeks to understand them ànd to regard them with as great evenness of mind as if he had before him phenomena of material Nature or geometrical figures. Secondly, he brings out all the points of view most important for the explanation of the feelings.

Spinoza entertained different cónceptions concerning the position and significance of feeling in the sphere of consciousness at different stages in his philosophical development. In his first work, the "Short Treatise" (ii. 16, 5), his conception is entirely intellectual. It is knowledge—ideas—which determine all the phenomena of psychical life. The will is only a consequence of the idea—an affirmation or rejection. At the same time, the ideas themselves are here said to be determined by the influence of objects, since he still retains his belief in the influence of one attribute on the other. In his work on the Cartesian philosophy he had already intimated that ideas themselves are expressions of our activity, so that we cannot distinguish between the genesis of ideas and their assertion or rejection. And in the definitive doctrine of the attributes, this thought is carried out still further, so that, indeed, understanding and will now become completely identical. Thought is mental activity, and all mental activity is thought: this is, roughly speaking, Spinoza's conception at this stage ; it is formulated in the Corollary to the 49th Proposition in the second book of the *Ethica: Voluntas et intellectus unum et idem sunt.* But in the third book, in which the natural history of the feelings is given, an entirely new conception of the will appears ; it is defined as the conscious impulse towards self-preservation (*Ethica*, iii. 9 Schol.). Far from being identical with knowledge, much less its effect, it is knowledge which is dependent on the will : "We neither strive for, wish, seek, nor desire anything because we think it to be good ; but, on the contrary, we adjudge a thing to be good because we strive for, wish, seek, or desire it." Here, then, impulse and will are identical, and ideas are dependent upon them. In his treatise on the course of Spinoza's development, which contains an illuminating discussion of this point, Tönnies conjectures, with great probability, that it was the influence of Hobbes which brought about this last change in

Y

Spinoza's conception.   Hobbes sets impulse and will in close connection with one another, and with the impulse towards self-preservation, while, at the same time, he emphasises the influence which the thought of an end exercises on the association of ideas. In Spinoza's work, as we have it, there is a manifest contradiction between the definition of the will given in the 49th Corollary of book ii. and that of the 9th Scholium of book iii., so that it seems extremely probable that two separate drafts were thrown into one, without the eradication of all traces of a difference of conception.

In his exposition of the psychology of the feelings in the third book of the *Ethica*, Spinoza starts from the impulse to self-preservation as the expression of the nature of every individual being.   If, in so doing, he has somewhat modified his psychology, he has changed nothing in his general philosophy.   In every individual being, infinite Nature, God Himself, is active.   Thus the striving of every individual being towards self-preservation is only a part of the infinite divine activity in all existence.   As early as the " Short Treatise " (i. 5) he, like Bruno, had seen in this impulse in all living creatures to self-preservation the revelation of the divine providence.   And this impulse is identical with the peculiar nature of things, and takes on a different character according to the nature of the individual being : existence is self-conservation.   This striving is called desire when it is attended with consciousness : by desire, then, we are to understand the nature of Man, in so far as this is conceived as determined to activity by a change of its condition.   If this desire be regarded from the mental side especially, it is called will.   Pleasure arises from the furtherance, pain from the hindrance, of this striving.   It must be carefully remarked that it is the *transition* to a more favourable (" more perfect ") condition that is attended with pleasure, while, again, it is the *transition* to a less favourable (" more imperfect ") condition that is attended with pain.   The conditions themselves, because at rest, are not attended with feeling. Moreover no express comparison of conditions is undertaken : feeling answers immediately to change of conditions.

As Spinoza here expresses what we now call the biological significance of feeling, *i.e.* its connection with the furtherance or hindrance of life, and as he was likewise well aware of the importance of the relation of contrast for the genesis of feeling (the law of relativity within the sphere of feeling), so, too, he has thrown great light on the third main point in the psychology of the feelings—the significance of ideas, and the association of ideas, for the development of the specific kinds of feeling. From desire, pleasure, and pain, he deduces, by means of the laws of the association of ideas, the special forms of feeling. We love that which causes us pleasure, but hate that which causes us pain. Further, we love that which furthers what we love, as we hate that which injures it. And when we imagine a being similar to ourselves as having a certain feeling, we ourselves involuntarily experience the same feeling. This may give rise to sympathy, but it may also give rise to envy and wounded ambition, if *e.g.* we wish to possess alone what is enjoyed by another, or if we wish another to feel precisely as we do. Spinoza proceeds to carry out his theory in detail according to these general principles. He founded the theory of evolution within the sphere of feeling, when he showed how, under the influence of ideas, and through various modes of combination and blending, our feeling is able to take on forms widely different from the elementary forms under which it started. Spinoza formulated the conditions of the growth of feeling. How far it is possible to adhere exclusively to the one starting-point he adopted, *i.e.* the individual's impulse to self-preservation, is a question which cannot be discussed here.

(*f*) *Ethic and Theory of Politics*

It is characteristic of Spinoza that while his thought has a practical motive, yet it soars high above the world of finitude and experience, in which alone practical motives and practical endeavour are possible. Spinoza denies the validity of any valuation (*Werthschätzung*) of Nature ; it follows its own eternal laws,—our ethical judgments, which rest upon a comparison of the more with the less perfect, according to our ideal of human life, are not adequate to the eternal essence of Nature, of which neither time, measure, nor number can be predicated. Spinoza emphasises the subjectivity of the ethical qualities no less energetically than that of the sense qualities had been emphasised since the time of Galilei. So long as Spinoza abides by his conception of existence " under the form of eternity " he can, strictly speaking, have no ethic ; nor does he

require any. Ethical questions can only arise in a world in
which the temporal relation holds good, where genesis and
development, change and opposition exist, where examples can
be followed and ends chosen. As Spinoza pertinently expresses
it : " Judgments on good and evil rest on comparison." In the
eternal unity of the infinite, divine nature with itself, however, all
comparison falls away, because all difference and opposition have
fallen away. The examination of Spinoza's theory of knowledge showed us that, regarded "under the form of eternity,"
all *riddles* vanish; we now see that all *duties* disappear likewise.

But as Spinoza distinguishes between the *natura naturans*
and the *natura naturata*, so also he distinguishes between the
purely theoretical and the practical standpoints. The practical
standpoint holds good only in the *natura naturata*. Spinoza
establishes an ethic with the same right with which he asserts the
significance of the empirical, of the finite world, and of the modes.
That he has an ethic involves no greater inconsistency than that
he has other concepts besides that of absolute Substance.

The possibility of an ethic stands, for Spinoza, in close
connection with his psychological doctrine of the feelings. The
foundation of ethics is the impulse to self-preservation, which
lies at the root of all our manifold feelings and passions. For
out of the impulse to self-preservation the desire to be no
longer agitated by the feelings and passions which external
causes arouse in us will be able to develop itself. As a part
of Nature—as a mode among other modes—man is dependent,
and is tossed about like the waves of the sea, without aim
or definite direction. We strive naturally to maintain our
being, to come to fuller inner activity. The fundamental
ethical virtue is strength of mind (*fortitudo*), an inner power
which makes men free and independent. Virtue is " the essence
itself or nature of man in so far as it has the power of
effecting certain things which can be understood through the
laws of its nature alone." In order to attain to this character
men must understand clearly that no feeling and no desire can
be restrained in us except by a stronger feeling or a stronger
desire. Spinoza grounds the proof of this proposition on the
law of inertia, which, in virtue of the identity of mind and
matter, finds its counterpart on the mental side of existence.
Ethical development is only possible because feelings can be
aroused in us which gradually crowd out the very feelings by

which they themselves were evoked. When, after a comparison
of the different forms and grades of human life, we form an
ideal of human nature (*idea hominis, tanquam naturae humanae
exemplar*), we call everything which leads us nearer to this
ideal, good, and everything which hinders us from reaching it,
evil, and a desire arises to approximate as nearly as possible
to it. Knowledge of good and evil—since it is concerned
with what really serves or injures us—is nothing but conscious
joy, because we are approaching our ideal, or conscious sorrow,
because we are withdrawing from it ; and this knowledge, precisely because it is identical with a feeling, can become a power
in the mind. Men soon perceive, however, that they are not able
to arrive at perfect strength and freedom of mind by self-help
alone. Their whole outer life must be ordered and secure.
This is especially true of the development of a true knowledge ;
this, too, can only be attained by means of united forces ;
as, on the other hand, there is nothing that unites men better
than the endeavour after such goods as may be common to all.
Those passions only excite strife among men which concern
something which the individual alone can possess. The more
the individual desires freedom and strength of mind, the less
strife will there be among men, and the more will they be
active in common, since they will all be striving after that which,
in very deed, beseems human nature. Nothing is so useful to
man as man. It would be best, since they seek a common
good, if all could be like *one* mind and *one* body. Those who
pursue their own true profit, therefore, wish nothing for themselves that they cannot equally wish for other men, and on that
account they are just, faithful, and honourable in their dealings.
The fortitude (*fortitudo*) in which virtue consists, appears not
only in the form of strength of mind (*animositas*), by means of
which each man directly develops his personality, but also as
generosity (*generositas*), since each person seeks to help others
and to bind them to himself in the bonds of friendship.

   Characteristically Spinozistic is the estimation of the
different feelings upon which he enters, after he has set forth
the type of human development. Joy is good, in and for
itself, sorrow, in and for itself, evil. Accordingly hate, fear,
contempt, pity, repentance, and humility are evil—in so far as
they are not elements necessary to the production of pleasure.
The reason given for this is that joy corresponds to a passage

to greater, while sorrow answers to a passage to lesser perfection. The intellectually free man, guided by true knowledge, fixes his gaze on the positive development of life in himself and others. " He thinks of nothing less than of death, and his wisdom is not a meditation upon death but upon life (*meditatio vitae*)." He strives with all his strength to requite the hatred, anger, and contempt of other men with love or generosity. He who meets hatred with hatred leads a miserable life ; but if the hatred is overcome by love, the conquered yield with joy, not from defect of strength, but from an increase of it. In no other way can a man better display his strength of mind than by so educating others that they live according to their own free knowledge.[71]

While Spinoza's ethic thus leads from the impulse to self-preservation, which was its fundamental assumption, to practical activity and the foundation of society, there is yet another tendency in his thought which, starting from the same point, leads in the direction of mysticism and individualism. We constantly meet with the assumption of his earlier psychological standpoint, *i.e.* that the real nature of man consists in pure knowledge ; the more this is able to develop itself the more the real nature of man emerges, and the more he is really self-active. The true impulse to self-preservation, therefore, leads to the development of knowledge. It was the knowledge, too, of the union in which our mind stands with the whole of Nature which appeared to Spinoza to be the only good of which external causes cannot rob us. This enables Spinoza to establish, almost in one breath (cf. *Ethica*, iv. 22, Coroll. with 26 Dem.), the two propositions, that the striving after self-preservation is the first and only foundation of virtue, and that the striving after knowledge (*conatus intelligendi*) is the first and only foundation of virtue. Side by side with his realistic psychology, in which Spinoza conceives feelings and passions as the positive powers of our nature, we find another conception, according to which feeling is defined as an inadequate or confused idea (*idea inadaequata siva confusa ;* see the explanation at the end of book iii. of the *Ethica*). According to this latter conception, with the fuller and clearer growth of knowledge, feeling disappears. The more we understand that we ourselves and our conditions are determined by the infinite nature, by God Himself, who moves in us, as well as in all things acting upon us, the more we regard ourselves not as a single, isolated, impotent being, but as included in God and identical with Him. We feel pleasure in this thought, since it is the fruit of the highest activity of our mind, and pleasure, too, at the thought of the Being who is the cause of the joy with which knowledge fills us : thus arises an intellectual love of God (*amor intellectualis dei*), which fills us with the highest peace. God no longer appears as an external object ; our own innermost power is a part of the infinite power which moves in all things, and our love to God becomes identical with the infinite love with which God loves Himself : God's love to man and the love of man to God is one and the same. We see ourselves and all things under the form of eternity. Spinoza, the mystic, is at variance with Spinoza, the psychologist ; for this intellectual love (the human and the divine) is exalted above all becoming and opposition, but Spinoza himself declares that feeling answers to a *transition*—to a step forwards or backwards ! Only when he explains feeling as unclear thought, and annuls the law of relativity, can he maintain the mystical conclusion of his ethics.

The fifth book of the *Ethica*, in which this mysticism is predominant, also contains Spinoza's doctrine of immortality. Through that intellectual love of God, founded in our union with the absolute Being, our true nature is expressed ; that is to say, it is not dependent on time, but is a part of the infinite intellect (*intellectus infinitus*), of the idea of God (*idea dei*), which remains constant, although individual mental phenomena arise and pass away, and which corresponds to the conservation of motion on the material side. As the immediate form of divine activity we are immortal. This immortality—which, however, is not a *continuous* but an *eternal* persistence, since the temporal relation has here no meaning whatever—seems to be only predicable of those in whom the highest knowledge and, with that, complete and clear self-activity, is developed.[72] Whether this persistence as an eternal element of thought (*modus cogitandi aeternus*) is personal or not, is not apparent from Spinoza's exposition ; in any case, his notion of immortality is very different from the popular one. In conclusion he remarks that the belief in the eternity of the mind is not a necessary condition for ethics, pointing out that he himself has developed his ethical system without the assistance of this belief.   Blessedness is not the reward of virtue, but is identical with virtue.   For only when we can feel joy in the highest activity of our mind are we in a condition to master our passions.

The deep and sound thoughts contained in Spinoza's ethics would have attained to a more complete development had he carried out his psychological theory in detail.   As it is now, intellectualism gains the upper hand with him, especially when he attempts to describe the highest forms of mental life. His ethic thus becomes an ethic for philosophers exclusively. The importance of immediate acquiescence and of artistic perception do not receive their due, although his " intellectual love," grounded on intuition, contains intimations of both.   No one with an unprejudiced mind, however, can study Spinoza's wonderful work without echoing Goethe's words, when he re-marked " how boundless is the disinterestedness conspicuous in every sentence, how exalted the resignation which submits itself once for all to the great laws of existence, instead of trying to get through life with the help of trivial consolations, and what an atmosphere of peace breathes through the whole book ! "

But peace, according to Spinoza, must be won by fighting. The individual wins it through the struggle with his passions, which develops a new and higher passion ; and men in combination win it thus ;—the rudeness of their natural condition, in which each man's right is coextensive with his might, is superseded by the installation of an authority which can soothe conflicting desires and bring into harmony the impulse to self-preservation of the different individuals.   In his civil philosophy, as in his psychology, Spinoza is decidedly influenced by Hobbes.   Only he does not feel Hobbes's blind and narrow-minded fear of the multitude.   He is logical enough to abide by the proposition that human nature is the same in all men, and to see that it is as necessary to be protected against those who rule as against those who are ruled.   We can no more assume the best motives in the rulers than in the multitude.   The belief that the multitude could not understand public affairs arises because they are kept in ignorance on the subject.   Spinoza is one of the first democratic jurists of modern times ; but since his " Political Treatise " was never finished, we are unacquainted with the details of his doctrine of democracy.   It is characteristic of the two thinkers that while

Hobbes asserts democracy to be always, in fact, an aristocracy —of orators, Spinoza declares a monarchy to be always an aristocracy—of officials. As a matter of fact, political functions must of course always be exercised by the few, but the question is : where may the ultimate power be said to reside ? According to Spinoza the matter may be summed up thus: the State is founded on the united power of the many, since this is united to form one single will, just as the power of the individual is augmented when it is united with the power of others. This "intellectual union," through which the unity of power is conditioned, can however only exist when the State aims at that which all men of sound reason acknowledge to be profitable. For the sake of peace men may put up with much, but if slavery, rudeness, and desolation are to be called peace, then is peace the most wretched state of mankind. The State must make men neither into animals nor machines, but must provide free scope for their mental and bodily activities, and ensure to them the free use of their reason. The power of the State has no other foundation than the free union of individuals, so that in becoming a member of the State the individual does not give up his natural right but, on the contrary, secures its confirmation and development. The State would defeat its own aim if it suppressed individual freedom of thought and speech, and, worse than all, it would turn the noblest and best men of the country into its enemies.

As Spinoza defends freedom of speech so, too, he defends complete freedom in religion. This is the chief subject of his " Theologico-Political Treatise." In it he attempts to show that religion is concerned neither with the State nor with science, and that the State, in accordance with its own nature and the end it has in view, must grant full freedom of development to the inner intellectual life. The State can control men's external actions only—not their minds. It can establish an external worship and, in this respect, its government is to be preferred to a hierarchy. But it turns its authority to a still better use when it makes the practice of religion to consist in works of love and justice. The mental nature (*ingenium*) of men is of so many different kinds that what one man holds in veneration excites the laughter of another. It were best, therefore, for every man to be allowed freedom of conviction, and the right to interpret religious documents

according to his own judgment (*ex suo ingenio*).   Religion is
distinguished from science by its practical character.   It rests,
not on truth, but on piety.   None of the prophets were men
of high intellectual gifts.   Their imagination was stronger than
their understanding.   Their function was to bring before the
nation, by means of pictures and symbols, ideas which should
induce them to live in obedience to God, as evidenced by
love towards their neighbours.   The majority, who are not
able to follow the ratiocinations of reason, must have historical
models for their guidance.   Only by this means will they
become obedient—not merely from fear, but of their own will
and submission.   Whatever theoretical opinions men have of
God—whether they believe Him to be fire, or breath, or light,
or thought—is a matter of indifference so long as they possess
in Him an example which can lead them in the right way.
While, according to Spinoza, the prophets did not perceive the
truth in its pure form, but only in pictures, the divine wisdom is
immediately revealed in Christ, the only man who was capable
of perceiving matters which are neither contained in the first
principles of our knowledge nor can be deduced therefrom.
In a letter (*Ep.* 73), Spinoza says he does not understand what
the Church means by the doctrine that God has taken upon
Himself human nature ; this seemed to him as impossible as
the squaring of the circle.   He believed, however, that God's
eternal wisdom which reveals itself in all things, and especially
in the human mind, has given a special revelation of itself in
Christ.   Spinoza would have the biblical writings subjected to
a strictly historical examination.   The Bible, like nature, must
be explained through itself.   Not till we are clear as to what
the Bible really teaches can we raise the question whether this
teaching be true or not.   As Spinoza had asserted the independence of natural science and of ethics, so here he asserts the
independence of the historical method.   His historical sense
expresses itself in the demand that in the exposition of a book,
all that is known of the personality of the authors be taken into
account.   We must also examine into the source of their
writings.   The examination which Spinoza himself made led
him to believe that the five books of Moses were written at the
time of the Exile.   Modern criticism does not, perhaps, go so
far as this, yet it has a precursor in Spinoza.
     Spinoza's philosophy of religion was the first of his doctrines

to bear fruit.   Before Lessing and Goethe and their successors, the speculative philosophers of the close of the eighteenth century had ranged themselves on his side ; his views had already spread over no small area in the Netherlands, so that not only did individuals appropriate his ideas to feed their inner life of thought and feeling, but religious sects, partly mystical and partly rationalistic in character, were formed, whose conception and application of Christianity sprang, through more or less middle terms and modifications, out of the writings of the solitary philosopher.   Till the end of the eighteenth century, Dutch orthodoxy found frequent occasion to condemn as heresy Spinozistic views.   In its more mystical form, religious Spinozism united with the influence of Jakob Boehme's writings which, since the end of the seventeenth century, had been eagerly read in the Netherlands.   Curiously enough, each of the three elements which, in Spinoza's thought, were characteristically woven into a unity, afterwards in turn found enthusiastic supporters : first the religious element in the Netherlands, then the idealistic, in the German Renaissance, towards the end of the eighteenth century, and, finally, the realistic, amongst the philosophers and scientific men of our own day.   And even thinkers who would never recognise him officially were deeply and strongly influenced by him.   This is especially true of the man who, by himself and by others, is often declared to be the antipodes to Spinoza, viz. of Leibniz.

(a) Biography and Characteristics

THE three great systems developed by Descartes, Hobbes, and Spinoza have, notwithstanding their many differences, this one thing in common—they all establish a strictly mechanical interconnection of Nature with regard to the material side of existence. In these systems were deduced the logical consequences of principles, the establishment of which had been made possible by the birth of the exact sciences. They were attempts to show the aspect presented by existence, when these principles are taken as absolutely valid of all material phenomena (leaving aside the question as to whether there are or are not other phenomena besides those of matter). To many men of the old school these new principles and systems appeared the essence of arbitrariness and godlessness. A reaction may be traced under different forms towards the end of the seventeenth century. From the point of view of philosophy that reaction is of the greatest interest which, while retaining genuinely scientific acquisitions, sought—not in external fashion, by means of a compromise, or a patching together of irreconcilable elements, but internally, through an examination of the presuppositions which underlie the mechanical conception of Nature—to find a way which should lead out beyond this view, and reconcile it with the ancient and mediæval conception from which men had so emphatically turned away. It is in this sense that Leibniz denotes a reaction against the three great thinkers we have named. Never, perhaps, was a reaction carried out so profoundly; although Leibniz, consciously or unconsciously, accommodated his phraseology to conservative opinions far more than, from his own standpoint, he was

justified in doing. Leibniz had from the outset taken objection to the modern ideas—in spite of all his admiration for
them and their supporters—because they threatened the æsthetic
and religious view of Nature. There was no place for the
concept of ends in the new-world conception, for the world
seemed to have become a mere machine. It was the task
of Leibniz' life to reconcile ideas taken from opposite regions
of the intellectual world, and, while labouring to attain this
end, he developed a wealth of ideas and points of view, of
discoveries and suggestions, unparalleled, perhaps, in the history
of thought. There was hardly any science which he did not
touch, either to produce something new, or to stimulate to fresh
activity, and although he worked on very different materials,
yet an inner agreement, a common type, characterises all his
thoughts.

GOTTFRIED WILHELM LEIBNIZ was born at Leipzig on
the 21st of June 1646. His father, a jurist and professor of
moral philosophy, died early, and the boy, who was for the
most part left to himself, elected to spend the greater part of
his time in his dead father's library, where he read as much as
was possible—at first, for the most part, romances and history,
afterwards scholastic works. In spite of all the hindrances
presented by foreign languages and the abstruse character of
the subject-matter, he tried to understand all that came into
his hands by his own unaided efforts. His friends, he tells
us in a biographical sketch, were at first afraid that he would
become a poet, afterwards that he would be a scholastic : "they
did not know that my mind could not be filled with one
single kind of thing." The struggle between the mechanical
and the teleological conception of Nature arose early in his
mind. He relates how, when quite a youth, he wandered in a·
forest near Leipzig, pondering whether he should remain true to
the scholastic philosophy, or attach himself to the new doctrines.
The desire to cultivate all sides of his nature, and to become
acquainted with the exact sciences, induced him to leave
Leipzig. On account of a sorrow which befell him, he gave up
the attempt to attain his doctorate in his native town. He
graduated as a "doctor juris" at Altdorf, and afterwards went to
Mainz, where, in spite of his youth, he obtained a post in the
service of the Elector. Plans for the improvement of legal
science and the codification of the laws, together with philoso-

phical and scientific studies, occupied him entirely for several years. He attempted to purge jurisprudence of scholastic barbarities, and was becoming increasingly convinced of the decided victory of modern physics over the scholastic philosophy of Nature. For some time, according to his own subsequent confession (in the *Nouveaux Essais*), he felt a strong inclination towards the "sect of the Spinozists." His ruling thought, however, is the defence of the view that Nature is determined by ends, in combination with the retention of mechanical physics. He eagerly defended the modern scientific conceptions against the men of an older generation, *e.g.* his teacher, Jakob Thomasius, and Hermann Couring, the famous jurist and physician. But he endeavoured to show that the mechanical conception of Nature, far from excluding the idea of a divine providence, on the contrary presupposes it. In a short treatise (*Confessio naturae contra atheistas*), and in the letters to Jakob Thomasius in the years 1668-69, this twofold endeavour is very prominent. Leibniz is here still a dualist ; he is still conscious of a chasm between the two principles he wishes to unite. As he himself has told us, the study of Kepler, Galilei, and Descartes caused him to feel as though "transported into a different world" ; but the old world had to be united with the new. A journey to Paris, undertaken in the service of his Government, afforded him opportunity for new studies. In addition to his practical business and to the remarkable proposal of the conquest of Egypt by the French, which he laid before Louis XIV. (in order to avert his lust of conquest from Germany), he buried himself, under Huyghen's guidance, in mathematical studies, which led to the discovery of the differential calculus, while, at the same time, he studied the Cartesian philosophy with great ardour. His standpoint in the year 1670 betrays the influence of Hobbes's works. In a treatise on natural philosophy (*Hypothesis physica nova*, 1671) he, like Hobbes and Gassendi, asserts the continuity of motion by means of the idea of tendencies to motion (*conatus*) throughout the smallest moments and in the smallest parts. This idea is connected with the discovery made in the following year of the significance of infinitely small quantities in mathematics. From this time forward he protests against Descartes' doctrine of the conservation of motion, and begins to assert in its stead the conservation of force. He finds the distinction between mind and matter to consist in this,—a tendency which does not pass over into motion can only, on the material side, exist for a single moment, but in the life of the soul, owing to memory and thought, it may extend beyond the moment. This thought finds pregnant utterance in the proposition that body is a momentary mind, or a mind without memory. In a letter written in the year 1671 he says: "As the activity of bodies consists in motion, so the activity of souls consists in effort (*conatus*) or, as it were, in a minimal or punctual motion, since the soul, strictly speaking, is only at a point in space, while the body occupies a place." In these declarations we have what might be called Leibniz' second philosophy. He is trying to get free of dualism, and he ranges himself on the side of continuity, attributing mental effort to the differentials of matter; but he is not yet clear as to the relation between the material and the psychical. The concept of effort (*conatus*) offers a possible point of union. Leibniz, however, does not here get beyond this vague indication. Of this alone he is sure, that the solution is to be found only by tracing back that which is given in phenomena to its elements and presuppositions.

As Leibniz occupied himself with different sciences so, too, he took pains to come into contact with leading men of different mental proclivities. In Paris he cultivated the society of Huyghens. Previously to this, he had addressed himself by letter to Hobbes, but no further correspondence between them seems to have ensued. During his stay in Paris his attention was directed to Spinoza, whose "Theologico-Political Treatise" had appeared a few years before, while the *Ethica* had only just become accessible to a small circle. Tschirnhausen, a mathematician and philosopher, who belonged to this circle, and who was among the most discerning of Spinoza's correspondents, became acquainted with Leibniz in Paris, and gave him some insight into Spinoza's opinions. Tschirnhausen informed Spinoza, through a mutual friend, that he had met in Paris with "a young man well versed in the different sciences and free from the usual theological prejudices, Leibniz by name, with whom he had contracted friendship, since he was a man who, like himself, laboured to develop his mind, and regarded this as all-important." Tschirnhausen considered his new friend worthy to become acquainted with the *Ethica*,

and begged the master for permission to show it to him, re-
minding him that Leibniz had already written a letter to him
in connection with the " Theologico-Political Treatise." Spinoza
answered : " I think I know this Leibniz from his letters. But
I do not know why he who was councillor in Frankfurt [Mainz]
has journeyed to France. As far as I could judge from his
letters he is a liberal-minded man, and well versed in every
science. Yet I think it would be imprudent to confide my
writings to him so soon. I should like first to know what he
is doing in France, and to learn what our friend Tschirnhausen
thinks of him when he has had intercourse with him for a
longer time and has learnt to know his character better."
Spinoza evidently mistrusted Leibniz, whose pliancy and
versatility were not altogether advantageous to his intellectual
character ; they left an impress on his mental life and activity
which was, certainly, the very antipodes to Spinoza's retiring
and concentrated intellectual life. Spinoza's mistrust proved
to be justified. For near as Leibniz is to Spinoza in his final
results and whenever he is strictly logical, yet in his later
writings he took every opportunity to differ from him, even
making frequent use of expressions which we should hardly
have expected from a man " free from the usual theological
prejudices." At this time, however, he was very anxious
to come in contact with Spinoza. After a residence of
four years in Paris (1672-76), where he had enjoyed intercourse with Antoine Arnauld, the great Jansenist theologian
and zealous Cartesian — an evidence of Leibniz' power of
appreciating different kinds of minds and of using them for his
own instruction—he went *viâ* England to Holland, where he
stayed two months, during which time he visited Spinoza
repeatedly and discussed philosophical subjects with him.
This personal relation between the two great thinkers, which
was so intimate that Spinoza finally overcame his scruples
and showed Leibniz the *Ethica*, was only discovered with
the last *trouvaille* of papers.[73] Leibniz himself, it is true,
mentions, in a single passage in the *Theodicée*, his visit to
Spinoza, but he makes it appear as though the conversation
had turned on everyday topics ! It was no recommendation
to have been so closely connected with Spinoza. We see, too,
that several of the letters in the posthumous edition of Spinoza's
works his friends published are abbreviated and the names

of the writers are frequently omitted.   Leibniz, who had waited
eagerly for its appearance, was much disturbed to find one of
his own letters (a very harmless one, certainly) printed with
his name attached to it.   Until recently, no one suspected that
Leibniz wrote several letters to Spinoza.   Spinoza's train of
thought exercised a great influence on Leibniz, more particularly in leading him definitely beyond the dualistic theory.
We recognise Spinozistic ideas again when Leibniz represents
to the Cartesians, at this time, that the difference between
mind and matter does not exclude the possibility of their
being qualities of one and the same being.   We have glosses
and excerpts of Leibniz which date from his first reading of Spinoza's *Ethica*.   He raises objections at once on
three points—all three of which are characteristic of his train of
thought.   The first is the assertion that there can only
be one single substance (*Ethica*, i. 5); the second is the
exclusion of the intellect and will from the *natura naturans*
(*Ethica*, i. 31); the third is the famous polemic against
final causes (appendix to book i.)   Leibniz was no more
a Spinozist than he was a Cartesian or a Hobbist.   But
he was strongly influenced by his predecessors.   As regards
Spinoza, the chief thing to remark is that Leibniz accepted,
and carried still farther, the identity hypothesis which
he had established.   There can hardly be a greater
misunderstanding than to suppose that, because Leibniz
asserted the plurality of substances, he disputed the hypothesis
of identity.   His aim, on the contrary, was to unite these
two views ; how far he succeeded in doing so is another
question.

Towards the end of 1676, Leibniz accepted the post of
councillor and librarian to the Duke of Hanover (Braun-
schweig-Lüneburg).   He became involved in a multitude of
administrative, historical, and political tasks, and his restless
eagerness to make progress on all sides entailed an enormous
amount of letter-writing.   His correspondence with more than
a thousand different persons is preserved in the library at
Hanover.   But as the main thought of his philosophy was
that existence is continuous and consists of a multitude
of individual beings, each with its own idiosyncrasy, in
reciprocal harmony with one another, so, too, we find an
inner connection between his labours in different spheres.

He had an eye for those small proportions and infinitesimal differences, which, when conjoined and summed up, may yet prove to be reality. His mathematics, his physics, and his philosophy all exemplify this characteristic. But he lays no less weight on the continuity, the inner connection between all things. His historical studies interested him on account of the connection of the past with the present, and a similar interest caused him to procure information about China through a Jesuit missionary. He had a sense for the practically useful, as well as for science and the Church. He promoted the development of mines in the dukedom, laboured for the establishment of academies, proposed the conversion of monasteries into scientific institutions, negotiated first with Bossuet concerning the union of the Catholic and Protestant Churches, and afterwards with the Protestant theologians for the union of the Lutheran and Reformed Churches. He laid before Peter the Great, whom he admired extremely, and with whom he had several times conversed, proposals of reform and measures for the furtherance of the science of language and physics. As a philologist he possessed so true an insight, and asserted the significance of experience in the study of speech with such energy, that Max Müller can say of him that, if he had been understood and supported by the scholars of his day, the science of language would have been established as an inductive science a century earlier. In the sphere of medicine, too, his ideas were significant. Small wonder that he says in a letter : " I cannot tell you how extraordinarily distracted I am. I set on foot investigations into the archives, fetch out old papers, and collect unprinted documents. I receive and answer letters in great numbers. I have so much, too, that is new in mathematics, so many philosophical thoughts, so many other literary observations which I should not like to lose, that I often do not know what to do first." Leibniz never succeeded in concentrating himself on a work which should be typical of his personality, and his line of thought. He was not, like Spinoza, " a man of one book." He has expressed his ideas in a multitude of letters and small treatises, which have not yet all appeared in print. The most important of his published writings on philosophy are to be found in Gerhardt's edition (seven vols.) ; but much still lies in the library at Hanover. An incredible power of work and mobility of thought characterised the man. And as, in his system, existence mirrors itself in innumerable ways in individual souls, so he felt the need of looking at his system from the very different standpoints with which he came in contact. During his correspondence with the Jansenist Arnauld, it became clear in his own mind. He had no objection to throwing it into a scholastic form, if haply it might find acceptance among his Jansenist friends, while he clothed it in a more popular dress when he philosophised with the Electress of Hanover or the Queen of Prussia, or when drawing up a sketch of his doctrine (the later so-called "Monadology") for Prince Eugene.

But we have not yet followed the development of Leibniz' philosophical views to the point where he could say he believed himself to have found "a new expression for the essence of things" (*une nouvelle face de l'intérieur des choses*). We saw that he took up the cudgels on behalf of mechanical physics, attempting, however, to reconcile it with the teleological view, at first dualistically, later (following Hobbes and Spinoza) in a more monistic manner. It was his conviction that "the moderns had carried reform too far," since they reduced everything to a machine ; but it was no less his conviction that hitherto people had only "exposed themselves to ridicule" when they tried to refute the strict mechanical connection even of the material events most closely connected with mental phenomena.

In a letter of 1697 Leibniz writes : "Most of my views are at length matured, after twenty years of deliberation, for I began to think at a very early age. . . . I have changed my views however, again and again, in accordance with the fresh knowledge I acquired, and it was not till about twelve years ago that I felt satisfied." These words refer to the year 1685. In that year Leibniz wrote a short treatise (*Petit discours de métaphysique*) which he sent to Arnauld at the beginning of 1686. According to this treatise, existence consists of individual substances ; in each one of these the world is expressed on one of the infinitely many possible sides from which it may be viewed in the divine thought ; every individual is an idea of God, actualised by means of a continual "emanation." Extension and motion, just like the sense-qualities, are nothing but phenomena. It is force only, not motion, which remains constant ; and force is identical with substance. Preliminary to this treatise was an earlier one (1680), in which it was shown that the essence of motion—motion, to which the modern systems reduced everything in Nature !—had not yet been adequately explained (*intima modus nondum patent*), and it was further asserted that being (existence, substance) and working are one and the same, also that all force or all effort is work.[74] The proposition that every substance works, and that everything which works is substance (*omnem substantiam agere, at omne agens substantiam appellari*), is perhaps the most important in all Leibniz' philosophy. It put an end to that mysticism or mythology which conceived the nature of things to be quiescent being, unchanging existence. It provided Leibniz with the means to unite teleology and mechanism, since he assumes that the forces which form the innermost nature of individual beings and phenomena and are that which, throughout all changes, remain constant, emanate from the divine Being, and work towards worthy ends. The divine aims, then, find their satisfaction in Nature, without interruption of its regular interconnection—even, indeed, by means of it. The advance of the *Discours* of 1685 on the treatise of 1680 consists more especially in this ;—that the *individual* character of the monads is asserted, and is conceived as analogous to the souls of men and of animals. Every individual being is a little world, developing itself according to its own laws by its own force, and is a special emanation of the divine force ; this development takes place, by reason of the common origin of all things, in harmony with the development of all other beings. With this Leibniz' system was complete. It was first published in a treatise printed in the *Journal des Savants* 1695 (*Système nouveau de la nature et de la communication des substances*). He did not use the name "monad" till later (1696). He can hardly have borrowed this appellation from Bruno, for history gives us no reason for supposing that Bruno exerted any direct influence on Leibniz, close as is the relationship between several of their ideas. It is more probable (as has been lately suggested) that he adopted the name from *van Helmont* the younger, mystic and chemist, with whom he had come into personal contact shortly before he first uses the term.

Leibniz contented himself with his own definition of

substance as that which works unceasingly. Even after the completion of his system, he persisted in his endeavour to formulate its fundamental ideas with the greatest possible distinctness. His comprehensive correspondence and his large personal acquaintance gave him ample opportunity for doing so. Thus, during his residence in Vienna (1714), he wrote a sketch of his doctrine of monads for Prince Eugene, which was published, after his death, under the title of *Monadologie.* Nor did he neglect to observe the tendencies of his own time. He was drawn into a discussion, which he carried on with great courtesy, with two leading thinkers. His criticism, in his *Nouveaux Essais*, of John Locke's attempt to deduce all knowledge from experience is brilliant and even at the present day, instructive, since especial emphasis is laid on the importance of the inner dispositions, of the conditions residing in the peculiar nature of the knowing being. As Locke died before Leibniz had completed his work, he refused to publish it, and on that account it did not exert so great an influence on philosophical discussion as it would otherwise certainly have done. It did not appear till 1765. The second contemporary, against whose views Leibniz felt compelled to take up his pen, was Pierre Bayle. Bayle had criticised the attempt of several theologians and philosophers to harmonise the assumption of an all-powerful, divine governance with the moral and physical evil in the world, asserting that, in view of the actual condition of the world, the assumption of two mutually opposing principles, one good and one evil, was much more susceptible of philosophical proof. In answer to this, Leibniz wrote his *Theodicée* (1710), in which he attempted to prove a harmony between theology and philosophy, and to establish the assertion that the actual world is the best possible world. This is Leibniz' poorest work; spun out and loose in form, vague and popular—in the bad sense of the word—in thought. In no other work does he so far accommodate himself to ideas which, in strict logical propriety, could find no place in his system. It was a misfortune that, during the eighteenth century, it was by this work that Leibniz became known. The *Nouveaux Essais* lay forgotten in the library at Hanover, and the splendid and original small treatises, published in journals, which expressed his own fundamental thoughts, were accessible only to a few.

There is no question that Leibniz' attempt to unite and reconcile religion and philosophy was honestly meant. It was the thought which occupied him throughout his life, from his youth up. But yet his was not, properly speaking, a religious nature. This is shown by the facility with which he could disregard confessional differences. It was natural, rather than positive, religion which he had at heart. And his sense for the individual and characteristic made it at once easy and interesting to him to familiarise himself with the different religious systems, just as his belief in the harmony of all individual peculiarities and efforts produced in him a wish for the reconciliation of the divided churches—a wish, however, which was not shared by men like Bossuet and Spener, who were unable to perceive any justifiable feature in confessions differing from their own. Arnauld admonished him to leave speculating as to the interconnection of things and turn to the true faith. Characteristic of Leibniz is a story of two brothers, which he was fond of telling : one of the brothers having gone over to Catholicism tried to convert his brother, who, on his part, was just as eager to win him back to Protestantism ; the result was that each convinced the other—and the end of it all was, that God had mercy on both, on account of their zeal. Leibniz cared for the inner force and inner striving of the monads, —not merely for the particular way in which this force expressed itself in individual monads, who were often inclined to look on this way as the only right one. The object of Leibniz' faith was the universal harmony, which was for him not merely a result in the future, but was already present in all minds, if only they could become conscious of it. In every book that Leibniz read—and he read many books— he found something interesting and instructive, and, since he knew how different things can appear from different standpoints, he was inclined to defend and excuse, even where he could not agree. He knew how to talk about what interested them to men in all ranks of life. His recognition of the monads extended even to the lower forms. He avoided killing animals, and if he had put an insect under the microscope to examine it, he always replaced it carefully on the leaf from which he had taken it. Gentle and gay, subject to no violent emotions, always occupied with thinking and studying—so he went through the world. His last years were spent in solitude. On account of his many occupations, he had had, as he himself said, no time to marry—until it was too late. While at one time he had been in favour at the Hanoverian court, and had risen to be a "Privy Councillor of Justice" he seems in his last years, after the death of his royal patron, to have fallen, to a certain degree, into disgrace. The clergy and the people suspected his orthodoxy because he did not attend church ; his name was put into Low German as Lövenix, *i.e. Glaube-nichts* [one who believes in nothing]. When he died (1716), only a few followed his bier. His motto was: "As often as an hour is lost, a part of life perishes." This was inscribed on his coffin together with a favourite symbol of his : a spiral with the motto, *Inclinata resurget.*

(b) The Doctrine of Monads

Now that we have gained some insight into the historical development of the Leibnizian philosophy, our next task must be to give a systematic exposition of it. The principal works on which this exposition will be founded are: *Discours de métaphysique* (1685), *Système nouveau* (1695), *Lettre à Basnage* (1698), *De ipsa natura* (1698), and *Monadologie* (1714). Together with these, however, must be taken a great number of letters and smaller treatises.

Leibniz founds his philosophy by means of an analysis of the fundamental principles of physical science. These principles he admits as freely as did Hobbes and Spinoza, but he considers them to be derived from still more fundamental presuppositions. Physics has its foundation in metaphysics. The chief thing for us, therefore, is to see how, according to Leibniz, the transition from physics to metaphysics is to be conceived.

Leibniz is entirely in agreement with the new science so far as its efforts are directed towards reducing everything in Nature to motion. But, as a philosopher, he asks : what reality does motion itself possess, and what is its cause? All motion is relative. If we believe that a thing moves, this depends upon the point of view from which it is regarded. True reality is not motion itself, but the force which is its cause, and which remains constant even though the motion cease. The Cartesians, who taught that the sum of motion in the world is always constant, while they asserted, at the same time, that motion passes over into rest, and the converse, were obliged to assume continual interruptions of continuity, for the transition from motion to rest as well as that from rest to motion were inexplicable. Only by means of the concept of force (or tendency, *conatus*) can we assert connection. There is, then, only a relative distinction between motion and rest : they are different phenomenal forms of force. It is force which remains constant. There is no such thing as absolute rest. Not even for the smallest moment that we can conceive, does a moving body occupy one and the same place in space. If we ask what this force is, Leibniz answers : it is that in the present state of things which brings about a change in the future (*ce qu'il y a dans l'état présent, qui porte avec soi un changement pour l'avenir*) (Lettre à Basnage). This it is which really exists. Leibniz also arrived at this concept by means of a criticism of the concept of atoms, as understood by the atomic theory of his day. The adoption of absolutely hard atoms would be in contradiction to the conservation of force and to continuity, since at every collision, force would be dissipated. The atoms must therefore (as Huyghens has already taught) be elastic, *i.e.* consist of parts ; absolute atoms, therefore, are a self-contradiction. If we thoroughly examine into the matter we shall find reality everywhere. "Atoms," says Leibniz, in a letter, "are only the result of a feebleness of our power of imagination, which is glad to rest, and is therefore in haste to make an end with divisions and analysis" (Letter to Hartsoeker, 1710). The difference between the solid and the fluid is relative, just as motion is relative. From this point of view, too, it is force only which possesses true reality.

That force is the true reality, Leibniz expressed in the language of his time by saying that force is substance, and that all substance is force. The concept of force, again, is closely connected with the concept of law, for force is nothing but that in a certain condition of things which brings about change in the future. Thus the presupposition of all applications of the concept of force is a connection according to law between the changing conditions. The principle of sufficient reason, which asserts that everything has a reason is, therefore, properly speaking, the fundamental proposition of Leibniz' philosophy, although he himself only expressly established it as a primary principle in his later works (the *Théodicée* and the *Monadologie*). And connected with this concept of law is, for Leibniz, another fundamental concept—that of *individuality*. For by individuality he understands the law according to which changes in the condition of a being take place. Each individual has its formula, so to speak, and as we can find the subsequent terms in a mathematical series when we have found the law of sequence for the first terms, so, too, with the inner changes of an individual being. It is in the law of sequence of these changes that individuality consists : *la loi du changement fait l'individualité de chaque substance particulière* (Lettre à Basnage). In the *Discours de métaphysique*, where the concept of individual substance was first introduced, Leibniz compares the relation between substance and its changing conditions with the relation between the subject and predicate of a logical judgment : as in a logical judgment it must be possible to find the predicate contained in the subject, as soon as we have a thorough knowledge of the latter, so he who knows the nature of the particular individual will, from this knowledge, be able to deduce all its changing conditions. These changes are continuous, for the ground of any one change is always to be found in the change which preceded it. Every one of these substances is, therefore, a little world in itself, developing itself from its own impulse and having an inner life of its own. Only by a miracle can such an individual substance arise or pass away, and every substance has its own inner law, differing from that of other substances.

If we ask why that which really exists (substance) must be individual, Leibniz replies : because only unities, individual beings, can exist. He finds fault with the Cartesians, because they not only attributed absolute reality to motion, but also extension, which they regarded as substance. As far back as the notes on Spinoza's *Ethica*, we find him writing : " It is not certain that bodies are substances ; it is different with souls." These words show the direction in which his thought was running. In his later works we constantly meet, under a great variety of forms, with the following train of thought : extension presupposes something which is extended, *i.e.* several times repeated. Extension means manifoldness, combination, aggregation. But the nature of a combination depends on its component parts. It is not the aggregation which possesses reality, but the units of which it is made up. If, then, there were no absolutely simple substances, there would be no reality. The assumption of the reality of extended matter, moreover, involves the difficulty that—according to the law of continuity—it can be divided *ad infinitum*. True unities cannot therefore be material, extended ; if, on the other hand, there were no such absolute unities in existence, matter would be mere appearance without any real significance. Only the absolutely simple and indivisible can be substance, and this cannot be material.

Before we ask what Substance then is, we must call attention to one other important definition. Leibniz started from the fundamental assumptions of physical science. Of these he regarded the principle of the conservation of force as the most important. This he considered to be the foundation of the laws of Nature (*fundamentum naturae legum*). This foundation of the laws of Nature can only, Leibniz thinks (see especially *De ipsa natura*, Erdmann's edition, p. 155), be explained by a teleological argument : It is necessary that the same amount of force be always preserved in the world ; but the ground of this necessity is that divine wisdom and order rules in the world ; the first principle or the first sufficient ground of mechanism is a final cause, a teleological principle. In a short treatise directed against the physicist PAPIN (*De legibus naturae*, Duten's edition, iii. p. 255), Leibniz expresses this in the following manner : Cause and effect must always correspond with one another ; they must be equivalent. If there were more in the effect than in the cause, we should get a *perpetuum mobile ;* if there were less in the effect than in the cause, the same cause could never again be produced. Nature would be in a state of constant retrogression, perfection would decline. Both of these alternatives are opposed to the divine wisdom and immutability. If, then, the two other possibilities being ruled out, there is equivalence in Nature between cause and effect, this, according to Leibniz, cannot be based on purely mathematical or mechanical grounds, but must be teleologically explained.[75]

The law, according to which the single individual beings, who are the true realities, develop their changes of condition, is, for Leibniz, a law according to which they progress to more perfect, not merely to new, conditions. The relation of cause to effect, that is to say, is here identical with the relation of means to an end. Existence, in its innermost essence, is so planned that the purely mechanical laws work towards that which is required by the laws of justice and love. In the indwelling law (*lex insita*) peculiar to the nature of each individual, both kinds of laws are, with respect to this individual, united. Leibniz is, as we see, so full of the principle of the conservation of force that he overlooks the fact that, teleologically, the point is, not that the same amount of force should be preserved, but that it should be preserved in a form favourable and serviceable to the existence of life and to its continuous development. The importance of this consideration, however, has only become clear in the light of modern investigations. Although Leibniz thus gives a teleological foundation to the mechanical connection of Nature, yet it is not his intention to reintroduce final causes or to allow an explanation of natural phenomena by means of an appeal to inner powers or adaptability to ends. In dealing with particulars, our procedure must be strictly mechanical ; only of mechanism as a totality, or rather of the first principles of mechanism, is it evident that they can only be understood when considered teleologically. The mechanical interconnection of Nature is the fact from which Leibniz' whole philosophy— no less than that of Hobbes and Spinoza—proceeds.

The technical name for the absolute individual which Leibniz considers to be the true reality is "monad." This Greek word means unity, and thus denotes the being on its formal side only. If we ask what this individual unity, with its inner conditions developing according to a definite law, really is, Leibniz answers we must think of it as analogous with our own souls. In the *Discours* this is not distinctly said. But in the subsequent correspondence with Arnauld we find the following passage : " The substantial unity presupposes a complete (*accompli*), indivisible and, by natural means, imperishable being, since its concept includes everything it may encounter. Nothing of this kind is to be found in figure or motion . . . but only in a soul or a substantial form similar to that which we call an ' I '" (Letter to Arnauld, Nov. 1686). Thus objective analysis is here completed by a subjective analysis. We find in ourselves, by means of self-observation, inner conditions (sensations, feelings, thoughts) which change, and an impulse or desire which causes us to pass over from one condition to another. By means of this subjective analysis we must make clear to ourselves, by way of analogy, the nature of the monads. Our soul is only a single monad, but we have no reason for believing that we stand alone in Nature. On the contrary, according to the law of continuity, by which all leaps in Nature are excluded, we are obliged to believe that there are infinitely many degrees of that kind of existence which we know through ourselves : *C'est partout et toujours la même chose, aux degrés de perfection près.* The law of analogy bids us do allegiance everywhere to the principle : " just as with us " (*tout comme ici*[76]). The law of analogy, according to which we conceive all other existence as differing in degree only from our own is, for Leibniz, only a special form of the law of continuity and, like it, originates in the principle of sufficient reason. If we assume no such general animation, in lower and higher degrees, it becomes altogether incomprehensible how sensation and consciousness can arise. Just as the origin of motion was inexplicable to the Cartesians, because they did not go back to force, so also the origin of consciousness was to them a riddle, because they took no account of the more obscure grades and forms of psychical life, of the impulses and efforts which only awake to clear consciousness in the higher grades of life. We are conscious in ourselves of a constant change between clearly conscious and dark and unconscious conditions. In analogy with this, we must conceive monads in all degrees of clearness and darkness. There are sleeping, dreaming, and more or less waking monads. The identity of Nature leads us to this assumption. For that part of matter which forms human bodies cannot be the only one which is gifted with the faculty of sensation and will. There must be something analogous to this (whether we call it soul or not) in the lower stages. In a letter, dated May 1704, Leibniz calls this application of analogy, *mon grand principe des choses naturelles.*

Leibniz consciously takes the same route as that which had been unconsciously taken by all mythologies and older speculative systems to arrive at the assumption that the spiritual rules in existence. He points out, with perfect clearness, the point at which all metaphysical idealism arises. And here, too, he is guided by the presupposition of the complete intelligibility of existence.   From this assumption there follows the continuity of all existence, and the analogy of all natures with our own.

But this point in the development of his thought was a turning-point for Leibniz.   Guided by the endeavour to find that which has real existence in material phenomena, he builds his philosophy on an analysis of the latter.   But now that he has become convinced that only beings having representations, in differing degrees of darkness and clearness, really exist, matter becomes, for him, *mere* appearance.   The seeming existence of bodies is a sense-phenomenon.   The senses, however, do not deceive us here, any more than they deceive us when we think the sun moves round the earth.   Phenomena are real in so far as they are bound together in a regular connection, and as a law determines their order of sequence.   This law is the mark of that which is reality for us.   It does not, however, oblige us to assume that anything else exists except monads and their representations.   At this point Leibniz might have entered upon an entirely new line of thought, *i.e.* an examination into whether, from the purely subjective standpoint, from the assumption that the world only exists in the form of representations, we should arrive at the same results as are given by the objective method which he had hitherto followed. Upon this new path Leibniz did not enter, and when, in his old age, he heard of Berkeley's attempt in this direction, it seemed to him utterly paradoxical (see the letter of the 15th March 1715, to des Bosses).   It is evident that Leibniz never clearly realised how great a difference there is between appearance *of something* and appearance *for some one*.   Both these relations may be contained in the concept "phenomenon"; Leibniz begins with the former and ends with the latter.   And only after he had established the concept of substance as force and individual unity, did he find—in accordance with the law of analogy—that its essence consists in representative activity.   But since this last assumption forms the final point of his thought-sequence we can understand how it was that he did not deduce all its consequences.[77] Leibniz continued to consider material phenomena as the expression of an objective order of things.   In virtue of the law of continuity everything in the material world is in reciprocal action ; modification of one part of the world extends to all parts. And from this it is concluded that each monad, in a darker or clearer manner, represents the *entire* universe, as every point of the physical universe feels everything that happens in the whole universe. This doctrine of a multiplicity of monads it is, which shows that Leibniz did not follow the purely subjective course, for, in that case, he would have had to deal with a single monad and its representation only. The assumption of a consciousness other than my own already presupposes the application of the conclusion from analogy on which Leibniz founds his metaphysical idealism.

Leibniz looked upon the discovery of small organisms made by Swammerdam, Leeuwenhook, and other investigators, by means of the microscope, as an empirical confirmation of his hypothesis that in all apparently dead masses, force, life, and soul exist. Here was a world of infinitesimally small beings revealed to him within the sphere of organic life, and he had himself helped to disclose the world of infinitely small quantities, as also in his philosophy he had asserted that behind seemingly homogeneous masses, true reality, consisting of individual beings with a nature akin to our own, is to be found. Arising and passing away, birth and death were for him nothing but phenomena, expressions of contractions or expansions, darkenings or illuminations going on in the monads. Absolute gulfs and differences (no less than homogeneous masses) vanished as he became increasingly convinced of the endless individual *nuances* of life. Leibniz alludes with evident satisfaction in all his subsequent expositions to the labours of his great contemporaries,—the natural philosophers above-mentioned.

On account of his concept of monads, Leibniz appears to stand in sharp antithesis to Spinoza. For the latter, there was only one single substance, and all individuals were related to it as waves to the sea. For Leibniz, true reality is a manifold of individual forces, each active according to its indwelling law, so that they all develop their effects out of their own original character. Leibniz himself often accentuated this contrast,—most clearly in a letter to Bourguet (December 1714). " I am at a loss to understand how they can deduce Spinozism from my doctrine. It is precisely by the monads that Spinozism is undone. For there are just as many true substances as . . . there are monads ; while, according to Spinoza, there is only one single substance. He would be right if there were no monads; then everything except God would be transitory and would be resolved into simple modifications." Thus Leibniz and Spinoza proceed from the same fundamental concept of substance. All determinations and conditions of substance must proceed from its own inner nature, and cannot be due to any external influence. Leibniz maintains this with regard to each of his monads as emphatically as Spinoza maintained it with regard to his one and only substance. The difficulty of this concept of absolute substance for Spinoza, lay in explaining how the multiplicity of the attributes and of individual beings is to be understood through the assumption of one single substance. The difficulty of the same concept for Leibniz lay in the explanation of the agreement between the states of the different monads, if each of these is only determined from within, and if none of them, to employ Leibniz' own metaphor, have holes, windows, or doors through which anything from outside can enter in. And, for Leibniz, there was the additional difficulty of reconciling the doctrine of monads with his theological presuppositions.

.   Leibniz believed that both these difficulties were solved by one single thought. That the conditions of the different monads should be found to be in harmony with one another, he takes as a matter of fact : there exists universal harmony or universal accord between all the beings in the world. It is evident that he here, as already hinted, proceeds from the perception of the general reciprocal action in the physical world, and from the empirical view—which, however, is supported by the conclusion from analogy—that the perceptions and representations of the separate individuals are so harmonious that a picture of the world can be constructed which, in its leading features, is common to all. But since true reality consists entirely of a multiplicity of self-dependent and independent beings which, as Leibniz says in a letter, must be considered little gods, because they have life in themselves, he is therefore, he concludes, obliged to assume a common founder of this harmony. "God alone," he says in the *Discours* (§ 32), "brings about the union or interconnection of substances, and through Him alone do the phenomena of one man coincide and agree with those of other men, so that our representations acquire reality." God has, from the beginning, so created the individual monads,

that the one takes account of the other ; their agreement springs
from their common origin.   They proceed from God through
an emanation or fulguration, as individualisations of the one
divine power, just as each single thought of ours is an emanation
of the force of our mind.   God perceives the world from
infinitely many different points of view, and each of these
different points of view He actualised, at the creation of the
world, in a single substance.   The states of the individual
monads correspond with one another as the different per-
spectives of a town, which we get from different points of view,
are in inner agreement with one another (*Discours*, § 14).
Thus both the spontaneity and the conformity of the monads
find their explanation in this, that the divine power and the
divine thought constitutes their innermost essence.   Their
harmony exists from the beginning ; it is " pre-established."
Each one of them is a particular concentration of the universe
that God's creating thought perceived ; it is a universe in
miniature and the universe consists of such concentrations.
Leibniz is a metaphysical Copernicus : he shows that the
world may be regarded from very many more points of view
than is generally conceived ; and that, in and for itself,
one point of view has as much authorisation and validity as
another.   The world, for him, is not something which lies
outside of, or between, individuals, but consists precisely of
these individuals.

Leibniz thus transfers the whole problem to the thought
of the creating Divinity.   From philosophy he passes over to
theology.   This, however, does not relieve him from difficulties ; for how does a world, which may be regarded from
infinitely many points of view, arise in the divine thoughts or
in the divine imagination ?   And these possible points of view
are no mere lifeless pictures in the divine imagination ; for as
Leibniz constantly asserts all possibility to be a little actuality,
a dawning reality, so here, too, he assumes an original impulse
or desire after existence (*inclinatio ad existendum, exigentia
existendi*) : the possibilities seek to press on to more complete
reality, which, however, is only granted to those who fit in
best in an harmonious world-system.   This is a mythological
prelude, which decides the struggle for existence before actual
existence begins, in order that the latter can be an harmonious
unfolding of the inner germ of every creature.   We shall

return to this point in our discussion of the *Théodicée*. It is
decidedly prejudicial to the clearness and significance of the
Leibnizian philosophy that, from beginning to end, theological points of view play so large a part in it. It by
no means furthers the solution of problems to clothe them in
theological form. A certain sentiment of piety causes us to
cease our questionings and objections sooner than we otherwise
should do, but such a cessation is no solution. It is easily seen
that, in the form in which Leibniz presented it, the problem is
insoluble. If the monads are absolute substances they cannot
have been produced. Only the appeal to a supernatural creation conceals this evident self-contradiction. As Leibniz excluded real reciprocal action from the monads, on account of
his concept of substance, so he ought, in consistency, to have
denied their origin in a substance different from themselves.
Malebranche has here found the right solution : God cannot
create gods ! The difference between Leibniz and Spinoza—
if we neglect this evident self-contradiction—practically falls
away, since the creation of the monads is not assigned once
for all to any one point in time, but goes on continuously ;
the emanation or fulguration of the monads proceeds uninterruptedly (*Discours*, §§ 14, 32 ; *Monadologie*, § 47). Leibniz
lays stress on the fact that it is the source, the efficient force,
which thus flows uninterruptedly from God into the monads ;
but Spinoza, too, explains the striving which moves every
individual being to self-assertion as a particular revelation of
the power which works in all individuals. Logically, Leibniz'
philosophy only differs here from that of Spinoza in that, in
it, the individual beings are placed more in the foreground,
while their common origin occupies the dark background
(which only gets more light thrown upon it when Leibniz is
seeking an alliance with theologians), while, with Spinoza,
individual beings are rather regarded as branches or ramifica-
tions of the infinite Being, who is his first and last thought.
The difference between the two systems may be reduced to
a difference similar to that which exists, according to Leibniz,
between two views of the world, owing to its rotation. For
both existence is a pyramid ; Spinoza regards it from the
apex and Leibniz from the base.[78] As already pointed out, it
throws a slur on Leibniz' intelligence as well as on his character that, in spite of this state of things, he should so frequently

have protested against Spinoza in terms which more or less accuse him of heresy.

Leibniz' theory of the relation between soul and body is simply a logical result of his doctrine of monads. What we call our body is a group of monads, each of which unfolds of itself, according to an indwelling law, and of its own power, just as do our souls. From the state of one monad we can, in virtue of the universal harmony, infer the states of other monads; this is popularly expressed by saying that one thing acts upon another. We say of the monad from whose states we can, by such an inference, deduce the states of the others that it acts. If the internal development of the individual monads is checked, this is the result of the darkness, of the chaotic condition of the elements within it. But since the nature of every monad, *i.e.* the degree of darkness or clearness, and the power to pass over into new states with which it is endowed, is, from the beginning, determined with regard to other monads, by the side of which it is placed in existence, so certain conditions of other monads correspond to these inner hindrances, and are therefore popularly called their causes. When Leibniz wishes to express himself quite popularly, he uses the metaphor of two clocks set together once for all to describe the relation between soul and body. In the same desire to accommodate himself to popular speech, he calls the body a composite substance. But this way of speaking is too rude to express his real conception. For matter is, for him, only a phenomenon, a world of external multiplicity, the states of which express to the senses the internal modifications of the monads, which constitute true reality. According to Leibniz' way of speaking a thing is " expressed " or " represented " by another, when the predicates of the two things stand in constant and regular relation to one another (Letter to Arnauld, October 1687). That which is concentrated, bound together in a unity, within the monads, appears to the senses as an extended manifold. In a letter of 4th November 1696 (to the Electress of Hanover) Leibniz writes : " Souls are unities ; bodies, multiplicities. Although unities are thus indivisible, yet they represent the multiplicities, in much the same way as all lines from the periphery meet together in the centre. It is this union which constitutes the wonderful nature of consciousness, and it is through this, too, that every soul is, as it were, a world for itself." The stringency with which Leibniz, in agreement with Hobbes and Spinoza, asserted the mechanical interconnection of Nature, made it impossible for him to retain the ordinary dualistic conception. According to his presuppositions and to his whole system, the identity hypothesis appeared to be the only possibility.

Leibniz has increased the difficulties to which this hypothesis is open by attributing absolute substantiality to the monads. From the stamp of unity which consciousness bears, he concludes, with dogmatic precipitancy, that a conscious being must be an absolute imperishable unity, which can receive nothing from without. Had he, instead of only conceiving the corporeal in analogy with the mental, *at the same time* conceived the mental in analogy with the corporeal, he would have perceived the necessity for assuming that individual consciousness, in spite of its wonderful character of unity, stands in reciprocal action with the rest of existence, in virtue of the very law of continuity which he himself so strongly emphasises, but which he was only able to apply to each individual monad, and not to the reciprocal relation of the monads. Development for Leibniz means no more than unfolding. In his view the individual organism has, properly speaking, no genesis; it exists from the beginning; its birth and growth only consist in its being relieved of its wrappings— in its dimensions being enlarged. Like so many other natural philosophers of his day, Leibniz subscribed to the so-called encasement theory (in which one germ is conceived as lying within the other throughout the sequence of generations). And in the same way, in the mental sphere, development admits of no acquisition of fresh content, but only of a clarifying of the content which was given—in a chaotic and obscure form certainly—at the beginning. Concentration cannot begin, according to Leibniz; new centres, new monads, cannot be formed. Here he cuts the knots. Perhaps those contained in the problem of individuality can never be undone by our thought, but to cut them is certainly not to undo them.

But this summary procedure is, like the protest entered against Spinoza, only a result of the energy with which Leibniz thought out the concept of individuality. In no other thinker does it occur with equal brilliancy and clearness. And the peculiar turn which he gave to the concept of substance by applying it to the individual elements of existence (the monads) is characteristic of the transition from the seventeenth to the eighteenth century. In the place of mystical resignation, and subjection to the absolute powers, we now have the free effort of each single individual after clearness, after the unfolding of its own nature. This is a revolution in the world of thought— a prelude to the revolution in the external world. There is *one* presupposition which Leibniz' system has in common with the other great systems, *i.e.* that of the complete rationality of existence. The principle of sufficient reason is his guiding principle in his theological speculation and in his monadology, as well as in his works on mathematics and natural science. He bequeathed this presupposition also to the new century, of which he was the typical forerunner.

(c) *Psychology and Theory of Knowledge*

It follows from the importance which attaches, for Leibniz, to the analogy from consciousness, as the foundation of his metaphysical idealism, that his real starting-point must be the same as Descartes, *i.e.* immediate self-inspection, inner experience. This gives us the first term of the analogy. Moreover Leibniz is quite clear that this is a starting-point for his thought, and has devoted great attention to it. The *Nouveaux Essais* are his most important work on this subject. We cannot do justice to it on the polemical side until we come to discuss Locke's theory of knowledge, against which it was directed. In this connection, however, it is important as giving Leibniz' own views on psychology and the theory of knowledge. Indeed it may be regarded as containing a verification of Leibniz' philosophical ideas in general; for he explains in the introduction that he desires to set aside his doctrine of monads and to take up his position on a strictly empirical footing.

The main question at starting is whether the soul is originally blank—like a *tabula rasa*. Leibniz had discussed this question long before, in the *Discours* (§ 27). He then found this notion of an unwritten tablet to be false. It rests upon inexact observation. The small, dark motions of the soul are overlooked, and note is taken only of that of which we are clearly conscious, which does not arise till later, when outer experiences have for a long time exerted their influence. Cartesians and empiricists are alike guilty of this mistake. The less difference and contrast there is between our sensations, the less any one particular element becomes prominent in comparison with the remaining content of consciousness; the darker, in a word, conscious life is, the easier it is to overlook it. More exact observation will be cautious in laying down limits. There are all possible grades of transition between darkness and distinctness. The dark modifications within us, which never come to clear consciousness, Leibniz calls "perceptions." Even in these, a manifold is united in one single state. At this stage are the lowest beings (in Leibniz' system : the monads of the lowest grade). The expression "consciousness" (*sentiment*) is not used by Leibniz until sensation (*perception*) becomes clearer and is accompanied by memory. The highest stage of psychical life is that of voluntary attention (*apperception*), or reflection, which is directed towards the obscure perceptions. (These three grades are best described in the short treatise : *Principes de la nature et de la grâce*, § 4 ; cf. *Monadologie*, § 14 *et seq.*) But activity, spontaneity, develops itself at all stages. We are active even in our darkest states. Just as there is no writing-tablet which does not, in virtue of its nature, exert an influence on that which is written, so our nature is preformed from the beginning. Involuntarily, instinctively, we use principles of which we can only later become aware. We reject that which is self-contradictory, even though we have never yet heard of the principle of contradiction. There are practical as well as theoretical instincts. The impulse to self-preservation and the desire to help others work involuntarily. There is altogether much more in us than we know. Here, as in material Nature, small magnitudes underlie that which becomes clear, and is given through the senses. No more than motion, can consciousness arise suddenly, or out of nothing. In accordance with the conservation of force (or properly speaking, according to the identity hypothesis as identical with this conservation), Leibniz believes in the uninterrupted existence of the life of the soul ; in states of consciousness or unconsciousness, distinctness or darkness. The apparent disappearance of psychical life is merely a change to a darker and more elementary form. To the question whether there are innate ideas, Leibniz answers, that there are innate tendencies and dispositions, which unfold as soon as experience offers them an occasion, and which underlie all theoretical and practical activity. As an example of the obscure elements which we are so apt to overlook, he mentions the usually weak sensations (now called common sensation) which correspond to the organic functions, and from time to time exercise influence on our condition. Our external senses are certainly more distinct; but since the sense-qualities are very different from the motions of matter answering to them, Leibniz assumes that our sensations are only apparently simple, being in reality just as composite as the corresponding motions. That which presents itself clearly to consciousness is, according to his view, always a combination, presupposing more obscure elements, *e.g.* the roar of the sea, in which the impressions of thousands of waves are united together into one single sensation. If we pay attention, we shall find that we are never without sensation. Our soul is continually active. We are always receiving small sensations, and these are constantly setting free our activity. We are never entirely indifferent; the opinion that there can be a state of indifference only expresses our inattention to small differences. Involuntarily we turn to the right or to the left, even when no external reason for our choice exists. Our nature is always working within us towards the attainment of greater satisfaction (*à se mettre mieux à son aise*). Continually making itself felt is a certain unrest, a lack of complete satisfaction, which drives us forward,— a spur which we usually only notice when the unrest amounts to pain. There are always small hindrances to overcome, and demands on our exertion of force are constantly being made. No feeling of pleasure is possible without such unrest, without minimal hindrances: this hidden spur remains even in joy, inciting us to continual progress. It is only by means of these small sensations (*petites perceptions*) that the connection between the different periods in the life of one and the same individual becomes clear; for clearly conscious states often appear to be contradictory. And as they explain at once the difference and the connection between the states of one and the same individual, so, too, they explain the difference as well as the connection between different individuals. Even if it were permissible to call the soul an originally unwritten tablet, yet it must be owned that no two tablets are ever exactly the same. If we take small *nuances* and differences into account we shall never, in the whole of Nature, find two things exactly alike. There are no two leaves which are precisely similar, much less two men. Here, too, the belief in sameness arises from our ignorance. In the obscure sensations, however, of which the individual is not conscious, the rest of existence reveals itself to him and determines him unknown to himself. By means of these sensations he is united with the rest of existence. And this union is not interrupted even in sleep. Between sleeping and waking there is only a difference of degree : the turning away of attention is a partial sleep.

Psychology is much indebted to Leibniz on account of the attention he drew to the importance of infinitely small quantities. He disclosed a new world to self-inspection, in which, however, it feels the want of an instrument answering to the microscope in the sphere of external observation. He indicated points of view, too, which made it possible to assert the continuity of the mental side of existence in a much higher degree than is permitted by the ordinary conception, or even than Leibniz himself believed, since his monads had no windows, and he thus debarred them from unconsciously receiving influences from the rest of existence. The elements of existence (the monads) are only distinguished from one another by the degree of distinctness or darkness of their inner states, and, in the same way, the states of one and the same individual are only distinguished by difference of degree. We notice here that we are entering upon the century of enlightenment. All the necessary conditions are believed to be present—it is only light that is wanted : it was on this optimistic faith that Leibniz and his successors built.

It must, however, be noticed that with regard to psychology proper, Leibniz hints at a much deeper view of psychical life than that from which Rationalism and the age of enlightenment proceeds. In the first place, the world has, for Leibniz, an infinite content, though given in an obscure form ; a complete understanding of it is therefore impossible to a finite being. Moreover he places alongside of sensations and representations, as an independent element, the impulse and tendency (*appetit*, *tendance*) to pass over to new sensations. To this

extent he regards effort or will as the essence of man ; moreover it is an effort that can never cease. His attitude towards
the passions is somewhat vacillating. Sometimes he regards
them as confused thoughts—according to which view they
must fall away on sufficient enlightenment—sometimes he
pronounces them different both from representations and from
feelings of pleasure and pain, and declares them to be tendencies
which are excited by ideas and accompanied by feelings of
pain ; and according to this view they are closely connected
with the never-resting effort or will.[79] Had Leibniz carried out
this latter point of view, he would have arrived at a more
realistic conception of mental development than that which
considers the latter to be exhausted by the concept of enlightenment.

Self-inspection gives us, as we have seen, the first facts
from which our thought proceeds, the first *truths of fact*. We
possess the first *necessary* or *a priori truths* in identical judgments, *i.e.* those judgments of which the subject and predicate
can be shown to be one and the same concept. Common to the
first truths of fact and the first *a priori* truths is their immediate
relation,—in the former of the understanding to its object, in
the latter of the subject to the predicate. This immediate
relation is, in both cases, the proof that we can arrive at
nothing more certain. Leibniz had long ago arrived at this
differentiation between *a priori* truths and truths of fact. We
find him making this distinction as early as 1678 (in a letter
of 3rd January to Conring), where he demands that all *a priori*
first principles should be reduced to identical judgments. He
therefore divides axioms into identical and *a priori*. The importance of identical judgments consists in this—that when
other judgments can be reduced to them, they invest them with
their own validity. Thus Leibniz demands that all our primary
assumptions should be susceptible of proof in so far as they
are not identical. He sympathises here with Locke's criticism of
" innate ideas," as far as he directs it against prejudice or
convenience. But Locke ought to have distinguished between
necessary and contingent truths. Even when a truth is
" innate " in Leibniz' use of the word, it must, in his opinion,
first be pointed out ; " innate " truths, just like other truths,
must be *learnt*. Enlightening the mind may be no easy task,
and perfect clearness is only to be found in identical judgments.

Leibniz has rendered a great service to logic by laying down the principle of identity, while the Aristotelian and scholastic logic had not got beyond the principle of contradiction. He sketched out a logic in which every judgment is formulated as a relation of identity, and thus anticipated a method which, in our time, has been adopted by the English logicians, Boole and Jevons. But this sketch was not published till 1840, and consequently exerted no influence. As the principle of identity in the sphere of abstract thought, so, in the world of experience, the interconnection according to law required by the principle of sufficient reason is the criterion of truth. And as Leibniz is the first to establish the principle of identity as a fundamental logical principle, so, too, he is the first to establish the causal principle as the special principle of relations given in matters of fact. He thus brings into prominence the principle that supports all real knowledge ; and as he, at the same time, makes a sharp distinction between this and purely logical principles, he was on the verge of a more thorough-going discussion of its nature. It must not be a principle of formal logic, nor must it be deduced from experience ; and yet it is to be a principle of reason and valid for all relations of fact (and that in the supernatural, as well as the natural, world !). How is this possible ? This problem Leibniz left to his successors. He contented himself with singling it out, by means of analysis, from the confusion—partly with general logical and partly with particular physical principles—in which it had appeared among his predecessors. He never even made any clear distinction between ground and cause, and hence we find that this principle is to be a principle of reason and yet valid of relations of fact ; and, in the last instance, that the laws of facts are regarded as witnessing to the divine reason, which is the author of the world.[80]

Leibniz was occupied throughout his life with planning a kind of thought-alphabet (*alphabetum cogitationum humanarum*), which was to be formed by means of a thorough-going analysis of our knowledge, so that it should exhibit the fundamental concepts by which this is conditioned. By means of a suitable system of signs we should be enabled at the same time to have a universal language, which should be for all concepts what the mathematical language of signs is for

magnitudes.   Thus it was to be at once a logic, an encyclopædia, and a grammar ; a means both of focussing what is
already known and of making new discoveries.   Gradually, as
the sharp distinction between *a priori* and contingent truths
dawned upon him, he limited his *ars combinatoria* or
characteristica universalis to the sphere of the former.   In
spite of many attempts the plan was never carried out, probably because he gradually came to see that, strictly speaking,
such a general language of signs already presupposes the
completion of our knowledge.   The plan, however, is characteristic of dogmatic philosophy.

(d) The Théodicée

As a thinker it was Leibniz' task to lead out beyond,
without interrupting, the mechanical conception of Nature.   He
attempted to do this by proving that the forces active in
mechanism are determined by ends, so that, regarded from
within, the whole graduated series of mechanical causes and
effects is a graduated series of means and ends.   The essence
of the world, at every point, is a striving, a development, a
progress.   In this thought, which brought into harmony not
only mechanism and teleology, but also the conditions of the
different monads and souls and bodies, he believed he also possessed a means to unite religion (positive as well as " natural ")
with reason.   It was his conviction that his philosophy
satisfied the claims which the most stringent orthodoxy could
make.   But, just at this time, the religious problem was being
accentuated by a contemporary author, for whom Leibniz entertained the greatest respect.   Pierre Bayle, as we have already
mentioned, asserted a want of harmony between religion
and reason, and found the doctrines of positive religion,
in particular, in contradiction to reason.   In so doing he
laid especial stress on the problem of evil, declaring the
Manichæan doctrine of two world-principles, one good and
one evil, to be far more in agreement with experience
than the orthodox doctrine, to which, however, he submitted
in devout obedience.   The Queen of Prussia, Leibniz' gifted
pupil, felt so much disturbed by Bayle's criticisms that
she begged Leibniz to refute them.   For this task Leibniz
believed himself well prepared.   Ever since he first began to

write he had had in view the problem of a Theodicy, *i.e.* the problem of how the belief in the origin of the world in an all-powerful, all-good, and all-wise being can be reconciled with the experience of the physical and moral evil there is in the world. Years ago he had planned a work on this subject. Bayle's *Réponse à un Provincial* and the solicitations of the Queen induced him to write and publish his *Essais de Théodicée sur la bonté de Dieu, la liberté de l'homme, et l'origine du mal*, which appeared in Amsterdam in 1710.

In reply to Bayle's assertion that the doctrines of religion are contrary to reason and yet must be believed, Leibniz makes the distinction between that which is *above* reason and that which is *contrary* to reason. This distinction is connected with his classification of truths into eternal truths (founded on the principle of identity) and truths of fact (which come under the principle of sufficient reason). Nothing which ought to be believed can conflict with the first kind of truths of reason. God's existence, for instance, is only possible if the content of the concept of God, *i.e.* the qualities attributed to God, are not mutually contradictory. A thought may, however, be exalted above that which is learnt from experience, since the logical necessity of the interconnection of phenomena, which we discover by means of the principle of sufficient reason, is always conditioned; the principles of natural science find their explanation, according to Leibniz, only in the thought of a providence, of a teleological principle. It is precisely the principle of contingent truths, *i.e.* the principle of sufficient reason, which leads us on beyond experience; since the harmony of the monads and the connection according to law of everything that happens can only be explained through an absolute Being, who has created the world by a reasonable choice. Every individual thing, every particular event, is in itself accidental; so that we can arrive at no conclusion as to the series of grounds or causes, to no complete satisfaction of the principle of sufficient reason, unless we go back to a first cause, which is the cause of itself. That the choice was a reasonable one is argued thus: besides the actually existing world, several others were possible; this one can therefore only have come into being because it is the best. But the best world does not mean a world without shadows or faults, but only one in which the deficiencies disappear in comparison with the perfections.   Every possible world consisting of finite beings must present imperfections, since finite nature involves limitations and cannot therefore completely embrace the divine nature.   From limitation (metaphysical evil) arises suffering (physical evil), and sin (moral evil).   Evil has thus, to a certain degree, its source in God : not in God's will, however, which wills the good always, but in God's reason, in which representations of possible worlds dwell from eternity.   God created the reality, but not the possibilities.   The source of evil is the imperfection which attaches to every possible world of limited beings : through the divine creative choice, however, this imperfection is reduced to the smallest possible minimum, and made to serve as a means and foil to still greater perfection. Carried out in a more mythological form and with greater vividness of colouring, Leibniz' conception was really the same as that of Jakob Boehme.   And they are neither of them far from Bayle since (as Leibniz himself remarked) they assume, as he did, two principles ; only while they believe they can unite these in the nature of one and the same God, Bayle found it necessary to assume two gods.   According to Leibniz and Boehme the possibilities press to the front in the divine nature and struggle with one another—a prelude to the struggle in actual existence.

Bayle had asserted that the strength of the Manichæan doctrine lay in the witness of experience to the unhappiness and sin in the world, while an *a priori* consideration of the world would rather lead us to dwell on its fundamental unity.   Leibniz had therefore to follow him into the sphere of experience.   Frequently, indeed, he contents himself with the explanation that this must be the best possible world, or otherwise God would not have chosen it.   He overlooks the objection which suggests itself (and which was raised many years later by Schopenhauer, Leibniz' antipodes) that even if the world chosen is the best this does not prove it was good enough to be actualised ! The impulse to existence, the striving after realisation which Leibniz attributes to the eternal possibilities (as he can never think of possibilities as anything but minimal realities) may be evil !   Leibniz must therefore attempt to show that the actual world is worthy of existence since a thorough and comprehensive view of it would reveal an overplus of light and perfection.   He exhorts us not to consider one single part of the

world only, but to think of the whole. A tone, in and for
itself discordant, may produce an excellent effect in a musical
ensemble. Cover a picture with the exception of one small
patch, and this will seem to be nothing but a senseless and confused juxtaposition of colours ; but, in the whole picture, it is
a factor in determining the general impression. A bitter
ingredient in a dish increases the excellence of its flavour,
while taken alone it would be disagreeable to the taste. How
far then are we to extend our view? Existence is infinite,
Leibniz answers. We can, therefore, never arrive at the fore-
thought, the end, which underlies all existence and whose
realisation conditions it. We know only a small and transient
part of the world,[81]—perhaps just that part in which the most
evil is to be found. Human ends and ideals ought not to be
looked upon as the only or, in the last instance, the most
important ones. God pursues ends which embrace the whole
universe, in which there are certainly many other beings besides men to be found. And shall this great, infinite work be
changed or recalled on account of our unhappiness and our
sin? especially since everything is so interconnected that
the historical development would have been quite different
if *e.g.* Tarquin's crime or the betrayal of Judas had been·
averted. God has placed individual beings in the world ; but
they themselves are the cause of their actions ; He created the
source, but not the stream. And although He knew what
would stream forth from this source, yet He has created it
because the world in which it exists is, on the whole, better
than any other. Without Judas' betrayal the atoning death
of the Saviour would not have taken place ; there is, therefore,
good reason for saying, in the words of the old hymn, " O felix
culpa ! " The reason why so many people have laid stress
on the evil in the world is because it attracts our attention, while habit weakens our sense of the good which we
enjoy. Hindrances and obstacles there must be, in order
that our activity may be constantly excited anew, and that we
should not become stupefied. Even the blessed and the angels
must encounter resistance if they are not to become " stupid."
Although existence in itself is continuous and harmonious, yet
it is expedient that apparent leaps, interruptions of the connection, dissonances should occur ; they exercise thought and
increase the beauty of the whole. Leibniz even tries to justify

the doctrine of eternal punishment: he believes in such a plenitude of light and perfection in existence as a totality that even if the majority of men were subjected to eternal torment yet, in comparison with the infinite sum of happiness, their pain would be infinitesimal!! Whether existence considered as a totality makes progress in perfection, or whether the perfection which it possesses is only a variation in form of changing conditions, is a question which Leibniz does not decide. But he has no doubt that the fundamental disposition of those who take a wide and intelligent view of existence will be joy at the beauty and perfection of things, and at their continuous development; a joy which is very different from the Stoics' patience in the face of necessity.

Leibniz unwittingly justifies Bayle far more than he intended to. Not only does he also, in a certain sense, assume two principles, but he is obliged to practically concede to Bayle that theological optimism is very difficult to maintain if we limit our considerations to *experience*. Leibniz' appeal to the infinity of existence and the limitation of our knowledge is practically a renunciation of proof: for how does he know anything about the aspect of things in other regions of the universe? He appeals to faith; thus pronouncing the question insoluble by way of reason. In a letter written at the same time as the *Théodicée* (to Bourguet, printed in Gerhardt, iii. p. 550 *et seq.*) he says too: "We can only see a very small part of the chain of things, and that part, moreover, which displays the most evil and which is therefore well suited to exercise our faith and our love to God." But the appeal from the particular to the whole does not undo the knot; for it is just in Leibniz' system, where body and soul are to be found at every point of existence, that it is impossible to justify the sacrifice of the individual to the whole. The suffering of individual monads does not disappear because it increases the beauty of the world-picture formed by all the monads in combination. The individual monads might well complain at the part allotted to them, and say they would rather not be than be in hell—even if this hell be indispensable as a kind of bass-tone in the great orchestra of existence. Leibniz' own sense for the infinitely little, for individual differences, ought logically to have weaned him from theological optimism.

(e) Philosophy of Law

Leibniz' ideas on ethics and the philosophy of law stand in close connection with his philosophy in general. His monadology culminates in the idea of existence as a " city of God," in which the fundamental principle is that of justice, according to which all the forces which underlie mechanism work. The teleological point of view is common to his conception of the world and to his ethics.

He finds the foundation both of ethics and of philosophy of law (both were included by him in the concept of natural right) in the immediate instinctive impulse towards happiness. Each separate feeling of pleasure corresponds to a progress, a " perfection," which consists either in an increase of power or in the attainment of greater harmony in that which is included under force. " Perfection," he says (in a small treatise " On Blessedness," one of the few works written in German which we have by him), " exhibits itself in power to work, as all being consists in a certain power, and the greater the power the higher and freer is the being. Moreover in all force, the greater it is, the more it reveals itself as one in many and many in one, since the one rules many besides itself and represents many. Now unity in multiplicity is nothing else than harmony." Leibniz means by this that the feeling of pleasure is conditioned by the fulness and harmony of the forces which support life, whether we are conscious of these conditions or not. Happiness consists in a continual feeling of pleasure. The condition necessary to the production of happiness is wisdom : enlightenment of the understanding and exercise of the will. But even the involuntary striving leads in this direction. Leibniz believes with Grotius—the " incomparable " Grotius as he calls him—in an involuntary impulse to further not only one's own happiness but also that of other men. Love is joy at the happiness of another, because we have made it our own ; even disinterested love is only possible because other men's happiness is, as it were, reflected upon ourselves. Leibniz, following Aristotle, takes justice as the fundamental ethical virtue, which he defines as the charity of the wise (caritas sapientis) : love selects the end, and wisdom knows how to find the right means and the right distribution.

Justice consists in giving every man his own, and in the right distribution of goods, both in the ordering of public affairs as well as in the lending of that which is at the disposal of individuals. justice in this sense (as law-giving and distributive justice) rests on the principle that all men should be benefited, and differs from law proper (*jus strictum*), the aim of which is to preserve peace in the community. (See the treatise, *De rationibus juris et justitiae*, 1693.)

There is something prophetic in Leibniz' philosophy of law, in spite of the fact that to a certain extent he employs antique and scholastic elements. In establishing the general good or happiness as the end of law and of morality, he is the precursor of so-called "utilitarianism." His ideas remind us of those of Cumberland, and he himself was agreeably surprised to meet in Shaftesbury—a contemporary younger than himself—with a line of thought akin to his own.

Although Leibniz' ethics and philosophy of law rest on a strictly psychological foundation, yet, in his opinion, they cannot dispense with theological sanctions. He agrees with Grotius that morality and law cannot be grounded in the arbitrary commandment of God. Like all highest principles and laws, however, the precepts of morality and law sprang originally from the divine thought, and they are maintained through the divine will. In disinterested love, certainly, the striving after the individual's own happiness is accompanied by the striving after the happiness of other men. But this is only the case in exceptional natures (*les âmes bien nées*). Without the supposition of divine rewards and punishments in a future life it could not be shown that the morally good and the most profitable are *always* coincident. Hence natural religion is necessary as a guarantee for morals; while, at the same time, it supplies the highest point of view of human morality and jurisprudence, since it extends our considerations to the divine law ruling throughout existence.

In Leibniz' philosophy of law, as in his whole system, the fundamental thought of a harmony existing between individual beings is prominent. This was the thought which guided his investigations in all spheres, and which he bequeathed to the new century, of which his system is in so many respects typical.

CHAPTER VII

CHRISTIAN WOLFF

WHAT Leibniz had expressed in letters and treatises only accessible and intelligible to a few, Wolff expanded and systematised, broadly and superficially, in his voluminous works. His influence was very great, for he introduced "rational thinking" into wide circles, and brought the "principle of sufficient reason" to bear in all departments. While Leibniz wrote, for the most part, in French or Latin (although for some time he had intended writing his *Théodicée* in German, on account of the philosophical "virginity" of that language), Wolff used the German language, and partly created German philosophical terminology. A popular "Wolffianismus" was an essential element in the German enlightenment of the eighteenth century. Many of the thoughts contained in the great systems of the seventeenth century found their way, through Wolff, to the educated public. Another group of ideas came, as we shall show in the following book, from England, through the movement started by John Locke.

CHRISTIAN WOLFF was born in Breslau in 1679; he studied mathematics and philosophy in addition to theology, and in 1706 became mathematical professor at Halle, although he lectured more particularly on philosophy. He was especially influenced by the works of Descartes and Leibniz, and also, through Tschirnhausen, by Spinoza, whose theory of knowledge Tschirnhausen (without mentioning Spinoza's name) had further developed in his *Medicina mentis*. Wolff himself disliked to be considered a disciple of Leibniz, and he certainly modified Leibniz' ideas in several ways; nevertheless the philosophy introduced by him at the German universities, and which prevailed till Kant's time, was correctly named the

2 B

Leibniz-Wolffian philosophy. The innermost kernel of the Leibnizian train of thought, his metaphysical idealism, the doctrine of monads, was, it is true, little suited to a popular systematisation such as it received at Wolff's hands. The tendency, however, to unite physical science with theology, by conceiving the world as a huge mechanism, designed to serve the divine ends, and brought into agreement with conscious life by means of a pre-established harmony, is always present in Wolff[82] as in Leibniz. The world is conceived as a whole, consisting of individual beings and determined according to law, the final ground of which is God. And the logical basis of the whole system is the principle of sufficient reason.

It is interesting to see that Wolff was not only the populariser of the dogmatic philosophy, but also its consummator. Leibniz took an important step when he established the principle of identity and the principle of sufficient ground as two separate principles, the former valid of all truths of reason, the latter of all truths of fact. Wolff seeks to deduce the latter from the former. He attempts to make it self-evident that everything that happens has a ground or cause, and he considers Leibniz was mistaken in giving no proof of the " principle of sufficient reason," which yet in his, as in the other great systems, occupied so conspicuous a place. Wolff's proof (see *Vernünftige Gedanken von Gott, der Welt, und der Seele des Menschen, auch allen Dingen überhaupt*, communicated to the lovers of truth by Christian Wolff, 1719, § 30) is as follows : " Where there is no reason, there is nothing by which we can understand why a thing is, and it must therefore arise out of nothing. . . . But since it is impossible that anything can come out of nothing, everything that is must have its sufficient reason why it is." It is easy to see that this proof moves in a circle ; for to say that something cannot arise out of nothing is to say that everything has a reason or cause, and this it was which was to be proved. By means of this train of thought, however, Wolff effected a complete systematisation of dogmatism. All certainty is reduced to the fundamental principle of contradiction, and philosophy becomes a system of laws, all of which have a purely logical foundation. The principle of contradiction contains, as must be carefully noted if we are to do Wolff no injustice, the guarantee of all empirical beliefs, as also of all inference. When I perceive something, I cannot, at the same moment, not perceive it: every perception must satisfy this requirement. Wolff does not, by any means, wish to reduce all science to formal logic. But he attempts to show that rational principles prevail everywhere. The reign of Rationalism had now begun.

Wolff made use of this principle not only in his conception of the world but also in theology. Just as, from the principle of sufficient reason, he deduces principles of physical science, such as the laws of inertia and continuity (Nature makes no leaps, or the transition from one state to another would otherwise be incomprehensible), so, too, he attempts to deduce from it not only the existence of God (the world must have its ground in that which has its ground in itself), but also the conditions to which every positive revelation must be subject. There must be definite signs by which revelation can be distinguished from vain imagination and false pretences. Revelation cannot be contrary to God's perfection, and must contain no contradictions. Although it is a miracle and, in so far, contrary to "contingent" truths (truths of fact), yet it must not be contrary to necessary truths: God can cause the sun to stand still, but He cannot change the relation of the diameter to the circumference of the circle. And Wolff asserts that a world in which miracles rarely happen is more perfect than one in which they occur frequently, for while miracles require power only, the order of Nature requires, in addition, a wisdom which concerns itself with the whole as such, and not merely with particulars. ·

Wolff was himself a victim to the principle of sufficient reason. The pietistic theologians of Halle considered the rationalism he promulgated dangerous, and the storm broke when, in a university lecture, he eulogised the philosophy of the Chinese Confucius, on account of its elevated morals. It is said that in order to win over King Frederick William I., use was made of Wolff's application of the principle of sufficient reason to human actions, it being represented to the soldier-king that, according to Wolff's doctrine, if his grenadiers deserted they could not be called to account for it. Wolff relates in his *Autobiography* how the King was shown a passage in the writings of his theological adversaries, where this conclusion was drawn from his determinism. In 1723 a royal cabinet order was issued, pursuant to which Wolff was dismissed from office on account of his impious doctrines, and was condemned, "on pain of the halter," to quit his Majesty's dominions within forty-eight hours. He went to Marburg, where he continued his activity till Frederick II., who was himself one of his admirers, recalled him to Halle, where he was active till his death (1754).

BOOK IV

ENGLISH EMPIRICAL PHILOSOPHY

INTRODUCTION

THE great systems proceeded from the conviction that there was material and clearness of thought sufficient for the erection of structures which should take the place of the mediæval conception of the world, overthrown by the inquiries of the Renaissance, and the birth of modern science. In a certain sense this confidence was not unfounded ; the new discoveries, methods, and principles had certainly thrown light on the direction in which men's thoughts concerning some of the most important problems were to move in the future, and the seventeenth century is especially important as having formulated, energetically and logically, the most important hypotheses touching the relation between mind and matter. The mere fact that several hypotheses were possible could not fail, however, to excite the attention of critical thinkers, and all the more because, though the very thinkers who had erected those thought-structures with so much confidence and genius had discussed the nature of thought and its mode of working, yet they had only done so by way of introduction to their own particular systems. With dogmatic haste they hurried on from the examination of thought to seek for the solution of the riddle of existence. The significance of the classical English school in the history of philosophy lies in the fact that it looked upon the examination of the development of human knowledge, and the forms and presuppositions which it has at its disposal, as a separate problem. John Locke and his successors assured to the problem of knowledge its independence over against the problem of existence, by which it had been altogether overshadowed in the great systems. They put the theory of knowledge before metaphysics. If (following Kant) we understand by dogmatism a movement which, without sufficient examination of the conditions and limits of our knowledge, uses our concepts to investigate the nature of things, while critical philosophy investigates the faculty of knowledge itself, before it proceeds to speculate concerning existence, then critical philosophy definitely begins with John Locke. Behind this purely philosophical antithesis between dogmatic and critical philosophy, however, lies a more comprehensive, historical antithesis. Philosophical systems are not the only object of criticism; critical investigation attacks every authority, every existing power. We have already seen that the concept of substance in philosophy was analogous to absolute authority in political life, and now comes the age of emancipation, simultaneously with that of criticism. The process of which Leibniz' monads are the symbol, *i.e.* the elevation of the individual to independence, becomes obvious in the clearness and simplicity with which Locke instituted the great inquiry of thought into the authorities and traditions which ruled within the spheres of science, education, the State and the Church. Leibniz and Wolff affirmed and applied the principle of sufficient reason. John Locke and his successors subjected all principles—finally even the principle of sufficient reason itself—to a thorough-going examination.

Side by side with this energetic handling of the problem of knowledge we find a no less energetic examination of the ethical problem. Ethics reached a more independent position in the English school than was possible in the great systems, the real interest of which led far beyond the bounds of human life. And, owing to the empirical method employed by this school, the basis of philosophical ethics was now subjected to a more thorough examination.

CHAPTER I

JOHN LOCKE

(a) Biography and Characteristics

THE first critical philosopher was born in the same year as the greatest of the dogmatists. JOHN LOCKE was born on the 29th of April 1632, in the neighbourhood of Bristol. His father was an attorney ; which, however, did not prevent his taking part in the Civil War, as the captain of a company of horse on the Parliamentary side. The education which the young philosopher received from his father was of such a nature that he could make use of his personal recollections in writing his epoch-making essay on education. The point that the relation of obedience necessary in childhood should gradually merge into a free relation of friendship (*Thoughts on Education*, § 40) was suggested by the bringing up the author had himself enjoyed. His experiences at school and at the university, on the other hand, are brought forward in his philosophy rather as examples of what to avoid. He was at Westminster for six years, where he learnt classics according to the strictly grammatical method, and was tormented by having to commit tasks to memory, and to compose Latin treatises on subjects which he did not understand. Physical science was not taught—only after supper in summer a little geography. His warnings against learning by rote and beginning with grammar in teaching languages were thus suggested by his own school experiences. When (1652) he went to Oxford he found Puritanism and Scholasticism in the ascendency. Locke felt himself unsatisfied with both of them. According to his own subsequent account, he owed his philosophical awakening to the study of Descartes' writings. Acquaintance with these was a great encouragement to him, since he had hitherto attributed his small progress in scholastic philosophy to a lack of philosophical ability. He also studied Gassendi and Hobbes, and they exercised great influence on his mental development.

At that time great tolerance was practised at Oxford. Freedom of thought was granted to all Protestants not only by John Owen, the Chancellor of the University, but also by Oliver Cromwell, the powerful Protector. This time left traces in Locke's thought which persisted throughout his life. With the Restoration, the Episcopal Church came once more into power. Locke's original intention was to enter the ministry, but his free "broad - church" views on Christianity now rendered this impossible. (In an essay of 1667 (afterwards enlarged to the famous *Letter on Toleration*, 1685) he denied, to each and all, the right to force on others speculative opinions, and definite forms of worship.) And in an essay entitled *Error* (which, like the above mentioned, is given in Fox Bourne's excellent *Life of Locke*, London, 1876) he says : " For he that examines and, upon a fair examination, embraces an error for a truth, has done his duty more than he who embraces the pro- fession of the truth (for the truths themselves he does not embrace) without having examined whether it be true or no." He lays chief stress upon the ethical side of religion, and demands as few dogmas and ceremonies as possible.) The Episcopal Church with its Thirty-Nine Articles and innumer- able ceremonies was thus closed to him.

He now determined to become a doctor, and studied medicine and chemistry. This laid the foundation of his friendship with ROBERT BOYLE, the famous chemist, and with SYDENHAM, the no less famous physician. Locke's philoso- phical endeavours are akin to those of his two friends. Boyle, who was six years older than Locke, championed the empirical method in chemistry against the alchemists and medical chemists who had other than strictly scientific ends in view. He was the first to show clearly what chemical analysis aims at, namely, the discovery of the elements of composite substances, *i.e.* those components which are demonstrably unresolvable. He predicted that the number of elements would be found to be much larger than was at that time believed, and he disputed the non-composite character of many substances which, till then, had been taken for elements. Sydenham followed the empirical method in therapeutics, and acknowledged the same principles as those which Locke had laid down in a small treatise *On Therapeutics*, in which stress was laid on the necessity of depending on observations rather than axioms. Locke often accompanied Sydenham in his visits to his patients.

The healing art, however, was not destined to be Locke's calling in life. (He made the acquaintance of the Earl of Shaftesbury, the famous politician under Charles II., and soon became associated with his family as the friend, secretary, doctor, and tutor of two generations. Locke's political views (as may be seen from the small treatises written in his younger days) were as free-thinking as his views on religion.) His convictions led him to attach himself with ardour to the side of the Whigs, and he became involved in their fate. The downfall of Shaftesbury in 1672 brought with it that of Locke, who was obliged to give up the posts which Shaftesbury's interest had procured for him. He spent the next few years travelling in France. His notes on his journeys are interesting historically, and witness to his great powers of observation, and the attention which he devoted to all sides of life. Afterwards, when his patron, having taken part in a conspiracy, had to flee to Holland, Locke believed that he was himself in danger in England and he too (1683) went to Holland, where a considerable number of Whig refugees gradually assembled. He had to remain in concealment for some time, as the English Government demanded his extradition. During these years he occupied himself with his writings, more especially with the *Epistola de tolerantia* (1685), which appeared several years later in English, and with his chief work *Concerning Human Understanding*. He was probably also busy at this time with preparations for the Revolution. He was intimately associated with the Prince of Orange and his wife, and in 1689 he returned to England with the Princess.)

Locke did not forget philosophy for politics, nor politics for philosophy. Early in 1690 appeared his chief work, the *Essay Concerning Human Understanding*, one of the most remarkable and pregnant works in the history of philosophy. It has its roots far back in Locke's mental evolution. He recounts in the preface that the work owes its existence to a discussion in which he and several of his friends had engaged. Since they had not been able to solve the problems which they had proposed to themselves, it occurred to him that it might perhaps

first be " necessary to examine our own abilities, and see what
objects our understandings were, or were not, fitted to deal
with." In a copy of Locke's essay, which is in the possession
of the British Museum, James Tyrell, Locke's friend, has
written : " I remember myself being one of those that met
there when the discourse began about the principles of
morality and of revealed religion." (Thus it was a discussion
on ethical and moral questions which led to the closer
investigation of knowledge.) The first beginning was made
in the winter of 1670-71. Locke occupied himself again
with this work during his stay in France and his banishment
in Holland, and he completed it in 1687. The following year
it was printed in an abridged form in the Dutch journal
Bibliothèque universelle, and in 1690 a complete edition in English
appeared. (It consists of four books : the first criticises the
doctrine of innate ideas and principles ; the second shows that
all ideas are gained from experience, and resolves composite
ideas into their constituent elements, in order that unity may
be more easily attained ; the third examines the influence of
speech on thought, disputes the scholastic philosophy of terms,
and emphatically asserts that generic concepts must not be
supposed, without further inquiry, to be valid of Nature also ;
the fourth distinguishes between the different kinds of
knowledge, and defines the limits of knowledge.) Thus the
theory of knowledge proper is contained in the fourth book.
This and the second book (on the empirical origin of ideas)
appear to have been written first ; the first (the criticism of
innate ideas) and the third (on speech) were added later.

Under King William, Locke had no small influence. He
was on intimate terms with the King and several of the leading
men. He filled various posts in which he exerted himself on
behalf of the freedom of the press, tolerance, rational currency,
trade laws, and the improvement of the poor-law system. In
his *Two Treatises on Government,* which appeared in 1690, he
confesses that, in addition to theoretical aims, he has also
attempted a defence of the Revolution which had brought about
the new order of things. Among his other writings (besides the
Thoughts Concerning Education, 1692) his work on *The Reasonableness of Christianity as delivered in the Scriptures* deserves
mention. (In his conception of Christianity Locke maintains, with
much emphasis, that the faith of the oldest Church is contained in

the sentence, "Jesus is the Messiah." He regards Christianity as the gospel of love ; he would not have men plagued with incomprehensible dogmas (of the Trinity, the Atonement, and Eternal Punishment) but would rather extend the law of Nature and Reason, since it is this which shows how men can win eternal blessedness.) He considered himself a believing Christian, and his letters, as well as his life, witness to religious inwardness. He read the Bible diligently, and, during his last years, was occupied with a commentary on the Epistle to the Corinthians. He felt most drawn, however, to those forms of Christianity which contained the least dogmatism and hierarchy. During his stay in Holland he lived for some time with a Quaker, with whom he contracted an intimate friendship. Afterwards, when in London, he accompanied King William when he went incognito to a meeting of the Quakers, in order to become acquainted with the sect. To an English Quakeress Locke wrote, that as women had been the first to see the risen Saviour, so perhaps now it is by women that the resurrection of the spirit of love must be proclaimed. He was the object of violent attacks from the theologians, and since the root of his theology was discovered to lie in his philosophy, this, too, was sharply attacked, especially by Stillingfleet, the Bishop of Worcester, whom Locke several times answered at great length. This was the last duel between scholastic and modern philosophy.)The displeasure at Locke's theological standpoint was increased by the fact that it approximated so closely to that of the Deists that a work such as John Toland's *Christianity not Mysterious*, which appeared in 1696, and which was publicly burnt at Dublin in the following year, seemed only to be its natural outcome. Since Locke's works were read by the undergraduates also, the heads of colleges at Oxford decided that Locke's *Essay* should not be recognised at the University. When Locke heard of this he remarked that though there may be people who put on blinkers or hide their heads, yet not every one would be content to dispense with the use of their eyes—and history has proved him to have been right.

Locke, who was never married, spent his last years in the house of Sir Francis Masham, at Oates, near London. Lady Masham was the daughter of Cudworth, the Cambridge philosopher, and was a highly gifted woman. After suffering from asthma for several years, he died there in 1704. A gentle disposition, great love to his friends, an honest seeking after truth, and a firm faith in the importance of personal and political freedom, are the traits most remarkable in Locke, as we know him from his books and letters. The words which he wrote the year before his death to a young friend, afterwards the Deistic writer Anthony Collins, are characteristic : " To love truth for truth's sake is the principal part of human perfection in this world, and the seed-plot of all other virtues."

(b) The Origin of Ideas

Since Locke's intention is to call human knowledge to account, his first task is to investigate the origin of the ideas with which it operates. Under " idea " he understands everything of which we can think. This task would be superfluous if there were innate ideas in the literal sense of the word, and it is against this view that he first directs his criticism. Men have thought, says Locke, that the idea of God is such an innate idea ; the most fundamental logical and moral principles have likewise been thought to be innate. Such propositions as : Everything is what it is, and We ought to do unto others as we would they should do unto us, are conceived to be indwelling in the human consciousness from the beginning. But, in that case, they must be the very first ideas which are present in consciousness. A man can easily convince himself that this is not the case by examining children, idiots, savages, and illiterate men. The consciousness of such beings contains only particular, definite, and concrete ideas and perceptions ; no general principles. Moreover experience shows us individuals and tribes without any idea of God at all, and without any moral ideas, properly so-called. If innateness is deduced from the fact that such ideas and principles are understood and accepted as soon as they are made clear to consciousness, this is an unwarrantable conclusion. What has to be pointed out and made clear is not innate but must be acquired. There is, of course, an original capacity of learning, and we rightly speak of natural laws or principles, since there are opinions at which men arrive by the natural use of experience and of their capacity of thought. Among such Locke reckons, in addition to logical and mathematical truths, the most important religious and moral opinions. A *natural* law, he emphatically asserts, is, however, by no means the same as an *innate* law. The doctrine of innate ideas arises for the most part from indolence ; from the wish to evade setting about an examination of the development of ideas.

This polemic seems to have been more especially directed against the scholastic philosophers, the Cambridge Platonists, and Herbert of Cherbury ; the latter is the only representative of the theory of " innate ideas" mentioned by name. Locke can hardly have been aiming directly at Descartes. Moreover the stricter explanation of the inappropriate expression " innate" which Descartes gives, sets him beyond the reach of Locke's criticism. (Locke himself used an expression which gave rise to misunderstandings, namely the old metaphor of consciousness as an unwritten sheet (*tabula rasa*). He did not (as has often been believed) mean by this to dispute that original faculties of the soul precede experience.' It is an unfortunate property of philosophical catchwords that they suggest ideas which are far too clumsy. Even after this emendation of the Lockian doctrine, Leibniz' criticism still holds good, viz. that Locke overlooks sometimes the significance of the obscure, more or less unconscious elements, sometimes the involuntary, spontaneous manner in which original inclinations make themselves felt. Even the moment of activity, which Locke acknowledges in the formation of certain ideas, was reduced and finally annulled by some of his followers. ,

Locke's own answer to the problem rests upon the doctrine that all ideas—by which he understands the whole content of consciousness—spring from experience, partly from outer experience (sensation), and partly from inner experience (reflection).) Outer experience arises when a stimulus or motion of any part of the body excites a perception in the soul. Inner experience arises because the soul also receives the impression of the activity which (*e.g.* in memory and comparison) is unfolded in the elaboration of the ideas given in outer experience. (By means of " reflection," then, we perceive our own states and activities, and by means of "sensation" the effects of other things. In all such immediate conception or perception of other things, consciousness is, for the most part, entirely passive. Still it is only the simplest ideas which arise by means of such immediate and passive perception.\

The simple ideas which arise by way of outer experience need no more resemble the qualities of the things which produce them than the word resembles the idea. Only the so-called primary qualities, density, extension, figure and motion cannot be separated from external things ; the secondary qualities, such as colour, taste, smell, etc., correspond only with the capacity which things possess, in virtue of their primary qualities, of exciting certain ideas in us. Locke seems to have adopted the terms "primary" and "secondary" qualities from Robert Boyle ; the doctrine itself, the authorship of which has been so often ascribed to Locke, originates, as we have seen, in Galilei, Hobbes, and Descartes. Locke does not inquire more closely into the problem here presented by the great difference existing between the outer cause and the inner effect.

Simple ideas are the material of consciousness, and are elaborated by the latter in different ways. The activity of consciousness displays itself firstly in the formation of *complex* ideas through the combination of simple ideas, secondly in the formation of *ideas of relations*, since it brings simple ideas into a certain reciprocal conjunction, and thirdly in the formation of *abstract ideas*, since it separates simple ideas from others with which they were actually presented. All ideas which do not spring from immediate impressions—however exalted and significant they may be—have arisen by means of the synthetising, uniting, and abstracting activity of consciousness, and are based on immediate perception. Of these three kinds of derived ideas the first two are the most interesting. They are formed, moreover, by the help of abstraction.)

Among complex ideas belong modes like space and time. In the formation of the idea of space we depend on the senses of sight and touch. We also make use of abstraction here, since we distinguish between space and solidity—a distinction which is about as clear as that between the bushel and the corn. We form the idea of time by the help of our inner sense, which shows us a succession of ideas. And since, as we know, our capacity of imagining the extension of space and time always remains the same, however many additions we may have made, this gives us the idea of immensity. Among the concepts of qualities must be reckoned the ideas of power and motion, as also all ideas of composite colours, forms, etc., and, within the sphere of the inner sense, ideas of conception, memory, thought, attention, etc.

While concepts of qualities offer no difficulty, it is otherwise with the *concept of thing, essence, or substance.* This, too, is formed by composition. Our idea of a thing or of a substance is the idea of the qualities or powers which we attribute to it. Curiously enough, however, we conceive the thing or substance itself as something different from the qualities and powers, namely as that which bears or supports them. Everything which we attribute to substance is derived from experience. This is true even of the idea of God, which is a substance-concept formed by extending and elevating the ideas of spiritual qualities taken from the inner sense.

As an example of *ideas of relation* that of cause and effect is mentioned. We construct this idea on the groundwork of the perception that qualities and things arise, and that their arising is due to the influence of other qualities and things. Other examples are the ideas of temporal and spatial relations, and of identity and difference. The moral ideas also come under ideas of relation, since they are formed from the simple ideas of our actions in conjunction with the idea of a law.

(c) *The Validity of Knowledge*

After the origin of ideas has been pointed out, arises the question as to their validity. Locke has not the least doubt that simple ideas possess real validity. They proceed from reality, and must therefore be in agreement with reality. The secondary qualities, certainly, do not *resemble* the things by which the ideas of them were excited, but they *correspond* to the things because they are their constant effects. The validity of the derived ideas cannot be established in this way, since they are formed by combination and comparison, that is to say, by our activity. To say that they contain no internal contradiction is an insufficient statement of their real significance. They are not copies of things, but their significance consists in this, that they are archetypes or patterns which consciousness employs when it arranges and names things (as in mathematics and moral philosophy). This, however, only holds good of ideas of modes and relations. The concept of substance, the idea of an unknown bearer of qualities, can, then, only possess validity if such a combination of qualities as is given in the concept is to be found in reality. The idea of a centaur is an untrue, the idea of God a true, idea of substance. The substance-concept itself is not the archetype, but its archetype must be outside us if it is to have validity. What, however, lies behind the qualities of things we cannot know. We know material as little as we know spiritual substance ; the Cartesians have no right, therefore, to affirm that matter cannot think.

Knowledge is the perception of the agreement or disagreement of ideas. In its simplest form it is intuition, immediate perception. At this point Locke is very near Descartes, *e.g.* when he says we have an intuitive knowledge of our own existence ; even doubt proves this ; for if I know that I doubt I possess a perception of the existence of the thing doubting, which is just as certain as the perception of the thought which I call doubt ! Besides our own existence we perceive, by means of such immediate intuition, the simplest fundamental relations between our ideas. When a group of intuitively known ideas are formed into a series we have a " demonstration." Every step of the demonstration is an immediate intuition. These two kinds of knowledge are the only ones on which we can strictly rely. All other knowledge is only supposition, more or less probable conviction ; our " sensitive " knowledge of external things is of this kind.

Demonstrative knowledge is concerned not only with mathematical propositions, but also with the existence of God —and this is the only case in which we are able, by way of demonstration, to know real existence beyond our own. Locke's proof of the existence of God is the usual one : from the world (or our own existence) he argues to God as its cause. His argument is of particular interest, however, because it rests on the principle of causality, which is declared to be an intuitive truth : we have immediate certainty that nonentity cannot produce any real being ! Hence, there must be an eternal Being. And this cannot be matter, Locke continues, for matter cannot produce understanding. The contradiction between this proposition and the one given above — that matter is, perhaps, able to think—is only an apparent one. For in the former proposition he was asserting that we do not know the innermost nature of matter ; while here he is dealing with matter as we know it.[83]

(Just as Locke's doctrine of the origin of ideas contains a sharp contrast between the passivity in the reception of simple ideas and the activity in the formation of secondary ideas so, in his doctrine of the validity of knowledge, we find a no less sharp contrast between "sensitive" knowledge, which can only give us probability, and intuitive and demonstrative knowledge, which afford complete certainty and necessity.' Curiously enough this contrast occurs in the establishment of the proposition, by the validity of which Locke's proof of the agreement of knowledge with reality is conditioned, *i.e.* in the establishment of the principle of causality. We form the concept of a causal relation by means of sensuous experience ; the validity of the principle of causality is proved by intuition. And yet Locke quietly uses this very proposition both when he is arguing from simple ideas to the things which produce them, and in his proof of the existence of God. The idea of God—like the idea of causality—is derived from experience, though with the assistance of the combining and extending (idealising) activity of the mind ; the existence of God, how-ever, is proved by ratiocination, while the validity of the causal relation is intuitively perceived. Locke's standpoint, as an empiricist respecting the origin of ideas, and as a rationalist with regard to their application, here comes out plainly. The naïveté with which he establishes and applies the causal proposition shows him still a dogmatist. By his demand for psychological explanation and epistemological confirmation, however, he led the way to critical philosophy. Locke's transitional position is to be seen most clearly in his concept of substance. This was the self-evident fundamental concept of the great systems, the last absolute halting-place of thought. Only Hobbes had attempted to shake it, and in this, as in several other points, was Locke's forerunner. Locke treats it with a certain irony, calls substance " I know not what," and compares belief in it with the Indians' belief in the necessity of the elephant to support the earth,—and yet he does not reject it. While he declares it to be a self-produced concept, just as are the concepts of mathematics and moral philosophy, yet he attributes to it an external archetype and an external ground.)

(d) *Philosophy of Religion*

Locke's religion did not conflict with his philosophy. It was not necessary for him to have recourse to the many prevarications of Leibniz in order to unite them. Believing that he had given a philosophical proof of the existence of God, he at the same time believed that he had established natural religion by way of the reason. By this means, too, he gained the theological presuppositions without which, according to his view, no ethic is possible. His ethic is a theological doctrine of blessedness: out of the natural impulse after happiness arises the law which specifies the conditions under which our own happiness, in conjunction with that of other men, is to be attained. This law, found by way of the reason, and expressed in the old saying, "We ought to do unto others as we would they should do unto us," must yet, if it is to be authoritative, be regarded as proceeding from God's will and upheld by the same.

Although Locke was of opinion that the State should extend its toleration to all who embraced natural religion, yet his own personal standpoint was that of a believer in revelation. In the spring of 1695 he wrote to Limborch: "This winter I have been carefully considering in what the Christian faith consists. I have drunk for myself from the Holy Scriptures, but I have held aloof from the opinions of sects and systems." He embodied the results of his investigations in his work on *The Reasonableness of Christianity.* (He regarded revelation as an extension of that natural religion which is founded in the reason ; on the other hand, reason must constantly control the faith in revelation. In his chief work (Essay iv. 18, 2) he defines faith as "the assent to any proposition, not thus made out by the deductions of reason, but upon the credit of the proposer, as coming from God, in some extraordinary way of communication." Reason must decide if anything be really a revelation, and faith can never convince us of anything contrary to reason ; for the knowledge we possess that a revelation comes from God can never be so sure as the knowledge which is founded on the agreement or disagreement of our ideas. Revelation is necessary. For although Nature affords adequate witness of God, men have often made a wrong use of their reason.   Out of laziness, sensuality, or fear, they fall under the dominion of superstitious priests, since the few who follow reason cannot gain any influence over the multitude.   The greater number of men have neither the time nor the capacity to follow the demonstrations of reason.   Hence Christ was sent to illuminate, to strengthen, and to help.   Faith in Him as Lord and Master contains the promise of eternal life. Even the most ignorant, even those whose lives are spent in toilsome labour, can understand Christ's teaching and example as they are given in the Gospels.   On the developments of the doctrines contained in the Epistles, Locke lays less weight. The dogma of the Trinity he is unable to find either in the Gospels or in the Apostles' Creed.

Locke stands side by side with Christian Wolff (who reminds us of Locke in several other points, *e.g.* the unsuccessful attempt to establish the causal proposition) as the founder of religious rationalism.   His writings, and especially his religious standpoint, influenced the great minds of the eighteenth century, of whom Voltaire and Frederick II. stand in the first rank.   Most remarkable of all, however, is it to see religious rationalism breaking out as a democratic movement — which indeed almost always happens with every fresh wave of religious feeling.   In his opposition to the theology of the Church, Locke had especially in view the needs of the ignorant and the wretched; he demands a Christianity that shall be accessible and comprehensible to them.   Nevertheless Locke's own standpoint was a dogmatic one : he attributed to " natural " religion such great certainty as regards demonstration, and such great necessity as the foundation of ethics, that he would even deprive those who reject it of the benefit of religious freedom !   Not only Catholicism and Protestantism but Rationalism also has its intolerance.

(e) *Philosophy of Law and of the State*

Locke's work on *Civil Government* is an occasional work.   In the preface he says that it is his intention "to establish the throne of our great restorer, the present King William, to make good his title in the consent of the people which, being the only one of all lawful governments, he has more fully and clearly than any prince in Christendom, and to

justify to the world the people of England, whose love of their
natural rights, with their resolution to preserve them, saved the
nation when it was on the very brink of slavery and ruin."
In the first part of the book Locke refutes the doctrine of the
Royalist, Filmer, that kingship is a patriarchal institution,
established by God.) 'Political power, says Locke, differs from
the power of a father over his children, from the power of a
master over his apprentices, and the power of a slave-owner
over his slaves.   It consists in the power to lay down laws, to
administer these laws, and to protect the community from
external acts of violence, but all this only for the sake of the
common good.   Such a power can only be set up by free
contract.   Now that we are no more in the state of nature,
this contract is implicitly made every time that a son takes the
place of his father in the community.   The contract rests
essentially on this—that the will of the majority shall be law,
because this is the only way in which society can act as a
totality.   The state of nature is certainly not, as Hobbes
thought, a condition of war ; but it involves evils which are
only to be met by firm laws, impartial judges, and an executive
power in the State.   The state of nature is itself a state
of freedom, but freedom can be better defended in a community.   Natural rights, therefore, are in no way abrogated
in the transition to a state of society.   The right of property
e.g. is a natural right, which is founded on the labour that men
expend in cultivating the earth, or in elaborating some other
material.   To the diligent, and not to the lazy, God has given
the world, and all economic value arises through labour.   The
State can therefore no more destroy than it can establish
the right of property ; its task is only to confirm and protect
it.   As with the right of property so also with personal freedom ; slavery is in contradiction to Nature and must therefore
not be supported by the State.

   The prominence which Locke gives to the legislative power
in his philosophy of the State has especial significance.) In
introducing a legislative power no arbitrary power is erected ;
it was in order to avoid this that the state of nature was
abandoned.   /All decisions are regulated by the greatest
possible consideration for the common good.   Only on
receiving the assent of the majority can taxes and duties be
levied ;   otherwise the right of property will be violated, for

that which another can take from me against my will, I do not really possess! Locke requires that the legislative shall be separated from the executive and judicial powers [84]; the legislative power, however, is supreme; with its establishment the form of government is given, moreover the legislator is above the executors of the law (*Of Government*, ii. 141, 143).

The highest power, however, remains with the people, and is applied when the executive power comes into conflict with the legislative. No power on earth, other than the people, can decide a conflict of this kind. In virtue of the ultimate, inalienable right—the right of self-preservation—the nation makes an appeal to heaven, and enforces its will. But this is no rebellion: rebellions are instigated by those who transgress the law. Nor does it lead to the dissolution of the State, for, in the first place, the assumption is that the majority of the people are conscious of the evils which are to be got rid of; and secondly, a nation does not break bounds so easily as some people believe.

Locke's free spirit of inquiry, together with his warm and practical sympathy in the great events of the contemporaneous history of his nation, led him to formulate the great principles of national freedom in a manner which was of marked importance, not only for subsequent doctrines of Rights and of the State, but also for the history of nations in the following centuries. Montesquieu and Alexander Hamilton were his pupils. Rousseau's doctrine of the sovereignty of the people found a support in him, and the North American and French Revolutions are illustrations of what Locke calls the "appeal to Heaven." The constitutional life of modern States is essentially based on Locke's principles. The limits of his whole philosophy of the State coincide with the limits of the constitutional question. Behind this rises the social question. By his derivation of the right of property from labour Locke had, without knowing it, raised this great problem, which, however, only gained a place in the first rank at a much later period.

CHAPTER II

(a) *The Doctrine of the Moral Sense*

ALL through the period of the Renaissance and the seventeenth century we may trace the impulse to self-preservation serving, under different forms, as the foundation on which men thought to build up the conduct of life. . With very few exceptions all attempts to find a foundation for ethics start from the individual, from his impulses and desires, from his existence and welfare. In principle it makes no difference here whether the existence of the individual in this world only is taken into consideration, or whether (as *e.g.* in Locke) his existence in another world is also included. In opposition to this point of view, which found in Hobbes its clearest and most logical defender, an appeal was made, within the sphere of philosophical ethics, to Reason, as the power which should regulate men's actions. Spinoza's profound attempt to exhibit the metamorphoses and transformations which the impulse to self-preservation may undergo was but little regarded. It is Shaftesbury's merit to have brought into prominence the significance of immediate feeling, determined by instinct, for ethical judgments. Shaftesbury initiated a well-timed opposition —and one which had important consequences—against the rising wave of Rationalism, and, as has so often been the case in modern times when a quickening stream of thought wells forth, it is classical influences which determine his ideas. The antique harmony and self-limitation, and the antique confidence in Nature, reappear in Shaftesbury, although mingled with some modern sentimentality.) ANTHONY ASHLEY COOPER SHAFTESBURY, born in London in 1671, was the grandson of

Locke's friend. Locke assisted at his birth in the capacity of physician, and was afterwards his tutor. Owing to the careful instruction which he received in classics they exercised the predominant influence on his mind. He had a governess who spoke Latin and Greek fluently, so that he learnt to speak these languages like his mother tongue. Sound Greek thoughts were impressed upon the boy's mind when he was still quite young. His further development was accomplished by means of journeys in Italy and France, which afforded him opportunities of gaining knowledge of the world and of cultivating his artistic interests. For some years he was a member of the House of Commons. King William valued him highly and offered him a post of great trust, which, however, he declined. His health was poor and he longed for a quiet literary life. He died in 1713 at Naples, at a comparatively early age.

Shaftesbury's works, the greater part of which he collected himself in three volumes, entitled *Characteristics of Men, Manners, Opinions, and Times* (London, 1711), are not written in the form of a quiet systematic development of a concept; they contain outbursts and reflections, many of them in the form of letters or dialogues, carried out often with great poetic feeling and impulse, but often, too, with sentimental rhetoric in place of sound reason. (In the good as well as in the less favourable sense of the word, he is the first philosopher of feeling. The importance of immediate feeling is defended in opposition to discursive reason, calculating egoism, and external sense-impressions. He asserts the union of the beautiful with the good under a revival of the antique conception of virtue as a harmony between the parts of the individual man and between men among each other. Finally, he asserts the independence of ethics over against religion, while at the same time it is his conviction that ethical feeling, through faith in the Divinity working in and harmonising all things, finds its consummation in religious feeling.)

Although Shaftesbury entertained the greatest esteem for his teacher, Locke, and directed his most severe polemic against Hobbes, yet he asserts (in his *Letters to a Young Man at the University*) that Locke had overthrown the basis of morality by his criticism of innate ideas. He admits that " innate " ideas, in one sense of the word " innate," are absurd. He himself uses this expression in the sense of " natural, agreeing with Nature, instinctive," in antithesis to that which is due to art, culture, and breeding (cf. *The Moralists*, iii. 2). The question does not turn, he says, on the moment at which one body quits another, or on the exact point of time at which our ideas were formed, but on whether men are so constituted that, in the course of development, certain ideas naturally arise. And we have no right to assert that we can only get the ideas of love and justice from experience and the catechism.) For, in that case, there must be a catechism which teaches the birds to fly and to build their nests, and a man and woman to find one another! According to Shaftesbury, who is here in agreement with Grotius, Cumberland, and Leibniz, there is an instinct which binds the individual to the race, an instinct which is just as natural as the instinct of propagation and the care for posterity. Man cannot exist and has never been able to exist apart from society. It is a mistake to oppose the state of nature to the state of society.) On a closer investigation of the development of the human race we shall find a whole series of different states of nature ; in none of them, however, did social life and the desires which support it entirely disappear. By this view (in *The Moralists*, ii. 4) Shaftesbury places himself in opposition to the contract theory of natural law, which regarded society as arising from the joining together of in-dependent individuals. (He goes back to the standpoint of obscure instinct, where the individual and the community are not yet contrasted ; while, at the same time, he perceives that the state of nature and the state of civilisation are relative concepts.) We have in this one of the most important germs of his thought. The mental atmosphere of the eighteenth century, however, was not favourable to its further development.

Although Shaftesbury attributes great importance to instinct, yet he does not overlook the significance of thought. By means of it we are enabled to reflect on our own inner conditions, which thus become objects of feeling and of judgment. He here appeals to Locke's inner experience.)/The special feelings, *e.g.* esteem or contempt, admiration for the noble and right, indigna-tion against the ignoble and false in thought and action, arise through reflection on the involuntary stirrings within us. These feelings are akin to æsthetic pleasure and displeasure, but differ from them in their active character, which impels to action. Shaftesbury calls such a feeling a " reflex affection " or a " moral sense." Because it springs from natural instincts it is itself natural, original (*Inquiry concerning Virtue and Merit*).)

There is, it is true, a "cool philosophy" which teaches that there is no natural faith, no natural justice, no real virtue, to be found, because self-love and the lust of power are the only active forces. Shaftesbury thinks that this doctrine may have arisen from dislike to the thought of being led by Nature to serve ends which lie beyond the Ego. He himself teaches that all beings strive after happiness. But it makes a great difference, he says, if we find our happiness in striving after common ends, or if we restrict our interests to our own advantage or even, perhaps, to our own self-preservation. There is no absolute opposition between the egoistic and the sympathetic feelings ; this is so partly because love and friendship bring with them self-satisfaction, since we participate in the happiness which we procure for others by means of a sort of reflex current, and partly because the conditions of our life are so intimately associated with those of other men that we cease to care for ourselves when we cease to care for common goods. What we have to do is to bring into harmony the different impulses which stir the heart. He is the architect of his own happiness who has laid for himself an inner foundation of order, peace, and harmony. (Happiness is within, not without us. The harmony and beauty of the feelings mould the forms and customs of the true social life ; that which satisfies the claims of the life of the community brings harmony also into the souls of individuals.) And therefore, writes Shaftesbury in the *Letters to a Young Student*, seek the beautiful in all, even in the smallest things ! He hints at the ideas of a modern evolutionary æsthetic when he says (in the *Miscellaneous Reflections*) that the forms which are ugly produce at the same time discomfort and disease, while those forms and relations which are beautiful are advantageous, since they make for efficacy and furtherance.

(The sense of order and harmony in which, according to Shaftesbury, the moral feeling consists, concerns itself not only with human society but also with the whole universe, and thus becomes religious awe. The order of Nature excites our admiration. Mischief and evil exist only in our limited view : our finite thought must often regard that as imperfect which would appear perfect if we could view it from the point of view of the totality. The universe encounters no external

resistance.   It follows its own inner harmonious order, which
has its ground in the thought of God.\ Thus ethics leads to
religion, and Shaftesbury advocates "a noble Theism, which
conceives God as the all-loving and all-protecting, and therefore
as the ideal example."   We should be beginning at the wrong
end if (with Locke) we were to attempt to base ethics on
religion.   In that case disinterestedness would vanish.   Virtue
is its own reward.   What more fitting reward could it have?

FRANCIS HUTCHESON (1694 - 1747), born of Scotch
parentage in the north of Ireland, who, after he had conducted
a private academy in Dublin, became Professor of Moral
Philosophy in Glasgow, threw Shaftesbury's ideas into a more
systematic form, by which means they attained a wider circulation.
In his *Inquiry into the Ideas of Beauty and Virtue* (1725) we
have an examination of the æsthetic and ethical feelings,
containing many interesting observations and more nearly
determining several points which Shaftesbury had left undecided.   His *System of Moral Philosophy* was published after
his death (1755).   He endeavoured to found ethics on the
observation of actual human nature.   He finds here, besides the
egoistic instincts, an involuntary desire to help and please
others ; while, on the other hand, he finds an equally
immediate feeling of joy and approval at actions springing
from this desire to help and give pleasure.   Reason is only
the faculty of finding the means to given ends ; it is useful
to sympathy and cannot be dispensed with, since, without
it, this immediate feeling would work blindly and short-
sightedly ; but it is not Reason alone which leads to an
estimation of human actions.   As little as the moral sense can
dispense with Reason, can it dispense with experience, through
which alone we can learn the effects or tendencies of actions.
The moral sense is only active when it has before it observations of human actions and of their effects.   In considering
how the moral sense works on the basis of such observations,
Hutcheson finds that, when the results are expected to produce
equally great degrees of happiness, that action is valued the
most the happy effects of which extend to the greatest number
of persons,—although, indeed, the character or the moral importance of the persons may be considered as outweighing
number,—and that in the case of an equally large number of
persons profiting by the effects of the actions, that action is

esteemed the highest which affords the highest degree of happiness. He condensed these observations into a principle which has since often been repeated : \that action is the best which procures the greatest happiness for the greatest number (*Inquiry*, ii. 3).[85]

The moral sense cannot be explained as arising from experience, for it expresses itself entirely instinctively and directly; neither does it come from education, habit, or association of ideas, for in none of these ways, in Hutcheson's opinion (*System*, i. 32, 57), can entirely new senses or ideas arise. He admits that, so far, the moral sense contains nothing mysterious. (He believes it to have been originally conferred by God, and he regards it as a proof of the wisdom of the Creator that the moral sense only justifies such actions which promote the welfare of others, or of ourselves in a manner which is in agreement with the welfare of others. But the moral sense is operative also in those who do not believe in a God.) The ethical is for Hutcheson as independent of theological ideas as it is of egoistical *arrière pensées*, although he admits that where the moral sense is blunted, the law of authority is the only means by which the struggle with the affections can be carried on. Further, the moral sense does not always work as immediate instinct. A feeling of duty may develop out of it when—even though the immediate impulse leads neither to action nor omission—consciousness becomes aware that, if a certain decision is not made, we shall be in conflict with the demands made by benevolence, and thus our inner serenity will suffer, and we may, perhaps, incur inner or outer unpleasantnesses. Thus, for Hutcheson, the feeling of duty is a secondary and vicarious feeling.

In dealing with individual ethical questions Hutcheson employs the principle of utility as a measuring-rod. His *System of Moral Philosophy* contains very many acute, humane, and free-thinking observations on particular moral, social, and political questions.

JOSEPH BUTLER, who after completing his studies at a Dissenting College became a member of the Established Church and died a bishop in 1752, an energetic thinker and an able observer, threw Shaftesbury's doctrine of the moral sense into a still more theological form than had been given to it by Hutcheson.)(In conjunction with this it must be noticed that

Butler had a very keen realisation of the dark side of life, and that he felt himself very far removed from Shaftesbury's enthusiastic optimism.

His conception of ethics is developed in his *Sermons* (1726). It is true that, like Shaftesbury and Hutcheson, he regards morality as intimately connected with the immediate relation of the individual to the race. But he emphasises, more strongly than they do, the unquestionably immediate inner needs which make themselves known through the moral sense, which he prefers to call conscience. We are too short-sighted to discover what brings happiness in individual cases. It is dispensed by the Ruler of the world. But we are so made that, without regard to consequences, we condemn falseness, violence, and injustice ; while, on the other hand, we approve love and benevolence. The principle of welfare established by Hutcheson is not applied here : Butler has in view only the inner subjective side of morality. He found fault with Shaftesbury's doctrine for not giving preeminence to the authority of conscience—of the inner moral feeling—above all other elements and impulses of the soul. Conscience is in its nature higher than all other faculties. It is destined to rule the world. By means of a subtle psychological analysis Butler shows that immediate satisfaction, such as is conferred by the moral feeling, differs from the feeling of pleasure reached by means of egoistical calculation : in the immediate instincts we do not consciously make ourselves our aim ; while, on the other hand, egoism proper presupposes experience of the pleasurable feelings resulting from immediate surrender to the passions, and the conscious erection beforehand of these as an aim ; but it is precisely this reflection and calculation which is likely to hinder the attainment of a complete satisfaction.

Although, according to Butler, obedience to the law of conscience carries with it immediate satisfaction, yet, so keen was his sense of the conflicting elements within human nature, he could not feel satisfied with Shaftesbury's joy over the harmony of our inner nature. If it were not expressly guaranteed to us that, in the long-run, the good and right will bring us a strictly personal satisfaction of our desire for happiness, we should never abide by them : " Though virtue or moral rectitude does indeed consist in affection to and pursuit of what is right and good as such, yet _when we sit down in a cool hour_, we can neither justify to ourselves this or any other pursuit till we are convinced that it will be for our happiness, or at least not contrary to it" (Sermon XI.). Shaftesbury had as little regard for "cool" hours as for "cool" philosophy. For Butler, in the last resort, it is only the prospect of a future life, afforded by religion, which can help us over such hours. Yet he knows of still another way in which ethics leads us to religion. The indwelling need of our nature to feel love and admiration, finds its highest possible object in God. Religion extends our feeling and changes its direction, but it does not create a new kind of feeling; our nature does not admit of transformation. Butler, then, extends the opposition between self-interest and admiring surrender from the ethical to the religious sphere, without, however, arriving at any definitive solution.

Butler's opposition to Shaftesbury is the opposition of the pessimist to the optimist. The early part of the eighteenth century was distinctly optimistic. Men looked at life and human nature through rose-coloured glasses and entertained great hopes of happiness and progress. Leibniz, Locke, and Shaftesbury all expressed this optimism under different forms. Shaftesbury and the free-thinkers eulogised natural religion, grounded in the contemplation of the unity and harmony of Nature, in opposition to the dark mysteries and inhuman dogmas of revealed religion. Personal temperament as well as theological conviction led Butler to attack this opposition. In his remarkable work, _Analogy of Religion, Natural and Revealed, to the Constitution and Course of Nature_ (1736), he seeks to show that the weightiest objections brought against revealed religion are equally valid against the faith of natural religion in a providential over-ruling of Nature. We can never discover by observation that Nature has a wise, righteous, and good cause. If we stumble at the doctrines of election and damnation, we must not forget that in Nature countless germs perish undeveloped, and that but few attain to complete moral development in this life! If we are offended at the doctrine of the Atonement we must remember that in Nature the innocent do actually suffer for the guilty! If Christianity be an offence, Nature must be an offence also. The mystery in both is, properly speaking, equally great. Butler himself is helped

over these difficulties—both with regard to Nature as well as
to Revelation—by the thought that in the natural as well as
in the supernatural world we are only parts of a vast un-
observable whole, which, from the place which we occupy, we
can never see in its entirety.

It is with such reflections as these that Butler meets that
smooth, superficial optimism which overlooks the real circumstances of the case.   It is just as possible to have an unthinking cult of Nature as an unthinking faith in Revelation ;
and the dogmatism of natural religion may be just as
dangerous as that of positive religion.   Butler's proposition,
however, may be converted, when it runs thus : Christianity
contains the same contradictions as Nature ; the question
then is : what solution of the riddle of existence is reached by
revelation, if this is only a kind of doubling or reflection of
Nature and her riddles?   The lance, which Butler put in rest
against his opponents, is turned against his own breast.

BERNARD DE MANDEVILLE, on the other hand (of French
extraction, born in Holland, established as a doctor in London,
died in 1733), the author of the *Fable of the Bees*, seems to
have avoided such self-injury.   The *Fable of the Bees* is a
poem which appeared in 1708 and was sold as a pamphlet in
the London streets.   It describes a colony of bees at the
zenith of their prosperity and power.   All work eagerly to
satisfy the common needs.   Restlessness, discontent, sensuality, vanity, and deceit prevail, but they all contribute to the
general advantage.   It is precisely the corruption in individual
parts of the State which makes the whole a paradise, just as
individual discords in a piece of music increase its harmony as
a whole.   Even the poor lived better than did the rich formerly.
But then came certain who began to cry: Down with corruption !   Let us at least be honest.   And the cry met with
approbation.   Those who had been foremost in deception were
now foremost in the cry for probity.   The gods heard their
cry.   Hypocrisy vanished.   Luxury ceased.   There were no
more predatory wars.   The dominion of the priests and of the
bureaucracy was curtailed.   The Commonwealth provided for
the needs of the poor.   They contented themselves with home
products and there was no further demand for the more costly,
imported   wares.   Hence   navigation   ceased.   Population
diminished—and at last the whole swarm retired into a hollow

tree. Contentment and honesty had been attained, but splendour and power had disappeared. The moral is clear enough : the happiness and morality of the individual is incompatible with the culture of the community.)

In a later edition (*The Fable of the Bees, or Private Vices Publick Benefits*, 6th ed. London 1732) Mandeville added notes, partly in the shape of a dialogue, in which he exhibits the very decided contrast that exists between his own and Shaftesbury's conceptions. No two systems, he says, can be more opposed than his lordship's and mine. (The selfish interests of man, his need of food and drink, his ambition and envy, his pursuit of pleasure, his laziness and impatience, these it is which lead to labour, to civilisation, and to social life. Contentment and virtue, on the other hand, tend to make men content with what they have. There is no original desire after the social life. Without hypocrisy no society can exist : let us only think of what the consequences would be if we were honestly to express all our ideas and feelings ! The task of the true statesmen is to make the community powerful, by letting the egoistic interests of men work together for the common good ; it would be foolish, therefore, to uproot the necessary evil. The ordinary virtues were invented by ambitious politicians, who could more easily secure the dominion and power to themselves if men could be made self-sacrificing and obedient, for only so is it possible to rule great numbers. A growing civilisation, however, brings to light the connection between the vice and continual discontent of the individual and the good of the whole. Philanthropy, which would abolish poverty, is injurious. In a special treatise (*On Charity and Charity Schools*) Mandeville dwells upon the danger of bringing greater enlightenment to the poor than is sufficient for their station : for then how are we to arrange for the doing of the lowest and least attractive work ? /We must choose between Nature and Culture, between moral and social progress. The mud in the London streets could not disappear unless the enormous traffic disappeared along with it. During the course of development, evil and good are inseparably bound up with one another.)

Mandeville thus rejects the harmony of Shaftesbury and Leibniz. He is the most powerful defender of pessimism in the eighteenth century, and deserves real credit for his treat-

ment of the problem of civilisation.   In order to be reconciled
with the theologians he declares that, since the author of Nature
is incomprehensible to us, we have no right to call Him cruel.
Indeed he even thinks himself to be working in the cause of
faith in revelation and Christian morality when he exposes the
vanity of the world and the insufficiency both of human reason
and of pagan virtue—in contrast to Shaftesbury, who favoured
deism and exalted pagan above Christian virtue (*Fable of
the Bees*, 6th ed. ii. p. 431 ff.).   This theological finale seems
somewhat loosely tacked on—but it was not without its effect.
The clergy attacked Shaftesbury much more vigorously than
Mandeville.

(b) *The Free-Thinkers*

Since the dawn of the Renaissance thought had been
trying its powers on the great problems of life under very
many different forms, and in very many different directions.
It was no wonder, therefore, that the conviction now began to
arise in more general circles that conceptions of life and the
conduct of life could dispense with the support of authority,
and that that insight into the laws of nature and human
life which men can obtain for themselves, by dint of their
own powers of intellect, is an all-sufficient guide.   Moreover
a class of men soon began to arise—in Italy from the fifteenth
century on, in more northern countries during the course of
the following centuries—for whom natural religion sufficed, or
who did not even require this in its usual form.   In and
after the sixteenth century the term " deist " was applied indis-
criminately to all those who believed in no " revelation " in
the orthodox sense of the word ; later, however, denial of
the miraculous intervention of God in the course of affairs
was regarded as the special characteristic of thinkers of this
type.   There was often no great distinction made between
deists and atheists.   Men were inclined to call each new philo-
sophico-religious view in turn " atheism."   With the beginning
of the eighteenth century the word " free-thinker " appears in
English literature.   By this is meant thought freed from the
trammels of authority.   Like the terms "deist" and "atheist" it
covers widely different views ; none of these expressions, therefore, are of any philosophical value.   It is, however, a sign of

the times that these so-called "free-thinkers" had become more numerous and more self-conscious since the beginning of the new century.   The deistic or free-thinking literature is, for the most part, of small value for philosophy.   This, however, does not diminish its great significance in relation to the history of civilisation, since it is a symptom of the extension of scientific and philosophical ideas, and indicates the general trend of thought in wider circles.   But to follow out such symptoms in detail is a task for the history of literature rather than the history of philosophy.   Leslie Stephen rightly remarks of the English deists (*History of English Thought in the Eighteenth Century*, vol. i. chap. ii.) that they were altogether inferior to their adversaries; while in France it was exactly the reverse.   The explanation of this is, without doubt, to be found partly in the greater opposition which the Catholic Church was able to offer, and which consequently stimulated its opponents and moved them to still greater exertions, and partly in the fact that in France dogmatic discussion was never purely abstract—opposition on religious and theoretical questions being closely allied with social and political antagonism.   Both these causes gave rise to an enthusiasm in which English deism was lacking.

Only one of all the men formerly known as the "English deists" has rendered contributions of any value to the history of thought.   This is JOHN TOLAND.   He was born in 1670, in the north of Ireland, and was brought up in the Catholic religion : this is all that we know of his childhood.   In the preface to his work, *Christianity not Mysterious* (1696), he says : "For being educated from my cradle in the grossest superstition and idolatry, God was pleased to make my own reason and such as made use of theirs the happy instrument of my conversion."   He finds no difference between the authority of the Pope and the authority to which the Protestant clergy lay claim.   Like the early Christians, he is only concerned with the choice between the clear teaching of Christ and the complicated doctrines of the learned.   What Toland regarded as Christ's clear teaching is to be gathered from the work above mentioned.   The physicist MOLYNEUX, Locke's Dublin friend, mentions Toland in his letters to Locke —at first with esteem ; in a letter of 6th April 1697 he calls him "a candid free-thinker and a good scholar."   (So far as I know, this is the first time the word "free-thinker" is used.) Later, however, he was disgusted by Toland's vanity, and his habit of carrying on propaganda in coffee-houses and other public places. The clergy and magistracy were no less offended. He was so zealously preached against that (as Molyneux relates) a pious man declined to go to church any more, on the ground that he heard more of one Toland than of the Lord Jesus. His book was burnt, and a member of the Irish Parliament would have had the author burnt with it.

After this Toland occupied himself with the history of literature and with politics. He appeared as defender of the Protestant succession, and thus gained the favour of the court at Hanover, where he met Leibniz. Toland also came into high favour with the gifted Queen Sophia Charlotta of Prussia, an Hanoverian princess and a pupil of Leibniz. The Queen liked to listen to discussions between the Berlin theologians, Leibniz, and Toland. In the preface to *Letters to Serena* (1704) Toland, mindful of this experience, extols the capacity of women for intellectual work. Serena is Sophia Charlotta. His activities as a publicist proved so remunerative that Toland was able to purchase a house in the country. Here his love of Nature could find satisfaction, and he was able to live "free from care as well as from ambition, with a book always in his hand or his head." Afterwards his circumstances became straitened, and his last years were troubled with poverty and illness. He died (1722) in a village near London.

Toland's attitude towards Christianity may be learnt from the above-mentioned book, in which he endeavours to prove that there is nothing in the Gospels which is *against* reason or *above* reason, and that the Christian doctrine cannot rightly be called a mystery. By reason he understands the mental faculty which, by means of a comparison between the doubtful and obscure and that which is clearly known, leads us to certainty. We must employ this faculty in religion also ; for it is this only, and not the authority of the Church, which can convince us of the inspiration of Scripture. The dogma of the creation and the account of the miracles are not in contradiction to reason. Because we cannot altogether understand a thing it does not follow that it is a miracle. In the New Testament, the word mystery is never used of that which, in and for itself, is incomprehensible, but always of that which, having been hidden, is afterwards revealed, and which can therefore now be understood. For why should God require us to believe what we are unable to understand? Our diligence would not be increased thereby, and we have reason enough, without that, to study to be humble. Priests and philosophers were the first to turn Christianity into a mystery.

Later deists, Collins, Tindal, Morgan, etc., went farther than Toland, and either attempted to explain miracles by natural causes or else denied them altogether. The dispute was carried on by them, as well as by their opponents, with great violence, and in a most unscientific manner. Both sides were lacking in historic sense. What the orthodox pronounced to be arbitrary miracles the deists declared to be no less arbitrary inventions of cunning priests.

Toland's most important work is his *Letters to Serena*. This is directed against the Cartesian conception of matter to which Spinoza, although not without hesitation, still adhered. Toland maintains that motion must be considered as an equally essential and original property of matter as extension and solidity. If we conceive matter as passive and at rest, then we must assume a supernatural cause by which it is set in motion. · A closer investigation will convince us that there is motion everywhere in Nature; it only appears to the senses as if at certain points there were cessation and rest; a thoughtful consideration will show us internal energy, *autokinesis*, in all things. Every motion must be explained out of another motion, and this is true of such motions, *e.g.* those of animals, as seem to arise of themselves, *i.e.* without cause. Consciousness denotes no interruption to the sequence of motions. We must assume that God created matter active. The order and harmony of the world proves that He guides the motions of matter; moreover without this belief the origin of organic life would be inexplicable.

This line of thought of Toland's influenced French materialism in the middle of the century. Quite new it was not: Leibniz had already modified the Cartesian physics in a similar direction, and with far more penetration. Toland, however, introduced the doctrine of the eternity of motion to much wider circles.

For the definitive unfolding of Toland's ideas we must turn to his *Pantheisticon* (1720). Here, in the guise of fiction, he describes how throughout the whole of Europe groups of unprejudiced men are to be found meeting together in simple social gatherings, where various important questions are quietly and sensibly· discussed. (They are called *pantheists* (which expression seems to have originated with Toland) because they believe that God is one with the ordering and creative power active throughout the universe, and can therefore only be distinguished in thought (*ratione*) from the world. They are altogether at variance with Epicurus, and are not materialists. In their opinion, all particular individuals, each one after its kind, have arisen out of motion and thought, which latter is the power and harmony of the universe. They have their own liturgy, and practise unconditional tolerance. They aim at the welfare of the State and of humanity, without regard to party. They keep their doctrine secret as an esoteric doctrine only accessible to the initiated ; for there are misguided and morose men who must be treated as a nurse treats a lisping infant. ' Toland wrote this work in a spirit similar to that in which, almost contemporaneously, the Masonic movement arose. New views require cultivation within restricted circles and, to a certain extent, new symbols also. The age of criticism and enlightenment, however, was not adapted to the foundation of such societies or to the creation of symbols likely to live. Free individualism and critical examination had (and have) a great work still to perform, and neither societies nor symbols are created by deliberate and conscious choice.

CHAPTER III

NEWTON AND HIS SIGNIFICANCE FOR PHILOSOPHY

As at the transition from the Renaissance to the seventeenth century it was necessary to intercalate an examination of the foundation of modern physics, without which the subsequent course of philosophical development would not have been intelligible, so here, too, at the threshold of the eighteenth century, we must turn our attention to a great figure in the history of physics, the greatest perhaps of any that it contains. In Newton not only did the ideal of inquiry which the new science had set up find its consummation, so that his work remains a model of general scientific method, but, in addition to this, his discoveries and results exercised great influence on subsequent philosophic development, in his own country as well as in France and Germany. Moreover, Newton had a peculiar philosophy of his own, which is of great interest for the history of philosophy, both as an expression of the conception of the world formed by a great investigator of Nature, and on account of the influence it exerted.

Isaac Newton was born on 25th December 1642, at Woolsthorpe, near Nottingham. While still a child he took a great interest in mechanics, and constructed machines, mills, and clocks. He was originally intended to be a farmer, but as he left the cows and sheep to take care of themselves when sent out to herd them, his wish was granted, and he was allowed to devote himself to study. He taught himself so much at the University of Cambridge that he soon surpassed his teachers. He was still quite young when he conceived the idea which led to his great scientific discoveries in mathematics, as well as in optics and astronomy. Like many other great minds in the history of science he ruminated for a long time over the ideas he had conceived so early, working at them in silence until he could carry them out to their fullest extent, and could adduce proofs of their validity.   The idea of the differential calculus, it seems, had occurred to him before Leibniz had come upon it, although the latter was before him in publishing his discovery ; in addition to this, his great discoveries are the composition of light and the law of gravitation, the nearer discussion of which, however, is not within our province.   His principal works are the *Principia philosophiae naturalis mathematica* (1687) and the *Opticks* (1704).   After holding a professorship at Cambridge for many years, he spent his later years in London, where he held a high post at the Mint.   He died full of years in 1727.

' The great philosophic importance of Newton's discovery of gravitation consists, before all else, in the verification of the fact that the physical laws which hold good on the surface of the earth are valid, throughout the universe, as far as we can know anything of it. ' Newton's fundamental thought which, as the story goes, occurred to him in a lucky moment, was as follows : we must extend what we see happening on the earth to spheres beyond it, and then see if the conclusions which we are thus enabled to draw are confirmed by observation.   Weight is greater in valleys than on the summits of mountains ; there is no reason, however, why we should suppose it to cease altogether in the moon or in one of the planets.   May not the motion of the moon be conceived as a falling motion, so that its line of motion deviates from that prescribed by the law of inertia just as far as is demanded by the law of falling bodies, according to the distance of the moon from the earth. In his chief work he has formulated as a special rule of investigation (*regula philosophandi*) the principle which guided his thought in framing this supposition: "Such qualities as cannot be diminished or increased and which belong to all bodies on which we can make experiment, must be regarded as qualities of all bodies whatsoever. . . . We must not, however, wantonly invent dreams, which contradict the evidence of experience (*tenor experimentorum*), nor must we forsake the analogy of Nature, since Nature is always simple and in agreement with itself. . . . In virtue of this rule we learn that all bodies gravitate towards one another."   In this rule of investigation Newton establishes the principle which serves as a guiding line to the whole of modern science and philosophy.   We

encountered it under different forms and in different applications in Copernicus, Bruno, Galilei, and Leibniz.   Newton
turned it to the most scientific use.
    This was a great extension of view.   It was now clear that
the fixed and law-abiding order of Nature prevails, not only
here on this earth, but also throughout the universe.   Thus the
mechanical conception of Nature founded by Kepler, Galilei,
and Descartes at once received confirmation and became more
comprehensive.   The world was now seen to be a huge
machine.   Men had, it is true, already had a suspicion that this
was the case ; but it was only now discovered how the machine
was held together.   It was natural that great reliance in the
scientific method and in the powers of the human mind which
had solved such a problem should spring up also in those who
were not able to understand for themselves how the solution
had been reached.
    Newton's method was no less important than his results.
The brilliant idea that, in virtue of the principle of actuality,
what is true in narrower spheres of experience may be extended
to wider, is only the first step.   The next step is the stringent
deduction of the consequences contained in the idea which has
been posited.   While the third step is the proof that that which
is thus found to follow logically from the idea is in agreement
with experience.   The combined use of deduction and induction makes Newton's *magnum opus* a model for all scientific
investigations which has never been surpassed.   First he
deduces the consequences of the assumption that all planets
move according to the same laws as falling bodies on the
surface of the earth, and then he shows that the consequences
are confirmed by actual experience.   Finally he concludes that
the same force works in both places.   From the phenomena he
reaches the law and from the law he arrives at the force.
    He calls this force attraction, expressly adding that by this
term he does not mean to assert anything as to its nature, but
merely to state that it causes a smaller body to approach a
larger one.   As a matter of fact he did not believe in force
working at a distance.   For both in the *Principia* (2, 11) and
in the *Opticks* (Query 18-24) he says, that centripetal force
should be called " impact " (*impulsus*) rather than " attraction "
(*attractio*), since the most probable hypothesis is the assumption
of an ether stuff which penetrates all things, and which is rarer

in the proximity of the heavenly bodies than at a great distance from them ; by this assumption, perhaps, not only weight but also light and warmth would be explained. His main point of view, however, is expressed in the Scholium generale (at the end of the third book of the *Principia*) : " The ground of the quality of weight I have not yet been able to deduce from phenomena, and I do not allow myself to invent hypotheses." Pemberton (*A View of Sir Isaac Newton's Philosophy*, London, 1728, p. 407) relates that Newton complained to him of having been misunderstood, as though he had intended the word attraction as an explanation, whereas he had only meant to turn men's attention to a force in Nature whose cause and manner of working must be the subject of much far-reaching investigation. Newton's doctrine, therefore, stands in no such irreconcilable antagonism to the Cartesian physics as the Cartesians themselves, as well as Leibniz, and many of Newton's friends, believed. In reality he agrees with Descartes in his general point of view, although, owing to his more perfect method, he corrected his views on special points. He was very unjustly accused of having wished to reintroduce the " hidden properties " of the Scholastics. He has satisfied his own requirement, *i.e.* to assume *verae causae* only.

Yet it is not only on account of his conclusions and of his method that Newton figures in the history of philosophy. Partly as a background to, partly as the consequence of, his physical theories is a conception of the world peculiar to himself. A brief notice of this may be of interest.

There is a remarkable connection between Newton's religious conceptions and his mathematical physics—a connection which is effected by means of his doctrine of space. (The most important passages occur in the Scholium after the definitions in the *Principia*, and Query 31 in the *Opticks*.) The popular conception (*vulgus*), Newton says, wrongly supposes that sensuous time, space, place, and motion are the true ones. They define the same according to their relation to sensuous things. But it has never been shown that any body exists in a state of absolute rest, so that we could use it as our starting-point in determining place, and in distinguishing between real and apparent motion. Before there could be real motion (that is to say such as is presupposed, *e.g.* by the law of inertia) there must be an absolute space and an absolute time which are not determined by their relation to anything external (*sine relatione ad externum quodvis*). There must be absolute, unmoving places if there is to be an absolute determination of space, but the senses are not able to show us such places. The absolute places (*loca primaria*) are places for themselves as well as for all other things. The true space and the true time are mathematical space and mathematical time, but these are not objects of the senses. Curiously enough we find in this great investigator of Nature the dogmatic tendency to leap from the phenomenal and relative to the absolute. He postulates a space in and for itself (a kind of *locus sui*), just as Descartes, Spinoza, and Leibniz postulated a cause in itself (*causa sui*). He regards the mathematical mode of thought not only as a method of conception which may guide us in calculating the relations of phenomena, but also as the *true* method of thought, in opposition to the sensuous or vulgar, which cannot reach beyond the relative. A mathematical abstraction is made into a true reality. In practical matters (*in rebus humanis*), it is true, we must not go beyond sensuous space and must forget that the senses are not able to show us absolute places ; but as thinkers (*in rebus philosophicus*) we must abstract from the senses !

Passages in Newton's works may be pointed out which indicate some vacillation on this point,[86] but the view of absolute, ideal space as a reality is bound up with the innermost essence of the Newtonian conception of the world. Space is for him not an empty form, but the organ by means of which God works as omnipresent in the world, and, at the same time, immediately perceives the conditions of things. It is an "unlimited and homogeneous sensorium." Extension, then, is for Newton (as for Henry More) no distinctive mark of material things. Matter is only that which has solidity as well as extension. In his conception of space on the physical side, Newton stands, by his own confession, nearest to Gassendi, while, as regards its religio-philosophical aspect, he was influenced by Henry More.

Newton proves the existence of God from the purposive and harmonious arrangement of the world, and in so doing he starts a theme which received a thousand variations in the course of the eighteenth century. Whence comes it that Nature does nothing

in vain, and always chooses the simplest ways ?   Whence come
all the order and beauty which we see in the world ?   The
motion of the planets round the sun in orbits which are concentric with that of the sun and which lie almost in the same
plane—in short, the whole wonderful conjunction (*elegantissima
compages*) of our solar system—cannot be explained according
to mechanical laws and cannot have had a purely natural
development.   Only by supernatural means can the masses,
distances, velocities, and densities of the different heavenly
bodies have been suitably arranged, and only by assuming a
supernatural force can we explain how it is that the planets
move in circles instead of following the law of gravity and
falling into the sun.   And besides all this there are the wonderful constructions, organs, and instincts of animals !   (In addition
to the Scholium generale of the *Principia*, and Query 28 and
29 of the *Opticks*, Newton discusses this subject in his letters
to Bentley ; cf. Brewster, *Life of Newton*, ii. p. 125 ff.)
    The world-machine, however, is, in Newton's opinion, not
quite perfect.   The attempt to prove the existence of God
from the purposiveness of Nature may easily become self-
contradictory ; for if Nature were created perfect its own indwelling force could keep it on its course, and continued
activity on the part of God would be superfluous.   This
possibility does not occur in Newton's theology, since, in his
view, irregularities have arisen in the system through the
reciprocal action of comets and planets upon one another,
which necessitates regulation by God.   This point was violently attacked by Leibniz, who scornfully compared Newton's
world-system to a clock which, from time to time, requires the
watchmaker.) Clarke, Newton's pupil, defended this doctrine,
maintaining that it ill beseems us to make God superfluous.
To sum up : first, God's existence is proved through the intelligence of the mechanism of Nature, but then the fear arises
that if this intelligence is too great, it will refute, rather than
prove, His existence, and this in spite of the fact that, properly
speaking, the intelligence must be infinitely great if it is to
afford a proof of the existence of a God !   This branch of
Newton's thought, in and for itself, would not have made him
famous.   Fortunately his own mind and his own method led
the great investigator of Nature out of and beyond his not very
happy philosophy.   Kant and Laplace showed that the solar

system may have developed its present form naturally, and the great French mathematicians, more especially Lagrange and Laplace, proved that the irregularities are periodical and equalise one another.   In Newton's doctrine and method lay a deeper philosophy than he himself was able to extract from it.   Kant and Laplace were better Newtonians than Clarke.   How dangerous an appeal to the supernatural in scientific matters may become may be seen from a passage of Maclaurin's—a pupil of Newton's and an excellent exponent of his doctrines —which makes short work of the whole question.   Speaking of the catastrophes which appear to have taken place in the world in bygone ages he says: "Since God has made the universe dependent on Himself so that He must renew it from time to time, it seems no very important matter whether these great changes are produced through the influence of external circumstances or through the same force which shaped things from the beginning."   All evolutionary theories are thus declared to be superfluous, a whole series of scientific problems are wiped out.   Nothing was further from the spirit in which· Newton's own doctrine was conceived.

CHAPTER IV

GEORGE BERKELEY

(a) Biography and Characteristics

WE must have patience for a while ere we follow the ideas established by Locke, Newton, and the deists on their wanderings through Europe. After it has shown the origin of these ideas, the history of philosophy turns to a thinker who gave them a new philosophical working-up, partly carrying them on, partly disputing them, and finally arriving far from the course of thought in which popular consciousness moves, and alone can move. The peculiarity in the case of GEORGE BERKELEY, —one of the most delicate and clearest minds known to the history of philosophy—however, is that though he took up the cudgels in support of the immediate practical consciousness in opposition to scientific abstractions and speculations, yet, in his own results, he came into the sharpest opposition to this consciousness and provoked it beyond measure by his paradoxes. In other respects also, Berkeley united in his mode of thought contrasts which might seem incompatible. Acute. criticism and childlike religious faith, the lust of inquiry and ardent missionary zeal, have never been so intimately and peculiarly bound together as in Berkeley.

GEORGE BERKELEY was born 12th March 1685 in Dysert, Co. Kilkenny. He belonged to an English family which appears to have come to Ireland immediately after the Restoration and was a collateral branch of the noble family of Berkeley. Swift, George Berkeley's friend, is said to have introduced him to the Earl of Berkeley with these words: " My lord, here is a young man of your family. I can assure your lordship that it is a much greater honour to you to be related to him than to him to be related to you." So much is certain, that the young man early displayed brilliant abilities. He studied at Dublin where, at that time, the works of Boyle, Newton, and Locke formed the basis of the instruction given at the University. He conceived the fundamental notions of his subsequent philosophy in early youth. In the *Commonplace Book* of these years, which FRASER has published in his excellent biography of Berkeley (*Life and Letters of George Berkeley*, Oxford, 1871), we see his ideas in successive stages of development. He early arrived at the conviction that if science and philosophy were freed from senseless abstractions and obscure words there would be an end to the quarrel between knowledge and faith. He exerted himself to lead men back to immediate experience and intuition. He strove to do away not only with any still surviving Scholasticism but also with that which had taken the place of the old dogmas. His central thought is the proof that, in the literal sense of the word, there are no such things as "abstract" ideas. Closely connected with this thought are his brilliant discoveries, and his personal conception of life.)

Berkeley's first work was the *New Theory of Vision* (1709); he here shows that in the perception of space the senses of sight and of touch are combined, and that space, in and for itself, is an empty abstraction, corresponding to no immediate perception. In the following year appeared his chief work, *Principles of Knowledge*, in which he first criticises the old theory of abstraction, and then endeavours to show that the concept of matter is an invalid abstraction, and that we have no-immediate objects of knowledge except our own sense-perceptions. How he effected the direct transition from this position to his religious ideas will be shown later. A few years after the appearance of this work he went to London, where he moved in literary circles and began his battle with the free-thinkers by an article in Steel's paper *The Guardian*. His polemic is somewhat childlike and naïve in character, *e.g.* when he wonders (in his *Remarks on Collins' Discourse of Free-thinking*) why, instead of seeking a substitute for supernatural bliss in the enjoyment of the senses, free-thinkers for the most part lead a retired life, devoted to study! (When, therefore, in another passage in this article Berkeley declares " If it were not for this thought (*i.e.* immortality) I had rather be an oyster than a man ! " he contradicts himself, unless he means to

say that the oyster is gifted with quite particular pleasures of
sense.)   The free-thinkers, he says, openly declare that they
have less reason to be virtuous than other men.   But they little
know the strength of passion who think that the beauty of virtue
is a sufficient counterpoise in the hour of temptation!   After
he had published a brilliant popular exposition of his philosophical ideas in the form of dialogues (*Dialogues between
Hylas and Philonous*, 1713), he spent several years travelling
in France and Italy.   The diary of his journals shows his
open mind and his keen sense for nature, history, and social
circumstances.   On his return he filled a clerical office in
Ireland, but he could not endure it there long.   He lost hope
in the realisation of his plans to lead men back to naturalness
and simplicity of thought and life in old Europe.   Europe was
too infirm with age for him.   In the new virgin country across
the Atlantic he anticipated a golden age for faith, science, and
art, as well as for life.   With this was united his zeal for the
spread of Christianity among the heathen, and a romantic sense
for wild nature.   He expressed these thoughts in a poem (" On
a Plan for the Transplanting of the Arts and Sciences to
America ").   He conceived the plan of founding a college in
the islands of Bermuda, for the training of American mission-
aries.   When, after wearisome exertions, he had obtained the
promise that the State would lend its support to the undertaking, he established himself in Rhode Island to direct the
preparations for the erection of the college.   The promise was
not kept and after a three years' residence in America he was
obliged to return (1731).   He never got over the disappoint-
ment of this great hope.   From this time forth he saw life in
less rosy colours.   Memories of the beautiful natural surroundings which were all about him in Rhode Island are reproduced
in the rich scenery of the dialogue *Alciphron* (1732), in which
he once more took up his polemic against the free-thinkers,
while at the same time he sought to give a clear and popular
exposition of his philosophical ideas.   In this work he
expresses an idea *a propos* of the difficulties common to
natural and revealed religion, similar to that which his friend
Butler developed in detail a few years later in the *Analogy*.
He directed his polemic against two different types of free-
thinkers : against the Mandevilles as well as the Shaftesburys,
and he is triumphant when he can show how little they agree

with one another (for the representatives of Mandeville declare natural, unsupported by supernatural, religion to be incomplete). Berkeley's Dialogues retain their interest to the present day, both on account of the philosophical and theological problems which they discuss and also for the beauty of their style and the great success of the dialogue form in which they are written.

As Bishop of Cloyne in the south of Ireland (since 1734) Berkeley showed himself equally zealous as a shepherd of souls, a philanthropist, and a patriot. He was loved and esteemed not only by the Protestants but also by the Catholics, who composed nearly five-sixths of the population of his bishopric. He advocated the admission of Catholics to the University. In his *Querist* (1735-37) he started a great number of social and patriotic questions. His interests even included medicine. He believed, as he tried to explain in detail in his last work (*Siris*, 1744), that he had found in 'tar-water' a panacea for different illnesses. This work is also remarkable for the mystico-platonic direction which his thought here takes. The last works from his hand are treatises on petrifaction and earthquakes. Nothing in the world of reality was indifferent or strange to this subjectivist and idealist. He spent his last years in Oxford, where he died in 1753.

From the chief aim which Berkeley set before him in his philosophy, his place in the history of thought forms an analogy with that of Leibniz. Both sought to lead thought out beyond a strictly mechanical conception of Nature, without however denying it. They set about testing the concepts with which Descartes, Spinoza, Newton, and, to a great extent, Locke also had operated with as great confidence as though they were realities. They regarded the world-scheme constructed by physics and philosophy not as a reality but as a phenomenon. (While, however, Leibniz dissolved the mechanical plan of the world mainly by the objective method, reducing motion to force, and making force identical with the subjective impulse of the monads towards new states, Berkeley took the subjective path, and sought to show psychologically how our ideas of space and matter—on which the whole mathematico-physical knowledge of the world rests—arise. Berkeley carries on Locke's examination into the origin of ideas, and discusses the question

as to what we can really know beyond the reality given in
our perceptions and ideas.   He follows out his logical consequences with a remorselessness which, in spite of his love of
truth, he would perhaps hardly have displayed, had it not been
that his lively religious faith was ever ready to supplement
immediately what his philosophical criticism had cut away.
Through the rejection of absolute space and absolute matter
to which his philosophy led him, he felt nearer to his God—
indeed he felt himself in immediate contact with Him,   His
fervent and primitive religious feeling could not rest content
with the watchmaker-theology, with the external relations
between God and the world to which Locke, Newton, and
most of the theologians and free-thinkers of that time subscribed.   Yet it is not as a religious thinker but as a psychologist and critical philosopher that he is of importance.
We shall only follow him here up to the door which leads him
into theology.   He himself regarded his philosophy as a
crusade, having for its object the re-conquest of the promised
land.   But as with the crusaders so with him—as a matter of
fact he worked for other aims and performed other tasks than
those which he had set before himself.

(b) On Space and Abstract Ideas

In his *Theory of Vision,* one of the most brilliant psychological works which has ever been written, Berkeley investigates the psychological nature of the perception of space.
He shows that distance and magnitude are not immediately
apprehended from the beginning.   The perception of distance
and of magnitude arises through the combination of sensations
of sight with sensations which are produced by movement or
straining of the eyes.   Berkeley calls these sensations of touch,
but they are now called sensations of movement, to which are
added memories and associations (or, as Berkeley calls them,
"suggestions") of sensations of touch which we have formerly
received through immediate perception of the objects.   The
idea of contact excited by the sensation of sight blends with
the latter in such a way that, afterwards, we immediately "see"
the object at a certain distance and of a certain magnitude.
The practical significance of the sensation of sight consists in
this ;—it enables us to foretell sensations of touch which we

should receive if we were in close proximity to the object. The combination of these two kinds of sensation, however, depends on experience and practice. We " see " distance and magnitude just as we " see " shame or sorrow in the face of a man. The sense of sight and the sense of touch have nothing in common with one another ; it is only habit which binds them together in a common result. But there is no real simple sensation answering to this result, *i.e.* space. Space corresponds only to a frequent subjective association of ideas furnished by the two different senses. In and for itself it is an empty word.

We see how seriously Berkeley takes Locke's requirement to test the validity of ideas by means of an examination of their origin. Space no longer hovers before us as something incomprehensible, general, above all sense ; its origin is traced back to a process of association. This is all that we know of it. Berkeley himself, however, also conceived it as a divine language of signs which is communicated to us by way of association.

In his investigation of abstract ideas (in the Introduction to the *Principles of Knowledge*) he directs his polemic against Locke, as the last important representative of the old abstraction theory, which attributes to us a " faculty " of abstraction in the sense of a faculty of forming ideas which contain only the characteristics common to several objects. Of the ideas of a green, a red, and a yellow thing, *e.g.* we are said to be able to " abstract " the idea of colour in general. That such ideas exist in our consciousness Berkeley does not dispute. We can, of course, divide an idea, *i.e.* think of one part of an object without the other parts ; but we can form no new ideas having for their content that which is " common " to several qualities ; we have words to denote this common element, but we can have no idea of it. He does not hereby deny that we are able to form general ideas, standing for a whole group of phenomena ; we can do this because an idea which, in and for itself, is concrete and particular is used to represent or stand for all other concrete ideas of the same kind. We think in examples !

Berkeley has rendered a valuable contribution to psychology in this investigation. While we leave it to that science to show wherein he still fails to reach a complete theory of

general ideas, we will pass on to consider the philosophical
consequences which he deduces from his psychological investigations.

(c) *Epistemological Consequences*

While—says Berkeley in the *Principles*—it never occurs
to men to attribute existence to the objects of the inner
sense when they are not perceived, the objects of external
sense are supposed to exist whether they are perceived
or not.   But this is an unprovable and improbable assumption.   Objects of knowledge exist, from the nature of the
case, only in so far as they are known ; there *esse* is *percipi*.
A closer scrutiny of the foundation of this opinion will show
us the old abstraction theory again.   For is it not the
most powerful of all abstractions to think of the object without
all that makes it an object for us ?   We ought therefore to
abstract from all our sensations.   It is true, they say we
should only abstract from the secondary qualities (colour,
taste, smell, etc.) and not from the primary (extension, solidity).
By matter men understand a something which possesses the
primary qualities only, a something that has extension and
figure and can move.   But they forget that the primary
qualities cannot be perceived apart from the secondary, and
that the former as well as the latter only exist for us by
means of sensation.   If *e.g.* we mean to say that extension
can exist outside consciousness then we must ask : is it
extension as the sense of sight or as the sense of touch shows
it us ?   Perhaps as they show it us both together ; but we
have already seen that the idea of extension only arises by
means of an association.   There cannot be an extended and
moving something which is neither great nor small, neither
far nor near, which moves neither quickly nor slowly.   Even
if there were firm, figured, and moving substances outside
consciousness how could we learn this ?   How can we appeal
to the senses to testify to something which cannot be perceived through the senses at all ?

But does not this do away with the difference between the
real and the imagined ?   Berkeley denies this decidedly.   I do
not deny real nature, he says ; I only deny abstract matter.
Everything which is seen, heard, felt, or perceived through any
of the senses I take to be real, but not matter, this unknown

somewhat—if indeed it may be termed somewhat—without sensuous qualities and inaccessible to all perception and apprehension through the senses. The difference between reality and imagination rests on the difference between sense-perception and memory or fancy. The sense-impressions make a stronger impression on us, are clearer, and occur in a definite order which we are not able to interrupt. Moreover we are conscious that we have not produced them ourselves. On this it is that my conception of reality rests, says Berkeley ; let others see to it if they can find anything more in theirs. Nor is the validity of physics shaken by this downfall of the concept of matter. For physics seeks to explain phenomena through other phenomena,—through causes which are themselves perceivable through the senses, not through belief in any mystical substance. To explain phenomena is to show that under such and such circumstances we have such and such sensations. Physics exhibits the definitive and regular connection in which our sensations occur, so that one sensation can stand as a mark of another. This enables us to reason backwards and forwards. By means of a careful observation of the phenomena accessible to us we discover the general laws of Nature, or establish certain formulæ for the phenomena of motion. Physics has to do neither with force nor with matter, but only with phenomena. Every demonstration of a law for the connection of phenomena, and every conclusion from such a law, ultimately rests on the presupposition that the author of phenomena always works in a uniform manner and observes general rules—an assumption which, according to Berkeley (*Principles*, § 107 *in fine*), is certainly not susceptible of proof.

What is the origin, then, of phenomena or sensations, in so far as I do not myself produce them ? While Berkeley holds that the causal proposition is insusceptible of proof where it is a question of the reciprocal relation of phenomena, he does not in the least question its validity in discussing the origin of our passively received sensations. There must be an activity which is in operation when we ourselves are passive. Now our own capacity of summoning up and modifying ideas is the only example of activity we have. In this capacity Berkeley finds our real nature expressed. The soul is the will, he says (*Commonplace Book*, p. 428). All inner activity, including thinking, Berkeley calls " willing " : " That of which

I think, whatever it be, I call idea. Thought itself or thinking
is no idea. 'Tis an act, that is a volition, or, as contra-
distinguished to effect, the will" (*Commonplace Book*, p. 460).
Its essence is not to be perceived, but to perceive (its *esse*
is *percipere*). The will is the only form of activity we know.
Berkeley is not always consistent in what he says of the
knowledge that we have of our will, *i.e.* of the real essence of
our mind. Of so much only he is certain—that the knowledge of our own active nature cannot be an idea, since all
ideas are passive. It is not an "idea" but a "notion" that
we have of ourselves. In one passage (*Principles*, § 27), however, he teaches that we know mind, or that which works, by
means of its effects (*i.e.* modifications of ideas); in another
passage (*Dialogues between Hylas and Philonous*, Dialogue
III., Fraser's edition, i. p. 326 ff.) he attributes to us an immediate knowledge of our mind and its ideas, since we perceive
them "by reflection." But by whatever means we perceive
our mind, we can only form the thought of the source of
phenomena in analogy with it. We conceive God as analogous
to our own mind, only with its powers infinitely increased.
The only real ideas are those which God gives us, and now we
can understand, too, how it is that things can exist even when
we do not perceive them : they exist potentially—as possibilities—in God, who is their continual cause (cf. *Commonplace
Book*, p. 489). The divine will reveals itself in the order and
connection of our sensations, but the divine Providence in the
purposiveness which Nature exhibits. If Nature differs in its
essence from God, it is a heathenish chimæra. According to
the ordinary conception, God first creates matter and then lets
it work on us. But why go this long way round? Why
should not God produce our sensations immediately? The
more we think clearly, the more we shall find ourselves in
direct relation with God. There are no secondary causes. In
God we live and move and have our being, says Berkeley,
and he believes he has a better right than Spinoza to say this.
Berkeley abandoned himself to this mystico-pantheistical conception more and more in the last years of his life, as may be
seen from *Siris ;* but we cannot here follow the shapes which
his thoughts in this direction subsequently assumed. We
can only draw attention to one point of similarity between
Berkeley and Leibniz in the transition from their empirical

to their speculative philosophy ; both make use of the principle of analogy, which is the principle of all metaphysical idealism. ⟩

It is Berkeley's especial merit that he persisted, with an energy unweakened by the paradoxical results to which his thinking led him, in asking : how do we know that things are anything more than our perceptions and ideas? By what right do we spring from consciousness, from the only thing which is immediately given, to things which are never given immediately? In Berkeley's own answer to this question, as may be seen from our account of it, he in no way reduces reality to a mere series of sensations. In the first place, he distinguishes between sensations and the mind : the essence of the former only consists in being perceived (*esse = percipi*) ; the essence of the latter consists in perceiving (*esse = percipere*), *i.e.* in working. In the second place, he acknowledges the principle of causation, and uses it to solve the problem under consideration. (But while the ordinary conception (popular metaphysics) starts by supposing that the cause of our sensations must resemble them, Berkeley proceeds from the assumption that the cause of our passive states must be thought of as analogous with the active principle within us. He is an idealist, but not a subjective idealist.⟩ His idealism, however, at once assumes a theological form. While he philosophises, his theological ideas lie in wait, and as soon as the plot thickens and a debatable question presents itself, they press forward to fill out what is lacking. On this account his thought stops short too soon. The theological ideas themselves are not criticised. His whole conception of the world becomes anthropomorphic. The uniformity of Nature is nothing but a uniformity of the divine will which holds phenomena together, and phenomena are only a collection of arbitrary signs. The principle of causality, too, is not examined more closely, and yet his whole solution of the problem rests upon it. To the latter point Berkeley's immediate successor laid his hand, continuing his work while he opposed it, just as Berkeley himself had done with regard to Locke's. ⟩

CHAPTER V

DAVID HUME

(a) Biography and Characteristics

THE great significance of English philosophy in the history of the development of human thought is that, in virtue of its empirical method, it calls to account not only the finished thought-constructions of speculative philosophers, but also the unconscious and untested assumptions on which the popular conception of the world and the special sciences rest. Thus Locke had demanded an exact explanation of the origin of our ideas in general, and Berkeley had pointed out how great a problem is contained in the ideas of space and of the material world if we attempt to supply this explanation. (This critical examination of knowledge reached its culminating point in the English school of the eighteenth century in the philosophy of David Hume.) He instituted an examination into the two concepts which formed the foundation of all earlier philosophy, and which neither Locke nor Berkeley had seriously attacked : *i.e.* the concepts of substance and cause, the two concepts which were the binding cement of all speculative, scientific, and popular thought-constructions.) On the principles of causality or of sufficient ground rested Leibniz' great system of harmony, Newton's world-mechanism, and the popular conception of a world of things subject to certain laws. All take the reasonableness, the rationality, of existence for granted ; all assume, more or less consciously, that existence contains within it something corresponding to our reason. It is this presupposition that Hume investigates. And he is the first to seriously undertake such an examination, and to descend to the depths out of which spring the forces which hold together the inner and outer world of our knowledge; depths far removed from the regions in which speculative philosophy, specific inquiry, and common sense move.   Hume himself felt, and characteristically expressed, the curious condition of loneliness and disintegration in which the thinker finds himself who perseveringly follows the problem of knowledge into these depths, and also the opposition which exists between the strictly theoretical and the instinctive, practical, and popular, conception of the world.   Only his ever-wakeful intellectual passion, together with his hope of winning renown if he followed the path consistently to the end, made it possible for him, according to his own confession (in the concluding section of the first book of his *magnum opus*), to complete his work.

In Hume's character intellectual ardour and ambition were united with good nature, benevolence, and forbearance towards weaknesses and prejudices, coupled with a certain easiness of disposition which refused to be disturbed by polemical discussions in the cause of literary interests.   He was born on 26th April 1711, as the second son of a landed proprietor, on the estate of Ninewells in the south of Scotland.   In his *Autobiography* he says: " I was seized very early with a passion for literature, which has been the ruling passion of my life and the great source of my enjoyments." ˉ His family wished to make a lawyer of him, but he felt " an insurmountable dislike towards everything except philosophy and learning." His ideal was an existence free from care, in which he would be able to satisfy his taste for critical investigation and to cultivate the acquaintance of a few chosen friends ; at the same time he was anxious that his literary activity should bring honour to his name.   While still quite a youth he believed himself to be on the track of new thoughts : a new " universe of thought " disclosed itself to him.   An attack of hypochondria (described by himself in a letter which is given in Burton's *Life and Correspondence of David Hume*, Edinburgh, 1846, vol. i. p. 30 ff.) interrupted his meditations for some time.   He was probably already feeling the curious contrast between the world of reflection and that of practical daily life, which he afterwards described in his great work.   He now resolved to abandon his studies and to become a merchant. Practical life, however, could not detain him.   He chose lonely

places in France in which to live while he wrote his great
work, *Treatise of Human Nature, being an attempt to introduce
the experimental method of reasoning into moral subjects.* It
appeared 1739-40 in London, and is in three parts, of which
the first treats of the understanding, the second of the passions,
and the third of the foundation of morality. It carried the
investigation of these different questions an important stage
further, and still stands in the first rank of philosophical classics.
At first, however, it was destined to have no result. " It fell,"
he says, " dead-born from the press without reaching such
distinction as even to excite a murmur among the zealots."
Hume's literary ambition, which led him to pronounce this
brilliant testimony to his mental abilities as " dead-born," had
fatal effects. He tried to win the fame which this had failed
to bring him by a series of essays, some on philosophy, others
on political economy and politics : he abandoned philosophy
altogether for some time and devoted himself to history ;
he even finally altogether denied the great work of his youth,
explaining—to avoid aspersions from his theological critics
(who, it seems, had after all begun to "murmur")—that he only
acknowledged the statement of his philosophical doctrines
given in the *Essays.* Excellent as many of these smaller
writings are, yet they could never attain to the place of importance in philosophical discussion which his chief work
might have occupied, if only he had used the literary fame
which was afterwards his to breathe life into the " dead-born "
child, instead of disavowing it, in order to avoid any disturbances it might cause him. As regards the problem of
knowledge in particular, Hume's philosophy, even in the
abbreviated and modified exposition given in the *Inquiry
concerning Human Understanding* (1749), was not without
influence on the later developments of thought, though the full
statement of it contained in the *Treatise,* which, strictly speaking, sunders the bond between our thoughts, indeed between
the elements of our nature in general, lay forgotten for many a
day. That the motive to Hume's disavowal of his early work
is the one here given may be seen from the recently published
Letters of David Hume to William Strahan (Oxford, 1888, p.
289 ff.). It is quite a mistake to suppose, as has sometimes
been suggested, that Hume had really changed his views on
the main points. It is, however, psychologically compre-

hensible that the highly strained intellectual condition in which he wrote his early work could not persist. After he had thought with—and indeed better than—the learned, he felt the need of talking with the unlearned. Having given a popular exposition of his philosophical and economic ideas in the *Essays*, he turned to history. " You know," he wrote to a friend, " there is no post of honour in the English Parnassus more vacant than that of history." The post of Keeper to the Advocates' Library, Edinburgh, which he obtained after violent opposition from the orthodox party, afforded him ample opportunities for research. His *History of England* gained him still more popularity than his *Essays* had done. As an historian he has the merit of having been the first to attempt to make history something more than a chronicle of wars, by taking account also of social relations, morals, literature, and art. The publication of his historical works began two years before the appearance of Voltaire's famous *Essai sur les mœurs.* While in his philosophical opinions he was a Liberal, his judgment of historical personages is biassed by Royalist and Tory views. Philosophy, however, was not altogether neglected at this time. He occupied himself, more particularly in his later years, with philosophico - religious studies. The results of these are embodied in the *Natural History of Religion* (1757) and his *Dialogues on Natural Religion*, which last work he withheld, from prudential reasons, so that it did not appear until a few years after his death.

Hume was not only a philosopher and an historian. He felt the necessity of taking part in practical life. As Secretary to the Embassy (1748) he travelled in Holland, Germany, Austria, and Italy. He afterwards exchanged his post of librarian at Edinburgh for that of secretary to Lord Hertford, who was sent as the English Ambassador to France after the Peace of Paris in 1763. By that time Hume had become famous, and he met with a brilliant reception at Court as well as in literary circles. He became the fashion, like Franklin afterwards, perhaps precisely because of his simple and unpretending exterior. After having spent three years in France he returned to England, taking with him Jean Jacques Rousseau, who had been exiled from Switzerland as well as from France, in order that he might procure him an asylum of refuge. Rousseau,

however, requited Hume's generous behaviour towards him
with the maddest suspicions, and after a scandalous rupture
between the two, Rousseau returned to France, where the storm
had now laid itself. After Hume had occupied the post of
Under-Secretary of State for Scotland for a year he resigned his
seat in Edinburgh and led a life of learned leisure in the
company of a few chosen friends, until, after a lingering illness,
which, however, did not deprive him of his cheerfulness and
peace of mind, he died on 25th August 1776.

(b) *Epistemological Radicalism*

All sciences—and the mental sciences not the least—stand
in a definite relation to human nature. From this proposition
Hume starts his examination of the understanding, and it
follows from it that the foundation of all human knowledge is
to be discovered by a study of human nature. But this study
must be carried out by means of the empirical method, which
had already been employed with success in the sphere of
physics, and the application of which to the study of human
nature had been introduced by Bacon, Locke, and Shaftesbury.
Appealing to experience to bear him out, Hume establishes as
his fundamental principle the proposition that all our ideas
are derived from impressions; ideas can never be *a priori.* When
we test the validity of an idea, therefore, the first thing we must
ask is: of what impression is it the after-effect? Hume finds
in the origin of impressions a problem insoluble by our understanding—a problem, however, the solution of which is not
necessary for the carrying out of his task (cf. *Treatise*, i. 3, 5 ;
in other passages, as ii. 1, 1, he expresses himself in the
ordinary manner). By means of this fundamental proposition
(which Berkeley had only applied to the ideas of space and of
matter) Hume now tests a series of important ideas. The idea
of a substance or of an essence must be declared invalid since
we have no impression corresponding to it. We immediately
perceive only particular qualities bound together more or less
firmly, but no "substance." The mathematical ideas of time and
space are formed by means of idealisation. Experience shows
us only an imperfect equality of time- and space-magnitudes ;
every measure we possess is imperfect. After experience has
afforded us opportunity, however, of comparing different grades

of similarity and different measures, we form the idea of perfect equality and of a perfect measure (*e.g.* of a perfectly straight line), while, once the power of imagination has been set going, it continues its course, even though experience lag behind. Since geometry is concerned with such ideal objects, its application to real objects can never be perfectly exact. Nor does the concept of existence—any more than that of substance and the mathematical concepts—correspond to any impression : to think of a thing and to think of it as existing is one and the same. Our idea of an object is still only an idea when we also think of the object as existing, and by thus thinking of it we endow the thing with no new quality.

In his examination of the validity of our knowledge in general, Hume distinguishes between the knowledge which consists only in the explication of the mutual relations of our ideas (the formal sciences, logic and mathematics) and the knowledge which leads us beyond the given impressions and convinces us of the existence of a something which is not given. This last kind of knowledge rests on the assumption of the validity of the causal relation, and Hume's great philosophical exploit consists in his establishment, in the most unmistakable manner, of the *problem* of causality—the problem on the solution of which every estimation of the significance of the exact sciences rests. At the root of all investigation lies the desire to discover what it is which holds the innermost parts of the world together, under every problem of the exact sciences lies the same fundamental problem, and Hume was the first to see this in its full extent. It must be remembered, however, that Hume never doubted that we must continue to make constant use of the causal proposition both in theory and in practice ; he only asks whether it can be *established*, and to this question he finds a negative answer only. He discovers that we are moved to assume the causal relation by the same thing that induces us to assume a something as existing, even though it is not given in experience. One and the same investigation—according to Hume's psychological method—throws light on the concepts both of cause and of belief.

We cannot appeal to immediate certainty or intuition to establish the validity of the causal relation, for we only have such intuition with regard to simple relations of similarity or of magnitude. Nor can we appeal to logical demonstration, for

we can hold all our ideas apart from one another.   The motion
of one billiard ball is an event which is altogether different from
the motion of another billiard ball.   There is no object which
we cannot easily think of one moment as existing and the next
as not existing.   Thus there is no self-contradiction in saying
that something begins without a cause.   The proofs which
former philosophers (Hobbes, Locke, Clarke—to whom Wolff
might also be added) have adduced are only apparent proofs.
For it is clear that if the principle of causality is founded in
the reason (either in intuition or demonstration), we shall come
into conflict with the "fundamental principle"; for then reason
would possess the faculty of producing entirely new ideas,
not derived from experience!   But is not the validity of the
causal relation founded in experience?   The answer to this is
that experience only shows us that one event follows another,
but does not exhibit to us the inner necessity of their union,
which is what is meant by "causal relation."   This holds good
whether we understand by experience inner or outer experience.
Hume is here especially refuting the opinion (held by Berkeley)
that, in the immediate consciousness of our will, we have a
conception of force or activity.   One particular experience is
not able to give us the idea of causality, and several experiences
together only give us a relation of succession.   After we have
very frequently seen one phenomenon follow another, we involuntarily expect the former the next time the latter occurs;
but this is custom and does not justify us in concluding from
the past to the future.

In his explanation of our tendency to pass beyond a given
impression and to believe in or expect something which is not
given, Hume emphasises firstly the experience that every strongly
excited state, or every strongly excited disposition or feeling in
consciousness, has a tendency to persist and to extend itself over
new ideas as they arise.   If consciousness has been heightened
or excited by any object, then every event in consciousness is more
lively than usual so long as the excitement lasts.   This is the
law which explains the idealisation of the mathematical ideas.
Secondly, he lays weight upon the fact that experience shows
us a tendency on the part of our ideas to mutually elicit each
other.   Every idea has an associative tendency; "a gentle force"
leads from the one to the other.   As different conditions of
such association Hume names similarity, temporal and spatial

coexistence, and causality.   An attraction within the inner
world here makes itself felt, which is no less important for
the inner world than physical attraction is for the outer.   Nor
is its nature less mysterious; its causes must lie in properties of
human nature unknown to us.(The bond which unites our
ideas is just as incomprehensible as that which unites external
objects ; and we can only know it from experience.   Indeed
Hume finds this associative connection not only incomprehensible
but even self-contradictory (in the Appendix to book i. of the
Treatise) : how can there be a *uniting principle* (*Tr.* i. 3, 4) or
principle of connection (*Tr.* i. App.) if all our impressions and
ideas are separate, independent existences?   Hume declares
this to be a difficulty too hard for his understanding.)

Both facts (which may be called expansion and association)
however are indubitable.   And by their help it is explained
how a lively impression which appears to us, precisely on
account of its liveliness, as the expression of a reality, is able
to impart its liveliness, and with this its stamp of reality, to
those ideas which it calls up by means of association.   What
we call belief is nothing more than the character of liveliness
which ideas are thus enabled to assume. : Belief is due to no
new and special impression, it only denotes the special manner in
which an idea appears to feeling or sentiment.   We cannot help
passing over to the idea associated with the lively impression,
and we cannot help holding to this idea and perceiving it in a
stronger light than usual ; and thirdly, since consciousness (as
evidenced in the ideas of the sense-qualities, of space and time
and of substance) has an inclination to take its own inner states
for external, objective phenomena, we can now understand how
we come to believe in a causal relation between things in the
world, although the necessity in question here only exists in us,
and is a need which is expressed by our inclination, owing to
psychological reasons, to pass over from one impression or
idea to another. ﹙Necessity is subjective, just as are the sense-
qualities, space and time. ﹚What we call reason [87] is only an
obscure instinct within us which arises because experiences are
repeated in definite order of sequence.   The origin of this
instinct, or the influence of custom, is just as incomprehensible
to us as is the fact of any connection at all between the
elements of our consciousness.   But since the mental activity
by means of which we conclude from the same causes to the

same effects is of the utmost practical importance, Nature
would not entrust it to the uncertain reason, but made it spring
from the certain, even though obscure, instinct which no critical
examination can move : " Nature is too strong for principle ! "

{ While dogmatic philosophy in its different forms believed
that, by the help of pure reason, it could construct thought-
sequences reaching far beyond sense, according to Hume's
investigation the imagination is the only faculty which can
lead us to believe in something which is not the object of
present perception.   On this rests also the belief in an outer
world, independent of consciousness.   We do not experience
the uninterrupted existence of objects, but only a certain
constancy and coherence.   This is enough for our imagination,
however, which continues its activity in the direction in which
it has once been started, and imagines as great uniformity and
as great coherence as it possibly can.   We fill out the intervals
between our impressions by the fiction of constantly existing
beings.}   The idea of the " I " or of the self may be explained
by exactly the same principle.   The invalidity of the substance-
concept has already been pointed out.   Our impressions and
ideas, says Hume, can exist very well without " inhering in " or
being supported by such a substance.   If any one wishes to
establish his belief in a soul-substance he must find an impression
on which this belief rests ; but this he cannot do, for all our
impressions change.   If we take the word substance in a vague
sense, *i. e.* in the sense of " something which may exist by
itself," why then should not our impressions and ideas, which
may each have separate existence, be substances ?   Hume
especially warns theologising metaphysicians against the belief
in a soul-substance, in which individual impressions and ideas
are said to exist as particular modifications, for by so doing
they give a dangerous support to Spinozism ; for just in this
way did Spinoza conceive the relation between God and the
things of the world !   But even if we abandon the idea of a
soul-substance and only ask how we come by the idea of the
" I " as the expression of our personal identity, we are involved
in many difficulties.   No impression or idea is invariable and
constant.   We always find a particular inner state, never " ourselves" as a totality.   The identity which we attribute to ourselves
is of the same nature as that which we attribute to external
objects : it is only a result of the ease with which we pass

over from one impression or idea to another, an ease which causes us to overlook the riddle contained in the fact that any element can pass over into another which is different from itself

Hume is a master in the art of raising problems. He is able, as are few others, to think out a concept or a relation so that its hidden difficulties are brought to light. By means of the energy of his thought he succeeded in bringing into prominence the fundamental concept, which underlies all the practical thought of man, all his exact science, all his speculation, and all his religion. He showed that there are problems enough for philosophy, even though the age of great systems be past. But to get a correct idea of Hume's significance we must study him in the *Treatise*. In the *Essays* [88] his investigation is limited to the causal concept, and we get no idea of the thorough-going manner in which he followed out the " uniting principle " in all its forms (in mathematical knowledge, in the concept of the " I ") nor of the method which he employed—especially of his sustained application of the law of expansion — from the abbreviated and modified sketch. Though he demonstrated the incomprehensibility of the uniting principle, yet he recognises its activity, firstly by assuming that we have ideas not only of particular things, but also of their relations (*e.g.* time and space, similarity and difference), secondly by accepting as fact the association of ideas, and thirdly by the stress which he lays on the tendency of the imagination to extend and widen itself, which tendency is one with the tendency of consciousness to preserve, in spite of all differences, its identity with itself. But all this, certainly, is strangely opposed to the absolute " substantial" distinction between particular sensations and ideas, which is the presupposition from which Hume starts—a presupposition which marks the limits of his thought. There would be more justification for saying that the *distinction* between the elements of our thought is incomprehensible ; for to comprehend is to unite, to find coherence !

(c) Ethics

The second part of Hume's *Treatise* treats of the feelings. It is of greater importance for the history of psychology ; we may notice it here, however, as forming the introduction to the

Ethics, which forms the third part of the work, and which Hume afterwards published in an abbreviated form as *Inquiry concerning the Principles of Morals* (1751). In his conception of the psychological nature of feeling Spinoza is his predecessor, and Hume was probably not uninfluenced by him, though his exposition is richer and more detailed than that of Spinoza. Both rest their views on the importance which ideas and their reciprocal associations have for the development of the feelings. Hume shows how one feeling unites with another by means of association between the ideas of their objects. On the question as to whether association takes place directly between feelings, he expresses himself uncertainly, generally attributing to feelings, as also to ideas, the tendency to reproduce other feelings (ii. 1, 4 ; cf. "Dissertation on the Passions" in the *Essays*), although in other passages (ii. 2, 8) he teaches that no association between feelings can take place if the ideas are not associated. This vacillation is probably due to the knowledge that feeling never remains entirely passive throughout these proceedings. Hume clearly perceived this, as may be seen in his doctrine of expansion, which is of so much importance for his theory of knowledge. As a psychologist he also exercised great influence by his emphatic assertion that only feeling—not pure reason—can produce actions of the will. He draws attention to the fact that impressions and ideas are easier to verify than impulses and inclinations, when these are not distinguished by their violence. Hence we are apt to overlook the first germ of the will. And just as will arises out of feeling only, and not out of the reason, so also it is feeling only which can check feeling and prevent action (ii. 3, 3). Here, too, he agrees with Spinoza on a psychological principle which is frequently overlooked in spite of its wide range. Feeling is an original and immediate state, but reason expresses itself through reflection and comparison, and thus can exert influence on feeling only so far as it is able to examine the ideas bound up with the feeling. It is an imperfection in Hume's psychology that he does not bring out the connection between feeling and the original instincts.[89] Shaftesbury had more insight here. Hume is inclined to regard instincts as secondary only (*e.g.* in his theory of knowledge he explains the causal instinct through custom). His empiricism limits his conception here. A kindred trait shows itself in his historical writings, to which it has been objected that they leave out of consideration the racial peculiarities of the nations which they describe.

The psychological examination of the relation of feeling to reason is of direct importance for Hume's ethics, since it contains the answer to the question whether morality rests on reason or on feeling. Reason ascertains relations or matters of fact only. But a moral judgment does not arise until a feeling is excited through the idea of an action, after all the relations and facts depending on this action have been brought out. It is only because our feeling has been set in motion that we call anything good or evil. The moral qualities (good or evil), therefore, are valid only from the standpoint of feeling beings, just as the sense-qualities only possess validity from the standpoint of sensuously perceiving beings.[90] This does not, however, deprive these qualities of their significance : we apply moral judgments in practice with the same certainty as sensuous qualities, although neither the one nor the other express objective and eternal relations. (See especially, besides *Treatise* iii. I, I, the essay on " The Sceptic.") Hume (who is in agreement with Spinoza on this point also) stands here in sharp contrast to those moral philosophers who would deduce morality from reason only, and who regard ethical principles as eternal truths—a standpoint which, even after Locke's time, was maintained by Clarke and Price (as Cudworth had maintained it against Hobbes).

The next question is : from what feeling does morality arise ? All actions and qualities which are objects of moral approbation have this common feature—that, directly or indirectly, they tend to the profit and advantage either of the agent himself or of others. This characteristic, independently of all education and authority, commands our approbation, our esteem—even perhaps our admiration. And since we approve actions by which we ourselves are not benefited, the feeling which lies at the root of this approbation cannot be egoistic in its nature. He who pronounces moral judgments abandons his private standpoint and adopts one which is common to himself and others. If we were guided in our judgments by self-interest alone, we could never arrive at any common estimation of worth. Even if the recognition of justice as a virtue were due, from the beginning, to the need of each individual to enjoy peace and security, yet interest in the general regulation of rights can only be explained through sympathy for that which supports

human life in general. The "first virtuous motive which
bestows a merit on any action" need not be the same as that
which afterwards underlies our judgment. It is sympathy
then, or "fellow-feeling," which is the real ground of morality.
Even the regard for those virtues (*e.g.* prudence in the conduct
of one's own affairs) which are only advantageous to the agent
are best explained through sympathy. Sympathy itself Hume
explains in accordance with the "fundamental principle" of
his theory of knowledge : it is due to the fact that when we see
or have a lively idea of the expressions or the causes of other
men's joy or pain, there arises in us also a lively feeling of joy
or pain ; also because a mere idea tends, on account of its connection with a lively impression, to pass over into *impression.*

Hume's ethic bears the stamp of a clear head and a warm
heart. But we must not look to him for explanation of deep-
lying ethical crises and oppositions. He does not even follow up
Hutcheson's interesting attempt to deduce the feeling of duty
from sympathy. The inner and outer opposition which the
ethical character may have to encounter in the course of its
development does not engage him. He is, however, completely
and clearly convinced that morality has human nature as its
foundation, and he indicates the distinction, so important in its
consequences, between the first motive for the development of
a quality of character or of an institution and the motive from
which the subsequent estimation of worth arises. If he has
frequently been called a sceptic, this appellation is certainly
not appropriate to him as a moralist. He devotes a special
investigation ("A Dialogue" in the *Essays*) to the discussion
of the objections based on the mutual contradiction existing
between the moral ideas, manners, and customs of different
peoples and times ; we might just as well, he says, find a
difficulty in the fact that the Rhine flows northwards and the
Rhone southwards ! Both rivers run according to the same
law—the law of gravity—in opposite directions, because of the
different slope of the ground. The fact that, under different
circumstances, men arrive at different results, is no reason for
supposing they could not have started from the same principle.
Everything which men have called good or evil has been something which has been regarded as either directly or indirectly
profitable or injurious. Differences, then, do not shake the
principle.

As a political economist Hume is Adam Smith's most important predecessor. In his economic writings he gives prominence to the importance of arousing the acquisitive instinct. Force never turned any man into a skilled labourer. New wants must arise before the desire for progress can arise. If no other wants developed themselves beyond those which could be satisfied by the poorest possible revenue from the soil, the latter would never be cultivated in the best possible manner. Agriculture only flourishes in reciprocity with trade and industry, and it is in this way that the middle class, which offers the surest and best support to public freedom, grows up. Hume did not examine any more closely than did his friend and successor, Adam Smith, the problem of the relation of the acquisitive instinct to sympathy. They both appear to have assumed that the results of the two motives are harmonious.

(d) Philosophy of Religion

Hume's chief contribution to the religious problem consists in his clear distinction between the question as to the possibility of founding religion by way of the reason and that of the actual origin of religion in human nature—a distinction to which we find analogies both in his theory of knowledge and in his ethics. The former question is discussed in his *Dialogues on Natural Religion*, the latter in the *Natural History of Religion*. As regards the latter, the historical question, Hume attempts to show that it is no necessity of the understanding which induces the belief in a divine Being. On the contrary, precisely that which to the thinker is a great stone of stumbling, *i.e.* the mischief and disorder found in Nature, is to the plain man a motive for belief. That belief is called out by feelings which arise in the course of life ; by hope and fear, suspense and uncertainty, and fear of the unintelligible. Together with these works the general propensity to conceive all other beings as resembling men. History seems to show that polytheism is the original religion. And this agrees with the natural course of development. Consciousness rises gradually from lower to higher grades, and since, in the violent agitation caused partly by fear, partly by enthusiasm, it enhances the object of the imagination and conceives it as more and more perfect and noble, it arrives at last at the idea of one only infinite and

incomprehensible God. ` The same process of idealisation goes
on here, within the sphere of religious feeling, as underlies the
construction of mathematical principles and the principle of
causality.   The transition from polytheism to monotheism
cannot be explained out of purely intellectual motives ; by the
way of feeling, however, men have arrived at the same result
as would have been reached by rational consideration : there
can only be *one* God.   After this exalted standpoint has been
reached, history shows that a reaction is apt to take place.
The necessity for mediating beings between this one, infinite,
purely spiritual God and the world makes itself felt.   Between
these two opposite poles—the conception of God as exalted
and imperceptible by the senses, and as limited and perceptible
—there is a constant vacillation.   On a close investigation
Hume finds the essence of religion to contain contradictory
tendencies and qualities.   Loftiness and vulgarity, belief and
doubt, purity and immorality, grandeur and horror, are curiously
mingled together.   There is so much that is unintelligible in
religion, and so much dissension between the different religions,
that Hume prefers to withdraw into the quiet, even though
obscure, regions of philosophy.   In the essay *On Miracles* Hume
discusses more particularly the question of the supernatural.
His chief thought here is that "no testimony is sufficient to
establish a miracle unless the testimony be of such a kind that
its falsehood would be more miraculous than the fact which it
endeavours to establish."   He maintains, however, that there is
no miracle which has been established by testimony of such
a nature.

As regards the question of the truth of religion, it is
difficult to discover what Hume's standpoint really is, since he
has thrown his examination of this question into the form of a
dialogue.   He takes up three different standpoints.   Demea
is the representative of a mystical orthodoxy, which relies partly
on *a priori* grounds of reason, partly on the postulate of feeling.
Cleanthes represents a rationalistic deism, which finds its chief
support in the purposiveness of Nature.   Philo is sometimes a
sceptic, sometimes a naturalist.   There can be no doubt that
Demea did not represent Hume's own standpoint.   It is
Cleanthes, according to his own confession, who is made the
hero of the dialogue ; but it is evident, and has indeed been
acknowledged by Hume himself (Burton, vol. i. p. 332 ; *Letters*

to Strahan, p. 330), that Philo's views interested him the most, although he is finally obliged to abandon his position. Philo's standpoint is unquestionably nearest to Hume's own. The chief thoughts which Philo brings forward are as follows : Who could blame us if, with respect to such great and difficult questions, we declared that we knew nothing ? For they carry us far beyond experience, and system is ranged against system ! Philo brings a series of objections against Cleanthes' argument from the order and purposiveness of Nature to the existence of God. (1) Why seek the cause of order and purposiveness outside the world ? There may be forces within the world itself by means of which, perhaps after many transformations and temporary accommodations, order and harmony are brought about. And as proficiency in the arts developed itself by means of frequent attempts and endeavours, so perhaps different world-systems may have succeeded each other until the present system, which offered the most favourable conditions for permanent existence, arose. (2) Experience shows us mind and thought as finite, limited phenomena. With what right do we explain the world as a whole by a part of itself? Thought itself, like all else in the world, requires explanation, and if we erect it into a final cause are we not in reality led to do so in order to satisfy our inclination to find our own nature behind things, just as we are inclined to find our own figures in the clouds? (3) Can there be a special problem concerning the world as a whole? When we have explained the origin of individual parts or phenomena the origin of all these parts collectively is not a special problem. That we conceive the same as a collective totality is only the result of an arbitrary act of consciousness. (4) From the world, as experience shows it us, with all its imperfection, its pain, and its need, we can certainly not conclude to a *perfect* cause. In one of his essays (*Of a Particular Providence and of a Future State*) Hume presents the following dilemma : if there is justice in this world there is no reason for us to seek another, and if there is no justice in this world we cannot suppose that it was created by God. Philo does not mean by this to deny the existence of God. He only protests against conceiving God in all too close analogy with man. He declares that in the long-run the difference between theists and atheists, dogmatists and sceptics, is only a difference of name ; for the theist admits that the divine mind differs widely from the human ; the atheist, that the ruling principle in the world has, after all, a certain analogy with the human mind ; the dogmatist confesses that his view involves great difficulties ; and the sceptic that, in spite of difficulties, we cannot remain in a state of pure doubt. The moral is that no preconceived opinions can blunt the natural love to our fellows and the sentiment of justice.

Hume's treatment of the religious problem indicates a great advance. His dialogues stand, as a lasting monument, beside Kant's criticism of theology in his " Critique of Pure Reason." To this day no real refutation of these works has appeared. Adequate treatment of the psychological side of religion demands greater depth and inwardness, however, than are to be expected from Hume's sober temperament, nor was the material at his command sufficient for the historical under-standing of religion. Nevertheless, in both these departments, he contributed thoughts which have been carried further by subsequent investigation. His sound empirical method lends lasting worth to his inquiries. He is the most important fore-runner of modern Positivism.

CHAPTER VI

THE development of philosophical thought in England during the eighteenth century touched its highest point in Hume. The conclusions from the positions taken up by Bacon and Hobbes and, more particularly, by Locke, had been pushed to their utmost; the line of thought entered upon had been carried up to its goal by means of the continuous activity of a succession of eminent thinkers. Only from quite new points of view which, however, lay beyond the horizon of the English school, and must and did come to it from quite another side, could the development be carried further. This, however, is not incompatible with the appearance—after Hume's time and before philosophical thought in England had entered upon that long pause which lasted until our own century—of a number of important works, partly completing and continuing, partly opposing and reacting against, Hume's teaching.

(a) Adam Smith

Hume's work in the field of ethics and of political economy was continued independently by his friend Adam Smith, born at Kirkcaldy, in Scotland, in 1723. He studied originally at Glasgow, where he heard and admired Hutcheson; afterwards he went to Oxford. To judge from the way in which he subsequently spoke of the English Universities in his famous work on Political Economy, life at Oxford was not congenial to him. Lord Brougham relates (*Lives of Philosophers of the Time of George III.*, p. 179) the story of Smith's personal experience of how narrow-minded university authorities could be. His copy of Hume's *Treatise*, which he was studying at the time, was confiscated, and he received a reprimand for reading such a book !—a characteristic trait of the way in which Hume and his works were regarded in the chief seat of English learning, where Hobbes and Locke had met with similar treatment before him. For many years (from 1751) Smith laboured as a professor in Glasgow. His course of moral philosophy consisted of four parts—natural theology, ethics, natural right (following Montesquieu's historical method), and political economy. Only the second and fourth parts appeared as independent works. Concerning his natural theology we know only as much as may be gathered from his papers. With regard to religion he was more conservative than Hume; his relation to him may perhaps be compared with that of Cleanthes to Philo (in Hume's Dialogue). In his lectures on natural right, according to the account of one of his hearers (quoted by Dugald Stewart: *Account of the Life and Writings of Dr. Smith*, p. xii.) he was chiefly concerned in tracing the successive development of public and private right under the influence of economic and industrial progress.[91] His works on ethics and political economy likewise show how eagerly he studied actual historical circumstances in order to illuminate questions of principle, and BUCKLE takes a too one-sided view when he says—in his otherwise instructive characterisation of Adam Smith in his *History of English Civilisation* —that his method was purely deductive. We have interesting writings of his on the origin of speech and the history of astronomy, which also witness to his historic sense. Some years after the publication of his *Theory of Moral Sentiments* (1759) he withdrew from his labours at the University and spent several years in France, where his acquaintance with Quesnay, Turgot, and Necker was not without significance for his study of political economy. After his return to England he lived for ten years in his birthplace, Kirkcaldy. Here he wrote the work which was to bring him his greatest renown, since the dawn of scientific economics is generally dated from its appearance: *Inquiry into the Nature and Causes of the Wealth of Nations* (1776). During the last years of his life Smith held a post in the Customs at Edinburgh, where he died in 1790.

The two works on which Adam Smith's fame as a thinker rests are curiously opposed to one another, for, while he bases his political economy on the acquisitive instinct, he takes sympathy as his foundation in his ethics.)

Buckle is of opinion that Smith posited two tendencies of human nature, each in its abstract form, in order to be able to proceed along a clear and deductive line of argument. Against this, however, is the fact that the opposition between the two works, although characteristic, is not absolute ; moreover Smith's method is not purely deductive. How Smith himself conceived the relation between his two works remains an unanswered question ; he entered upon no psychological and historical investigation of these two tendencies of human nature. Injustice has often been done him by neglect of the fact that he is the author not only of the work on the Wealth of Nations but also of that on the Moral Sentiments.

As a moralist Smith asserts with great emphasis that the ethical feeling only arises when men live in the society of other men. A natural instinct to imitate the gestures and behaviour of others, to put oneself in their place, to feel and to suffer with them then makes itself felt. This is an involuntary inclination which not even the most egoistical of men can altogether suppress. This instinctive sympathy acquires its more definite character through the ideas which arise of the causes and effects of other men's feelings and actions. We approve the feelings of another when we are conscious that, under similar circumstances, we should have feelings of the same kind and strength. The feeling must stand in a certain proportion to the cause which evoked it if we are to be able to sympathise with it. But if the feeling of another becomes the motive for actions which affect a third person, we put ourselves in the place of this third person also, and we can then only sympathise with an action if its effect stands in fit proportion to the original cause of the motive. In benevolence and philanthropy we sympathise with the giver as well as with the recipient. In gratitude and revenge sympathy for the agent ceases if the effect is disproportionate to the original cause. In opposition to Hume, Smith maintains that regard to the utility of the qualities of character of which we approve is not the original ground of our approbation. It is a moment which supervenes later in support of it, but it is an " after-thought "—a thought which succeeds the involuntary judgment which arises when we put ourselves in the place of the agent and in that of those affected by him.

Our first ethical judgments are passed on other men, whose behaviour we observe as impartial spectators. We soon discover, however, that other men observe and judge our behaviour in the same manner, and we then learn to judge of this ourselves—at first from the standpoint of others. Only when we live together with others do we thus learn constantly to hold a mirror before our own actions. We are split up into two persons—one acting and the other looking on. And this inner spectator does not remain a mere representative of outer censors ; we naturally attribute to him a greater knowledge of ourselves than that which others can have of us, and we involuntarily set up this inner spectator as a judge, to whose superior wisdom and justice we appeal from the short-sighted and unjust sentences of those around us. On the other hand, remorse may arise when our will conflicts with that which the inner impartial spectator is able to approve, even when no man knows what is going on in our hearts. Smith could have better explained the deepening and idealisation of the ethical feeling here described if he had applied Hume's doctrine of the tendency of the imagination to hold fast to and to strengthen its objects. Smith's exposition, however, although several middle terms are wanting, is of extraordinary interest, and denotes considerable progress in the understanding of the development of the ethical feeling. He rejects the view of a particular, original, moral sense, finished and complete once for all, as also the explanation of all morality in egoism or in pure reason. He does not deny the great importance of reason for moral development ; but the only moral experiences from which general moral principles of reason can be deduced must, in his view, be gained by means of involuntary and instinctive sympathy with the circumstances and behaviour of other men. Only in the generalisation—and not in the involuntary perception of good and evil—does reason co-operate. On this point he agrees with Hutcheson, whom he praises as having been the first to see it clearly. In the latter part of the *Theory of Moral Sentiments* Smith gives an excellent criticism of earlier theories, which is still of great interest.

The opinion that Smith's two great works stand, not merely in contrast, but even in actual contradiction to one another has been occasioned by the great stress which he lays, in his discussion of national prosperity, on the importance of allowing free play to the acquisitive instincts of the individual. The source of all wealth is thrift and industry, and these only develop where the acquisitive instincts are unsuppressed. The impulse which induces us to be thrifty, says Smith, is the desire to better our condition—a desire which is indeed for the most part quiet and passionless, but which nevertheless accompanies us from the cradle to the grave. How the individual can best satisfy this desire he himself will be able most easily to discover. The State must not interfere here, either with commands or with prohibitions. Let every man buy in the cheapest market, whether abroad or at home. Supply and demand will regulate everything in the best possible manner. Under the influence of the relation between supply and demand, division of labour has arisen. This is a necessary condition of all development of civilisation, since by means of it, the individual himself, as well as others, find it advantageous to restrict their work to that which is best suited to their capacities. This appears in large things as well as in small. What is prudence in every small household can scarcely be folly in a great kingdom. The task of the Government is only to protect from external violence, to maintain peace at home, and to establish and preserve such public works and institutions as it would not be to the interest of private persons to carry on. By this last qualification Smith confesses that there are tasks which cannot be executed by the reciprocal action of single individuals, each prompted by his selfish instincts. Moreover it is worthy of note that Smith himself stands in the position of the "impartial observer" when writing his work on political economy. Far, however, from having set aside his ethical standpoint, it is this which underlies it. If he praises the system of freedom it is because it is noble and generous. If he demands that every individual shall be free to go wherever he thinks his interests lead him it is because he believes that the individual is "led by an invisible hand to pro- mote an end which was no part of his own intention. . . . By pursuing his own interest he frequently promotes that of the society more efficiently than when he really 'intends' to promote it." We must notice the little word "frequently." This passage from Smith has been quoted (as Knies, *Die politische Ökonomie vom Geschichtlichen Standpunkte*, Neue Aufl. Braunschweig, 1883, p. 226, points out) with the omission of 'frequently,' and this has given his doctrine the appearance of being a doctrine of the absolute harmony of the egoistical interests,

which would make all sympathy and all ethical action superfluous, even injurious. Then indeed Smith's two chief works
would stand in irreconcilable contradiction to one another.

In order rightly to understand Smith's importance as a
political economist we must remember how great a burden
weighed on all civil life at that time, even in the most advanced
countries. He defends the cause of the diligent and thrifty
citizen against ignorant, extravagant, and overbearing governments ; arguing from the evidence of experience that, in spite
of war and extravagance, England had advanced in prosperity
through the good management of private persons and through
their unceasing endeavours to improve their own circumstances.
He demands recognition of the work which, though done in
obscurity and on a small scale, yet, taken together, forms the
sum-total of the nation's strength. And he rejoices over the
increase of wages in the immediately preceding period, because
labourers form the largest part of the community. Thus we
see that, even in his work on political economy, Smith's views
are of an ethico-social nature, although he lays greater weight
on production than on distribution, and takes it too much for
granted that the point of view of domestic economy can be
transferred, without modification, to political economy.

(b) *Hartley, Priestley, and Erasmus Darwin*

If DAVID HARTLEY is mentioned among Hume's successors,
it is not because he was particularly influenced by Hume, but
rather because he shed fresh light on the questions with which
the latter occupied himself. He himself states that he received
his chief inspiration from Newton and Locke. He was born
in the neighbourhood of York in 1705. He first studied
theology, but gave this up as he found himself unable to sign
the Thirty-nine Articles. He then devoted himself to medicine.
Quite early in life he conceived the plan of writing a work in
which to weave together his ideas on religion, philosophy, and
physiology. He took the central thought of this work from an
attempt of a little-known author called Gay, to explain all the
higher feelings as having arisen, by means of association, from
the lower ones. Hartley's work, *Observations on Man, his
Frame, his Duty, and his Expectations*, appeared in 1749.
Hartley was active in his profession and is described as " a

noble and philanthropic man" (*d.* 1757). His significance in
the history of psychology rests on his attempt to explain all
complex psychical phenomena by the association of simple
sensations and ideas. All thought and all feeling, even the
most ideal and exalted, has developed in this manner, and the
power which our will can exercise over our ideas, feelings, and
actions has also arisen by association. The laws of association
are, according to Hartley, the highest mental laws of Nature.
It is true that Hartley defines association as a union of ideas
given together or in immediate succession (*Observations*, London,
1792, vol. i. p. 66); but he also describes the phenomenon which
is now called association by similarity (vol. i. p. 291 ff.), and
he likewise mentions a direct "coincidence" of ideas which
appears in intuitive certainty, the foundation of all other
certainty. The counterpart to association in physiology is the
union of several vibrations in the molecules of the brain, since,
after repetition, such vibrations coalesce into one single vibra-
tion. Hartley has no theory to bring forward with regard to
the reciprocal relation of ideas and vibrations; in the last
resort they are closely connected, but he subscribes neither
to materialism nor to spiritualism. By means of the laws of
association, according to Hartley, psychical life develops, step
by step, from the lower to the higher forms. In this way
are formed complex ideas which can become such complete
unities that the simple ideas of which they are composed are
no longer perceivable—just as a composite substance may
possess qualities other than those of its elements. Further,
activities which were originally undertaken with full consciousness, become by repetition unconscious or, as Hartley calls
them, "secondary automatic activities." Finally, the liveliness
and strength with which certain ideas occur may afterwards
pass over to others by means of association with the ideas
connected with them. On these three secondary laws rests all
mental development, and especially the process by which the
primitive, sensuous, feelings and expressions of the will yield to
more ideal expressions. In this way egoism can be refined
and exalted, and disinterested and universal sympathy may be
developed. On the other hand, envy and cruelty may, in like
manner, develop themselves according to these laws.

　　Hartley reminds us of Spinoza in his conception and
manner of exposition. He carried the psychology of associa-

tion an important step onwards by establishing the theory of psychical complexes, having properties other than those of their elements ; and by the prominence into which he brought the phenomenon of the transference of motives. And Hartley, no less than Spinoza, is convinced that by means of such psychological laws the transition between the greatest mental contrasts is possible ; self-preservation may pass over, through association and transference of motives, into mystical self-forgetting. Love to God, says Hartley, arises partly from egoistical grounds ; but since God is the cause of all things, infinitely many associations will unite in the idea of Him, and this idea will become so predominant that, in comparison with it, ideas of all else, even of ourselves, are as nothing. A curious combination of mysticism and realism is to be found in Hartley as in Spinoza ; the former, however, is lacking in the surpassing clearness of the latter.

Hartley's theory attracted little attention until, towards the end of the century, it was adopted and popularised by JOSEPH PRIESTLEY (1733-1804), a natural philosopher and theologian, famous for his discovery of oxygen, for his assault on the doctrine of the Trinity, and for his enthusiasm for the French Revolution. Priestley describes his general standpoint as materialism ; he believes, however, in accordance with a theory set up by the Jesuit Boscovich, that the essence of matter consists in force—attractive or repulsive—and that atoms must be conceived as centres of force, since this is all, as a matter of fact, that we know about them. Solidity is only a quality we perceive by the senses, which does not express the nature of matter, but only an effect of the same on the senses. If this be so, there is no ground (as Priestley argues at length in his *Disquisitions on Matter and Spirit*, London, 1777) for assuming two different substances ; the physical and psychical forces may very well belong to the same substance. Priestley is convinced that this conception agrees far better than the spiritualistic—which is taken from heathen philosophy —with the original Christian conception.

Hartley's theory was also taken up by another natural philosopher, ERASMUS DARWIN (1731-1802), the grandfather of Charles Darwin, a doctor, who displayed talent as a naturalist, a poet, and a philosopher. In his chief work, *Zoonomia, or the Laws of Organic Life* (London, 1794), he explains the origin of instincts through experience and association, under the influence of the impulse to self-preservation and accommodation to circumstances. He goes farther than Hartley, since he lays especial weight (see especially the curious 39th chapter of Part I.) on the fact that, in this way, acquired qualities may be transmitted ; the psychological doctrine of association is thus extended to a biological doctrine of evolution, which has not a little in common with the hypothesis of the development of species brought forward some years later by Lamarck ; and, together with this, it prepared the way for the great hypothesis with which the name of Darwin must ever be connected.

(c) Reid and the Scotch School

Thomas Reid and his successors took up a very different position towards the philosophy of Locke and Hume. In opposition to the persevering analysis, which was at once the strength and the greatness of the English School, but which entailed the danger of undermining the confident, popular conception of the world no less than the speculative and religious conception of it, they appeal to the judgment of the naïve consciousness and of common sense. Philosophy is called upon to give an account of what this judgment contains, and to systematise this content. Exhausted and rendered doubtful by analysis, men turned back to the immediate, and demanded that it should have its due. This is a reaction which appears under different forms in the course of the century, and is a premonition of the thorough-going reaction against the whole tendency of the eighteenth century, which took place at the beginning of the new century—a reaction which was in many respects fruitful and justifiable, since it maintained the rights of historical matters of fact, but which, at the same time, frequently showed itself extremely uncritical when it had to decide in particular cases what had been given as actual matter of fact. The Scotch School (as the school of thought founded by Reid is called, because, though indications of it are to be found in Hutcheson and Smith, it only gained the ascendency in Reid's time and at the Scotch Universities) has rendered good service to mental science by its sound descriptive psychology ; it suffers, however, from the faults of mistaking description for explanation, and of subordinating theoretical standpoints to description. THOMAS REID (1710-96), the most important thinker of this school, was first preacher and afterwards professor at Aberdeen and Glasgow. He relates in his principal work, *Inquiry into the Human Mind on the Principles of Common Sense* (1764), that he had been an adherent of the philosophy of Locke and Berkeley until Hume's *Treatise* had shown him that it led to dangerous consequences, *i.e.* to the subversion of all science, of all religion, of all virtue, and of all common sense! He had thereupon subjected the whole movement to a critical examination, and had discovered it to be in contradiction to experience; he disputes it, therefore, on empirical grounds. He intends to follow the method of Bacon and Newton. Reid afterwards elaborated, with special regard to the psychological side of the question, the argument given in a shorter form in the *Inquiry* in his larger works, *Essays on the Intellectual Powers of Mind* (1785), and *Essays on the Active Powers of Mind* (1788).

Underlying all our knowledge, according to Reid, are certain instinctive presuppositions, which are unassailable by doubt. They also govern with irresistible power the opinions and conduct of all men in the ordinary circumstances of life. They are the principles of common sense, which are older, and therefore possess greater authority, than all philosophies. They are elements of our original constitution as it came from the hand of God.

First among these original principles stands the belief in a material external world, and in the existence of the soul. Every sensation which I receive arouses, through natural suggestion, the belief in an external object of sensation, as also of an I (*ego*) which experiences the sensation. Between sensation and memory, on the one hand, and imagination, on the other, there is not only a quantitative, but also a qualitative difference, which cannot be explained any further. Belief in that which is sensed or remembered is a simple act of consciousness, which admits of no nearer description, nor can it be explained through association. We certainly have here a very remarkable feature in our nature : by a natural kind of magic sensation summons up a something in our consciousness which we have never yet experienced and which we are nevertheless able at once to perceive and to believe! Akin to this sensuous perception ("perception" which includes, besides "sensation," the " natural suggestion " above mentioned) is the causal instinct, a natural, although inexplicable, propensity to believe that those conjunctions of phenomena which we have observed in the past will also persist in the future. This is the principle on which all science, as well as all superstition, rests ; we may call it the inductive principle. All common sense acknowledges it, and we should send anybody who did not acknowledge it into a lunatic asylum. As an example of an original principle in the practical sphere we have the moral sense. " As by the external senses," says Reid, " we have not only the original conception of the various qualities of bodies, but the original judgment that this body has such a quality, that such another ; so by our moral quality we have both the original conceptions of right and wrong in conduct, of merit and demerit, and the original judgments that this conduct is right, that is wrong ; this character has worth, that demerit."

The testimony of Nature makes itself known in the moral sense in the same way as it does in the external senses. First principles in the practical, as well as in the theoretical sphere, possess intuitive evidence, which permit of no resistance, if only the mind is mature, quiet, and unprejudiced.

Reid and the Scotch School indicate a reaction against Hume similar to that, in its time, of the Cambridge School against Hobbes. It is characteristic of this reaction to appeal, not to eternal truths, but to the testimony of experience. It believes indeed—and this is its great mistake—that it can directly read eternal truths in the simplest perceptions, and it believes, too, in as many original instincts as there are unintelligible phenomena—a very convenient method of explanation ! At the same time it gives a much wider extension to intuition than did Descartes, Locke, and Leibniz, who restricted this term to the simple perception of resemblance and difference. The most complicated acts of consciousness were declared to be intuitive, and were thus regarded as vindicated. This movement could not but lead to the checking of all inquiry and analysis. And, as a matter of fact, it did not touch Hume at all, for he had himself declared that in practice he bowed to " the principles of common sense," but that he found it uncommonly difficult to *prove* them. Reid's justification against Hume lies in the fact that the latter overlooked the original and invariable connection of phenomena, which is just as much a fact as every particular phenomenon in itself. But he disqualified himself for any scientific refutation of Hume by his appeal to common sense, which was virtually the abandonment of philosophy.

Nor are the reasons for the long ebb in the history of English philosophy which set in after Hume far to seek. As already stated, the tendency of thought represented by the English School had now exhausted itself ; the line had become extinct. On the other hand, interests partly political, partly religious, were once more pressing to the front. Once again, after the long interval during which men were reaping the after-effects of the Revolution of 1688, did politics claim their highest powers in her service, while religious feeling, which had been partially suppressed by latitudinarianism and deism, blazed up again in methodism, which embodied a strong and very popular reaction against the rationalism of the preceding period. These circumstances, however, cannot be further discussed here. Leslie Stephen gives a most excellent characterisation of them in his *History of English Thought in the Eighteenth Century.*

BOOK V

THE FRENCH ENLIGHTENMENT PHILOSOPHY AND ROUSSEAU

GENERAL CHARACTERISTICS

PHILOSOPHICAL thought had been carried by David Hume to a point whence further progress was only possible through the adoption of entirely new points of view. No answer was forthcoming to the question propounded in Hume's *Treatise* in 1739 until Kant's *Critique of Pure Reason* in 1781. The interval which lies between these two great works is of importance in the history of thought chiefly because, in it, philosophical thought was turned into a weapon of warfare. The peaceful work of thought was interrupted by the sound of the signal to turn out and do spiritual battle with the traditions and institutions of former times, which the impatient spirit of man was now calling into question. Within the sphere of material nature the new science had led to a magnificent result —magnificent not only on account of the width of its horizon, but also on account of its exact foundation. Within the mental sphere men possessed in the principle established by the English School, *i.e.* that the validity of every idea must be attested by its origin in experience, a means by which all ideas for which respect was claimed could be put to the test ; while, in the social and political sphere, the principles of natural right, which had emerged in the hard struggles of the sixteenth and seventeenth centuries, provided a standard of measurement which was boldly applied to the principle of authority, hitherto the support of the social order. Had, then, a sufficiently exhaustive examination been made to warrant the advance to practical application? There was of course no other right than that which life's own mighty impulse gives. Solitary thinkers would hardly have come to a definitive settlement, but their time had gone by for the present. Some years before Hume went to France in order to procure greater solitude for the composition of his great work, two

French youths had visited England, not, however, to mature their thoughts in solitude, but, on the contrary, to open their hearts and minds to the intellectual forces at work in England, and to participate in the vigorous movement which had been able to develop itself in the healthy atmosphere of England.

Voltaire and Montesquieu brought home with them from England, as though from an entirely strange world, new ideas on philosophy, religion, the Church and the State. They had a travelling acquaintance with English thought and circumstances, and their aim was, not to keep what they had learned to themselves in order to develop it further, but to let it pass out into the world in as free, easy, and simple a form as possible, there to awaken, to stimulate, and to transform. And to this end not only the methods and results of English investigation were employed, but the whole development of thought, beginning with the Renaissance, and passing on through the great systems to empirical philosophy, furnished means for carrying on the battle. Behind the violent and ruthless criticism which was turned against everything traditionary, lay a dogmatism which believed itself to have finished with all that essentially concerned the conceptions of the world and of life. A man must stand very firmly himself to be able to overthrow the powers that be. He must have great confidence in his own standpoint who is ready suddenly, in a moment, to close his account with everything that history has produced in the mental and social spheres. But so it is everywhere in history : on the day of judgment there is no time to wait till all the premises are set in order. Christianity and the Church did not delay the destruction of ancient civilisation until they could completely make good their own superiority. The civilisation of antiquity was blown up. Spiritual currents are remorseless. When a spiritual need has been stemmed for a long time there comes a moment when it breaks through, however much of value it may destroy in its path. That classical culture had not really been overthrown by the Church was shown by the Renaissance, and that the philosophical and political revolution of the last decade of the eighteenth century had not really conquered the old order of things, was shown by the Romantic reaction at the beginning of the nineteenth century. Men had not really finished philosophising in the study when they began to philosophise first in the salons, and then in the streets and lanes. The philosophic incompleteness of the thought-weapons with which they entered the field does not, however, deprive the historical mission of the men who opened the battle of any of its significance. Where life is at stake, men must use what weapons they have. And though the French philosophers of the middle of the eighteenth century do not always impress us as possessing intellectual superiority, though, on account of their eager attempts to simplify and popularise, they often make the great small, and profane what is really sublime, yet behind their dogmatism, their short-sightedness, and their trivialities lies a fervent faith in light, in progress, and in humanity, for the sake of which they must be forgiven much. The words with which Voltaire commemorates a young and noble thinker (Vauvenargues) who died young : " From whence didst thou get thy mighty flight in this age of trivialities ? " might be taken as a motto for the whole movement. The strongly subjective undercurrent must more especially be kept in view when we are treating the French philosophy of the eighteenth century in a history of philosophy rather than in one of literature or civilisation ; what rises to the surface may often appear trivial and insignificant. Yet *one* man there was in whose tempest-tossed spirit the subjective undercurrent was almost entirely in the ascendency, so that he had the power, in a hitherto unknown degree, of defending the right of immediate feeling, of the individual disposition, the right of Nature against culture and reflection, the right of the great, simple, human values of life against every kind of aristocracy and refinement. In JEAN JACQUES ROUSSEAU a new element in life, a new side of spiritual life, came into prominence, and ranged itself against the new critical wisdom as well as the old order of things. He proved that living human feeling goes deeper than any relation of authority, or any critical reflection, that no thought and no tradition can make its support superfluous, and that it is the foundation of all that makes life valuable. Never before had the significance of feeling been brought out with such simplicity and purity, although mysticism had often spoken a word in its behalf. It is not so much on account of his ideas and theories, but rather on account of his personality (in spite of all weaknesses) that Rousseau forms a great turning-point in philosophy : the problem of worth took with him the foremost place, which, up to his time, had been occupied almost exclusively by the problems of existence and of knowledge. And in attacking the old order as well as the new criticism he showed that there is something which will not surrender its rights to either of them. Among the French philosophers of the eighteenth century he is the one who most clearly prognosticated the future, and bore within himself the seed from which it was to spring. He is also the one among the thinkers of his time who was most interested in childhood.

There is very good reason historically why the radical consequences—in their negative as well as in their positive form—should have been drawn in France and not in England, where the main principles arose. TAINE in his brilliant work *L'ancien régime* has pointed out that the French language and the French spirit had acquired such a polish at court, in the salons, and by means of classic art, as to fit it to become the organ of simple and clear ideas, of a school of thought which is ready to discuss the greatest problems with the smallest possible preparation, and that is concerned not to enlarge its sphere, but only to work up that which it has already acquired. The classical spirit and the polish of the language do not, however, afford a sufficient explanation. They explain the form only, not the content or direction. The real reason why the practical consequences of the English philosophy were drawn in France and not in England must be sought in the fact that on French soil, unlike England, the old order confronted the new with unyielding antagonism, and that it was at the same time both more hollow and more rotten than in England. In England, society had taken up the new forces into itself, and was in a position to use them for the production of a continuous development. In France the old order of society had been carried through so consistently that it had either to destroy all criticism or be destroyed by it itself.

CHAPTER 1

VOLTAIRE AND MONTESQUIEU

IN his *Lettres sur les Anglais* (1732) VOLTAIRE (born 1694, died 1778) introduced his countrymen to a new physics, a new philosophy, and a new constitution of society. He contrasted Locke and Newton with Descartes ; Socinians, Quakers, and other Dissenters with Catholics ; representative government with absolute monarchy. Even where he drew no direct comparison, but restricted himself to mere description, his intention was plain enough ; nor was it misunderstood. The book was burnt. Many Frenchmen considered Voltaire (as afterwards Montesquieu) a bad patriot, merely because he admired the English character. These letters, however, indicate a turning-point in the history of civilisation, *i.e.* the inoculation of English ideas on the Continent. Voltaire afterwards published a good popular exposition of Newton's theory of physics (*Éléments de la philosophie de Newton*, mis à la portée de tout le monde, 1738) which did much towards effecting the dissemination and ultimate victory of the new natural philosophy. He is important, not as an independent thinker, but as a great paraphrast and populariser. The title of one of his most important works, *Dictionnaire Philosophique portatif* (1764), is in this respect characteristic. The views it sets forth were ready to his hand ; all he had to do was to clothe them in a form in which they could easily be disseminated. He commends Locke because he has given us the history of the mind, while so many earlier *raisonneurs* have offered us its romance, and because he derived everything that is in the understanding from sensation. Voltaire, however, is inclined to go still further, and to regard all memory and thought as nothing more than continued and modified sensation. When Condillac (of whom we shall have more to say presently) had propounded this theory, Voltaire accepted the utterances of "the great philosopher" (Art. "Sensation" in the *Dict. phil.*). But if everything is derived from the senses what, in that case, can we know of the eternal and infinite, and of the nature of the soul? Almost nothing. Peculiar to Voltaire—in contradistinction to Locke as well as to Condillac—are the sceptical results which he derives from the proposition that everything in consciousness arises out of sensation. Officially, to be sure, he informs us, with an irony which cannot be misuuderstood, that revelation has taught us that the soul is a spiritual substance. His real views as to the limits of the human mind (see Art. "Bornes de l'esprit humain" in the *Dict. phil.*) are, however, expressed in the concluding words of his article on the "Soul" in his Philosophical Dictionary: "God has given thee understanding, O Man! for thy own good conduct, and not to penetrate into the essence of the things which He has created." Everything is derived from sensation ; on this point Voltaire entertains no doubts. But how about sensation? Locke, to Voltaire's great joy, had declared that there is nothing against the view that God has endowed matter with the capacity of sensation. That this endowment could only, according to Locke, have taken place by means of a miracle, Voltaire does not stop to consider ; he seizes upon the remark and continually uses it as a weapon against the spiritualists. And yet, at the same time, running through his system is the endeavour to reduce everything to the two principles : God and matter. Of spirits as middle terms he has no need. But what then is matter? That, indeed, we know as little as we know what the soul is. Voltaire, however, does not question its existence ; he even attributes everlasting existence to it. "No axiom," he says (Art. "Matière" in the *Dict. phil.*), "has ever been more generally received than this, that *nothing arises out of nothing.* Indeed the contrary is incomprehensible." And he attempts to show that religion does not suffer from the assumption of an everlastingly existing matter, ordered by God to serve ends. "We of the present day are so happy as to know by faith that God created matter out of nothing, but," etc. It is true that the assumption of an eternally existing matter presents difficulties of its own, and we must not flatter ourselves that they can be surmounted ; philosophy cannot explain everything. The belief in an eternally existing matter, ordered by God, does not, however, involve any ethical difficulties : our duties remain the same whether it be an ordered or a created chaos that lies under our feet ! Voltaire maintains that speculative and dogmatic results are of little importance within the practical and moral sphere. It is, perhaps, on this point that he is of the greatest importance philosophically; here, too, his scepticism shows itself as something other than mere cynicism. His appearance as defender of the oppressed and the unjustly condemned is quite sufficient witness to the practical earnestness which Voltaire could display when it was needed. His deeds show that, however frequently irony or malice may have prompted him to attack the teaching of revelation, his whole will was engaged as soon as he opposed practice to speculation. With regard to the belief in immortality he seems to have held that it was necessary for the preservation of morality among mankind ("Le bien commun de tous les hommes demande qu'on croye l'âme immortelle," *Lettres sur les Anglais*, xiii.).

Nevertheless he attempted to find a ground for the belief in God (although here, too, he relies on "*le bien commun*"),[92] starting (like Newton) from the purposiveness of Nature. He defends the theory of final causes (*causes finales*), only we must fix our eyes on those effects which at every time and at every place are invariably the same—not those which are particular or secondary. Voltaire took a malicious pleasure in bringing into prominence the dark side of existence, and he attacks optimism which, fastening its gaze on the great laws ruling the whole, overlooks and despises the suffering and unhappiness which may accrue to the individual in virtue of this general order of things. The destruction of Lisbon by an earthquake afforded him, as is well known, especial occasion to mock at this best of all possible worlds. He strikes at the heart of Leibniz' optimistic system when he makes Candide (who is scourged at an *auto-da-fée* which takes place as a day of expiation after the destruction of Lisbon) say to himself: "If this is the best world, what must the others be like ? " Voltaire was indignant because Leibniz and Shaftesbury and afterwards —in verse—Pope, had pronounced everything good, adding that we cannot require of God that He should alter His eternal laws for the sake of such a miserable creature as man. "It must be confessed at least," he says (Art. "Tout est bien" in·

the *Dict. phil.*), "that this pitiful creature has a right to cry out humbly and to endeavour while bemoaning himself to understand why the said eternal laws do not comprehend the good of every individual." For Voltaire himself the answer to the latter question was given in his doctrine of God and matter, which may have been occasioned by his contemplation of the evil to individuals involved by an order of nature according to law. He believes in a good God, but the suffering in the world convinces him that this God is not omnipotent, but has to overcome unceasing opposition, and this opposition he ascribes to eternally existing matter. Morality, for him, was the essence of religion. "After our own holy religion," he says, beginning with his usual official obeisance (Art. "Religion" in the *Dict. phil.*), "which is indubitably the only good one, what religion would be the least objectionable? Would it not be the simplest? that which should teach much morality and very few dogmas? that which would tend to make men just without making them absurd?" He denounces as superstition everything in religion connected with the worship of a highest Being. The idea of simplicity, employed by the thinkers of the Renaissance in deciphering the natural world, was now, by the thinkers of the Enlightenment, applied to the supernatural world. With regard to positive religion, Voltaire's criticism is confined to dogmas as he found them : he makes no inquiries as to their genesis, their origin in human emotional impulses, or the symbolical value as expressions of dearly bought spiritual experiences which they may possess. He made sport of the islands sown at random in the ocean of religion, and does not remember that what thus seems on the surface scattered, contradictory, and lawless may have a deep underlying connection, and is, perhaps, the effect of volcanic forces working in the depths. The unconscious or semi-conscious, the involuntary and spontaneous, and the obscure movements of feeling he could not understand. He saw everything in full daylight. Dawn and twilight he regarded as indications of ambiguity, madness, stupidity, absurdity, or baseness. In the face of such his only alternative was that a man must be either a fool or a knave (*fou, fripon*) to believe in it. Superstition is begotten by the madness and stupidity of fanaticism, amounting sometimes to insolence (*insolente imbécillité*) ; but then come the knaves and use this madness for their own ends.[93] An elementary psychology of religion, which undeniably satisfies the principle of simplicity and is, in the highest degree, "*portatif*"!

Voltaire was persuaded that the moment had arrived when all prejudices could be abolished. Not that he considered all prejudices bad : some are sanctioned by reason (Art. "Préjugés" in the *Dict. phil.*). But he did not doubt the all-sufficiency of reason, as then understood. He rejoices (in the letters to d'Alembert) because the "age of reason" has now come. He perceived the decline of the power of the Church on all sides— in the consciousness of the educated as well as in the State. There were, it is true, limits to the extension of the enlighten- ment : the *canaille*, "cobblers and maidservants," could not participate in it. Voltaire consoled himself however : "The important point, however, is not so much to hinder our lackeys from attendance at the mass or the sermon ; but to deliver the fathers of families from the tyranny of impostors and to spread abroad the spirit of toleration." [94] He little thought that soon lackeys, too, would begin to philosophise ; had not he himself made philosophy "*portatif*"? He was never able to rise above the dualism between "the classes" (*honnêtes gens*) and "the masses"(*canaille*). Here, too, he seized upon salient contrasts, and was not able to discover the underlying, though often enough hidden, connection. It must not be forgotten, however, that just in his time the cleft between the different parts of the nation was greater and wider than any we now know, and that Voltaire considered the solution of the question to lie in the care of the great masses being undertaken by an enlightened tyranny.

MONTESQUIEU (1689-1755) possessed essential qualities in which Voltaire was lacking—more particularly a mode of thought which led him to see things in their definite mutual connection and never to lose sight of this for the sake of any particular point. He rises high above the usual line of thought of the eighteenth century in the idea which underlies his chief work (*Esprit des lois*, 1748), *i.e.* that institutions and laws are not arbitrary products but presuppose—if they are to be able to exist and work—certain definite natural conditions. He showed the connection that exists between the law on the one hand and the climate, customs, manner of living, religion, and national character in general on the other. "Laws," he says (*Esprit des lois*, i. 3), "should be appropriate in such a manner to the people for whom they are framed, that it is a mere accident if those of one nation suit another." The modern historical school has in Montesquieu one of its most important precursors. He aims, however, at arriving at general ideas through the study of historical relations. He is able at several points, precisely because he carried out his historical method, to exhibit the sophistry of the defence which had been set up for traditional abuses, *e.g.* in his investigation of personal and political freedom. And his admiration for antiquity and for England moved him to ideal descriptions which were so many condemnations of the existing state of affairs in France. Just as immediately on his return home he transformed his garden into an English park, so, too, his political ideas took on an English colouring. It must be carefully noticed here that his famous description of the English constitution (*Esprit des lois*, xi. 6) is based on his study of Locke's treatise *Of Civil Government*, rather than on any more penetrative examination of English constitutional life in its connection with the history and the customs of the nation. Now Locke's treatise was a theoretical vindication of the Revolution; it aimed, not at describing what historically existed, but at establishing the right to further develop the historically existing in a definite direction. Montesquieu, indeed, goes still farther than Locke in his sharp tripartite division of power into the legislative, the judicial, and the executive. He did not see that, as a matter of fact, this tripartite division only partially applies to a definite period of English history, *i.e.* to the time immediately following the Revolution. Before that, the King had had the larger share of the legislative power, and afterwards Parliament acquired a constantly increasing share in the executive power.[95] And yet Montesquieu regarded this system as originally Germanic: "this beautiful system was discovered in the forests." He knew it only as it appeared when fully developed, and as the external form of the political life of the nation; the self-government in smaller spheres which is the basis of the English parliamentary constitution escaped his notice. Just as Voltaire fastened upon Locke's and Newton's results without the power of comprehending the spirit of inquiry in which they had been conceived, so Montesquieu took the form of the English constitution and systematised it, without including herewith the firm basis which was its real support. Regarded from this side, he is akin to the French Enlightenment philosophers and finds his place in their ranks. In him, too, we can trace the "classical spirit." Albert Sorel appositely remarks of him : " He did not trace the historical developments of governments. . . . He exhibited them as established, complete, definitive. . . . Without chronology and without perspective, everything lies in the same plane. The unities of time, place, and action are transferred from the theatre to the legislature." Montesquieu did not suppose, however, that English forms could be transplanted to France just as they were. His thought turned rather in the direction of a resuscitation of the old French monarchy, with an enlightened bureaucracy, and, more particularly, with an independent judicature. The spirit of the age, however, crept into his work, introducing tendencies which conflicted with his historical method, while it exercised so great an influence on his readers that the book acquired a revolutionary significance which was quite foreign to the spirit in which it had been conceived.

CHAPTER II

CONDILLAC AND HELVÉTIUS

THE epistemological and psychological basis of the French Enlightenment philosophy was worked out by CONDILLAC (1715-
1780), a peaceable thinker, in holy orders from his youth, who
was entrusted with the education of an Italian prince, and was
presented in his old age with an abbey and its revenues.   In
his chief work (*Traité des sensations*, 1754) he establishes, with
much breadth and clearness, and by the deductive, rather than
the inductive method, the proposition that everything in our
consciousness, not only all content—as Locke had taught—
but also all its activities and forms of thought, are nothing
but transformations of simple passive sensations (*sensations
transformées*).   Each sense-perception occurs as a purely passive
modification of consciousness.   If the modification is strong
enough to exclude all other sensations, attention arises.   If we
have two sensations at the same time, we say that we compare
and judge.   Memory is only an after-effect of sensation.
Abstraction is the singling out of one sensation from other
sensations.   The condition of all comparison, judgment,
memory, and abstraction, is attention, which is, therefore, the
fundamental phenomenon of knowledge.   By its help we are
able to apprehend clearly and separately what first appeared
as a chaotic manifold.   On such differentiated, and therefore
clear, perception of this originally chaotic manifold—that is to
say, on analysis—all knowledge rests.   After we have established,
by means of speech, a sign for each of the elements presented
by analysis, we are able, by combining these signs, and replacing
some by others denoting the same thing, to develop a logical
calculus, a scientific language, of complete clearness and
accuracy.   Only by means of a sign-language can analysis be

performed ; this, however, reacts on the sign-language, and all science is, properly speaking, a system of signs, the signification and reciprocal relations of which are perfectly clear. Languages are analytic methods ; for man, led by his impulse to make gestures or utter cries when his attention is excited, involuntarily analyses. Afterwards, conversely, science, *i.e.* exact analysis, becomes identical with a perfect speech.

Condillac's theory of knowledge is the most vigorous attempt that has been made to deduce everything from ex- perience in such a manner as, while exhibiting the possibility of erecting a science on the basis of experience, shall yet conceive experience itself as altogether passive. His doctrine gained many adherents on account of its clearness and simplicity ; it supplanted Cartesianism in the public schools and academies. It was the philosophy which was taught at the close of the century—during the Revolution and under the Empire—until new tendencies made themselves felt. In his *Traité des sensations* Condillac employs, as his method of exposition, the fiction of a statue whose senses awake to activity one after another. Only one single sensation arises at a time, so that Condillac can examine the way in which conscious life successively develops itself and, under the influence of external impressions, acquires its different faculties (attention, comparison, memory, etc.), which cannot therefore be original dispositions bestowed by Nature. Especially charac- teristic is his attempt to describe attention as a purely passive condition, and also his description of comparison as simultane- ous attention to two impressions. The gradual development of the different faculties proceeds under the influence of the instincts and wants of men. Instincts and wants arise through com- parison of feelings of pleasure and pain, which are a particular kind of sensation. Instead of equipping us with a multitude of original faculties, the author of Nature gave us feelings of pleasure and pain to arouse attention, and, with this, to set in motion analysis—at first in its simpler, later in its higher forms.

Although Condillac's doctrine, regarded from one essential side, presents a sharp contrast to Cartesianism, yet it is not wanting in points of contact with the latter, not only on account of the great importance it attributes to the analytic method, but also because of the spiritualistic mode of con- ception on which it ultimately rests. For Condillac asserts decidedly that sensation is different from motion, and that the latter can only be the occasional cause of the birth of sensation in a soul which is something other than body. It is true that we know (Condillac, like Locke, admits this) the substance of the soul as little as we do that of the body.   Nevertheless, the possibility of comparison (according to Condillac, the faculty of having two sensations simultaneously) presupposes one *single* substance as the bearer of sensations. (See especially *De l'art de raisonner*, i. 3, and *Discours préliminaire du cours d'étude*, Art 4.) With this exception, Condillac's doctrine deals with our sensations only; these are nothing but the "statue's" own states ; if the first sensation is the scent of a rose then the soul is the scent of a rose and nothing more.   Extension, which Condillac considers to arise from the sense of touch, and not at all, in the first instance, from that of sight, is only the most constant element of our sensations, around which other elements collect ; but are we therefore justified in regarding it as the expression of absolute reality ?   Extension is a sensation which, like all other sensations, is aroused in us by a something, the essential nature of which we do not know (*Traité des sensations*, i. 1 ; ii. 11 ; iv. 5).   Condillac was evidently influenced by Berkeley ("Barclai" as he calls him), at any rate by his *Theory of Vision*, although it is doubtful whether he was acquainted with his chief works : his doctrine of abstraction shows no sign of it.

We have already seen that Voltaire referred to Condillac as "the great philosopher." As may often happen in troublous times, the results arrived at by a peaceable thinker were employed as weapons of war.   His doctrine of the transformation of sensation was adopted, but his spiritualism was left disregarded. HELVÉTIUS (1715-71), on the contrary, wrote his works (*De l'esprit*, 1758 ; *De l'homme*, 1773-74) in direct concurrence and in growing sympathy with the free movement. *De l'esprit* was treated as one of the most godless of books. It was condemned by the Archbishop of Paris, by the Pope, and by the Parliament of Paris, and Helvétius, who had hoped to gain literary fame by his work, was obliged to spend some time abroad, where he was well received, especially by Frederick the Great.   The latter entertained the highest esteem for his disinterested character and wrote to d'Alembert after his death : " I have learnt with the greatest pain of his death.   His character always excited my admiration.   We ought perhaps to wish that he had taken his heart, rather than his head, as his guide." Helvétius was a free-thinking, tender-hearted, and benevolent man, who employed the riches he had amassed as farmer-general in the service of literature and philanthropy.   The contemplation (as appears especially in his posthumous work *De l'homme*) of the degradation and internal disintegration of his fatherland filled him with sorrow and wrath.   His writings proceed from the conviction that the exclusion of individuals from active participation in public life must lead to unhappy results.   Character finds no sufficiently great motives and objects for action.   Both literature and morals must suffer under such a state of affairs.   For both talent and virtue, intellect (*l'esprit*) as well as integrity (*probité*), are conditioned and developed by the form of govern-ment, which also determines education.   This is the great and profound thought from which Helvétius' works start.   He carries on Condillac's theory of the development of all our faculties through experience and external influences.   Even self-love is acquired, for we could not feel love unless we had first felt pleasure and pain.   Susceptibility to pleasure and pain is, therefore, the only gift with which Nature has directly endowed us.   It arouses and sharpens attention, and determines our actions.   What it is that will attract our attention depends upon our education—taking this word in its widest sense, so that it includes everything in our environment and circum-stances which has influenced our development, even down to the smallest trifles.   In virtue of this interpretation of the word Helvétius is able to assert that no two men ever received precisely the same education (*De l'esprit*, iii. 1).   All men are equally gifted, but the conditions of their development are different.   Helvétius derives all differences of character from education, and, since this is dependent on public relations and the form of government, we see how far his theory prompted his sorrow and anger at the internal condition of France.

Moral depravity consists not so much in the excesses to which individuals are addicted, as in the general cleavage between individual and social interests.   It is hypocritical of moralists to attack the private vices of single individuals instead of at once directing their attack towards public abuses and oppression in high places.   Morality, the art of making laws, and pedagogy, are not endeavours in three different spheres; they all rest on the same principle : *i.e.* on the principle of public utility, utility to the greatest possible number of men who are bound together in one State (*De l'esprit*, ii. 17). On this interest rests all that is recognised as good and virtuous (*probité*). Most men only recognise as good that which is in harmony with their own limited interest. Only comparatively few—especially under bad social and political conditions—possess the enlightened pride, the spiritual nobility, to let their moral judgments be determined by considerations of public utility, without being led astray by their own narrow interests or their immediate surroundings. Such a nobility of soul in no way presupposes the abandonment of self-love, for this is an impossibility. But it does presuppose that our own, is inseparably connected with the public interest, more especially by means of the impulse towards power and honour. " No one," says Helvétius (*De l'homme*, v. 1), " has ever contributed to the public good to his own hurt. That citizen who risks his life, like a hero, in order to cover himself with glory, to earn public esteem, and to free his fatherland from slavery, follows the feeling which, for him, is associated with the greatest pleasure. A good man, therefore, only obeys a noble interest." It is not clear whether, according to Helvétius, the desire for power and honour takes on another complexion when it is indissolubly united with regard for " *le bien public* " from that which it has when it stands alone, and therefore seeks to find satisfaction by any means whatsoever. The expression " nobility of soul " (*noblesse de l'âme*) seems to presuppose that feeling must have undergone a certain metamorphosis when, thanks to a good education, it has succeeded in so closely uniting the idea of justice with the idea of power and happiness that they completely fuse into one single idea (note 33 to *De l'homme*, sect. 4). In Helvétius (as in Condillac) we look in vain for a more exact investigation of the way in which, under the influence of ideas and their associations, the feelings are modified—an investigation which had been begun by Spinoza, Hume, and Hartley.

It is a leading principle with Helvétius that we can only recognise such ideas and qualities of character as agree with our own ideas and feelings. We only recognise intellect (*esprit*, in the sense of capacity to form new thought-connections) when the new thought-connections which we encounter present a certain analogy with our own thoughts, and are in harmony with our own interests. And what is true of the recognition of mind holds good also of the recognition of integrity (*probité*). Unless our own interest is set in motion we recognise nothing. But, according to Helvétius, interest is of two kinds : " Some men there are animated by noble and enlightened pride, maintaining their minds in that state of suspension (*état de suspension*) which allows the free entrance of new truths. Among such belong a few philosophic minds and a few youths, too young still to have formed their opinions so fixedly that they blush to change them. . . . There are others—and amongst these I reckon most men—who are animated by a less noble vanity. Such men can only esteem in others ideas conformable with their own, and calculated to justify the high opinion they all have of the justice of their minds." (*De l'esprit*, ii. 3 ; cf. *De l'homme*, iv. 6. " The man of genius has as his only protectors and panegyrists youths and a few enlightened and virtuous men.") Besides ignoble vanity, however, Helvétius mentions laziness as a hindrance to the recognition of new ideas and new virtues. According to his view, both these hindrances can only be conquered by a feeling of sufficient strength to rouse men out of their apathy and narrowness. Both of Helvétius' works (the tendency of which is often misunderstood) investigate the conditions for the arising of great minds and important qualities of character, and for the recognition of the same when they have arisen, and he finds the fundamental condition to lie in the intimate association of individual with public life. His theories of the original sameness of individuals, of the fundamentality of self-interest, and of the omnipotence of education, all seem to emphasise one and the same fundamental thought.

Helvétius' religious standpoint is deistic, with especial prominence given to the unknowableness of God. He polemicises against theological morality, which attacks private vices only and not the seat of the evil, *i.e.* the relations of public life, and against the clergy, whose interest cannot coincide with that of the nation as a whole. . There is, moreover, a polemical undercurrent running through all his works—in *De l'homme* still more strongly than in *De l'esprit*, although Diderot was right in describing the latter as dealing a smashing blow to all prejudices.

CHAPTER III

LA METTRIE, DIDEROT, AND HOLBACH

As early as Voltaire we find physical science and its results together with empirical philosophy, playing an important rôle But the influence of physics does not become predominant until the appearance of a group of French philosophers who, while they adopted Locke's doctrine that everything in consciousness is derived from sensation, are yet mainly concerned with material nature, which they seek to show to be the only real Nature. Their philosophy professes to be a simple logical consequence of the doctrine of physics. They carried on Hobbes's materialistic tendency, though, while Hobbes had employed the method of deduction, their procedure is in the main inductive. Their appearance testifies to the growing energy with which the methods and results of physical science claimed a share in determining conceptions of life and of the world. And the more impossible they found it to explain or to justify ecclesiastical dogmas and existing institutions in accordance with the fundamental principles of physical science, which they regarded as eternal truths, the more must these dogmas and institutions have seemed to them purely arbitrary — the work of stupidity, fanaticism, or fraud. Voltaire's dilemma—folly or knavery—was here pushed to its extremest consequences, and was thrown down with a passionate defiance and passion to which Voltaire, who never quitted the atmosphere of the court and of the salon, was a stranger. And yet these writers, too, were aware that their ideas could never find access among the great majority of men.

The revolutionary tendency of these authors—their conviction that if this earth is to be reformed heaven must be reformed first—does not deprive their work of philosophical value. They disputed the spiritualistic doctrine, not indeed with deductive arguments superior to those already contributed by Hobbes and Spinoza, but with a greater wealth of particular experiences. They rely not only, like the thinkers of the seventeenth century, on the general principles of a mechanical physics, but also on the results reached by the science of organic life during the preceding century. In this connection LA METTRIE (1709-51), who was, properly speaking, the founder of French materialism, is specially to be noticed. He was originally a military doctor, but he lost his appointment, partly on account of his attack on the prevailing medical system, partly because of his *Histoire naturelle de l'âme* (1745), in which he first gave expression to his views. For some time after this he resided in Holland, but was obliged to flee from thence to Prussia, owing to the indignation excited by his work entitled *L'homme machine* (1748). He found a refuge with Frederick the Great, to whom he became reader, and with whom he appears to have been on very confidential terms. He died suddenly in 1751. Evil tongues (especially Voltaire's) attributed his death to the result of overeating; it was more probably a case of poisoning. La Mettrie's character attracts us by its boldness, and by a certain amiable frivolity. But he could be insolent instead of bold, and wanton instead of frivolous, and his philosophical fame could not but suffer from this unfavourable side of his character, unmistakable traces of which are to be found in his works. In recent times, ALBERT LANGE in his *History of Materialism*, and DUBOIS REYMOND in his brilliant essay, have prepared the way for a juster estimation of La Mettrie.

La Mettrie wished to build on experience and perception, and to employ the comparative method. In natural philosophy he is a pupil of BOERHAVE, the famous doctor who applied the fundamental principles of the Cartesian physics to the study of organic life. The title of La Mettrie's well-known work *L'homme machine*, points back to Descartes, and the book might very well have been written by one of the elder Cartesians—if he could have given up the soul-substance with its occasional pushes of the pineal gland. La Mettrie seeks to show, by means of the comparative method, that the difference between man and the lower animals is merely quantitative, and that there is therefore no ground for the assumption that, in the case of man, an entirely new kind of substance is added. In order not to misunderstand La Mettrie we must remember that he wrote not only *L'homme machine*, but also a work entitled *Les animaux plus que machines*. After having brought out the affinity between the structure and manner of working of the human and the animal organism, his object is to bring forward evidence to show that that which is operative in both does not differ in its essence. He goes still further. He brings out not only the similarity between man and animals, but also that between man and plants (*L'homme plante*). And from the whole graduated series which the study of the structure and the functions of living beings reveals to us, he draws the conclusion that the psychical life which is to be found at the top of the scale cannot be entirely wanting at the bottom. He extends the capacity of feeling to all living things, even, indeed, to all material things: everything in the universe is full of souls, and he refers here (*Les animaux plus que machines*, Œuvres philos., Berlin, 1755, ii. p. 82) to Leibniz' slumbering monads. But this graduated series of La Mettrie's does not consist of ready-made forms. He believes—in adherence partly to Maillet, the natural philosopher ridiculed by Voltaire, partly to Epicurus and Lucretius—in a development from lower to higher forms. He seems (*Système d'Épicure*, §§ 13, 32, 33, 39) to believe in an eternal organic germ out of which have proceeded, through reciprocal action with external circumstances, and in an ascending scale of perfection, the different forms of life. The impelling force is desire—want. A higher psychical life only arises where there are other than purely vegetative wants. Plants do not require souls properly so-called. The transitional forms between plants and animals possess the more intelligence the more they are obliged to move in order to procure their food. And man occupies the highest place because he has the most wants (*L'homme plante*). We meet here with an interesting anticipation of the idea of the struggle for existence. And it is not impossible that, by his pronouncement that " beings without wants are also without mind," La Mettrie gave Helvétius the *motif* of his leading thought.

The side of La Mettrie's doctrine which we have hitherto been describing is interesting even if we altogether neglect the materialistic conclusions which he himself deduced from it. The necessity of the materialistic conclusion lay, for him, in this : that we see around us nothing but matter under constantly changing forms. He admits indeed that we cannot know the real nature of matter. But we know its qualities, *i.e.* extension, motion, and sensation. That sensation is a quality of matter he deduces from experience, which shows us that certain organic states are always accompanied by sensation. He appeals here especially to the comparative examination which has shown us psychical life varying according to the organisation. If the soul were not material, *i.e.* extended, how should we be able to explain the fact that enthusiasm heats us and, on the other hand, that the heat of fever influences our ideas ? (*L'homme machine*, Œuvres iii. p. 75 ff.) All our thoughts must be modifications of matter. And since, as a matter of fact, an enormous number of thoughts find a place in our brain, it follows that these must be extremely small, in order to be able to " lodge " there (*Traité de l'âme*, § 103 : De la petitesse des idées)! La Mettrie considers the assumption of a spiritual substance to be a useless and self-contradictory hypothesis ; for his part he will content himself with the teaching of anatomy and physiology—and he really believes he does this. He maintains that the question as to the truth of materialism must be decided on purely theoretical grounds. The grandeur of our mind does not depend on our being able to apply to it the senseless word " incorporeal," but on its power, its reach, its clearness. It need not blush because it was born in the mire. La Mettrie was right in thinking that materialism may be united with practical idealism. His own moral philosophy, in so far as he has such, is certainly very far from bearing this stamp. The measure of righteousness is the good of the community he says ; but he only really employs this measure to establish a distinction between debauchery (*débauche*), *i.e.* that feeling of pleasure which is injurious to society, and enjoyment (*volupté*), *i.e.* that feeling of pleasure which involves no harm to others. But once having made this distinction, he gets no farther than enjoyment, and gives minute directions with regard to this (*L'art de jouir*) in which sentimentality and sensuality are combined in a manner which excites our disgust.

In DENIS DIDEROT (1713-84) the French literature of the eighteenth century touched the zenith at once of philosophical thought and of the revolutionary spirit. He was a warm-hearted man with a great power of working himself into subjects and circumstances of the most diverse kinds—a French Leibniz, who was able to detect life everywhere, and who combined a keen eye for particulars with the feeling of the necessity of understanding the connection of the whole. The poet in him was often at issue with the philosopher ; many of his thoughts express, with the crassest narrow-mindedness, the mere mood of the moment, without any attempt to find a bond of connection which might unite them with other thoughts which he also intended to maintain. The most exalted ideas and moods serve him as occasions for cynical rejoicing over the rude and the mean. In his works, too, sentimental out-pourings stand side by side with the development of thoughts full of genius. His literary career was very varied. His contemporaries knew him only as a writer of comedies, as the author of some works on natural philosophy displaying a deistical tendency, and as the editor of the great *Encyclopædia*, in which, on account of the censorship of the press, he was obliged to play the part of a smuggler whenever he wanted to bring forward his own ideas. The *Encyclopædia* took up most of his time and energy. He carried it through, in the teeth of all opposition, with indomitable perseverance. The versatility of his interests is displayed here on a large scale, for not only did he write a series of philosophical articles but he also contributed articles on hand-industries and on factories which are based on thorough personal knowledge. This work denotes a turning-point in the history of civilisation, for by its means knowledge and enlightenment were conveyed to a wide circle of readers. Diderot could not, however, exhibit his own views in it. These are to be found in his correspondence (*i.e.* in the letters to Mademoiselle Voland, which give an interesting as well as a humorous description of the Radical salons in Paris) and in his dialogues (especially the *Entretien entre d'Alembert et Diderot* and in *Le rêve d'Alembert*) which appeared first in 1830 (under the title *Mémoires, correspondances, et ouvrages inédits*). It was not till the appearance of these works that the real Diderot was known. We shall concern ourselves here with his purely philosophical ideas only. Danish literature has recently received a valuable addition in Knud Ipsen's work on Diderot (*Diderot, hans Liev og hans Gerning*, Köbenhavn, 1891).

In his early writings Diderot still, in accordance with the popular theology of the day, employed the idea of God to explain what science seemed unable to explain. But it became increasingly evident to him that such an explanation is something quite other than what science understands by explanation. In his work *Interprétation de la nature* (1754) he asserts that the true method is a combination of perception and thought, induction and deduction, acting and reacting on one another, by which we pass from experience, through reason, back to experience again. He here repeats, too, in a more realistic spirit, questions on which he had already touched—particularly the great question as to how the purposive phenomena in Nature are to be explained. Instead of appealing to a cause beyond Nature he suggests the possibility that, from all eternity, elements endowed with the capacity of life and consciousness may have existed in the chaos of matter, and that these elements have gradually collected and, having passed through many grades of development, have at length become animals and men, while the formations and combinations less capable of sustaining life have been gradually scattered. Like La Mettrie, Diderot seems to have come upon these ideas partly under the influence of Lucretius, and partly in carrying out Leibniz' doctrine of a continuous and ascending scale of monads. This doctrine he combined with the results of the investigations of minute organisms arrived at by the naturalists of his day. If we must not exactly describe Diderot as Leibniz' disciple,[96] yet the influence which the founder of the doctrine of monads exercised upon him may be clearly traced. It is true he might have borrowed the idea of motion as an original quality from Toland, and it is also true that he might have taken the conception of the state of rest as a state of energy or tension (*nisus*), expressed in the short paper *Principes philosophiques sur la matière et le mouvement*, from others just as well as from Leibniz. But when Diderot, in his brilliant dialogue, " A Conversation between d'Alembert and Diderot," not only, like La Mettrie and several of his contemporaries among the natural philosophers, conceives the capacity of receiving sensations, sensibility, to be a general and essential quality of matter, but also, in the further carrying out of this thought, establishes a distinction between potential and actual sensibility (*sensibilité inerte—sensibilité active*), analogous to the distinction between "dead" and "living" force, we can hardly help recognising here the influence of one of the most important of Leibniz' ideas.   For Diderot, the life and the intelligence of Nature are everlasting.   They are never mere results or products of purely mechanical effects.   They existed in germ from the beginning ; it is only a question of whether the conditions necessary for development arise.   A transition from potential to actual forms takes place every time that the organism conveys nourishment to the blood and nerves! However great importance is to be attributed to external conditions, yet Diderot regards the inner original conditions as the essential ones.   The belief that out of one dead particle, by the addition of one, two, or three dead particles, a living system can be formed, is a huge absurdity!   A change in the disposition of particles able to produce consciousness!   No ; that which possesses life and consciousness has always possessed them, and will always possess them.   Why should not all nature be the same in kind?   The difference between the lower and higher grades, then, is only that that which, in the higher grades, exists in a concentrated form is, in the lower grades, scattered over a manifold of elements (Lettre à Mademoiselle Voland, 15th October 1759).   This thought is elaborated in the "Conversation between d'Alembert and Diderot," and in "D'Alembert's Dream," two dialogues which in virtue of their form, as well as of their content, rank among the classics of philosophy.

D'Alembert raises an objection which received no answer. Even if we attribute to the particles of matter an original capacity of receiving sensations (in potential form) how, by the conjunction of such particles, can a consciousness arise which has its seat in no one of these particles, but which corresponds to the aggregate of all the particles!   "Listen, philosopher," says d'Alembert, "I see the aggregate well enough, the web of small beings each one capable of feeling, but a living being, a whole, a system, a self with the consciousness of its own unity!   That I do not see; no, that I do not see."   It is thus clearly stated that here—in the origin of consciousness—lies a problem which is by no means solved by assuming sensibility to be a general property of matter. Diderot, then, acknowledges that the monads do not admit of a mechanical interpretation ; it is impossible to deduce the unity which characterises consciousness by the method of mechanical combinations. He does not always, however, retain the clear insight which sometimes illuminates him like a flash of lightning. Memory and comparison, in his view as in Condillac's, follow, as a matter of course, from particular sensations. Yet the objection raised showed how clearly Diderot had thought out the matter. He did not tread the ordinary path of materialism.

The difficulty of explaining the origin of consciousness falls the more easily into the background with Diderot, since all finite individuals, in virtue of their inner connection, form one great whole. " Do you not admit that everything in Nature is connected, and that it is impossible that there can be any break in the chain ? What do you mean, then, by your individuals ? There are no individuals, none at all. There is only one single, great individual ; the whole ? " So he passes from one extreme point of our knowledge to the other, from individuality to totality. For one moment he pauses, amazed at what he catches sight of there ; but his thought moves in altogether too violent oscillations for the problem to have time to establish itself.

Diderot's ethical ideas betray similar oscillations. He assumes a critical attitude towards Helvétius' attempt to explain all feeling as arising from the endeavour to further our own interest, and he believes a basis for the recognition of right and good is to be found in human nature—a basis which is never entirely lacking in any man. He defended this thesis with great enthusiasm in Holbach's salon, and in his earlier writings (especially in his elaboration of one of Shaftesbury's works) he develops the view that there is a special moral sense. But his letters clearly show that he afterwards abandoned this view. That which is called a moral instinct, and which appears in our involuntary actions or judgments of actions, is, in fact, the result of an infinite number of small experiences which began with life itself. A crowd of different motives here come into play, none of which, however, need come into consciousness in the moment of acting or judging. Everything in us rests on experience (*tout est expérimental en nous*); but we need not be conscious of these experiences (Lettres à Mdlle. Voland, 2nd Sept. 1762, 4th Oct. 1767). Among these unconscious or forgotten motives are also to be found those which concern ourselves, especially the desire for honour and imperishable fame (Diderot carried on a lively correspondence with the sculptor Falconet on the significance of this motive). We find, in Diderot, signs of an examination into the history of the development of the moral feeling, and it is especially interesting to note that his great enthusiasm for the " motives of great and noble minds" is not in the least degree weakened by his view that these motives are the fruit of a development on the soil of experience. But he did not succeed in applying this view in all cases—especially when he stands face to face with the precepts of ordinary social morality. Only in the individual—not in society—does he find a natural development. Society as it existed exhibited rules and institutions which appeared to him so contrary to reason, especially when he compared them with accounts of the life of savage peoples, that he could only suppose them to have arisen out of superstition and lust of power. Between the savage and the civilised man he could find no natural middle terms. How can a morality which is contradictory to nature have arisen, except through the slyness and arbitrariness of rulers? "Examine carefully all political, civil, and religious institutions; unless I am very much mistaken you will find that for centuries long the human race has bowed under a yoke imposed upon it by a parcel of rogues. Beware, above all things, of those who will introduce order. To set in order always means to set oneself up as ruler over other men by placing hindrances in their way" (*Supplément au voyage de Bourgainville*). It would be difficult to find a clearer evidence of how completely Diderot's time was lacking in the faculty of discovering historical connection. Even Diderot with his great aptitude for living into and feeling all sorts of circumstances could find no other explanation but arbitrariness and lust of power. The interval between the longing and striving of the individual and that exhibited by society, between the powers which each man felt within him and the narrow room in which the existing order allowed him to exercise them, was too great to render an understanding possible. From the future everything might be hoped, but the past held nothing beyond—knavery. Religious faith in particular seemed to Diderot nothing but a source of evils. It is something more than a joke when he says in a letter that he lays the blame on the gods rather than men.

Belief in God is no harmless matter ; it begets evil in two ways.   In the first place, it inevitably involves a form of worship, when ceremonies and theological dogmas soon take the place of natural morality, and deform its precepts.   Secondly, since the great suffering there is in this world is contrary to the idea of a good God, men are reduced to all sorts of absurdities and contradictions in order to palliate this fact. In the latter case religion is contrary to reason, in the former to morality (Lettres à Mdlle. Voland, 20th October 1760 and 6th October 1765).

Such questions were frequently discussed by Diderot in Holbach's *salon*, of which his letters give us a vivid picture. HOLBACH (1723-89) was a German Freiherr who had settled in Paris when quite young, and had drawn around him some of the leading Radical writers.   He occupied himself with chemistry, and also (probably under Diderot's influence) took up philosophic studies.   There can be no doubt that the views expressed by Diderot in the course of his frequent visits to Holbach, furnished the latter with the groundwork of the most important of his works, which has been called the Bible of materialism, *i.e.* the *Système de la nature*, which appeared pseudonymously in 1770.   The author states in the preface, too, that he has received the assistance of several friends.   In addition to Diderot, the mathematician LAGRANGE, who was tutor in Holbach's family, is said to have lent his aid.   Holbach himself supplied the systemisation.   For the book is materialism reduced to system, a task which neither La Mettrie nor Diderot, who were partly of a more inquiring, partly of a more playful turn of mind, had attempted.   It contains no really new thoughts. Its significance lies in the energy and indignation with which every spiritualistic and dualistic view was run to earth on account of its injuriousness both in practice and in theory.

Holbach shows at length that it would be necessary to believe in spiritual causes—in a God in relation to the world, in a soul in relation to the body—only if material nature were dead, passive, and incapable of moving itself.   But if there is no rest in Nature, if motion is a fundamental property of matter, where, in that case, is the necessity of spiritual causes? Moreover they explain nothing, and the appeal to them is only an expression of our ignorance ; we interpolate the soul or God where we are unable to discover the natural cause.   As

a matter of fact this appeal is merely a survival of the way in
which savage man explained natural phenomena through the
intervention of spirits. Every time that science attempts to
give a natural explanation, theology contends for a supernatural explanation. We know nothing of the spiritual except
that it is a quality connected with the brain. If any one
asks how the brain came by this quality, the answer is : " It is
the result of a disposition or combination peculiar to living
beings, in virtue of which a lifeless and insentient matter ceases
to be lifeless and obtains the capacity of feeling by being
taken up into the living being. This is what happens to milk,
bread, and wine, when these are taken up into the human
system " (*Système de la nature*, i. p. 105). We have already
met this comparison in Diderot. Holbach, however, as far as
we can see, did not agree with Diderot's view that the capacity
of receiving sensations is a fundamental property of matter ;
he mentions it, indeed, but retains the view that the capacity
of feeling originates in a combination of elements, each of
which, taken by itself, is not possessed of this capacity. On
this point there is a difference between Holbach and Diderot
which involves further consequences. For Holbach explains
thought (consciousness) itself as a motion, not, of course, a
molar motion, but a molecular motion, of the same kind as that
which underlies fermentation, nutrition, and growth—" motions
not indeed visible, but which we can infer from their effects "
(i. p. 15). In this motion, as in others resembling them, lies
much that is mysterious ; but the mystery does not vanish
when we assume a spiritual substance : " Let us rest content
with the knowledge that the soul is moved and modified by
those material causes which work upon her " (i. p. 118). All
science, then, is physics. Even ethics is only applied physics.
The imaginary duties and virtues, which were derived from the
relation of men to beings outside Nature, are now supplanted
by duties and virtues which are grounded in man's own nature.
The laws of Nature show us the way we must pursue to gain
our end. In this way the concept of duty arises out of the
concept of Nature ; for duty indicates precisely the way we
must necessarily take in order to reach our end (ii. p. 229).
Every individual seeks his own happiness ; Reason, " which is
nothing but physical science, applied to the behaviour of men
in society " (ii. p. 186), teaches him, however, that he cannot

be happy if he separates his own happiness from that of other men—for this is the decree of fate (*ordre du destin*)—while, on the other hand, he who makes others happy cannot himself be unhappy. In the last chapter of the work, which contains an "outline of natural law" (*abrégé du code de la nature*), these thoughts are expressed in enthusiastic language, in which some have thought they recognise the accents of Diderot.

The assumption of a twofold kind of being, spiritual and material, is, according to Holbach, the source of the greatest evils for men. At first, it is true, men arrived involuntarily at the belief in spirits; they did not know the causes of things and they very naturally, therefore, conceived them as personal beings. But it was priestly lust of power which first systematised this belief. The priests, moreover, recognised very clearly the power that the mysterious exercises over men. Accordingly they led them from the belief in visible gods (the sun and other natural objects) to the belief in invisible gods. Spiritualism is theoretically so unfounded that there can be no doubt "that this system is the fruit of a very deep and very interested theological policy" (i. 97): for now there is an invisible part of man which in a future world can receive its reward or its punishment! The theologians are the real makers of gods (*fabricateurs de la divinité*). "If we go back to the beginning we shall always find that ignorance and fear have created gods; fancy, enthusiasm, or deceit has adorned or disfigured them; weakness worships them; credulity preserves them in life; custom regards them and tyranny supports them in order to make the blindness of men serve its own ends." This passage (ii. p. 200) is an epitome of Holbach's philosophy of religion. He makes no distinction between natural and positive religion. If once the idea of God is admitted, a form of worship becomes a necessity; in this way the priests obtain the power, natural morality is defaced and persecution follows. At the same time ruminations on the reconciliation of evil with the existence of God lead to sophistical speculations. Holbach's line of reasoning here reminds us forcibly of Diderot's, which probably influenced the composition of this section. In religion, as in society, they encountered historical facts for which no natural basis could be found and with which they immediately felt themselves in irreconcilable contradiction. Hence they snatched at the theory of arbitrariness, which was apparently so simple.   Indeed it is so simple that it reminds us of the mythological theories of the childhood of the human race, which was precisely what the system of Nature was to exterminate : Holbach, with his cunning priests, introduced a new kind of mythological beings.

He touched a great problem : What value do religious ideas possess if they must no more, as in the childhood of the race, be used to fill up the lacunæ in our knowledge ?   The enlighten-ment philosophy was unable, however, on account of its im-perfect understanding of the forces of the religious life to supply an answer to this question.   If the belief in a divine world had really only been imposed from without on men,— had they been talked into it or had it arisen in any other way than out of the forces and needs of the human spirit itself,— there would be no religious problem, properly speaking, in existence.   It needed a new generation and a new age to take up this question again.   Rousseau—whose loneliness in his own age arose because he felt the sting of this problem earlier than any one else—was the only man to try his powers upon it.

Before we pass on, however, to describe this remarkable man, we must observe with regard to the *Système de la nature* that in the concept of Nature on which it rests there is a certain ambiguity.   On the one hand, Nature is defined as a being which exists in itself, is its own cause, its own eternal substance—that is to say, in accord with Spinozism. On the other hand (often in the same breath even, *e.g.* ii. p. 189) it is admitted that, in experience, we know efficient causes only, not first causes.   Here the concept of Nature is grounded on experience, there on a thought-construction.   But what validity has it in either of these forms ?   How far can experience take us ?   What authorisation do thought-construc-tions possess ?   Of its own enlightenment the enlightenment philosophy entertains no doubt ; does it not exist to enlighten others ?   And yet the future of philosophy rested on the discussion of such questions.   But the mental atmosphere of France was too disturbed to allow of its being undertaken.   In a remote university town in Germany, however, it was already in full course when the *Système de la nature* appeared.

CHAPTER IV

JEAN JACQUES ROUSSEAU

ROUSSEAU'S great work consists in this, that he brought into prominence the deep-lying foundation by means of which a decision could be arrived at between the enlightenment philosophy and the existing state of things. He asserts Nature and immediate feeling to be the basis of all determinations of worth, and demands of all culture and reflection which would transcend this basis that they exhibit their authorisation for doing so in developing and perfecting it; if they hinder and disfigure it they are evil. He is the first, in modern times, to state the problem of civilisation. Since the Renaissance the work of culture had proceeded briskly in all spheres; now a voice was raised asserting that there was something false in the whole movement. Rousseau's first philosophical work was occasioned by the offer of a prize on the part of a French provincial academy for the solution of the problem contained in the question "whether the restoration of the sciences and arts has contributed to purify manners?" The question pierced Rousseau's soul like a flash of lightning.

It seemed to him, he tells us, as if he saw an entirely new world, and as if he himself had become a new man! This new world was the world of personality, of living feeling, of the inner life. He suddenly perceived the incongruity between the world on one side, and the existing order and its critics on the other. Whether it was his original intention to answer the question in the negative, or whether Diderot's daughter is right in declaring that it was her father who advised him to do so, is a matter of no moment. The negative answer is only a formal paradox which Rousseau limited and explained in his correspondence and in his later works. The violent collision between

feeling, which in the long-run always determines our estimations, and the whole of the brilliant intellectual and æsthetic
development could only have taken place in Rousseau ; his personality and career had prepared the way for it.   JEAN JACQUES
ROUSSEAU was born 28th June 1712, of a fairly well-to-do
family in Geneva.   His up-bringing fostered imagination and
indefinite feeling ; while still quite young he developed what he
himself has called a romantic spirit (*esprit romanesque*) which
made him long for something transcending the present, and
find his greatest enjoyment in the world of possibilities.   After
a restless youth, characterised by the same romantic spirit as
that which coloured his imagination, he went to Paris, where
he managed to support himself by teaching, secretarial work,
and afterwards more especially by transcribing music.   Copy-
ing was to him what polishing optical glasses was to Spinoza.
He achieved a success with an opera and was drawn into a
dispute on the rival merits of Italian and French music.
There was nothing to indicate that he was destined one day to
become famous in the world of thought and to turn the course
of intellectual life into entirely new channels.   He had previously had opportunity of acquiring a certain amount of
general culture, and had also dabbled in philosophy.   As co-
operator in the great *Encyclopædia* he had the *entrée* into the
circle of " philosophers," who looked upon him as one of
themselves.   He was led into the paths of authorship by
writing the above-mentioned prize-essay.   His name became
known, and as he continued to discuss the problem which had
dawned upon him so suddenly, his attitude towards both the
great dissentient powers of the age—the assailants as well
as the defenders of the existing order—became increasingly
polemical.   A new prize-essay (*On the Origin of the Inequality between Men*) was the occasion of a detailed eulogy
of the state of Nature at the expense of civilisation.   As he
had formerly denied that the restoration of arts and sciences
had been beneficial, so now he denied that the substitution
of social and civilised life in place of the state of Nature had
been good.   Both these prize-essays show Rousseau on his
negative side only.   A new chapter of his life began when he
was able to retire into the solitude of the country.   His
Encyclopædist friends failed to understand him.   Something
was fermenting within him of which they, in spite of all their

criticism and talent, had no perception. Rousseau's enthusiasm and feeling for Nature which supported him during the
latter part of his life under great bodily sufferings, and in spite
of real and imaginary persecutions, are intimately associated
with his propensity to live in immediate feeling. His inner
life was so overwhelming that he found it difficult to clothe his
emotions in words. He was seldom, at any rate, able to find
the right word at the right moment, and this made him feel ill
at ease in drawing-rooms. To the acute, the refined, and the
articulate, in which the intellectual movement had culminated,
he opposed the simple, the broad, and the indefinite. He was
interested in the chaotic beginning of life, in the elements
which had not yet formed any clearly shaped world. While
wandering through the forests of St. Germain or Montmorency,
rhapsodising on freedom, he believed himself to be leading the
life of primitive man, before civilisation had destroyed the happy
state of immediacy.

The primitive and elementary, the great and simple relations of life, commanded his respect and afforded him joy.
He understood what was stirring in the breasts of the
stragglers in the army of civilisation, those whose enlightenment the Encyclopædists regarded as hopeless and whom
Voltaire spoke of as "*la canaille.*" He found in immediate
feeling something which all men may have in common, however diverse the development of their intellectual life. His
own ideas were the children of his feeling. He says of himself in the *Confessions*, that he felt before he thought. And in
his highest moments,—in the moments that came to him on
his lonely wanderings,—his heart swelled to such fulness, such
a host of vague feelings stirred within him, to such a degree
did he struggle to transcend all limitations, that no idea, no
representation, was adequate to the expression of his feelings.
He became convinced of the independence of feeling not only
through these states, in which it was almost entirely predominant, but also through its influence on ideas. His expectations of the future were gloomy, his memories of the past
cheerful ; the content was determined by the nature of his
mood. He thus learnt from personal experience the psychological truth that feeling is just as much an original and independent side of psychical life as knowledge, and that its
relation towards the latter is by no means merely passive and

receptive. The dark side of Rousseau's character shows itself
partly as sentimentality, partly as suspicion amounting to
madness. An unedifying example of the way in which feeling
can excite ideas, and, in order to find expression and interpretation, can weave them into a complex system, is offered by
one of Rousseau's latest works, *Rousseau juge de Jean Jacques*,
in which he describes the systematic persecutions on the part
of those who had once been his friends to which he believes
himself exposed. We find the same systematic construction,
which is here based on morbid feeling, in his famous works :
his philosophy, in fact, is what he himself says of his religious
beliefs, merely an exposition of his feeling (*exposition du
sentiment*).

Rousseau has developed the conception of life which he
opposes to the over-refinement and corruption of civilisation
in three works. In *La nouvelle Héloïse* (1761) he describes
strong and deep love, the beauty and dignity of marriage and
family life, the nobility of resignation, the fervour of religious
faith, the magnificence of Nature—subjects which had become
strange to the age in which he lived, which elicited from him
tones which had a new sound in the ears of his generation, and
which formed a great turning-point in poetical literature. In
Émile (1762) he expounds a system of education which, instead
of suppressing Nature, subserves the course of natural development, and at the same time he takes the opportunity to
develop his religious views. Finally, in the *Contrat social*
(1762), he unfolds his doctrine of an order of society which
must dissolve the tyranny under which man at present groans.

With these works Rousseau considered his mission accomplished. It was not granted to him, however, to lead the
peaceable life according to nature. His *Émile* was burnt in
Paris and a warrant of arrest was issued against its author.
Now began the unhappy period of Rousseau's life. He took
refuge in Switzerland, but there also he found no rest. Neither
in Geneva nor in Berne would the Government tolerate him ;
and in Neufchâtel he was insulted by the populace on account
of his religious views. He next accepted Hume's offer to find
him an asylum in England, but owing to his morbid state of
mind he soon grew suspicious of his English friends, and fled to
France once more, where he wandered about from place to
place till a sudden illness put an end to his life in 1778.

In order to discover Rousseau's real attitude towards the problem of civilisation we must not only take account of the paradoxical expressions contained in the two prize-essays, but must compare these with various passages in his letters and with the contents of his later writings. We then, in my opinion, find an astonishingly clear and important thought-sequence, the evidence of a deep psychological insight into the conditions of man's mental life.

He paints the state of Nature out of which man is torn by civilisation in anything but ideal colours. It is true he rejects Hobbes's description of it as a war of all with all, because, in his opinion, war presupposes wants which do not arise in the natural state, and also implies greater intercourse among men than would have been possible at such a stage. He considers, too, that Hobbes overlooked sympathy, which is a spontaneous and original human sentiment. For him, however, the state of Nature is a purely instinctive condition, the advantage of which over civilisation consists in the fact that between wants and the capacity to satisfy them there is a relation of equilibrium. Men are guided by the impulse to self-preservation (*amour de soi*), which they easily find means to satisfy. Emotion, imagination, and reflection have no meaning. It is only society and civilisation that arouse the faculty of comparison and reflection. But now the condition of equilibrium is disturbed. The impulse to self-preservation is satisfied at the expense of others, and so becomes egoism (*amour propre*).[97] There arise ideas of goods which cannot be attained, and with these the disproportion between needs and capacities comes into play. Men now begin to ponder on the value and significance of life, instead of following instinct. Disgust with life and suicide, which are unknown in the state of nature, become frequent. Fear of the future and of death disturbs all settled peace. Doubt, that insupportable condition, takes the place of the happy thoughtlessness of the natural state.

These disintegrating and unhappy effects, however, do not, according to Rousseau, immediately make themselves felt. If he were asked to say which stage in human development is to be regarded as the happiest, he would point, not to the primitive condition, but to the state of dawning social life and dawning civilisation which lies between the indolence of the primitive state and the petulant activity of our own self-love. This period was the real youth of the world, and ought never to have been abandoned. In it reflection and refinement had not yet exercised their corroding influence, while instinct had begun to yield before thought and feeling.[98] The most dangerous stage is the third ; here the destructive forces are in full activity. It is the stage of corrupt and refined civilisation.

If, however, we ask of Rousseau whether he thinks that men ought to return to that condition which lies so near the primitive state, his answer is that it is impossible—as impossible as to live one's own childhood over again.[99] We cannot remove error by returning to the state of ignorance. When once reflection has supplanted instinct the only thing to do is to substitute true and natural, in the place of false, knowledge. " Since men are corrupt it is at any rate better that they should be instructed than ignorant," says Rousseau in a letter (to Scheib, 15th July 1756), and with these words he practically justifies the Enlightenment, for they assert that intellectual culture does not increase but rather lessens depravity. He desires a civilisation which does not dissipate and weaken feeling and power ; a social life which does not take away our independence and exhaust itself in outward show. Only within himself, he says, can a man find peace. He only has lived much who has _felt_ life. Civilisation, however, brought doubt, enervation, outward show, and restlessness, while at the same time, owing to division of labour, it brought us slavery. Social unhappiness originated when one man perceived that he could use the labour of others, and when he employed the superfluous store which he had been able to accumulate for the maintenance of others. All these evils must be got rid of by means of a new order of life both for the individual and for society.

Rousseau's ideas concerning "the new world " fall under three heads, _i.e._ education, religion, and the State. He has expressed these ideas in _Émile_ and in the _Contrat social._ They met with opposition from the adherents of the old order, and derision from the adherents of the new. His works were burned by the authorities. Voltaire calls him an arch-fool (_archifou_). Diderot dubbed him "the great Sophist." And very naturally ; for neither side had pursued the problem to such a depth as Rousseau, neither had felt its innermost sting as he had. The supporters of the existing order relied upon a supernatural sanction, while the Encyclopædists believed themselves to have discovered the true enlightenment, and to have made it accessible to those who deserved it. Whereto, then, these paradoxes and schemes for the future?

In his theory of education Rousseau maintains that Nature must be given free play, and that the art of the educator consists in removing hindrances, and securing the best possible conditions under which the faculties and impulses may develop according to their own nature. No external culture must be imposed from without, either in the guise of authority or of enlightenment. Childhood, like every other period of life, has its end in itself, and must not be treated as a mere preparation. The child is unknown to us because, hitherto, he has only been regarded from the standpoint of the adult. He has a natural right to free self-development. Wrap him, therefore, in no swaddling clothes, suckle him with his own mother's milk, pamper him not, let him follow his own instinct of self-preservation and make his own experiences, teach him nothing that he can learn for himself, preach him no sermons, excite in him no wishes and needs before they can be satisfied! The longer mental development can be postponed the better. See to it that the mind is full-grown, so that its powers are not stunted by a too early use of them. Where possible, guide the child till his twelfth year so that he shall not know his right hand from his left; all the quicker will the eyes of his reason open when the time is come! Let him grow up—without prejudices, without habits, and without learning! Only in this way can we learn to know the child's own particular nature. The germ of character needs time to unfold itself; only when it has unfolded can we treat it rightly. Impulse and desire similarly require time to arise, and we shall only excite his disgust if we force upon the child what he is incapable of appreciating. In other words, education should be negative, not positive. "By positive I mean," says Rousseau (in the *Lettre à M. de Beaumont*, the great apology for *Émile*), "that system of education which aims at prematurely forming the mind and imparting to the child the knowledge of the duties of the man. By a negative education I mean that which aims at perfecting the organs, the instruments of our knowledge, before imparting knowledge, and which prepares the way for Reason by exercising the senses. Negative education is not inactive, far from it; it imparts no virtues, but provides against vice ; it does not teach the truth, but it guards from error ; it prepares the child for everything that can lead him to the truth when he is capable of understanding the truth, and to the good when he is capable of loving the good."

The conception of a negative education expresses Rousseau's fundamental thought in a remarkably striking manner. Culture must be natural development, not a sheath or heavy frame imposed from without. Only that culture is genuine which is Nature itself on a higher level of development. He therefore enjoins caution in introducing culture. Rousseau has a deeper insight into the characteristics of mental life than the adherents either of authority or of " Enlightenment." He regards that only which has developed naturally and which is the product of self-activity as genuine. Only by means of such a genuine development of culture can we abandon the quiet and careless age of instinct and yet retain the harmony between wants and capacities, between thought and feeling, between the outer and the inner. Like so many mystics he has a fine sense of the conditions of intellectual growth. His establishment of such a concept as that of negative education betrays this sense and is Socratic in character. And yet Rousseau shows himself a true child of his age. He has no real confidence in the involuntary use of our powers, for he sets a prudent tutor and a whole system of intrigues and prearrangements in motion in order that *Émile* may be exposed to no influences other than those which are supposed to be suitable to his age. This systematic construction within all spheres is characteristic of Rousseau. His vivid feeling and enthusiasm showed him things that are hidden from others ; but he cannot advance beyond the main outline : when he proceeds to carry out his thought in detail, we see how far removed he is from the real world. Instead of letting himself be guided in particulars by real experience, he gives free rein to his constructive powers. Even in *Émile's* wooing and marriage " *le gouverneur* " is always in the background arranging everything—and by no means always in a negative and indirect manner.

It is in accordance with the fundamental notion of Rousseau's theory of education that the conception of religion is not to be inculcated upon the child from without, but must be elicited from his own heart under the influence of its needs.

In the famous section on "The confession of faith of the Savoy pastor," which is interpolated in *Émile*, Rousseau gives us his religion. His religious ideas contain nothing new. He finds his feeling expressed in those of "natural religion" or "deism." He attempts no proof of the validity of these ideas, but lays them down as dogmas. Matter cannot get its motion from itself; the first cause of motion must be a personal will. In opposition to Condillac's doctrine, he maintains the essential difference between feeling and thought, while in opposition to materialism, he asserts the distinction between mind and matter as that of two different substances. In Rousseau's working out of these points several interesting observations occur, and it is of special interest historically that Rousseau's countryman, CHARLES BONNET, almost at the same time criticised in his psychological works (the most important of which is his *Essai analytique sur les facultés de l'âme*, Copenhague, 1760) Condillac's attempt to reduce all psychical life to passive sensation. We have, however, no ground for supposing that Rousseau was acquainted with these works. We find in Nature a striving after ends and a unity throughout the whole plan which witness to the activity of a personal God. Rousseau dissociates himself here, however, from the current "watch-maker philosophy" of the time by asserting that this harmony and purposiveness in Nature is not his ground for believing in God. The converse is rather the case. His belief springs out of an immediate necessity of feeling. The state of doubt is to him insupportable. When his reason wavers his faith decides the matter on her own account. And not until he has thus been led by subjective feeling to believe, can he find indications in Nature which point in the same direction as his dogmas.

Although the "Savoy pastor" constantly attempts to show how natural and reasonable his assertions are, yet, on the other hand, he is always explaining that he does not wish either to philosophise or to dogmatise, but merely to describe what he feels, and he invites his hearers to seek in their own feelings for a confirmation of his assertions. Decision must be made from the practical standpoint of feeling. He would never have pondered on the existence of God were it not that he had been forced to do so "from the feeling of the relation in which God stands to him."[100] It is more particularly, however, in his famous letter to Voltaire (18th Aug. 1756), occasioned by the latter's

poem on the destruction of Lisbon, that Rousseau defends the
inner subjective origin of faith; he does not believe in God
because everything in the world is good, but he finds some
good in everything because he believes in God.   He rests his
defence of optimism against the criticism of Voltaire contained in this letter, principally upon the fact that the great
elementary relations of life contain sources of joy and satisfaction to which the *blasé* man of the world is a stranger.   He lays
especial weight upon "the sweet feeling of existence" (*le doux
sentiment de l'existence indépendamment de toute autre sensation*).   At the same time he assumes that the ills of the
individual may be necessary for the world as a great whole,
and he finds ultimate consolation in the belief in immortality.
The real foundation of the optimism which, in spite of his
weak health and his narrow circumstances, he defends against
a Voltaire living in honour, riches, and magnificence, is his own
personal surrender to the religious sentiment.   It is this which
enables him to rejoin to Voltaire, "You enjoy, but I hope"!
In the matter of content Rousseau's religion did not differ from
that of Voltaire; "natural religion" was common to both.
But what a difference in sincerity and frame of mind!
Rousseau's transference of the religious problem from the sphere
of external observation and explanation of the world back to
inner personal feeling and to the way in which this is determined
by life, marked an epoch.   The goal which Pascal, on account
of his Catholic dogmatism, was unable to reach, Rousseau
approached more nearly, in spite of his deistic dogmatism.
For he, too, is a dogmatist in virtue of the haste with
which he casts anchor in the spiritualism of the Cartesians
and in the theology of the deists.   Here, as so often in
philosophy, it is not his results but his motivation which is
new and of lasting value.   And the motivation is closely bound
up with the relation of dependence—of such importance for
Rousseau's personality and mode of thinking—in which ideas
stand to feeling and wants.   The last word of the "Savoy
pastor" is as follows: "Keep thy soul in such a condition that thy
wish is always that God exists ; then wilt thou never doubt it!"

   That Rousseau's dogmas take the particular form in which
he exhibits them is, however, not merely a consequence of the
manner in which he interprets his feeling.   He subjects ideas
to a criticism.   In a letter (to M——, 15th January 1769) he

says he has thought out the different systems, and has decided in favour of the one which seemed to him to involve the fewest difficulties. Thus he here concedes to thought a reciprocal influence on the postulate of feeling. If *e.g.* his experience of the suffering there is in the world did not destroy his belief in a good God this was because, in virtue of the doctrine of two substances (mind and matter), he assumed that matter imposes limits to the carrying out of the divine ends. He believed, not in a creation, but in an ordering of already existing and perhaps eternal matter. The God who orders and guides is good, but He is not omnipotent (see the above-mentioned letter and the *Lettre à M. Beaumont*). Here too, then, Rousseau arrives at the same results as Voltaire, although the two men envisage the problem of evil in the world in a very different temper of mind. Rousseau's religion consists, properly speaking, in joy and enthusiasm at finding in the world traces of a power which works for good. He does not believe that prayer can have physical effects. His prayer is an outburst [101] of enthusiasm, in which joy in Nature passes over at its height into a hymn of praise to " the great Being " who works in all things and for whom thought can find no adequate concept ; this enthusiasm finally becomes an ecstasy, in which his fervour and depth of feeling are beyond words, for feeling soars beyond all limits (3rd letter to Malesherbes). The independence of feeling over against knowledge which Rousseau here asserts comes to light in the fact that, at its height, feeling can find no ideas which express it satisfactorily. From this it is only a step to the confession that all religious ideas, all dogmas, are symbols—a step, however, which Rousseau was precluded from taking by his deistic dogmatism.

He opposes his natural religion, which he regards as independent of all tradition, to positive religion. He is persuaded that had men only remained faithful to the guidance of their hearts they would never have had any other religion but this. But he cherishes the conviction that, in his religion, he has room for the real essence of Christianity. To the Archbishop of Paris he writes : (*Lettre à M. de Beaumont*) : " Monseigneur, I am a Christian, and a Christian at heart, according to the teaching of the Gospels. I am a Christian, not as a pupil of the priests, but as a pupil of Jesus Christ. My Master speculated very little concerning dogmas ; He enjoined good works rather than many articles of faith ; He demanded belief in that only which was necessary to make men good." He thus left the riddle of Christianity unanswered ; it did not concern the important point, *i.e.* the essence of morality. If we lay weight on that which transcends this essence and on definite dogmatic formulæ we shall end in unreasonableness, falsehood, hypocrisy, and tyranny. And are we to believe that it is God who demands all this dogmatic learning, and over and above that, has condemned those who have no wish for such learning to hell fire ? These positive dogmas are only to be learnt out of books which men have written and men have vouched for. The Gospel is the most sublime of all books, but still it is but a book. Not on the leaves of a book but in the hearts of men has God written His law (Letter to Vernes, 25th March 1758). Rousseau had been persuaded in his youth to go over to Catholicism. Afterwards he returned to Protestantism and took part in its worship, reserving to himself the right of the Protestant laity to freely subject all dogmas to the test of the approval of conscience and of the heart. He was naturally accused by both Churches of heresy, while the Encyclopædists regarded him as a hypocrite or a muddle-headed fellow who would end his days as a Capuchin. He calls himself the only man of his age who believed in God.

The third sphere in which Rousseau believed he descried a new world was the social and political. Here, too, it is evident that he has not abandoned the hope that in place of the stunting and suppression of Nature might be substituted a development in which Nature would come by her rights. In his *Contrat social* (i. 8) he expresses himself emphatically on the progress which has been made since man gave up the natural condition and, in accordance with a (tacit) contract, entered upon social life. " Although in the civil state he is deprived of many advantages that he derives from Nature, he acquires equally great ones in return : his faculties are exercised and developed; his ideas are expanded; his feelings are ennobled; his whole soul is exalted to such a degree that, if the abuses of this new condition did not often degrade him below that from which he has emerged, he ought to bless without ceasing the happy moment that released him from it for ever, and transformed him from a stupid and ignorant animal into an intelligent being and a man."

Rousseau's theory of the philosophy of rights forms the conclusion of a long series of attempts begun during the struggle for the Reformation, which all aim at constructing the State out of the free transference of the power of individuals. The idea of the social contract did not originate with Rousseau, but he availed himself of it in order to be able to depict society as having arisen in accordance with nature ; in the state of nature men had lived in isolation, the only transition to civil life which could make the State natural, therefore, is voluntary association, free transference. By means of the latter the nation as such comes into existence, since the individual transfers his absolute power over himself to the people as a whole. The sovereignty of the people is absolute and inalienable. Rousseau transfers Hobbes's conception of absolute sovereignty to the people as a whole. He agrees with Hobbes that the sovereignty can have one seat only, but instead of assuming, as he does, that, with the social contract, an immediate subjection to the governing power takes place, he, like Althusius, of whom his language reminds us,[102] proclaims the principle of the sovereignty of the people, and assumes that the "general will" includes within it the will of all individuals. Like Althusius, too, he distinguishes between the form of the State and the form of government, and while he admits only one single form of the State, he recognises various forms of government. The best is that of an elective aristocracy. But he rejects the division of power, and denies that the sovereignty can be exercised through representatives. The highest power is and remains with the people, who must from time to time assemble in order to give laws. As soon as the people are assembled all jurisdiction ceases, all executive power is suspended. The legislative power—as identical with the nation itself—is sovereign ; the executive is its handmaid. The legislative power is the heart, the executive is the brain ;—a man may continue to live when the latter is injured, provided the former be unhurt.

The condition for the exercise of the sovereignty of the people is, according to Rousseau, that the whole nation can be assembled. On this account the State must not be large. Rousseau's ideal states were—in addition to Geneva, his fatherland—the city-states of the ancients. The only form under which the sovereignty of the people can exist in a large state is that of a federal constitution.

Rousseau had written a treatise on this form of constitution which he entrusted to a friend, who destroyed it on the outbreak of the Revolution, for fear it should work mischief! It was, as Rousseau remarks, "an entirely new subject, the principles of which had yet to be established." Shortly before the French Revolution this subject was discussed in *The Federalist* by Alexander Hamilton, the founder of the constitution of the North American Union. The leaders of the French Revolution, who took many of their catchwords from other passages of the *Contrat social*, disregarded both the above-mentioned indication of how the advantages of a large state may be combined with those of a small one, those of centralisation with those of decentralisation, and also the practical attempt in this direction which was being made on the other side of the ocean.[103] They contented themselves with that part of Rousseau's doctrine which demands that the individual should merge his will completely in the general will, which announces itself in the decisions of the majority and has full power over the life and property, the education and religious exercises of all citizens. Hobbes makes the individual abdicate in favour of the sovereign governing power, while Rousseau makes him abdicate in favour of the sovereign democracy.

There is a decided discrepancy between Rousseau's essay on the origin of inequality (1755) and his *Contrat social* (1762)—a discrepancy, however, of which he himself was very well aware. On a closer examination it becomes evident that he meant the later exposition to complete and improve upon the earlier. He shows in the *Discours* that economic inequality originates in the division of labour, and that it was only after this, that the formation of the State by contract sanctioned and emphasised the distinction between rich and poor. "Laws," he says (*Discours*, p. 95), "gave the weak new burdens and the strong new powers ; they irretrievably destroyed natural freedom, established in perpetuity the law of property and of inequality, turned a clever usurpation into an irrevocable right, and brought the whole future human race under the yoke of labour, slavery, and misery."

Here then the original contract is conceived as sanctioning inequality. In the *Contrat social*, on the other hand, he says (i. 9) : " Instead of destroying natural equality, the fundamental

pact, on the contrary, substitutes a moral and lawful equality
for the physical equality which nature imposed upon men, so
that, although unequal in strength or intellect, they all become
equal by convention and legal right."

Rousseau adds in a note that it is a sign of a bad government when this equality is merely apparent ; he confesses that
the social state is, as a matter of fact, advantageous to men
only so far as they all have something, and none of them has
too much.   There can be no doubt that Rousseau intends in
these words to show how the later exposition may be reconciled
with the earlier.   Moreover it is true, as he says, that law and
right may be used in both ways, *i.e.* both to confirm as well as
to annul existing relations of inequality.   In the *Discours* he
is considering the matter from the first point of view only, which,
in the old state of society, was also the more apparent ; in the
Contrat social, which describes an ideal, and therefore dis-
regards actual relations,[104] he takes up the other side, and lays
especial stress on what ought to be done ; precisely because the
course of things (even in the state of nature, as the *Discours*
shows) always tends to destroy equality, precisely on that
account—he says in the *Contrat social* (ii. 11)—must the
legislative power always strive to maintain it.   It must see to
it that no man becomes rich enough to be able to buy another,
and none poor enough to be forced to sell himself.   That this
view contains nothing visionary has been shown by later times,
for the equalisation of social extremes has become increasingly
recognised as an essential duty of the State.   Rousseau was no
socialist, but he had a clear perception of the influence of social
inequalities and of the evils arising out of the system of private
property.   He transcends in a higher degree than any former
teacher of natural right, mere formal, political principles, and
behind all constitutional questions he found the social question.
For *one* subject only was he, like all his contemporaries, blind,
i.e. for the importance of free associations.   Once the State
has arisen, it must regulate everything.   Rousseau here comes
into conflict with himself.   For in *Émile* it was precisely on
individual development, on the evolution of the natural character
of each man, that he laid weight ; but how is this possible under
the tyranny of the " general will " ?   We must not be astonished
that Rousseau did not perceive the great problem here involved ;
for, in his time, the arbitrariness of the old *régime* was at its

height, and neither the general nor the individual will could make itself felt; he aimed at emancipating them both—and he could afford to leave it to the future to reconcile them with one another.   He had set the age in which he lived problems enough.

In the history of philosophy Rousseau occupies a position which offers a certain analogy with that of Leibniz.   Both emphasise the ethical problem ; they are neither of them content with the mechanical explanation of Nature and with the mechanical ordering of society, but seek to discover the significance of Nature and of society for human feeling, the source of all estimation of worth.   And closely connected with this with both of them is the emphasis they lay on the rights of individuality, and their sense of the inner infinity of every individual.   But these thoughts were carried out by these two very different minds in very different manners.   Leibniz attempted to retain the scientific conception of Nature by conceiving the laws of Nature which it had discovered as expressions of the harmony between the self-development of innumerable individual beings.   The gradual transition from darkness to clearness was the fundamental law of all development in this harmonious world-picture.   For poor Jean Jacques it was not so easy to find the harmony, either within or without his *ego*. In his ecstatic moments he believed in it,—saw it before his mental eyes.   But his monads had within them a dark depth which so far from becoming illuminated became ever darker, and neither in the world, nor in society, was he able to reduce all things to an intellectual harmony.   His feeling was too strong to be explained as confused thought.   Hence he maintained the rights of the irrational.   By way of personal experience of life he finally arrived at the same result which Hume had reached by way of epistemology ; for Hume, too, had asserted that all our knowledge is based upon unprovable assumptions.   Whether regarded from the practical or theoretical side, therefore, philosophy offered no lack of problems to him who should succeed in carrying it further.

NOTES

NOTES

1. p. 16. As, in addition to older authors, G. SPIEKER, *Leben und Lehre des Petrus Pomponatius:* Munich, 1868, p. 8 and f. See, on the other hand, F. FIORENTINO, *Pietro Pomponazzi:* Florence, 1868, p. 30. Fiorentino thinks, however, that Pomponazzi's later works disclose a less zealous subjection to faith,—an effect of constant and continuous criticism.

2. p. 29. In my treatise, "Montaigne's Betydning i Etikens Historie," *Det nittende Aarhundrede*, 1876 ("The Significance of Montaigne in the History of Ethics," *The Nineteenth Century*, 1876), I have already developed this view of Montaigne. In his work, *Skepticismen som Led i de aandelige Bevägelser siden Reformationen:* Kòbenhavn, 1890 (Scepticism as a Factor in the Intellectual Movement since the Reformation: Copenhagen, 1890), STARCKE has described Montaigne entirely from the negative and sceptical side. As I tried to show in my treatise, *Trivlens Historie i nyere Tid:* Tidskueren, 1891 (The History of Scepticism in Modern Times), there is no doubt that Starcke, in his excellent book, lays too great stress on the sceptical ideas of a series of authors in the sixteenth and seventeenth centuries.—DILTHEY ("Auffassung und Analyse des Menschen im 15. und 16. Jahrhundert," *Archiv für die Geschichte der Philosophie*, 1891, p. 647 and f.) emphasises, as I do, the fact that Montaigne's scepticism only serves as a means to prepare the way for the belief in Nature.

3. p. 30. "Qui se présente comme dans un tableau cette grande image de nostre mère nature en son entière majesté ; qui lit en son visage une si générale et constante variété ; qui se remarque là dedans, et non soy, mais tout un royaume, comme un traict d'une poincte très délicate, celuy-là seul estime les choses selon leur juste valeur" (*Essais*, i. 25).

4. p. 36. Almost contemporaneously with Vives' work appeared another psychological work, which also exercised great influence on the conceptions of the following age, although it possesses neither such lasting interest nor such important principles as the former, namely, MELANGTHON'S *Liber de anima:* Vitebergae, 1540. Melancthon is much nearer Aristotle than Vives ; his exposition is far more theological, and he cannot compare with the Spanish psychologist in the art of observation and description.

5. p. 40. On Luther's shifting standpoint with regard to philosophy, see F. BAHLOW, *Luther's Stellung zur Philosophie:* Berlin, 1891.

6. p. 48. O. GIERCKE (*Johannes Althusius und die Entwickelung der naturrechtlichen Staatstheorien:* Breslau, 1880, p. 58) points out that this doctrine of ephors originated with the *Monarchomachen*, indeed with

504	A HISTORY OF MODERN PHILOSOPHY

Calvin himself, who regarded the magistracy as a divine institution, although he adds that where there are magistrates, *e.g.* the Spartan ephors, the Roman tribunes, and the estates of modern kingdoms, to defend the right of the people against the cupidity and caprice of princes, it is their duty as well as their right to set aside the will of princes, when it is unconstitutional. Cf. also LOBSTEIN, *Die Ethik Calvins*, p. 117 and f.

7. p. 55. Grotius establishes the wrongfulness of lying by means of a tacit contract, which coincides with the origin of speech (*De jure belli ac pacis*, iii. 1, 11). P. C. KIERKEGAARD'S theory (in his dissertation, *De vi atque turpitudine mendacii*), which grounds the condemnation of lying in the necessity of preserving confidence in the sense of words, reminds us of Grotius' doctrine, when this is stripped of its setting in the mythological theory of contract.

8. p. 57. Cf. HENRY MAINE, *International Law :* London, 1888, p. 23 and f.

9. p. 60. On the tendency to a universal theism in the Italian Renaissance cf. BURCKHARDT, *Die Kultur der Renaissance in Italien*, 4th ed. vol. ii. p. 236 and f. ; 300 and f. On Franck and Coornhert cf. the interesting characterisations of DILTHEY in the *Archiv für Gesch. d. Phil.* 1892, pp. 389-400 ; 487-93.

10. p. 65. *Autobiography of Edward Lord Herbert of Cherbury*, edited by Sidney L. Lee : London, 1892, p. 248 and f.

11. p. 76. Boehme's expression is "Auswickelung." The term " Entwickelung" did not appear till later (in the eighteenth century, in Tetens). Cf. EUCKEN, *Geschichte der philosophischen Terminologie :* Leipzig, 1879, p. 127.

12. p. 80. Aristotle expounds his scheme of the world in his work *On the Universum* (περὶ οὐρανοῦ). See especially i. 3, 8, 9 ; ii. 1, 4, 6.

13. p. 88. Cf. *De docta ignorantia*, ii. 2, 3. I do not enter further here into the modifications of Cusanus' ideas which appear in his later works (*Possest* and *De apice theoriae*), in which he emphasises particularly the activity of the highest principle and conceives this principle as the unity of possibility and actuality, and afterwards more especially as force (*posse*). Cf. on this point, F. FIORENTINO, *Il resorgimento filosofico nel Quattro cento :* Napoli, 1885, p. 136 and f. ; AXEL HERRLIN (*Studier i Nicolaus af Cues' Filosofi, med särskilt afseende på dens historiska betydelse :* Lund, 1892, p. 22 (Studies in the Philosophy of Nicolaus Cusanus, with especial reference to its historical significance) denies that the standpoint of the *Possest* is other than that of the *Docta ignorantia*. But it seems to me that Fiorentino's view is confirmed by the fact that in the *Docta ignorantia* (i. 26) Cusanus expressly declares that the Infinite neither begets, nor is begotten, nor proceeds (*Infinitas neque generans, neque genita, neque procedens*), while in the *Possest* he attributes very great importance to its activity. I admit that too much weight must not be laid on this distinction, since in all his works Cusanus operates with the relation *complicatio-explicatio*, and, so far, he can at no stage abstract from working and proceeding.

14. p. 88. RICHARD FALCKENBERG (*Grundzüge der Philosophie des Nicolaus Cusanus :* Breslau, 1880, p. 54) points out that the relation *complicatio-explicatio* has quite another meaning when applied to God's relation to the world (where it denotes the transition from a higher to a

lower) than when it is used in reference to the world (where it denotes the transition from lower grades of Nature to higher).

15. p. 90. LUDWIG LANGE (in his interesting treatise, "Die geschichtliche Entwickelung des Bewegungsbegriffes," *Philosophische Studien*, Herausg. von W. Wundt, iii. p. 350) remarks that, as the precursor of Copernicus, the idea of the relativity of place and of motion must lie especially near to Cusanus. But the converse is really rather the case: it was the idea of the relativity of place and of motion which made him the precursor of Copernicus.

16. p. 93. With regard to PARACELSUS (whose real name was Theophrastus Bombastus von Hohenheim) I must refer my readers to CHR. SIGWART'S excellent characterisation (*Kleine Schriften*, i.). Paracelsus was born in 1493 at Einsiedeln in Switzerland, and, after a very unsettled life, died at Salzburg in 1541. On his significance as chemist and physician see ERNST V. MEIER, *Geschichte der Chemie*, Leipzig, 1889, pp. 57-61.—JULIUS PETERSEN, *Hovedmomenter af den medicinske Lägekunsts historiske Udvikling* (The Chief Moments in the Historical Development of the Healing Art of Medicine), Köbenhavn, 1876, pp. 21-24.—CARDANUS (born at Pavia, 1501, died in Rome in 1576) is more interesting in his *Autobiography*—remarkable on account of its candour, and one of the most important documents belonging to the period of the Renaissance—than he is in his works, of which the most important (*De subtilitate*) is a chaotic mixture of profundity, fantasticalness, and superstition. He credits himself with great powers of observation (*De vita propria*, Kap. 23) both in science as well as in practical matters; indeed he even, in a chapter in the *Autobiography* especially dedicated to the recital of his scientific merits (*De vita propria*, Kap. 44: Quae in diversis disciplinis digna adinveni) says of himself that within the sphere of natural science he had "reduced the observation of things in Nature to a definite art and method, which, before him, had been attempted by no one." This honour, however, history has not confirmed to him.

17. p. 96. FIORENTINO has collected the manuscripts which contain Patrizzi's observations on Telesio's book, and Telesio's reply to the same. See the addenda to the second volume of his work, *Bernardino Telesio. Studi storici su l' idea della natura nel risorgimento italiano*: Firenze, 1872.

18. p. 98. *De rerum natura*, vii. 2 (cf. v. 7). In one single passage Telesio has defined *sensus* without the interpolation of *perceptio* as a middle term, for in viii. 21 he explains *sentire* as "a rerum viribus exile quid pati." There lies here, then, an ambiguity in the word *pati*.

19. p. 101. It may appear as a contradiction that wisdom is declared to be the universal virtue (*virtus universalis*, ix. 6), and magnanimity as the whole of virtue (*virtus tota*, ix. 22), since the two virtues are not identical. Telesio must have meant that wisdom is a co-operative condition in every individual virtue (since it is always a question of finding the means to self-preservation), but that magnanimity (which is called the summit of all virtues, *omnium virtutum veluti apex*) completes the list of virtues as that quality of character in which all virtues in their most perfect form are contained. I do not here discuss Telesio's polemic, grounded in a misapprehension, against Aristotle's doctrine of virtue as habit. That a naturalistic tendency must be the source of this polemic (FIORENTINO, *Bernardino Telesio*, i. p. 316 and f.) I am not able to perceive.

20. p. 104. JOACHIM RHETICUS, *Narratio prima* (in the Thorn edition of Copernicus' work, *De revolutionibus orbium coelestium*, 1873, p. 490).—KEPLER'S utterance on Copernicus is quoted by RENSCHLE, *Kepler und die Astronomie:* Frankfurt, 1871, p. 119.—GALILEI on Kepler: *Opere*, Firenze, 1842, and f. ; vii. p. 55.

21. p. 107. Copernicus laid down the principle of simplicity in his first sketch (*Commentariolus*, see PROWE, *Nicolaus Coppernicus* : Berlin, 1883, i. 2, p. 286 and f.), as also in his great work *De revolutionibus* (i. 10). The Principle of Relativity, *De revolutionibus*, i. 5, 8.

22. p. 107. This was the chief difficulty which deterred Tycho Brahe from fully concurring with Copernicus. See his letter to Kepler, December 1599 (*Kepleri Opera omnia*, ed. Frisch, i. p. 47). Galilei also found this the greatest difficulty in the Copernican system, and strove to eliminate it in his " Dialogues on the World-Systems."

23. p. 108. This explanation, which Bruno and Galilei adopted from Copernicus, and which he himself probably took from Plutarch (who says somewhere that the earth draws heavy things to itself, not because it is a centre, but because it is a totality) is, as EMIL STRAUSS, Galilei's German translator, remarks (*Galilei's Dialoge*, Uebers. von E. Strauss : Leipzig, 1891, p. 499), the antique surrogate of a theory of gravitation.

24. p. 109. GIORDANO BRUNO, *Cena de le ceneri*, iii. (Opere italiane, ed. Lagarde, Gottinga, 1888, i. pp. 150-2).—KEPLER, *Opera*, ed. Frisch, i. p. 245 and f.

25. p. 110. The chief sources for the life of Bruno are the papers of the Inquisition during his trial in Venice, which were first published by DOMENICO BERTI in his biography of Bruno (Turin, 1868). Berti afterwards published fragments of the trial in Rome.—CHR. SIGWART has collected evidences of Bruno's appearance at the German Universities (*Tübinger Osterprogramm*, 1880, and *Kleine Schriften*, i.).—DUFOUR (*Giordano Bruno à Genève*, Genève, 1884) has published documentary evidence of Bruno's sojourn in Geneva.

26. p. 115. Berti (*Giordano Bruno da Nola*, nuova edizione, Torino, 1889, p. 196 and f.) agrees with some German authors in believing that Bruno influenced Shakespeare either through mutual acquaintances or by his works. Shakespeare did not come to London until a year after Bruno had left it. As ROBERT BEYERSDORF (*Giordano Bruno und Shakespeare* : Oldenburg, 1889) has shown, however, such influence is highly improbable. The point seems to me to be decided by the fact that there is no trace in Shakespeare of the new astronomical ideas of which Bruno was the prophet. And yet what scope they would have afforded to the Shakesperian imagination ! Beyersdorf very neatly sets forth the different views taken by Bruno and Shakespeare respectively of the idea of the continuous change and flux of natural phenomena. The poet saw in it a witness to the poverty and nothingness of human existence, while to the thinker it revealed the unity and eternity of Nature, glorious in the midst of change. It should be noticed here, however, that Bruno, as will be shown in more detail below, also perceived the bitter and painful side of the struggle of opposites. This comes out especially in his *De gl' Heroici Furori*, and here Bruno differs—in spite of all his Neo-Platonism—from Plato.

27. p. 121. A friend of Berti's took advantage of the Revolution of 1849 to make copies of the papers giving an account of Bruno's trial at

Rome, but had not time to finish them. Until recently it was supposed that the remainder of the papers connected with the trial must be among the archives of the Inquisition in the Vatican. But the inquiry of Dr. Güttler, a German student of Bruno, solicited from the Vatican a definite statement that neither the papers nor the confiscated manuscripts are to be found in the archives and that it is not known what has become of them. See on this point *Archiv für Gesch. d. Phil.* vi. p. 344 and f.

28. p. 121. SCHOPPE, a German *savant*, who had become converted to Catholicism and was an eye-witness of Bruno's condemnation and death, in a description glowing with hatred towards heresy, names among "abominable and altogether absurd doctrines" the hypothesis of countless worlds. If, at the Pope's command, the Inquisition had taxed Bruno with the fact that the eight propositions, selected from his writings, had been already declared, by the oldest Church, to be heretical, it is quite possible that the hypothesis of a plurality of worlds may have been included among these old heresies. Galilei was indeed afterwards obliged to abjure, on the Holy Writ, the doctrine of the motion of the earth. By the Protestants the belief in a plurality of worlds was considered heretical. MELANCTHON combats it as a godless doctrine, since Christ could not have died and risen again several times over (*Initia doctrinae physicae*, Corp. Ref. xiii. p. 220 and f.); CAMPANELLA, on the other hand, tries to prove in his *Apologia pro Galilaeo* (Francofurti, 1620, pp. 9, 51) that this doctrine is not heretical.

29. p. 128. Bruno had already, in his *De l' infinito universo e mundi* (ed. Lagarde, p. 343 and f., 363) rejected the fixed spheres on physical and epistemological grounds. In the *De immenso*, i. 5, he finds his view confirmed by Tycho's investigations. Tycho himself drew the same consequences from his doctrine as did Bruno. Thus he says in a letter to Kepler, dated April 1598 (*Kepleri Opera*, ed. Frisch, 1858, i. p. 44): "In my opinion, the reality of all the spheres, however they may be conceived, is to be excluded from the heavens; this I have learnt from all the comets which have appeared since the new star of 1572, and which are in truth heavenly phenomena" (according to the old view comets were due to the evaporation of the earth, and moved within the sublunary world only). As F. TOCCO (*Opere latine di G. Bruno esposte e confrontate con le italiane*, Firenze, 1889, p. 318 and f.) remarks, Bruno's acquaintance with Tycho's works was probably not first hand, since he nowhere uses the excellent argument against the fixed spheres afforded by the "new stars," which Galilei himself used later. Bruno also nowhere mentions Tycho's peculiar world-system.

30. p. 133. An interesting anticipation of Goethe's famous words, "IHM ZIEMT'S, die Welt im Innern zu bewegen," occurs in the *De immenso*, v. 12. "God or Reason does not stand without and let the world move round; for the inner principle of motion which is the real nature, the real soul, which possesses everything, that lives in His bosom and in His body, must be WORTHY of Him" (DIGNIUS ENIM ILLI DEBET ESSE internum principium motus, etc.). Of this principle, which lies at the root of the impulse to self-preservation of every creature, Bruno uses, in the last work we possess from his hand, viz. the *Summa terminorum metaphysicorum*, dictated during his sojourn in Zurich in 1591, the expression VOLUNTAS NATURALIS; cf. *Cena*, ed. Lagarde, p. 163 and f.; 183 and f.; *De l' infinito*, p. 370 and f.

31. p. 135. With regard to the question as to the relation between the spiritual and the material Bruno expresses himself differently in his different works. In the *Cena*, p. 189, he does not inquire into whether spiritual substance can be transformed into material substance and the converse or not. In the *De la causa*, p. 235 and f. (cf. *Spaccio*, p. 409), it is said that spiritual *just as much as* material substance persists through all change. At the same time the *De la causa*, pp. 261 and 280 and f., maintains the absolute unity of substance, explaining the difference between spiritual and material substance as due to a differentiation (explication) only. Finally, in the *De gl' Heroici Furori*, p. 721, he expressly denies the transformation from material to spiritual and the reverse. Not only the contrast between spirit and matter, but also that between freedom and necessity must, according to Bruno, fall away in the highest principle, as he shows in a series of remarkable propositions in the *De immenso*, i. 11, 12.

32. p. 139. Bruno's atomism or doctrine of monads is to be found in the didactic poem *De triplici minimo*, which appeared at Frankfurt in 1591. It occupies, as LASSWITZ (*Geschichte der Atomistik :* Hamburg and Leipzig, 1889, i. pp. 359-399) points out, an interesting place in the history of the development of modern atomism. Lasswitz, however, it seems to me, has not perceived the contradiction between Bruno's polemic against infinite divisibility and his doctrine of the relativity of the concept of atoms. FELICE TOCCO who first (in the *Opere latine di G. Bruno*) supposed Bruno to have applied his atomism within the psychical sphere also, afterwards modified his opinion (in a work entitled *Opere inedite di G. Bruno :* Napoli, 1891). He here taxes Bruno with inconsistency in not assuming psychical as well as material atoms. But the great question is whether the concept of atoms can be suitably applied to the spiritual side of existence at all ; and it was, perhaps, a true instinct which deterred Bruno from undertaking such an application, even though, had he only held fast to the relativity of the concept of atoms, it could not have embraced all the consequences which, at the first glance, it might appear to do. TOCCO (*Opere latine di G. Bruno*, p. 353) remarks, with regard to the expression "monas monadum" (of God) that it is not clear whether God thus becomes separated from the other monads or whether He is to be conceived as their substance, but Bruno himself has clearly expressed his view, for he says: "God is the monad of monads, *i.e.* the essence of all essences" (*Deus est monadum monas, nempe entium entitas.—De minimo*, ed. 1591, p. 17). The universum is called monad : *De gl' Heroici Furori*, p. 724. This use of the word monad is only comprehensible if we bear in mind the relativity of the concept.

33. p. 139. On the transmigration of souls, Bruno says (*Spaccio*, p. 410) that if we cannot believe it, it is at least worth consideration. In his trial at Venice, too (see BERTI, *G. Bruno*, 2nd ed. pp. 402-408), he expresses himself with a certain hesitancy on the subject. His fullest discussion of the relation between the world-soul and the individual souls occurs in the *Cabala*, pp. 585-588.

34. p. 152. In the *Apologia pro Galilaeo :* Francofurti, 1622, p. 54, CAMPANELLA says that modern investigations may perhaps oblige us to believe that there are several suns in the universe, so that this does not, as has hitherto been supposed, contain two centres, *i.e.* the sun and the earth, but many. He withholds his judgment, however. In the *Realis philo-*

sophia (1623, p. 10) he is also in doubt. Afterwards, however, he interpolated in his *Universalis philosophia seu metaphysica* (Parisiis, 1638, iii. p. 71) some remarks in which he shows how the matter would have to be conceived should Galilei be right (*posito quod vera sint Galilei dogmata*), but he adds : "Sentence has now been passed in Rome on Galilei, and thus what I wrote before [these remarks] is established." A curious kind of verification !

35. p. 176. The first work on the history of philosophy in which Galilei is given the place due to him, in virtue of his clear consciousness of the method of thought, is J. F. FRIES' *Die Geschichte der Philosophie, dargestellt nach den Fortschritten ihrer wissenschaftlichen Entwickelung*, vol. ii. : Halle, 1840. Later PRANTL ("Galilei und Kepler als Logiker," *Münchener Sitzungsberichte*, 1875) discussed his doctrine of method and showed how it eclipses that of Bacon ; and TÖNNIES ("Über die Philosophie des Hobbes," *Vierteljahrschrift für wiss. Philos.* iii.), and NATORP (*Descartes' Erkenntnisstheorie :* Marburg, 1882, chap. vi.) have shown the important position Galilei holds at the opening of modern philosophy, in contradistinction to the traditional beginning which starts with Bacon and Descartes.

36. p. 180. Galilei, *Opere :* Firenze, 1842 and f. ; xiii. p. 200 and f. The German translation of the *Discorsi* (in the *Klassikern der Naturwissenschaft*, No. 24, p. 57) has here an inaccuracy which annuls the simplification of circumstances aimed at by Galilei. Galilei's words, "dum externae causae tollantur" (if only external causes are excluded), are rendered as "while external causes are added." Galilei's mental experiment comes out most clearly in another passage in the *Discorsi* (*Op.* xiii. p. 221): "Mobile quoddam super planum horizontale projectum *mente concipio*, omni secluso impedimento" (*I conceive* a moving body, under the exclusion of every obstacle, thrown along a horizontal plane). For the history of the law of inertia cf. WOHLWILL, "Die Entdeckung des Beharrunggesetzes," *Zeitschrift für Völkerpsychologie*, xiv.-xv.

37. p. 183. It is NATORP'S merit to have been the first (in his work on Descartes' Theory of Knowledge) to call attention to this section of the *Saggiatore* (*Opere di Galilei :* Firenze, 1842 and f. ; iv. pp. 332-338). The new doctrine was dangerous because it was believed that the denial of the reality of the sense-qualities contradicted the Catholic doctrine of the Eucharist, according to which the host retains its sensuous qualities after its substance has been transformed. Later both Descartes and Leibniz had to encounter much unpleasantness over this question.

38. p. 185. As PRANTL shows ("Ueber Petrus Ramus," *Münchener Sitzungsberichte*, 1878).

39. p. 187. Cf. FREUDENTHAL, "Beiträge zur Geschichte der englischen Philosophie," *Archiv für Gesch. der Philos.* iv.-v.—CROOM ROBERTSON in the *Academy*, 1892, p. 110.

40. p. 193. It may be mentioned here as a curiosity that just as there are people who think that not Shakespeare, but another, perhaps Bacon, wrote the "Shaksperian" tragedies, so quite recently a sagacious critic has convinced himself that Bacon is not the author of the *Novum organum*, and has dallied a moment with the possibility that Shakespeare may have written it ; he is not bold enough, however, to decide in favour of this possibility. See *Archiv für Gesch. d. Philos.* i. p. 111.

41. p. 200.   On Bacon's relation to Plato see *Nov. org.* i. 105-124 ; ii. 7-13.—In the *De augmentis scientiarum*, iii. 4, Bacon says : " It is evident that Plato, that sublime spirit who surveyed all things as it were from the summit of a mountain, recognised in his doctrine of ideas that ' forms ' are the proper objects of science."

42. p. 213.   *Discours de la méthode* (1637), 2. partie.—*La vie de Monsieur Descartes* [par A. Baillet] : Paris, 1691, i. pp. 51-71.—MILLET, *Histoire de Descartes avant* 1637 : Paris, 1867, p. 100 and f.

43. p. 219.   In the exposition here given I have followed Descartes' original sketch of a doctrine of method, given in the *Règles pour la direction de l'esprit*, the careful study of which work will dispel many of the usual misunderstandings relating to Descartes.   Compare also the *Third Meditation* and the answer to the second group of objections, in which Descartes, in answer to a challenge he had received, attempted a systematic exposition of his ideas.   To the question as to how general propositions can be framed from particular intuitions Descartes only gives the following answer : " It lies in the nature of our mind to form general propositions from the knowledge of individual things " (*Resp. ed. sec. obj.*).

44. p. 221.   At the close of the *Third Meditation* he says : "There only remains then the possibility that the idea of God is innate in me in the same sense in which the notion of myself is innate."   This is for Descartes something more than a comparison.   For I cannot—he thinks—be conscious of myself as a limited and imperfect being, without an unconscious application of the idea of a being exalted above all limitation (*Third Medit.*). —To Hobbes's objection : " There are no innate ideas, for what is innate must always exist," Descartes answers (*Resp. tertiae*, x.) : " When we say an idea is innate, we do not mean that it is always before us,—for in this sense there would be no innate ideas at all—but only that we possess in ourselves the capacity to develop it."—In the *Notae in programma quoddam* Descartes says : " When I observed that there were thoughts in me which proceeded not from external objects or from the determination of my will, but only from my capacity to think, I called those ideas which are the forms of such thoughts " innate," to distinguish them from others which come from without or are produced by myself.   In the same sense we say that generosity or certain illnesses like gout or the stone are innate in certain families, by which we do not mean that the children suffered from these illnesses in their mother's womb, but only that they were born with the disposition or capacity for developing them."

45. p. 222   Cf. NATORP'S excellent exposition (*Descartes' Erkenntniss-theorie*, p. 55 f. ; 76 f.).   Natorp explains that Descartes does not make such an external use of the concept of God in his theory of knowledge as most expositions of his doctrine lead us to think.   Natorp does not here bring out with sufficient strength what, in my opinion, is the point to be most emphasised, *i.e.* that this epistemological application of the concept of God was entirely unnecessary, for Descartes made use of the axiom of causality in order to prove the reality of the concept of God ; if the causal axiom is *presupposed* as valid, the validity of the theory of knowledge requires no theological guarantee.

46. p. 224.   Properly speaking, it is not individual bodies but matter as a whole which Descartes calls Substance in the stricter meaning of the word. Cf. *Synopsis Meditationum : Corpus quidem in genere sumptum* esse

substantiam, idque nunquam etiam perire ; *sed corpus humanum* . . . non nisi ex certa membrorum configuratione aliisque ejusmodi accidentibus esse conflatum ; mentem vero humanam non ita ex ullis accidentibus constare, sed puram esse substantiam.—There arises here for Descartes (as for Spiritualism in general) the great problem as to how the assumption of individual soul-substances can be harmonised with the doctrine of the continuity of matter. As I have shown in my Psychology (English translation, cf. p. 55 and f.) every hypothesis encounters a difficulty here, although, of course, in the case of the spiritualistic hypothesis it becomes especially prominent.

47. p. 225. The strict concept of substance is found in Descartes' *Medit.* iii., *Princ. phil.* i. § 51, and especially in *Epist.* i. 8 and ii. 16. The lax concept of substance is found *Resp. sec.* and *Princ. phil.* i. § 52.— Descartes himself draws attention to the double sense of the word substance (*Ep.* ii. 16 ; *Princ. phil.* i. 51).

48. p. 233. For Harvey's discovery and its previous history see P. HEDENIUS, *Om upptachtan af blodomloppet* (On the Discovery of the Circulation of the Blood), *Upsala Universitets Årskrift*, 1892. Descartes supposed that the warming of the blood in the heart caused it to be pressed into the body ; he had therefore not adopted Harvey's view of the heart as a contracting muscle. Harvey, too, held to the old doctrine of the warming of the blood in the heart, but did not apply it in this way.

49. p. 235. Descartes' localisation of the soul in the pineal gland was altogether arbitrary and was criticised by the anatomists of his day. THOMAS BARTHOLIN (*Anatomia*, Lugd. Batav. 1651, p. 356 f.) objects, firstly, that the nerves do not end in the pineal gland, secondly, that this is so small that the ideas would become mixed with one another (!), and thirdly, that they are situated where "the excreta of the brain" are accumulated NIELS STEENSEN remarked in his excellent lecture given at Paris, and which is published in WINSLÖV'S *Exposition anatomique* (part iv.), that since it is not known with what the cavities of the brain are filled, the doctrine of the animal spirits may be just as good as the doctrine of the excreta of the brain. Against Descartes, to whose general method he attributes great merit, he objects that the pineal gland is not connected with any canal, and that it does not move freely, but is in contact with the other part of the brain.—In our own day an attempt has been made to prove that the pineal gland is a rudimentary form of an organ for the sensation of warmth which is found in lower animals.—On Descartes' services to nerve physiology cf. HUXLEY, "On the Hypothesis that Animals are Automata."

50. p. 248. Malebranche must be regarded as a precursor of Hume in virtue of his denial of a necessary connection of phenomena. It may even be that Hume took some of the *motifs* of his theory of causality from Malebranche, whom he studied eagerly (as may be seen from the *Treatise*, (i. 3, 14 ; 4, 5).—MARIO NOVARO, in his *Die Philosophie des Nicolaus Malebranche* (Berlin, 1890, pp. 45-50), has drawn an instructive parallel between Malebranche's and Hume's theories of causation. We might also find parallels to Hume in the philosophy of Guelincx, but it is hardly possible that Hume was acquainted with it.

51. p. 260. *Vita Thomae Hobbes* (Autore Rd. B. ; Richard Blackbourne), 1681, p. 14 f. In his *Vita carmine expressa*, p. 119, Hobbes

describes how after he had long been ruminating on the nature of things he discovered that there is only one single real thing in the world [*i.e.* motion], although this is "falsified" (*sic*) in many ways.—F. TÖNNIES, whose energetic inquiry has recently shed so much light on Hobbes and his philosophy, found a MS. (see his "Anmerkungen über die Philosophie des Hobbes," *Vierteljahrschrift für wiss. Philos.* iii.-v.) containing an essay by Hobbes, which, judging by its content, must have been written between the time when the importance of the deductive method and, with that, the importance of motion, became clear to him, and the time when the subjectivity of the sense-qualities dawned upon him.   This essay, which is of interest in reference to the historical development of the principle of the subjectivity of the sense-qualities, has been published by Tönnies in his edition of Hobbes's *Elements of Law* (Oxford, 1888).   Hobbes asserts that as early as 1630 (that is to say before he had become acquainted with Galilei) he had become convinced of the subjectivity of the sense-qualities. Cf. TÖNNIES in the *Vierteljahrschrift*, iii. p. 463 f.—CROOM ROBERTSON, *Hobbes* (London, 1886), p. 35.

52. p. 266.   Cf. Hobbes's treatise *Of Liberty and Necessity*, 3rd ed. London, 1685, p. 314, where, with regard to the definitions of spontaneity, reflection, will, propensity, impulse and freedom, he says : "Could there be any other proof beyond that afforded by each man's experience by reflection on himself and consideration as to what he himself means when he says an action is spontaneous," etc.

53. p. 267.   In the *De corpore*, ix. 9, Hobbes deduces the axiom that all change (including qualitative change) is motion from the causal axiom and the law of inertia.   His "proof" of the causal axiom is as follows (*Of Lib. and Necess.* p. 315) : "If a thing had no cause it might arise at one moment just as soon as at another ; there must, therefore, be a cause why it arises precisely at *this* moment"!   As Hume pointed out, Hobbes here presupposed exactly what was to be proved.   Analogous with this is his proof of the law of inertia (*De corpore*, viii. 10).   If a body at rest were surrounded by empty space there would be no reason why it should move itself in one direction more than in another, and it would therefore not move at all, unless some external cause arose.   He here evidently assumes that there are no "immanent" causes.   It is possible that this proof of the law of inertia originated with Galilei.   See the last "Dialogue on the World-System."   First Day.

54. p. 268.   Hobbes demands for the perfect understanding of a phenomenon the proof of continuous progression from cause to effect. This *continua progressio* (*De corpore*, ix. 6) reminds us of Bacon's *latens processus continuatus* (*Nov. org.* ii. 5-7).   I think it not improbable that Bacon's doctrine of the continuous process may have emerged in Hobbes's thought after he had been led, by another path, to the idea that all change is motion.   He takes as his deductive principle what, according to Bacon, is the result of an induction from many instances.   It is also not improbable that the title of the second part of the *De corpore*, *i.e.* Philosophia prima, was borrowed from Bacon, since by this name he denotes the science of general principles, which was to be valid within all spheres (*De augm.* iii. 1).

55. p. 275.   In the *De corpore*, xxv. 5, Hobbes raises the question whether the proposition that all sensation arises by means of a reaction on a

stimulus is convertible, so that we can say, everything which reacts also feels : " Scio fuisse philosophos quosdam [he is probably thinking of Telesio and Campanella] eosdemque viros doctos qui corpora omnia sensu praedita esse sustinuerunt ; nec video, si natura sensionis in reactione sola collocaretur, quo modo refutari possint. Sed etsi ex reactione etiam corporum aliorum phantasma aliquod nasceretur, illud tamen remoto objecto statim cessaret." In the sequel he distinguishes between *phantasma* and *sensio*, so that the latter presupposes memory and comparison. These remarks are of interest in two connections: (1) from Hobbes's axiom (p. 299) that consciousness is motion, and *nothing else but motion*, it follows, strictly speaking, with necessity that all motion must be (or have) consciousness. This inference is drawn by Hobbes's spiritualistic opponent, HENRY MORE (*De anima :* Rotterodami, 1677, lib. ii. cap. i. p. 64). And in modern times it has been drawn by MOLESCHOTT and HEINRICH CZOLBE (cf. vol. ii. of this work). Hobbes only apparently escapes it : he thinks that to *sensio* proper (as distinct from *phantasma*) a longer persistence of motion and a repetition of the impression is requisite ; but continued and repeated motion is still nothing but motion, and Hobbes holds fast to the axiom : *motus nihil generat praeter motum ;* (2) the *phantasmata* of which Hobbes speaks would answer to the so-called *petites perceptions* of Leibniz, and the difference between *phantasma* and *sensio* corresponds to the Leibnizian difference between "perception" and "sentiment." So that we have here another point besides that mentioned on p. 334 in which the influence of Hobbes on Leibniz may be traced.

56. p. 287. The State archivist A. D. JÖRGENSEN gives, according to my view, a far too crude account of Hobbes's philosophy of the State, especially in his comparison between Hobbes and Bishop Vandal (*Peter Schumacher Griffenfeldt*, i. p. 218 f. : Copenhagen, 1893). The ethical limitation of the physical right of the Prince occurs in Hobbes as well as in the Lutheran theologian. Hobbes even lays it down in such a way as to make the absolute sovereignty the means and not the end. Cf. *e.g. De cive*, xiii. 3, "The State is instituted for the good of the citizens" (*Civitas civium causa instituta est*). In the older edition of the *Leviathan* (ed. 1651, p. 193) the hope of influencing the Prince is expressed somewhat more strongly than in the later edition (ed. 1670, p. 172).

57. p. 288. FREUDENTHAL (*Archiv für Gesch. der Philos*. vi. p. 191 f. ; 380 f.) was the first to bring Lord Brooke's work to light and to show how much of interest it contained.

58. p. 288. On Culverwel see M. M. CURTIS, *An Outline of Locke's Ethical Philosophy :* Leipzig, 1890, pp. 9-13.

59. p. 296. COLERUS (*La vie de B. de Spinoza, tirée des écrits de ce fameux philosophe et du témoignage de plusieurs personnes dignes de foi, qui l'ont connu particulièrement :* à la Haye, 1706, p. 14) considers Spinoza to be merely a pupil of Descartes in philosophy. LEIBNIZ (*Opera Philos*. ed. Erdmann, p. 139) says of him that he only developed some of the seeds sown by Descartes. This was for long the prevailing opinion, and some authors in their works on the history of modern philosophy still keep to it.—JOËL (*Beiträge zur Geschichte der Philosophie :* Breslau, 1876) shows, in opposition to this, what a great and lasting effect Spinoza's studies of Jewish theology and philosophy of law have exerted.—CHR. SIGWART (*Spinoza's neuentdeckter Trahtat :* Gotha, 1868) and AVENARIUS (*Über die beiden ersten Phasen des*

Spinosischen Pantheismus: Leipzig, 1868) point out—on the evidence of Spinoza's early work, *Tractatus (brevis) de Deo et Homine ejusque Felicitate,* published by van Vloten (*Ad Benedicti de Spinoza opera quae supersunt omnia supplementum :* Amstelodami, 1862)—the probability that Spinoza was influenced by Giordano Bruno.—Finally, FREUDENTHAL (*Spinoza und die Scholastik,* in the congratulatory address to Zeller) has called attention to the great extent to which Spinoza uses scholastic concepts and proofs, especially in the *Cogitata metaphysica,* which forms a supplement to Spinoza's summary of the Cartesian philosophy, although also in the *Ethica.* —A good biography and characterisation of Spinoza is given by F. POLLOCK (*Spinoza : his Life and his Philosophy:* London, 1880).—In my *Spinoza's Liv og Läre* (Spinoza's Life and Doctrine): Copenhagen, 1877, I have given a popular description of Spinoza and his philosophy. Later, continued study has led me to adopt views on some points other than those advocated in this work. I take this opportunity to make the following correction with regard to the picture used as the title-vignette in this book. It has since been proved that this picture, which was taken from van Vloten's *Supplement,* represents, not Spinoza, but Tschirnhausen, the mathematician and philosopher, who was one of his friends. A good and, according to all accounts, faithful portrait of Spinoza is found in van Vloten and Land's new edition of Spinoza's works.

60. p. 299. I must also protest against A. D. JÖRGENSEN'S reflections (*Nich. Steensen,* p. 57) on Spinoza's attitude towards experience. On this point, however, the section on Spinoza's "Theory of Knowledge" will contain all that is necessary.

61. p. 300. "Studie zur Entwickelungs-geschichte des Spinoza," *Vierteljahrschrift f. wiss. Philos.* vii. pp. 161, 334.

62. p. 306. In their work, *Spinoza's Erkenntnisslehre in ihrer Beziehung zur modernen Naturwissenschaft und Philosophie* (Berlin, 1891), BERENDT and FRIEDLÄNDER make an interesting attempt to arrive at a nearer determination of the relation between *ratio* and *scientia intuitiva.* In their view, *ratio* corresponds to scientific knowledge, *scientia intuitiva* to the artistic conception through which, without denying the firm mechanical interconnection of Nature, we apprehend immediately the essence of things. Ratio gives us the qualities of things ; intuition gives us their essence. And from Spinoza's teaching that *conatus* and *virtus* are nothing else than the essence of the individual in question (*Ethica,* iii. 7 ; iv. Def. 8), these authors deduce the conclusion that, according to Spinoza, the essence of things lies in the will ; they find here a kinship between Spinoza, Kant, and Schopenhauer. This is, in my opinion, to attribute too æsthetic a character to Spinoza's *scientia intuitiva.* It is nearer to mysticism than to æsthetics. And, as has already been indicated in the text, the discursive intellect does not entirely disappear in the *scientia intuitiva.* When Spinoza says that intuitive knowledge proceeds (*procedit*) from a complete idea of the nature of certain divine qualities up to a complete knowledge of the nature of things (*Ethica,* ii. 40, Schol. 2) we are led to think of Stuart Mill's so-called inverse deductive method ; for the *modi* (the existence of which, according to Ep. x., can only be known *empirically*) have here to be deduced from the attributes (*i.e.* the general laws or forms). Further, in my opinion, it is no mere accident that Spinoza did not convert the proposition that will is the essence of things.

He has nowhere taught the absolute identity of essence and will. In the most important passage (*Ethica*, v. 29 Schol.) he is not talking of the will as the object of intuition at all. On the whole, however, Berendt and Friedländer's work is a justifiable and successful attempt to exhibit Spinoza's fundamental thoughts in their lasting significance, which is of especial importance for our age.

63. p. 309. The first book of the " Ethics " develops the concepts of Substance and of God in a series of definitions, axioms, and propositions.— With regard to the connection between the concepts of Substance, of God, and of Nature, cf. AVENARIUS, *Über die beiden ersten Phasen des Spinozischen Pantheismus*, where it is clearly shown that all three concepts, if they were consistently carried out, would, with Spinoza, meet in a single point. Yet Spinoza has hardly kept the three streams of thought so sharply distinguished from one another as is the case in Avenarius' exposition. With regard to the relation between substance and modes we must notice, in addition to the first book of the *Ethica*, Ep. 12 (in van Vloten and Land's edition) where a distinction is made between abstract and substantial conception, and Ep. 50, where it is asserted that all determination is negation. The expressions *natura naturans* and *natura naturata* occur in the Renaissance philosophers, the Mystics (Meister Eckart), and the Scholastics. According to SIEBECK (*Archiv für Gesch. der Philos.* iii. p. 370 and f.) they come from the Greek φύσις (as φύον and as φυόμενον), and were introduced into Latin by the translation of Greek philosophical writings, probably in the thirteenth century.

64. p. 310. When Spinoza's Definition (in the first book of the " Ethics ") runs : " Per attributum intelligo id, quod intellectus de substantia percipit, tanquam ejusdem essentiam constituens " (cf. also Ep. 9 of Land and Vloten's edition), is it possible that by *intellectus* he means here the *intellectus infinitus ?* Cf. *Ethica*, ii. 7 Schol. : " Revocandum nobis in memoriam est id, quod supra ostendimus, nempe quod quicquid *ab infinito intellectu* percipi potest tanquam substantiae essentiam constituens, id omne ad unicam tantum substantiam pertinet." If this were so, any doubt as to the objectivity of the attributes would be impossible. Yet in the passage to which "supra ostendimus" refers (*i.e.* i. 30), Spinoza expressly distinguishes between *intellectus finitus* and *intellectus infinitus*. Hence it is probable that in bk. i. Def. 4, the concept of *intellectus* is quite undetermined. It is exactly characteristic of his dogmatic standpoint to make no distinction *here* between the limits of the *intellectus finitus* and the *intellectus infinitus*.

65. p. 310. In opposition to this view of the Spinozistic concept of attributes maintained by the elder Erdmann, cf. H. BROCHNER, *Benedict Spinoza :* Copenhagen, 1857, p. 47, etc.—I am at a loss to understand how MOURLY VOLD (*Spinoza's Erkendelsesteorie*[Spinoza's Theory of Knowledge]: Christiana, 1888, p. 242) can mention Bröchner among those who explain the attributes " as necessary for our understanding, but, for God, accidental predicates." It is precisely against this view that Bröchner polemicises.

66. p. 312. In my *Spinoza Liv og Läre* (Spinoza's Life and Doctrine, 1877, p. 100) I have already pointed out this confusion in Spinoza. It is also brought out by WINDELBAND, *Geschichte der neueren Philosophia*, i. (1878) p. 211 and by TÖNNIES, " Studie zur Entwickelungs-geschichte des Spinoza " (*Vierteljahrschrift für wiss. Phil.* 1883) p. 176, etc.—MOURLY

VOLD (*Spinoza's Erkendelsesteorie*, p. 202) denies the confusion and considers the doctrine of attributes as necessarily arising from the attempt to found a "correspondence between idea and object." If he thus admits that the doctrine of attributes has, with Spinoza, *also* a psycho-physical significance, and finds in this double meaning no difficulty, he himself is guilty of the same confusion as Spinoza. For theory of knowledge and psycho-physics are really two different things, as may be seen from the fact that "objects" are physical as well as psychical; the problem of knowledge is concerned with the knowledge of the psychical as well as of the physical.

This confusion in Spinoza comes out clearly if we compare *Eth.* ii. Schol. 7, where the relation between the idea of the circle and the actually existing circle is used to explain the relation between the attributes, with ii. Schol. 17. Where a distinction is made between the idea of Peter (*idea Petri*) which corresponds to Peter's own body as its mind (*mens Petri*), and the idea of Peter (*idea Petri*) which Paul has, the first *idea Petri* has a psycho-physical, the last an epistemological significance. Spinoza's most inappropriate habit of calling the mind (*mens*) the *idea corporis*, has fostered the confusion. This confusion flourishes among the German speculative philosophers (Schelling and Hegel) and it has also crept into Vold's otherwise able and interesting work.

67. p. 315. H. MORUS, *Demonstrationis duaı um propositionum, quae praecipuae apud Spinozium* (sic) *Atheismi sunt columnae, brevis solidaque confutatio* (*Opera philosophica*, Londini, 1679, vol. i. p. 619).—There is an instructive essay on the different interpretations of the Spinozistic concept of God by J. H. LÖWE (*Über Spinozas Gottesbegriff und dessen Schicksale* ; an appendix to his work on Fichte's philosophy : Stuttgart, 1862) in which, however, More's characteristic explanation is not mentioned.

68. p. 315. Cf. on this question ED. ZELLER'S remarks in the *Vierteljahrschrift für wiss. Philos.* i. p. 285 f.

69. p. 317. Spinoza makes this confession in the last letter which we have in his handwriting (15th July 1676), written in answer to Tschirnhausen, a philosopher and mathematician, who, with great acuteness, had asked how we can deduce the figure and motion of corporeal things from the general concept of extension. Tschirnhausen draws attention to the fact that this difficulty did not exist for Descartes, since he believed God to have created matter in motion ; but Spinoza, for whom extension is a divine attribute, lacks the concept of force which was conceived by Descartes in theological form. Spinoza declares the definition of matter as extension to be inadequate, and promises a closer examination of the question, which, however, his illness did not allow him to fulfil.

70. p. 320. In *Eth.* ii. 18 the only law mentioned is the one we now call the law of contiguity. But the law of similarity is presupposed in *Eth.* iii. 27, and in *Tract. theol. polit.* cap. 4 it is mentioned as an example of a mental law of Nature.

71. p. 326. A more detailed account of Spinoza's Ethics than I can here give is to be found in my *Spinoza's Life and Doctrine*, pp. 120-146.

72. p. 327. When in *Eth.* v. Schol. 38 and Coroll. 40 it says the *intellectus*, not the *imaginatio*, is eternal, it seems as if only those individuals who rise above the standpoint of imagination (of sensuous perception) become organs of the divine activity of thought, and can no more cease to be than can motion. An expression in the "Short Treatise"

(Part ii. Preface No. 15) to the effect that the mind can become eternal if it unites itself, by means of knowledge and love, with the absolute Substance, points this way. The thought which we meet with here in Spinoza appears again and again in the history of philosophy. I cannot here enter further into the question, and must restrict myself to some bibliographical references. PLATO'S *Republic*, vii. p. 534 C.—CHRYSIPPOS (*Diog. Laert.* viii. 157).—MAIMONIDES (see Joël, *Zur Genesis der Lehre des Spinoza*, p. 66).—SALOMON MAMION, *Lebensgeschichte*, written by himself: Berlin, 1792, ii. p. 178 f.—GOETHE, *Gespräche mit Eckermann*, 4th Feb. and 1st Sept. 1829.—WILHELM VON HUMBOLDT (see Haym, *W. v. Humboldt*, p. 637 f.).—J. G. FICHTE, *Die Thatsachen des Bewusstseins*: Stuttgart and Tübingen, 1817, p. 197 f.—C. H. WEISSE, *Die philosophische Geheimlehre über die Unsterblichkeit des menschlichen Individuums.*—LOUIS LAMBERT (See Ravaisson, *La philosophie en France au 19ᵉ siècle*, p. 223).

73. p. 336. See on this point LUDWIG STEIN, *Leibniz and Spinoza. A Contribution to the History of the Development of the Leibnizian Philosophy*: Berlin, 1890 (especially chap. iv.).

74. p. 340. The essay of 1680 has no title. Erdmann, who was the first to unearth it from the library at Hanover, entitled it (in his edition of Leibniz, *Opera philosophica*, 1840), *De vera methodo philosophiae et theologiae*, and attributed it to the years 1690-91. That its origin was earlier, however, is shown both by internal and external evidences, and more especially by a comparison with the *Petit discours de métaphysique*, written in 1685 and submitted to Arnauld in the following year. Cf. with regard to this, SELVER, "Der Entwickelungsgang der Leibniz'schen Monadenlehre bis 1695" (*Philosophische Studien*, published by W. Wundt, iii.) p. 443.— LUDWIG STEIN, *Leibniz und Spinoza.*—In his excellent sketch of the evolution of the Leibnizian philosophy, Stein lays too great weight on the influence which the study of Plato had on Leibniz. It is certainly very significant that during the years which were of such importance for the maturing of his philosophy, Leibniz should have occupied himself so much with Plato, and quoted, amongst others, the well-known passage from the *Phaedo* on final causes no less than twelve times. But this is to be regarded rather as a symptom than as a cause. The conviction of the existence of final causes was present in Leibniz from the beginning; it sprang out of his religious presuppositions, and throughout his youth he had sought a means to reconcile it with his theories of physical science. Plato could give him nothing new here. Stein's explanation appears to me particularly forced where he deduces the Leibnizian proposition of the identity of substance with force from Plato's doctrine (only given in one single passage) of the "Ideas" as active forces. Leibniz had occupied himself with the concepts of "force" and "effort" ever since 1670, and he transfers these concepts from his physico-mathematical studies to his philosophy, and uses them to give life to the concept of substance. Several authors have described the progress made by Leibniz in the year 1680 as a substantialisation of force, but in my opinion it would be more correct to reverse the relation and to speak of a conversion of substance into force. The treatise of 1680 did, as a matter of fact, effect a dissolution of the Cartesian and Spinozistic concept of substance.

75. p. 346. In a recently published fragment by Leibniz, the connection between his doctrines of the soul and body, of teleology and mechanism,

and of God and the world, is brought out in a most instructive manner: "Anima quomodo agat in corpus. Ut Deus in mundum: id est non per modum miraculi, sed per mechanicas leges; itaque si per impossibile tollerentur mentes, at manerent leges naturae, eadem fierent ac si essent mentes, et libri etiam scriberentur legerenturque a machinis humanis nihil intelligentibus. Verum sciendum est, hoc esse impossibile, ut tollantur mentes salvis legibus mechanicis. Nam leges mechanicae generales sunt voluntatis divinae decreta, et leges mechanicae speciales in unoquoque corpore (quae ex generalibus sequuntur) sunt decreta animae sive formae ejus, contendentis ad bonum unum sive ad perfectionem . . . . Omnia in tota natura demonstrari possunt tum per causas finales, tum per causas efficientes. Natura nihil facit frustra ; natura agit per vias brevissimas, modo sint regulares." (E. BODEMANN, *Die Leibniz-Handschriften der kgl. öffentlichen Bibliothek zu Hannover:* Hanover and Leipzig, 1895, p. 89.)

76. p. 348. The "tout comme ici" of Leibniz has the same source as Holberg's "ganz wie bei uns," viz. the comedy, *Harlequin empereur de la lune* (Gherardi's *Théâtre italien,* vol. i.). See *Nouveaux Essais,* iv. 16, 12 (Erdmann, p. 391 f.): "On diroit quasi que c'est dans l'Empire de la lune de Harlequin tout comme ici."—Besides this passage the following are to be noticed in connection with the law of analogy: Letter to Arnauld, Nov. 1686 (Erdmann, p. 391 f.); *De ipsa natura* (Erdmann, p. 157); *Nouveaux Essais,* i. 1 (Erdmann, p. 205) and iii. 6, 14 (Erdmann, p. 312); passages in letters (Gerhardt, ii. p. 270: iv. p. 343).

77. p. 349. The latest and, in many respects, the most interesting and instructive exposition of the doctrine of monads (EDWARD DILLMANN, *Neue Darstellung der Leibnizischen Monadenlehre:* Leipzig 1891) seems to me entirely to overlook the great importance which the law of analogy has for the subjective conclusion of the monadology. Dillmann considers the capability of having ideas to be given from the beginning in the concept of monad, and takes the concept of "appearance" in Leibniz only in the subjective sense (appearance for). This view, however, is already refuted by the fact which Dillmann himself acknowledges, *i.e.* that Leibniz assumes, without any more exact foundation, that the monad represents the universe according to the standpoint of *its body,* and that he rests the assumption that the monad represents the *entire* universe on this—that every body, in virtue of the law of continuity, is affected by every modification in every other part of the world whatever (cf. Dillmann, p. 301 f. ; p. 342 f.). According to Dillmann's hypothesis it would be incomprehensible that Leibniz should have expressed himself, as soon as he heard of them, so decidedly against Berkeley's ideas.

78. p. 353. On the different ways in which the relation between Leibniz and Spinoza has, in the course of time, been conceived, see the first chapter in L. STEIN's *Leibniz und Spinoza.* C. DILLMANN finds agreement as to principles between the two systems, but, at the same time, thinks that Leibniz' doctrine of the relation between God and the world is unassailable, and does not emphasise the passages in which Leibniz protests against Spinoza (*Neue Darstellung,* p. 472 and f.). Dillman lets himself be betrayed by his great and justifiable admiration for Leibniz into apologies for unmistakable contradictions and evident accommodations.

79. p. 360. On the distinction between "perception" and "appétit" see the *Monadologie,* § 15.—Passions as "pensées confuses," *Réplique aux*

réflexions de Bayle (Erdmann, p. 188*a*) ; as "tendances ou des modifications de tendances," *Nouv. Ess.* ii. 20, 9 (Erdmann, p. 249*a*).

80. p. 361. Cf. an essay (without title) printed in Gerhardt's edition, vii. p. 300 f., where it is first said that all contingent data must have their reason, since the creative will, which reveals itself through them, is not arbitrary but acts according to reason, and then : " It is therefore certain that all truths, even the most contingent, have an *a priori* motivation (*probatio*) or a reason why they should much rather be than not be. And it is just this which is asserted in the usual saying that nothing happens without a cause (*causa*), or (*seu*) nothing is without a reason (*ratio*)."

81. p. 365. Leibniz first made use of the law of contrast in a letter written in defence of Optimism at the beginning of the year 1670 (Gerhardt's edition, i. p. 61). He developed it later (as *lex laetitiae*) in *De rerum originatione* (Erdmann, p. 149 f.). This æsthetico-psychological argument is of antique origin ; it is to be found in Plautinus and, curiously enough, it is repeated by Augustine. On the other hand, the prominence given to the infinitude of existence is modern. Leibniz remarks that Augustine does not yet know "la grandeur de la cité de Dieu" (*Théodicée*, § 19) ; cf. *Causa dei asserta*, §§ 57, 58.

82. p. 370. In the preface to the first edition of his " Rational Thoughts " WOLFF says : " I did, indeed, at first intend to leave the question of the association of the body with the soul and the soul with the body quite undecided ; but as, contrary to expectation, I was naturally led by reasons set forth in another chapter, to the pre-established harmony of Mr. Leibniz, I have retained this and have put it in such a light as this ingenious discovery has never yet enjoyed." In the preface to the second edition he expresses himself still more exactly as to the relation of his doctrine to that of Leibniz. Leibniz, he says, united idealism (the uninterrupted connection of mental phenomena) with materialism (the uninterrupted connection of material phenomena) without subjecting either to a closer examination. Wolff believed himself to have done this, and he came to the conclusion that the dualists are in a position to unite the theory of the idealists with that of the materialists. The following is the really correct description of the difference between Leibniz and Wolff on this point : Leibniz holds the hypothesis of identity (although with modifications), while Wolff supports dualism (although with the assumption borrowed from the identity hypothesis, that mental and material phenomena, each for themselves, stand in uninterrupted connection). The greater number of the objections usually raised against the identity hypothesis apply to the Wolffian theory, which is well called "Duplizismus"—a quite unsuitable name for the real identity hypothesis.

83. p. 386. Molyneux, Locke's friend, explains the apparent contradiction between these two propositions (of which the first occurs in Essay iv. 3, 10, and the latter in Essay iv. 10, 5), thus : In the former passage God is said to be able to endow matter with capacity of thought in a supernatural manner, while in the latter it is matter apart from such supernatural influence which is under discussion (Letter to Locke, 22nd December 1692). Locke declares this view to be quite correct (Letter of 20th January 1693). *The Works oj John Locke*, 9th ed. London, 1794, ix. pp. 293-303.

84. p. 391. Locke nowhere formally establishes this triad. Where he

speaks of the necessity of abandoning the condition of nature (*Civil Government*, ii. §§ 124-126) he names the legislative power, impartial judges, and the executive power as the three requirements.   Later (§ 136) he emphasises the necessity of the legislative being kept distinct from the judicial power, since otherwise the way would be opened for arbitrariness.   But when (cap. 12-13) he sets up three powers in the State, and examines into their mutual relation, the triad here consists of the legislative, the executive, and the federative powers.   By the last, Locke understands an authority which represents the State in its external relations and in its dealings with communities, with regard to which it is still in the state of nature.   But since, he goes on to say, the executive and federative powers are best united in *one* hand (§§ 147, 148) the distinction between them practically falls to the ground ; and as, in other connections, he lays great weight on the separation of the legislative from the judicial power, the triad is, in so far, certainly recognised by him.   In the doctrine of the division of political power, moreover, Locke has predecessors in Buchanan, Hooker, and Sidney (cf. O. GIERCKE, *Joh. Althusius*, pp. 157, 163 f.).

85. p. 397.   I take the opportunity here of referring to an interesting theory of Hutcheson's for which I had no space in the text.   In his *Inquiry* he has given a sketch of an ethical algebra, in which he attempts to formulate exactly the elements involved in an ethical judgment.   These elements are : the personal welfare of the agent, the welfare of others, the "ability " of the person willing, his self-love and his goodwill towards others. By taking "ability" into account Hutcheson revives a significant thought of Aristotle's, which I have attempted to carry out still further in my article on "The Law of Relativity in Ethics " (*Internat. Journal of Ethics*, vol. i.) ; cf. my notice of Meinong's "Theory of Worth " in the *Göttingischen gelehrten Anzeigen*, 1896, No. 4, pp. 310-312.

86. p. 411.   In the Scholium after the definition he speaks of "*true*, absolute, and *mathematical* space" (and likewise of time).   "Ordinary people (*vulgus*), on the other hand, conceive magnitudes only in relation to sensuous things (*ex relatione ad sensibilia*)."   At the close of Definitio 8, however, the "true, physical" manner of conception is opposed to the *mathematical: vere et physice*, in opposition to *mathematice tantum !*   In connection with this must be taken the fact that Newton considered the central point of the world to be at rest (*Principia*, iii. 10 ; cf. 12 Coroll.), although he had founded his view of absolute space on the impossibility of proving that any body is in a state of absolute rest.

87. p. 431.   As may be seen from the text, Hume uses "reason" in two different meanings.   According to one meaning reason is an instinct, a product of habit, and, as such, a product of Nature, *e.g. Treatise*, i. 3, 16 (*in fine*).   In the *Inquiry concerning Human Understanding*, § ix. (*in fine*) reason of this kind is called "experimental reasoning."   According to the other meaning, reason is opposed to Nature (see *Treatise*, i. 4, 2): "Nature is obstinate and will not quit the field, however strongly attacked by Reason."   It here denotes "subtle reasoning " (*Treatise*, i. 4, 1).   The phrase "Nature is too strong for principle"! occurs in the *Inquiry*, xii. (of the academical or sceptical philosophy).

88. p. 433.   ED. GRIMM (*Zur Geschichte des Erkenntnisproblems :* Leipzig, 1890, pp. 571-586) draws an interesting comparison between Hume's two works.   I cannot, however, agree with Grimm that Hume's

repudiation of his early work was really owing to his having changed his standpoint. The motive was, there is no doubt, the same which caused him to delay the publication of his *Dialogues on Natural Religion* till after his death, *i.e.* the desire to escape the attacks of the orthodox (cf. *Letters of David Hume to Strahan:* Oxford, 1888, p. 289 f. ; 303-330).

89. p. 434. Only in one single passage (*Treatise*, ii. 3, 9) does Hume say that feelings or "affects" may arise not only through experience of good and evil, but also from a "natural impulse or instinct," which instinct he at the same time declares to be "altogether inexplicable." As examples of such feelings he names desire for revenge, the wish for the happiness of our friends, hunger, and other bodily instincts.

90. p. 435. Cf. an interesting passage in a letter to Hutcheson : " I wish from my heart that I could avoid drawing the conclusion that morality, which in your opinion is determined by feeling, concerns only human nature and human life. This is often brought as an objection against you, and its consequences are very significant" (Burton, *Life and Correspondence of David Hume:* Edinburgh, 1846, i. p. 119).

91. p. 442. This is verified by the recent discovery of the third part of Smith's lectures (*Lectures on Jurisprudence, Police, Revenue, and Arms*, by Adam Smith. Reported by a student in 1763. Edited by Edwin Cannan, Oxford, 1896), which are, for the most part, the history of social institutions. These lectures give us not only the third part of Smith's course, but also the first version of the fourth.

92. p. 461. " Il est absolument nécessaire pour les princes et pour les peuples, que l'idée d'un être suprême créateur, gouverneur, rémunérateur et vengeur soit profondément gravée dans les esprits " (Art " Athéisme " in the *Dict. Phil.*). At the conclusion of this article he says there are now fewer atheists than formerly, because true philosophers acknowledge final causes. " God is preached to children by the priests, but Newton reveals Him to the instructed."

93. p. 462. In the *Lettres sur les Anglais* xiii. he says (speaking of Socrates' faith in his dämon) : " Il y a des gens à la vérité qui prétendent qu'un homme qui se vantait d'avoir un génie familier, était indubitablement un fou ou un fripon, mais ces gens-là sont trop difficiles." In the *Essai sur les mœurs et l'esprit des nations* (tome ii. chap. 9) he writes : " Christianity must certainly be divine, puisque dix-sept siècles de friponneries et d'imbécillités n'ont pu la détruire." Shortly before, the expression " insolente imbécillité " is used of a legendary.—Art. "Fanatisme" in *Dict. Phil.* : " Ce sont d'ordinaire les fripons qui conduisent les fanatiques."—Religious and ecclesiastical characters were not the only objects of Voltaire's ridicule. Even old Socrates has to serve as a butt. In other passages he falls upon Spinoza and Maillet, the natural philosopher, whose anticipation of the evolutionary hypothesis was ridiculed by Voltaire, and all because it seemed to him incomprehensible, stupid, or fraudulent.

94. p. 463. Cf. D. Fr. STRAUSS, *Voltaire*, 3 ed. p. 330 f.

95. p. 464. GNEISST (*Das Self-Government in England*, 3. Aufl. S. 944) remarks : " The spokesman of the new doctrines [*i.e.* the new political doctrines in France], Montesquieu, had before him not the English constitution but Blackstone's Institutes, in which the historical process of development of the whole and the intermediate construction of self-government are wanting. It was precisely this which made his exposition

acceptable in French eyes." An error has crept in here, for Blackstone's work did not appear till 1765, while the *Esprit des lois* was published in 1748. The reverse is really the case : Montesquieu's theory influenced Blackstone, and thus in no small degree determined political development in England ; cf. F. C. MONTAGUE's introduction to his edition of Bentham's *Fragment on Government* (Oxford, 1891, p. 68). Montague makes, at the same time, the apposite remark that Montesquieu must no doubt have been induced, by the sight of the system of suppression of the continental governments, to emphasise the division of power more strongly than was in keeping with the English constitution and English theories. *The Federalist*, Nos. 47-51, contains an interesting examination by MADISON and HAMILTON, the founders of the constitution of the United States, of Montesquieu's doctrine of the division of power, and a special discussion as to how this could be carried out when we allow for the fact that the legislative power always displays a tendency to appropriate the executive power also.

96. p. 477. F. PAPILLON, in his *Histoire de la philosophie moderne dans ses rapports avec le développement des sciences de la nature* : Paris, 1876, ii. p. 194, traces Diderot's philosophy direct from that of Leibniz. Against this view see KNUD IPSEN, *Diderot :* Köbenhavn, 1891, p. 206 f. and 210, where he points out, and there can be no doubt rightly, that the collection of extracts and notes which is to be found among Diderot's works under the title *Éléments de physiologie*, shows how great and direct an influence his study of physics had exercised upon him.

97. p. 489. The difference between *amour de soi* and *amour propre* is developed by Rousseau in his *Discours sur l'inégalité* (note 12), and after-wards in *Émile*, and in *Rousseau juge de Jean Jacques* (London, 1780, p. 20 and f.). These developments, in which the influence of ideas on feeling comes out very clearly, call to mind the teaching of Joseph Butler, although we have no reason for supposing that Rousseau was acquainted with it.

98. p. 490. *Discours sur l'inégalité :* Amsterdam, 1755, p. 80. "Lettre à M. de Beaumont" (*Petits chefs d'œuvre :* Paris, 1859, p. 304 f.). While this happy condition is here described as immediately following on the primitive, animal state, in other passages (*e.g.* in the letter to Marshal Luxembourg, 20th Jan. 1763), Rousseau describes a much more advanced civilisation, which still bears the stamp of simplicity, but which becomes demoralised by the introduction of the customs and wants of a large civilised country. Such, in Rousseau's opinion, was the civilisation of Switzerland in his own time, and it was on this account that he resisted so strenuously the introduction of French customs (*e.g.* comedy). This question brought Rousseau into sharp disagreement with Voltaire, and occasioned his *Lettre à d'Alembert.*

99. p. 490. Compare the letter to Mdlle. D. M. 7th May 1764 : "On ne quitte pas sa tête comme son bonnet, et l'on ne revient pas plus à la simplicité qu'à l'enfance ; l'esprit une fois en effervescence y reste toujours, et quiconque a pensé, pensera toute sa vie. C'est-là le plus grand malheur de l'état de réflexion," etc.

100. p. 493. "Souvenez-vous toujours que je n'enseigne point mon senti-ment, je l'expose," *Émile* iv. (éd. Paris, 1851, p. 326). "Je ne voulais pas philosopher avec vous, mais vous aider à consulter votre cœur" (p. 344). "Je ne raisonnerai jamais sur la nature de Dieu, que je n'y sois forcé par

le sentiment de ses rapports avec moi" (p. 327). Here we have almost an anticipation of Schleiermacher's conception of dogma as having arisen out of reflection on states of religious feeling.

101. p. 495. Cf. besides the third letter to Malesherbes, also the *Confessions*, xii. (éd. Paris, 1864, p. 608): "I can find no more worthy adoration of God than the silent admiration which the contemplation of His works begets in us, and which cannot be expressed by any prescribed acts. In my room I pray seldomer and more coldly; but the sight of a beautiful landscape moves me, I cannot tell why. I once read of a certain bishop who, when visiting in his bishopric, encountered an old woman whose only prayer consisted in a sigh of 'Oh!' The bishop said to her, 'Good mother, always pray like that; your prayer is worth more than ours.' My prayer is of that kind."

102. p. 497. GIERCKE calls attention to this in his Monograph on Althusius (p. 201). As far as I remember, Rousseau mentions Althusius in one passage only, and that not in the *Contrat social*, but in the *Lettres écrites de la Montagne* (6th letter).

103. p. 498. *Contrat social*, iii. 15.—In most of the recent editions a note is added to this chapter, describing the fate of Rousseau's treatise on federation. On Alexander Hamilton cf. my treatise, *Hamilton og den nordamerikanske Unionsforfatning* (Hamilton and the Constitution of the United States of North America): Tilskueren, 1889. Cf. some interesting remarks on this point in JOHN MORLEY'S *Rousseau:* London, 1891, ii. pp. 166-168.

104. p. 499. That Rousseau was very well aware of the abstract and ideal character of the ideas contained in the *Contrat social* may be seen from the book itself, where (iii. 8) he shows at length that not every form of government is suitable to every country; this may also be gathered from many passages in his letters, as well as in his defence of the *Contrat social*, contained in the *Lettres écrites de la Montagne*, see *e.g.* Lettre vi. (éd. Amsterdam, 1764, p. 219): "Je ne sors pas de la thèse générale. . . . Je ne suis pas le seul qui *discutant par abstraction* des questions de politique ait pu les traiter avec quelque hardiesse."

INDEX

ABBOTT, Edwin, 192
Abelard, 186
Abstraction theory, 419 f
Actuality, principle of, 127
Æsthetic, theory of, 395
Agricola, 185
Althusius, life and works, 46 ; theory of the State, 47 ff ; also 263, 283, 497
Analogy, law of, 348 ; principle of, 422 f
Analytic method, 176
Animal spirits, 233 ff, 238
Animism, theory of, Telesio's, 97 ff, 152 ; Kepler's, 171 f ; of Spinoza, 319 f
"Apperception" in Leibniz, 357
Aquinas, Thomas, 6 f, 14, 20
Archimedes, 163, 173
Aristotle, his philosophy, 7 ff ; commentators, 13 f ; conception of the world, 79 ff, 83 ; doctrine of elements, 92, 95 ; of "forms," 7, 14, 94, 162 ; fundamental virtue, 367 ; opposition to, 9 f, 140, 173, 178, 186
Arnauld, Antoine, 216, 225, 237, 242, 336, 339, 342
Ars combinatoria, 362
Association, with Hume, 430 f ; with Hartley, 447 f ; see Ideas
Atheism, 315, 402
Atom, concept of, 344
Atomism, Bruno's, 141 ; Gassendi's, 258 ; atomists, 129, 133
"Attraction," 409, 431
Attributes, Spinoza's, 308, 309 ff, 317
Augustine, 154, 255
Authority, principle of, 262 ; in ethics, 397, 402
Automatism, with Descartes, 233 f ; with Pascal, 253 f ; with La Mettrie, 474
Avenarius, 514, 515
Averroës, 14

BACON, Francis, predecessors, 183 ff ; life and personality, 189 ff ; method of knowledge, 193 f ; "idols," 195 ff ; "first philosophy," 203 ; theology, 204 f ; ethics, 206 ; also 93, 102, 157, 164, 260, 266, 287, 302, 428, 441, 450

Bahlow, 503
Baillet, 510
Bartholin, Thomas, 511
Basso, Sebastian, 228, 257
Bayle, Pierre, 254 f, 341, 362
Berendt, 514
Berkeley, George, life and characteristics, 414 ff ; on space and abstract ideas, 418 ff ; epistemology, 420 ; also 249, 349, 424, 450, 468
Berti, 506, 508
Beyersdorf, 506
Blackbourne, 511
Bodemann, 518
Bodin, Jean, concept of sovereignty, 45 ; doctrine of the State, 46 ; *Colloquium heptaplomeres*, 60 ff ; also 76
Boehme, life and works, 69 f ; problem of religion, 71 ; of evil, 72 ff ; also 78, 129, 136, 255, 331, 364
Boerhaves, 473
Bonaventura, 85
Boole, 361
Bossuet, 242, 338, 342, 493
Boyle, 378, 384
Brahe, Tycho, 109, 119, 128, 151, 152, 169, 171, 179, 180
Bröchner, xvii. 515
Brooke, 288, 306
Bruno, life and characteristics, 110 ff ; world-scheme, 123 ff ; conception of God, 128 ff ; stages of development, 130 ; conception of law, 131 ; of the world-soul, 132 f ; conservation of matter, 134 ; concept of substance, 135 ; of God, 136 ; of unity and manifold, 136 f ; individualism, 138 ; concept of atoms, 138 ff ; theory of knowledge, 140 ff ; ethical ideas, 144 ff ; also 102, 109, 149, 165, 167, 168, 181, 197, 210, 257, 295 f, 340, 506
Buckle, 442 f
Burkhardt, 11, 504
Butler, 397 ff

CABBALA, 289
Calvin and Calvinism, 43, 113, 143, 289.
Cambridge school, 288 ff, 383

END OF VOLUME I

Printed by R. & R. CLARK, LIMITED, Edinburgh.

Lightning Source UK Ltd.
Milton Keynes UK
UKHW02f1946030818
326743UK00013B/857/P

9 781330 053522